PEASANT RUSSIA, CIVIL WAR

Orlando Figes is Professor of History at Birkbeck College, London. He was born in 1959 and took a double-starred First in history at Gonville and Caius College, Cambridge in 1982. He was made Research Fellow at Trinity College in 1984, completing his PhD in 1987. He joined Cambridge University's History Faculty as a University Assistant Lecturer in 1987 and was Lecturer in History and Teaching Fellow of Trinity College between 1987 and 1999.

Also by Orlando Figes

A People's Tragedy:
The Russian Revolution 1891–1924
(NCR Book Award, Los Angeles Times Prize, 1997)

Interpreting the Russian Revolution:
The Language and Symbols of 1917
(with Boris Kolonitskii)

PEASANT RUSSIA, CIVIL WAR

The Volga Countryside in Revolution (1917–1921)

Orlando Figes

PHOENIX PRESS

PHOENIX PRESS
5 UPPER SAINT MARTIN'S LANE
LONDON WC2H 9EA

The lucky historian
gets all the glory,
The sadder the epoch
the better the story.
(Pavel Kogan)

A PHOENIX PRESS PAPERBACK

First published in Great Britain
by The Clarendon Press in 1989
First issued in paperback with corrections in 1991
This paperback edition published in 2001
by Phoenix Press,
a division of The Orion Publishing Group Ltd,
Orion House, 5 Upper St Martin's Lane,
London WC2H 9EA

A CIP catalogue record for this book is available from the British Library.

Printed and bound in Great Britain by
Butler & Tanner Ltd, Frome and London

ISBN 1 84212 421 8

ACKNOWLEDGEMENTS

MOST of the research for this book was completed in Moscow between September 1984 and December 1985. At the Main Archival Administration (GAU), where I worked in TsGAOR and TsGANKh, Liudmila Evgen'evna Selivanova, Tat'iana Feliksovna Bavarova, Ol'ga Mikhailovna Gibayants, and Elena Aleksandrovna Tiurina organized the delivery of many invaluable materials. Thanks are also due to the State Archive of Kuibyshev *oblast'* (GAKO), the Lenin Library, and the Institute for Scientific Information in the Social Sciences under the Academy of Sciences (*INOIN*). In the West, I have relied most heavily on the British Library, Cambridge University Library, the Library of Congress, and the New York Public Library.

I wish to thank the Master and Fellows of Trinity College, Cambridge, for supporting my work as a graduate student and electing me to a Research Fellowship in 1984. I am also indebted to the British Council, which sponsored several trips to the Soviet Union in 1984–5 and 1988.

The second section of Chapter 5 originally appeared in *Soviet Studies* (vol. 40, no. 1), whose editors kindly allowed the materials to be reproduced here in a slightly altered version. At Oxford University Press special thanks are due to George Tulloch, who made careful corrections to the final draft. I am also grateful to Stella Gutteridge, of the Geography Department at the University of Cambridge, who drew the excellent maps.

This is my first book, and it naturally bears the influence of the people who have taught and encouraged me. Norman Stone gave me, and many others at Cambridge, an approach to the study of European history that has stood me in good stead ever since. Teodor Shanin advised and inspired my work from the start: he gave me the passion and conviction required to argue my case. Viktor Danilov, above all, taught me to understand the complexities of Russian agrarian history which make its study so fascinating, and difficult.

I wish to thank a number of people who read and commented on parts of the manuscript at various stages of its life. Alec Nove read several chapters of an early draft, as well as the doctoral dissertation upon which Chapters 2, 3, and 5 were based. The dissertation was also read by John Barber, whose criticisms proved particularly useful during the later revisions of these chapters. Jana Howlett, who taught me Russian, read parts of the early drafts. Tim Mixter, Esther Kingston-Mann, Dan Field, Carol Leonard, Larry Epstein, and Sheila Ogilvie read and commented on conference papers which later became parts of the book. Special thanks are due to Jim Scott and Norman Stone, who read the complete manuscript. Needless to say, none of the people mentioned above is responsible for any shortcomings that may remain in the text.

I have benefited from discussions with John Channon, Don Raleigh, Hiroaki Kuromiya, David Shearer, Johnathan Aves, and Viktor Kabanov. Unfortunately, Kabanov's book on the peasant economy under war communism was published shortly after the completion of my manuscript. Our points of view coincide on a number of issues, and I have tried to make this clear wherever possible in the footnotes.

Last, but by no means least, I wish to thank Stephanie Palmer, who saw this book through from its early stages and put up with its difficult author.

O.F.

October 1988

CONTENTS

ILLUSTRATIONS

Plates (between pp. 208 and 209)

Figure (p. 202)

MAPS

TABLES

GLOSSARY OF RUSSIAN TERMS USED IN THE TEXT

arshin: measurement of length, equivalent to 71 cm.

artel' (pl. *arteli*): type of collective farm (*kolkhoz*)

bedniak: poor peasant

Cheka: Chrezvychainaia Komissiia; Extraordinary Commission for Struggle against Counter-Revolution and Sabotage

Chreznalog: Revolutionary Tax

desiatina (abbr. *des.*): measurement of land area, equivalent to 1.09 hectares, or 2.7 acres

funt: measurement of weight, equivalent to 0.41 kg.

guberniia: province (subdivided into *uezdy* and *volosti*)

khutor (pl. *khutora*): peasant farm or homestead with enclosed arable and domestic buildings

khutorianin (pl. *khutoriane*): farmer of a *khutor*

KNV: komitet narodnoi vlasti; committee of people's power (Samara province, 1917)

kolkhoz: *kollektivnoe khoziaistvo*; collective farm

kombed: *komitet bednoty*; committee of the rural poor

kommuna: type of collective farm (*kolkhoz*)

Komsomol: Kommunisticheskii soiuz molodezhi; Communist League of Youth

Komuch: Komitet chlenov Uchreditel'nogo Sobraniia; Committee of Member of the Constituent Assembly (anti-Bolshevik government, 1918)

kontributsiia: revolutionary tax

kop: copeck (1/100 rouble)

kustar' (pl. *kustari*): handicraftsman

mir: village commune

Narkomprod: Narodnyi komissariat prodovol'stviia; People's Commissariat of Provisions (RSFSR)

Narkomtrud: Narodnyi komissariat truda; People's Commissariat of Labour (RSFSR)

Narkomzem: Narodnyi komissariat zemledeliia; People's Commissariat of Agriculture (RSFSR)

narodnyi dom: people's house

NEP: New Economic Policy

NKVD: Narodnyi komissariat vnutrennikh del; People's Commissariat for Internal Affairs

obshchina: land commune

otrub (pl. *otruba*): peasant household farm with enclosed field strips

otrubnik (pl. *otrubniki*): farmer of an *otrub*

prodrazverstka: Bolshevik food levy

promysly: rural trades

pud: measurement of weight, equivalent to 16.38 kg.

raion: region (intermediary territorial-administrative division between *volost'* and *uezd*)

razverstka: levy, or tax quota

rb: rouble

revkom: revoliutsionnyi komitet; revolutionary committee

Revvoensovet: Revolutionary Military Soviet (of the Red Army)

RSFSR: Rossiiskaia Sovetskaia Federativnaia Sotsialisticheskaia Respublika; Russian Soviet Federative Socialist Republic

samosud: mob law

sazhen': measurement of length, equivalent to 2.13 m.; 2,400 square *sazhen'* = 1 *desiatina*

seredniak: middle peasant

skhod: village or communal gathering

soiuz frontovikov: union of front-line soldiers

sovkhoz: sovetskoe khoziaistvo; soviet (state) farm

sovnarkhoz: sovet narodnogo khoziaistva; local economic soviet (council)

Sovnarkom: Sovet narodnykh komissarov; Council of People's Commissars (RSFSR)

ssypnoi punkt: grain collection station

starosta: village elder

tovaroobmen: commodity exchange (under Narkomprod)

trudpovinnost': labour duty (under Narkomtrud)

TsSU: Tsentral'noe statisticheskoe upravlenie; Central Statistical Administration (RSFSR)

uezd (pl. *uezdy*): district; subdivision of *guberniia*

vershok: measurement of length, equivalent to 4.4 cm.

versta (pl. *versty*): measurement of distance, equivalent to 1.06 km.

VIK: *volostnoi ispolnitel'nyi komitet soveta* (*volispolkom*); *volost'* soviet executive committee

voenkom: voennyi komitet; military committee

volost' (pl. *volosti*): rural district; subdivision of *uezd*

VTsIK: Vserossiiskii tsentral'nyi ispolnitel'nyi komitet; All-Russian Central Soviet Executive Committee of Soviets

zemstvo: local self-government organ (pre-1917; under Komuch)

LIST OF ABBREVIATIONS

DGS	A. Okninsky, *Dva goda sredi krest'ian: Vidennoe, slyshannoe, perezhitoe v Tambovskoi gubernii s noiabria 1918 goda do noiabria 1920 goda*, Newtonville, Mass., 1986 (originally Riga, 1936).
DSV	*Dekrety Sovetskoi vlasti*, 10 vols., Moscow, 1957–76.
ISG	*Izvestiia samarskogo gubprodkoma* (Samara), 1918–19.
KK	V. V. Kabanov, *Krest'ianskoe khoziaistvo v usloviiakh 'voennogo kommunizma'*, Moscow, 1988.
MZR 1	*Materialy po zemel'noi reforme 1918 goda*, vyp. 1, *Raspredelenie zemli v 1918 godu*, Moscow, 1919.
MZR 6	*Materialy po zemel'noi reforme 1918 goda*, vyp. 6, *Otchuzhdenie i ispol'zovanie sel'sko-khoziaistvennogo inventaria*, Moscow, 1918.
PSG	*Protokoly saratovskogo gubernskogo s"ezda sovetov krest'ianskikh deputatov, proiskhodivshego v g. Saratove s 25-go maia po 2 iiunia 1918 g.*, Saratov, 1918.
PSS	V. I. Lenin, *Polnoe sobranie sochinenii*, 5th edn., 55 vols., Moscow, 1958–65.
PVO	S. P. Rudnev, *Pri vechernikh ogniakh: Vospominaniia*, Newtonville, Mass., 1978 (originally Kharbin, 1928).
PVS	*Protokoly 2-go samarskogo gubernskogo krest'ianskogo s"ezda s 20 maia po 6 iiunia 1917 g. i protokoly obshchegubernskogo vsesoslovnogo s"ezda s 28 maia po 6 iiunia 1917 g.*, Samara, 1917.
RR	V. P. Danilov, *Rural Russia under the New Regime*, trans. with an introd. by O. Figes, London, 1988 (originally *Sovetskaia dokolkhoznaia derevnia: Naselenie, zemlepol'zovanie, khoziaistvo*, Moscow, 1977).
SEV	V. P. Antonov-Saratovskii (ed.), *Sovety v epokhu voennogo kommunizma (1918–1921): Sbornik dokumentov*, 2 vols., Moscow, 1928–9.
SGB	*Biulleten' saratovskogo gubprodkoma (statisticheskii otdel)* (Saratov), 1918.
SS	*Sovetskoe stroitel'stvo* (Samara), 1918–19.
SU	*Sobranie uzakonenii i rasporiazhenii raboche-krest'ianskogo pravitel'stva*, Moscow, 1917–24.
GAKO	Gosudarstvennyi Arkhiv Kuibyshevskoi Oblasti (State Archive of Kuibyshev *oblast'*).
TsGANKh	Tsentral'nyi Gosudarstvennyi Arkhiv Narodnogo Khoziaistva (Central State Archive of the National Economy).
TsGAOR	Tsentral'nyi Gosudarstvennyi Arkhiv Oktiabr'skoi Revoliutsii (Central State Archive of the October Revolution).
f.	*fond* (collection).
op.	*opis'* (inventory).
d.	*delo* (file).
l.	*list* (folio).

NOTE ON DATES

All dates before 1 February 1918 are given according to the Julian (Old Style) calendar, which ran thirteen days behind the Gregorian (New Style) calendar in use in western Europe. The Gregorian calendar was adopted in Russia on the day following 31 January 1918, which was declared to be 14 February. All dates after this are given in the New Style.

1
Introduction

> Nothing would so certainly have altered the course of the Russian revolution as a higher level of education and material well-being among the peasantry.
>
> W. H. Chamberlin, *The Russian Revolution*

MANY historians outside the Soviet Union have sought to explain why the Bolsheviks won the civil war. Some have focused on the military history of 1918–20. Others have connected the victory of the Red Army to the growth of the Soviet state. But none has made a detailed study of the relationship between the Bolsheviks and the peasantry, the overwhelming majority of the Russian population, during the formative years of the Soviet regime.[1] None has seriously investigated the ways in which the Bolshevik victory was made possible by the transformation of the Russian countryside in the years leading up to and during the revolution. That is the purpose of this book.

Nearly all of the following narrative takes place behind the military lines. The civil war is treated here not so much as a straight military conflict as part of the revolutionary process itself—the process of state destruction and political reconstruction, related to the transformation of social relations. This is not to deny the importance of the military struggle: the civil war, like any war, had to be won by superior military force. But it is to emphasize that in a civil war any military victory will be short-lived unless it is backed by political power. The Russian civil war was, to borrow the phrase of Clausewitz, no more than the continuation by military means of the political struggles begun in 1917. The tasks of military organization were inextricably connected with the broader purposes of state-building and socio-economic control.

The peasantry, in this respect, presented a particular problem. On the one hand, the support of the peasants was essential to the conduct

[1] Four in five subjects of the Russian Empire on the eve of the First World War were registered as peasants. The urban working class, the main social basis of support for the Bolshevik party in 1917, numbered, properly speaking, only 3 to 4 million people out of a total population of 160 million. Soviet historians have produced much larger estimates of the 'proletariat' (up to 18 million), by including building and transport workers, domestic servants, artisans, agricultural labourers, and peasant workers in industry. By the end of the civil war the size of the urban working class had been halved compared with 1913.

of any military campaign. The Red Army was made up largely of peasants, and the White Army contained significant numbers of them. Both armies were fed and transported by peasants. Most of their footwear and saddlery, and a good share of their clothing, was manufactured by peasant craftsmen. Even their military performance depended upon a wide variety of labour services by the peasantry, such as the clearing of snow from roads and railways, the breaking-up of ice on rivers, and the digging of fortifications and graves. On the other hand, in the early stages of the civil war the two main protagonists had neither the political authority, nor the means of coercion, to ensure the mobilization of the peasantry and its property for their respective military campaigns. The officers and civilian leaders of the White movement were too closely associated with the old landowning class and the urban bourgeoisie to have any real influence over the peasantry once the agrarian revolution had been completed in 1917–18. But the division of the gentry estates, the destruction of the old state apparatus in the rural areas, and the establishment of the *volost'* soviets, which at the beginning of the revolution were decentralized organs of peasant self-rule, not only undermined the counter-revolution and the restoration of parliamentary rule; they also complicated the Bolsheviks' own tasks of military and political organization in the countryside. To be sure, the Bolsheviks had stolen some of the traditional peasant support for the Socialist Revolutionaries (SRs) during the autumn of 1917 by legalizing the peasant seizures of the gentry estates and declaring 'All power to the soviets!'. But once this had been done, they had no further means—apart from propaganda—of mobilizing peasant support for their own political campaign against the Whites and the SRs. The Bolsheviks were a party of the urban working class and had no traditions of political organization in the countryside (the whole of the Volga region had only fourteen non-metropolitan Bolshevik party cells in August 1917).[2] Orthodox Leninist ideology was committed to the collectivization of agricultural production in large mechanized farms, and was opposed in the long term to the survival of the peasant family economy. The policies of war communism (1918–21), which many Bolsheviks viewed as the quickest path to socialism, were bitterly resented by the peasants, who were widely expected—by Marxists and non-Marxists alike—to rise against the Bolshevik regime, as the peasants of the Vendée and other regions of revolutionary France had risen against the Jacobins.

How did the Bolsheviks ever win the civil war, given these problems in the rural sector? Why did the peasantry of central Russia remain, on

[2] V. V. Anikeev, 'Svedeniia o bol'shevistskikh organizatsiiakh s marta po dekabr' 1917 goda', *Voprosy istorii KPSS*, 1958, no. 2, p. 133.

the whole, loyal to the Bolsheviks, whose policies and methods of rule were so alien to the well-being of the peasant family farms? This book is the history of a 'missing counter-revolution'.

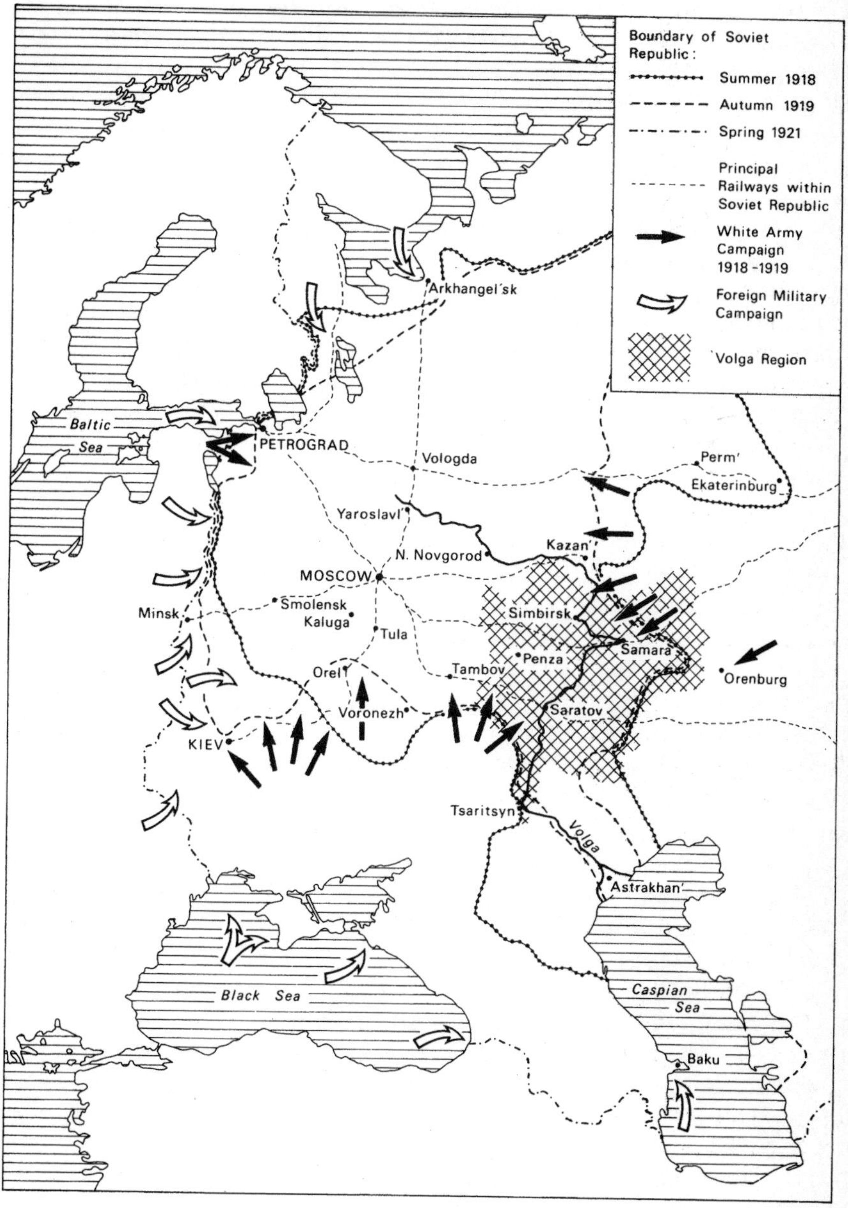

Map 1. *The Russian civil war*

Geography provides part of the explanation for the Bolshevik victory. The Bolsheviks retained control of the industrial heartland of central Russia, whose web of railways, converging on Moscow, enabled the Red Army to operate on internal lines (see Map 1). The anti-Bolshevik armies were dispersed on several fronts, and were largely dependent upon military units whose commitment to the overthrow of the Soviet regime was unreliable. The Don Cossacks, as Peter Kenez has pointed out, 'fought well when they were defending their own territory, but when Denikin ordered them to march north against Moscow, their enthusiasm quickly faded'.[3] The Bolsheviks also benefited from the simple fact that it was more prestigious to rule from Moscow (and to have possession of Petrograd) than it was to issue decrees from such far-flung 'capitals' as Samara, Arkhangel'sk, Omsk, or Ekaterinodar. Starting from the hungry north gave the Red Army the added advantage that every advance into the White-occupied agricultural regions of the south would improve the food situation; by contrast, the Whites 'had to carry with them food not only for themselves, but also for the population of the territories wrested by them from the Reds'.[4]

The political skills of the Bolsheviks were another important factor in their victory. The ideological commitment of the Bolsheviks to a clear revolutionary goal, the charismatic leadership of Lenin and Trotsky, the Bolsheviks' brilliant use of propaganda, the superior organization of the Red Army, and, above all, the disciplined strength of the Bolshevik party itself gave the Reds a decided advantage over their enemies. The anti-Bolsheviks were hopelessly divided between those who supported the democratic forces of the February revolution and those who wanted a return to the monarchy, or some other authoritarian order. None of the White armies was able to build effective institutions of government in the areas under its nominal rule. This was partly the result of the White generals' habitual mistrust of political methods and politicians, a mistrust which had been reinforced by the Provisional Government's 'betrayal' of the army in 1917. But it was also the result of a deeper social division between the peasantry and the *burzhui* (the propertied classes), who were seen to epitomize in social terms the anti-Bolshevik movement. It is symbolic that at the critical stages of their campaigns the armies of Kolchak and Denikin were crippled by peasant uprisings behind the White lines. The Red Army also suffered from peasant uprisings, but at the critical

[3] P. Kenez, *Civil War in South Russia, 1919–1920: The Defeat of the Whites*, Berkeley, Calif., 1977, p. 21.

[4] D. D. F. White, *The Growth of the Red Army*, Princeton, 1944, p. 122. White paraphrased the argument of Pavel Miliukov in *Rossiia na perelome*, vol. 1, Paris, 1927, p. 177.

moments the rural areas behind the Red lines remained solid.[5] The peasants' dislike of the Bolsheviks, it would seem, was not as powerful, and certainly not as ingrained, as their hatred and fear of the old political order.

The strategic advantages and superior political skills of the Reds are not sufficient, however, to explain the outcome of the civil war. In a military struggle for power in the wake of a social revolution the victor must involve representative groups in its own projects of political reconstruction. To a large extent, the victory of the Bolsheviks in the Russian civil war may be explained by their ability to integrate lower-class elements into the construction of the Soviet regime through the local soviets and mass-membership organizations (e.g. the party, the Red Army, and the Komsomol, or Communist youth league).[6] In this respect, they had a clearer understanding than their political rivals of the relationship between civil war and the process of state-building. The civil war, as Sheila Fitzpatrick has remarked, 'was not an unforeseeable act of God for which the Bolsheviks were in no way responsible'.[7] During the winter of 1917–18 the Bolsheviks had knowingly risked—and perhaps even sought—civil war by seizing power on the eve of the Second Soviet Congress (25 October), by closing down the SR-dominated Constituent Assembly (6 January), and by signing the 'shameful peace' of Brest-Litovsk (3 March). Indeed, in so far as they lacked a national base of political support during the winter of 1917–18, the Bolsheviks, as Fitzpatrick explains, stood to benefit from the consequences of a civil war:

> A civil war, if the Bolsheviks could win it, represented the best hope of consolidating the new regime, whose position at the beginning of 1918 was extremely precarious. The predictable costs of a civil war—social polarization, violence, wartime emphasis on unity and discipline, wartime centralization, and emergency rule—were costs that the Bolsheviks were ready or even anxious to pay. The benefit, of course, was that the Revolution should have its 'heroic period' of struggle and emerge strengthened and legitimized by victory.[8]

If the civil war gave the Bolsheviks the chance to build a new state apparatus, then who were the social élites of the emergent regime in the rural areas? To extend its influence to the countryside the Soviet

[5] W. H. Chamberlin, *The Russian Revolution 1917–1921*, vol. 2, Princeton, 1987 (Originally New York, 1935), p. 455.

[6] I have found Theda Skocpol's comments *(States and Social Revolutions*, Cambridge, 1979, pp. 161–73, 206–35) very useful in formulating my ideas on this theme.

[7] S. Fitzpatrick, *The Russian Revolution 1917–1932*, Oxford, 1982, p. 65.

[8] S. Fitzpatrick, 'The Civil War as a Formative Experience', in A. Gleason, P. Kenez, and R. Stites (eds.), *Bolshevik Culture*, Bloomington, Ind., 1985, p. 74.

government would have to find supporters among the rural population capable of integrating the peasantry into the new regime and neutralizing peasant resistance.

Orthodox Soviet historians under Stalin and (to a lesser exent) Brezhnev approached this issue within the framework of Lenin's writings up to and including 1917–18.[9] In these writings (especially those before 1905), Lenin emphasized the development of capitalism in Russia and its effects on the socio-economic differentiation ('disintegration') of the peasantry. He believed that the emergence of an agrarian capitalist class (the 'kulaks') and its socio-economic exploitation of the weakest peasantry had already created the conditions for a socialist revolution in the countryside. During the 'bourgeois-democratic' stage of the agrarian revolution (spring 1917 to summer 1918) Lenin argued that the peasantry was acting as a united class for the seizure of the gentry estates and the democratic election of the village soviets. But he maintained that the urban-proletarian revolution would necessarily give rise to a conflict in the countryside between the 'rural proletariat' (the poor and landless peasants) and the 'rural bourgeoisie' (the 'kulaks', the clergy, and the rural intelligentsia hostile to Bolshevik power). According to Lenin, this 'socialist stage' of the revolution began in the countryside during the early summer of 1918, when the civil war proper commenced, and the Bolsheviks established committees of the rural poor (*kombedy*) to expropriate the property of the 'kulaks' under the 'food dictatorship'. Thus, the consolidation of the Soviet regime in the countryside after the summer of 1918 is presented by Soviet historians as the victory of the 'rural proletariat' (under the leadership of the Bolshevik party) in the class, or civil, war against the 'rural bourgeoisie' and the anti-Bolshevik parties.

The standard of historical scholarship within this orthodoxy has not been very high. Documents have been deliberately selected to support the orthodox Soviet viewpoints. The perceptions of contemporary Soviet and Bolshevik officials have been cited without reservation as objective evidence of actual social conditions. The peasantry has been inappropriately analysed in 'class terms' derived from the observation of West European industrial societies. Very little attempt has been made to observe the peasantry during the revolution through its own historical records (e.g. the minutes of communal and

[9] See e.g. *Istoriia grazhdanskoi voiny v SSSR*, 5 vols., Moscow, 1937–60; B. M. Morozov, *Sozdanie i ukreplenie sovetskogo gosudarstvennogo apparata (noiabr' 1917 g.–mart 1919 g.)*, Moscow, 1957; I. I. Mints, *Istoriia Velikogo Oktiabria*, 3 vols., Moscow, 1967–73; E. G. Gimpel'son, *Sovety v gody interventsii i grazhdanskoi voiny*, Moscow, 1968; V. M. Selunskaia, *Rabochii klass i Oktiabr' v derevne*, Moscow, 1968; ead., *Izmeneniia sotsial'noi struktury sovetskogo obshchestva, oktiabr' 1917–1920 gg.*, Moscow, 1976.

village meetings). Political events in the capital and changes of Bolshevik policy towards the peasantry have served instead of meaningful social processes as the major divisions of historical periodization. This, for the most part, has been a lifeless 'pseudo-history' written by bureaucrats.

The historical orthodoxy was seriously challenged, however, in the period following the Twentieth Party Congress (1956) by a group of younger Soviet historians under the influence of Lenin's post-revolutionary writings. The weakness of the 'kulaks', the continued domination of the middle peasantry, and the failure of the poor peasants to develop a 'proletarian' consciousness after 1918 encouraged Lenin to reconsider the characteristics of Russian peasant society and the significance within it of capitalist relations. Whereas Lenin had previously emphasized the predominance of capitalism in rural Russia, he now stressed its limited nature and interaction with other types of rural social relations. He characterized the post-revolutionary countryside as a complex of five interlocking socio-economic structures: patriarchalism, petty-commodity production, capitalism, state capitalism, and socialism. Within this multistructured system (*mnogoukladnost'*), the spontaneous capitalist tendencies of the peasantry were checked and balanced by the state and the collective social-levelling mechanisms of the peasant commune (*mir, obshchina*). This understanding was essential to Lenin's conception of the New Economic Policy (NEP) during the 1920s, when the government sought to encourage the collectivism of the peasantry and its integration into the socialist regime through the regulation of the market economy and the establishment of agricultural co-operatives.[10]

Lenin's last writings provide an interesting theoretical base on which to analyse the peasantry in the revolutionary period. They have greatly influenced the works of V. P. Danilov on the peasantry during the 1920s,[11] and A. M. Anfimov on rural Russia before the revolution.[12]

[10] V. I. Lenin, *Polnoe sobranie sochinenii* 5th edn., 55 vols., Moscow, 1958–65 (henceforth referred to as *PSS*), vol. 43, p. 158. For further discussion see S. Cohen, *Bukharin and the Bolshevik Revolution*, Oxford, 1980, ch. 5; T. Cox, *Peasants, Class and Capitalism*, Oxford, 1986, pp. 20–79; V. P. Danilov, *Rural Russia Under the New Regime*, trans. with an introd. by O. Figes, London, 1988 (originally *Sovetskaia* dokolkhoznaia derevnia: naselenie, zemlepol'zovanie, khoziaistva, Moscow, 1977, henceforth referred to as *RR*), pp. 30–4.

[11] See e.g. *RR*; V. P. Danilov, *Sovetskaia dokolkhoznaia derevnia: sotsial'naia struktura, sotsial'nye otnosheniia*, Moscow, 1979; id., 'Zemel'nye otnosheniia v sovetskoi dokolkhoznoi derevne', *Istoriia SSSR*, 1958, no. 3; id., 'O kharaktere sotsial'no-ekonomicheskikh otnoshenii sovetskogo krest'ianstva do kollektivizatsii sel'skogo khoziaistva', in *Istoriia sovetskogo krest'ianstva i kolkhoznogo stroitel'stva v SSSR*, Moscow, 1963; id., 'K kharakteristike obshchestvenno-politicheskoi obstanovki v sovetskoi derevne nakanune kollektivizatsii', *Istoricheskie zapiski*, vol. 79, Moscow, 1966; id., 'K voprosu o kharaktere i znachenii krest'ianskoi pozemel'noi obshchiny v

Danilov and Anfimov have stressed the primitive and complex nature of agrarian capitalism in Russia—its interconnection with natural-patriarchal and neo-feudal social forms, and its geographical limitation to certain areas of commercial agriculture on the periphery of central Russia. They have underlined the strength of the peasantry's traditional institutions, their ability to survive under capitalism, and their potential for socialist development. More recently, Soviet historians and historical anthropologists have examined the peasant commune and other institutions during the nineteenth century, highlighting the complexities of Russian rural society and the traditions of peasant self-organization.[13] However, with the exception of V. V. Kabanov's work, there has been little attempt by Soviet historians to re-evaluate in the light of Lenin's last writings the system of rural social relations during the revolutionary period itself.[14]

Until very recently, Western historians have been unable to work on the revolutionary period in Soviet archives. This is a severe handicap for the historian of the Russian peasantry, given the political bias and urban orientation of the published Soviet (and *émigré*) sources and the general unreliability of rural statistics during the revolution. A major publication was Teodor Shanin's *The Awkward Class*,[15] which developed some of the Neo-Populist theories of the late nineteenth and early twentieth centuries in an attempt to explain the particular characteristics of Russian peasant society—its inability to become 'capitalist' and failure to fit into the communist system. Shanin's views of Russian rural society as a particular culture on the periphery

Rossii', in *Problemy sotsial'no-ekonomicheskoi istorii Rossii*, Moscow, 1971; id., 'Obshchina u narodov SSSR v posleoktiabr'skii period: K voprosu o tipologii obshchiny na territorii sovetskikh respublik', *Narody Azii i Afriki*, 1973, no. 3.

[12] A. M. Anfimov, 'K voprosu o kharaktere agrarnogo stroia Evropeiskoi Rossii XX v.', *Istoricheskie zapiski*, vol. 65, Moscow, 1959; id., *Zemel'naia arenda v Rossii v nachale XX veka*, Moscow, 1961; id., *Rossiiskaia derevnia v gody pervoi mirovoi voiny*, Moscow, 1962; id., *Krupnoe pomeshchich'e khoziaistvo Evropeiskoi Rossii*, Moscow, 1969; id., *Krest'ianskoe khoziaistvo Evropeiskoi Rossii 1881–1904*, Moscow, 1980; id., *Ekonomicheskoe polozhenie i klassovaia bor'ba krest'ian Evropeiskoi Rossii 1881–1904*, Moscow, 1984.

[13] V. A. Aleksandrov, *Sel'skaia obshchina v Rossii (XVIII v.–nachalo XIX v.)*, Moscow, 1976; M. M. Gromyko, 'Territorial'naia krest'ianskaia obshchina Sibiri (30–e gg. XVIII v.–60e gg. XIX v.)', in *Krest'ianskaia obshchina v Sibiri XVII v.–nachala XX v.*, Novosibirsk, 1977; L. S. Prokof'eva, *Krest'ianskaia obshchina v Rossii vo vtoroi polovine XVIII v.–pervoi polovine XIX v.*, Leningrad, 1981; L. I. Kuchumova, 'Sel'skaia pozemel'naia obshchina Evropeiskoi Rossii v 60-e–70-e gody XIX v.', *Istoricheskie zapiski*, vol. 106, 1981; B. Mironov, 'The Russian Peasant Commune after the Reforms of the 1860s', *Slavic Review*, vol. 44, 1985.

[14] V. V. Kabanov, 'Otkiabr'skaia revoliutsiia i krest'ianskaia obshchina', *Istoricheskie zapiski*, vol. 111, Moscow, 1984; id., *Krest'ianskoe khoziaistvo v usloviiakh 'voennogo kommunizma'*, Moscow, 1988 (henceforth referred to as *KK*); id., *Oktiabr'skaia revoliutsiia i kooperatsiia (1917–mart 1919g.)*, Moscow, 1973.

[15] T. Shanin, *The Awkward Class*, Oxford, 1972.

of Western capitalism have been immensely influential on the study of the Russian peasantry during the pre-revolutionary period. Moshe Lewin's *Russian Peasants and Soviet Power*,[16] which shares a number of Shanin's views, has had a similar influence on the study of the Soviet peasantry during the 1920s. However, we still lack a detailed study of the peasantry during 1917–21. Graeme Gill's monograph focused on the breakdown of political relations between the Provisional Government and the peasantry during 1917, but said little about the development of peasant institutions and social relations in the rural localities.[17] Some of the general studies of the revolution and civil war have included useful information about rural affairs, but they have lacked detailed social analysis to support their generalizations. Too many Western historians have portrayed the consolidation of the Soviet regime in the countryside as an imposition of power by 'outside' forces without satisfactorily explaining how—or by whom—this was carried out.

The following study—the first detailed non-Soviet history of the peasantry during 1917–21—examines the social forces behind the consolidation of the Bolshevik dictatorship in the countryside. The archival records of the village communes and soviets and higher government bodies, upon which this book is based, suggest that neither the orthodox Soviet interpretation ('class struggle'), nor the standard western one ('imposition by outsiders'), is able to explain satisfactorily the complex social changes underlying the emergence of the new regime. The key to the problem lies in a much broader range of socio-economic, cultural, and institutional relations, which must be seen in the context of Russian social development since the turn of the century, and, in particular, since 1914. These relations may be grouped in the following general analytical categories, requiring study as a complex whole:

1. Relations between the peasants, grouped by socio-economic status, sex, age, literacy, social 'standing', etc.
2. Relations between the peasantry and non-peasant rural groups (e.g. squires, merchants, craftsmen, clergymen, the rural intelligentsia, in-migrant townsmen).
3. The relationship between the village community and the peasant households (i.e. the conformity of peasant social behaviour).
4. Relations between neighbouring village communities.
5. Peasant–state relations.

16 M. Lewin, *Russian Peasants and Soviet Power: A Study of Collectivization*, London, 1968.

17 G. J. Gill, *Peasants and Government in the Russian Revolution*, London, 1979.

1. THE RUSSIAN PEASANTRY ON THE EVE OF THE REVOLUTION

The basic institution of the Russian peasantry, the peasant household, was both a farm (*khoziaistvo*) and a domestic family unit (*dvor*). The peasant family was always the main, and usually the only, labour force on the farm (i.e. hired labour was an exception).[18] It consumed directly the greater part of the farm product, or used the money received from its sale to purchase goods on the market. Many peasant families, especially during the winter season, fabricated household goods from their own agricultural products (*promysly*) and other raw materials, such as simple furniture, agricultural tools, shoes, clogs, and vodka. The domestic economy (housework, work in the yard, crafts) and the field economy were thus closely intertwined.

The typical peasant household of European Russia consisted of a hut or house (*izba*), with a number of outbuildings attached to it in an enclosed formation around a central yard.[19] Some of the outbuildings were used for storage of food and clothes, some for stalling young animals, and some for sleeping space in the summer. During the winter the peasants and the animals slept indoors—the peasants on high platforms over the stove in the hut, and the animals in the adjoining outbuildings. At the back of the homestead there was a small kitchen garden, rarely larger than an acre in size and usually considerably smaller, in which the peasant family grew fruit and vegetables and sometimes specialist crops, such as tobacco or flax.

The living conditions of the majority of the peasants were, by any standards, wretched. An English Quaker relief worker in Samara province in the Volga region described some typical conditions in the early part of 1924:

> Actual living conditions are almost indescribably miserable, and even those of the richer peasants would be utterly condemned in any part of England . . . The best houses have some appearance of solidity and comfort, being built of trimmed logs, well jointed, with a short iron roof, inner walls lined with matchboarding, and floor boards well raised from the ground. The average log hut has a thatched roof, unlined walls, and floor boards often laid onto the earth. Meanest and most wretched of all is the mud hut, with walls that crack in summer and are washed away in the spring floods, and a floor of beaten clay or earth . . . A brick house, or one with two stories, is rarely seen. More often than not the cowshed and stable are built against the side of the hut, and the

[18] The vast majority of peasant households comprised blood relatives or relatives by marriage. However, it was not unusual for a household to adopt a non-related member, and customary law in many places recognized the rights of adopted sons to be equal to those of kin.

[19] An excellent description of peasant housing conditions in central Russia during the mid-19th c. may be found in S. Hoch, *Serfdom and Social Control in Russia*, Chicago, 1986, pp. 56–64.

horse and cow are the first to greet newcomers as they enter the door. Chickens and goats, and even pigs, sheep and heifers, where they exist, are often co-habitants of the one room that serves as living room and kitchen, adding their quota of moist warmth and close stale smell. The lack of a convenient water supply makes cleanliness difficult even in the summer, and in the winter water is avoided as much as possible. Winter indeed throws into relief the miserable conditions . . . The husbandman sits discussing local politics and farmers' questions with neighbours, all smoking vile-smelling, home-cured tobacco screwed up in newspaper. The housewife is busy spinning flax or hemp . . . and the children sit dumbly around the wall. Doors are kept vigorously closed, windows are hermetically sealed, and the atmosphere cannot be described, its poisonous quality can only be realised by experience. The only light during the long evening comes from a paraffin lamp, often home made . . . The universal habit of chewing sunflower seeds and spitting the husks onto the floor adds to the untidiness and filth of the hut.[20]

The economy of the typical peasant farm may be characterized as a semi-natural system of small-scale agricultural production. The main productive forces were natural (land, physical labour, and animal draught-power), rather than man-made or industrial (e.g. tools, machines, irrigation systems, and other 'capital' inputs).[21] Hard physical toil with simple hand tools and inadequate draught-power was the basis of peasant farming in Russia, as it still is today in most of the Third World. Few peasant households in Russia were lucky enough to claim the possession of more than one horse, or any of the modern farming tools commonly found in Europe at the end of the nineteenth century. The light wooden scratch-plough (*sokha*), similar to the *aratrum* of the Roman Empire, dominated peasant farming in central and northern Russia until the present century.[22] The small hand sickle was still used on most peasant farms in Russia at the time of the revolution, more than a half-century after it had been superseded by the scythe and the heavy reaping hook in the rest of Europe.[23] The other main tasks of field-work—sowing, threshing, and winnowing—

[20] *Some Notes on Social Conditions in Soviet Russia*, The Friends' Council, London, 1925, pp. 6–7.

[21] V. P. Danilov stresses this contrast to differentiate between peasants and capitalist farmers. This marks a clear break from the traditional Soviet-Marxist emphasis on commoditization (integration into the market) and the system of production relations in making this distinction. See my article, 'V. P. Danilov on the Analytical Distinction Between Peasants and Farmers', in T. Shanin (ed.), *Peasants and Peasant Societies*, 2nd edn., Oxford, 1987, pp. 121–4.

[22] On the history of the *sokha* and other tillage implements see R. E. F. Smith, *Peasant Farming in Muscovy*, Cambridge, 1977.

[23] *RR*, pp. 268–9; E. J. T,. Collins, 'Labour Supply and Demand in European Agriculture 1800–1880', in E. L. Jones and S. J. Woolf (eds.), *Agrarian Change and Economic Development*, London, 1969, pp. 79–92.

continued to be done by hand long after suitable machines had been introduced into western Europe.

Because of the overwhelming importance of human toil in the peasant household economy, the productive capacity of the latter was greatly influenced by demographic factors. It was not coincidental that the richest peasant households were also often found to have the largest number of able-bodied workers relative to the number of consumers. Some Russian agrarian economists at the turn of the century, such as A. V. Chayanov, N. P. Makarov, and A. N. Chelintsev, went as far as to argue that the family structure of the peasant household was at least as important as the ownership of means of production in determining the production and socio-economic status of the family farm.[24] One does not have to go as far as that, however, to appreciate the significance of the household family structure in the peasant economy. Households with a relatively large number of female or dependent members (i.e. young children and old people) were often found to be weaker in the agricultural economy (though not necessarily in handicrafts). A household with several adult male workers was likely to prosper, whereas the custom of partitioning the family property on the marriage of each of the sons (*razdel*) broke up or parcellated the means of production of the household and hence weakened it. This weakening resulted not only from the parcellation of property, but also from the break-up of the family work-force, since the labour co-operation of the family members was an additional production value, over and above the sum of its parts.[25]

The production of the peasant family farm was oriented towards the creation of use values (the farm income measured mainly in terms of its value for domestic consumption needs), as opposed to profit values. Unlike the capitalist agricultural enterprise, or the proto-industrial household, the typical Russian peasant farm was only marginally integrated into the market economy. The majority of the arable in peasant use was held in communal tenure, rather than rented or purchased. The size of the peasant farm's marketable agricultural surplus was normally small, while some of the household goods it required could be fabricated at home or obtained through natural exchange. The peasant farm rarely hired waged employees, since the family's labour was usually adequate, while the assistance of neighbours could be sought during the peak periods of the agricultural cycle. The comparative independence of the peasant farm from the market

[24] A. V. Chayanov, *The Theory of Peasant Economy*, ed. D. Thorner, B. Kerblay, and R. E. F. Smith, Manchester, 1986; N. P. Makarov, *Krest'ianskoe khoziaistvo i ego evoliutsiia*, vol. 1, Moscow, 1920; A. N. Chelintsev, *Teoreticheskie osnovaniia organizatsii krest'ianskogo khoziaistva*, Khar'kov, 1919.

[25] *RR*, pp. 240–58.

sheltered it from the adverse economic pressures of the dominant social system within which it was integrated. This helps to account for the survival of small- and medium-scale family farming under the capitalist system. A decrease in the profitability of agricultural production, brought about by a fall in food prices or a rise in capital rents, could be counteracted on the peasant family farms, but not in the capitalist enterprise, through overproduction (producing more commodities, and thereby increasing the exploitation of one's own family's labour at deflated monetary values).[26] The relative independence of the peasant farmers from the market also helps to account for their ability to retreat into subsistence production and autarky during periods of economic crisis and dislocation between town and country, such as the Russian revolution and civil war.

The vast majority of Russian peasant households were settled in self-governing village communes. Nearly all the arable land in European Russia was held and administered within the repartitional land commune (*peredel'naia pozemel'naia obshchina*), whose territory usually coincided with that of the village commune (*mir, sel'skaia obshchina*). Only in the extreme north-west and parts of the Ukraine was a significant proportion of the peasantry's land in hereditary tenure. In the Volga region repartitional communal land tenure was universal until the Stolypin land reforms (1906–11), which encouraged the peasants to leave the system of strip-farming in the commune and consolidate their arable holdings (*otruba*) or set up fully enclosed farmsteads (*khutora*).[27]

Through the communal assembly of household elders (*mirskii skhod*) and the general village assembly (*sel'skii skhod*), the peasant commune (i.e. the village commune and the land commune) regulated the entire spectrum of rural affairs. It set the common patterns of cultivation and grazing necessitated by the open-field system. It periodically redistributed the household arable strips (usually in three fields) according to the number of labourers or consumers ('eaters') in each peasant household. It managed the woods and the pasture, hired shepherds and watchmen and purchased the village bull. It organized the maintenance of roads, bridges, and communal buildings (including the school and the church). It collected state and communal taxes and

26 This phenomenon was discussed equally by Chayanov ('self-exploitation'), Kautsky ('over-work and under-consumption'), and Lenin ('plunder of labour'). See Chayanov, ch. 2; K. Kautsky, *Die Agrarfrage*, Stuttgart, 1889, pp. 106–16; *PSS*, vol. 19, p. 343.

27 In 1905 all the allotment land in the middle Volga and the Volga-Don region was registered in communal tenure. In the trans-Volga region the proportion was 99 per cent. In 50 provinces of European Russia 83 per cent of the allotment land was in communal tenure (D. Atkinson, *The End of the Russian Land Commune 1905–1930*, Stanford, 1983, p. 4).

carried out the mobilization of soldiers and labour teams. It maintained public order, arbitrated minor disputes, and administered local justice. It regulated public and religious holidays. It was responsible for fighting fires and coping with other natural calamities. And it organized simple welfare schemes and forms of neighbourhood co-operation (*pomoch'*) on behalf of soldiers' wives, widows, orphans, and other dependants. In some places this even included the collective cultivation of part of the arable to provide communal grain stores.[28]

The commune was more than a neighbourhood association of peasant households. It represented the peasant world in microcosm, and could engender strong feelings of solidarity among the fellow villagers (*odnosel'chane, zemliaki*), who were bound together by their common ties to the land and the community. The commune set the social customs and the moral standards of peasant life, within which even the most entrepreneurial farmer was forced to operate; and it enforced these behavioural norms through a wide variety of informal social controls, such as 'village opinion', 'mob law' (*samosud*), 'rough music' or *charivari* (noisy nocturnal processions designed to keep awake and humiliate those who had digressed local norms), and the patriarchal sanction of village elders.[29] These controls served to integrate the peasant community into a cohesive body capable of defending itself against outside interests, such as the state, the landlord, and other village communes. It was characteristic that decisions at the communal and village assemblies were passed unanimously,[30] usually after several hours of apparently chaotic shouting and drinking among the peasant men, although the actual power to influence the decisions lay in the hands of a few of the more substantial peasant farmers. This was a political culture dominated by patriarchal hierarchies, the force of tradition, and the need for general consensus.

The Emancipation decrees of the early 1860s liberated the peasant

[28] On *pomoch'* see M. M. Gromyko, 'Obychai pomochei u russkikh krest'ian v XIX v. (K probleme kompleksnogo issledovaniia trudovykh traditsii)', *Sovetskaia etnografiia*, 1981, nos. 4–5. On collective cultivation in the commune see my article on 'Collective Farming and the 19th-Century Russian Land Commune: A Research Note', *Soviet Studies*, vol. 38, no. 1, 1986, pp. 89–97.

[29] Mironov, pp. 444 ff. On the *samosud* and *charivari* see C. Frierson, 'Crime and Punishment in the Russian Village: Rural Concepts of Criminality at the End of the Nineteenth Century', *Slavic Review*, vol. 45, 1986; S. Frank, 'Popular Justice, Community and Culture among the Russian Peasantry, 1870–1900', *Russian Review*, vol. 46, no. 3, 1987.

[30] 'Communal measures are generally carried . . . by acclamation; but it sometimes happens that there is such a diversity of opinion that it is difficult to tell which of the two parties has a majority. In this case the Elder requests the one party to stand to the right, the other to the left. The two groups are then counted, and the minority submits, for no one ever dreams of opposing openly the will of the *mir*' (D. M. Wallace, *Russia*, Princeton, 1961, p. 278).

commune from the local structure of feudal power and integrated it into a new structure of state administration in the *volost'* township. The 'rural society' (*sel'skoe obshchestvo*), which became the new official term for the village commune, was made collectively responsible before the state for the redemption payment of the nobles' land received during Emancipation as well as the other traditional obligations of the commune. The society was to elect representatives who, along with the village elders (*sel'skie starosty*) and the tax collectors, attended the *volost'* assembly. The latter had its own elder (*starshina*) and a court, which administered justice according to local customary law. The *volost'* administration stood at a level below the gentry-dominated *zemstva* in the district towns. The continued autonomy of the communes in the most important areas of rural administration (e.g. land use, tax collection, military recruitment) created serious problems of political decentralization, giving rise to an increasing level of central government intervention in the countryside, from the land captains (*zemskie nachal'niki*) of the 1890s to the rural officials who implemented the Stolypin reforms after 1906.[31] The 1917 revolution in the countryside reflected the reaction of the peasantry against the encroaching power of the state in its affairs.

In recent years there has been considerable historical controversy in the West concerning trends in the late nineteenth-century peasant economy. The traditional view of the peasantry being impoverished by over-population, labour immobility, technological stagnation, declining productivity, and increasing state taxation has been challenged by a number of historians whose data suggest much more buoyant levels of agricultural productivity and lighter rates of state taxation.[32] There is not enough space here to review the debate in full. However, we do need to consider, if only in passing, some of the regional aspects of the

[31] See G. Yaney, *The Urge to Mobilize: Agrarian Reform in Russia, 1861–1930*, Urbana, Ill., 1982; D. A. J. Macey, *Government and Peasant in Russia, 1861–1906*, De Kalb, Ill., 1987.

[32] For a classic statement of the traditional view see A. Gerschenkron, 'Agrarian Policies and Industrialization in Russia, 1861–1917', in *Cambridge Economic History of Europe*, vol. 6, pt. 2, Cambridge, 1965, pp. 706–800. For the revisionist view see J. Y. Simms, 'The Crisis in Russian Agriculture at the End of the Nineteenth Century: A Different View', *Slavic Review*, vol. 36, 1977, pp. 377–98; E. M. W. Wilbur, 'Was Russian Peasant Agriculture Really That Impoverished?', *Journal of Economic History*, vol. 43, no. 1, 1983, pp. 137–47. In loose support of the revisionist view see P. Gregory, 'Grain Marketings and Peasant Consumption in Russia, 1885–1913', *Explorations in Economic History*, vol. 17, 1980, pp. 135–64; id., 'Russian Living Standards during the Industrialization Era, 1885–1913', *Review of Income and Wealth*, vol. 26, 1980, pp. 87–103. For criticism see G. M. Hamburg, 'The Crisis in Russian Agriculture: A Comment', *Slavic Review*, vol. 37, 1978, pp. 481–6; E. Müller, 'Der Beitrag der Bauern zur Industrialisierung Russlands, 1885–1930', *Jahrbücher für Geschichte Osteuropas*, no. 27, 1979, p. 202; J. Sanders, ' "Once More Into the Breach, Dear Friends": A Closer Look at Indirect Tax Receipts and the Condition of the Russian Peasantry, 1881–1899' *Slavic Review*, vol 43, 1984, pp. 657–66.

debate,[33] since these will be of considerable significance to the following study of the Volga region.

Whatever its general direction, the development of the agricultural economy in the Russian Empire during the late nineteenth century was characterized by highly unequal rates of regional growth. The problems of peasant impoverishment were most acute in the central black-soil regions of Russia and the Ukraine—the old, densely populated areas of serfdom and small-scale peasant farming. The traditional agricultural system of these regions was little affected by the development of agrarian capitalism until the turn of the century. The landowners were accustomed to feudal practices on their estates, and were slow to take up the opportunities of the Emancipation (e.g. the receipt of redemption payments for the land transferred to the peasants; the development of the labour and land markets) in order to transform themselves into large-scale capitalist farmers, as the Junkers had done after the Prussian Emancipation earlier in the nineteenth century. The peasants were similarly held back by the inefficiencies of communal land use (e.g. strip-intermingling, distance to plots), technological backwardness, the declining significance of handicrafts, slow rates of capital accumulation, high birth rates, and correspondingly high rates of taxation. The social-levelling mechanisms of the commune and the customs of family ownership hindered the formation of a class of rich, entrepreneurial peasant farmers. Hence, capitalist relations of production among the peasantry were interconnected with—and dominated by—natural-patriarchal relations: labour tended to be hired without the use of cash; peasant or 'kulak' usurers were obliged to operate within customary norms; and so on.

In these central regions the development of the peasant economy during the post-Emancipation period was closely related to peasant–gentry land relations. The Emancipation had left the mass of the peasantry in a position of economic dependence upon rental contracts with the landowners. Unable or unwilling to intensify their production through the cultivation of root-crops in modern field rotations, the peasants of central Russia responded to the growth of the population by expanding their area of production—renting more land from the gentry, or bringing more pasture and fallow under the plough (and thus worsening the problems of soil erosion, inadequate fertilization, and 'depecoration', or the declining ownership of livestock). By the end of the nineteenth century, 38.3% of all privately owned land (i.e.

[33] On this see S. G. Wheatcroft, 'The Agrarian Crisis and Peasant Living Standards in Late Imperial Russia: A Reconsideration of Trends and Regional Differentiation', paper presented to Conference on the Peasantry of European Russia, 1800–1917, University of Massachusetts at Boston, 1986.

excluding peasant communal land), including two-thirds of the arable land in private ownership, was rented by the peasantry.[34] Table 1 shows the changes in the distribution of land tenure and land ownership among the social estates of European Russia during 1877–1905. The growth of the population and the expansion of peasant demand for rentable land increased rental prices by a factor of more than seven between 1861 and 1900.[35] This critically worsened the position of the peasant *darstvenniki*—those who had chosen in 1861 to take, without any obligation to pay redemption fees, one-quarter of their former serf allotment, on the assumption that land rents would remain lower than the level of redemption payment. It is not surprising that the areas of greatest agrarian unrest during 1905–7 were also those with the highest proportion of *darstvenniki*, impoverished by the increase of land rents.[36]

TABLE 1. *Land tenure and land ownership of the social estates in European Russia, 1877 and 1905* ('000,000 *des.* and %)

Social estate	Land in 1877		Land in 1905		% change 1877–1905
	des.	%	*des.*	%	
Peasant and Cossack communal land	123.3	58.5	163.4	67.9	+32.5
Private noble land	73.1	34.7	53.2	22.1	−27.2
Private land of merchants and industrial companies	11.5	5.5	16.7	6.9	+45.2
Other private land	2.8	1.3	7.2	3.0	+157.1
Total	210.7	100	240.5	100	+14.1

Source: T. Shanin, *The Roots of Otherness: Russia's Turn of Century*, vol. 1, *Russia as a 'Developing Society'*, London, 1985, p. 137.

In the peripheral regions around the central black-earth zone (the Baltic, western Ukraine, south Russia, the Volga steppe, and western Siberia), there was an altogether different pattern of agrarian development during the late nineteenth century. In these regions the remnants of feudalism and the traditions of the peasant communal system were less in evidence. The weakness of the commune and the semi-capitalist nature of agricultural practices were reflected in the concentration of land ownership and a relatively high degree of socio-economic differentiation among the rural population, compared with

[34] Anfimov, *Zemel'naia arenda*, pp. 149–72.
[35] T. Shanin, *The Roots of Otherness: Russia's Turn of Century*, vol. 1, *Russia as a 'Developing Society'*, London, 1985. p. 147.
[36] P. N. Pershin, *Agrarnaia Revoliutsiia v Rossii*, 2 vols., Moscow, 1966, vol. 1, p. 15.

the central zone. In the Baltic provinces the serfs had been emancipated in 1817 without land or the right to migrate, so that landlords with access to the west European grain markets were able to develop large-scale commercial farms with cheap wage-labour. In the western Ukraine it had become an established practice for many peasants to rent their land to commercial grower-processors of sugar-beet and vodka, working as wage-labourers in these 'factories in the fields'. In the south-eastern Volga steppelands and western Siberia serfdom had never taken root. The larger holdings of the colonists of these new lands were from the start geared towards the commercial cultivation of wheat, tobacco, cotton, fruit, and other cash crops. The export and internal market potential of the south-eastern and eastern regions was greatly increased by the construction of the trans-Siberian railway and the rapid industrialization of northern-central Russia during the 1890s, with the consequence that more nobles, merchants, and wealthy peasants purchased land in the expanding frontier zones to set up capitalist farms.

The expansion of the commercial agricultural sector in these frontier zones of central Russia undermined the fragile position of the peasant farmers, who had come to depend upon land rentals to meet their subsistence needs. The increasing profitability of agriculture during the inflationary 1900s meant that landowners tended to withdraw their land from peasant renters in order to cultivate it themselves on a capitalist basis, or to rent it at more profitable rates to larger 'kulak' farmers.[37] It is no coincidence that the agrarian unrest of 1905–7 was greatest in the band of provinces situated directly between the old, over-populated areas of serfdom in central Russia (where land rents were high) and the new, expanding zones of commercial agriculture on the periphery (where wage-labour was cheap)—Saratov and Samara in the Volga region; Voronezh, Kursk, Chernigov, and Tambov in the southern-central zone; and Poltava, Ekaterinoslav, and Kherson in the south-west. The agrarian disorders of 1905–7 were the crisis-protest of a traditional peasantry, impoverished by feudalism and threatened with extinction by the primary stages of capitalist development.

The experience of the 1905–7 peasant movement—the seizures of land, the refixing of rental and wage-labour contracts, the clashes with state officials, and so on—gave the revolutionaries of 1917, the elder sons and younger brothers of the 1905 generation, inspiration and guidance.[38] The bitter disappointment of defeat and the barbaric

[37] R. T. Manning, *The Crisis of the Old Order in Russia: Gentry and Government*, Princeton, 1982, pp. 162–3.

[38] On the relationship between 1905–7 and 1917–21 see T. Shanin, *The Roots of Otherness: Russia's Turn of Century*, vol. 2, *Russia 1905–7: Revolution as a Moment of Truth*, London, 1986.

brutality with which the government had eventually suppressed the agrarian uprisings of 1905–7 strengthened the peasants' desire for vengeance in 1917 and their determination not to accept any compromise with the forces of the old order. After 1907 it was commonly perceived by the landowners, caught in a frenzy of panic land sales, that the next—and imminently more powerful—revolutionary outburst by the peasantry would only be a question of time. Conflicts with state officials during the enclosure of the Stolypinite plots were commonplace between 1906–14. Passive peasant opposition to the big gentry estates continued to manifest itself long after 1907 in rental disputes, illicit timber-felling and pasturing, etc. An increasing number of landowners detected undertones of peasant hostility after 1907. As A. N. Naumov, the provincial marshal of the nobility of Samara province noted upon returning to his estate after the peasant uprisings: 'Instead of the peasants' previous courtesy, their friendliness, bows and willingness to pull off the road [upon encountering the vehicle of a local nobleman], animosity could now be clearly seen on their faces, and their greeting accentuated their rudeness . . .'[39]

2. THE VOLGA REGION

One of the main difficulties of writing a history of the peasantry is the fact that no two villages, however close in geographical terms, were ever exactly alike in terms of their natural conditions, their population, and their social and economic organization. Naturally, the problem of diversity is faced by every historian, whose inclination must inevitably be towards generalization. But the problem is confronted in an especially acute form by the historian of the peasantry, since small-scale farming is so heavily dependent upon the local environment.

The following study has been limited to one area of Russia, the Volga region (see Map 2), in order to facilitate a closer examination of the local variations in peasant life during 1917–21 than has so far been accomplished by Western historians.[40] For our purposes, the Volga region has been taken to include Samara, Saratov, Simbirsk, and Penza provinces (*gubernii*), together with the Autonomous Republic of Volga Germans[41]—an area, in total, roughly equivalent to the size of West Germany today. The population of the region in 1920 was as follows:

[39] Cited in Manning, p. 147.

[40] Gill's *Peasants and Government* takes very little account of regional or local variations in peasant organization. A welcome addition to the literature is H. Altrichter's study of the peasantry in Tver' province during 1917–30 (*Die Bauern von Tver: Vom Leben auf dem russischen Dorfe zwischen Revolution und Kollektivierung*, Munich, 1984).

[41] Strictly speaking, the four provinces were divided between the 'middle' and the 'lower' Volga regions. However, in the Soviet historical literature the demarcation

Map 2. *The Volga region and surrounding area*

Samara province, 2.780 million (2.443 million rural); Saratov province, 3.079 million (2.634 million rural); Simbirsk province, 1.622 million (1.427 million rural); Penza province, 1.748 million (1.597 million rural); the Autonomous Republic of Volga Germans, 0.450 million (0.415 million rural).[42]

between these regions is ambiguous. Samara (today Kuibyshev) and Saratov provinces and the Autonomous Republic of Volga Germans are sometimes counted as part of the 'lower Volga' and sometimes as part of the 'middle Volga'. Simbirsk (today Ul'ianovsk) and Penza provinces are not always included in historical studies of the middle Volga, although Kazan' province sometimes is. This study draws most of its data from Samara and Saratov provinces. References are also made to the surrounding provinces of Tambov, Voronezh, and Kazan', and to the regions around Ural'sk and Ufa.

[42] *Itogi perepisi naseleniia 1920 goda*, Moscow, 1928, pp. 71, 75.

For most of the civil war the Volga region remained under Soviet rule (see Map 1). However, the influence of Moscow was never very strongly felt in the region, on account of its geographical separation from the capital, the breakdown of official communications, and the proximity of the military fronts. For four months during the summer of 1918 a large part of the Volga region was brought under the nominal control of the anti-Bolshevik Samara government, led by the mainly Right SR delegates of the disbanded Constituent Assembly (Komuch). In the following spring Kolchak's White army came within striking distance of the Volga, before being pushed back by the Reds. Shortly afterwards, in July 1919, Denikin's White army occupied the south-western districts of Saratov province, although it too was repulsed by the Reds during the autumn. Both the Reds and the Whites were acutely conscious of the strategic importance of the Volga region. It separated the two largest White armies—Kolchak's in Siberia and Denikin's in South Russia—and prevented these from joining forces for a march on Moscow. It was the most important source of food in the Soviet Republic until the Red Army captured western Siberia and the northern Caucasus in 1919–20. The Volga itself was a vital river for commercial shipping, connecting the industrial heartland of northern-central Russia with the agricultural regions of the south-east, the oilfields of the Caucasus, and the minerals of the Urals. All the main railways between Moscow, Siberia, Central Asia and the Caucasus ran through Samara or Saratov. More than any other in the Soviet zone, the Volga region stood between the Bolsheviks and military-political defeat. As one Soviet historian has recently concluded, 'it was precisely in the territory of the Volga and the Urals during the summer and autumn of 1918, and the spring and summer of 1919, that the fate of the revolution was decided'.[43]

In historical terms, the Volga region was remarkable for the revolutionary traditions of its peasantry. From the 'peasant wars' of Stepan Razin and Emelian Pugachev in the seventeenth and eighteenth centuries to the revolutions of 1905–7 and 1917–18 itself, the Volga peasantry distinguished itself in the vanguard of the struggle against the gentry and the state. As much private property was destroyed by the peasants during 1905–7 in the four Volga provinces (Samara, Saratov, Penza, Simbirsk) as in the fifteen remaining provinces of European Russia, whose records were collated in 1907 by V. V. Veselovskii.[44] Peasant representatives from Saratov province were noted as active participants in the Peasant Union and vociferous

[43] A. L. Litvin 'Itogi i zadachi izucheniia grazhdanskoi voiny v Povolzh'e'; *Voprosy istorii*, 1988, no. 7, p. 141.

[44] Manning, p. 143.

proponents of revolutionary views at national peasant assemblies.[45] It is hardly surprising that the Populists and Neo-Populists (SRs), a large proportion of whose leading figures came from the Volga region (e.g. Chernyshevskii, Radishchev, Chernov, Breshko-Breshkovskaia, and Kerensky), considered Saratov their 'Athens on the Volga'.[46]

How are we to explain the outstanding traditions of peasant resistance on the Volga? The answer appears to lie in a combination of factors associated with the intermediate position of the Volga region between the old areas of serfdom in central European Russia and the peripheral zones of the south-east, which, as we have already noted, experienced a very different historical development.

The Volga region evolved within the Russian Empire as a 'semi-frontier' zone between the black-soil regions of European Russia and the Asian steppe. The main provincial centres of the Volga were all founded as military fortresses during the period of Muscovite expansion into Asia, following the defeat of Kazan' and Astrakhan' by Ivan IV in the 1550s. The indigenous peoples of the Volga 'wild lands'—Mordvinian, Chuvash, Tatar, Kalmyk, and Bashkir farmers and pastoralists—were gradually forced eastward into the steppe by Cossacks, *odnodvortsy*,[47] and Russian noblemen, most of whom settled in the fertile black-soil regions on the right (western) bank of the Volga River. Saratov province remained the eastern territorial limit of Russian ethnic hegemony until the colonization of Siberia in the late nineteenth century (see Table 2). During the eighteenth century the European settlement of the Volga region was increased by the establishment of the German colonies;[48] by the imposition of serfdom in the north-western areas; and by the arrival of Russian and Ukrainian runaway serfs, debtors, political fugitives, Old Believers, and escaped convicts, seeking refuge in the remote areas by the Volga River, bordering the 'kingdom of the nomads'. The presence of these people, the volatility of the Cossacks, the grievances of the non-European

[45] See A. Studentsov, *Saratovskoe krest'ianskoe vosstanie 1905 goda*, Penza, 1926, pp. 42 ff.

[46] M. Melanchon, 'Athens or Babylon: The Birth and Development of the Socialist-Revolutionary and Social-Democratic Parties in Saratov, 1890–1905', paper presented to Conference on the History of Saratov Province, University of Illinois, 1985.

[47] Homesteaders granted land in the border areas in return for military service to the Tsar.

[48] The Volga German colonies were established during the reign of Catherine the Great on the steppelands between Kamyshin and Novouzensk in order to settle the area and improve the farming techniques of the neighbouring Russian population. By the middle of the 19th c. there were more than 100,000 Germans (mainly from the Palatinate, Hesse, and the Rhineland) in the Kamyshin and Novouzensk districts. After 1917 this area was reformed as the Autonomous Republic of Volga Germans. Stalin disbanded the Republic during the Second World War and sent many of its inhabitants to labour camps. Others emigrated to Europe and the USA.

Table 2. *Ethnic distribution of the Volga population, 1897*

Native language	% population			
	Penza	Saratov	Samara	Simbirsk
Russian (incl. Ukrainian and White Russian)	83.0	83.0	68.9	68.1
Mordvinian	12.8	5.1	8.7	12.4
Tatar	4.0	3.9	6.0	8.8
Bashkir	—	0.05	2.1	—
Chuvash	—	0.6	3.3	10.5
German	0.04	6.9	8.1	0.04
Jewish	0.03	0.1	0.06	0.03

Source: *Pervaia vseobshchaia perepis' naseleniia Rossiiskoi Imperii 1897 g.*, St Petersburg, 1903–4, vols. 30 (pp. 98–101), 36 (pp. 56–9), 38 (pp. 62–3, 78–81).

population against Russian rule, the newness of serfdom, and the consequent weakness of the state in the Volga region all helped to turn it into a bastion of banditry, libertarianism, and anti-centralism. This was the heartland of the uprisings led by Razin (1670–1) and Pugachev (1773–5), whose mythical raven images continued, until the beginning of the present century, to be seen at night by the peasants, flying on carpets up and down the Volga River, announcing the advent of the peasant revolutionary utopia.[49]

The establishment of serfdom in the Volga region was limited to the black-soil northern and western areas, closest to central Russia. In the southern and eastern steppelands, where the soil was lighter and the presence of the state much weaker, serfdom gave way to the tenancies of State and Crown peasants.[50] It is generally understood that the burdens of the latter were not as onerous as those of the serfs, and that this distinction continued to be true after the Emancipation. This may partly account for the quieter character of the peasant movement in Simbirsk and Samara provinces during 1861–3 and 1905–7, compared with the peasant movement in Saratov province. Whereas serfs accounted for 81% of the peasantry in Saratov province, in Simbirsk province as many as 49% of the peasants were Crown peasants, while in Samara province 64% of the peasants were State peasants.[51]

The north-west and the south-east of the Volga region constituted two very distinct agrarian civilizations. In the old and over-populated north-western areas of serfdom the black soil was up to one *arshin* (71

[49] See P. Longworth, 'The Subversive Legend of Stenka Razin', in V. Strada (ed.), *Russia*, Turin, 1975, vol. 2, p. 29.

[50] L. N. Iurovskii, *Saratovskie votchiny*, Saratov, 1923, p. 52.

[51] Iu. I. Smykov, *Krest'iane Srednego Povolzh'ia v period kapitalizma*, Moscow, 1984, p. 44.

cm.) in depth. The soil became shallower towards the Volga River, and in the woodland regions of the north (in Simbirsk and Kazan' provinces) became a greyish-white sterile soil, known as *podzol.* Because of the abundance of rivers, lakes, and woodlands dividing the arable territory in the north-west, the village settlements tended to be smaller than in the south-east (although they were larger than the villages of central and north-western Russia). Whereas the average village of the north-western Volga districts contained between 300 and 450 inhabitants at the turn of the century, the average village of the south-east numbered between 500 and 750 inhabitants, since the dearth of rivers afforded few places for settlement. Many villages on the south-eastern steppe contained several thousand inhabitants.

The high population density and the relatively small size of the average peasant allotment in the north-western Volga districts resulted in the adoption of more intensive methods of cultivation than in the sparsely populated areas of the south-east. Up to 9 *pud* (147.4 kg.) of rye or wheaten seed was sown per *desiatina* (1.09 ha) in the north-western districts, compared with only 3 to 5 *pud* per *des.* in the south-eastern steppe. Despite considerable improvements during the nineteenth century, the harvest yields of the Volga peasantry remained at a very low level compared with western Europe. The average rye yield in the north-western districts of Saratov province, whose harvests were commonly found among the highest in Russia, was only 48 to 56 *pud* per *des.* during the 1897–1900 period. Meanwhile, in Germany the average yield of rye was approximately 89 *pud* per *des.*[52]

In the south-eastern steppelands cereal farming was carried out on an extensive basis, and the pastoral economy remained an important sector. The light sandy soil was of a poor quality and its high salt content tended to make it crack in the sun. The climate of the south-eastern steppe is dominated by the Asiatic high-pressure system, which produces extremes of temperature in the summer and winter, early frosts in the autumn, and gusting winds in the spring that blow away the top soil and damage tender young crops. Summer droughts are a regular occurrence in the south-east.[53] Because of the scarcity of rivers, lakes, and woods for settlement on the steppe and, consequently, the large size of the villages, many peasants within the communal system were forced to travel enormous distances to farm their allotment land. Some of the larger communes in the south-east

[52] *Materialy dlia otsenki zemel' Saratovskoi gubernii*, vyp. 6, *Osnovaniia otsenki i normy dokhodnosti zemel'nykh ugodii*, Saratov, 1908, pp. 189–90; B. R. Mitchell, *European Historical Statistics 1750–1970*, Columbia, 1978, pp. 87, 113.

[53] On steppeland farming conditions see J. Long, 'Agricultural Conditions in the German Colonies of Novouzensk District, Samara, 1864–1914', *Slavonic and East European Review*, vol. 57, no. 4, 1979, pp. 531–51.

covered a land area of literally hundreds of thousands of hectares. During the 1920s one in three villages in Samara province was separated from its arable by an average distance of more than 10 km. The peasant farmer in the commune who had 16 *des.* of land in three fields travelled on average each year 1,898 *versty* (2,011 km.) to and from his plots.[54] In some of the Volga German colonies the problem was so acute that the villagers migrated in caravans to their fields during the sowing and harvest seasons.[55]

These distinctions between the agrarian systems of the north-west and the south-east help to explain the unrest of the Volga peasantry during the late nineteenth and early twentieth centuries. The problems of that band of provinces between the central Russian zone of former serfdom and the peripheral regions of commercial farming, which, as we have seen, accounted for the peaks of agrarian unrest during 1905–7, were nowhere more in evidence than in the Volga region.

On the one hand, the problems of peasant impoverishment in the old north-western areas of the Volga region were probably just as acute as in the central zone of Russia itself. The abundance of land and the low level of rents at the time of the Emancipation had encouraged a large number of peasants (*darstvenniki*) in the Volga region to accept the 'beggarly allotments': 45% of the land received by the peasantry in this form after 1861 was situated in the four Volga provinces; in parts of Saratov province more than 50% of the post-Emancipation peasantry lived from these tiny plots.[56] The steep growth of the population in the Volga region during the late nineteenth century undermined the position of such smallholders by rapidly pushing up land rents. Because of the general weakness of rural industry in south-eastern Russia, many of the poorest smallholders had no alternative source of on-farm income, and were thus forced into wage-labour on the gentry estates, or into migrant labour on the capitalist farms in the south-eastern steppelands. This had the effect of deflating agricultural wages, so that many labourers left the countryside to work in the fast-expanding industrial centres of northern and central Russia.

On the other hand, the growth of large-scale gentry commercial agriculture and of peasant semi-capitalist farming threatened the

[54] *RR*, p. 137.

[55] H. P. Williams, *The Czar's Germans*, Denver, 1975, p. 132; Baron A. F. Haxthausen noted a similar form of 'nomadic' agriculture among the Volga Russians during the early 19th c. (*Studien über die innern Zustände, das Volksleben und insbesondere die ländlichen Einrichtungen Russlands*, vol. 2, Hannover, 1847, pp. 10, 28).

[56] P. A. Zaionchkovsky, *The Abolition of Serfdom*, Gulf Breeze, Fla., 1977, pp. 157, 169; T. Mixter, 'The Polarization of the Saratov Countryside: Peasants in the Revolution of 1905–1907', paper presented to Conference on the History of Saratov Province, University of Illinois, 1985.

traditional peasant economy more immediately in the Volga region than in central Russia.[57] In the south-eastern Volga districts the difficulties of extensive steppeland farming gave rise to centrifugal social pressures[58] in the commune during the late nineteenth century: the weakest peasants were forced into wage-labour, while a stratum of rich, entrepreneurial peasants was formed and expanded rapidly during the Stolypin land reforms (see Table 3). Meanwhile, many of the Volga

TABLE 3. *Land in Private Peasant Ownership, Volga Region, 1877–1914 (des.)*

Province	1877	1905	Land purchased by individual peasants 1905–14
Penza	53,854	118,156	63,300
Samara	365,372	803,053	243,272
Saratov	84,410	247,300	61,123
Simbirsk	57,465	145,414	99,948

Sources: *Statistika zemlevladeniia 1905 g.*, 50 vols., St Petersburg, 1906, vol. 2, pp. 12–13; vol. 12, pp. 12–13; vol. 22, pp. 12–13; vol. 28, pp. 12–13; A. M. Anfimov and I. F. Makarov, 'Novye dannye o zemlevladenii Evropeiskoi Rossii', *Istoriia SSSR*, 1974, no. 1, p. 97.

landowners were also drawn into large-scale commercial farming after the mid–1890s on account of the reduction in transportation costs brought about by the construction of the railways, and the increase of food prices brought about by the recent wave of urbanization in Europe. Much of the land that the nobles had formerly rented to the peasants was now withdrawn from the market, or leased out at higher capital rents to the bigger farmers. A large number of landowners chose to rent land to the peasants in return for labour service (*otrabotka*), or to put it into sharecropping systems, instead of the old system of cash rent, in order to expand their own demesne and ensure a fixed supply of cheap peasant labour. This practice, reminiscent of the methods of the Prussian Junker farms, was especially common on the gentry estates specializing in labour-intensive crops (e.g. sugar-beet, flax) on the

[57] See T. S. Fallows, 'Forging the Zemstvo Movement: Liberalism and Radicalism on the Volga, 1890–1905', Ph.D. diss., Harvard University, 1981; Mixter.

[58] In the *Development of Capitalism in Russia* (*PSS*, vol. 3, pp. 76 ff.) Lenin highlighted the south-eastern districts of the Volga as an area of extreme socio-economic differentiation as a result of capitalist development. It is true that the socio-economic differentiation of the population in this region was very pronounced, but it is not at all clear whether this resulted from the development of capitalist relations or from the natural difficulties of peasant farming on the steppe. Large-scale ownership of livestock, moreover, might have been expected in a region, such as this, where pastoralism remained important.

borders of the over-populated black-soil regions, where the employment of peasant labour teams was more economic than the purchase of expensive machinery. Such exploitative methods severely undercut the position of the small peasant farmers in these regions, who had come to depend upon the rent of private land, since they were now squeezed between the high cash rents of the older feudal system and the low wages of the capitalistic one. It was these peasants who took the lead in the agrarian unrest of 1905–7 and 1917–18.

3. THE ORGANIZATION OF THE BOOK

Chapter 2 examines the breakdown of state power in the countryside and the transformation of agrarian relations during 1917. The chapter analyses the forms of revolutionary organization, from the village commune to the provincial peasant assembly, which enabled the rural population to dismantle the apparatus of the old regime in the localities and begin, on its own initiative, the tasks of the revolution—the seizure and redistribution of the gentry estates, the establishment of democratic organs of power, and the reorganization of rural life according to local concepts of social justice.

During its first months of power, the Soviet government in Petrograd and (after March 1918) in Moscow had very little influence on the revolution in the countryside. The village communes and the *volost'* soviets restructured the rural system of social relations on the basis of the local population's own understanding of property rights, civil liberty, economic freedom, and social welfare. The nature of these reforms was determined by the balance of autonomous social forces in the rural localities and by the need of the communities for consensus and order. Chapter 3 examines this system of 'peasant rule' during the first six months of 1918—a remarkable, if brief, interlude between the collapse of the old regime and the construction of the new. The chapter analyses the composition and functioning of the local rural soviets, and asks how far they represented a 'village democracy', and how far an oligarchy of peasant patriarchs. It examines the problems of the market economy and of food distribution during the grain crisis of 1918. It investigates the communal land redivisions, and assesses their ability to solve the problems of small-scale peasant farming. Finally, the chapter examines the peasantry's relations with the non-farming inhabitants of the village (e.g. craftsmen, the rural intelligentsia), and asks to what extent the 'peasant rule' represented a stable social system.

It was widely expected that the peasantry would prove an anti-Bolshevik force after October 1917. The Volga region, with its strong traditions of Populist-SR organization and its stratum of semi-capitalist peasants, was a prime candidate in this respect. The elections to the Constituent Assembly in November and December 1917 had resulted in a large peasant majority for the SR parties in the Volga provinces. Yet, when the Bolsheviks closed down the new parliament in January 1918 the Volga peasantry failed to respond to the calls of the SR leaders to rise against the Soviet regime. Chapter 4 attempts to explain this. It argues that the Bolsheviks' fear of a counter-revolution by the 'kulaks' during the spring and summer of 1918 was quite unfounded. The number of rich peasants hostile to the revolution was insignificant, and the ability of the SRs to stir anti-Bolshevik sentiments among the peasantry severely restricted. The failure of the Right-SR-dominated Komuch in Samara during the summer of 1918 is explained by its inability to gain the support of the peasants, who as yet had very little experience of the oppressive policies of the Bolshevik regime, and were wary of supporting a government whose military officers were largely drawn from the old landowning class.

The second half of the book (Chapters 5 to 7) examines various aspects of the relationship between the peasantry and the Bolsheviks during the civil war (1918–21), a period when the new state regime developed in the provincial towns and started the 'reconquest' of the countryside. Chapter 5 examines the socio-political forces underlying the emergence of the Bolshevik regime in the countryside. It focuses on the disastrous attempts by the Bolsheviks to divide the village on class lines through the committees of the rural poor—the *kombedy*—established in June 1918. It gives a detailed analysis of the results of the 1919 soviet election campaign, which, it is argued, greatly extended the influence of the Bolshevik party in the local soviets and, especially, in their executives. It provides a new interpretation of the rural social groups who supported the Soviet regime and joined the Bolshevik party. Finally, the chapter offers some general conclusions on the nature of peasant–state relations at the end of the civil war.

Chapter 6 is concerned with the policies of the Bolshevik government (war communism) to mobilize the resources of the peasantry for the civil war campaign. It focuses on the Bolshevik food procurements, and assesses their impact on the agricultural economy and the development of peasant–state relations. It highlights the natural-autarkic forms of the rural economy that developed in response to the breakdown of market relations between town and country. It describes the first wave of Soviet collectivization after 1918, and accounts for the failure of the new socialist farms to attract the smallholding peasants. The chapter also looks at the Red Army campaigns to mobilize peasant soldiers, and accounts for the willingness of the peasantry to support the Red Army under certain conditions.

The policies of war communism were seen by the Bolsheviks not only as a temporary military expedient, but also as a means of socialist transformation in the countryside. The government's trade monopolies and food requisitionings were designed not only to service the cities and the Red Army, but also to weaken the market economy and expropriate the rich peasant farmers. The collective and state farms that were established under the protection of the Bolshevik government after 1918 were intended not only to transfer land and property to hungry proletarians, but also to challenge the domination of the peasant family farms, whose interests were seen at that time to be inimical to the development of socialism. The policies of war communism drew up the basic lines of confrontation between the peasantry and the new regime. They marked out the Bolsheviks as an alien and coercive force in the countryside. The brutal requisitionings of food, the forcible mobilization of peasants by the Red Army, and the use of mass terror against the villages of peasant deserters were met by many different forms of passive peasant resistance and sabotage, interspersed by sporadic peasant revolts. However, as long as the Whites remained in the field, the peasants were reluctant to challenge the Soviet regime. Large-scale peasant rebellions against the Bolsheviks did not take place until the closing period of the civil war. Chapter 7 examines the various forms of peasant resistance to the Bolshevik regime in the Volga region, explains their origins, and assesses the reasons for their ultimate defeat.

2
The Emergence of Peasant Autonomy

> Traditional political authority has eroded or collapsed; new contenders for power are seeking new constituencies for entry into the vacant political arena. Thus when the peasant protagonist lights the torch of rebellion, the edifice of society is already smouldering and ready to take fire. When the battle is over, the structure will not be the same.
>
> E. Wolf, *Peasant Wars in the Twentieth Century*

In the revolutions of 1917 the role of the peasantry, the vast majority of the Russian population, was decisive. Without the simultaneous rising of the peasants, the revolution in the cities could not have been accomplished. By undermining the old agrarian order, upon which the political and military supports of the Tsarist state had been based, the peasants enabled the Bolsheviks, with the support of only a minority of of the population, to consolidate their power in the capital and the other major cities.[1]

The importance of the peasantry's contribution to the revolution stemmed from the widespread and destructive nature of the agrarian revolution. Prior to 1905, peasant uprisings in Russia had failed because they had been local in character (as Trotsky put it, 'a cretinous localism has been the historical curse of peasant risings').[2] But the peasant movements of 1905–7, and especially 1917, developed on a national scale. Bit by bit, as the result of a multitude of 'revolutions' at the village level, the old agrarian system was dismantled. The political impotence of the peasantry was, if only temporarily, transcended. This was not because the organization of the isolated villages had been made any easier (indeed, the breakdown of the communications system during the revolution made it significantly harder); nor can it be fully explained by a deterioration of the peasant economy, or an increase in exploitation, although both were undoubtedly noted as a result of the Stolypin land reforms and the First World War, and both may be assumed to have precipitated peasant disquiet.[3] It was because

[1] On the role of the peasantry in modern social revolutions see B. Moore, *Social Origins of Dictatorship and Democracy*, Harmondsworth, 1967; T. Skocpol, *States and Social Revolutions*, Cambridge, 1979.

[2] L. Trotsky, *1905*, 4th edn., Moscow, 1925, p. 54.

[3] On the Russian peasantry during the war see A. M. Anfimov, *Rossiiskaia derevnia v gody pervoi mirovoi voiny*, Moscow, 1962. This subject has not received the attention it merits from Western historians. N. Stone's *The Eastern Front 1914–1917*, London, 1975,

thousands of peasant revolts had acted in unison at a time when the dominant social classes and the power of the state had been weakened by internal divisions, by the war, and by the workers' revolution. The peasants grew in confidence as it became apparent in the rural localities that the landowners were no longer able to mobilize against them the machinery of the state.

The peasant revolution, which we shall be examining in this chapter, destroyed piecemeal the old state apparatus in the countryside—the provincial governors, the district *zemstva*, the *volost'* administration (*uprava*), the land captains, and the police officials (*strazhniki*, *uriadniki*). It replaced them with a network of *ad hoc* peasant committees (and later soviets), elected by the communal or village assembly. These committees passed their own 'laws', sometimes authorized by district and provincial assemblies, empowering the local peasantry to carry out a revolution on the land—to regulate rental contracts with the landowners, to establish pasture and timber-felling rights on the estates, to mow the landowners' meadows, to enforce fixed-price sales of gentry seed and livestock, and, finally, to seize and redistribute parts of the estate lands themselves. Despite the calls of the Provisional Government to delay any revolutionary actions until the convocation of the Constituent Assembly, it was clear that the peasants were beginning to take the law—and much of the property of the landowners and the church—into their own hands. As the Nizhegorod provincial commissar put it in the summer of 1917: 'the local peasantry has got a fixed opinion that all civil laws have lost their force and that all legal relations ought now to be regulated by peasant organizations'.[4]

A similar tendency towards localist solutions was noted among factory workers in 1917–18.[5] The slogan 'All power to the soviets!' was being widely interpreted as an invitation to the masses to take power into their own hands, electing their own organs of self-government (soviets). During the early revolutionary period (1917–18) Lenin supported the decentralization of power as a means of completing the destruction of the old state apparatus. The localism of the soviets was

contributes some interesting ideas on the peasant sector and the national war economy. But the crucial questions (peasant–gentry and peasant–state relations) are still begging discussion.

[4] Cited in L. Trotsky, *The History of the Russian Revolution*, trans. M. Eastman, London, 1965, vol. 3, p. 882.

[5] See W. G. Rosenberg, 'Russian Labor and Bolshevik Power: Social Dimensions of Protest in Petrograd after October', in D. H. Kaiser (ed.), *The Workers' Revolution in Russia, 1917: The View From Below*, Cambridge, Mass., 1987, p. 105; J. D. White, 'The Sormovo-Nikolaev zemlyachestvo in the February Revolution', *Soviet Studies*, vol. 31, no. 4, 1979, pp. 475–504.

said to be 'completely natural, since Tsarist and bourgeois centralism had engendered in the masses a hatred and disgust of all central authority'. But as the civil war demanded the reconstruction of a strong state apparatus, Lenin later condemned the localism of the soviets as a 'reactionary utopianism' and 'an illness of the transitionary period',[6] the period between the destruction of the old state and the building of the new.

1. THE END OF THE OLD REGIME

During the second half of March 1917 news of the February revolution in Petrograd and the abdication of the Tsar filtered down to the villages of the Volga by word of mouth, by telegraph, and by newspapers. Soviet historians tell us that the news was greeted by the peasants with excitement and pleasure. Many villages sent a couple of messengers to the nearest town just to confirm the rumours. Others sent proclamations of good will towards the new government with expressions of hope for a bright future without oppression.[7]

During the following weeks open assemblies were held in almost every village to discuss the current situation and to formulate resolutions on a broad range of local and national issues. These assemblies were important in two new respects. Firstly, they discussed a much wider range of issues than the village assemblies before 1914. The personal fortune of the Tsar and his family, the future of the war campaign, the position of the church, the rights of the gentry squires, the price of foodstuffs, and many other general issues were debated at these assemblies. The excitement of the revolution must have played a major part in broadening the political horizons of the peasantry. But it should also be borne in mind that, as a result of the First World War, a large number of new responsibilities had been imposed on the village assembly, from the compulsory collection of foodstuffs for the government to the billeting of refugees and prisoners of war. The peasants were no longer able to view the decisions of the village assembly solely in the light of their own local lives. They were forced to view them in the context of national and international affairs, if only because their sons were fighting in western Russia and Romania.

Secondly, the village assemblies which met during the spring of 1917 marked a process of democratization within the peasant community. Whereas village politics before 1914 had been dominated by the communal gathering of peasant household elders (*mirskii skhod*), the village assemblies which came to dominate politics during 1917

[6] *PSS*, vol. 36, p. 351.

[7] V. V. Vas'kin and G. A. Gerasimenko, *Fevral'skaia revoliutsiia v Nizhnem Povolzh'e*, Saratov 1976, pp. 141–75.

comprised all the village inhabitants (*obshchie skhody, obshchie sobraniia*) and were sometimes attended by several hundred people. The patriarchal domination of the peasant household elders was thus challenged by junior members of the peasant households (including the female members), landless labourers and craftsmen, village *intelligenty* (e.g. scribes, teachers, vets, doctors), soldiers on leave, and other 'respected citizens' (e.g. the clergy and well-loved gentry squires) who had formerly been excluded from the communal gathering. This process of democratization requires detailed study.[8] It stemmed partly from the obligation of the peasant patriarchs to involve a wider range of village inhabitants in the process of decision-making as the political and social responsibilities of the village broadened during the First World War and the revolution, when the state administration was destroyed. But it mainly resulted from the return of the peasant soldiers during 1917–18, since many of them established new family households (with rights of representation at the *mir*), partitioned from larger, patriarchal family households.[9]

The spirit of democracy in the villages soon spread to the *volost'* townships, where the old organs of state administration (*upravy*) were gradually supplanted by *ad hoc* peasant committees. The first elements of the old organs to be removed were generally the land captains, the *volost'* elders, and the police officials, although some of them managed to gain a position in the newly elected peasant committees. This was most commonly noted in the early weeks of the revolution, when the district and provincial authorities issued decrees to maintain the former structure of power in the *volost'*. Many villages were uncertain whether the new order in the cities would last and dared go no further than re-elect the old organ, or elect a mixed one with old and new members. Others retained the old organ, but put it under the control of a peasant committee.[10] Gradually, as the first uncertain weeks of the revolution passed, the peasants began to remove from office the land captains, the police officials and the *volost'* elders. In some places the latter were arrested and imprisoned or expelled from the *volost'*. In others they were driven out of office by a communal boycott of the *volost'* taxes (*sbory*), which left the officials

[8] V. V. Kabanov makes a passing reference to the topic in his essay on the commune during the October revolution ('Oktiabr'skaia revoliutsiia i krest'ianskaia obshchina', *Istoricheskie zapiski*, vol. 111, Moscow, 1984, p. 106).

[9] See *KK*, pp. 220–9; T. Shanin, *The Awkward Class*, Oxford, 1972, pp. 157–9.

[10] V. Krasnov, 'Iz vospominanii o 1917–1920 gg.', *Arkhiv russkoi revoliutsii*, vol. 7, Berlin, 1923, p. 122; G. J. Gill, *Peasant and Government in the Russian Revolution*, London, 1979, pp. 33–4; Vas'kin and Gerasimenko, pp. 148–79, 158–62; L. S. Gaponenko (ed.), *Revoliutsionnoe dvizhenie v Rossii posle sverzheniia samoderzhaviia: Dokumenty i materialy*, Moscow, 1957, pp. 422, 440.

unpaid. In the Volga region the removal of these officers quickened after the Samara peasant assembly of March 1917 and the Saratov peasant assembly of April had passed formal resolutions suspending the land captains and the Tsarist police.[11] 'In the villages of Saratov', reported one newspaper on 17 March, 'the *volost'* elders are, to a man, disappearing and peasants are arresting the village elders.'[12]

The Provisional Government was concerned to influence and contain the process of democratization in the *volost'* townships. Its prime concern in the rural areas was to keep the flow of food coming into the cities, to prevent a gentry counter-revolution, and to hold off the land question until the convocation of the Constituent Assembly. For this it was necessary to establish order in the countryside and to integrate the democratic initiatives of the peasantry into the work of the government. On 20 March the Provisional Government ordered its provincial and district commissars to set up temporary *volost'* committees in preparation for the institution of *volost'*-level *zemstva*, the great democratic hope of Russian liberal progressives. The committees were to include peasants, landowners, and 'all the intellectual forces of the countryside'. They were designed to counteract the prolific growth of the *ad hoc* peasant organs of self-rule at the *volost'* level. They were to be responsible for the entire spectrum of local governmental duties, especially food procurement and public order, and were to be answerable to the government district commissars (the majority of whom had formerly been the chairman of their district *zemstvo* board).[13]

Despite these measures, the higher authorities proved generally unable to influence the formation of the *volost'* committees, which tended increasingly to be set up by the peasants, the rural *intelligenty*, and the other democratic elements of the villages in their own fashion. The provincial and district government commissars rarely took the lead in forming the *volost'* committees: if the latter were authorized by any higher authority, then it was most likely to be some sort of district 'executive committee' (*ispolnitel'nyi komitet*) acting on the instructions of a district or provincial Committee of Public Organizations (*komitet obshchestvennykh organizatsii*), or a peasant assembly. The great majority of the *volost'* committees were elected in a spontaneous fashion by a peasant assembly or an informal village meeting. The idea

11 A. V. Shestakov (ed.), *Sovety krest'ianskikh deputatov i drugie krest'ianskie organizatsii*, 2 vols., Moscow, 1929, vol. 1, pp. 89, 97, 110 ff.

12 *Saratovskii listok* (Saratov), 17 Mar. 1917, p. 2.

13 Gill, p. 25; W. G. Rosenberg, 'The Zemstvo in 1917 and its Fate under Bolshevik Rule', in T. Emmons and W. S. Vucinich (eds.), *The Zemstvo in Russia: An Experiment in Local Self-Government*, Cambridge, Mass., 1982, pp. 386–7, 390; K. G. Kotel'nikov and V. L. Meller (eds.), *Krest'ianskoe dvizhenie v 1917 g.*, Moscow/Leningrad, 1927, pp. 403–4.

of the 'committee' had, as John Keep put it, a 'fashionable ring' in peasant circles during 1917.[14] Literally hundreds of different peasant committees and executives were set up in the villages and *volost'* townships during the spring. There was nothing systematic about their organization. Some of the committees were representative of an entire *volost'*, while others were elected by no more than a handful of people in a single village. Many of them were highly unstable in their membership, lasting often no more than a few days. But this fluidity was itself a reflection of the creativity of the peasant revolution, which in its early stages was bound to be expressed in a wide variety of local and experimental forms. The committees made up in revolutionary verve what they lacked in systematic organization. They were broadly representative, in form and content, of the rural masses, and were motivated, for the most part, by the democratic driving-force of the peasant revolution. They sabotaged the work of the district *zemstva* which were dominated by hostile gentry interests. They transformed themselves into autonomous local 'governments', sometimes with their own police, a peasant court (*mirovoi sud*) and various subcommittees to deal with social and agricultural affairs. Some of the *volost'* committees, especially those which were re-elected while the rear-garrison soldiers were on leave during Easter, were transformed into exclusively peasant organs. A report to the State Duma in May was anxious that the peasants no longer 'elect *intelligenty*. They grow in their conviction that they should direct their own affairs . . . They even boycott the managers of credit co-operatives, schoolmasters, and, in particular, schoolmistresses'.[15]

A similar clash of interests between the peasantry and the Provisional Government was noted in relation to the provisions committees (*prodovol'stvennye komitety*) and land committees (*zemel'nye komitety*). The former, which had been established in March to administer the government procurements of grain, were generally unable to involve the peasantry in their work because they were seen to be dominated by the merchantry and the landowners. Many of the *volost'* committees forbade the peasants to sell their grain to the government through the provisions committees.[16] The land committees, which were intended by the government to protect the estates until the resolution of the land question by the Constituent Assembly, tended, in fact, to be dominated by the peasantry; many of them began to reform the system of land relations in a radical way.[17] The

14 J. L. H. Keep, *The Russian Revolution: A Study in Mass Mobilization*, London, 1976, p. 218.

15 Cited in Vas'kin and Gerasimenko, pp. 176–7.

16 Ibid., pp. 165–77, 189–90.

17 There is a wide divergence of opinion among Soviet historians about the *volost'* land committees. Some have argued that the committees were dominated by the

Government tried to curtail the activities of the land committees by cutting their grants, but this appears to have had little effect: the number of land committees continued to grow, since they were financed mainly by local communal taxes. By the beginning of June there were 232 land committees in Penza province and over 300 committees in Saratov province. In Simbirsk province there were 153 land committees, of which only 39 had been financed by the central exchequer. Many local land committees had been established before an equivalent body existed at the corresponding district or provincial level. In Buzuluk *uezd*, for example, most of the *volost'* land committees were established before May, whereas the Buzuluk district land committee was not established until 17 June, and the Samara provincial land committee not until 14 July.[18]

This administrative conflict, or power struggle, between the local peasant organs and the centralized authorities of the state did not bode well for the *volost'*-level *zemstva*, whose institution on 21 May was expected to lay the foundations for the integration of the peasantry into the democratic republic. The legislation envisaged the substitution of the *volost'*-level *zemstvo* for the *ad hoc* peasant committees and soviets which had sprung up since March. The official responsibilities of the *zemstva* were comprehensive: the collection of taxes; the procurement of grain at fixed prices for the government; the distribution of goods and provisions; the management of roads, schools, and hospitals; and, with the help of the land committees, the supervision of all agrarian relations until the convocation of the Constituent Assembly. The new organs were to be headed by an

'kulaks' and acted in the interests of the Provisional Government (P. N. Pershin, 'Krest'ianskie zemel'nye komitety v period podgotovki Velikoi Oktiabr'skoi Sotsialisticheskoi Revoliutsii', *Voprosy istorii*, 1948, no. 7, pp. 70–83; E. A. Lutskii, 'Politika sovetskoi vlasti po otnosheniiu k zemel'nym komitetam', *Trudy moskovskogo istoriko-arkhivnogo instituta*, vol. 13, 1959, p. 138). This was the established view during the Stalinist period. Others have argued that the committees were used by the landowners as a brake on the peasant movement: see V. I. Kostrikin, 'Iz istorii zemel'nykh komitetov Riazanskoi gubernii (mart–oktiabr' 1917 g.)', *Trudy moskovskogo istoriko-arkhivnogo instituta*, vol. 9, 1957, pp. 5, 9, 12–13; O. N. Moiseeva, *Sovety krest'ianskikh deputatov v 1917 g.*, Moscow, 1967, pp. 113–14. Recently, a number of Soviet historians have returned to the view, originally expressed in the 1920s, that the committees were, for the most part, democratic organs which helped to organize the peasant movement against the landowners: see A. Alaverdova, 'Ocherk agrarnoi politiki vremennogo pravitel'stva (fevral'–oktiabr' 1917 g.)', *Sotsialisticheskoe khoziaistvo*, vol. 2, 1925, p. 148; Shestakov (ed.), *Sovety krest'ianskikh deputatov*, vol. 2, p. 108; V. I. Kostrikin, *Zemel'nye komitety v 1917 g.*, Moscow, 1975, pp. 130–8; G. A. Gerasimenko, 'Vliianie posledstvii stolypinskoi agrarnoi reformy na krest'ianskie organizatsii 1917 goda (po materialam Saratovskoi gub.)', *Istoriia SSSR*, 1981, no. 1, pp. 45–6. My own view is that this last interpretation may be equally applied to most of the committees established at the *volost'* level during 1917.

18 Kostrikin, *Zemel'nye komitety v 1917 g.*, pp. 101–2, 130–8.

executive (*uprava*) elected at a *volost'* gathering (*skhod*) of peasant delegates from every ten households (*desiatidvornik*), *zemstvo* councillors (*glasnye*), and other 'respected citizens'. The *upravy* were to function within the former structure of *zemstvo* power at the district and provincial levels, but they were to report to the district commissar instead of the land captain.[19] No significant element of democracy was added by the legislation to the new *volost'* authorities, which were legally powerless to initiate any major project of social reform.

In this form, the *volost'*-level *zemstva* stood little chance of success. The legislation was attempting to impose a centralized structure of state authority directly on top of the peasant communes, whereas the latter had only recently pulled down the old structure of the state in the *volost'* townships and, through the peasant committees, were beginning to enjoy the taste of freedom from state intervention. In many of the *volosti* where there was a large number of gentry and merchant *zemstvo* councillors, or 'Third Element' *zemstvo* personnel (e.g. doctors and teachers), who were likely to dominate the *volost' zemstvo*, the peasants were known to be hostile towards the establishment of the new administrative structure, since they viewed it as a challenge to the *ad hoc volost'* committees which had been elected by themselves. The same tendency was noted in the *volosti* where a peasant soviet had been established during the spring, or where there was a large contingent of peasant soldiers on leave.[20] In these areas the elections of the *volost'*-level *zemstva*, which were finally held during August and September, were marked by a bitter struggle between the peasant communes and the higher *zemstvo* authorities. The leaders of the peasants refused to allow the candidates who had been nominated by the district *zemstvo* boards to stand for election. They destroyed electoral lists and ballot papers, and harassed electoral commissioners. Some communes organized a boycott of the elections. Others turned them into a street-fight. In Saratov province more than one-third of the elections had to be rescheduled because of such disruptions. A large number of the elections which were completed suffered from bribe-taking and an extremely low turn-out. In Saratov province only one in five peasants took part in the elections; in Samara province only one in four. This was partly because the elections had been called at the busiest period of the agricultural season. But it was also because many of the peasantwomen, who were legally entitled to vote for the first time, proved unwilling or unable to

[19] Shestakov (ed.), *Sovety krest'ianskikh deputatov*, vol. 1, pp. 338–44; Moiseeva, pp. 44–5; A. I. Lepeshkin, *Mestnye organy vlasti sovetskogo gosudarstva (1917–1920 gg.)*, Moscow, 1957, p. 92.

[20] Lepeshkin, pp. 93–6; Rosenberg, 'The Zemstvo in 1917', pp. 393–6; Keep, p. 169.

do so, because of pressures from their menfolk. Another explanation may be the complexity of the electoral system and the procedures of secret balloting and slate-voting, which were alien to the open-voting customs of the peasantry in the communes.[21]

In many areas the establishment of the *volost'*-level *zemstva* followed the same pattern as the establishment of the *volost'* committees. The government intended the *zemstva* to be managed by the well-to-do citizenry as organs of the state. Yet they were easily dominated by the local peasant communes and tended to function as independent revolutionary 'governments'. As we will discover, there was in fact a significant element of continuity between the committees, the *zemstva*, and the soviets which were elected at the *volost'* level during successive stages of the revolution. This continuity, which may be noted in both the personnel and the policies of the different *volost'* organs, is hardly surprising, although it is denied by Soviet historians, who are eager to emphasize the distinctive and revolutionary character of the soviets.[22] From the spring of 1917, the state was powerless to control the organization of power in the rural localities. The influence of the well-to-do *intelligenty*—a tiny minority of the rural population—was all the time declining as the peasantry's drive towards social dominance (*vlast'*) gained momentum. In this context, any institution at the *volost'* level, whatever its social composition, was forced to function in the interests of the peasantry, if it was to have any chance of survival. To be sure, the return of the peasant-soldiers from the army during 1917–18 radicalized the *volost'* institutions and sped up the formation of the soviets, but it did not alter the basic structure of power relations in the rural localities, or at least not until 1919–20.

S.P. Rudnev, the owner of an estate near the village of Durasovka (Beklemishevo *volost'*, Karsun *uezd*, Simbirsk *guberniia*), who enjoyed a privileged position among the peasants during 1917–18 (chiefly because he left them most of his property), gave a detailed description of the Beklemishevo *zemstvo* in his memoirs.[23] The *zemstvo* was

[21] G. A. Gerasimenko, *Nizovye krest'ianskie organizatsii v 1917–pervoi polovine 1918 gg. (Na materialakh Nizhnego Povolzh'ia)*, Saratov, 1974, pp. 180–4; Rosenberg, 'The Zemstvo in 1917', pp. 396–8; P. A. Butyl'kin and G. A. Gerasimenko, 'Osushchestvlenie agrarnykh preobrazovanii v Nizhnem Povolzh'e', in *Leninskii Dekret o zemle v deistvii*, pp.151 ff.; M. Gaisinskii, *Bor'ba bol'shevikov za krest'ianstvo v 1917 g.: Vserossiiskie s''ezdy Sovetov krest'ianskikh deputatov*, Moscow, 1933, p. 119.

[22] Two exceptions are: V. V. Grishaev, *Stroitel'stvo sovetov v derevne v pervyi god sotsialisticheskoi revoliutsii*, Moscow, 1967; and S. L. Makarova, 'Oprosnye listy Narodnogo Komissariata Zemledeliia i moskovskogo oblastnogo ispolnitel'nogo komiteta kak istochnik po istorii agrarnoi revoliutsii (noiabr' 1917–iiun' 1918)', kand. diss., Moscow, 1970.

[23] S. P. Rudnev, *Pri vechernikh ogniakh: Vospominaniia*, Newtonville, Mass., 1978 (orginally Kharbin, 1928) (henceforth referred to as *PVO*), pp. 81–5.

elected during the summer of 1917 by the peasants and other 'citizens', excepting the landowners. The *uprava* consisted of five or seven members (the author's memory was uncertain) who were all 'young "middle peasants", but people who farmed and were not without energy'.[24] From Rudnev's own village two members were elected: one the son of the Beklemishevo church elder (*tserkovnyi starosta*), the other a young peasant, who became the chairman of the *zemstvo*. None of the former district or provincial *zemstvo* councillors (*glasnye*) was elected. Nor were any of the 'village conservatives (*stolpy*) or rich men' elected.[25] Although the peasants did not permit the landowners to vote in the *zemstvo* elections, they allowed them to attend the meetings of the *zemstvo*. These invariably took place on a Sunday afternoon in front of the building of the former *volost'* administration. The chairman of the *zemstvo* executive and his secretary sat behind a table. In front of them, on two rows of benches, were the remaining (four or six) *zemstvo* representatives. Behind them stood the peasant crowd, grouped around their respective village elders, who acted as spokesmen before the executive. Seven villages were represented at the assembly (although not all the villages had a representative on the executive). By the side of the executive sat the landowners who had been invited to attend the meeting: the Rudnevs, a Pole named Iatskovskii, and usually one other small landowner by the name of Isaichev. Rudnev recalled that his family 'took part neither in the discussion, nor in the voting, but the peasants sought our advice and undoubtedly respected it'.[26]

The *zemstvo* meeting proceeded in the manner of a general peasant assembly. The opinion of the village elders was sought on each issue by the executive after a suitable period had been allowed for discussion among the peasant crowd. If there was disagreement between the village elders, then the elders went to one side and negotiated among themselves in the hope of coming to a common decision. If this could not be done, then the elders were asked by the executive to discuss the matter at a gathering of their village and report back at the next meeting of the *zemstvo*. If at the next meeting there was still disagreement between the elders then a general open vote—by shouting, by a show of hands, or by standing in sides—would be organized. Like the *volost'* committees and the soviets of 1917–18, the *volost' zemstvo* was a decentralized system of power: the influence of the village elders on the floor of the assembly was much greater than the influence of the *volost'* executive. Moreover, as Rudnev pointed out,

[24] Ibid., p. 82. [25] Ibid. [26] Ibid., p. 83.

the *zemstvo* had neither the authority nor the strength to force the new 'citizens' of the villages to comply with their own resolutions. Even the resolutions which had been made in accordance with the opinions of the village elders and their communes were frequently known to carry no weight, since, I repeat, there was no power or authority to enforce these resolutions.[27]

The *zemstvo* police (*militsiia*) was said to be 'completely isolated from the village' and without any of the powers of intervention previously enjoyed by the land captain or the communal arbitrators (*mirovye posredniki*). The peasant court (*mirovoi sud*) was not informed of a single law infringement.[28]

2. PEASANT ASSEMBLIES

The district and provincial peasant assemblies of 1917 served as an important focus for the articulation of peasant grievances and aspirations. They were a sort of 'political apprenticeship',[29] in which the peasantry learned how to organize and legitimize its interests at a territorial level which had previously been dominated by state organizations. As the power of the state collapsed in the provinces during 1917, the political initiative passed to these district and provincial assemblies, which began to turn themselves into autonomous 'governments', authorizing the peasant seizure of private property in the rural localities.

The earliest peasant assemblies of 1917, during March and April, expressed support for the Provisional Government and drafted temporary proclamations on the land question. The Saratov peasant assembly in April, which was attended by more than 400 delegates, resolved to improve food deliveries to the government and issued a declaration, in broadly SR phraseology, calling for the abolition of rights of land ownership on the convocation of the Constituent Assembly. In the mean time, the seizure of private land was condemned, but measures were taken to allocate the uncultivated spring fields to the landless peasants.[30] The Samara peasant assembly in March, which was attended by only twenty-five delegates, most of them SR *intelligenty*, agreed to do 'everything possible . . . for the better provision of grain for the Motherland and the maintenance of civil order in the countryside prior to the resolution of all matters in a legal form'. The assembly passed a series of temporary land measures, including: the prohibition of land sales and of peasant separations from the commune; the

27 PVO, p. 85. 28 Ibid., p. 81.

29 M. Ferro, *October 1917: A Social History of the Russian Revolution*, trans. N. Stone, London, 1980, p. 120.

30 Shestakov (ed.), *Sovety krest'ianskikh deputatov*, vol. 1, pp. 110–14. See also D. Raleigh, *Revolution on the Volga: 1917 in Saratov*, Cornell, 1986, pp. 181–2.

transfer of a small amount of church land to the poorest peasantry; and the reduction by 75% of all land rents on the estates.[31]

The cautious character of these measures failed to prevent the growing impatience of certain sections of the peasantry. During March there were reports that the peasant communes in the Volga region were already engaged in disputes with the landowners over rent, the allocation of war-prisoners, the woods, and common rights of pasture. During April some of the peasant communes began to enforce fixed-price purchases of seed from the squires. Others began to mow the gentry meadows, or to confiscate the spring arable.[32] Many such actions were supported by a 'resolution' or 'decree', passed by a peasant committee. Some were even endorsed by a regional or district peasant assembly.

On 20 May the SRs in Samara convoked a second peasant assembly, attended by 516 delegates. The minutes of this assembly are particularly interesting for the light they shed on peasant political attitudes. G. M. Sokolov, one of the SR leaders, gave the opening address in praise of 'patience and patriotism', which was followed by two days of discussion and resolutions formally expressing support for the Provisional Government.[33] On the third day the impatience of the peasant delegates began to make itself apparent, however, when the land question came up for discussion. The speeches of the SR leaders calling for patience and moderation were met from the floor by hostile voices calling for an immediate resolution of the land question. Egorov, a peasant delegate, warned the assembly not to trust the advice of the SR party leaders in the city:

> Igaev [a member of the Popular Socialist party] speaks of judicial rights. I am no judge and don't know the law. When I was a boy my father told me that I was a peasant. I believe that land means freedom. It is wrong to pay the landowners for the land. Will we be any better off if we wait for the Constituent Assembly to resolve the land question? In the past the government decided the land

[31] Shestakov (ed.), *Sovety krest'ianskikh deputatov*, pp. 94, 97; Gaponenko (ed.), pp. 693–7; N. A. Kravchuk, *Massovoe krest'ianskoe dvizhenie v Rossii nakanune Oktiabria*, Moscow, 1971, pp. 139–40; A. D. Maliavskii, *Krest'ianskoe dvizhenie v Rossii v 1917 g. mart–oktiabr'*, Moscow, 1981, p. 230.

[32] E. I. Medvedev, *Oktiabr'skaia revoliutsiia v Srednem Povolzh'e*, Kuibyshev, 1964, p. 37; A. S. Konkova, 'Bor'ba partii bol'shevikov za trudiashcheesia krest'ianstvo Samarskoi gubernii v period podgotovki Oktiabr'skoi revoliutsii', *Trudy moskovskogo istoriko-arkhivnogo instituta*, vol. 13, Moscow, 1959, p. 113; Shestakov (ed.), *Sovety krest'ianskikh deputatov*, pp. 99–100. See further T. Galynskii, *Ocherki po istorii agrarnoi revoliutsii Serdobskogo uezda, Saratovskoi gubernii*, Serdobsk, 1924, pp. 111–17; Vas'kin and Gerasimenko, pp. 199–200; *1917 god v Saratove*, Saratov, 1927, p. 78.

[33] *Protokoly 2-go samarskogo gubernskogo krest'ianskogo s''ezda s 20 maia po 6 iiunia 1917 g. i protokoly obshchegubernskogo vsesoslovnogo s''ezda s 28 maia po 6 iiunia 1917 g.*, Samara, 1917 (henceforth referred to as *PVS*), pp. 3, 8, 11.

question for us, but their efforts led us only into bondage. Now the government says there must first be order. We are always being told 'later, later, not now, not until the Constituent Assembly' . . . The land question must be resolved now, and we should not put our trust blindly in the political parties.[34]

On 25 May the impatience of the peasant delegates turned into anger when the assembly was read a circular from the Ministry of Internal Affairs, ordering the provincial commissar in Samara to prevent any confiscation of private property by the peasants. The Committees of People's Power (*komitety narodnoi vlasti*—KNV) in the districts of Nikolaevsk and Novouzensk were singled out for criticism, since they had already endorsed the peasant seizures of uncultivated private land. Not surprisingly, then, it was the delegates from these districts who tended to be the most vehement in their rejection of the circular. One delegate accused the Provisional Government of 'returning to the ways of the old regime'. A second warned that the circular 'should not tie our hands; if we agree to it, then we might as well go home now'. And a third delegate concluded confidently that 'the Minister who issued the circular must learn that the life of our villages is governed by the resolutions of our own assemblies and that these circulars should not be in disagreement with our resolutions, or else they will be repealed'.[35]

Under popular pressure, the SR leaders at the assembly agreed to organize a series of countermeasures against the Ministry. A telegram was sent to Petrograd demanding the circular be withdrawn. A second 'circular' was issued by the assembly itself and sent to the local KNVs advising them 'not to follow the circular of the old government[!], but to follow the instructions of the Samara peasant assembly in March and the resolutions of this assembly'.[36] The assembly declared the provincial KNV executive the highest authority in Samara province. The provincial commissar, who was appointed by the Provisional Government, was recognized 'only on condition that he is elected by the KNV executive, to which he is completely subordinate'.[37] The assembly then issued a series of far-reaching temporary land reforms, similar to those passed by the All-Russian Peasant Soviet Assembly in Petrograd (4 to 28 May). Until the convocation of the Constituent Assembly, all private land was to be placed under the control of the land committees or the KNV and was to be used for the general needs of the people. Any private land left uncultivated by its owner was to be confiscated and distributed on an equal basis among the peasants after the KNV and the land committees had accounted the war-prisoners,

[34] *PVS*, pp. 43–4. [35] Ibid., pp. 53–4.
[36] Ibid., p. 55. [37] Ibid., pp. 103, 106.

the livestock, and the available tools in the villages. The landless peasants would be the first to receive an allotment of the private land, followed by the rest of the peasantry. If any land was left over, it could be rented by its former owner at the price the latter had charged the peasants before its confiscation! The assembly passed these resolutions as fully binding 'laws' and warned that if any peasant commune infringed the resolutions it would 'be subject to the severest punishment'.[38]

In effect, the Samara peasant assembly had declared itself an autonomous 'government'. Its delegates returned to their villages with a set of 'laws' empowering them to confiscate any uncultivated private land. During the weeks immediately following the assembly there was a marked increase in the number of peasant land seizures in Samara province. The landowners claimed that the peasants had been influenced by the resolutions of the assembly and by Bolshevik leaflets.[39] The Ministry of Internal Affairs outlawed the resolutions of the Samara assembly in orders of 15 and 20 June. But neither the KNV executives nor the district land committees were prepared to act on these orders and they refused to send them to their own lower-level organs. The Nikolaevsk district KNV executive sent its own order around the localities, in which it declared itself at the head of an autonomous peasant dictatorship: 'All orders of the KNV are compulsory! The orders of any other institution or organization which negate the orders of the KNV and which are not issued by it must not be enacted.'[40] At least one of the Ministry's spies in Samara had read the writing on the wall. He wrote back to Petrograd: 'the local powers like to think on all questions that . . . their orders are equal to, or even better than, the orders of the Provisional Government . . . The psychology of local constituent power is beginning to rule.'[41]

The Samara assembly was just one among several in the Volga region during the early summer marking a downturn in the credibility of the Provisional Government and the formation of a 'peasant dictatorship' at the district and provincial levels. We shall not dwell here upon the peasant assemblies in Kazan' and Simbirsk provinces, which both took place during May.[42] Instead let us turn to the Penza provincial peasant

[38] Ibid., pp. 112–14. The resolutions are also reported in *Pobeda Velikoi Oktiabr'skoi sotsialisticheskoi revoliutsii v Samarskoi gubernii: Sbornik dokumentov*, Kuibyshev, 1957, pp. 59–67; Kostrikin, *Zemel'nye komitety v 1917 g.*, pp. 172–3; Maliavskii, pp. 232 ff; Kravchuk, pp. 141 ff.

[39] E. I. Medvedev, 'Zavoevanie i uprochenie vlasti rabochikh i krest'ian v Samarskoi gubernii', in D. A. Chugaev and V. S. Vasiukov (eds.), *Ustanovlenie sovetskoi vlasti na mestakh v 1917–18 gg.*, Moscow, 1959, pp. 298, 305.

[40] Kostrikin, *Zemel'nye komitety v 1917 g.*, pp.174–8.

[41] Ibid., pp. 178–9.

[42] On the Kazan' congress see Moiseeva, pp. 65 ff.; I. M. Ionenko, *Krest'ianstvo*

assemblies (7 to 10 April; and 11 to 15 May), which were praised by Lenin himself as a model of political organization.[43] They underwent a similar process of radicalization to the one just outlined in Samara province. The first assembly elected a thirty-eight-man commission (20 peasants, 12 soldiers, 6 assembly nominees) to draw up a series of temporary land measures: all private land was placed under the control of the local peasant committees; land sales, the renting-out of land, the enclosure of allotment land and the employment of wage-labour were all prohibited; and, finally, controls were established on the allocation of seed, tools, livestock, and war-prisoners. One of the delegates to the assembly claimed in a newspaper article entitled 'Peasant Revolution' that, in so far as the landowners had been deprived of a labour force, the peasantry had in fact gained control of the private estates. However, it was only the second assembly that gave full authorization to the peasant committees to confiscate the private property of the landlords.[44]

The Volga peasant assemblies of the early summer were among the most radical and far-reaching in the whole of Russia during 1917. This partly reflects the highly organized and violent nature of the agrarian struggle in the rural localities of the Volga region. It also reflects the organizational strength of the socialist parties in the Volga region, since they were largely responsible for the convocation of the peasant assemblies and the formulation of their resolutions. However, the relationship between the SR party leaders and the peasant delegates at these assemblies became increasingly strained as the mood of the latter grew more radical. Such tensions were apparent on the opening day of the Samara peasant assembly (20 May), when the party factions, numbering ninety-six representatives, demanded full voting rights and a budget to develop their political work. A number of the peasant delegates argued that the parties should have no more than an advisory voice on general issues. One delegate, named Ushakov, said he was not against the socialist parties, but that whereas the peasants and workers worked together, the political parties only argued among themselves. The parties gained full voting rights, as well as 23 of the 100 places on

Srednego Povolzh'ia nakanune Velikogo Oktiabria, Kazan', 1957, pp. 95 ff.; *Revoliutsionnaia bor'ba krest'ian Kazanskoi gubernii nakanune Oktiabria: Sbornik dokumentov*, Kazan', 1958, pp. 96–100. On the Simbirsk congress see *Bor'ba za ustanovlenie i uprochenie sovetskoi vlasti v Simbirskoi gubernii: Sbornik dokumentov*, Ul'ianovsk, 1958, pp. 45 ff.

[43] *PSS*, vol. 31, p. 378.

[44] Cited in A. S. Smirnov, 'Krest'ianskie s''ezdy Penzenskoi gubernii v 1917 g.', *Istoriia SSSR*, 1967, no. 3, p. 21. See also *Podgotovka i pobeda Velikoi Oktiabr'skoi sotsialisticheskoi revoliutsii v Penzenskoi gubernii: Sbornik dokumentov*, Penza, 1957, pp. 53–5.

the provincial KNV executive.[45] But later the same day, tensions resurfaced during the election of the executive presidium. M. T. Igaev, the leader of the Popular Socialists, suggested that the election of two candidates, Khlopotin and Luk'ianov, should be made conditional upon some 'proof of their worthiness'. I. V. Mashkov, a peasant delegate on the executive, stood up and accused Igaev of double standards:

> Khlopotin and Luk'ianov are peasants, so Igaev suggests postponing their election as permanent members until someone has checked their mandate . . . but he does not suggest the same for [S. A.] Volkov. Why? Because Volkov is an *intelligent*, as is Igaev himself. It is clear from what he has said that the *intelligenty* should be elected without checking their mandates, whereas we peasants have to have ours checked before we can be elected. But Igaev and Volkov have no authority because no one elected them.[46]

Technically, Mashkov was correct: Igaev and Volkov held mandated places for the Popular Socialist party. But the chairman of the assembly, the SR leader, Sokolov, made a powerful speech defending the record of all the socialist leaders and this was enough to sway the rest of the peasant delegates. The eleven-man presidium of the executive, when it had been elected, comprised 4 socialist party representatives (in the leading positions), 4 peasant delegates, 2 representatives of the Muslim minority and a chairman of one of the district KNVs.[47]

Despite this victory, the peasant delegates continued to voice frustration with the socialist party leaders who sat on the assembly executive. One delegate spoke about the *intelligenty* of the political parties in the same breath as the police and commissars of the government. He drew hoots of laughter from the assembly floor when he suggested that men should have to wear felt boots, like the peasants, to be allowed to serve as a judge. Another delegate, a Bolshevik, from Natal'ino *volost'* (Nikolaevsk *uezd*) condemned the paper resolutions of the assembly officials and called on the peasants to take the land without delay. When he was opposed by Igaev, who warned that an early land division would drive home the soldiers from the front, the peasants shouted 'Deception! Deception!' Egorov, who had already spoken against Igaev for using too many juridical terms, again took the stage amidst cheers of support: 'the soldiers have been cheated out of the land on four occasions and now they are impatient. Now they say to all the party activists and to all those who would only make fine speeches in support of the peasants: "go into the villages and

[45] *PVS*, pp. 29–31. [46] Ibid., p. 8. [47] Ibid., p. 9.

carry out the struggle for the land there!" '[48] At this highly charged moment a representative of the SR party stood up and began to read out a list of figures purporting to show that in fact there was not a great deal of private land still to be transferred to the peasantry, but the peasant delegates shouted him down with roars of anger.[49] As this sad figure left the rostrum, it must have appeared to many of the leaders of the moderate socialist parties that their romance with the peasantry was beginning to turn sour.

This impression was strengthened by the next provincial peasant assembly during August, when the right-wingers of the Samara SR party were repeatedly attacked by the maximalists (leftist SRs) for their failure to defend the position of the Samara KNVs and the soviets against the Provisional Government, whose circulars were said to 'go against' the decisions of the peasant assembly in May–June. The rightist SRs assured the assembly that the government had condemned only 'unorganized activities, whereas those in our province can not be described as such, because they are decided by local committees'.[50] This convinced the majority of the delegates that the government was not in fact 'stopping them from acting, while some believed it was relying on them'.[51] The resolutions of the rightist SRs expressing confidence in the Provisional Government were passed, despite the criticisms of the maximalists. Yet there was still an underlying feeling that the rightist SRs on the executive presidium had not been active enough in carrying out the land measures agreed at the last assembly to prove beyond doubt their independence from the Provisional Government. On the demand of the maximalists, a committee was established to supervise the work of the executive in the areas of land reform and political agitation (including the setting up of *volost'* soviets). Much more significant, however, was the fact that most of the peasant delegates had voted for the resolution in support of the Provisional Government only because they had been assured by the rightist SRs that the government had authorized the local committees to carry out the land seizures, on condition they were done in an organized manner. Thus the delegates returned home in the conviction that they had been instructed to complete the revolution on the land through their own local committees, without necessarily waiting for the Constituent Assembly.[52] It is to this revolution that we turn next.

48 PVS, p. 28.
49 Ibid., p. 37. See also Shestakov (ed.), *Sovety krest'ianskikh deputatov*, vol. 1, pp. 104–5.
50 Cited in Ferro, p. 121.
51 Ibid., p. 124.
52 Ibid., pp. 125, 307 n. 31.

3. THE JACQUERY AND ITS ORGANIZATION

Although there are no reliable figures on the different forms of peasant struggle during 1917, it is generally agreed that the level of unrest was highest in the central black-earth zone and the Volga region.[53] These regions were the most densely populated in Russia and they contained the largest number of private estates. The figures of the Main Administration of Militia Affairs show that peasant 'disturbances' were most frequently reported in the provinces of Kazan' (271 reports), Riazan' (242), Penza (233), Tambov (200), Saratov (179), Kursk (161), Orel (146), and Samara (141). Only three other provinces (Tula, Smolensk, and Khar'kov) reported more than one hundred such incidents.[54] The figures of S. M. Dubrovksii, which are generally much higher, show that Riazan', Penza, Tambov, Kazan', and Orel provinces were the most disturbed during 1917, while Saratov, Samara, and Simbirsk provinces followed closely behind.[55]

The peasant movement appeared to many people as a violent and anarchic 'jacquery' without proper organization.[56] Take the description of it by an SR party leader at the Samara provincial peasant assembly in May 1917:

In many villages and *volosti* there are disputes about the distribution of the land and the meadows between the large committees, which grant themselves rights over the private land, and the smaller committees, which, although they may have an equal claim to the land, are given only distant and inferior land to farm. Many *volost'* committees, without waiting for legislation, have already begun to divide up the land and cut down the trees. The village, *volost'*, and district committees fight among themselves. The district committees do not recognize the authority of the provincial committee. In short, disorder reigns

[53] The figures, which are based on the reports of the government's commissars to the Main Administration of Militia Affairs (GUDM) tend to underestimate the true level of peasant unrest, since the commissars, who wanted to play down the problems of their area, gave only a very general outline of the peasant movement with illustrative examples. Many of their reports never reached Petrograd because of the difficulties of communication. On the status of this evidence see Maliavskii, pp. 55–8; S. P. Melgunov, *The Bolshevik Seizure of Power*, Oxford, 1972, pp. 198–204. Over the years, Soviet historians have supplemented the GUDM figures on the basis of newspaper reports and other government sources. Their estimates vary widely, since each historian has a different understanding of what constitutes the peasant movement. I. I. Mints (*Istoriia Velikogo Oktiabria*, 3 vols., Moscow, 1967–73, vol. 2, pp. 838, 1120–6) has registered 4,285 peasant risings in Russia from Mar. to Oct., whereas Maliavksii (p. 378) lists 16,298 disturbances in the same period.

[54] Mints, vol. 2, pp. 1120–6.

[55] S. M. Dubrovskii, *Die Bauernbewegung in der russischen Revolution 1917*, Berlin, 1929, pp. 98–9.

[56] For a discussion of the term 'jacquery', and its application in Russia see T. Shanin, *The Roots of Otherness: Russia's Turn of Century*, vol. 2, *Russia 1905–7: Revolution as a Moment of Truth*, London, 1986, pp. 79–83.

everywhere and there is a smell of anarchy in the air, from which Heaven preserve us![57]

A similar impression of the peasant movement is given by modern Soviet historians. One has described the movement in Saratov province as 'an anarchic outburst of devastation and unorganized confiscation'.[58] By depicting the peasant movement as a sudden and violent rising without organization, Soviet historians underline the peasantry's need of Bolshevik leadership and state organization during the consolidation of the agrarian revolution.

Lenin himself was more sympathetic towards the spontaneous initiatives of the peasantry during 1917–18. He emphasized the rational methods of organization utilized by the local peasantry, as in the case of the Penza peasant assemblies. The reports of the Provisional Government also emphasized the 'organized nature' of the peasant land seizures.[59] How did this organization manifest itself?

Firstly, there was a general pattern in the intensity of the movement which followed changes in the agricultural seasons. During April, when the peasants were preparing the spring fields, there was a marked increase in the level of unrest. The month of May, when the peasants were busy in the meadows, witnessed a lull in the movement. But it revived during June and July, before the harvest. The decline in the level of unrest during August was probably due more to the demands of field work than the effects of government repression (a factor which Soviet historians have tended to stress).[60] The sharp increase in participants in the movement, and its more violent nature, during September and October should be explained by the collapse of the government, the publication of the Decree on Land, and the return of the peasant-soldiers from the front and the rear-army garrisons. As we shall see (ch. 3, sect. 4), the peasant-soldiers tended to be more radical and aggressive than their fellow villagers and often took the lead in the march on the estates.

Secondly, the form of the peasantry's actions was also influenced by seasonal factors. The early months of 1917 were bitterly cold. In Simbirsk province the average temparature between January and March was −13°C, compared with −7°C during the same months of

57 *PVS*, pp. 57–8.

58 G. A. Gerasimenko, 'Klassovaia bor'ba v derevne i nizovye krest'ianskie organizatsii v 1917–pervoi polovine 1918 goda (Na materialakh Nizhnego Povolzh'ia)', kand. diss., Saratov, 1973, p. 296.

59 *Ekonomicheskoe polozhenie Rossii nakanune Velikoi Oktiabr'skoi sotsialisticheskoi revoliutsii*, Leningrad, 1967, pt. 3, p. 402.

60 See e.g. Kravchuk, pp. 172–91. Maliavskii (p. 378) has recently suggested that the lull in the peasant movement during Aug. was slighter than previously thought by Soviet historians.

1916.[61] It is not surprising, then, that the felling of the gentry's woods played a prominent role in the peasant movement during these months.[62] During the spring sowing season the most common forms of peasant unrest involved the renting of gentry land, the allocation of war-prisoners, and the distribution of seed and tools. The communes passed resolutions which enforced fixed-price rentals of land and purchases of seed and tools from the landowners. They grazed their cattle on private pastures. And they organized communal work-teams to plough and sow the private lands that had been left uncultivated. During the high summer season the number of different forms of peasant struggle increased. The peasants mowed the private meadows; harvested the gentry fields; accounted and confiscated bits of private land; forcibly seized livestock and tools from the estates; and, if the squire had fled, sometimes even burned the manor house.

Thirdly, the peasant struggle took on different forms in the various ecological zones. Saratov province, with its many different soil-types and systems of land use, provides a good testing-ground to look at these variations. As in 1905–7, the peasant struggle was most intensive in the black-soil districts of the north-west: in Balashov, Serdobsk, Atkarsk, and Petrovsk. These districts contained the largest number of gentry estates and the highest population pressure on the land. The peasant economy was entirely dominated by agriculture. In the south-eastern districts (Kamyshin, Tsaritsyn) the land was of poorer quality. The population pressure on the land was less and there were fewer gentry estates than there were large private farms owned by peasants and merchants. Pastoralism and its related industries (e.g. leather-working, wool-weaving) played an important role alongside wheat farming. For these reasons, the peasant movement was less intensive in the south-east and assumed particular forms. Up to one-third of the agrarian disturbances involved conflicts between the peasant communes and enclosed peasant farms (*khutora, otruba*).[63] Conflicts with merchants and traders were also frequently noted. In the larger villages (large villages were more common in the south-east than in the north-west) there was often a high level of political organization in the revolutionary movement: leaflets were distributed; rent strikes were organized; officials' wages were left unpaid; the vaults of savings banks

[61] *Trudy TsSU: Statisticheskii sbornik za 1913–1917 gg.*, vol. 7, vyp. 1, Moscow, 1921, p. 254.

[62] Vas'kin and Gerasimenko, p. 200; Kotel'nikov and Meller (eds.), (table) *vedomost'* (Mar.).

[63] V. I. Kostrikin, 'Krest'ianskoe dvizhenie nakanune Oktiabria', in *Oktiabr' i sovetskoe krest'ianstvo*, Moscow, 1977, pp. 37–8; I. V. Igritskii, *1917 god v derevne*, Moscow, 1967, p. 70; Gerasimenko, *Nizovye krest'ianskie organizatsii*, p. 175.

and insurance companies were looted; and in some localities a 'peasant republic' was proclaimed.[64]

The most important organizational aspect of the peasant movement was the role of the commune. The land commune was the main institutional link between the peasants and their former landlord. Indeed, it was not until 1918 that the communes ceased to be delineated by their type of land use rights under serfdom (e.g. one village could contain a commune of former serfs, a commune of former State peasants, and a commune of Crown peasants). For this reason, the peasants viewed the land commune as the most obvious means by which to reorganize relations with their former landlord during the revolution. Through the commune the peasants could make an exclusive claim to the land of their former lord on the principle of 'Ours was the lord, ours is the land'. According to the Kuznetsk land department (*zemel'nyi otdel*), this principle was applied universally during 1917–18:

> the population divided the estates of the former landowners on a historical and geographical basis. Take, for example, the former estate of Petrov near the village of Ivanovo, where the inhabitants of Ivanovo declared that they alone had rights to its property. If an estate was equally distant from several villages, then the rights to its property were assumed only by the village which under serfdom had been owned by the forefathers of the landowners.[65]

The organizational methods of the land communes in their struggle against the landlords presupposed at many points the collective participation of the entire village community. To begin with, a gathering of the community, or its elders, would elect a committee to represent the commune before the landlord (e.g. in the negotiation of rent, in the enforced fixed-price purchases of seed, etc,). It would possibly also appoint a number of watchmen to 'protect' the property of the estate until its final confiscation.

In many villages the peasants were hesitant to challenge the property rights of the local squire, because they respected or feared his authority and power. Some villages continued to be wary even after they had received the assurances of the Soviet government in the October Decree on Land. S. P. Rudnev, the landowner from Beklemish-

[64] *1917 god v Saratove*, p. 78; Kotel'nikov and Meller (eds.), pp. 16–17, 94, 154, 225, 272, 330. A similar correlation has been noted between the large size of the village and the level of political organization during 1905: see T. Mixter, 'The Polarization of the Saratov Countryside: Peasants in the Revolution of 1905–1907', paper presented to Conference on the History of Saratov Province, University of Illinois, 1985; Shanin, *Revolution as a Moment of Truth*, p. 134. On the effects of large village size on Soviet political organization see *RR*, p. 167. This is also discussed in ch. 5, sect. 2, below.

[65] TsGANKh, f. 478, op. 1, d. 202, l. 7.

evo whom we encountered above, recalled that his family spent the summer and autumn of 1917 just as they had always done: 'the men went drinking and hunting; guests from Simbirsk came to stay; we went to Nazhim and the Molochnyi Khutor for picnics and mushroom-picking . . . Austrian prisoners of war worked our estate'.[66] Many other landowners must have had a similar experience, since a significant portion of them remained on their estates after 1917 (see ch. 3, sect. 4).

Elsewhere the peasants took the earliest opportunity to establish their claims to the private land. In the early stages of the revolution the estate land tended to be expropriated or put under the control of the commune through written resolutions (*prigovory*) presented to the landowners. These named in detail the areas of land which were subject to the various conditions set out. They invariably left the squires who had not already fled to the towns a generous amount, or 'norm', of the land in recognition of their former property rights and their future consumption needs, although the land was often situated at the farthest extremities of the village terrain. The peasants were wary of demanding more than they could justify as a 'fair share' of the private land, especially since the Provisional Government had expressly forbidden the seizure of private property. By formulating their demands in written resolutions, the peasants were 'legitimizing' them in a pseudo-legal form—a form which, in their own eyes, distinguished organized 'confiscation' from unorganized 'seizure', rightful 'expropriation' from unrightful 'theft'. The nature of such resolutions, which were also characteristic of the 1905–7 peasant movement, is suggested by the following petitions from landowners to the Serdobsk district *zemstvo*:

A resolution of the Cherkass committee in the spring took nearly all my land away and I was left only 30 *des.* of spring fields and 36 *des.* of fallow, the largest part of which is situated a long distance away beyond the Khoper River, whither it is difficult to carry tools, and, moreover, the soil there is much worse than it is in the nearby plot, which was manured daily, but which the committee took away. A second resolution took away a field of boon of 28 *des.* and some other meadows sown with lucerne, of about 40 *des.* in size . . . I was left two gardens sown with herbs and a field of 5 *des.* sown with lucerne . . . Now the committee is hiring labourers and war-prisoners, and is allowing the peasants to graze their cattle in the woods . . . and is felling the trees. (E. V. Radchenko)

I own 22 *des.* 600 sq. *sazhen'* of land . . . All the arable is farmed by hired labourers. In the spring of 1917 the peasants of Khananeevka village, Buturlin' *volost'*, took away the war-prisoners I had hired and resolved that I may employ labour only from Buturlin' *volost'* at the price of 1 rb. per *des.* per worker

[66] *PVO*, p. 79.

per day, on my food *(na svoikh kharchakh)*. These conditions have prevented me from getting my spring fields sown. (P. S. Monakhov, 5 June)

A resolution of the Davydovka *volost'* executive committee on 10 April ordered our convent to rent to the peasants 15 *des.* of our spring fields. On 19 May we received a communication from the same committee that, for our own needs, we may keep 15 *des.* of fallow land, but that a further 30 *des.* of land must be given to the peasants of Pleshcheevka village . . . Now the peasants are requisitioning grain from our convent: 600 *pud* has been taken for the local villagers at 1 rb. 52 kop. [per *pud*], but grain from the peasants is requisitioned at 2 rb. 50 kop. (The nuns of Panovka convent)[67]

From the summer, the actions of the peasant committees became more assertive. The resolutions of the district and provincial peasant assemblies and the publication of the October Decree on Land assured the peasants that their claims to the private lands were both legal and just. The return of the peasant-soldiers during the autumn and the onset of the new agricultural year, beginning with the autumn sowing, instilled a growing feeling of impatience in the villages, which was only aggravated by the failure of the *volost'* land committees to complete the expropriation of the private lands. The initiative now passed to the individual communes which had a claim to the property of the estates. The vast majority of the private land which was expropriated during 1917–18 was first placed under the control of the nearest peasant commune. When the gentry estates were transferred to the control of the *volost'* land authorities during the spring of 1918, only a very small number of them were still found to have their livestock, tools, and buildings (see ch. 3, sect. 3).

How did the communes actually take control of the gentry estates? The majority of the estates were expropriated just before the start of the autumn or spring sowing.[68] A general gathering of the peasants resolved to place under the control of the commune all or part of the estate property. At a selected time, the peasants assembled their carts in front of the church and moved off towards the manor, armed with guns, pitchforks, axes, and whatever came to hand. The squire and his stewards, if they had not already fled, were arrested and forced to sign a resolution placing the property of the estate under the control of a village committee. The peasants loaded on to their carts the contents of the barns and led away the cattle, excepting the property which had been left for the use of the landowner and his family. Pieces of large agricultural machinery, such as harvesters and winnowing machines,

[67] Cited in Galynskii, pp. 111–13, 115–16.

[68] Approximately 80 per cent, according to my calculation from 233 enquiries (*oprosnye listy*) completed by the *volost'* administrations in Penza and Saratov provinces during the spring of 1918 (TsGANKh, f. 478, op. 1, dd. 149, 150, 154).

which the peasants could not move or could not use on their small farms, were usually abandoned or destroyed. The Saratov provincial land department left a vivid account of this plundering of the estates in December 1917:

As far as the manor buildings are concerned, they have been senselessly destroyed, with only the walls left standing. The windows and the doors were the worst to suffer; in the majority of the estates no trace is left of them. All forms of transport have been destroyed or taken . . . cumbersome machines like steam-threshers, locomotives, and binders were taken out for no known reason and discarded along the roads and in the fields . . . the agricultural tools were also taken; anything that could be used in the peasant households simply disappeared from the estates. On the estates that used to have collars and harnesses for 100 or 200 horses, such as those belonging to the Ikoninkovs and the Gagarins, it is now difficult to find enough harnesses for a single horse and cart.[69]

From a different perspective, the following account, written in January 1918 by a small landowner in Samara district about the expropriation of his farmstead (*khutor*), is also evocative:

Yesterday, 26 January, at 12 noon the entire commune of Kolybelka, led by the chairman of the village committee, appeared at my *khutor*. They arrested me and my family, as well as two policemen who happened to be at my house, and left a guard with us with a warning not to go out of the house. They also placed armed guards around my farm and made threats to my labourers. Then they took away all my grain and seed, except 40 *pud* of rye, and locked up my barns. I asked them to weigh the grain they had taken, but they refused as they loaded up their 56 carts until they were overflowing . . . That night some of the peasants returned, broke the lock on the barn and took away my scales and tubs with weights of 5 *pud* measure.[70]

It was very rare indeed for the squire himself to be harmed during these proceedings. However, the destruction and burning of manor buildings (*razgrom, pogrom*) did become increasingly common, especially during the autumn and winter of 1917–18. In Penza province it was reported that one-fifth of all the manors had been burned or destroyed during September and October alone. In the following spring it was claimed that the manor houses had been destroyed in 89 out of 159 *volosti* in the province. A year later, in February 1919, the Insaro district land department in Penza province reported that there were only two manor houses left in the entire district which had not yet been destroyed.[71]

[69] TsGANKh, f. 478, op. 1, d. 202, ll. 7–8.
[70] GAKO, f. 81, op. 1, d. 119, l. 209.
[71] TsGANKh, f. 478, op. 1, dd. 149, 150; op. 6, d. 1015, l. 194.

Judging from the eighty-nine reports made by *volost'* authorities in Penza province during spring 1918, there were three main causes of the *razgromy*. The first and most common (noted in 20 reports) was the peasants' impatience with the slowness of the higher authorities in starting formal procedures for the expropriation of the estates. At the Saratov peasant soviet assembly in May 1918 one of the leaders of the provincial land department lamented that 'if only the land had been taken into account from August [1917], there would not have been so much chaos and destruction' on the estates.[72] The failure of the *volost'* land departments to transfer the property of the estates to the peasant communes at the earliest opportunity encouraged the latter to take it for themselves. This was registered by the *volost'* land departments as the 'plunder' or 'misappropriation' (*raskhishchenie*) of the estate property by the peasant communes, since it pre-empted the land reform work of the *volost'* authorities and resulted in the unequal distribution of the estates' property among the various communes. As far as the latter were concerned, however, this was no more than the rightful expropriation of the property which, historically speaking, should have belonged to them. As we shall discover in the next chapter (sect. 3), this conflict of views between the *volost'* land authority and the individual communes was to play a dominant role in rural politics during the period of the land reforms.

A second common cause of the *razgromy* (noted in 12 reports) was described in the following terms by the *volost'* authorities: 'the peasants do not understand the meaning of the Decree on Land'; 'the peasants are not politically aware' (*nesoznatel'nye*); 'the peasants take a very localist view' (*mestnichestvo*); and so on. These reports also implied that a case of *razgrom* had been recorded because one or more of the communes had seized the property of an estate without waiting for the resolution of the land question by the *volost'* authorities. For this reason, the reports have a similar set of implications as the first group of reports on the *razgromy*.

A third common explanation of the *razgromy* (noted in 14 cases) was the peasantry's 'hatred of the landowners', or its 'animosity towards the old order'. In two further reports the peasants were said to be motivated by their 'hatred of the bourgeoisie' (a number which underlines the inappropriateness of the Marxist-Leninist interpretation of the agrarian revolution). If the landlord had fled to the town, then, by destroying his manor, the peasants could make his return unlikely. If, on the other hand, the landlord had not fled, then the

[72] *Protokoly saratovskogo gubernskogo s''ezda sovetov krest'ianskikh deputatov, proiskhodivshego v g. Saratove s 25–go maia po 2 iiunia 1918 g.*, Saratov, 1918 (henceforth referred to as *PSG*), p. 133.

peasants in this way might encourage him to do so. The manors of the most unpopular landowners, especially those who had been staunch supporters of the old regime, were the most likely to be destroyed. In June 1917 the villagers of Bor-Polianshchina (Buturlin' *volost'*, Serdobsk *uezd*) forced their way into the manor of V. V. Saburov, whom they brutally killed. This was retribution for the bloody part played by D. I. Saburov, the former land captain, in the suppression of the peasant uprising in 1906. For three days after the murder, the peasants ran riot on the estate. The farm buildings and the manor house, which boasted a large library, were burned. Food and livestock to the value of 125,000 gold rb. were taken away.[73]

Who led the seizures? An historian of the 1905–7 peasant movement has suggested that the peasantry tended to fight the landowners as a collective group of the whole village or commune, rather than in social subgroups. She has also argued that when the peasants did act in the latter manner, they tended to do so according to the form of the action itself, rather than the level of 'class-consciousness' supposedly held by the peasants within each of the subgroups. Thus, the richer peasants, who were the best equipped with horses and carts, most often led the march on the estate, but they seldom took part in a *razgrom*.[74] Both points are borne out by the evidence from 1917. Only two of the eighty-nine reports on the destruction of the manors in Penza, which we considered above, mentioned the initiative of the 'kulaks' or the richest peasants. As might be expected, the reports most often implied (seventeen times) that the poorest peasants were the main instigators of the *razgromy*: five times 'on account of hunger'; once 'on account of hatred of *barshchina*';[75] eight times as 'the least politically conscious [*nesoznatel'nye*] peasants'; and thrice as the 'land hungry'. In two reports it was claimed that peasant-soldiers had instigated the *razgrom*.[76]

Whatever the roles played by the particular socio-economic subgroups—the rich, the poor, the mobile, the literate, the young, or those experienced in earlier uprisings—it is clear that the peasantry

[73] Galynskii, pp. 117, 141, 172.

[74] M. Perrie, 'The Russian Peasant Movement of 1905–07: Its Social Composition and Revolutionary Significance', *Past and Present*, vol. 57, 1972, pp. 138, 142. In the villages of Kondol' and Viazemka (Petrovsk *uezd*) the rich peasants were reported to have said to the others: 'we have no power, go and take the land yourselves'. In the village of Elizavetino (Vol'sk *uezd*) the white-bearded and rich peasants were said to be opposed to the villagers' plan to seize gentry land: 'leave things as they are and don't touch the land of the squire!' (cited in M. O. Sagrad'ian, *Osushchestvlenie leninskogo dekreta o zemle v Saratovskoi gubernii*, Saratov, 1966, pp. 43–4).

[75] Rent in the form of labour service, or *corvée*.

[76] TsGANKh, f. 478, op. 1, d. 149, ll. 79, 83, 135, 139, 159, 180, 204, 221, 238, 247, 249; d. 150, ll. 21, 65, 85, 93, 96, 118, 137, 150, 169.

generally organized its collective forces through the politico-social structures of the village and the commune. It was common for a village or communal gathering to demand the participation of all its adult male members in the march on the manor. The aims of this were to make the village responsible collectively for its action and to ensure the equal distribution of the expropriated property. Anyone who did not take part in the march would automatically forfeit his (and his family's) share of the property. He might also be made to pay a heavy fine. It was not unknown for several village communes to act in co-ordination in the confiscation of an estate. An example of this was reported from Marianovka *volost'* in Karsun *uezd*:

> on 15 November the inhabitants of Marianovka, Fedorovka, and Berezniaki began the destruction and the independent seizure of the property from the estate of Arapov. All three communes held auctions in their respective villages for the livestock, the tools, and the buildings, but the household utensils were pillaged. The money which was raised was divided among everyone.[77]

Together with the gentry estates, the private peasant farms (*khutora*) and enclosed holdings (*otruba*) also fell victim to the peasant movement. If, in 1916, between 27% and 33% of the peasant households in Russia farmed arable in private enclosed tenure, then six years later less than 2% continued to do so in the major agricultural regions, and only in the far north-west was there still a significant number of separate holdings outside the commune.[78] The communal movement against the separators was most intense in the south and south-east, where the Stolypin land reforms had gained most ground before the revolution. Between 1916 and 1922 the share of peasant land within private household enclosures fell from 19% to 0.1% in Samara province; from 16.4% to 0% in Saratov province; and from 24.9% to 0.4% in the Stavropol' region.[79] Nearly all of these losses were incurred during 1917. In March 1917 there were 144 *volosti* in Saratov province with enclosed peasant holdings, but by the following October these types of holding had been totally liquidated in 74 of the *volosti* and partly liquidated in the remaining 70 *volosti*.[80] Such figures suggest that attacks on the household enclosures represented an important element of the peasant movement. Although Soviet historians during the 1920s considered that no more than 6% of the cases of

[77] Cited in Kabanov, 'Oktiabr'skaia revoliutsiia',

[78] V. P. Danilov, 'Ob istoricheskikh sud'bakh krest'ianskoi obshchiny v Rossii', *Ezhegodnik po agrarnoi istorii*. vyp. 6, *Problemy istorii russkoi obshchiny*, Vologda, 1976, pp. 106–8.

[79] P. N. Pershin, *Uchastkovoe zemlepol'zovanie v Rossii*, Moscow, 1922, p. 8.

[80] E. I. Medvedev, *Krest'ianstvo Srednego Povolzh'ia v bor'be za zemliu v mirnyi period revoliutsii 1917 goda*, Kuibyshev, 1981, p. 42.

rural unrest during 1917 involved the peasant enclosures, modern Soviet historians have estimated that such cases accounted for up to 20% of the agrarian unrest in European Russia, and up to 33% and 44% in certain areas of the south-east.[81] The latter figures, which are used to support the argument that the peasant attacks formed part of a general 'proletarian' struggle against the 'rural bourgeoisie', are possibly too high.

According to the Saratov provincial commissar, the communal war against the separators was even more bitter than the war against the gentry estates. If the separators refused to return to the commune, it was not unknown for the latter to bar them from using the roads, the wells, the church, and all the other amenities of the village. It was also common for the separators to be disallowed from voting for any of the *volost'* authorities. Some communes legitimized violent acts of revenge and 'mob law' (*samosud*) against the private farmers. In Vol'sk *uezd*, for example, 160 peasants from Tersa commune marched on one of the leading *otrubniki* in the region and dragged him to a village gathering, where, in front of other separators, they tied him to a stake and beat him to death with clubs. A resolution was then passed, which the separators were forced to sign, calling for the liquidation of all the enclosed holdings. According to a local police official, 'the *skhod* always assembles before an attack like this and resolves that all the private holdings must return to the commune before the next sowing'.[82]

How are we to explain the bitterness of these struggles? To begin with, we must date the communal war against the separators not from 1917, but from 1906, when the Stolypin land reforms were introduced. The Volga region registered higher rates of land enclosure after 1906 than almost any other region of Russia. The figures of P. N. Pershin, which are somewhat exaggerated, show that between 1907 and 1916 as much as 1,927,000 *des.* of communal allotment land in Samara

[81] The earliest Soviet estimate (Shestakov (ed.)), *Sovety krest'ianskikh deputatov*, pp. 254–6) was based upon materials of the Main Land Committee, communicated to the All-Russian Soviet of Peasant Deputies in August 1917 by the SR N. Ia. Bykhovskii. Bykhovskii said that 5.5 percent of rural disturbances involved the peasant household enclosures. A decade later S. M. Dubrovskii (*Krest'ianstvo v 1917 g.*, Moscow/Leningrad, 1927, p. 56) offered the estimate of 6 per cent. Both figures have been attacked as too low by T. V. Osipova—Bykhovskii's on the basis of alleged SR bias, and Dubrovskii's because, whereas the attacks on the estates were reported individually, the incidents involving the enclosed allotments were reported in groups. Osipova offered the estimate of 20 per cent for European Russia (*Klassovaia bor'ba v derevne v period podgotovki i provedeniia Oktiabr'skoi revoliutsii*, Moscow, 1974, p. 169). For the figures relating to the south-east see n. 63 above.

[82] Vas'kin and Gerasimenko, p. 216; Gerasimenko, 'Vliianie posledstvii', pp. 39–40, 42, 47; id., *Nizovye krest'ianskie organizatsii*, p. 209.

province was enclosed, a figure representing 24.8% of the allotment land in 1917. In Saratov province 739,000 *des.* of communal allotment land was enclosed (19.3% of the allotment land in 1917), according to the figures of Pershin, although a more accurate estimate may be 661,658 *des.* (17.2%).[83] The Stolypin land enclosure movement in the Volga region was marked by frequent struggles between the communes and the machinery of the state which was used to enforce the rights of the separators to 'opt out' of the communal system. Most of the separations were done by individual households without the agreement of the communal assembly (i.e. by the order of the land captain and the district *zemstvo* land organs): 84% and 93% of the separations in Samara and Saratov provinces, respectively, fell into this category. The figure for European Russia was 26%.[84]

The resolutions of the peasant communes against the separators during 1917 displayed a detailed knowledge of the land which had been enclosed since 1906. This is not surprising, since nearly all of the consolidated land had once belonged to the commune, or had been rented by it. The peasants believed that the land of the gentry should 'belong to the people', but they considered that the land of the separators was already, and always had been, the property of the people. Thus, during 1917–18 the communes tended to divide, and there-after to farm, the estate land separately, lest the authority of the land-owner should be restored, whereas they nearly always divided the land of the separators along with the rest of the communal allotments (the latter was only kept apart if it had been purchased by the separator).

The peasantry's dislike of the separators was rooted in the traditional legal customs of family ownership and communal land tenure. As early as 1906, a correspondent of the Free Economic Society reported from Saratov province that the peasantry was 'very hostile' to the Stolypin land measures (the Law of 9 November 1906), since it feared the social effects of primogeniture and a free trade in land:

> the peasant elders will sell up and their children become paupers. The peasants say no one should sell land—let them trade what they like, but not land. Let him have land who will work it . . . for it must be defended against squires taking money out of the country and from merchants trading in land. Of this the peasants are convinced, and both rich and poor are united in solidarity.[85]

[83] Pershin, *Uchastkovoe zemlepol'zovanie*, pp. 50–1. The percentages are calculated from *Trudy TsSU: Statisticheskii Sbornik za 1913–1917 gg.*, pp. 178, 186, 188. The revised Saratov figure is from M. Ia. Kosenko, 'Agrarnaia reforma Stolypina v Saratovskoi gubernii', kand. diss., Saratov, 1950, p. 109. On Pershin's methods of calculation see Danilov, 'Ob istoricheskikh sud'bakh', pp. 103–6.

[84] Kosenko, p. 109; E. I. Medvedev, *Krest'ianstvo Srednego Povolzh'ia v bor'be za zemliu*, p. 40.

[85] *Agrarnoe dvizhenie v Rossii v 1905–1906 gg.*, St Petersburg, 1908, pp. 151–2.

At the end of the civil war a large portion of the peasantry was to express frustration with the system of communal land tenure (see ch. 3, sect. 3). But during the revolutionary period the universal division of the land on local egalitarian principles continued to represent the basic ideal of the majority of the peasants. The realization of this goal, which could only be achieved through the land commune, demanded a high level of solidarity among the fellow villagers. Hence in the summer of 1918 the Atkarsk district land department published an appeal

> 'to all the peasants farming an *otrub* to return to the commune and enjoy equal rights with all other citizens in order to unite the entire peasantry during this difficult time and to annul all the divisions between us!'[86]

It is very doubtful whether any of the land communes consciously organized their struggle against the 'traders in land' as a 'proletarian' struggle against the 'rural bourgeoisie', in the manner suggested by modern Soviet historians.[87] Many of the enclosed holdings were actually smaller than the neighbouring communal allotments (a phenomenon noted in twenty out of forty-seven provinces in European Russia)[88] and were relatively weak in economic terms. In the Volga steppe regions, where many of the enclosed holdings were situated, only 3.1% of the peasant enclosures were consolidated in one plot (this figure includes the *khutora*); 58.6% were divided into two plots; and 38.3% were divided into three or more plots.[89] The large number of peasant enclosures established in the south-east under Stolypin may be explained by the presence of the Volga Germans and the relatively fast rate of socio-economic polarization in this region and, in particular, by the problem of distance in the communal system of land use. On the other hand, without several adult males, without three or four horses, a couple of well-built carts, and some advanced agricultural machinery, without fencing, irrigation and sufficient stocks of fertilizer and reserve grain, it was very hard for a peasant family on its own, without the advantages of communal life, to farm an enclosed holding of 20 or 30 *des.* on the steppe, with its harsh climate and poor soil, its lack of fresh water sources and woods, its few roads and poor communications and, last but not least, the enormous distances between market centres. The steppeland village—with its church, its schoolhouse and

86 Cited in Pershin, *Uchastkovoe zemlepol'zovanie*, p. 36.

87 A recent exception is the work of V. V. Kabanov (*KK* pp. 71–83), whose views on this subject largely coincide with my own.

88 *O zemle: Sbornik statei o proshlom i budushchem zemel'no-khoziaistvennogo stroitel'stva*, Moscow, 1921, p. 15. Lenin acknowledged that a significant number of the *khutora* and *otruba* were established by weak peasant households (*PSS*, vol. 23, p. 270).

89 Pershin, *Uchastkovoe zemlepol'zovanie*, pp. 14–15.

its well, its small shops and trades, and its networks of neighbourhood co-operation—must have appeared as an oasis of civilization in the arid wilderness. 'To be without the village was simply not to be!' declared one of the characters in a novel by J. Ponten about German peasant life in the Novouzensk district.[90]

It is not surprising, then, that a large number of the peasant households which consolidated private plots after 1906 decided to remain in the village commune (*otruba*): in Samara and Saratov provinces the proportion was estimated to be 78%.[91] Many of the smaller *otrubniki* in the south-east voluntarily broke up their private plots and returned to the communal system during 1917 in order to share in the division of the estates. A contemporary study of the agrarian revolution in Zadonsk *uezd* (Voronezh province) noted that in one-third of the villages all the *otrubniki* broke up their holdings voluntarily during 1917, and 70% of the *khutora* followed their example.[92] The more stable *khutoriane*, who tended to resist the communes,[93] should be seen as the victims of a strong collective village bonding against 'outsiders', especially when the private farmers were members of an ethnic minority, such as the Volga Germans, rather than the targets of a proletarian struggle against the bourgeoisie. In 1917 the statistician G. I. Baskin showed that in the villages of Samara province situated less than 25 *versty* from a market centre only 58% of the peasants expressed hostility towards the *khutoriane*, whereas in the more remote villages as many as 66% of the peasants expressed such hostility.[94] If this was part of a struggle against the bourgeoisie, then we would expect to find the reverse correlation, with a larger proportion of the peasants expressing hostility towards the *khutoriane* in the villages closer to the market centres.

Like the agrarian revolution itself, the movement against the peasant separators was guided by the principles of communal land tenure. These principles were pragmatic and flexible (as any practicable set of rules has to be during a revolution). They were not a dogmatic charter of social revenge. The success of the peasant revolution demanded a high level of social conformity. There was no doubt that the peasant communes would demand the destruction of all large-scale private farming. But the principles of communal land tenure, like the Land Code of 1922, did not preclude the freedom of the

[90] J. Ponten, *Der Sprung ins Abenteuer*, Stuttgart, 1932, p. 14.

[91] Pershin, *Uchastkovoe zemlepol'zovanie*, pp. 16–17.

[92] V. Keller and I. Romanenko, *Pervye itogi agrarnoi reformy: Opyt issledovaniia rezul'tatov sovremennogo zemleustroistva na primere Zadonskogo uezda Voronezhskoi gubernii*, Voronezh, 1922, pp. 103–4.

[93] Gerasimenko, 'Vliianie posledstvii', p. 47.

[94] G. I. Baskin, *Printsipy zemel'nogo naseleniia v sviazi s otnosheniem naseleniia k raznym formam zemlevladeniia i zemlepol'zovaniia*, Samara, 1917, pp. 16–18.

small peasant farm to choose its own form of land use, provided it did not employ the wage-labour of other families. So, the peasant communes and their soviets during the spring of 1918 fully recognized the rights of the separators' hamlets (*vyselki, poselki*) to farm a share of the allotment land; and they supported the establishment of the 'communes' (*kommuny*) with enclosed household tenure. Indeed, it was often not until the summer of 1918, when the regional land authorities began to organize inter-village and inter-*volost'* land redivisions, that the hamlets and 'communes' with enclosed household tenure were forced to merge with the neighbouring land commune in order to simplify territorial boundaries.[95] This balance between the ideals of collective organization and freedom of land use was neatly encapsulated by a resolution of the Dubovo-Pobedimov *volost'* soviet (Bugul'ma *uezd*) in March 1918:

> Today, in free Russia, everyone should be equal and united and there should be no disputes between the members of the communes and the separators . . . the members of the communes should accept all the separators into their family on an equal basis and should cease all oppressive measures against them, since these only play into the hands of the enemies of the people![96]

4. THE ESTABLISHMENT OF THE *VOLOST'* SOVIETS

'The terrible days of the October revolution in Petersburg and Moscow passed me by', recalled S. P. Rudnev, the landowner from Simbirsk province whom we encountered earlier,

> I lived through them in Durasovka without knowing what had happened; there all was quiet, and only a faint echo of the storm that was rumbling in the capital cities could be heard . . . The news which came from the town and the railway stations . . . did not communicate more than one-tenth of what had actually happened.[97]

Thousands of Russian villages must have had a similar experience of the October revolution.

Modern Soviet historians have depicted the 'October days' in the countryside as a dramatic break from the past—a fundamental socio-political revolution, liberating the working peasants, granting them land and uniting the agrarian movement with the Bolshevik revolution in the cities. This interpretation is a political fantasy, a deliberate misrepresentation of the social and political processes which constituted the revolution in the rural areas. The establishment of the

[95] GAKO, f. 81, op. 1, d. 119, ll. 165–8.
[96] TsGAOR, f. 393, op. 3, d. 359, l. 202.
[97] *PVO*, p. 91.

volost' soviets represented a major discontinuity neither in the social life of the villages, nor in the development of the peasantry's political institutions since the spring of 1917. Lenin himself was later to stress that 'the October revolution of the cities came to the countryside only in the summer and autumn of 1918'.[98]

The decisive break in the peasant revolution was the confiscation of the gentry estates. Indeed, it was not uncommon for the peasants to date 'the revolution' from the day the estate in their locality was taken over by the commune. Hence, some of the *volost'* soviets replied to the enquiries of spring 1918 in Penza province that the estates in their locality had been expropriated 'on the day of the revolution', although the day which was cited did not always fall on the 25 October, or on the date when Soviet power was established at the local level (from the village to the provincial capital).[99] Table 4 shows that there was no real

TABLE 4. *Dates of establishment of* volost' *soviets and confiscation of gentry estates, Saratov and Penza provinces, 1917–1918*

	Soviets established		Estates confiscated	
	Saratov	Penza	Saratov	Penza
March – October 1917	40	—	—	—
October	11	—	14	37
November	7	—	7	5
December	34	—	12	7
January 1918	95	30	4	8
February	62	128	2	3
March	16	82	1	9
April	11	15	3	22
May	—	2	—	—
'In spring'	—	—	11	24

Sources: Figures on the establishment of the soviets are from G. A. Gerasimenko, 'Klassovaia bor'ba v derevne i nizovye krest'ianskie organizatsii v 1917–pervoi polovine 1918 goda (Na materialakh Nizhnego Povolzh'ia)', kand. diss., Saratov, 1973, p. 261 (Saratov); P. N. Abramov, 'K voprosu o vremeni sozdanii pervykh volostnykh sovetov', *Istoriia SSSR*, 1960, no. 5, p. 159 (Penza). Figures on the confiscation of the estates are from S. L. Makarova, 'Oprosnye listy Narodnogo Komissariata Zemledeliia i moskovskogo oblastnogo ispolnitel'nogo komiteta kak istochnik po istorii agrarnoi revoliutsii (noiabr' 1917–iiun' 1918)', kand. diss., Moscow, 1970, p. 199.

correlation between the dates of the expropriation of the estates and the establishment of the *volost'* soviets. The majority of the estates were expropriated in time for the winter or spring sowing, whereas the

98 *PSS*, vol. 37, p. 141.
99 TsGANKh, f. 478, op. 1, d. 149, ll. 184, 249; d. 150, l. 21.

majority of the *volost'* soviets were set up during the winter months. Only a handful of soviets, most of them badly organized and short-lived, had been established before October 1917.[100] News of the October revolution and the Decree on Land undoubtedly helped to change the mind of those peasant communities, which had previously been hesitant to take the law into their own hands. The peasants' conviction that they were entitled to confiscate the property of the estates was probably strengthened by the peasant and soviet assemblies which met during the weeks immediately after October. Many of these assemblies were radicalized under the influence of the Left SRs, the Bolsheviks and the soldiers who had returned from the front and the rear army garrisons.[101] However, the fact remains that the majority of the estates were confiscated by the peasant communes and the village committees, and not by the *volost'* authorities. There is little evidence to suggest that the establishment of the *volost'* soviet had any direct influence on the expropriation of the estate. A Soviet historian has collected evidence which gives, for the same *volost'*, both the date of the soviet's election and the confiscation of the estates. In 14 of the 27 *volosti* for which she has managed to find the relevant data, the estates were accounted after the establishment of the soviet; and in the 13 remaining *volosti* they were accounted before the establishment of the soviet.[102] In other words, there was no significant correlation between these two events. This is supported by the findings of the enquiries of spring 1918 in Penza province: by the end of April, only 54% of the *volost'* soviets had accounted the estates under their official jurisdiction; 18% of the *volost'* soviets reported that the estates were still under the control of the individual communes; while 17% of the *volost'* soviets had no idea who controlled the estates. The *volost'* soviet was found to be more likely to control the expropriated land in the smaller *volosti* (or in the *volosti* with a relatively small number of estates), where the power of the soviet was readily felt, and less likely

[100] Butyl'kin and Gerasimenko, pp. 147, 150; Vas'kin and Gerasimenko, pp. 191–2; E. I. Medvedev, Krest'ianstvo Srednego Povolzh'ia v bor'be za zemliu, p. 43; *PVS*, pp. 16–17.

[101] On the soviet and peasant assemblies in Samara during Dec. and Jan. see GAKO, f. 81, op. 1, dd. 1, 2; E. I. Medvedev, 'Zavoevanie i uprochenie', pp. 323–4. On the assemblies in Saratov see Gerasimenko, 'Klassovaia bor'ba', pp. 248, 255, 257–60; *Godovshchina sotsial'noi revoliutsii v Saratove*, Saratov, 1918, pp. 15–16; V. P. Antonov-Saratovskii, *Pod stiagom proletarskoi bor'by: Otryvki iz vospominanii o rabote v Saratove za vremia s 1915 g. do 1918 g.*, Moscow/Leningrad, 1925, vol. 1, pp. 222–30. The influence of the Saratov Congress of *Volost'* Representatives (30 Nov–4 Dec.) is much vaunted by Soviet historians, but doubted by O. H. Radkey, *The Sickle Under the Hammer: The Russian Socialist Revolutionaries in the Early Months of Soviet Rule*, New York, 1973, pp. 267–70.

[102] Makarova, pp. 202–3.

to control it in the larger *volosti* (or the *volosti* with a relatively large number of estates), where the village communes tended to dominate and the whole structure of power was more decentralized. Nearly all the *volost'* soviets lamented that the individual communes had taken away the movable property of the estates prior to the establishment of soviet power.[103]

Modern Soviet historians have associated the establishment of the *volost'* soviets with a class war between the poor peasants, in support of Soviet power, and the rich peasants or 'kulaks', in support of the *volost' zemstvo*. Although there were such conflicts, they were not as common as Soviet historians would have us believe. P. N. Pershin, for example, cited the report of the Efimovka *volost'* delegate at the Novouzensk soviet assembly in January 1918 as evidence of a general 'kulak' war against the soviets. There was, indeed, a report of a struggle in Efimovka *volost'*, but it was not representative of the general situation: the minutes of the Novouzensk soviet assembly reveal that only 5 of the 31 *volost'* delegates reporting on the establishment of their soviet referred to any dissension or violent conflict.[104]

In the overwhelming majority of cases, the transfer of power from the *volost' zemstvo* or committee to the soviet was peaceful and quick. According to the estimates of two Soviet historians, 98.5% of the *volost'*-level *zemstva* (in eleven provinces of central Russia) conceded power voluntarily to the soviet.[105] In Saratov province 79% of the *volost'*-level *zemstva* were abolished on the same day as the soviet was elected; only 12% continued to function alongside the soviet in a system of dual power.[106] The spring enquiries of 1918 in Penza province showed that in only 5 out of 172 *volosti* was there a similar system of dual power.[107] Many of the *volost'*-level *zemstva* were simply renamed 'soviets' or re-elected, with a few minor changes of personnel, following the declaration of Soviet power in the district town.[108] An equally large proportion of the *volost'* soviets continued, throughout 1918, to use the stationery, stamps and seals of the old *volost' zemstvo* executive. The mandate commissioner of the Saratov soviet assembly reported in May 1918 that more than one-third of the

103 TsGANKh, f. 478, op. 1, dd. 149, 150.

104 P. N. Pershin, *Agrarnaia Revoliutsiia v Rossii*, 2 vols., Moscow, 1966, vol. 1, p. 474; *Otchet novouzenskogo soveta soldatskikh, rabochikh i krest'ianskikh deputatov*, Novouzensk, 1918, pp. 3–7.

105 Grishaev, *Stroitel'stvo sovetov*, p. 21; Makarova, p. 145.

106 Butyl'kin and Gerasimenko, p. 152.

107 TsGANKh, f. 478, op. 1, dd. 149, 150.

108 *Sovety v oktiabre: Sbornik dokumentov*, Moscow, 1928, p. 170; V. N. Aver'ёv, 'Likvidatsiia burzhuaznykh organov mestnogo samoupravleniia', *Sovetskoe Gosudarstvo*, 1936, no. 4, p. 114; Grishaev, *Stroitel'stvo sovetov*, pp. 23, 26; Kabanov, 'Oktiabr'skaia revoliutsiia', p. 107.

delegates had arrived at the assembly with their mandate stamped by the old *zemstvo* authority, while another one-third had arrived with their mandate stamped by the village elder (*sel'skii starosta*). Some of the other mandates had been stamped with the seal of the *zemstvo* executive which had then been corrected by hand with the word 'soviet' (*sovet*).[109] Such alterations have been interpreted by some Soviet historians as a trick by the 'kulaks' to hide behind the mask of 'soviet power'.[110] But the real explanation is more simple—a shortage of paper and seals!

A large number of the *volost'* soviets were elected at a meeting of the *volost' zemstvo*. The latter was usually abolished at the same meeting. The following three examples were all taken from Samara district during January 1918 (after the closure of the Constituent Assembly):

1. A meeting of 16 *zemstvo* councillors (*glasnye*) in the village of Zubovka resolved on 26 January by 12 votes to 4 in favour of soviet power. The *zemstvo* was disbanded, a soviet was elected, and a delegate was sent to the district soviet assembly in Samara with a mandate for the reconvening of the Constituent Assembly.
2. A meeting of 37 communal representatives, called by the *volost' zemstvo* executive in the village of Chernorechenka on 25 January, resolved to abolish the *volost' zemstvo* and elect a soviet executive.
3. In the village of Trost'ian the following resolution was passed before the *volost' zemstvo* was disbanded and a soviet executive elected:

> a full meeting of the *zemstvo* assembly . . . on 17 January, attended by one delegate from every ten households, *zemstvo* councillors, members of the peasant council, and all interested persons, regardless of estate or sex, . . . got down to discuss the question of the recognition of the power of the workers', soldiers' and peasants' soviets, or the recognition of the old powers—that is, the *volost' zemstvo* authority and the Constituent Assembly . . . We resolved in general agreement by a direct, secret and fair ballot, with 133 votes for and 61 votes against, to recognize the power of the soviets.[111]

The majority of the *volost'* soviets were elected at an open gathering of the population with open voting by a show of hands, by shouting or by standing in groups. Like the committees of 1917, the *volost'* soviets arose directly from the intimate political world of the peasant

[109] *PSG*, p. 25.
[110] See e.g. M. I. Kubanin, 'Predposylki kombedov', *Na agrarnom fronte*, 1934, no. 11, p. 69; P. N. Abramov, 'Sovetskoe stroitel'stvo na sele v dokombedskii period', *Voprosy Istorii KPSS*, 1960, no. 6, p. 69; E. I. Medvedev, *Oktiabr'skaia revoliutsiia v Srednem Povolzh'e*, pp. 78–9; E. N. Gorodetskii, *Rozhdenie sovetskogo gosudarstva 1917–1918 gg.*, Moscow, 1965, p. 114.
[111] GAKO, f. 81, op. 1, d. 119, ll. 176–7; d. 119a, ll. 187, 159.

communes. The peasants selected their representatives by name and patronynmic, because they knew them as fellow villagers. This close link with the communes accounts for the soviets' 'all-peasant' nature which Lenin characterized as the basis of soviet democracy in 1917–18.[112]

However, on account of the shortages of qualified personnel in the rural localities, most of the new soviets were forced to include some of the people who had previously held office in the *volost'* committee or the *zemstvo*. This was not the manifestation of a 'kulak' or 'bourgeois' master-plan to take over the soviets, but the inevitable outcome of the needs of the peasantry for literate administrators. Many of the *intelligenty* continued to perform valuable tasks of organization in the villages after 1917; they were committed to the peasantry and to the revolution, if not to the Bolsheviks (see ch. 3, sect. 4). The agronomic personnel of the *volost'* land organs, for example, remained basically unchanged during 1917–18, despite the alteration in their official title from the *zemstvo* land 'committee' (*zemel'nyi komitet*) to the soviet land 'department' (*zemel'nyi otdel*). The enquiries of spring 1918 in Penza province showed that 13.4% of the *volost'* soviet executives retained the *zemstvo* land committee without even changing its name. In Saratov province a similar pattern was noted.[113] In the next chapter (sect. 1) we shall see that the more sophisticated the organizational structure of the *volost' zemstvo* had been, the more likely the soviet was to resemble it in its own form and composition.

The revolution in the countryside resulted in a complete breakdown of the local state apparatus. The peasant committees and soviets, which, as Emma Goldman observed, were really no more than the *mir* in 'an advanced and more revolutionary form',[114] assumed all the responsibilities of government in the *volosti*. The district and provincial organs of power were gradually democratized from below by the inclusion of large numbers of *volost'* delegates, so that they tended to become local revolutionary bodies, rather than a part of the central state structure. By the end of the summer, the Russian state had fragmented into a collection of autonomous local 'republics'—informal 'governments', elected by the *demokratiia*, which enacted their own revolutionary 'laws' without regard to the interests of the national state. The liberals of the Provisional Government viewed this process of fragmentation—the collapse into a system of *mnogovlastie* ('multi-power')—as the

[112] *PSS*, vol. 37, pp. 141–4, 313; vol. 38, pp. 192–3; etc.
[113] TsGANKh, f. 478, op. 1, dd. 149, 150. Makarova (p. 155) made a similar calculation and offered the lower figure of 11.7 per cent.
[114] Cited in P. Avrich, *The Russian Anarchists*, Princeton, 1967, p. 252.

beginning of anarchy. But the Bolsheviks championed it during 1917 as the essence of Soviet power. On 26 January 1918 the editor of *Pravda* wrote in a leader entitled 'What does "All power to the soviets!" mean?': 'The Russian state is being transformed into an organization of soviet commune-republics. The Tsarist administrative divisions have been broken down and these commune-republics are all to a certain extent autonomous . . . The soviets act as local "governments".'[115]

The decentralized system of Soviet power that had emerged during 1917 as a result of the destruction of the state was not, in the long term, compatible with the principles of Democratic Centralism propounded after 1918 by the Bolshevik party. During the autumn and winter of 1917–18, however, Lenin recognized that the decentralization of power went hand in hand with the spontaneous revolutionary initiatives of the masses and the final destruction of the old regime: 'the masses could not but want to establish a new government on the basis of their own experience. The slogan "All power to the soviets!" meant, in real life, that the people in the localities wanted to become experienced in government by making their own mistakes.'[116] The Bolsheviks' use of the slogan 'All power to the soviets!' was a brilliant example of their revolutionary pragmatism. The localist initiatives of the soviets sprang from the demands of a social revolution in a country without a state and in the throes of a socio-economic crisis dislocating the countryside from the towns. The Bolsheviks could not alter these facts. They knew that they could not win the hearts of the peasantry through the seizure of power in Petrograd, since, as Lenin acknowledged, 'from the government, which for centuries had been seen by the people as an organ of oppression and robbery, we inherited the peasantry's hatred and mistrust of everything to do with the state'.[117] However, the Bolsheviks understood that the decentralization of the soviets was a pre-condition of their own consolidation of political power at the national level. None of the other socialist parties came to grips with this dialectic of the October revolution. The agrarian revolution and the establishment of the *volost'* soviets, which made the peasantry autonomous in the rural localities and gave them social dominance (*vlast'*) over their class enemies, made it possible for the Bolsheviks to destroy the Constituent Assembly—the last major institution of the old state and a refuge of the SRs—without a peasant counter-revolution.

The majority of the peasants had voted for the SRs in the elections to the Constituent Assembly (although it is not known how many of the

115 *Pravda*, no. 9, 26 Jan. 1918.
116 *PSS*, vol. 37, p. 21.
117 Ibid., vol. 36, p. 184.

votes were cast for the Right SRs and how many for the Left SRs, who had supported the October coup).[118] However, although many of the more politically conscious (*soznatel'nye*) peasants were hostile to the Bolsheviks, it is probably fair to say that the majority were, and would continue to be throughout the civil war, in favour of a government by an alliance of the major socialist parties—a government, with peasants in its central executives, to organize and defend the gains of the social revolution. The political struggles between the socialist parties left most peasants cold, and strengthened their scepticism towards the political parties. A peasant elder from Saratov province neatly summarized these feelings when he said: 'some say one thing, some say another; but they are all chiefs *(nachal'niki)*. We will be for none of them but will wait and see who is right'.[119] Very few peasants were willing to join the Right SRs in the fight for the restoration of the Constituent Assembly. The middle peasants, whose support was essential to any mass movement against the Bolsheviks, had got the bit of the social revolution between their teeth, and were not ready to fight the political battles of any party in Petrograd. The question of state power had, moreover, been complicated by the establishment of the *volost'* soviets and the October Decree on Land, which reduced the immediate appeal of the Constituent Assembly. Thus, the Buzuluk district peasant assembly on 16 January called for the restoration of the Constituent Assembly, 'but only if it stands firmly for the realization of the cherished wishes of the toiling people, and only if it stands firmly for the consolidation of the ground we have already gained'.[120] In a similar vein, one of the delegates at the Novouzensk district soviet assembly reported on 26 January that his village, Aleksashkino, 'recognized the authority of the soviets and now wants a Constituent Assembly, not as a political master (*vlastelin*) of the Russian land, but only as an executive of the people's will'.[121] The Constituent Assembly remained a popular political symbol of 'the revolution'. But it was only a national parliament, dominated by the political parties, and did not decide the matters of immediate concern to the peasantry. For better or worse, the land question was already being resolved in the localities by the communes and the soviets. The peasants were no longer prepared to wait for the legislative blessing of the Constituent Assembly. It is probable that a large number of the peasants would

118 For details of the elections in the Volga region see O. H. Radkey, *The Election to the Russian Constituent Assembly of 1917*, Harvard, 1950, pp. 78–9.

119 Cited in Keep, p. 159.

120 Cited in E. I. Medvedev, 'Zavoevanie i uprochenie', p. 321.

121 *Protokoly novouzenskogo soveta*, n.p., 26 Jan. 1918, p. 3.

have supported a system of councils in the localities (soviet power) in conjunction with a national parliament (the Constituent Assembly). But very few were prepared to fight for the latter at the expense of the former. The centre of power was now inside the village.

3
Six Months of Peasant Rule

> Turning the landlords out of office has killed the peasant's ancient dread of government . . . Government to him is no longer an invincible force, above, aloof and beyond control . . . In the villages, the officials dress like peasants, talk like peasants, and live like peasants.
>
> Jack Belden, *China Shakes the World*

THE first six months of Soviet rule represent a unique period in the history of the Russian peasantry. During these months, from the establishment of the *volost'* soviets in the winter of 1917–18 to the outbreak of the civil war at the beginning of the following summer, the countryside was governed by the peasants themselves. The destruction of the state and the decentralization of power, which culminated in the October revolution and the closure of the Constituent Assembly, left the peasantry in a position to complete the social revolution in the villages. How was this social revolution carried out? What did it hope to achieve? And to what extent was it able to solve the problems which had caused the revolution? These are the central issues of this chapter.

The peasant rule of these months did not leave any major aspect of rural life untouched. The land system, the market economy, the church, the judiciary, the schools, and the surrounding power structures in the district and provincial centres were all profoundly influenced. Most of the reforms of this period either strengthened the traditional practices of the village commune, or sought to bring into effect peasant ideals based upon the egalitarian and collectivist principles of the commune. Private land ownership was abolished. Every peasant family was granted the right to work a share of the land with its own labour, and to sell or exchange its product on the market (provided the provisions needs of the village community had been met). Communal land tenure was strengthened and extended to cover new rural groups, such as the landless labourers of the pre-revolutionary period and even some of the gentry.

In their first six months of power, the Bolsheviks had little option but to leave the control of the rural localities to the peasant communes and the local soviets. Until the complete demobilization of the army and the mass influx of urban workers into the countryside during the spring and summer of 1918,[1] the Bolsheviks had far too few supporters

[1] See ch. 6, n. 1.

in the countryside to contemplate building up their own structures of power. They were obliged to accept the autonomy of the communes and the local soviets as a minimum condition of the peasantry's neutrality during the political conflicts of 1917–18. Two of the earliest decrees of the Soviet government gave the rural soviets the right in their own localities to manage the private land and to supervise the distribution of food.[2] Lenin himself arguably favoured the development of the decentralized soviet system during the winter of 1917–18, since at this stage he believed the revolution was directed against the 'bourgeois state apparatus'; and the soviets were still thought to be capable of bringing into effect the stateless 'primitive democracy', which Lenin had outlined in *State and Revolution* (1917).[3] Even as late as 8 March 1918, at the Seventh Party Congress, Lenin spoke about the emergence of 'a new type of state . . . without bureaucracy, without police without a standing army'.[4]

It was only during the spring of 1918, as the food supply crisis in the cities became more critical and the country moved closer to open civil war, that the Bolsheviks became concerned with the need to construct a centralized state apparatus. At the Seventh Congress Lenin had concluded that it would be premature to proclaim the 'dying away of the state'.[5] The Bolshevik leaders were considering the best means to strengthen the state's control of the local soviets through proletarian forces. However, it was not until the beginning of the civil war, during the early summer of 1918, that the Bolsheviks took their first initiatives to build up an apparatus of state control in the rural areas with the declaration of the 'food dictatorship' (13 May), the institution of the *kombedy* (11 June), and the proclamation of the first Red Army conscription (12 June).[6] These measures marked the beginning of the end of the peasant self-rule in the Volga region.

1. THE STRUCTURE OF SOVIET POWER IN THE COUNTRYSIDE

The Soviet Constitution of July 1918 outlined a clear and uniform structure of rural administration for the whole of the Soviet Republic. The 'rural', or village, soviets (*sel'skie sovety*) were to be elected in every rural settlement by the entire population over 18 years of age (excluding persons hiring labour for profit or living on unearned

[2] *Dekrety Sovetskoi vlasti*, 10 vols., Moscow, 1957–76 (henceforth referred to as *DSV*), vol. 1, Moscow, 1957, pp. 17–20; *Sobranie uzakonenii i rasporiazhenii raboche-krest'ianskogo pravitel'stva*, Moscow, 1917–24 (henceforth referred to as *SU*), 1917–18, no. 1, art. 6.

[3] *PSS*, vol. 33, p. 91.

[4] Ibid., vol. 36, pp. 50–1.

[5] Ibid., pp. 53–4.

[6] *DSV*, vol. 2, Moscow, 1959, pp. 261, 264–6, 416–19, 428–9.

income, the clergy and former police officials). Settlements with less than 100 adult inhabitants were ordered to merge with a neighbouring community for the election of a soviet. Each member of the rural soviet, which was to comprise between three and fifty members, was supposed to represent 100 franchised inhabitants. Settlements with over 1,000 inhabitants were to elect an executive committee (*ispolkom*) of up to five members. This was to meet at least twice a week. One rural soviet member in every ten (and at least one member of each rural soviet) was to attend a *volost'* assembly, which, according to Article 57 of the Constitution, represented the highest authority within the *volost'*. It was obliged to meet at least once a month. The assembly elected an executive committee (*volispolkom*, or VIK) of up to ten members, which served as the responsible organ between convocations of the *volost'* assembly. The VIK was answerable to the *volost'* soviet assembly, but it was expected to carry out the orders of the higher soviet and military authorities, particularly the district (*uezd*) soviet, which was attended by rural soviet delegates (one for every 1,000 inhabitants) and representatives of the factories and towns (usually one for every 200 electors).[7] This dual obligation of the VIKs was to play a crucial role in the social and political history of the early Soviet period.

The tidy political structure of the Constitution did not reflect the variety of local soviet forms in the countryside prior to July 1918. The structure of Soviet power in the rural localities did not begin to resemble the Soviet Constitution until 1919–20. During their first few months of power the soviets developed in an *ad hoc* and heterogeneous fashion. The Samara provincial soviet executive (*gubispolkom*) even promulgated its own 'Constitution of provincial power' (January 1918), which recognized the provincial assembly as the highest authority in the province and instituted eleven regional 'soviets of provincial commissars'. The new structure was reminiscent of the KNV network of 1917.[8] In Saratov province there was no official provincial authority until September 1918: the district soviets chose not to elect one, since they preferred to remain autonomous authorities.[9] The same was true in the south-eastern territories of Samara province, where the Nikolaevsk district authorities established a 'Socialist Labouring Commune', and the Pokrovsk regional authorities an 'Autonomous

[7] A. I. Lepeshkin, *Mestnye organy vlasti sovetskogo gosudarstva (1917–1920 gg.)*, Moscow, 1957, pp. 167–70; M. Vladimirskii, *Organizatsiia sovetskoi vlasti na mestakh*, Moscow, 1919, pp. 10–11.

[8] E. I. Medvedev, 'Zavoevanie i uprochenie vlasti rabochikhi krest'ian v Samarskoi gubernii', in D. A. Chugaev and V. S. Vasiukov (eds.), *Ustanovlenie sovetskoi vlasti na mestakh v 1917–18 gg.*, Moscow, 1959, p. 342.

[9] V. P. Antonov-Saratovskii (ed.), *Sovety v epokhu voennogo kommunizma (1918–1921): Sbornik dokumentov*, Moscow, 1928–9 (henceforth referred to as *SEV*), vol. 1, p. 143.

Republic', during the early months of 1918. Similar republics were formed at this time in the provinces of Kazan', Tver', Viatka, Altai, Kursk, and Kaluga. In the last named there was a 'republican federation of autonomous *volosti*'. State representatives from Moscow were forced to negotiate their business separately with each *volost'* authority, even if only to cross the *volost'* boundaries.[10]

Let us look more closely at the different forms of soviet organization in the countryside during this period.

There were relatively few village-level soviets during the first year of Soviet power. In Tambov province only forty-one out of the eighty-seven *volost'* soviet chairmen who replied in April 1918 to an enquiry of the People's Commissariat of Internal Affairs (NKVD) were able to report the existence of one or more 'rural soviets' in their locality. No more than eight could report that there was a soviet in every village of their *volost'*. In Kamyshin district only one-third of the villages had a soviet in March 1918.[11] Many villages did not elect a soviet until the autumn of 1918, while others continued without one throughout the civil war.[12]

In many of the villages without a soviet, especially in the smaller ones, the peasants elected a commissar, a chairman, or a *starosta* who, together with a scribe, served as the executive of the communal or village assembly.[13] These latter institutions invariably performed the functions of the missing soviet. Indeed, the earliest village soviets tended to function heavily under the influence of the peasant commune, and were often no more than a committee of its representatives. In this context it is significant that the number of village soviets at their first registration in 1922 (110,000) closely correlated with the number of rural communes in 1917 (120,000). Some villages with two communes even elected two 'communal soviets'.[14] The meetings of the soviet and the commune constantly overlapped: the

[10] See F. V. Chebaevskii, 'Stroitel'stvo mestnykh sovetov v kontse 1917 i pervoi polovine 1918 gg.', *Istoricheskie zapiski*, vol. 61, Moscow, 1957, pp. 252–4; E. G. Gimpel'son, *Sovety v pervyi god proletarskoi diktatury (oktiabr' 1917 g.–noiabr' 1918 g.)*, Moscow, 1967, pp. 299–302; *SEV*, vol. 2, p. 189.

[11] V. V. Grishaev, *Stroitel'stvo sovetov v derevne v pervyi god sotsialisticheskoi revoliutsii*, Moscow, 1967, pp. 27–8.

[12] Lepeshkin, p. 170; P. N. Abramov, 'Oprosnyi list volostnogo soveta (1918 g.)', *Istoricheskii Arkhiv*, 1960, no. 3, p. 200. In the German Volga region there were few soviets at any level until the autumn of 1918 (E. Gross, *Avtonomnaia Sovetskaia Sotsialisticheskaia Respublika Nemtsev Povolzh'ia*, Pokrovsk, 1926, p. 13).

[13] In Voronezh province this was noted in 11 out of 87 *volosti* (Grishaev, *Stroitel'stvo sovetov*, p. 35). See further Chebaevskii, pp. 250–1; Lepeshkin, p. 170; *SEV*, vol. 2, p. 215.

[14] V. Gorokhov, 'Organizatsiia territorii sel'skikh sovetov', *Sovetskoe stroitel'stvo*, *1929*, no. 2, p. 18; V. V. Kabanov, 'Oktiabr'skaia revoliutsiia i krest'ianskaia obshchina', *Istoricheskie zapiski*, vol. 111, Moscow, 1984, pp. 109–10.

former were sometimes called a *sovet*, sometimes a *sobranie*, and sometimes a *skhod*. Some village soviets even named themselves 'communes'.[15] The protocols of the Kolyvatkino village soviet (Dubovo-Umet *volost'*, Samara *uezd*) during the spring of 1918 were recorded under a wide variety of different titles: 'communal meetings' (*sobraniia obshchestva*); 'general meetings' (*obshchie sobraniia*); 'village meetings' (*sel'skie sobraniia*); and 'rural soviets' (*sel'skie sovety*).[16] The differences between these meetings are hard to distinguish: the meetings of the village soviet tended to be smaller than the other meetings, but it was usual for both to share the same venue (a particular building, a street or a field), to be dominated by the same people, and to discuss a similar set of issues. The Khvatovo village soviet (Khvatovo *volost'*, Vol'sk *uezd*) resolved a number of matters which were traditionally associated with the communal gathering: it employed shepherds and watchmen from the immigrant population; purchased a 'communal horse'; raised a communal tax to repair the village road; and, in preparation for the repartition of the land, took a census of the 320 households 'in our commune'.[17] Other village soviets passed resolutions on the methods of land use in the commune, on the organization of social welfare schemes, and on the maintenance of the church. Some village soviets even authorized household partitions and mergers—a task which had formerly fallen exclusively under the jurisdiction of the peasant commune.[18]

The dominant influence of the commune on the earliest forms of soviet organization was underscored by two important territorial-administrative changes during the spring of 1918. To break down the large, unwieldy *volost'* structures of the Tsarist system of administration, the Soviet government issued a Decree on 27 January 1918 which granted every village the right to request a separation from the *volost'* territorial-administrative unit within which it found itself.[19] These requests were to be considered by the *volost'* soviet assembly and the district soviet executive. However, in spite of these regulations, only a very small number of the *volosti* which were reformed during the spring of 1918 actually received any authorization from the district soviet; some were reformed without the authorization of the VIK.[20] Hundreds of new *volosti* were established in this fashion during the spring of 1918. The number of *volosti* in Voronezh province

15 TsGAOR, f. 393, op. 13, d. 609, ll. 15 ff., 53 ff.
16 GAKO, f. 81, op. 1, d. 119, ll. 110–19.
17 TsGAOR, f. 393, op. 3, d. 332, ll. 267–70.
18 Ibid., d. 331, l. 58; GAKO, f. 81, op. 1, d. 119, ll. 131, 137; d. 119a, l. 183, etc.
19 *SU*, 1917–18, no. 21, art. 318.
20 Vladimirskii, *Organizatsiia sovetskoi vlasti*, p. 23.

increased from 244 during 1917 to 315 by the end of 1918. In the Soviet Republic (RSFSR) the number of *volosti* increased from 10,606 during 1917 to 12,363 by the beginning of 1922.[21] This proliferation of new *volosti* may be partly explained by the over-large size of many of the old *volost'* units, which inevitably resulted in the representatives of the outlying villages having to travel large distances to attend the *volost'* assembly. It was certainly true that a large number of the communes which had requested to separate from the old *volost'* authority were situated a long way from the *volost'* township. However, a significant portion of these requests had been made by the wealthiest or the most land-extensive communes with the motive of breaking away from the old *volost'* authority in order to safeguard themselves against a general redistribution of property (see sect. 3 below).

A second and integral part of this process was the merger of several neighbouring communes which had previously been divided by their status under serfdom or during the Emancipation (i.e. the communes of former serfs, of 'cut-off' peasants, etc.). These mergers sometimes produced a commune which was large enough by itself to form a new *volost'*. L. N. Kritsman showed that in six out of eleven *volosti* in Penza, Kursk, Tambov, and Tula provinces, the number of land communes declined between the censuses of 1917 and 1920 (from 131 to 79); only in one *volost'* did the number increase (from 11 to 12). In the five remaining *volosti* the number of land communes remained constant.[22]

The size of the village soviets and of the *volost'* soviet assemblies was highly variable. This was an unavoidable outcome of the traditional peasant political practices that dominated the election of the soviets in the early period of Soviet rule (see ch. 5, sect. 2). The peasants selected their representatives by name and patronymic from among their fellow villagers, regardless of strict numerical limits. Because the majority of the representatives were peasant farmers, the attendance of the village soviet meetings tended to be highly irregular, especially during the busy periods of field work. For this reason, a large number of 'reserve' soviet members had to be elected in order to share out the time-consuming burdens of village politics more equally among the households. This tended to result in the election of extraordinarily large village soviets, far in excess of the size set out by the Soviet Constitution. The stipulation of Article 57 that the village soviets were to comprise between three and fifty members was often interpreted by the peasants to mean that they were entitled to elect

21 Grishaev, *Stroitel'stvo sovetov*, p. 41; Gorokhov, p. 18.
22 L. N. Kritsman (ed.), *Materialy po istorii agrarnoi revoliutsii v Rossii*, vol. 1, Moscow, 1928, tables 1 and 2.

any number of soviet representatives between those two figures, regardless of the size of the village.[23] The *volost'* soviet assemblies were also known to have their own norms of representation, which tended, for similar reasons, to be more generous than the norms set out by the Soviet Constitution. One Soviet historian has noted the following variety of norms of representation at the *volost'* soviet assemblies of one district: from three to ten delegates per village; three delegates per 1,000 inhabitants; one delegate per 200 inhabitants; five delegates per village; and one delegate per ten households.[24]

The *volost'* soviet assembly was, like most peasant meetings, normally held on a Sunday afternoon. Too large to be contained in one building, the crowd sprawled out along the village streets, or, in the tradition of the communal assembly, met in an open field. The chairman of the VIK played a dominant role. He drew up the agenda, initiated the discussion on most issues and formulated the resolutions.[25] In spite of his tremendous influence, however, the chairman (like the VIK) was subordinate to the will of the assembly. Hence, the Raznochinsk VIK resolved in March 1918 that: 'since several resolutions have been refuted and opposed at open peasant meetings, our soviet should be declared an advisory body'.[26] At this stage of the revolution the most important issues (e.g. land use, taxation) were decided by a general *volost'* assembly, or by open village meetings.[27]

There was considerable variation in the size of the VIKs and their methods of formation. Although a NKVD circular of April 1918 stipulated that the VIKs were not to exceed five members, a study of 85 VIKs in Voronezh province, carried out during April and May, discovered that 22 of these VIKs contained between 5 and 9 members, while a further 8 contained between 10 and 84 members. The same study discovered that only 52 of the VIKs had been elected at a general *volost'* assembly (i.e. one attended by representatives of all the villages). As many as 20 VIKs had been elected at a meeting of the main village, the *volost'* township, with no more than a few representatives of the other villages present. In a number of cases the village soviet of the *volost'* township simply declared itself the VIK.[28] This was to be a common phenomenon in areas situated near the civil war front, where a VIK or a revolutionary committee (*revkom*) had to be set up in a

23 Vladimirskii, *Organizatsiia sovetskoi vlasti*, p. 11.

24 Grishaev, *Stroitel'stvo sovetov*, p. 30.

25 TsGAOR, f. 393, op. 3, d. 333, ll. 39 ff.; GAKO, f. 81, op. 1, d. 119, ll. 131 ff.

26 Cited in G. A. Gerasimenko, 'Klassovaia bor'ba v derevne i nizovye krest'ianskie organizatsii v 1917–pervoi polovine 1918 goda (Na materialakh Nizhnego Povolzh'ia)', kand. diss., Saratov, 1973, p. 360.

27 GAKO, f. 81, op. 1, d. 119, ll. 18, 180; d. 119a, ll. 113, 173, etc. See also Kabanov, 'Oktiabr'skaia revoliutsiia', pp. 110–11.

28 Lepeshkin, pp. 125–6; Chebaevskii, p. 251.

hurry and there was no time to hold a full *volost'* meeting. It was also common in situations where the *volost'* township was controlled by a left-wing faction of workers or soldiers, while the outlying villages were dominated by the traditional agrarian élites.[29]

TABLE 5. *Volost' soviet departments, Penza province, April–May 1918*

Department	No. of *volosti*
Land	133
Provisions	106
General/Executive/Administrative	45
Internal/Internal Order	26
Charity/Welfare	26
Justice	25
Finance/Savings	15
Education	11
Economical/Agricultural	8
Labour	5
Audits/Inspection	3
Woods	2
Military	1
Births, deaths, and marriages	1
Total no. of *volosti*	172

Source: TsGANKh, f. 478, op. 1, dd. 149, 150.

During the early years of the revolution the VIKs had an enormous variety of different departments to deal with special matters. It was only after 1919 that the internal structure of the VIKs started to become more uniform. Table 5 shows the departments registered by 172 VIKs in Penza province in the NKVD enquiries of spring 1918. The overwhelming majority of the VIKs (141 out of 172) had at least one special department; most of these had either two (45) or three (47). Nearly all the VIKs (as well as a large number of the individual communes) had a special committee to manage the private land. The majority also had a provisions committee to procure and distribute grain. Another very common department (which was sometimes the only one) appeared under a variety of different titles: 'general' *(obshchii)*; 'administrative' *(administrativnyi)*; 'executive' *(ispolnitel'nyi)*; 'internal' *(vnutrennii)*, etc. A significant number of the VIKs (28) had more than three departments. Some were highly complex and sophisticated organizations. The VIK in Zolotoe (Kamyshin *uezd)*,

29 TsGAOR, f. 393, op. 3, d. 325, ll. 147, 174, 178, 240–417; TsGANKh, f. 1943, op. 3, d. 223, l. 250.

wealthy locality with a remarkable tradition of peasant organization, boasted a fabulous array of different departments: an 'agricultural and land department' (10 members); a 'committee for the welfare of the families of soldiers and immigrants' (7); a 'medical commission' (7); a 'cultural and educational committee' (18 members and 10 communal delegates); a 'veterinary section' (5 and 3); a 'technical department' (9 and 3); an 'agronomy department' (9 and 3); a 'savings and financial department' (10 and 1); an 'insurance department' (8 members); a 'provisions committee' (8); a 'production control board' (8); an 'auditing commission' (5); and a 'revolutionary court' of two, with one permanent judge.[30] Zolotoe was an exceptional case. The peasants were hard-working and comparatively wealthy. The church, the school, the Peasant Union, and the *volost' zemstvo* all had strong roots in this region. Nevertheless, other rural communities without the advantages of Zolotoe also had complex structures of soviet organization. The VIK in Chernovka (Buzuluk *uezd*) had its own special 'commissariats' for land, provisions, labour, education, trade, and the welfare of the families of soldiers. It also nominated commissioners from time to time in order to account the population and the availability of agricultural tools and livestock; to requisition surplus grain; to prevent the uncontrolled felling of timber; to set up tool repair shops; to control the movement of goods through the railway station; to mobilize soldiers; to form a Revolutionary Tribunal; and so on.[31]

The VIKs employed a wide variety of different means to maintain public order and administer justice. Most of these entailed the democratic election of a police force and a court, although a number of soviets refused to set up either, since they saw them as a symbol of Tsarist state oppression (see Table 6).

The taxes raised by the village communes provided the principal source of income for the VIKs. The main expenditures of the latter were: the salaries of the executive members and the administrative staff; the heating and maintenance of buildings; and the employment of watchmen, police, postmen, drivers, etc. The real value of the salary of the soviet executive members was constantly in decline, as a result of inflationary pressures.[32] Many VIK members were left without a

30 TsGAOR, f. 393, op. 3, d. 333, ll. 219–21. On the background of Zolotoe see A. N. Minkh, *Istoriko-geograficheskii slovar' Saratovskoi gubernii*, vol. 1, Saratov, 1900, pp. 323–32; *Iz revoliutsionnogo proshlogo Kamyshina (1905–1920 gg.)*, Kamyshin, 1964, pp. 41, 49, 71–2, 76.

31 GAKO, f. 3134, op. 2, d. 21, ll. 24 ff.

32 The monthly salary of a *VIK* chairman, for instance, ranged from about 375 rb. to 720 rb. during Jan. 1918, and from about 1,800 rb. to 2,400 rb. during the following June (GAKO, f. 3134, op. 2, d. 21, l. 10; TsGAOR, f. 393, op. 3, d. 328, ll. 108–9; d. 332, l. 219; d. 333, ll. 55, 219, etc.).

TABLE 6. *Police and judicial institutions under the VIKs, Penza province, spring 1918*

Description by VIK chairman	No. of reports
Police institutions	
No police force exists	44
No police force exists and none is needed	20
There is an elected police force	3
The soviet keeps order	47
The local organizations keep order	1
There is a *militsiia*[a]	38
There is a red guard[b]	16
Various socialist brigades keep order	3
Police forces are sent from the district town when necessary	8
Total	180
Judicial institutions	
The *volost'* court was abolished in 1917[c]	96
A court has not yet been elected	7
There are elected peasant judges	22
There is a *narodnyi sud*[d]	107
There is a *mirovoi sud*[e]	6
The judges are nominated by the soviet	3
There is a VIK department of justice	6
Judges are sent from the district town when necessary	3
There is a revolutionary court	1
Total	251

[a] The Soviet *militsiia* of this period was an unsalaried volunteer force (the 'People's Militia'). It was only very slowly transformed into a salaried and permanent militia under the control of NKVD. See further G. Leggett, *The Cheka: Lenin's Political Police*, Oxford, 1981.

[b] The red guards were formed by the VIKs, and were usually made up largely from ex-servicemen. Many of the red guards became regular units of the Red Army during April and May 1918. In central Russia and the Volga region the number of red guard units fell sharply during these two months (*Grazhdanskaia voina i voennaia interventsiia v SSSR: Entsiklopediia*, Moscow, 1983, p. 299).

[c] The *volost'* courts were established during the 1860s. They comprised four members, elected for a period of one year. See further P. Czap, 'Peasant-Class Courts and Peasant Customary Justice in Russia, 1861–1912', *Journal of Social History*, vol. 1, 1967.

[d] The *narodnyi sud* ('People's Court') was instituted in November 1917 (*SU*, 1917, no. 4, art. 50). It comprised one judge and two jurors, elected at the *volost'* soviet assembly.

[e] The *mirovoi sud* was a Justice of the Peace, appointed by the district *zemstvo* board.

Source: TsGANKh, f. 478, op. 1, dd. 149, 150.

salary because the communes refused to pay the *volost'* taxes (for many peasants the non-payment of government taxes represented the essence of freedom).[33] Some poor destitutes were prepared to work for the soviet in return for no more than a ration of food and some other meagre payments in kind (see sect. 4 below). Table 7 shows that the

TABLE 7. *Methods of financing the VIKs, Penza province, April–May 1918*

Method	No. of *volosti*
Collected through the commune	
Head tax	62
Land tax	32
Voluntary donations	10
Raised by the soviet	
Requisitioning of property	2
Sale of estate property	10
Tax on traders	12
Loans	3
Other sources of finance	
Finance from the district soviet	14
Revenue left by *zemstvo*	3
'As before 1917'	1
No finances	52
Total No. of VIKs responding	172

Source: TsGANKh, f. 478, op. 1, dd. 149, 150.

majority of the VIKs selected a universal tax (e.g. a per capita tax, or a land tax) with embryonic forms of progressive taxation (e.g. the exclusion of war-invalids and widows). Such taxes were noted in the commune before 1917. As in many peasant societies, they were commonly seen to uphold a notional equality among the village households, giving every member of the village, including the poor, an equal entitlement to use the general services (e.g. schools, roads, barns, watchmen) provided by the revenues of the tax, since everyone had paid an equal share.[34] Very few soviets were able or willing to put all the burden of taxation on the 'kulaks' and the richest peasant stratum, as suggested by the higher Soviet authorities. During the spring of 1918 the Soviet government promulgated a tax on the rural bourgeoisie (*kontributsiia*) to increase local soviet revenues. But the VIKs managed to raise only a tiny fraction of the levy. By November 1918 no more

33 N. G. Sokolov, 'Nalogovaia politika v derevne v pervye gody sovetskoi vlasti (1917–1920 gg.)', *Istoricheskie zapiski*, vol. 113, Moscow, 1986, p. 77.

34 B. Mironov, 'The Russian Peasant Commune after the Reforms of the 1860s', *Slavic Review*, vol. 44, 1985, p. 460. See generally J. C. Scott, *The Moral Economy of the Peasant*, New Haven, 1976.

than 1,469,697 rb. had been collected from the four Volga provinces. In Buzuluk district only 9 of the 55 VIKs bothered to collect the *kontributsiia* at all. Many village soviets were opposed to any form of state taxation. They impeded the collection of the *kontributsiia* by destroying tax notices, misleading the tax inspectors, and causing a multitude of further delays.[35]

The social composition of the *volost'* soviets in their first months of power has been the subject of much controversy among Soviet historians. During the early months of 1918 Lenin stressed the all-peasant nature of the *volost'* soviets, which he believed represented the general interests of the peasant masses.[36] This interpretation has informed the works of the majority of Soviet historians.[37] But others have stressed the influence of the 'kulaks' and the richest peasantry in the pre-*kombed* soviets.[38] Recently, a third interpretation has been put forward by G. A. Gerasimenko and V. P. Sem'ianinov on the basis of their own studies of the Volga region.[39] They argue that the 'local' soviets (they do not specify whether they mean the village soviets or the VIKs) were, to begin with, controlled by the poor peasants, but that during the spring of 1918 the 'kulaks', who had been unable to prevent the establishment of the soviets, began to subvert them instead. This was facilitated, it is argued, by the mass withdrawal of the poor peasantry from the soviets on account of the low wages paid. Gerasimenko and Sem'ianinov put forward evidence purporting to show that the composition of the VIKs changed frequently during the spring, on account of these financial difficulties. The 'kulaks' are said to have become increasingly dominant in the soviets, since they were willing to work without pay. Variations in the size of the VIKs were to be expected of course, since the majority of the VIK members were farming peasants themselves and were not able to attend soviet meetings regularly. However, the authors' own illustrations show that in Penza province as many as 66.4% of the VIKs remained unchanged in their composition (over an indeterminate period) and only 15.4%

[35] TsGAOR, f. 393, op. 3, d. 323, ll. 153–4; *Vlast' sovetov*, no. 2, 30 Jan. 1919, p. 3; Sokolov, p. 87.

[36] *PSS*, vol. 37, pp. 312, 313, 315, etc.

[37] See e.g. Gimpel'son, *Sovety v pervyi god*, pp. 212–13; P. N. Abramov, 'Sovetskoe stroitel'stvo na sele v dokombedskii period', *Voprosy istorii KPSS*, 1960, no. 6, p. 69; Grishaev, *Stroitel'stvo sovetov*, p. 30.

[38] A. S. Bystrova, *Komitety bednoty v Viatskoi gubernii*, Kirov, 1956, p. 8; A. M. Dedov, *Komitety derevenskoi bednoty i ikh rol' v ukreplenii sovetskoi vlasti*, Moscow, 1958, pp. 6, 28; *Soiuz rabochikh i krest'ian v pervye gody sovetskoi vlasti (1917–1922 gg.)*, Yaroslavl', 1958, p. 63.

[39] G. A. Gerasimenko and V. P. Sem'ianinov, *Sovetskaia vlast' v derevne na pervom etape Oktiabria (Na materialakh Povolzh'ia)*, Saratov, 1980. See also V. P. Sem'ianinov, 'Volostnye sovety Srednego Povolzh'ia v dokombedskii period, noiabr' 1917–iiun' 1918 gg.', kand. diss., Saratov, 1977, pp. 21, 104–9, 158.

changed their composition 'frequently' or 'very frequently'. These figures underline the stability, rather than the instability, of the Penza soviets, given the observations made above and the fact that at this stage of the revolution the soviets were inevitably searching for new organizational forms. Gerasimenko and Sem'ianinov are unable to give any firm evidence showing that the 'kulaks' were becoming more numerous in the soviets. Their claim that the 'kulaks' gained control of the soviets during May, when the first three-month term (*srok*) of the latter ran out and new elections were held, is absurd. There were no fixed terms for the soviets before the July Constitution and the first official decision to re-elect the village and *volost'* soviets was not taken until November 1918 (see ch. 5, sect. 2).[40] Even if the VIKs had been re-elected after a strictly limited three-month term, only a fraction would have been re-elected during May, since, as we have seen, the *volost'* soviets were established at various times during the winter and spring of 1917–18.

The 'kulak interpretation' of the soviets originated in Bolshevik propaganda during 1918. It was common for the Bolshevik press and the leading Soviet officials in the provincial towns to condemn any local soviet as a 'kulak' one, if it was deemed not to have acted upon the orders of the higher authorities with sufficient zeal. A local soviet which ignored the decrees of the Soviet government, or turned them into cigarette paper, because it was hostile to any state authority (or because there was a shortage of paper!) would be automatically condemned as an enclave of 'kulak' interests. Such misunderstandings tell us a great deal about the cultural divide between the Bolsheviks and the peasantry. The former mistook the everyday acts of peasant disobedience, which one would expect to find in a revolution, for organized acts reflecting political or 'class' interests. A delegate of the Romanovka VIK told the Novouzensk soviet assembly in August 1918 that his soviet had been 'until recently in the hands of the kulaks, the pot-bellies (*tolstopuzye*) and the saboteurs, who disobeyed all the decrees of the central authorities'. The delegate from the D'iakovka VIK declared in a similar vein that his soviet 'used to be controlled by the kulaks and acted just as it wanted and did not fulfil the orders of the *narkomy* [people's commissariats]'.[41] Obviously, some of the soviets included members of the former propertied classes (*byvshie*), if only because of the desperate need for experienced and literate administrators in the rural areas. But there is no evidence to suggest

[40] B. M. Morozov, *Partiia i sovety v Oktiabr'skoi revoliutsii*, Moscow, 1966, pp. 213, 264, 385–6.
[41] TsGAOR, f. 393, op. 3, d. 325, ll. 169, 151.

that these soviets were more likely to counteract the measures of the central government than any other soviet.

Lenin's characterization of the *volost'* soviets during this period as general peasant institutions is substantially correct. The close interconnections between the soviets and the peasant communes underlined the 'peasant' nature of the former. The non-farming members of the villages, who were to play such an important role in the *kombedy*, occupied only a secondary position in the village soviets, although in the larger *volost'* centres, some of which were, properly speaking, market towns or small industrial centres, the landless elements did play an important part in the VIKs (see ch. 5, sects. 1 and 2). In the Volga region, however, there were very few *volost'* townships which were not themselves agricultural communities with their own peasant commune. Here the VIKs remained essentially 'peasant' in their composition. This was even reflected in their everyday methods of work. A. Okninsky, a former Tsarist official who for two years held a post in the Podgornoe VIK in Tambov province, recalled how for most of the working day the VIK members sat around in the office talking, playing cards, drinking vodka, smoking home-grown tobacco, and chewing sunflower seeds. The typical day of the VIKs was marked by a constant coming-and-going of the peasants with oral and semi-literate petitions for a ration of food, a horse or a plough, or some other petty favour.[42]

There is little reason to doubt that the first six months of Soviet rule witnessed a sharp upturn in the participation of the peasantry in village politics. During the spring period of field work (April-May) there were inevitably problems of peasant absenteeism from the soviet meetings. During May the VIK in Bobrovka (Samara *uezd*) had to impose a fine of 3 rb. on every member who failed to attend a meeting 'without a satisfactory reason'. The *volost'* soviet assembly in Dubovo-Pobedimov (Bugul'ma *uezd*) resolved on 26 May to increase the salaries of the VIK members to 90 rb. (this was still a very low wage) in order to increase the attendance of the VIK meetings.[43] The VIK in Chernovka (Buzuluk *uezd*) complained that the delegates of the outlying communes regularly failed to attend the *volost'* soviet assemblies. It resolved that on the first occasion of their absence the delegates should be reprimanded; and on the second occasion 'the commune, from which the member was elected, should be told to elect

[42] A. Okninsky, *Dva goda sredi krest'ian: Videnno̲e, slyshannoe, perezhitoe v Tambovskoi gubernii s noiabria 1918 goda do noiabria 1920 goda*, Newtonville, Mass., 1986 (originally Riga, 1936) (henceforth referred to as *DGS*); GAKO, f. 81, op.1, d. 119, l. 29.

[43] TsGAOR, f. 393, op. 3, d. 359, ll. 209–10.

another representative'.[44] Nevertheless, the great majority of the available sources suggest that the communal and *volost'* assemblies took place more frequently during the spring of 1918 than either before or after. The VIK in Chernovka (Buzuluk *uezd*) met on 12 occasions between January and May 1918; during the same period there were 22 'general *volost'* meetings' or soviet assemblies, attended by anything up to 1,000 peasants. In Antipovka *volost'* (Kamyshin *uezd*) there were no less than 71 general meetings or *volost'* soviet assemblies, some of them attended by several hundred inhabitants, from January to mid-June.[45] This upsurge in the level of political activity in the rural localities reflects the importance of the tasks of social reconstruction facing the peasantry during these months—the tasks of land reform, food distribution, and the regulation of trade and social relations. But it also highlights the popularity of the village and *volost'* soviets during this period among the peasantry—a popularity stemming from the social and political freedom which the Russian peasantry, for the first time in three hundred years, experienced through the soviets.

2. THE *VOLOST'* SOVIETS AND THE FOOD CRISIS

The most urgent task facing the *volost'* soviets on their assumption of power was the resolution of the food crisis. Many peasants believed in soviet power during the spring of 1918 for no other reason than that the local soviet had promised them grain. In attempting to fulfil this promise, the local peasant officials who controlled the *volost'* soviets came up against a fundamental problem of government (should compulsion be used to provide for the poor?), which they had previously only had to face at the level of village politics. At the heart of the problem stood a basic clash of interests between the stable peasant farmers, who generally wanted a return to the pre-war free market economy, and the poor and landless inhabitants of the village, who would not be able to feed themselves unless the soviets took it upon themselves to control local prices and redistribute food the population on an equal basis. This clash of interests was intersected by a broader conflict between the food requirements of the local population and the restoration of commodity exchange between town and country. The resolution of the hunger crisis therefore put to the test several important aspects of peasant class organization in the context of the revolution: the relation between the peasant households, the village community, and the *volost'* soviet; the solidarity of the village communities; and the articulation of peasant interests *vis-à-vis* other social groups as well as the state. The solutions of the

44 GAKO, f. 3134, op. 2, d. 21, l. 6.
45 Ibid., ll. 2–150; TsGAOR, f. 393, op. 3, d. 333, ll. 39–168.

village and *volost'* soviets to the food crisis contrasted strongly with the provisions policies of the Bolsheviks implemented after May 1918 (see ch. 6, sect. 1).

The severity of the food crisis should not be underestimated. The 1917 harvest in the Volga region was estimated to be 55% smaller than the average gross harvest of the region during the 1909–13 period. Allowing a per capita consumption norm of 10 *pud* per head and excluding all fodder needs, the Samara population was estimated to have started the 1917–18 agricultural year with a 4 million *pud* grain deficit. The Saratov population started the year with a forecast deficit of 12.2 million *pud*, half the gross harvest in Saratov province during 1917.[46] The increase of the peasants' agricultural area, as a result of the land seizures, together with the transfer of war-prisoners from the estates to the peasant farms, encouraged the latter to increase their autumn sown area during 1917. In Saratov province 40% of the rural soviet respondents in an enquiry of the provincial provisions committee reported an increase in the autumn sown area of the peasantry; only 19% reported a decrease. In total, the 1917 autumn sown area was 14.3% larger than in 1916.[47] The grain stocks of the peasantry would have been further reduced by the grain procurement campaign of autumn 1917: 1.736 million *pud* of grain and fodder was exported from Saratov province; 2.948 million *pud* of grain and fodder was exported from Samara province.[48] By the time of the spring sowing of 1918, there must have been many peasant communities without enough grain to feed themselves and their cattle, let alone sow the fields (see Table 8). At the end of March 1918 the provincial provisions commissar in Samara, Miaskov, warned the People's Commissariat of Provisions (Narkomprod) that the peasant farmers had enough seed to sow only one-quarter of the available spring arable and that, unless a large quantity of seed was imported, 'any hunger riot may take place'.[49] Replying to a questionnaire of May 1918, 95% of the rural soviet respondents in Saratov province claimed that the spring seed stocks were inadequate. Wheaten seed stocks were inadequate in all the households of the community, according to 17.7% of the soviet respondents, as were oats (according to 26.6% of the respondents) and millet (19.5%).[50] The worst-affected regions were those in which

[46] N. Orlov, *Deviat' mesiatsev prodovol'stvennoi raboty Sovetskoi vlasti*, Moscow, 1918, pp. 281–2, 285.

[47] *Biulleten' saratovskogo gubprodkoma (statisticheskii otdel)* (Saratov) (henceforth referred to as *SGB*), no. 1, 15 May 1918, pp. 1–4; *Izvestiia samarskogo gubprodkoma* Samara (henceforth referred to as *ISG*), nos. 6–7, 1918, pp. 39–40.

[48] *Trudy TsSU: Statisticheskii ezhegodnik 1918–1920 gg.*, vol. 8, vyp. 2, Moscow, 1922, sect. xi, p. 2.

[49] TsGANKh, f. 1943, op. 4, d. 116, l. 7.

[50] *SGB*, no. 1, 15 May 1918, pp. 12 ff.

Table 8. *Peasant grain and potato supplies, requirements, and balance, Samara province, 15 April 1918* (*'000,000 pud*)

	Bugul'ma	Buguruslan	Buzuluk	Nilolaevsk	Novouzensk	Samara	Stavropol'
Supply after sowing							
Spring grains	+0.1	—	−4.4	−3.6	+0.6	−0.9	−0.8
Rye	+2.2	−0.3	−1.4	−0.3	+0.7	+0.6	+1.7
Potatoes	+0.4	−0.5	−1.6	−0.3	−1.2	−0.5	−0.4
Required until harvest							
Spring grains for food	0.5	0.7	1.7	2.8	2.4	1.0	0.4
Spring grains for feed	0.5	0.9	1.1	1.3	1.4	0.6	0.4
Rye for feed	1.3	1.9	1.5	0.4	0.3	0.7	1.1
Balance							
Spring grains	−0.9	—	−7.2	−7.7	−3.2	−2.5	−1.6
Rye	+0.9	−2.2	−2.9	−0.7	+0.4	−0.1	+0.6
Total	0.0	—	−10.1	−8.4	−2.8	−2.6	−1.0

Note: The table uses a government consumption norm of 10 *pud* per capita p.a. and estimates the general grain requirement to be 27.3 million *pud*. A second set of figures by the Samara provincial provisions committee was based upon a lower consumption norm; it estimated the overall deficit to be 9 million *pud*. A third set of figures was based upon the assumptions that the peasants concealed from 25% to 50% of their grain and that the harvest of 1917 was between 10% and 20% larger than the amount shown in local figures. This put the grain deficit between 1 million and 14 million *pud* (*ISG*, nos. 1–2, 1918, pp. 18–19).

Source: *ISG*, nos. 1–2, 1918, p. 18.

the spring grains had failed during 1917. Thus, in Khvalynsk district only 35% of the rural soviet respondents could report by the end of May 1918 that all the spring fields had been sown; in the district of Kuznetsk the proportion was as small as 13%.[51]

An important feature of the 1918 grain crisis was the sharp regional variations in its intensity. Three of the seven districts of Samara province were reported to have a grain surplus during March, whereas the remaining four districts were in a hopeless situation. Novouzensk district was said to have an unofficially recorded surplus of 2 million *pud* of grain as late as June 1918: the Samara provisions organs had been unable to collect the grain on account of the civil war against the Ural'sk Cossacks and the difficulties of transportation in this remote region.[52] In Buzuluk district, on the other hand, the 1917 harvest was estimated at only 8 million *pud* of grain and potatoes (on a sown area of 950,000 *des.*). This was barely enough to recover the seed. By January 1918 some sections of the immigrant population were already said to be starving and there were sporadic hunger riots. The district provisions commissar petitioned the higher authorities on several occasions for an extra 3 million *pud* of grain to feed the Buzuluk population until the next harvest; but only 180,000 *pud* was delivered.[53]

The reaction of the *volost'* soviets to the grain shortages varied and developed within every region, in response to the severity of the crisis. A Soviet historian has presented figures which purport to show that the *volost'* soviets of Saratov province took simple and radical measures to resolve the food crisis: 60% of the soviets, it is said, carried out grain requisitionings from the 'kulaks'; 14% imported foodstuffs from other regions; 9% raised a mill tax; 7% organized charity schemes; 3% confiscated gentry grain; and the remaining 7% of the soviets were said not to have taken any measures.[54] However, on a closer examination of their meetings, it appears that the *volost'* soviets took neither simple nor radical measures to ease the food crisis. In fact, they developed a wide variety of complex and often very cautious strategies, whose main purpose seems to have been to feed the local population without causing a civil war between the rich and the poor. A typical chronological sequence of the soviets' policies was as follows: they appealed to the richer communes to lend some of their grain to the poorer ones; they organized charity schemes; they levied taxes to procure grain from Siberia, the Kuban', and other grain-surplus regions; they imposed controls on the movement of grain between the

51 SGB, no. 2, 1 June 1918, pp. 6–9.
52 TsGANKh, f. 1943, op. 3, d. 223, ll. 42, 47, 51.
53 Ibid., ll. 60–1.
54 Gerasimenko, 'Klassovaia bor'ba', p. 351.

villages and its export from the *volost'*; they regulated the activities of the mills; they struck off members of the in-migrant population from the rations lists; they set fixed prices on the main foodstuffs; and they established a provisions consumption norm. It was usually only as a last resort, when starvation was imminent, that the soviets began to requisition the surplus grain stores of the richer peasant households, with, if necessary, the use of armed force. Let us look in detail at the different policies of the soviets at each successive stage of the deepening crisis.

Rejecting the wartime market controls of the Imperial and Provisional governments, the *volost'* soviets favoured a policy of free trade during the winter of 1917–18, as long as there was food on the market and the soviet was able to support the poor.[55] Contrary to the arguments of Soviet historians, this standpoint was not exclusive to the soviets in the grain-surplus localities. Many soviets viewed the free market as the best means to ensure that the provisions needs of the population were met. The mainly Bolshevik VIK in Bazarnyi Karbulak (Saratov *uezd*), a *volost'* whose population was almost entirely engaged in the leather-working industry, promulgated a free trade in all goods during January 1918, after a series of hunger murders, 'in order to increase the food supply'.[56] The VIK in Chernovka (Buzuluk *uezd*) resolved on 10 March to revert to a policy of free trade, since its earlier attempts to close down the markets had only worsened the local food crisis. Like many other soviets, the Chernovka VIK limited the free market to the local citizenry; all foodstuffs imported for sale at free prices were to be confiscated.[57] In Antipovka *volost'* (Kamyshin *uezd*) a meeting of 136 peasants agreed on 20 January to institute a free trade in grain until 1 March, since, in the words of the resolution, 'it has proved impossible for the soviet to purchase grain at fixed prices'. The same meeting made a number of recommendations for the prices of various goods (8 rb. per *pud* of rye; 10 rb. per *pud* of wheat), and agreed to distribute 200 *pud* of wheaten flour to the poor and the soldiers in the 151st Regiment of the Red Army, which was billeted in a nearby garrison.[58]

In spite of the increasing level of state intervention in the market after May 1918, the free, or 'black', market exchange of foodstuffs continued to play a predominant role in the Volga countryside, as it did in the whole of Russia, during the civil war. During the hungry days of

[55] GAKO, f. 81, op. 1, d. 119a, l. 121; *Serdobskaia zhizn'* (Serdobsk), 19, 1918, pp. 9–10.

[56] TsGAOR, f. 393, op. 3, d. 338, l. 41.

[57] GAKO, f. 3134, op. 2, d. 21, l. 50.

[58] TsGAOR, f. 393, op. 3, d. 333, ll. 59–65.

spring 1918 this trade was mainly in unmilled cereals. This was a good indication that the rural population, which had access to the local mills, accounted for a large portion of market demand. The speculators and bag-men (*meshochniki*) from the cities generally preferred cereal products which were ready for consumption (flour, hulled millet, and groats). This is supported by Table 9, which shows that the free market prices of grain (in so far as they could be evaluated during this period,

TABLE 9. *Estimated increase in free market cereal prices, Saratov province, 1917–1918* (% of July 1917 prices)

	Rye	Common millet	Wheat	Wheaten flour	Hulled millet
July 1917	100	100	100	100	100
August	120	111	129	130	132
September	165	157	160	153	176
October	246	239	209	186	207
November	269	272	240	230	243
December	362	282	292	286	275
January 1918	460	390	351	345	306
February	558	450	404	383	340
March	668	500	467	432	379
April	776	556	555	520	422
May	927	691	669	622	513
June	1,371	914	815	738	681

Source: *SGB*, no. 9, pp. 2–10.

when goods were partly bartered or sold in several different currencies) increased faster in the basic food staples (rye and common millet) than in the prepared cereals and wheat (the latter was an export crop in most of the Volga region).

As the number of local peasants who depended upon purchasing grain increased, so the *volost'* (and district[59]) soviets began to take meaures to curb the rising prices of grain. On 19 March, the VIK in Antipovka (Kamyshin *uezd*), which, as already shown, had previously permitted a free trade in grain, resolved to set all the prices on essential foodstuffs, since, in the words of the resolution, 'the poor can no longer afford to buy grain'. The price of rye flour was set at 10 rb. (approximately one-third the free market price) and hulled millet at 18 rb. (approximately half the free market price). Free market prices could

[59] See *Vestnik Komissariata Vnutrennikh Del*, no. 14, 27 May 1918, p. 14; *PSG*, pp. 24, 39; *Protokol kamyshinskogo uezdnogo s''ezda krest'ianskikh deputatov i predstavitelei razlichnykh politicheskikh grupp, uchrezhdenii i organizatsii, 10-go marta 1918 g.*, Kamyshin, 1918, pp. 50–1.

still be charged to non-residents of the *volost'*, but a market salesman caught charging free prices to local inhabitants would be arrested. At another meeting of the soviet, on 1 May, a second market 'control' was instituted to deflate food prices: local resident purchasers at the market were entitled, by presenting the relevant receipt, to force a salesman to sell his foodstuffs at the same price he had charged on the previous market day.[60] This was a simple solution, to be sure, but it must have given rise to numerous disputes between peasants.

In the early stages of the food crisis, the soviets' various strategies of food distribution were heavily dependent upon the voluntary co-operation of the wealthy peasantry. In Chernovka *volost'* (Buzuluk *uezd*) a voluntary land tax was imposed (1 *pud* of grain per *des.*) as a way for the stable peasantry to help support the landless population.[61] In Poretsk *volost'* (Ardatov *uezd*) a 'general meeting of the wealthy class' on 25 April agreed to make a voluntary donation of 20,000 rb. in aid of the poor. This was really quite a considerable sum. Two representatives of the soviet assembly were given the money to purchase grain from the district authorities in Ardatov, but they returned empty-handed.[62] The Borodachei village soviet (Krasnyi Iar *volost'*, Kamyshin *uezd*) passed the following resolution on this matter during April 1918:

> we ask the wealthy citizens of Borodachei to lend the commune 1 *pud* of rye per 100 *pud* of surplus rye; those who are willing to may lend more. The grain will be collected in the communal store and will be used to feed the people who have no grain of their own. The grain will be returned in the autumn of this year when the harvest is collected and not later than 1 September.

The soviet made a list of 'the households genuinely in need of grain'. Then a second resolution was passed to permit the farmers who had lent the required amount of surplus grain to sell the remainder of their surplus at free market prices.[63]

In many localities these voluntarist principles continued to predominate well into the grain crisis, since the peasant communes jealously guarded their grain surpluses against the claims of the *volost'* authority. A good illustration of this is in Elshanka *volost'* (Buzuluk *uezd*), where the VIK suggested at the soviet assemblies of 16 and 21 April that every village commune should elect two representatives to collect surplus grain for the poor. The VIK also suggested that the communes should open their grain stores for inspection by the *volost'* provisions committee. Armed force would be used, if necessary,

[60] TsGAOR, f. 393, op. 3, d. 333, ll. 117, 135–6.
[61] GAKO, f. 3134, op. 2, d. 21, l. 55.
[62] TsGAOR, f. 393, op. 3, d. 359, ll. 15–17.
[63] Ibid., d. 333, l. 205.

against any commune which refused to allow the committee to inspect its barns. At the next *volost'* soviet assembly, however, all the delegates from the separate communes declared their opposition to the VIK proposals. Instead, it was unanimously resolved that a voluntary loan would be collected from the villages, with receipts from the VIK given to every creditor.[64]

It is worth mentioning briefly that similar voluntarist principles were applied by the village and *volost'* soviets during the Bolshevik food procurement campaigns of 1918–21 (see ch. 6, sect. 1). The majority of the village communes carried out the Bolshevik grain levies in the manner of a traditional communal tax, levied equally from each household in the commune, and not as a compulsory tax on the village rich (as the regulations of the grain monopoly required). The district provisions commissar in Vol'sk emphasized in a report of December 1920 that this voluntarist approach had disastrous consequences for the state procurement of foodstuffs:

> several communes in the *volosti* pass very nice resolutions, in which it is set out in words that the peasantry understands its obligations towards the military and labour fronts; but, in fact, instead of fulfilling their government *razverstka* [levy], they agree to collect on a voluntary basis anything from 10 to 20 *funt* of grain from each person. In this way, the communal *razverstka* of, say, 5,000 *pud* is left unpaid, while perhaps 300 *pud*, and a maximum of 500 *pud*, is collected through donations.[65]

Although the peasant communes recognized the obligation to give up any surplus food to the Red Army, they were never prepared to subordinate their own consumption needs to those of others. 'Localist tendencies' were noted at every level of the food supply system during the civil war, but they were especially apparent during the food crisis of spring 1918. The majority of the VIKs attempted to stop foodstuffs and other valuable items being exported from their *volost'* by setting up road blocks guarded by an armed patrol (*boevaia druzhina*) or a red guard. This was also done by the VIKs which simultaneously supported a free market in grain within the *volost'* territory.[66] Some of the village soviets also tried to stop the export of foodstuffs from their localities. This often resulted in a conflict between the VIK and the villages concerned. Sometimes the latter broke away from the *volost'* authority to form a new *volost'* (see sect. 1 above). At a *volost'* soviet assembly in Lipovka (Samara *uezd*) on 29 March the commune of

64 GAKO, f. 81, op. 1, d. 119, ll. 139–41, 170.

65 *Materialy k XIII-mu vol'skomu uezdnomu s''ezdu sovetov 12 dekabria 1920 g.*, Vol'sk, 1920, p. 69.

66 GAKO, f. 81, op. 1, d. 119, ll. 43, 186; TsGAOR, f. 393, op. 3, d. 340, ll. 291–2; *PSG*, p. 22.

Dmitrievka, the largest and richest in the *volost'*, tried to break away from the assembly in order to form its own *volost'* authority. It was no coincidence that six weeks previously the Lipovka *volost'* assembly had passed a resolution to redistribute all the grain in the *volost'* among the communes. The Lipovka assembly passed a resolution of censure against the delegation from Dmitrievka and rejected its demand: 'Dmitrievka is the most wealthy village and does not want to give the other villages any grain; it has still not carried out an inspection of its own grain stores. If Dmitrievka is allowed to form a new *volost'*, the villages remaining in the old *volost'* will be left in a very poor state.' In the end, of course, there was little the Lipovka authorities could do to prevent the breakaway of Dmitrievka. When the latter ceased to pay its *volost'* taxes, the Lipovka *volost'* soviet assembly could only bar the inhabitants of Dmitrievka 'from all the activities of the soviet'.[67]

Another interesting example of the sort of conflicts which could take place between the *volost'* authority and the individual villages is in Mariinovka *volost'* (Saratov *uezd*). By February 1918 the shortages of food had already incited hunger riots in the villages of Khanenevka and Nikolaev. The *volost'* soviet assembly called for a 'voluntary collection' of the grain surpluses which had been registered at the end of 1917. Five of the poorer villages refused to give up their grain and began to take the law into their own hands. On 4 March the peasants of Aleksandrovka commune seized one of the local mills and, with the peasants from Khanenevka, Nikolaev, and Kuvyka, marched westward towards the village of Rybushka in order to seize the grain surpluses of the latter in the name of the *volost'* soviet. However, their march was intercepted by 'almost half of the male population' of the village of Konstantinovka, a crowd of a hundred or so. A general fight broke out, which was joined on the side of Konstantinovka by the peasants of the nearby village of Teplovka. The records of the VIK in Mariinovka suggest that the three richest communes in the *volost'* (Rybushka, Konstantinovka, and Teplovka) had entered 'an alliance to protect their own interests'. Situated in the western corner of the *volost'*, bordering on Atkarsk district, they certainly had a larger amount of land than the other five communes: in Teplovka, for instance, the average household allotment of arable in 1911 was 13.2 *des.*, whereas in Khanenevka it was only 5.4 *des.*[68] Beaten in battle, the peasants of Mariinovka and Nikolaev held a general meeting, which disallowed the three richest communes from using the *volost'* institutions in

[67] GAKO, f. 81, op. 1, d. 119a, ll. 16, 22–3, 32.

[68] *Spiski naselennykh mest Saratovskoi gubernii: Saratovskii uezd*, Saratov, 1912, pp. 24–6, and map.

Nikolaev (a school, an agronomic centre, and a hospital). The same meeting organized an 'armed brigade of local soldiers' which, during the following months, made several unsuccessful efforts to wrest the grain surpluses of the three western communes.[69]

A very common symptom of this type of localism was the refusal to feed the in-migrant townsmen and refugees who had flooded into the villages since 1917. A study carried out by the Central Statistical Administration (TsSU) in 1922 suggested that the majority of the peasant communities were willing to give both land and food to those in-migrants who were returning to their native village.[70] However, a more hostile reception awaited those in-migrants who could not claim any such link with the community (*ne zdeshnie, chuzhie*), yet who still hoped to sit out the hungry years in the countryside. Some VIKs, it is true, did follow the resolutions of the higher authorities, which spoke in favour of awarding the in-migrants a ration of food on an equal basis with the rural poor.[71] The VIK in Elshanka (Samara *uezd*) even took measures to billet some of the in-migrants in nearby soviet mills.[72] However, the allocation of land and food fell mainly under the jurisdiction of the village communes, and so the majority of the VIKs were likely to leave the fate of the in-migrants up to them.[73] Others simply endorsed the views of the communal delegates at the *volost'* soviet assemblies. At an assembly in Voskresenskoe (Samara *uezd*) on 20 April the provisions commissar of the VIK asked the peasant delegates if they wanted the in-migrants to be included on the rations list. The peasants' unanimous response was not to include the in-migrants, 'but only natives of the *volost'*'.[74] In Bogdanovka (Samara *uezd*) a *volost'* assembly on 2 January petitioned the Samara soviet 'to resettle all in-migrants outside the *volost'*, since there is no grain for them here'. Three months later the in-migrants had still not been resettled and the assembly was forced to grant them a ration of 10 *funt* of flour per month, although this was to be done only 'for as long as the grain can be found'.[75] The Chernorech'e and Natal'in *volost'* soviets also resolved to petition the Samara authorities to resettle their in-migrant population. Meanwhile, the two soviets decided they could

[69] TsGAOR, f. 393, op. 3, d. 338, ll. 233, 323; see also GAKO, f. 3134, op. 2, d. 21, ll. 94–5.

[70] Ia. Bliakher, 'Sovremennoe zemlepol'zovanie po dannym spetsial'noi ankety TsSU 1922 g.', *Vestnik statistiki*, vol. 13, 1923, nos. 1–3, p. 143.

[71] GAKO, f. 81, op. 1, d. 119a, l. 163; TsGAOR, f. 393, op. 3, d. 336, l. 111; *Plennyi i bezhenets*, nos. 3–4, p. 3.

[72] GAKO, f. 81, op. 1, d. 119, l. 128.

[73] TsGAOR, f. 393, op. 3, d. 338, l. 261.

[74] GAKO, f. 81, op. 1, d. 119, l. 87.

[75] Ibid., ll. 32, 42, 195.

not be responsible for feeding the in-migrants.[76] In Antipovka (Kamyshin *uezd*) various peasant meetings during February and March 1918 passed resolutions rejecting the demands for food made by the 1,200 in-migrants who had settled in the locality. The indigenous population of 6,000 was itself said to be 'in a desperate situation', while the soviet had only 2,000 *pud* of grain left for distribution. Petitions were sent to the Kamyshin authorities asking them to 'remove the in-migrants to a village which has surplus grain'. But nothing was done. Then, in April, a 'final resolution' was passed: those in-migrants who were able to find work on the local peasant farms would be granted rights of habitation in the *volost'*, whereas the others would be left to fend for themselves (see also secs. 3 and 4 below).[77]

As the food crisis deepened, the village and *volost'* soviets organized their own grain procurements from Siberia, the Kuban', and other regions. Some soviets employed black-marketeers and bag-men to import the grain. Others purchased it at 'special prices' from traders arrested by soviet armed patrols on the roads. The VIK in Antipovka struck one such deal with a 'kulak', by the name of Timofei Nashniasev, whom the red guard had caught trying to export 400 *pud* of oats. Nashniasev was allowed to export his oats on the condition that he imported an equivalent amount of wheat and sold it to the soviet at 15 rb. per *pud*.[78] A much more common method of importing the food was for the village or *volost'* assembly to levy a tax or make a collection of money or goods and to send two or three young delegates to purchase foodstuffs from other localities. In Trost'ian *volost'* (Samara *uezd*) the peasants pooled the money which had been gained from the sale of the property of the estates to purchase foodstuffs.[79] In other places a head tax (usually between 2 rb. and 10 rb.) was collected by the communes for the purchase of grain.[80] On rare occasions these taxes were progressive, with the richest peasants being asked to pay more in return for less grain.[81] But in the majority of cases it was the communes themselves which served as tax units, with each being given an amount of grain in proportion to the capital it had invested.[82] In some villages the peasants had already organized 'credit companies', 'savings associations', 'societies of self-help', and 'people's' or 'soviet'

[76] GAKO, f. 81, op. 1, d. 119a, ll. 77, 188.

[77] TsGAOR, f. 393, op. 3, d. 333, ll. 68, 116, 133, 138; *Tablitsy statisticheskikh svedenii po Saratovskoi gubernii po dannym vserossiiskoi sel'vko-khoziaistvennoi i gorodskoi perepisei*, Saratov, 1919, pp. 50–1.

[78] TsGAOR, f. 393, op. 3, d. 333, l. 93.

[79] GAKO, f. 81, op. 1, d. 119a, l. 165.

[80] Ibid., d. 119, ll. 110, 177, 195; TsGAOR, f. 393, op. 3, d. 359, ll. 344, 358.

[81] TsGAOR, f. 393, op. 3, d. 333, l. 57.

[82] GAKO, f. 81, op. 1, d. 119a, l. 90; TsGAOR, f. 393, op. 3, d. 359, l. 55.

banks, through which the financing of the grain imports was arranged.[83] S. P. Rudnev, the ex-landowner from Simbirsk, recalled how in January 1918 he was entrusted by the peasants to organize the purchase of 5,000 rb. worth of grain from a trader in the Bugul'ma region. An armed detachment of fifteen ex-servicemen (deserters from the army) was sent, according to Rudnev's instructions. It lost its purchase to a soviet road-block brigade (*zagraditel'nyi otriad*) near Bugul'ma. But a second detachment of twenty peasants from the neighbouring village to Rudnev's accomplished the same mission and caught up with the first detachment, which then went back to purchase more grain.[84]

This spontaneous reorganization of the market economy by the village communities and the local soviets was commonplace during the 1917–21 period. Beneath the state structures of food distribution and trade control which the Bolsheviks and, to a lesser extent, the Komuch tried to build up during these years, there was a flourishing free market exchange of goods and services which was mostly organized by the village and *volost'* soviets themselves. This was a form of rural self-organization which one would expect to find in the conditions of 1917–21, when the economic ties between town and country were disrupted and the old market structures were attacked by the state (see ch. 6, sects. 1–3). The higher provisions authorities were powerless to stop this proliferation of commodity exchange between the localities, especially during the earlier period when the Bolshevik state organs of food control were still in embryonic form. Miaskov, the provincial provisions commissar in Samara, was asked by Narkomprod in April 1918 to combat the chaotic movement of grain across the Urals, which was said to be disrupting the state's procurement programme: he replied that nothing could be done, since all the peasant trade 'delegations' travelled with certificates from their local soviet.[85] Indeed, it was often the district peasant assemblies that put forward the idea of organizing the food importations; they also issued the *volost'* soviet delegations with 'government passes' for the railways and the territorial borders.[86] Sometimes the district soviet provisions departments themselves took part in a free market exchange with the *volost'* soviet delegations: few would take cash from the *volost'*

[83] GAKO, f. 81, op. 1, d. 127, l. 11; d. 119, l. 12; TsGAOR, f. 393, op. 3, d. 323, l. 362; *ISG*, nos. 4–5, p. 30.

[84] *PVO*, pp. 106–10.

[85] TsGANKh, f. 1943, op. 4, d. 116, l. 17.

[86] GAKO, f. 81, op. 1, d. 127, l. 11; TsGAOR, f. 393, op. 3, d. 359, l. 197; d. 323, l. 362; *Izvestiia saratovskogo gubprodkoma*, no. 1, 14 July 1918, p. 9.

delegations, but a large number were prepared to give out grain in exchange for wool, cloth or leather.[87]

In their struggle against the food crisis, many VIKs were forced to establish a *volost'* consumption norm of grain, fodder, and seed. The stable peasant farmers, whose interests would be threatened if the consumption norm was set too low, usually succeeded in getting the VIK to institute a higher norm than the one suggested by the district and provincial provisions authorities. However, as the food crisis deepened the VIKs came under increasing pressure from the poor to lower the consumption norm. Generally speaking, the majority of the VIKs attempted to balance these two conflicting interests; the production needs of the peasant farmers had to be recognized, but efforts also had to be made to feed the landless inhabitants. It is understandable why, at the height of the food crisis, some of the landless elements preferred to form their own organs of power (culminating in the *kombedy*) than to continue under the peasant-dominated soviets. In Saratov the provincial provisions committee established the consumption norm until the next harvest at 15 *pud* of grain per peasant, 40 *pud* per horse, and 12 *pud* per cow. The Samara provincial peasant assembly of January 1918 passed similar norms.[88] In Lipovka (Samara *uezd*) a *volost'* assembly on 2 February resolved to issue the provincial norm only to the landless residents without grain, whereas the peasant households which had their own grain stores were allowed a consumption norm of 24 *pud* per person, 60 *pud* per horse, 36 *pud* per cow, and 8 *pud* of seed per *des.*.[89] In Kandabulak *volost'* (Samara *uezd*) a general meeting on 6 February passed the following norm, which was to last until the next harvest: 15 *pud* of grain and 12 *pud* of flour per person; 10 *pud* per horse in households with up to four horses (5 *pud* per horse in households with more than four horses); 5 *pud* per cow (up to three cows per household); and 13 *pud* of wheat per household for the spring sowing. In Trost'ian *volost'* (Samara *uezd*) a soviet assembly on 26 April set the norm for the year at 15 *pud* of grain and 12 *pud* of flour per peasant, and 60 *pud* of grain per horse.[90] Similar norms were set by the *volost'* soviets in Saratov province.[91]

It was essential for the enforcement of the *volost'* soviet norms that the VIK established some control of the local mills. The closure of the steam-mills, because of shortages of fuel, complicated this process,

[87] TsGAOR, f. 393, op. 3, d. 359, ll. 15–17, 358–9; *ISG*, nos. 4–5, pp. 30–1; *PSG*, pp. 21, 30, 102.
[88] TsGANKh, f. 1943, op. 4, d. 117, ll. 19–23.
[89] TsGAOR, f. 393, op. 3, d. 330, ll. 2–3; GAKO, f. 81, op. 1, d. 119, l. 121.
[90] GAKO, f. 81, op. 1, d. 119a, l. 92; d. 119, ll. 183, 172.
[91] TsGAOR, f. 393, op. 3, d. 338, l. 197.

since the peasants reverted to the old windmills and horse-drawn mills which produced flour in quantities that were far too small to be detected by the *volost'* soviet authorities. Moreover, whereas the average *volost'* might have one or two steam-mills, there were far too many windmills for the VIK to be able to keep a check on each one. Most of the windmills were still controlled by the individual communes, or by private merchants, whose interests were too well organized to be controlled by the new VIKs. One way for the VIKs to curtail the activities of the windmills was to prohibit the transportation of grain between the villages. A number of VIKs attempted to do this by setting up road patrols,[92] although this rarely had much effect because of the ease with which the patrols could be bribed. A more effective control was for the soviet to take over the steam-mills and to subsidize their prices for milling grain in order to compete with the windmills. The money and the grain (*gartsevyi*) which were earned by the soviet mills (typical rates for milling were 2 to 3 rb. per *pud*, or 2.5 *funt* per *pud*) were usually used to feed the people on the soviet rations list. This strategy, which was adopted by most of the VIKs, had two great drawbacks. Firstly, the soviet steam-mills were constantly being shut down because of the shortage of fuel; rising fuel costs pushed up the prices of the soviet mills, making them uncompetitive against the windmills. Secondly, the soviet mills were obliged to keep a register of all their transactions in order to prevent the peasant farmer from milling more than his consumption norm. This increased the attraction of the windmills, which were less efficient, but more discrete. It also increased the level of corruption at the soviet mills. In some localities the employees of the soviet mills were replaced more than thirty times between 1918 and 1921.[93]

It was also essential for the enforcement of the consumption norms that the soviets brought under control the peasants' domestic production of moonshine, or home-brewed vodka (*samogon*). This was a very hard task during this period, when the power of the VIKs was so weak: a bottle or two of vodka could usually be used to bribe the rural soviet official. Some VIKs were prepared, however, to take a tough line on the vodka question, if only on paper. The VIK in Elkhovka (Samara *uezd*) resolved on 21 February that any peasant household caught brewing vodka would be fined up to 500 rb. On its second offence, the household would be fined again and then 'thrown out of the

[92] Ibid., d. 333, l. 233; d. 340, l. 19.

[93] GAKO, f. 81, op. 1, d. 119a, l. 171; TsGAOR, f. 393, op. 3, d. 331, ll. 19–20; d. 336, l. 39; *Biulleten' saratovskogo gubernskogo soveta narodnogo khoziaistva* (Saratov), no. 11, 20 Dec. 1918, pp. 4–5; *Otchet pugachevskogo uezdnogo ekonomicheskogo soveshchaniia*, Pugachev, 1921, pp. 26, 28.

commune'. These fines were to be paid at all costs, 'even if the household has to sell its livestock and property'. The vodka which was taken from the household was to be poured away and the stills destroyed. The same VIK resolved that any peasant found in a drunken state would be fined 50 rb. or sent to prison for one month. Anyone who denounced a vodka producer would be rewarded 250 rb.[94] Some of the communes also took measures against the vodka trade. A gathering of sixty-seven peasants from the commune of Kolyvan' (Dubovo-Umet *volost'*, Samara *uezd*) resolved on 28 April to fine any household caught distilling vodka 300 rb. On its second offence, the household would be fined 1,000 rb. or have its best worker imprisoned for one year.[95]

Once the consumption norms had been established, the *volost'* soviet was in a position to start accounting the surplus grain in the communes in order to purchase it and resell it at the prices which had been fixed to favour the poor. This process was usually done with extreme caution, since it was only with the co-operation of the local communes that the VIK was able to push through a general redistribution of the surplus grain. A resolution on the food crisis, passed by the VIK in Poretsk *volost'* on 27 March, was typical of the sort of political compromise which was made during this period: 'the will of independent peasantry and the poor population of our *volost'* must be considered; the former obviously want to store their grain in case of a future famine, but the poor, who have neither bread nor wages, insist that the grain should be distributed at once at the cheapest prices'.[96] Like most of the soviets, the VIK in Poretsk tried for as long as possible to balance these two interests. The requisitioning of grain from the independent peasantry did not begin until the grain stores at the disposal of the soviet ran out and there was nothing left with which to feed the landless inhabitants on the soviet's rations list.

In accounting the grain stores of the independent peasant farmers, the *volost'* soviets were dependent upon the co-operation of the communes themselves. The decision to redistribute the grain was taken at a general *volost'* assembly of the communal representatives, who agreed to call a gathering in their respective communes to elect an audit committee. The decision to redistribute the grain had to be affirmed at the *volost'* assembly. Thus, an assembly in Starodvorian (Samara *uezd*) on 7 February resolved:

94 GAKO, f. 81, op. 1, d. 119, l. 162. Neil Weissman has argued mistakenly that the soviet 'authorities mounted no systematic effort against illegal alcohol' during the civil war ('Prohibition and Alcohol Control in the USSR: The 1920s Campaign against Illegal Spirits', *Soviet Studies*, vol. 38, no. 3, 1986, p. 350).

95 GAKO, f. 81, op. 1, d. 119, l. 118.

96 TsGAOR, f. 393, op. 3, d. 359, l. 10.

to propose to all the rural communes in the *volost'* that they find out at a communal gathering *[mirskii skhod]* if their citizens are willing to collect their grain surpluses . . . and to express their decision in the form of a resolution *[prigovor]*, which is to be delivered to the soviet before 10 February; otherwise the soviet will use its right to proceed with the requisitioning of grain which was given to it by the provincial peasant assembly in Samara from 12 to 17 January 1918, and it will use armed force if necessary. The adoption of such extraordinary measures will be announced to the population, if need be, at a general assembly on 11 February.[97]

In fixing the prices of the surplus grain, it was also common for the *volost'* soviet to confer with the communes. Thus, the Elshanka soviet assembly (Saratov *uezd*) passed a resolution on 11 February to requisition any grain surpluses at 15 rb. for wheat and 12 rb. for rye: 'and if these prices are supported by the majority of the communes, then the elected executive of the *volost'* soviet shall have the right to bring the prices into effect; otherwise, whatever prices are agreed on by the majority of the communes shall come into effect'.[98] The final account of the grain stores of the peasant farms was carried out by a commission of the VIK with the help of the communes' audit committees. The account of the grain surpluses and the allocation of the taxes was a social, as well as an economic, matter. The peasants often preferred to measure the grain in subjective terms ('by eye'), instead of using weights.[99] In this way, the entire village could be involved in the assessment of the surplus of each household. The surplus of an unpopular household was often seen to be 'larger' than it actually was, whereas the surplus of a popular household tended to be overlooked.[100]

There was a notable reluctance among the communes and the soviets to requisition the grain of industrious and respected family farmers. It tended to be the farmers who hired wage-labour or those who refused to give up their grain voluntarily who were the first to be subjected to the food tax. Barn owners, free traders, black-marketeers, vodka distillers,and the peasants who had failed to sow all their seed were also in the front line.[101] The VIK in Lipovka (Samara *uezd*) made an interesting distinction in this respect at a *volost'* soviet assembly on 2 February. The surpluses of the peasant family-labour farms were to be purchased 'at the current [market] prices', whereas those of the

[97] GAKO, f. 81, op. 1, d. 119, l. 90.
[98] TsGAOR, f. 393, op. 3, d. 338, l. 196.
[99] GAKO, f. 81, op. 1, d. 119a, l. 11.
[100] On the social forces at play within the village during the grain procurements see A. M. Bol'shakov, 'The Soviet Countryside, 1917–24', in R. E. F. Smith (ed.), *The Russian Peasant*, London, 1977, pp. 47–8.
[101] GAKO, f. 81, op. 1, d. 119, ll. 112, 117; d. 119a, ll. 11, 15, 50, 65, 109.

farms which had employed wage-labour were to be purchased at the lower prices, fixed by the soviet, of 2 rb. 30 kop. for rye and 3 rb. 36 kop. for wheat. It is interesting to note that these prices were roughly equivalent to the prices in this region at the time of the 1917 harvest—a symbol, perhaps, of the peasants' belief that the entrepreneurial peasant, who was able to store grain, should not be allowed to speculate on the increase of food prices. The soviet also resolved that the farms which had employed wage-labour were to be taxed on their earnings from the requisitioned grain (30 kop. per *pud* of rye and 36 kop. per *pud* of wheat). The receipts from this tax were to be used to purchase more grain for the poor.[102]

It is important to underline that, in contrast to the grain procurement campaigns of the Bolshevik 'food dictatorship', the village and *volost'* soviets of this period organized their grain procurements in the manner of a traditional communal tax. The task of distributing the grain among the households was usually left to the village communes themselves. Thus, the VIKs demanded that only the overall surplus of the commune be delivered to the soviet for redistribution to the grain-deficit communes.[103] The use of armed force against the communes or peasant farms which were thought to be withholding a surplus of grain was always a final resort. Thus, at a *volost'* soviet assembly in Staryi Buinsk (Buinsk *uezd*) on 20 March a large majority of the delegates twice rejected the use of an armed brigade (*druzhina*) against the grain hoarders. The assembly resolved instead to proceed 'by further appeals for the voluntary surrender of the grain at fixed prices'.[104] It was normal for several warnings to be issued to the hoarders at the *volost'* assembly before a brigade was set up to take the grain by force.[105]

A number of peasant delegates at the Saratov provincial soviet assembly at the end of May 1918 stressed that the *volost'* soviets were, for the most part, able to take the grain of the hoarders without serious conflict. Progressive self-taxation, legitimately backed by the use of coercion, was understood by the majority of the peasantry to be an integral element of the social revolution which it was carrying out in the rural localities through the soviets. It is probable that these principles could have been extended to the national domain, once the immediate food crisis had been overcome. As we shall discover, the disappointing results of the Bolshevik procurement campaign after the big harvest of 1918 were not caused by the failure of the peasantry to fulfil its obligations: they were caused by the political failure of the

102 GAKO, f. 81, op. 1, d. 119a, ll. 11–12.
103 Ibid., d. 119, l. 39; TsGAOR, f. 393, op. 3, d. 359, l. 197.
104 GAKO, f. 81, op. 1, d. 119, l. 52.
105 Ibid., d. 119a, ll. 61, 109.

Bolsheviks to organize the procurement system on an efficient basis without the use of brutal force (see ch. 6, sect. 1). A warning of what was to come was sounded at the Saratov provincial soviet assembly. Some of the delegates were angry because the urban food squads (*prodotriady*) and some brigades of the Red Army had been using violence indiscriminately to requisition grain. The Khvalynsk delegate complained that 'bad people . . . not from here, not from Khvalynsk, were sent to take our grain, and they knew nothing about how to tax the peasants'. They soon resorted to robbery, bribe-taking, and the use of torture against any peasant farmer who could not give them grain or vodka. 'The confidence of the poor peasants in the district has been lost', concluded the delegate from Khvalynsk, 'and wherever the Red Army travels the population flees into the ravines and woods.'[106]

3. LAND REFORM

In peasant societies the significance of the land is felt in almost every aspect of life. The land is the natural environment of the peasantry's existence and the primary means of its agricultural production. The tenure of land is the main criterion of peasanthood, and 'position in the hierarchy of the peasant sub-groups is, to a large extent, defined by the amount of land held'.[107] The reform of the land system is thus a crucial moment in the history of the peasantry because it affects the whole development of rural life.

Before 1917 the peasantry's regulation of the land system was circumscribed by the surrounding power structure of the state. The territorial rights and the fiscal obligations of the communes were fixed by the Emancipation decrees of the 1860s. Peasant land tenure rights and the rights of private land ownership were fixed by written law. A communal resolution to redivide the allotment land required by law the consent of two-thirds of the household elders. This was difficult to attain, since the richest elders, who were usually opposed to a redivision, had a dominant influence in the village. The destruction of the state during 1917 swept aside these constraints. Rights of private land ownership were abolished. New regulations made the redivision of the land dependent upon only a simple majority in the commune. Free from intervention, the peasants were left to reform the land system according to traditional egalitarian norms. Not even the *volost'* soviets were well enough prepared to influence the course of the land reforms in 1918.

The traditionalism of the peasant revolution was nowhere better

[106] *PSG*, pp. 31, 34, 49–50, 52.
[107] T. Shanin, 'The Peasantry as a Political Factor', *The Sociological Review*, vol. 14, no. 1, 1966, p. 7.

illustrated than in the land reforms. The peasants aimed to restore the idealized 'good life' of the village commune, a life which had been irrevocably lost in the modern world. They appealed to the ancient peasant ideals of truth and justice (*pravda*) which, since the Middle Ages, had been inextricably connected in the dreams of the peasants with land and freedom (*zemlia, volia*).[108] The village commune was the focus of the peasantry's traditions, the voice of its social ideals. It provided the organizational structure and the ideological basis of the peasant revolution, whose climax was the land reforms. These were implemented in the form of a traditional repartition of the communal land. The land was retained in small parcels, or strips, distributed among the households in the commune on an equal basis. Every family household, including those of the former landowners, was given the right to cultivate with its own labour a share of the land. The land rights of the marginal social groups were considered in the light of local peasant customs.

The peasants believed that the land question would be resolved as it had been in their own subversive folklore before the revolution. The myth of the Tsar's 'golden manifesto' confirming the peasants' domain of the land and dividing it, once and for all, within a 'universal commune' of Russia was transposed to the Constituent Assembly, which the peasants expected to come to a final resolution of the land question. The closure of the Constituent Assembly and the approach of the civil war cast a shadow of doubt over the fate of the land. The peasantry's fear that the gentry squires would return and its continued expectation, long after the publication of the Law on the Socialization of Land (19 February 1918), that a final repartition would later be organized at the national level are sufficient to explain the piecemeal and temporary nature of the peasant land reforms in 1918. The resolution of the Balashov district peasant assembly in April 1918 was typical in this respect: 'In the very near future there should be a radical, full and final equalization of the land. [The assembly therefore resolved on a] temporary repartition of the land, without specified duration, until the final enactment of the Law on the Socialization of Land.'[109]

The majority of the communes carried through several land repartitions during 1917–21. The land reforms should not be conceived

[108] See H. Wada, 'The Inner World of Russian Peasants', *Annals of the Institution of Social Science*, vol. 20, Tokyo, 1979, pp. 61–94.

[109] Cited in *Materialy po zemel'noi reforme 1918 goda*, vyp. 1, *Raspredelenie zemli v 1918 godu*, Moscow, 1919 (henceforth referred to as *MZR 1*), pp. 1–2; P. N. Pershin, *Agrarnaia Revoliutsiia v Rossii*, Moscow, 1966, vol. 2, p. 223. It should be noted that the Instructions on the enactment of the Law on the Socialization of Land, published on 11 Apr., ordered only a temporary equalization of land use.

as a single historical feat, but as a protracted period of land redistribution, whose height of activity came in 1918. The most intensive process of land redistribution was noted in the densely populated black-earth region of central Russia. This may be explained by the large number of landed estates in the region, by the difficulties of integrating the confiscated arable into the open three-field system, and by the constant influx of soldiers and townsmen into the countryside of central Russia, each with a claim to readjust the existing distribution of arable strips. The correlation between the population and the intensity of the land reforms was also reflected in the different regions of the Volga: 82% of the villages in the middle Volga carried out at least one land repartition during 1917–22, compared with only 48% of the villages in the less densely populated regions of the lower Volga. In the central black-earth zone of Russia 94% of the villages carried out at least one land repartition.[110] In the densely populated district of Zadonsk in Voronezh province only 2 of the 432 villages failed to carry out a land repartition between 1917 and 1920. Of the 430 villages which did carry out a land repartition: 7% repartitioned it once; 23% twice; 66% three times (annually); and 4% four times. The most intensive repartitioning occurred in the communes which had not redivided the land since 1861 (they represented roughly one-quarter of the total): 88% of these communes carried out three or four repartitions, whereas only 66% of the communes which had redivided the land betwen 1861 and 1917 carried out as many repartitions. The busiest period of the redivisions in Zadonsk district was in 1918–19, although, as in the rest of Russia, some communes continued to repartition the land into the 1920s.[111]

The repartitions followed a seasonal pattern. As soon as the snow melted and the arable could be marked out in the mud the peasants started to divide up the spring fields in time for the new sowing. During the mowing season the meadows and the pasture were divided. It was usually not until August, after the harvest, that the communes began to divide the fallow land and the autumn fields.[112] The arable fields were generally divided for a period of one agricultural season. This enabled the communes to accommodate the increasing demands on the land of the peasant-soldiers and the townsmen, whose arrival in the village did not necessarily coincide with the beginning of the

110 Bliakher, p. 141.

111 V. Keller and I. Romanenko, *Pervye itogi agrarnoi reformy: Opyt issledovaniia rezul'tatov sovremennogo zemleustroistva na primere Zadonskogo uezda Voronezhskoi gubernii*, Voronezh, 1922, pp. 100–2.

112 Pershin, *Agrarnaia revoliutsiia v Rossii*, vol. 2, p. 225; Iu. V. Fulin 'Osushchestvlenie Dekreta o zemle v tsentral'no-zemledel'cheskom raione', in *Leninskii Dekret o zemle v deistvii*, p. 98.

agricultural year. It also enabled any additional bits of private land which had not been expropriated before the previous sowing to be included in the communal stock of land (*zemel'nyi fond*). The first to be divided was the private land of the gentry, the church, and state institutions, followed by the peasant consolidated plots and any arable purchased through the peasant Land Bank. In many localities the communal allotments were not redivided because enough private land had been confiscated to satisfy the needs of the poor.[113]

Since the spring repartitions commenced in the middle of an agricultural year, it had to be decided what should be done with the confiscated land which had already been sown or prepared during the previous autumn. In many communes this land was divided at once among the landless peasants, or the peasants without sufficient means of production to plough the spring arable. In other communes it was divided among all the peasants, regardless of their economic status. A minority of the communes left these fields undivided in order to farm them as a collective, or else to turn them over to the landless peasantry to farm them collectively. This was most commonly noted in localities where the *volost'* soviet had taken control of the estates from early on. The seed and tools were provided by the commune or the soviet, and part of the harvest was used to pay the landless peasant workers; the rest of the harvest was taken by the soviet provisions committee and stored in the communal barns. If the landowner who had prepared or sown the arable during the previous autumn remained in the locality, then he was sometimes allowed to reap the harvest himself provided he surrendered an agreed amount of it in tax. This was commonly noted when the spring sowing campaign was seen to be critical, because of the food shortages, and the local peasantry lacked sufficient means of production to cultivate the gentry fields (which were often a long way from the village). If the land was taken away from the landowner, then he was commonly compensated for the labour and expenditures which he had put into the preparation of the fields in the form of a cash payment, a share of the harvest, or part of the arable itself.[114]

The spring fields of the landowners which had not been previously prepared caused fewer problems, and were invariably divided among the peasantry. Because it was still by no means certain that the power of the landowners would not be restored, the peasant communes tended to keep the estate land in a separate *fond*. Many peasants believed they would have to answer for the land they had gained since 1917 because it had not been given to them by the Tsar himself. Others

113 *MZR* 1, pp. 6–9, 11.
114 Ibid., pp. 11–12; Pershin, *Agrarnaia revoliutsiia v Rossii*, vol. 2, p. 238.

Others believed they would lose the land because the Bolshevik government would be defeated.[115] The separation of the ex-estate land from the communal allotments was often necessitated by the physical distance between them. It simplified the redivision of the land and enabled the spring sowing to go ahead without delay, when the ex-estate land was simply divided among the landless and poorest peasant households.[116] However, in many villages the fear of the return of the landowners was such that the ex-estate land was retained in a separate *fond* even if it bordered on the communal allotments. The land would be redivided each season and, in order to share the burden of risk, every peasant household would be obliged to receive a share. Sometimes this land was farmed by the peasant households without a common system of crop rotation, so that it even looked different from the communal allotments. The separation of the ex-gentry land from the communal allotments was retained in many villages until the mid–1920s.[117]

The peasants were much less fearful of the private peasant farmers (*khutoriane, otrubniki*) whose land they had expropriated. They nearly always broke up the consolidated plots and included them in the general redivision, although sometimes the property of the *khutora* was auctioned separately in order to raise money for the social needs of the village.[118] One study showed that 90% of the villages in Saratov province broke up and divided the *khutora* during 1918.[119] A survey by the TsSU in 1922 showed that 83% of the villages in the middle Volga and 90% of the villages in the lower Volga claimed to have included the *khutora* and the *otruba* in the communal repartitions since 1917. This represented a much higher proportion than in the black-earth zone of central Russia (64%) and the RSFSR (54%).[120] It was often the case that the VIK was more favourably disposed than the individual communes towards the retention of the private plots.[121] The Soviet land laws of October 1917 and February 1918 guaranteed the right of the peasant family-labour farm to cultivate the land in private, as well as in communal, tenure. Moreover, the prime concern of the VIKs was the resolution of the food crisis and the need to sow the maximum spring arable with the minimum disruption to the system of land relations, whereas the communes were engaged in a territorial struggle

[115] See *DGS*, p. 27; *KK*, pp. 50–2.
[116] TsGANKh, f. 478, op. 6, d. 1015, ll. 118, 120; TsGAOR, f. 393, op. 3, d. 359, ll. 56, 75, 85, 97; *MZR*, 1, p. 2. The last source suggested that this policy was deliberately planned in order to facilitate the sowing.
[117] Keller and Romanenko, p. 103.
[118] TsGAOR, f. 393, op. 3, d. 333, l. 100; d. 337, ll. 196, 201, 205, 207, 208, etc.
[119] Gerasimenko, 'Klassovaia bor'ba', pp. 303–4.
[120] Bliakher, p. 140.
[121] GAKO, f. 236, op. 1, d. 160, ll. 3–4, 7; TsGAOR, f. 393, op. 3, d. 333, l. 223.

with the private farmers over the land. Most resolutions of the *volost'* soviet assemblies achieved some sort of compromise between these two principles: the farmers of the consolidated land would be recognized as 'toiling people' (*trudiashchiesia*) and allowed to remain on their plots (within the limits of the local landholding norm), provided they did not 'hinder the interests of the communes'.[122] A typical formula was passed by the Menzelinsk peasant assembly on 3 April 1918:

> as long as their plots do not aggravate the problem of the intermingling of strips, the *otrubniki* and the *khutoriane* are to be left where they are until the enactment of the Law on the Socialization of Land, when their plots will be distributed equally, like the peasant allotment land. If their plots intersect the allotment land, then the *otrubniki* and the *khutoriane* are to join the nearest land commune and are to have the right to resettle in any of the surrounding villages where they will be allocated land on an equal basis with the local peasant farmers.[123]

Most repartitions of the peasant allotment land dated from the early summer of 1918 and resulted from the initiatives of the communes themselves.[124] Generally speaking, the land which had been purchased through the Land Bank or which had been rented from the landowners was the first to be redivided. A survey of the TsSU in 1922 discovered that 98% of the villages in the middle Volga and all the villages in the lower Volga included the former type of land in the communal repartitions after 1917. The figure in the central black-earth region was 92% and in the RSFSR 74%. All the villages in both the Volga regions (compared with 80% of the villages in the RSFSR) claimed that they had included the land purchased by the peasant associations (*tovarishchestva*) in the communal repartitions during the revolutionary period.[125] Other sources, however, suggest that the communes may have been more liberal in their attitudes towards these peasant entrepreneurs. In Penza province it was known for a *tovarishchestvo* to retain the land it had purchased before the revolution by forming itself into a separate settlement whose land rights were recognized by the surrounding communes.[126] In some localities the communes even recognized the property rights of individual peasants who had purchased land before 1917; when this land was confiscated the former owners were compensated. There is little evidence to suggest that such

122 Cited in *MZR 1*, pp. 9–10.
123 TsGANKh, f. 478, op. 6, d. 1015, l. 120.
124 *MZR 1*, pp. 2–4.
125 Bliakher, p. 140.
126 *MZR 1*, pp. 8–9.

policies were exclusive to localities under the influence of the SRs, as Soviet historians have argued.[127]

The repartitions of the communal land may be divided into two broad categories: general repartitions of all the arable land (the 'black repartition', or *chernyi peredel*); and partial redivisions of individual household allotments (*skidka-nakidka*). The former was the most radical type of land redivision. It predominated in the most densely populated areas, such as the black-earth centre, where, as we have already seen, the rate of communal repartitioning was most intensive. In the district of Zadonsk (Voronezh province) 84% of the villages carried out a 'black repartition' during 1918.[128] In some villages the population pressure on the land was so great that the wasteland (*gulevishche*) was also divided. The partitioning of the woodlands, despite their nationalization in May 1918, was widespread in these regions.[129] The household garden plots, which were traditionally not subject to the communal redivision, were also included in some 'black repartitions'.[130]

The partial redivision of the household allotments (*skidka-nakidka*) was more common in land-extensive regions. Sections of the household strips (*otrezki*) were cut from the plots of the richest peasants and reallocated to the poor. The opposition of the dominant or the richest peasants to a full repartition of the land partly explains the frequency with which the *skidka-nakidka* was noted in these regions, though modern Soviet historians have probably overstressed this factor. The People's Commissariat of Agriculture (Narkomzem) explained the preference of the peasants for the partial redivisions by the shortage of time between the agricultural seasons and by the lack of agro-technical means in the localities (e.g. maps, pencils, agronomists) to complete a full repartition. It also pointed out that a large number of the peasant communities consciously selected a partial redivision so as not to destabilize the agricultural system at a time when the food crisis made it vitally important 'to facilitate the sowing of the largest possible arable area'.[131]

The decision to repartition the allotment land was always finalized

[127] See A. V. Shestakov (ed.), *Sovety krest'ianskikh deputatov i drugie krest'ianskie organizatsii*, Moscow, 1929, vol. 1, p. 100; T. Galynskii, *Ocherki po istorii agrarnoi revoliutsii Serdobskogo uezda, Saratovskoi gubernii*, Serdobsk, 1924, p. 162.

[128] J. L. H. Keep, *The Russian Revolution: A Study in Mass Mobilization*, London, 1976. p. 402.

[129] GAKO, f. 81, op. 1, d. 119a, l. 81; d. 119, ll. 96, 102; *MZR 1*, p. 16; *Rezoliutsii i postanovleniia 7-go buzulukskogo uezdnogo s''ezda sovetov 20–24 oktiabria 1919 g.*, Buzuluk, 1919, p. 7.

[130] GAKO, f. 81, op. 1, d. 119, l. 18; TsGAOR, f. 393, op. 3, d. 333, ll. 143, 267; *Sel'sko-khoziaistvennyi listok* (Balashov), 7 July 1918, p. 2.

[131] *MZR 1*, pp. 3–4.

by a resolution of the communal gathering. 'The commune', declared the Ardatov district land department in May 1918, 'has full power to distribute the land between the members of the settlements according to its own discretion . . . the land is divided in the manner customary to peasant households in the commune.'[132] The resolution of the village commune specified the bits of land which were to be included in the repartition, the methods of division, and the people who were eligible to receive a share of the land. A general meeting of the peasants in the village of Kandeevka (Samara *uezd*) on 25 April resolved

> to distribute all the arable, the fallow, the meadows, and the pasture; to distribute the meadows and the wasteland according to custom, but the arable is to be divided from the fallow of 1918 according to the number of souls in the village. The smaller side [i.e. the minority] lodged a complaint against the resolution.[133]

This is a good example of the pressures involved in the decision to carry out a 'black repartition'. The interests of the minority, which probably comprised the wealthiest peasant farmers, were insufficient to prevent the implementation of a popular reform.

An example of a more complex land division is the resolution of 6 May passed by the very large village commune in Antipovka (Kamyshin *uezd*):

> to distribute the land according to the number of souls in the village, counting only the adult men and also the widows of soldiers; to allocate a garden plot 16 *sazhen'* in size to all the peasants except the women. The garden plots will be allocated first to the gardeners and to anyone who wants to swap his arable land for a garden plot. The account of the garden plots will be done by the Commission which has the right to mark out three different categories: (1) 5 *sazhen'* of arable in exchange for 1 *sazhen'* of garden; (2) 3 *sazhen'* of arable for 1 *sazhen'* of garden; (3) 1 *sazhen'* of arable for 1 *sazhen'* of garden. The arable will be divided into two fields and the methods of its division will be worked out by the Commission.

This system of exchanging the arable land for an extra garden plot was unusual. It may be explained by the presence of a large number of in-migrant townsmen and landless peasant labourers who lacked sufficient means of production to cultivate the fields. It must have resulted in the wealthier peasant farmers consolidating a larger share of the arable land. The Commission noted in the resolution comprised twelve elected 'dividers' (*delenshchiki*), who were later to be entrusted with the registration of the arable land and its division into eight sub-regions, differentiated by their proximity to the wells, the rivers and

132 Cited in Kabanov, 'Oktiabr'skaia revoliutsiia', p. 117.
133 GAKO, f. 81, op. 1, d. 119, l. 175.

the grazing areas. Every peasant household was to receive a share of the land in each of these subregions.[134]

The land rights of the different social groups of the village were also decided by the communal assembly. These decisions were, for the most part, independent of the instructions of the higher Soviet authorities, although many of them were influenced by the resolutions of a peasant or soviet assembly at the district level. In general, the communal assembly recognized the right of every family household in the village to farm a share of the land with its own labour (the more complex question concerning the land rights of the non-peasant groups will be discussed in detail in sec. 4 below). But the enactment of this principle was conditioned in each commune by a number of local factors and customs. The following communal resolutions are representative:

We resolved, by a majority of voices [votes], to divide the fallow land from this year according to the number of people of both sexes—that is on an equal basis to everyone, without exception, who lives in our commune, including prisoners of war and the people who have gone missing, until we find out what happened to them. If a family loses one of its members, because of death, marriage, or some other reason, then we will carry out a *skidka-nakidka.* We resolved to start the division as quickly as possible, and to divide the land for six years. (21 May, Korolevka, Lipovka *volost'*, Samara *uezd*).[135]

All the land will be divided, beginning with the fallow, between all the people—that is on an equal basis between adults, old people and children, including temporary residents in the commune, except immigrants, until the general-state division of the land. Those who are unable to work their piece of land with their own labour may cultivate it through labour exchange or association (*tovarishchestvom*), but they do not have the right, under any circumstances, to sell the land or sharecrop it. (25 May, Petropavlovka, Petropavlovka *volost'*, Samara *uezd*).[136]

1. The allocation of the land for 1918 will begin with the fallow and each *desiatina* will cost 3 rb. 50 kop. for the half year.
2. The allocation of the meadows for the spring of 1918 will be done in accordance with the number of people [in the households].
3. So as not to disrupt the farms which already have meadows, we resolved to allow them to graze their cattle on the commons and in the places where the commune may decide . . . .
5. The hamlets of P——and B——have an equal right to the land and the meadows with ourselves—that is as the commune decides and they must pay an equal amount of taxes to the *volost'* soviet.

134 TsGAOR, f. 393, op. 3, d. 333, ll. 141–4.
135 GAKO, f. 81, op. 1, d. 119a, l. 64.
136 Ibid., l. 102.

6. All strangers who live and farm in our commune should have equal rights with members of the commune.
7. The members of the commune who are at present living in the town of Samara have forfeited their rights to the meadows until they return to Kolyvan' and begin to farm again. (27 February, Kolyvan', Dubovo-*Umet volost'*, Samara *uezd*).[137]

We resolved to repartition the meadows according to a norm of workers and consumers among all the citizens, except the *intelligenty*, who will receive an allotment only in special circumstances after a check has been made on their sown area and their grain, but then the size of their allotment will be fixed according to the norm, even though they are not workers. (July 1919, Kazenno-Maiantka, Balakovo *uezd*).[138]

Once the necessary resolutions on the details of the land repartition had been passed, the peasants went into the fields (*polia*) and divided them into sections (*iarusy*), differentiated by their soil quality, their flatness, their distance from the village and from water supplies, etc. The *iarusy* were subdivided into strips (*polosy*) and furrows the width of a plough (*gony*). These divisions were made without technical means, simply by pacing out the distances and using markers, or by coming to an agreement on the relative sizes and merits of the *iarusy* through open discussion. Some communities appointed an adjudicator to equalize the *iarusy* 'by eye'. The division of the land was inevitably accompanied by arguments. If opinion remained divided about the relative values of two different *iarusy*, then the commune was obliged to allocate each household a strip in both. This sometimes resulted in the parcellation of the land area to an absurd degree: in the most densely populated communes the arable strips were not as wide as 1 *arshin* (71 cm.); they had to be marked out 'by the span', or 'by the foot'. The peasants of these communes were later to complain that their strips were too narrow to accommodate a simple harrow.[139]

The allocation of the strips between the peasant households was completed by the casting of lots. The peasants believed that 'equality of chance' was the 'ultimate guarantee' of fairness, since 'however much care was taken to equalize plots, some were inevitably considered better than others'.[140] Each household received a number of strips in accordance with the number of allotment units it could legitimately claim. The most common allotment unit was the number of 'souls' or 'eaters' (consumers) in the peasant household. A survey of the TsSU in 1922 discovered that 91% of the villages in the middle

137 GAKO, f. 81, op. 1, d. 119, l. 112.
138 Ibid., f. 193, op. 2, d. 159, l. 87.
139 Galynskii, p. 162.
140 *RR*, p. 126.

Volga region had redivided the land on this basis. In the lower Volga region only 57% of the villages had redivided the land according to a consumption norm. This may be explained by the land-extensive nature of this region, which assigned greater significance to the production side of the peasant household. The remaining villages in the lower Volga had repartitioned the land according to the number of male souls in the peasant households. In the middle Volga only 6% of the villages had redivided the land in accordance with the number of males, while no more than 2% had repartitioned it by the number of adult male workers.[141] The higher Soviet authorities condemned the use of allotment units based upon the productive capacity of the peasant households (e.g. the number of male workers, the holding of cattle). They encouraged the communes to use an allotment unit based upon the balance of workers and consumers in the peasant households, as set out in the Law on the Socialization of Land. But this proved to be too complex for the communes. The latter had always divided the land in accordance with the number of 'eaters' or the number of male souls, and they were unwilling to break with tradition at the behest of the government.

The meadows and the pasture were usually left in communal use (i.e. were not partitioned), in accordance with traditional custom. Since the pasture was situated in dozens of different locations, it would have been highly complicated and uneconomical to subdivide it any further. Some communes, however, did divide the meadows for the purposes of mowing. Each peasant household was given the right to mow a fixed area of the meadows in accordance with the number of animals it had to feed, or the number of family members.[142] The former method was condemned by the higher authorities, since it tended to favour the wealthiest peasants. But the communes which divided the use of the meadows in this manner were concerned not to disrupt the economy of the strongest peasant farmers, upon whose harvests the resolution of the food crisis would depend.

So far we have focused entirely upon the activities of the village communes. This is quite proper. The commune provided the ideological kernel and the basic organizational structure of the land reforms.[143]

[141] Bliakher, p. 141.

[142] *MZR 1*, pp. 14–15; Pershin, *Agrarnaia revoliutsiia v Rossii*, vol. 2, p. 276.

[143] For ideological reasons, the majority of modern Soviet historians have underplayed the role of the commune and have overplayed that of the soviets in the land reforms. This was not the case before the Stalinization of the historical profession (see e.g. Keller and Romanenko, pp. 95–115). Against the current of modern Soviet orthodoxy, Danilov has emphasized the significance of the commune both during and after the revolution. See his 'Zemel'nye otnosheniia v sovetskoi dokolkhoznoi derevne', *Istoriia SSSR*, 1958, no. 3; 'Obshchina u narodov SSSR v posleoktiabr'skii period: K voprosu o tipologii obshchiny na territorii sovetskikh respublik', *Narody Azii i Afriki*, 1973, no. 3; 'K

But what was the role of the *volost'* soviets in the communal repartitions? Although they stood on the bottom rung of the new state apparatus, they lacked the means to influence the general direction of the communal repartitions. The resolutions of the *volost'* soviet assemblies invariably left the repartition of the allotment land to the responsibility of the communes themselves. The Trost'ian *volost'* soviet assembly (Samara *uezd*) on 19 May resolved by 113 votes against 34 to carry out a 'black repartition' and 'to allow each commune to decide by itself, after a democratic vote, how to carry out the division of the land, whether by the ownership of livestock, or whether by some other method'.[144] A similar resolution was passed by the VIK in Sofyn' (Samara *uezd*) on 24 March: 'to hand over responsibility for the repartition of the land to the communes; any payments made by the peasants for the arable should be decided by the commune and then handed over to the soviet'.[145] A third example is the Elkhovka *volost'* soviet assembly of 8 April, which resolved 'by a majority of voices [votes] to concede the right to distribute the land in the communes to the local village meetings; if any land needs to be distributed between neighbouring communes, then this will be done by the *volost'* land commission'.[146] An instructor of the Kuznetsk district land department claimed that it was unheard of a VIK land department taking any responsibility for the repartitions of the communal land: 'the communal repartitions are carried out entirely independent of the district and *volost'* [land] committees; the villages manage the repartitions themselves and they claim rights over any private land which they formerly rented'.[147]

Although the VIKs had no direct role to play in the communal repartitions, they were assigned a number of important functions by the communes themselves during the land repartitions. Firstly, the communal delegates at the *volost'* soviet assemblies were told about any resolutions on the land question which may have been agreed by a peasant assembly at the district or regional level (*raion*).[148] They

voprosu o kharaktere i znachenii krest'ianskoi pozemel'noi obshchiny v Rossii', in *Problemy sotsial'no-ekonomicheskoi istorii Rossii*, Moscow, 1971; 'Istochnikovedcheskie i arkheograficheskie problemy istorii russkoi obshchiny posle Oktiabr'skoi revoliutsii', in *Severnyi arkheograficheskii sbornik*, Syktyvkar, 1977. See also id., 'Ob istoricheskikh sud'bakh krest'ianskoi obshchiny v Rossii', *Ezhegodnik po agrarnoi istorii*, vyp. 6, *Problemy istorii russkoi obshchiny*, Vologda, 1976, pp. 106 ff.; *RR*, pp. 101–42.

144 GAKO, f. 81, op. 1, d. 119a, l. 173.
145 Ibid., l. 109.
146 Ibid., d. 119, l. 160.
147 TsGANKh, f. 478, op. 1, d. 202, l. 1.
148 An intermediary territorial-administrative level between the *volost'* and the district (*uezd*).

passed their own resolutions on the general principles of the land redivision, which often served as a guide for the individual communes. A typical example of this sort of 'land charter' was passed by the Bogdanovka *volost'* soviet assembly (Samara *uezd*) on 2 April:

> In view of the need to allocate land to any persons who do not have it for the spring sowing of this year, our assembly resolved that the rural soviets should be able to judge how to transfer land from those who have it to those who do not.
>
> The payment for this land: invalids and wounded poor peasants—no payment; members of the poor population who have their own labour force at the time of the autumn ploughing—10 rb. for each *des.* of ploughland.
>
> Former government officials and people who have not farmed previously are not entitled to receive ploughland.
>
> Note: the payment for ploughland taken from peasants should be decided by the rural commune.[149]

This resolution is particularly interesting because of its specific denial of the land rights of former government officials and its insistence that only people with experience of farming should receive an allotment. The money raised by the payments in the above resolution was probably paid to the land department of the VIK. A second typical example was passed by the Poretsk *volost'* soviet assembly (Ardetov *uezd*) on 9 April:

> [we resolved] to defer the partition until the fallow field [autumm] because of the lack of time and technical means, which makes the division of the spring fields on the lines laid out by the instructions of the land committee and the Law on the Socialization of Land quite impossible. We decided therefore to resolve the land question by local means, bearing in mind the following general conditions and principles:
>
> In the first place, the land may be tilled by anyone who already does so, but only as much land as he is due in accordance with the number of souls in his family and the means at his disposal, the surplus being transferred to the land reserve.
>
> In the second place, the land may be given to any person who does not already have any land, but is able to work it with the labour of his family. In the third place, the land may be given to any person who has the seed to sow it, or who is able to sharecrop it, but this can not be done with strangers, but only with fellow villagers.
>
> Any person who receives a plot of land, but who is not able to plough it before the start of sowing on 15 April and who does not inform the rural soviet by that date will be fined by an amount to be decided by a meeting of the Peasant Union.
>
> Any remaining land will be ploughed by the local commune or the soviet.

[149] GAKO, f. 81, op. 1, d. 119, l. 41.

Since the soviet does not have the means to plough the remaining land, it would be desirable to levy a tax of 1 rb. per head on every household which receives an allotment.[150]

An interesting aspect of this resolution is its clear ranking order for the allocation of land rights. The demand for an allotment of land in Poretsk *volost'* was obviously greater than the supply. The *volost'* soviet assembly was concerned to ensure that the maximum arable area was sown in order to combat the food crisis. Hence anyone who received an allotment of land, but failed to work it, was subject to a fine. A third example of these 'land charters' was passed by the Kandabulak *volost'* soviet assembly (Samara *uezd*) on 9 April:

1. Under no conditions may any land which has been ploughed for 1918 be sold, leased, or mortgaged. Note: any land which is sold, leased, or mortgaged without the permission of the *volost'* and the rural soviets will be immediately confiscated and transferred to the communal land reserve for redistribution to the poor peasant soldiers, widows, invalids, and anyone else who does not have any ploughland.
2. Citizens who employ hired labour to plough their land will have their surplus land taken away and redivided among the soldiers, the invalids, etc. Note: citizens will otherwise be left with as much land as they can farm with their own labour.
3. Citizens who have land in more than one commune will lose one of their allotments. Note: citizens who plough this land with their own labour may keep both allotments.
4. Any land which is confiscated and redistributed between the invalids, the soldiers and the poorest members of the villages will be paid for, the amount decided by the rural soviets.
5. Anyone who does not have a family who receives an allotment on the discretion of the rural soviet will be given communal assistance in the form of seed, cattle, and tools.
6. To allocate the land between the soldiers, the widows, and the invalids and the poorest citizens a special commission will be selected from these groups in order to assess the individual needs of these people and to prevent any bribe-taking.[151]

This resolution is particularly interesting because of the light it sheds on the peasantry's perception of what constitutes just and unjust wealth. The entrepreneurial farmer was allowed to retain as much land as he was able to cultivate with his own family labour, even if this land was situated in two separate communes. Land was to be confiscated only from those who had employed wage-labour, or who had sold or subrented their communal allotment: these were the two most

[150] TsGAOR, f. 393, op. 3, d. 359, l. 9.
[151] GAKO, f. 81, op. 1, d. 119, l. 184.

common criteria used by the peasantry to define the 'kulak' (see ch. 4, sect. 1).

A second function of the *volost'* soviets was the arbitration of land and property disputes between the peasants and communes. The VIKs received many petitions from widows and landless labourers who required some basic means of production, which their commune was withholding from them. The VIKs were sometimes able to satisfy these demands, if they had their own land *fond* and a store of tools and livestock. Other petitions were concerned with more complex disputes involving several households or communes. These were usually discussed at the *volost'* soviet assembly. A good example is the Ten'evka *volost'* soviet assembly (Samara *uezd*) on 26 March, which discussed a land dispute between two communes. During the autumn of 1917 a group of peasants from Ten'evka had rented some arable from a peasant of Fedorovka commune. The Fedorovka commune had redivided this land at the beginning of March 1918. The assembly ordered the Fedorovka commune to return the land to the Ten'evka peasants, and to give the peasant who had leased it out a second allotment instead. The Ten'evka peasants were ordered to pay him 30 rb. in compensation for the loss of his original allotment. The same assembly considered the petition of a peasant named Igor' Fedorov from the village of Ten'evka. He had signed a contract with Andrei Gubanov from Fedorovka to rent two of his arable strips (a total land area of 2,500 sq. *sazhen'*) until 1922. The Fedorovka commune had reallocated these strips to Osip Bikipeev during the land redivision at the beginning of March. Since the latter already had 8 *des.* of spring arable, the assembly ordered the Fedorovka commune to return these two strips to Fedorov, and to allocate to Bikipeev two alternative strips. Fedorov was ordered to pay 18 rb. 75 kop. to Bikipeev in compensation. Several similar disputes were discussed at the Ten'evka assembly. Some concerned the claims of wealthy peasants that their commune had taken from them an unfairly large portion of their land. Others concerned disputes between villages over grazing rights.[152] The peasants, it seems, had an inexhaustible appetite to discuss the minor details of their neighbours' land relations.

A third task of the *volost'* soviets was to defend the landed interests of the communes against those of communes in neighbouring *volosti*. Land conflicts between the *volosti* were commonplace during 1918; some of them continued for several years.[153] In Penza province 13% of the VIKs responding to the enquiries of NKVD in spring 1918 referred

[152] Ibid., d. 119a, ll. 131–44.
[153] *Agrarnaia politika Sovetskoi vlasti (1917–1918 gg.)*, Moscow, 1954, p. 349.

to specific instances of conflict over land with neighbouring *volosti*.[154] In Simbirsk province it was calculated that one-fifth of all government work in the field of land relations during 1919 involved the resolution of inter-*volost'* land conflicts.[155] Many such conflicts broke out spontaneously between the communes of neighbouring *volosti*. They usually involved some disputed meadows or woodlands which had been annexed by one of the communes during the land repartitions (the meadows and woodlands were often situated at the extremities of the communal territory).[156] Sometimes the dispute was about a piece of arable which had been rented by one commune before the revolution and redivided by another during 1918.[157]

The majority of such conflicts were not spontaneous, however. They arose when the higher soviet authorities attempted to carry out a land equalization between the *volosti*. This was usually done by a district or regional assembly of the land committees of the VIKs. The estimated total area of arable land was divided by the population to arrive at a regional or district land norm, and on the basis of this the assembly ordered the land-surplus *volosti* to transfer part of their land to the land-deficit ones.[158] The plan was absurd. It inevitably meant that the land-surplus *volosti* would transfer the least suitable land to their poorer neighbours. This would have increased the distances from the land-deficit villages to their newly gained land, which could only have resulted in a decline of the sown area. More importantly, the redistribution would have unavoidably broken up the traditional territorial boundaries of the village communes. It was even proposed to resettle part of the population of the land-deficit *volosti* in the communes of the land-surplus ones! The inevitable outcome of these plans was to incite a mounting level of opposition from the communes concerned. Those which stood to lose the most land took the lead. They falsified the figures on the land and the population which the higher authorities demanded from them. They boycotted the regional or district assembly, and passed resolutions to defend their historic claims to the land. And they issued threats, sometimes backed up by physical violence, against the communes of the neighbouring *volosti*.[159]

[154] TsGANKh, f. 478, op. 1, dd. 149, 150.

[155] *KK*, p. 108.

[156] TsGANKh, f. 478, op. 6, d. 1015, l. 112; GAKO, f. 81, op. 1, d. 119a, l. 99; TsGAOR, f. 393, op. 3, d. 337, l. 17; *Vestnik Komiteta Uchreditel'nogo Sobraniia* (Samara), no. 56, 14 Sept. 1918, p. 3; Galynskii, p. 163.

[157] GAKO, f. 81, op. 1, d. 119, ll. 124–5.

[158] See e.g. GAKO, f. 81, op. 1, d. 119, ll. 165–8; P. A. Butyl'kin and G. A. Gerasimenko, 'Osushchestvlenie agrarnykh preobrazovanii v Nizhnem Povolzh'e, in *Leninskii Dekret o zemle v deistvii: Sbornik stalei*, Moscow, 1979, p. 163; E. I. Medvedev, 'Agrarnye preobrazovaniia Oktiabr'skoi revoliutsii v Srednem Povolzh'e', in *Leninskii Dekret o zemle v deistvii*, p. 130.

[159] See e.g. Keller and Romanenko, pp. 10–13; *PSG*, pp. 40, 43; *Agrarnaia politika*

The three functions of the *volost'* soviets which we have outlined so far were all essentially positive from the viewpoint of the local communes. The soviets articulated the interests of the latter, organized them as a cohesive body, and defended them against the interests of communes in other *volosti*. There were many other points, however, where the activities of the *volost'* soviets were opposed by the local communes.

One point of conflict arose over the recovery and redistribution of the property which the communes had taken from the private estates. The majority of the land departments of the VIKs found the estates denuded of all their movable property when they began to make their detailed accounts of them (see ch. 2, sect. 3). In the general interests of the *volost'*, the land departments took measures to prevent any further 'pillage' and to recover the lost property for redistribution among the communes. On 29 January the peasant section of the Buguruslan district soviet sent a circular to the VIKs in which it was stated that the wealthy peasants should be fined for any property they had taken from the estates; the poor peasants were to be given a chance to return any 'stolen' property, but, failing that, were to be made to do community work.[160] The *volost'* land departments (under the *zemstvo* and the soviet) went to extreme lengths to persuade the communes to return the property they had taken from the estates or to put it to proper use. They tried to negotiate settlements at the *volost'* assembly, whereby the property would be returned, or taxed, or redistributed, under the supervision of the land department, among the poorest peasants. They declared an amnesty for the return of the property. They instructed the red guards, the patrols, and the police to protect the estates and to carry out house-searches of suspected peasants. In extreme cases, the entire commune was barred from using the services of the *volost'* township, or struck off the provisions list for kerosene, salt, sugar, cloth, and other goods which were hard to come by. Despite these measures, no more than a handful of the VIKs were able to retrieve the missing property. Of the 266 VIKs in the four Volga provinces which replied to the NKVD enquiries in spring 1918, only 30 (11.3%) were able to claim that they had control of the tools and livestock of the former private estates.[161]

A typical example of the difficulties faced in this matter by the land

Sovetskoi vlasti, pp. 272, 347–8; *Izvestiia (Kamyshin)*, no. 88, 3 Oct. 1918, p. 2; Galynskii, pp. 159–60; E. I. Medvedev, 'Agrarnye preobrazovaniia', p. 132.

160 GAKO, f. 81, op. 1, d. 127, l. 12.

161 TsGANKh, f. 478, op. 1, dd. 149, 150; S. L. Makarova, 'Oprosnye listy Narodnogo Komissariata Zemledeliia i moskovskogo oblastnogo ispolnitel'nogo komiteta kak istochnik po istorii agrarnoi revoliutsii (noiabr' 1917–iiun' 1918), kand. diss., Moscow, 1970, p. 262; Sem'ianinov, p. 96.

departments is the conflict between the Shirokopol' *volost'* soviet and the local commune of Dmitrievka (Petrovsk *uezd*) over the former estate of the Akitov family. On 22 May the *volost'* soviet assembly resolved to divide the property of the estate among all the communes of the *volost'*. It was found, however, that all the movable property had already been taken by the commune of Dmitrievka; the horses and cows had been sold to the poor peasants of Dmitrievka at prices agreed by the communal assembly. On 27 May the *volost'* assembly reviewed the situation. The Dmitrievka commune was ordered to return the property to the VIK in Shirokopol', where it would be sold to the poor population at prices agreed by a special soviet commission. A number of delegates at the assembly complained that the Dmitrievka commune had not distributed the livestock fairly among its own people, so a second commission was appointed to look into this. The assembly agreed to allocate the four brothers of the Akitov family a *khutor* of their own, each provided with two horses and one cow from the former estate. When the *volost'* assembly reconvened on 30 May it was reported that the Dmitrievka commune had returned only a small fraction of the property, and that it had refused outright to allocate any land or livestock to the four Akitov brothers. The situation was discussed and it was decided that nothing more could be done to retrieve the other property. The livestock and tools which had been returned were auctioned to the poor peasants.[162]

The *volost'* soviets and the communes each had their own view on the best methods of distributing the movable property of the estates. Many village communes either distributed the tools and livestock among the poor peasants, or sold them at prices fixed by the commune for the different categories of the poor population. A small number of the village communes pooled the tools and livestock in order to cultivate the fields of the estate as a collective team (*supriaga, obshchestvennaia zapashka*). The harvest was used to feed the poor population, the wives and widows of peasant-soldiers, and other dependants.[163] Many villages auctioned the property of the estate. S. P. Rudnev recalled the auction of his livestock in the village of Durasovka during February 1918:

> The prices were fixed unbelievably low and there was an immense crowd (only residents, the fellow villagers, were allowed at the auction); the auction went very quickly without a hitch . . . none of the richest peasant's wanted to come to the auction as they did not want to purchase someone else's property; only one, Mal'tsev, could not resist purchasing a beautiful horse for 70 rb. which in

[162] TsGAOR, f. 393, op. 3, d. 336, ll. 149–56.
[163] Ibid., d. 325, l. 153; d. 333, ll. 39 ff.; d. 336, l. 284.

peace time would have cost ten times as much. After that, Mal'tsev began to avoid us . . . the horse he had bought, like most of the horses bought at the auction, died[164] during the following autumn . . . [165]

Finally, in many villages there seems to have been no formal system of redistributing the property from the estates; it was simply passed or sold from one peasant to another. The Kuznetsk district land department described this in January 1918:

the livestock and the tools were passed around as gifts or sold at very low prices. The peasants who had the property of the former landowners feared the revolution would not last long, and so they tried to sell the property as quickly as possible. The cows and the pieces of furniture were sold in the neighbouring villages; small pieces of livestock and domestic fowl were cut up and preserved in cold hiding places. Sometimes the cows were also cut up, even the pedigree stock.[166]

Many of the redistributive methods of the *volost'* soviets in this field resembled those of the communes outlined above. Most of the soviets distributed the livestock on an egalitarian basis, according to the number of horses and cows in each commune.[167] Others hired out the tools and livestock at fixed prices. The prices fixed by the Sofyn' *volost'* soviet (Samara *uezd*) on 24 March were 1 rb. per *des.* for iron harrows and seed drills, and 50 kop. per day for iron ploughs. Wooden harrows were sold for 3 rb. a piece, and wheels were sold at a price agreed by the land department, but not more than 10 rb. each.[168] In Kurmanaevka *volost'* (Samara *uezd*) the land department hired out 58 iron harrows and seed drills from the estates at 1 rb. per harrow and 5 rb. per seed drill. A further fifty-four wooden harrows were distributed among the communes without charge. The livestock was auctioned and the proceeds used to purchase grain from Siberia.[169] Some of the other redistributive methods of the soviets, however, came into conflict with the traditional principles of the village communes. The Balakovo regional land department tried to make the award of the livestock and tools from the estates to the poor peasants dependent upon the peasants' joining a household which already owned a horse.[170] In the districts of Novouzensk and Nikolaevsk some of the VIKs promulgated norms of livestock ownership and requisitioned by

[164] There was an epidemic during 1918–19 which killed many horses in this region (see ch. 6, sect. 2), although Rudnev claimed that his horses died because the peasants could not afford to feed them. He recounted that many of the horses kept returning to the estate, where they knew they would be fed! (*PVO*, p. 104).
[165] *PVO*, pp. 102–4.
[166] TsGANKh, f. 478, op. 1, d. 202, ll. 7–8.
[167] GAKO, f. 81, op. 1, d. 119a, ll. 30, 168.
[168] Ibid., l. 111.
[169] Ibid., d. 119, l. 212; d. 119a, ll. 2–4.
[170] TsGAOR, f. 393, op. 3, d. 323, l. 21.

force the 'surplus' animals of the wealthier peasant households. By the admission of Soviet historians, this resulted in the economic ruin of many middle peasant households and a number of peasant uprisings.[171] Finally, some of the VIKs kept the pedigree livestock and the tools from the estates in a special reserve. The tools were hired out to the poorest peasants from special shops (*prokatnye punkty*) and were later transferred to the collective farms, in spite of the complaints of the peasant communes (see ch. 6, sect. 4).[172]

A second point of conflict between the *volost'* soviets and the communes arose over the control of the woodlands. A Decree of the Soviet government on 27 May 1918 nationalized the woodlands and placed them under the control of the *volost'* soviets. The latter were to provide the peasants with timber and heating materials, according to the government's norms.[173] For the peasants, however, the woodlands were more than a source of timber and fuel. They were a place to graze young animals, to hunt and to fish, to pick mushrooms and berries, to gather wax and honey, to manufacture resin, to strip bark for cord-making, to court and to make love. Free access to the woodlands was a major aspiration of the peasant revolution. As soon as the woods had been taken out of the domain of the gentry, the church, or the state, the communes declared them to be the 'property of the people' (*v obshchenarodnoe dostaianie*), whereby they meant the people in the commune.[174] The communes organized labour teams to fell the timber for the village and trading purposes. They included the grazing areas of the woodlands in the communal land repartitions. Some communes even cleared the woodland in order to bring it under the plough.[175]

Some *volost'* soviets condoned the peasantry's localist conception of the nationalization of the woods. Thus the VIK in Kashirsko-Khutorskoe *volost'* (Samara *uezd*) defended the peasants' felling of the Dut'mlianskii woods in the neighbouring *volost'* of Spasskoe on the grounds that 'the Dut'mlianskii woods belong not only to the people in Spasskoe *volost'*, but to all the common people'.[176] The majority of the

171 E. I. Medvedev, *Oktiabr'skaia revoliutsiia v Srednem Povolzh'e*, Kuibyshev, 1964, pp. 115–16; Pershin, *Agrarnaia revoliutsiia v Rossii*, vol. 2, pp. 377–8; *Ocherki istorii kuibyshevskoi organizatsii KPSS*, Kuibyshev, 1960, p. 224.

172 *Materialy po zeml'noi reforme 1918 goda*, vyp. 6, *Otchuzhdenie i ispol'zovanie sel'sko–khoziaistvennogo inventaria*, Moscow, 1918 (henceforth referred to as *MZR 6*), pp. 6, 10, 13; E. I. Medvedev, *Oktiabr'skaia revoliutsiia*, p. 198; Galynskii, pp. 178 ff.

173 *Sbornik dokumentov po zemel'nomu zakonodatel'stvu SSSR i RSFSR, 1917–1954 gg.*, Moscow, 1954, pp. 32–3.

174 GAKO, f. 193, op. 2, d. 159, l. 84; *Protokol kamyshinskogo uezdnogo s''ezda krest'ianskikh deputatov i predstavitelei razlichnykh politicheskikh grupp, uchrezhdenii i organizatsii, 10-go marta 1918 g.*, 1918, p. 20.

175 GAKO, f. 193, op. 2, d. 159, l. 82; f. 81, op. 1, d. 119, l. 139; TsGAOR, f. 393, op. 3, d. 323, ll. 89–90, 314; d. 333, l. 255; *Kommuna* (Samara), no. 172, 10 July 1922, p. 4.

176 GAKO, f. 81, op. 1, d. 119, l. 199.

VIKs, however, did take some measures to counteract the peasants' illegal felling of the woods. Some VIKs established a woodland guard to combat the peasant teams.[177] Others appointed a commission to search the yards of the peasant households for illegal timber: heavy fines were imposed on the rich peasants; the poor peasants were forced to do community work for the soviet (such as the felling of trees). Peasants caught trading in timber with other communities could expect to be severely reprimanded and even dispatched to the district authorities.[178] Despite these measures, the VIKs made little headway in their struggle against the peasant wood-cutting teams. It was simply impossible to supervise the whole of the area covered by the woodlands. The mass felling of trees continued unabated throughout this period, intensifying during the winter months and decreasing during the summer. The armed patrol of the Buguruslan district woods department was called out by the VIKs on average sixteen times per week between October and December 1918.[179] The Simbirsk provincial land department reported that during 1918 more than 100,000 pine trees had been illegally cut down by the villagers in the Shemurshinskii forest of Buinsk *uezd* alone.[180] This 'universal and merciless abuse of the woodlands' was explained by the Menzelinsk district land department in terms of the 'absence of any real soviet authority in the rural areas and the peasants' poor understanding of the meaning of national property'.[181]

A third point of conflict between the *volost'* soviets and the communes arose when the former began to take steps to equalize the land tenure of the individual communes. The procedures for this were similar to those of the regional and district land assemblies during the inter-*volost'* land redistributions. The land department of the VIK declared its intention at the *volost'* soviet assembly to redraw the boundaries of the settlements in order to equalize the land in each commune on the basis of a *volost'* land norm. The land-surplus communes would eventually be ordered to transfer specified pieces of land to the land-deficit communes.[182] This reform in fact turned out to be well beyond the technical means of the average *volost'* land department. The VIKs did not have enough qualified agronomists to carry out the boundary changes. A course on the socialization of the

177 Ibid., d. 10, l. 306; d. 119a, l. 100; TsGAOR, f. 393, op. 3, d. 323, l. 90.

178 GAKO, f. 3134, op. 2, d. 21, l. 139; f. 81, op. 1, d. 119, l. 81.

179 TsGAOR, f. 393, op. 3, d. 323, l. 314,

180 *Protokoly i doklady VII-go simbirskogo gubernskogo s''ezda sovetov*, Simbirsk, 1919, app. 3, pp. 46–7.

181 TsGANKh, f. 478, op. 6, d. 1015, l. 121.

182 See e.g. TsGAOR, f. 393, op. 3, d. 332, ll. 55, 67, 69, 72–4; d. 337, ll. 225–30, 247, 248; GAKO, f. 81, op. 1, d. 119, ll. 172–3; Galynskii, p. 163.

land organized by the Balashov district land department in February 1918 and aimed directly at increasing the number of rural agronomists attracted no more than fifteen people from the fifty *volost'* townships in the district.[183] A similar course held in Saratov during July, which was supposed to be attended by two delegates from every *volost'* centre, managed to attract only 400 people from five provinces (and over 1,200 *volost'* townships).[184] The Saratov provincial land department sent 166 agronomists to help the land departments in the VIKs, but they achieved very little.[185] In Kuznetsk district it was reported that the instructors, faced by local conditions, were forced to 'worry more about getting the land sown than dividing it equally'.[186] Another problem was the complete lack of technical means: the Saratov provincial land department had given each agronomist only a quarter of a pencil and three or four pieces of paper to last for a period of six months.[187] The VIKs had accurate figures neither of the land nor of the population in the communes. At the Saratov peasant soviet assembly in May it was stated that many of the *volost'* land departments were forced to use maps and land figures dating back to the 1870s. Since then, much of the woodlands, the pasture, and the wasteland had been converted into arable.[188] Thus the VIKs were almost entirely dependent upon the figures provided by the communes themselves, though the latter obviously tended to inflate the figures relating to their population and to deflate the figures relating to the area of their arable land. Many communes refused to provide any figures.[189] The Soviet statistician, N. M. Vishnevskii calculated in 1922 that, as a result of such falsification by the communes, the 1917 census had underestimated the arable in Russia by as much as 15%.[190]

The efforts of the *volost'* soviets in this field of land redistribution caused widespread discontent not only in the communes with 'surplus' land, but also in those with an average amount of land. The communes were not accustomed to the transfer of land between themselves, and were generally unwilling to see the breakup of their

183 *Izvestiia* (Balashov), no. 48, 8 Apr. 1918, p. 3.

184 TsGAOR, f. 130, op. 2, d. 441, l. 12; M. O. Sagrad'ian, *Osushchestvlenie leninskogo dekreta o zemle v Saratovskoi gubernii*, Saratov, 1966, p. 20.

185 Ibid., p. 58.

186 TsGANKh, f. 478, op. 1, d. 202, l. 1; see also TsGAOR, f. 393, op. 3, d. 323, l. 1.

187 A. Berzin, 'Itogi i blizhaishie perspektivy zemleustroistva', in *O zemle*, p. 170.

188 *PSG*, pp. 134–5.

189 See e.g. TsGANKh, f. 478, op. 6, d. 1015, l. 115; TsGAOR, f. 130, op. 2, d. 441, l. 15. On the communes' methods of 'hiding' the land surpluses see N. M. Vishnevskii, *Statistika i sel'sko-khoziaistvennaia deistvitel'nost'*, Moscow, 1922, p. 34.

190 Vishnevskii, pp. 40–1. For similar criticisms of the census data of 1917 and 1919 see A. E. Lositskii, 'Publikatsii TsSU o zemlevladenii i ugod'iakh', *Sel'skoe i lesnoe khoziaistvo*, 1923, no. 7.

traditional territorial boundaries.[191] A good illustration of this is the petition of the villagers of Gnilusha in Zadonsk district (Voronezh province) to the VIK in Teshevka, which had instructed the redistribution of Gnilusha's 'nearest and most arable land' to the neighbouring villages. The demands of the petition included: 'the return of our ancient domain of Volkhovikovo'; the alteration of the village boundaries 'in the most convenient way for us'; and the 'allocation of some water-meadows in a situation convenient for our use'.[192] Another good illustration is in Elshanka *volost'* (Samara *uezd*), where four of the communes broke away from the *volost'* authority during the early stages of the inter-communal land redistribution. Their motive seems to have been the consolidation in their domain of some water-meadows along the banks of the River Boka. The VIK complained that 'none of the communes pays any attention to the orders of our *volost'* soviet and the whole of the *volost'* is in chaos, although we are unable to do anything against these communes since we have no armed force'.[193] Situations like this often resulted in the complete breakdown of the *volost'* authority, with the land-extensive communes breaking away from the assembly to form a new *volost'* authority rather than submit to a redistribution of their surplus land. A good example is in Elshanka *volost'* (Saratov *uezd*). On 11 February the land department of the VIK made its proposals to the *volost'* soviet assembly concerning the redistribution of the land between the ten communes. The delegates of the five land-extensive communes demanded the right to form a new *volost'*. The assembly broke up without reaching an agreement, and the five communes went ahead with their own plans.[194] A slightly different type of power breakdown was noted in Kamyshin district, where many of the *volosti* were said to have as many as three or four different '*volost'* soviets' all issuing their own resolutions on the land question.[195]

Soviet historians have laid a great deal of stress on the 'class struggle' between rich and poor peasants during the land redivisions. Yet the records of the village and *volost'* soviets leave little evidence to suggest that such a struggle played anything more than a very minor role. Indeed, the records of several district soviet land departments testified, to the contrary, that the communal repartitions 'took place very peacefully' (Melekess *uezd*), or 'were carried out very quietly, without

[191] The main exception arose over land previously rented by one commune to another, or when an inter-communal redistribution could help to solve the problem of strip-intermingling: see *MZR 1*, p. 8.
[192] Cited in Keller and Romanenko, p. 91.
[193] GAKO, f. 81, op. 1, d. 119, ll. 135–6.
[194] TsGAOR, f. 393, op. 3, d. 338, l. 198.
[195] *Izvestiia (Kamyshin)*, no. 86, 1 Apr. 1918, p. 1.

a single drop of blood' (Buguruslan *uezd*). In Simbirsk province it was said that 90% to 95% of the communal land redivisions had been completed peacefully.[196] During the redivisions the peasants naturally had disputes about particular bits of land. These sometimes ended in violence. Yet this was hardly a symptom of the 'class struggle', but merely a part of the everyday rough-and-tumble one would expect to find among peasants during such vital moments as the redivision of the land. Rudnev emphasized in his memoirs that the class tensions of the peasantry during 1918 were less apparent between the villagers, than they were between the villagers and outsiders—soldiers, landless refugees, and other 'free riders', whose poverty and rootlessness led them into conflict with the stable peasant farmers.[197] There is some truth in Rudnev's statement, as we shall see when we consider in detail the clash between the communes and the *kombedy* during the summer and autumn of 1918 (see ch. 5, sect. 1). Generally speaking, it is fair to conclude that the different socio-economic subgroups of the farming peasantry all recognised the authority of the village commune during the land redivisions. The main form of social conflict was between the communes themselves.[198] It was often the case that the interests of the richer communes were pitted against those of the poorer ones. But this, again, was not the 'class struggle' diagnosed by Soviet historians, since the form of the struggle was institutionalized within a patriarchal framework: the fellow villagers of diverse socio-economic groups fought together against a similar grouping of peasants from a neighbouring village commune. Moreover, the disputes were not always motivated by socio-economic interests; territorial and historical claims often played a key role. The Buzuluk land department emphasized this point:

> the Soviet government made a terrible mistake by allowing the villages to change their territorial boundaries without any real supervision by the higher authorities; an unbelievable number of new *volosti* have been formed without any good reason; as a result, the villages have become embroiled in all sorts of violence, in street battles and even in murders over the distribution of . . . schools, hospitals, post offices, agronomic centres, experimental farms, mills, estates, and so on.[199]

[196] TsGAOR, f. 130, op. 2, d. 441, l. 15; f. 393, op. 3, d. 325, l. 30; TsGANKh, f. 478, op. 6, d. 1015, l. 112.

[197] *PVO*, pp. 87–8.

[198] See e.g. TsGANKh, f. 478, op. 6, d. 1015, l. 91; d. 154, ll. 15–16; TsGAOR, f. 393, op. 4, d. 110, l. 164; op. 3, d. 331, ll. 19–20; d. 334, l. 259 ff; GAKO, f. 81, op. 1, d. 119, l. 203; *Svobodnyi zemledelets* (Saratov), no. 10, 1 Apr. 1918, p. 7; *Izvestiia* (Kamyshin), no. 89, 4 Oct. 1918, p. 1; A. Manuilov, 'Melkaia arenda zemli', in *O zemle*, pp. 107–8; Keller and Romanenko, pp. 32–3.

[199] TsGAOR, f. 393, op. 3, d. 323, l. 109. Danilov has noted that the formation of

It is impossible to give a full and accurate evaluation of the amount of land transferred to the peasantry as a result of the revolution.[200] The quality of the statistics which were available to the local soviet authorities during the revolutionary period was, as we have already seen, very low. The data of the 1917 census on the land ownership of the gentry are, for obvious reasons, questionable. The 1905 land census, meanwhile, needs to be supplemented with figures of the considerable changes in land tenure between 1905 and 1917. About 20% of the land in European Russia west of the Volga River and as much as 38% of the land in European Russia east of the Volga was simply unaccounted in the official land statistics of the early twentieth century.[201] Without detailed maps and statistics for each locality, it is impossible to evaluate how much of the land was fit for cultivation, how much of it was wasteland, how much belonged to the state land reserve, how much to the towns, and how much remained the property of the monasteries or the squires. The collection of these details, some of which may still be found in scraps in the local soviet archives, is a task for future historians.

These difficulties are compounded by the fact that only a fraction of the private land was transferred directly to the peasantry during the revolution. In central Russia the portion was very large indeed. But in the Ukraine, the Don, the Kuban', the Caucasus, the Urals, Siberia, the Far East, Kazakhstan, and Central Asia the land reforms could not begin until the end of the civil war. In remote regions the feudal land structures were not fully broken down until the land reforms of 1925–8.[202] The Volga region occupied an intermediate position in this respect. In the north-western regions of the Volga, which were closest to the central Russian zone and furthest from the military operations of the civil war, a very large fraction of the land was transferred to the peasantry during the revolutionary period. In the south-eastern regions of the Volga, on the other hand, many communes (52%) were unable to carry through a land repartition because of the proximity of the civil war front. The low density of the population and the large distances between the villages and the private estates also inhibited the land redivisions in this area. In 1920 Narkomzem registered as much as

subvillages, or hamlets (*poselki, vyselki*), by rich peasant factions represented a major form of land conflict in the bigger villages, whose soviets tended to be controlled by the poor peasants (*RR*, p. 167).

[200] For a detailed discussion of this problem see V. P. Danilov, 'Pereraspredelenie zemel'nogo fonda Rossii v rezul'tate Velikoi Oktiabr'skoi revoliutsii', in *Leninskii Dekret o zemle v deistvii*, pp. 261–310. [201] Ibid., p. 265.
[202] Ibid., p. 263.

500,000 *des.* of ex-estate land in the southern districts of Samara province which had still not been divided and brought into use by the neighbouring communes.[203] It is not known whether this land was occupied by the collective and state farms, which were concentrated in these south-eastern districts (see ch. 6, sect. 4).

Despite these statistical difficulties, it is possible to say with conviction that the Volga peasantry gained a relatively large amount of land as a result of the revolution, compared with the other regions of European Russia. This is to be expected, given the land-extensiveness of the Volga region and its large number of private estates before 1917. Table 10 compares two sets of Narkomzem figures showing the amount of land gained by the peasantry in the Volga provinces and various other regions of the RSFSR. The first two columns, which show the absolute and percentage increase in the area of peasant land use between 1917 and 1919, are based upon the data of enquiries completed by local Narkomzem officials during the spring and summer of 1919. V. P. Danilov, the leading historian of the Soviet peasantry who brought these figures to light, considers them to be 'sufficiently reliable, though incomplete and not entirely free from defects'.[204] The next three columns, which show the amount of agricultural land per capita in each province before and after the revolution, and the percentage increase, are based upon data found in the records of the land-accounting subdepartment of the Narkomzen department for land reorganization (*zemleustroistvo*). These data were compiled from the detailed reports of the district land departments. The two sets of figures give remarkably similar results in terms of the percentage increase of peasant land use in the different regions. The wide divergence of the figures for Samara province, which is the only major exception, may be explained by territorial boundary changes.[205]

The significance of the Volga peasantry's land gains during the revolution undoubtedly weakened the social basis of the anti-Bolshevik struggle in this region. The success of the Bolsheviks in holding on to the Volga region may be explained by their ability to play on the peasantry's fears that the gentry would return. This should not lead us to the conclusion, however, that the Volga peasantry was fully satisfied with the system of land relations which resulted from the revolution. On the contrary, the increased dominance of the communal system highlighted its shortcomings in the field of peasant land

203 TsGANKh, f. 478, op. 3, d. 1157, l. 58.
204 Danilov, 'Pereraspredelenie', p. 289.
205 The Republic of Volga Germans was established on the former territory of Samara province. Samara's control of the districts of Novouzensk and Nikolaevsk (Pugachev) was extremely weak. The land statistics of Novouzensk district are not included in the table under Samara province (Danilov, 'Pereraspredelenie', p. 286).

TABLE 10. *Land gained by peasantry during the revolution in various areas of Russia*

Province or area	Increase of peasant land area (*des.*)	% increase	Agricultural land per head		% increase
			Before 1917	After 1917	
Samara	5,481,912	127.7	2.24	3.37	50.5
Saratov	2,275,664	84.5	1.00[a]	2.00[a]	100.0[a]
Simbirsk	412,626	20.3	1.23	1.47	19.5
Penza	879,524	45.9	1.00	1.47	47.0
German Volga	—	—	3.02	3.29	8.9
Tatar ASSR	—	—	1.35	2.10	55.6
Astrakhan'	2,236,359	18.9	12.43	13.86	11.5
Voronezh	865,299	23.6	1.23	1.31	6.5
Tambov	1,024,036	28.8	1.03	1.30	26.2
Riazan'	787,527	60.3	0.64	0.97	51.6
Nizhegorod	180,258	7.9	1.19	1.29	8.4
Viatka	202,778	3.2	2.12	2.26	6.6
Moscow	225,414	17.8	0.82	0.99	20.7
Tver'	311,518	9.7	1.78	2.00	12.3
Iaroslavl'	222,297	12.0	1.44	1.58	9.7

[a] Approximate.

Sources: V. P. Danilov, 'Pereraspredelenie zemel'nogo fonda Rossii v rezul'tate Velikoi Oktiabr'skoi revoliutsii', in *Leninskii Dekret o zemle v deistvii*, pp. 284–7; TsGANKh, f. 478, op. 6, d. 1701, l. 276.

use. The peasantry soon became disillusioned with the ideal of the land commune as a remedy for all its problems.[206] A survey done by the TsSU during 1922 showed that the peasantry was dissatisfied with the distribution of the land and the system of communal land tenure in 42% of the villages of the middle Volga region and in 44% of the villages of the lower Volga region. In the central agricultural region the proportion was 62% of the villages; and in the RSFSR as a whole it was 54% of the villages.[207]

What were the causes of the peasantry's dissatisfaction? The highest rates of peasant discontent were found in the areas where the repartitioning of the land had been the most intensive (e.g. the central agricultural region).[208] The most heavily populated, these areas had suffered most from the in-migration of demobilized soldiers and townsmen. In some localities the land gains of 1917–18 were cancelled out by the increase of the population, giving rise to new problems of land hunger. At a conference of land administrators in Simbirsk province in December 1918 it was stated that 'the population is not entirely happy with the temporary repartition of the land . . . since there are still family farms without enough land; the population, believing the redivision to be incomplete, is waiting for something else'.[209] Because of the constant influx of in-migrants, many communes in these areas carried out annual repartitions during 1917–21. The deleterious effects of frequently repeated land redivisions were well known and widely discussed among economists and peasants alike. The constant redivision of the land delayed the commencement of field work and thus reduced the area of land that could be farmed in each agricultural season. It also discouraged the peasants from applying manure fertilizer to their allotments, since it was not certain that the allotments would remain in the hands of the same farmers from one redivision to the next. This resulted in a decline of productivity and an increase in the instability of the communal system of land use. Narkomzem was forced to introduce several pieces of legislation during 1919 and 1920 to slow down the rate of repartition-

206 Danilov claims to have detected this disillusionment from as early as 1918 ('O kharaktere sotsial'no-ekonomicheskikh otnoshenii sovetskogo krest'ianstva do kollektivizatsii sel'skogo khoziaistva', in *Istoriia sovetskogo krest'ianstva i kolkhoznogo stroitel'stva v SSSR*, Moscow, 1963, p. 139). My own impression is that it did not become widespread until the end of the civil war.

207 Bliakher, p. 146.

208 Dorothy Atkinson missed this simple point ('it is not easy to interpret the 1922 responses'), because she misunderstood the figures of the TsSU survey. These showed that the central agricultural region experienced one of the highest rates of partitioning (in 94 per cent of the villages), not 'the lowest (6 per cent)', as Atkinson stated (*The End of the Russian Land Commune 1905–1930*, Stanford, 1983, p. 184).

209 TsGANKh, f. 478, op. 6, d. 1015, l. 43. See further *KK*, pp. 57–8.

ing and to link the redivisions with a programme of land improvements carried out by local agronomists.[210] It is unclear whether this legislation had the intended effect. The reports of local Narkomzem agronomists at the end of 1920 suggested that the rate of land repartitioning had decelerated during the course of that year. But many communes were continuing to repartition the land annually. In Samara province this was explained by the civil war, which in some areas had prevented the communes from carrying out a repartition at an earlier date. In Penza province the continuation of the reforms was explained by 'qualitative and quantitative inequalities resulting from the earlier repartitions'. In Saratov province the continued repartitioning was explained by the failure of 'the temporary redivisions to solve the fundamental problems of peasant land organization'. As the agronomist in Saratov province concluded, if was futile trying to 'tell the peasants that the repartitions are economically harmful, since the peasants will simply reply that the land was also divided by their fathers and their grandfathers'.[211]

The main reasons for the peasantry's dissatisfaction was that the land reforms had tended to aggravate the problems of communal land organization. The most serious problem in the Volga region was the distance the peasant farmers had to travel from the village to their plots. The incorporation of the land from the estates into the communal land *fond* could only increase the average distance, since the demesne was usually separated from the village commune. Some sources also noted an increasing level of inter-communal land rent, which, like inter-communal land redivisions, would have had the same effect.[212] In a number of villages of Saratov and Penza provinces it was noted that the land redivisions had resulted in some of the peasant farmers having to travel up to 50 miles between the village and their plots.[213] This obviously had a bad effect on the level of agricultural output. At the Kamyshin district assembly of *volost'* land departments in February 1919 many of the delegates complained that the remote fields in the communes had had to be left unsown during the previous autumn because of shortages of seed, draught power, and, above all, transport. In Miroshnikov *volost'* more than 600 *des.* had been left unsown because of the distance to the plots. In Lemeshkin *volost'* the autumn sown area of 1918–19 was said to be down by 40%

[210] *SU* 1919, nos. 39–40, art. 384; 1920, no. 35, art. 170; 1920, no. 52, art. 226; *Agrarnaia politika Sovetskoi vlasti*, pp. 138, 418. For a discussion of these and other measures see Kabanov, 'Oktiabr'skaia revoliutsiia', pp. 128–9; *KK*, pp. 64 ff.; D. J. Male, *Russian Peasant Organization before Collectivization*, Cambridge, 1971, pp. 58–9.

[211] TsGANKh, f. 478, op. 6, d. 2010, l. 45, 56, 63, 69.

[212] Manuilov, pp. 105, 108.

[213] Kabanov, 'Oktiabr'skaia revoliutsiia', pp. 120–1. See also *KK*, p. 53.

on the previous agricultural year, owing to the 'incorrect repartitioning of the land, and the problems of narrow strips and distances of more than 20 or 30 *versty* to the plots'. In the communes of Rudnian–2 and Podkuev (Rudnian *volost'*) more than 2,600 *des.* of winter arable had been left unsown because of the distance to the plots.[214] Two further points were mentioned by the delegates which help to account for the reduction of the sown area. First, many communes were afraid that the gentry squires might return; this helps to explain why the fields of the estate, which were generally the furthest from the village, tended to be left unsown. Second, the communes tended to allocate the new land, which was furthest from the village, to the poorest peasants who did not have the means to travel to the allotments; this resulted in the increase of subrent and sharecropping relations between the poor peasants and the wealthiest farmers. Some sources noted an increase of illegal land sales which also transferred the land from the poorest to the richest peasant farmers. Many of these sales and subrent relations were hidden in the form of fictitous 'household mergers'.[215]

The peasantry's dissatisfaction with the communal system was reflected in two main social trends: an increase in demands to leave the commune and to set up a private farmstead; and a demand for land reorganization work within the communes themselves. The TsSU survey of 1922 showed that part of the peasantry—especially in the middle and rich peasants groups—wanted to leave the commune and set up a private farmstead (*khutor*); this was the case in 28% of the villages of the middle Volga region and in as many as 50% of the villages of the lower Volga region.[216] It was one thing to wish to go private, and another to have the means to do so, however. It turned out that only the richest peasants had the means to break from the commune during the early 1920s.[217] The position of the middle peasantry continued to be dependent upon the commune itself. 'By custom, by tradition and by habit, the peasants hang onto their commune', reported an agronomist from Samara province at the end of 1920, 'even in those localities where the Stolypin reforms had taken root among the ordinary peasants.'[218]

Within the commune, an increasing number of the peasants became

214 TsGANKh, f. 478, op. 6, d. 1015, ll. 86, 88.

215 *Stenograficheskii otchet 7–go syzranskogo uezdnogo soveta s 4–go po 5–e iiulia 1920 g.*, Syzran', 1920, p. 12; *Kommuna* (Samara), no. 164, 1 July 1919, p. 4; *Izvestiia* (Kamyshin), no. 89, 4 Oct. 1918, pp. 1–2; no. 105, 23 Oct. 1918, p. 4; S. S. Maslov, *Rossiia posle chetyrekh let revoliutsii*, Paris, 1922, pp. 123–4. On similar illegal land sales during the 1920s see *RR*, pp. 95–6.

216 Bliakher, pp. 147, 149.

217 Maslov, p. 122; *RR*, pp. 146–53.

218 TsGANKh, f. 478, op. 6, d. 2010, l. 58.

aware of the need to rationalize the land system during these years. The majority of the available sources suggest that the peasantry was on the whole becoming more receptive to the introduction of modern agro-technical methods and eagerly sought the services of agronomists. This was partly due to the influence of the demobilized peasant-soldiers, who had become acquainted with the better farming methods of the peasantry in eastern Europe and western Russia. Several agronomists from northern Russia reported in 1919 that the peasants were willing to pay high prices for agronomic work. In one village of Moscow province it was noted that the peasants had paid their blacksmith an enormous amount to make a copy of a seed drill which they had seen in the soviet hire shop.[219] Agronomists reporting from the Volga region at the end of 1920 agreed that their work was in great demand. The peasantry was particularly interested in the introduction of multi-field crop rotations with rootcrops, early fallow systems and autumn preparation (*ziab'*), mineral fertilizers, the breakup of large communes into smaller land units (*poselki, vyselki*), and the broadening of the household strips.[220] The TsSU survey of 1922 showed that in 35% of the villages of the middle Volga and 40% of the villages of the lower Volga the peasantry wanted the introduction of a multi-field crop rotation system. In 32% of the villages of the middle Volga and as many as 56% of the villages of the lower Volga the peasantry wanted to break up the commune into smaller land units (the main effect of this would have been to reduce the average distance from the village to the plots).[221] These results boded well for the Leninist co-operative plan in the field of land reorganization, a plan which V. P. Danilov has described in the first volume of his book on the Soviet peasantry during the 1920s.[222] The old peasant superstition that the size of the harvest was decided by the will of God was at last beginning to be eroded.[223]

4. A VILLAGE DEMOCRACY OR A DICTATORSHIP OF THE FARMING PEASANTRY?

The revolution increased the social dominance of the peasant family farm and the land commune in Russian rural society. But how did it affect the non-farming inhabitants of the village who did not belong to the land commune (e.g. craftsmen, traders, occasional labourers, members of the rural intelligentsia)? Under the conditions of the civil

[219] Maslov, pp. 113–16.
[220] TsGANKh, f. 478, op. 6, d. 2010, ll. 27, 45, 54, 55–60, 62–7, 68–70, *KK*, pp. 100–105.
[221] Bliakher, p. 147.
[222] *RR*, pp. 158 ff.
[223] See Ia. A. Iakovlev, *Nasha derevnia: Novoe v starom i staroe v novom*, Moscow, 1924, pp. 98–102, *KK*, pp. 90–110.

war, when the countryside was cut off from the towns, the skills of these people would have been especially valuable in the social reconstruction of the rural areas. The revolution in the villages depended upon the integration of the rural population. If the peasants were to let their spontaneous desire for social revenge against the *burzhui* run wild, then there was a danger that the *burzhui* would become a fifth column of the counter-revolution. If, on the other hand, the peasants failed to appease the landless elements, then the latter would—and did—become a hostile subclass, whom the Bolsheviks would mobilize to divert the revolution to their own ends.

This section looks at some of the social relations between the peasantry and the non-farming groups of the village (ex-landowners, landless labourers, in-migrant townsmen and refugees, peasant-soldiers, priests, and schoolteachers). The position of the village craftsmen will be examined at a later point (ch. 6, sect. 3). This analysis will help us to understand the socio-political dynamics of the peasant system of rule and the basis of its transformation under the Bolsheviks.

A revolution is an excellent vantage point from which to survey the system of social relations. It is unwise, however, to assume that popular actions in a revolution are necessarily or especially characteristic of the social system as a whole. Revolution is a 'moment of truth', when latent social tensions are laid bare by the dominant political conflict. But it is also a moment of chaos, when such tensions may be expressed in extreme and regrettable forms.

Former landowners

The mandates and resolutions of the peasant assemblies of 1917 were in no doubt about the justice of confiscating the land of the gentry without compensation.[224] However, most of the peasant communities also recognized the right of the ex-landowner to farm a share of his former land with the labour of his family. Indeed, this right was enshrined in the October Decree on Land and the Basic Law on the Socialization of Land.[225] A survey in Moscow province on the eve of the October revolution showed that 79% of the peasantry believed the landowners and their families should be allowed to farm a share of the land. Not surprisingly, peasants who lived in enclosed farmsteads were even more resolute in support of this issue.[226]

224 See E. A. Lutskii, 'Krest'ianskie nakazy 1917 g. o zemle', in *Istochnikovedenie istorii sovetskogo obshchestva*, Moscow, 1968, pp. 145 ff.

225 *DSV*, vol. 1, p. 19; *Sbornik dokumentov po zemel'nomu zakonodatel'stvu SSSR i RSFSR 1917–1954*, no. 8, pp. 23 ff. See further E. A. Lutskii, 'Leninskii Dekret o zemle', in *Leninskii Dekret o zemle v deistvii*, pp. 34–5.

226 Kabanov, 'Oktiabr'skaia revoliutsiia', p. 124.

It is well known that a significant portion of the former landowners remained in the villages and continued to enjoy rights of land use after 1917.[227] A recent article by John Channon has estimated that the number of such landowners during the mid–1920s was in the region of 100,000 (400,000 people including their families); that represents 11% to 12% of the landowners before 1917. Most of them were small landowners, whose economic activities during the 1920s were no more exploitative than those of the richest peasant stratum.[228]

The landowners had a number of different motives to remain in the village. In political and economic terms, they faced much better prospects in the countryside than in the town, especially if the peasantry was prepared to grant them a share of the land. Although the larger landowners were invariably hostile to the new government, most of the smaller ones preferred to join the green army of peasant 'toilers' than the White ones of Denikin and Kolchak. Naturally, the decision of the individual landowner was dependent upon his relations with the peasantry before 1917. The class hatred of the peasantry was strongest towards the largest landowners in the most densely populated regions. The estates of these landowners were most commonly destroyed, forcing the latter to flee to the towns. Some returned to their former villages as officers of the anti-Bolshevik armies (see ch. 4, sect. 2). Towards the smaller landowners, by contrast, the attitude of the peasantry was much more charitable, provided the former showed no counter-revolutionary tendencies. In areas where there was a shortage of economic means to cultivate the land, the peasantry was known to be especially generous. There is no evidence to suggest that the peasantry took an active part in the persecution of the small landowners during the Cheka's 'red terror' campaign of autumn 1918.[229]

The decision of the peasant communes to allocate the former landowners an allotment during the land redivision is not hard to comprehend. The former landowners, whose fortunes could easily be restored by a change of the political climate, continued to be feared and respected by the peasantry. For this reason, many communes not only recognized the former landowners as equal citizens (granting them the right to farm a communal allotment with family labour), but also left

[227] See e.g. N. I. Nemakov, 'K voprosu o zemlepol'zovanii byvshikh pomeshchikov v pervoi desiatiletii sovetskoi vlasti', *Vestnik moskovskogo gosudarstvennogo universiteta*, 1961, no. 2, pp. 21–8; V. M. Selunskaia, *Izmeneniia sotsial'noi struktury sovetskogo obshchestva, oktiabr' 1917–1920 gg.*, Moscow, 1976, pp. 197–8; *RR*, pp. 96–8.

[228] J. Channon, 'Tsarist Landowners After the Revolution: Former Pomeshchiki in Rural Russia during NEP', *Soviet Studies*, vol. 39, no. 4, 1987, p. 584.

[229] See e.g. Galynskii, pp. 171–3.

them a significant portion of their former property. The Bogdanovka village soviet (Samara *uezd*) left Kirilin, the ex-landowner,

a manor house with a barn, stables, and a bath-house
4 horses
1 cow with calf
10 chickens
1 mowing machine with rake
1 iron plough
1 iron harrow
1 winnowing machine
1 seed drill
1 cultivator
several carts and a tarantass
harnesses, collars, and saddles.

The following resolution was then passed:

to grant Kirilin the full rights of a household farmer [*khoziain*] on an equal basis with the other household farmers of the village, and to give him enough seed and grain and to leave him 8 cartloads of hay for his cattle . . . the agricultural tools should stay with Kirilin for safe-keeping, but other citizens have the right to use them.[230]

A similar resolution was passed by the Alekseev *volost'* soviet assembly (Samara *uezd*): the three brothers of the Nikitin landowning family were recognized as 'semi-toiling peasants' and allowed to keep from their former estate:

4 working horses
3 milking cows with 2 calves
3 oxen
a mowing machine
a harvesting machine
a seed drill
3 iron ploughs
6 harrows
9 *des.* of arable land.

The Nikitins' barn was locked and sealed and the keys returned to the former owners. A commission was elected to supervise the distribution of grain from the barn to the hungry villagers.[231] It is significant that in both these cases the former landowners were entrusted by the peasants to look after part of the property that had been confiscated from them by the commune (Kirilin retained his tools for 'safe-

230 GAKO, f. 81, op. 1, d. 119, l. 36.
231 Ibid., f. 236, op. 1, d. 159, l. 1; f. 81, op. 1, d. 119, ll. 12–13; f. 185, op. 2, dd. 13, 89.

keeping'; the Nikitins kept the keys of their former barn). This highlights the assimilation of the small gentry farmers into the peasantry. Many landowners were registered as 'peasant souls' by the communes during 1918. Others were given tasks to perform in the soviet and social institutions.[232]

The story of S. P. Rudnev is a good illustration of the peasantry's attitude toward those landowners who remained in the village. Rudnev stayed in Durasovka because he thought

> the disturbances of the revolution would be less harsh in the countryside than in the towns; the economic conditions of the village, with its almost natural economy, would also be better. I was sure that if the peasants and the landowners could get on without the old hostilities, then it would be ... advantageous for both sides, since a social revolution, and this undoubtedly was one, demands the constant creativity of new social relations ...[233]

The Rudnevs continued to work their large estate, with the help of war-prisoners, until the winter of 1917–18, when they turned the land over to the local peasantry and kept for themselves an allotment of 20 *des.* nearby the manor house. The peasants came to help the Rudnevs in the fields during the summer of 1918, and were paid in the form of a grand dinner at the manor house: 'there was plenty of vodka, fruit liqueurs, and kvass. Not only the peasants of Durasovka, but also those of Beklemishevo and Butyrka wanted to help. They were all peasants or young boys before the call-up age. Many of them, I am sure, could never have seen a spread like that before ...'[234] The harvest yield of the Rudnevs' allotment was much bigger than that of the surrounding peasant farms. The Durasovka commune worked out the size of the harvest and the consumption needs of the family, and passed a resolution ordering the Rudnevs to sell the surplus at fixed prices to the commune. Their prestige enhanced by the success of their farm, the Rudnevs worked out a scheme to harvest the peasant fields in collective teams. Unfortunately, the harvest had not been completed before the pillage of the manor house by a passing Red Army unit forced the Rudnevs to flee the village.[235]

Landless labourers

During the revolution the Russian peasantry aimed to strengthen the agricultural and social system based upon the smallholding peasant family farm. In the peasant mandates which constituted the October

[232] TsGAOR, f. 393, op. 13, d. 578, l. 186; TsGANKh, f. 478, op. 1, d. 149, ll. 153–4; *DGS*, pp. 59–62; Galynskii, p. 173.
[233] *PVO*, pp. 70–1.
[234] *PVO*, p. 90.
[235] *PVO*, pp. 112–29.

Decree on Land the abolition of wage-labour and the allocation of the land on a family-labour norm were inextricably connected. The Law on the Socialization of Land strictly prohibited wage-labour relations except on model farms and peasant farms without adult male labour.[236] Wage-labour relations, which were associated with large-scale capitalist and gentry farming, could have no part to play in the ideal socio-economic system of the peasantry. The army of landless labourers, which had been amassed as a result of the impoverishment of the smallholding peasantry prior to 1917, would have to be broken up and reintegrated into the ranks of the toiling peasantry.

During the land reforms the peasant communes gave a high priority to the allocation of land and other means of production to the landless labourers of the locality. However, many of the new peasant farms were too weak to remain independent of the richer peasant farmers. Although the censuses of this period noted a sharp decline of long-term (*srokovoi*) money-based wage-labour relations, other sources noted a simultaneous increase of daily (*podennyi*) and contract (*sdel'nyi*) hiring-labour relations without cash payments.[237] Sometimes the weakest peasant farmers leased or sold their land to richer neighbours before turning to non-agricultural occupations, such as domestic manufacturing or off-farm employment (e.g. barge-hauling, timber-felling, speculative trade, employment in the soviet). More often, the weakest farmers were forced to sharecrop their newly acquired land with a wealthier household, hiring means of production from the latter at unfavourable rates. The peasant communes, which themselves employed a large number of wage-labourers (e.g. shepherds, watchmen, messengers), did very little to impede these exploitative relations, since their prime concern was to support the stable peasant farms. The VIKs, on the other hand, did sometimes try to intervene in the labour market on the side of the poor. They fixed the prices and conditions of labour; regulated sharecropping and rental contracts; merged the weakest households with stronger ones; and even allocated tools and livestock to groups of poor peasants for the collective cultivation of the

236 *DSV*, vol. 1, p. 19; *Agrarnaia politika Sovetskoi vlasti*, pp. 131–9, 144–7.

237 *SGB*, nos. 3–4, 1 July 1918, p. 8; *Otchet saratovskogo ekonomicheskogo soveshchaniia*, Saratov, 1922, pt. 2, p. 49. Hidden and natural forms of labour hire were not included in the census data, which, according to S. G. Strumilin, showed a fall in the number of wage-labourers (*batraki*) from 2 million to 816,000 ('Dinamika batratskoi armii v SSSR', in *Naemnyi trud v sel'skom khoziaistve: Statistiko-ekonomicheskii sbornik*, Moscow, 1926, pp. 12–15). V. K. Bazarov estimated the number of wage-labourers in 1920 to be 899,000 ('K voprosu o razvitii batrachestva v poslerevoliutsionnye gody, in *Sel'skoe khoziaistvo na putiakh vosstanovleniia*, Moscow, 1925, pp. 383–4).

land.[238] In the semi-natural economy of this period, it was unrealistic to expect such measures to have much effect. Of the 1,119 village respondents from Saratov province who replied to an enquiry of the provincial provisions committee in the spring of 1918, as many as 969 (86.6%) testified to the continuation of contract- and day-labour hire. The respondents stressed that the inflation of prices, the influx of urban workers, and the general shortage of housing had resulted in the substitution of a natural system of labour hire (with the labourers paid in land or food) for the old cash system of wage-labour:

there is no wage-labour, but those who do not have an allotment or a horse work without pay and are given 1 *des.* of inferior land with 7 *pud* of seed. (Ekaterinoslav-Maza *volost'*, Khvalynsk *uezd*)

to quote a daily price for labour is impossible, because the system has transferred to flour. One man without a horse hired for the whole of the spring sowing will receive 3 *pud* of flour. A boy with a horse who is hired to do the harrowing will also get 3 *pud* of flour, as well as food at work. (Bulgakovka and Sinodskoe *volosti*, Vol'sk *uezd*)

Prices for hired labour are set by the commune only for cripples, widows, and orphans. (Kozlovka *volost'*, Petrovsk *uezd*)

Some of the respondents also emphasized that, by combating wage-labour hire, the soviets unavoidably handicapped the weakest peasant households:

It is possible to find hired labour, but it is expensive. The rich and the middle peasants are able to sow their own land, but the poor peasants do not have enough labour and can not afford to hire it, so they are going hungry. The landless soldiers go from barn to barn and steal grain. (Kniazevka *volost'*, Petrovsk *uezd*)

The soviet has decreed that you have to work on your own without hired labour, even if you starve as a result: from now on, everyone must be equal! Our comrades have decided to work the land with their own labour, and so many households have no choice but to leave some of the land unsown. (Beguchevka *volost'*, Petrovsk *uezd*)[239]

Only the peasant households of at least average economic strength could expect to maintain the status of an independent family farm. Without a horse or the basic tools, the weakest peasant farms were unable to support themselves through agriculture during the economic crisis of 1917–22. Those household farms which had been partitioned

[238] TsGAOR, f. 393, op. 3, d. 325, l. 417; d. 337, l. 228; d. 340, ll. 25, 32, 38; *Protokoly i doklady VI-go atkarskogo uezdnogo s''ezda sovetov 15–19 oktiabria 1918 g.*, Atkarsk, 1918, p. 138; *Izvestiia* (Balakovo), no. 8, 26 Jan. 1919, p. 3; no. 24, 2 Feb. 1919, p. 4.

[239] *SGB*, nos. 3–4, 1 July 1918, pp. 8–12.

from stable peasant households by soldiers on return from the war faced similar difficulties.[240] The census data of the TsSU showed that the number of smallholdings with less than 2 *des.* of arable in Saratov province increased by 13.4% between 1917 and 1919; the proportion of these households without a horse remained at a very high level (69% in 1917 and 54% in 1919). Most of the households with less than 2 *des.* had a cow (57% in 1917 and 62% in 1919), from which a small living could be made.[241] However, without a horse their lives must have been very difficult, and many households must have been forced into liquidation.[242] Some of these people became dependent upon the soviet for employment, or joined the red guards (and then the Red Army), where a basic provision of food and clothing was assured. Trotsky recalled that most of the first volunteers in the Red Army were 'vagabond, unstable elements . . . [who were] so numerous at that time'.[243] An English visitor in Russia gained a similar impression: 'the hard conditions of life in Russia and increasing poverty led many family men with dependants to seek employment in the red guard because the wages were good and the conditions as to food and clothing were excellent . . . Many joined towards the end of 1917–18 who saw no alternative but starvation.'[244] In Chapter 5 we shall see that the political recruits of the *kombedy* were largely drawn from similar social groups. The destitution of these people often resulted in their treating the stable peasant farmers with less respect than the latter merited. This was to create serious problems for the Bolshevik government in the rural localities.

In-migrants and refugees

The military and political upheavals of 1914–21 uprooted and dispersed throughout the Russian countryside millions of people. Approximately half the population of the major cities, including many of the skilled workers, moved into the countryside after 1918 to set up rural trades and industries, or simply to sit out these difficult years close to the sources of food (see ch. 6, sect. 3).[245] Some were returning from towns where they had gone after 1914 as factory workers or migrant labourers. They were registered as 'absent householders' in their village, where they retained the right to an allotment of land.

240 On these newly partitioned households see T. Shanin, *The Awkward Class*, Oxford, 1972, pp. 157–9.

241 *Trudy TsSU: Ekonomicheskoe rassloenie krest'ianstva v 1917 i 1919 g.*, vol. 6, vyp. 3, Moscow, 1922, pp. 142–3.

242 See *KK*, pp. 225–7.

243 L. Trotsky, *How the Revolution Armed*, trans. B. Pearce, London, 1979, vol. 1, p. 5.

244 J. Rickman, *An Eye Witness from Russia*, London, 1919, p. 14.

245 D. Koenker, 'Urbanization and Deurbanization in the Russian Revolution and Civil War', *Journal of Modern History*, vol. 57, no. 3, 1985.

Others were factory workers organized into brigades for the procurement of grain. A number of them decided to remain in the countryside during the summer holidays (or on unofficial leave from their factories) in order to purchase foodstuffs (see further ch. 6, sect 1). In the areas near the civil war front many of the migrants were refugees: Austrian, German, and Turkish prisoners of war; Volga and Black Sea Germans who had been interned during the war; noblemen, Tsarist officials, merchants, and professionals fleeing Bolshevik rule; etc. Finally, everywhere soldiers returning from the war found their progress held up in the countryside because of the difficulties of transport.

The Volga region was a busy crossroads for these various migrant groups. The main railways between the industrial centres of the north and the fertile agricultural regions of the south-east all traversed the Volga River at Kazan', Samara, Simbirsk, or Saratov. The Volga itself was a busy waterway linking the industrial north with the Caspian Sea. The outbreak of the civil war in the Volga region during the summer of 1918 and the destruction of the main railways and bridges by the forces of the Komuch on their eastward retreat after the Red Army's capture of Samara in the following October brought the civilian transport system to a halt.[246] Thousands of refugees, demobilized soldiers and prisoners of war encamped in the railway stations of the Volga region in the distant hope of getting on a train going to some point nearer their destination. Other migrants lived along the railway sidings, on the river banks by the main wharfs, or in suburban areas. Some found their way into a camp for refugees, where they might expect to receive a meagre ration of food. Others tried to settle in the villages as wage-labourers, or minor officials of the soviet (e.g. clerks, postmen, stable-workers).[247] Unavoidably, a large number of these migrants could find no means to support themselves other than by joining the Red Army, where they could at least expect a ration of food and a uniform.[248]

Because they were constantly on the move, it is impossible to be precise about the number of migrants in the country areas at any one time. One village near a main line of transportation could have several thousand migrants, whereas a remote village might have none. Official statistics are a poor source of information, because it was in the interests of the communities to exaggerate the number of temporary

[246] It took a middle-ranking government official three days during Nov. 1918 to travel between Samara and Syzran', a distance of about 130 km. His methods of transport were train, boat, horseback, sleigh, and foot (TsGAOR, f. 393, op. 3, d. 323, l. 354). On the transport crisis generally see further ch. 6, sect. 1, below.

[247] TsGAOR, f. 393, op. 13, d. 578, l. 341; d. 581, l. 197; *DGS*, pp. 13 ff., 33–5.

[248] Rickman, p. 14; V. I. Lebedeff, *The Russian Democracy and its Struggle against the Bolshevist Tyranny*, New York, 1919, p. 10.

residents (in order to reduce their fiscal obligations). The census of summer 1917 in Saratov province registered 16,302 refugees (*bezhentsy*) in the villages (0.6% of the rural population).[249] But a little more than a year later, in the autumn of 1918, the authorities estimated that there were as many as 150,000 refugees from as far afield as central Europe, Turkey, and the western Russian provinces in the camps of Saratov province.[250] The number of in-migrant townsmen in the villages was too large to enumerate.

TABLE 11*a*. *The agricultural labour force, hired labour, in-migrants, and prisoners of war in regions of Samara province, February 1918*

	Woodland (north) (A)	Woodland-steppe (south) (B)	Steppe (south-east) (C)
Population	668,055	635,552	128,832
% workers	44.6	44.0	42.8
% half-workers	22.3	19.5	17.5
% dependants	33.1	36.5	39.7
Spring ploughland per worker (*des.*)	1.8	2.5	4.6
Hired labour[a] as % workers	5.9	5.9	10.8
Hired labour[a] as % half-workers	1.8	4.1	14.3
In-migrants as % workers	2.7	3.5	3.1
In-migrants as % half-workers	3.2	3.6	3.5
Prisoners as % workers	0.4	1.6	2.2

[a] Permanent and seasonal.

Source: Chislennost' sel'skogo naseleniia v Samarskoi gubernii, Samara, 1920, pp. 9–12.

TABLE 11*b*. *In-migrants and prisoners of war as percentage of workforce, grouped by proximity to market*

Proximity to market	(A)	(B) and (C)
Close		5.7
Medium		2.9
Close and medium	2.9	
Distant	1.7	2.3

Source: As for Table 11*a*.

[249] *Tablitsy statisticheskikh svedenii po Saratovskoi gubernii po dannym vserossiiskoi sel'sko-khoziaistvennoi i gorodskoi perepisei*, p. 139.

[250] *Plennyi i bezhenets*, nos. 1–2, 1–15 Nov. 1918, pp. 54–8.

The figures of G. I. Baskin (Table 11) from Samara province are the best available information on the number and geographical distribution of the in-migrants in the rural localities. The in-migrants were concentrated in the zones close to market centres, as opposed to those further away from them. They settled mainly in the woodland-steppe regions of the south and the land-extensive steppeland districts of the south-east, where there was the greatest demand for hired labour,[251] as opposed to the northern woodland regions. During 1918–20 the in-migrants also played a prominent role in the collective and state farms, which in Samara province were mainly located in the steppeland regions of the south-east (see ch. 6, sect. 4).

There are a number of conflicting reports on the attitude of the peasantry towards the in-migrants. A survey of the TsSU in 1922 found that 62% of the villages in the middle Volga region claimed to have allocated the in-migrants a share of the land during the revolutionary period. All but one of the villages (84 out of 85) claimed to have allocated land to those families which had returned during 1917–22 after a period of absence in the city.[252] It is likely, however, that the respondents to this survey exaggerated from hindsight the goodwill of the villagers, for the contemporary records of the village and *volost'* soviets suggest that the in-migrants were, for the most part, unwelcome.

In the land-extensive regions the communes were inclined, at least in the early months of 1918, to give the in-migrants an allotment of land. Some were pressurized into doing so by the VIK or the higher soviet authorities (which generally supported the land rights of in-migrants according to the Law on the Socialization of Land). The land area set aside for the in-migrants was very small: in Zadonsk *uezd* it was only 4% of the allotment area in the communes (36% of the total number of communes) which had established a land reserve for the in-migrants.[253] The land was usually of inferior quality, and was invariably situated in the most distant part of the communal terrain. It was often the case that a number of conditions were applied to the tenure of this land, as in the commune of Rakovka (Samara *uezd*): 'all strangers living in the village of Rakovka will be thrown out if there is not enough land, according to the land norm, for the peasants of the village; but if there is a surplus of land, then the strangers will be

[251] TsGAOR, f. 393, op. 4, d. 110, l. 142; *Protokoly zasedaniia kamyshinskogo uezdnogo ispolkoma sovetas 22 Marta po 1 iiunia 1918 g.* (5 Apr.); *PSG*, pp. 32–3; *Izvestiia* (Saratov), no. 258, 20 Nov. 1919, p. 2; *Chislennost' sel'skogo naseleniia v Samarskoi gubernii*, Samara, 1920, p. 1.

[252] Bliakher, pp. 143–4.

[253] Keller and Romanenko, pp. 109–10.

moved out on to these plots. In future, the strangers will not be given land in the commune'.[254]

As the number of in-migrants in these regions increased, so the communes had no choice but to refuse them an allotment of land. This had been the policy of the communes in the over-populated regions since the early months of 1918. A. Okninsky recalled that in his village in Tambov province the peasantry became hostile towards the in-migrants only after the return of the peasant-soldiers. This suggests that the agricultural labour of the in-migrants was needed until then. After the return of the soldiers the peasants were concerned to keep only those in-migrants

> who had some useful skill, such as carpenters, blacksmiths, wheelwrights, coopers, makers of felt boots, etc. . . . the others, who did not have any of these skills, had to live on occasional earnings from helping those peasant families which for some reason or other were unable to cultivate their own plots. But not all the in-migrants were able to do this and many of them lived in desperate need. At the end of the summer of 1918 I saw several in-migrant families walking across the fields after the rye harvest collecting any ears of grain that had been dropped during the harvest.[255]

These in-migrants could not expect a food ration from the commune or soviet (see sect. 2 above), or even the right to live in the village. The latter restriction was mainly explained by the housing crisis, which resulted from the recent increase of the rural population and the dilapidation of the peasants' huts during the war. The peasants petitioned the higher authorities, which had directed the migrants into the rural localities because of the overcrowding of the district towns, to remove the temporary residents to other villages, or to house them in military barracks. At the Balashov district soviet assembly in April 1918 this issue caused a bitter dispute between the *volost'* delegates and the district land department. The latter wanted the assembly to pass regulations to keep down the price of food and accommodation rental for the in-migrants. The former argued that these prices were so low that they would encourage thousands of further in-migrants. The assembly hall had to be emptied on more than one occasion after disruptions from the floor. Although a resolution was passed in the form suggested by the land department, there was general agreement that it would be a dead letter in the localities.[256]

The peasantry's hostility towards the in-migrants, which contravened the village tradition of welcoming strangers with bread and salt, should be seen in the context of the peasantry's mistrust of the

254 Cited in E. I. Medvedev, *Oktiabr'skaia revoliutsiia*, p. 111.
255 *DGS*, pp. 175–6.
256 *Izvestiia* (Balashov), no. 48, 8 Apr. 1918, p. 4; no. 56, 30 Apr. 1918, p. 3.

towns—a mistrust that was heightened during this period (from 1917 to the summer of 1918) on account of the unstable political climate and acute inflation of industrial prices. Just as the workers believed (or were told by the Bolsheviks) that the peasants were withholding their grain, so the peasants believed that the workers were withholding their industrial manufactures (indeed, there is evidence to suggest that the peasantry was not altogether mistaken).[257] Only this could explain the shortages of kerosene, tobacco, tea, cotton, and other essential items in the rural areas. Some peasant resolutions of this period complained that the towns were 'full of kulaks and speculators', or that 'the worker lives like a lord (*khodit barinom*) while the peasant works all day and is always in need'.[258] The social tensions between the rich and poor villagers were seen to be caused by the inflation of industrial prices, for which the workers and the merchants were held responsible. The peasants saw the solution to this problem in the re-establishment of the pre-war system of market relations between town and country, with 'equal' prices for industrial and agricultural goods.[259] The fair trade between town and country remained one of the peasantry's principal demands under war communism (when the prices of grain were fixed at much lower levels than the prices of industrial goods).[260] A good illustration of the peasants' reasoning may be found at the Trost'ian *volost'* soviet assembly (Samara *uezd*) on 26 April. The peasants (182 householders attended the assembly) expressed concern about the rising cost of industrial manufactures, which, it was said, was forcing the peasant farmers to sell their grain at prices which the landless inhabitants could not afford. In order to prevent a 'war between peasant brothers', it was resolved to call on the cities to carry out a 'black repartition' of all commercial property:

> we appeal to all the peasants and workers in the city of Samara to confiscate all the goods from the shops, the factories, and the houses of the landowners and all the other enterprises and to place all these goods under the control of the

[257] In some factories during this period the workers 'devoted much of their workday to producing goods such as primus stoves, candlesticks, and kerosene lamps that had no relationship to normal production but that could be exchanged for food in the villages . . . There were also many cases of "sabotage" by hungry workers and soldiers who stole industrial products, materials, and tools to sell or exchange for food and fuel' (W. J. Chase, *Workers, Society and the Soviet State: Labour and Life in Moscow, 1918–1929*, Urbana, Ill., 1987, pp. 19–20). In some factories the workers divided the products of their labour between them, in the manner of a 'black repartition', in the understanding that this was the meaning of workers' control (oral communication by Johnathan Aves, University of London).

[258] *PSG*, pp. 21–2, 98. See also TsGAOR, f. 393, op. 3, d. 335, ll. 25–6.

[259] See e.g. the resolutions in *PSG*, pp. 99–101.

[260] See e.g. *Protokol 5-go s''ezda upolnomochennykh potrebitel'nykh obshchestv Serdobskogo uezda*, n.p., 1919.

provincial soviet executive committee; and also to cancel all the bank accounts, leaving the depositors no more than 3,000 rb. per family member; and also to give the provincial soviet the right to fix the prices on all these items, though they must not exceed the pre-war prices, namely: 20 kop. per *arshin* of simple cotton and no more than 5 rb. per *arshin* of heavy cloth . . . and no more than 2 rb. per *pud* of grain. If this is done then the peasants will not hide their grain in order to sell it privately, but will sell it to anyone. This is the only way to save the poor from hunger and to end the animosity between the rich and poor peasants.[261]

Peasant-soldiers

The return of the peasant-soldiers from the army during the winter and spring of 1917–18 had a profound effect on the course of the revolution. These young men presented themselves as the natural leaders of the revolution in the villages. Lenin saw their return as an essential precondition of the consolidation of Soviet power.[262]

The transformative effect of the modern conscript army in peasant societies is well known. True, during peacetime the Tsarist army had based itself on the traditional social structures of the peasantry as well as elements of the peasant economy.[263] But the experience of the army during the First World War transformed the parochial outlook of its peasant conscripts. It taught them the principles of large-scale organization with formal hierarchies and abstract rules; it taught them 'to think in wide national, and not village-limited terms'.[264] It acquainted them with modern technologies and military skills. And it introduced them (the first predominantly literate generation of male peasants in Russia) to a new vocabulary and new ideologies.

The mood of the soldiers on their return from the army was radical and volatile. Hunger and exhaustion, rather than Bolshevik or Left SR propaganda, had turned them into revolutionaries, though most of the soldiers belonged in spirit, if not in name, to one of these two political camps.[265] The slogan calling for the robbery of all stolen (i.e. private) property (*grab' nagrablennoe!*), whose appearance in the countryside was associated with the return of the peasant-soldiers, is probably the best reflection of the mood of these men. The knowledge of the ex-servicemen of the world outside the village connected the peasant

261 GAKO, f. 81, op. 1, d. 119a, l. 171.

262 PSS, vol. 36, pp. 85–6.

263 See J. Bushnell, *Mutiny and Repression: Russian Soldiers in the Revolution of 1905–1906*, Indiana, 1985, pp. 11–15, 18.

264 Shanin, 'The Peasantry as a Political Factor', p. 21.

265 On the politics of the demobilized soldiers see esp. M. Frenkin, *Russkaia armiia i revoliutsiia 1917–18*, Munich, 1978, ch. 7; O. H. Radkey, *The Sickle Under the Hammer: The Russian Socialist Revolutionaries in the Early Months of Soviet Rule*, New York, 1973, pp. 257–79; D. J. Raleigh, *Revolution on the Volga: 1917 in Saratov*, Cornell, 1986, pp. 328–9.

revolution with the broader currents of revolutionary change at the national level. They were the best suited to attend the higher soviet assemblies as delegates of their villages. They were the most able to formulate the peasants' resolutions in the terms of the dominant power structure. Thus, whereas the peasant mandates of 1917 translated the principles of state land-ownership into local 'peasant' terms (e.g. the land being 'in the hands of the people'), the mandates of the peasant-soldiers revealed a clear grasp of the principles of state land-ownership, as specified in the Decree on Land.[266]

From the beginning, then, the peasant-soldiers formed a powerful socio-political group in the villages. They played a leading role in the expropriation of the private estates and the establishment of the soviets. They were to dominate the first generation of peasant officials in the soviets and the socialist party cells (see ch. 5, sect. 2). During the spring of 1918 they established their own social institutions, which often wielded a powerful influence at regional and district soviet assemblies.[267] The largest such organization was the Union of Front-Line Soldiers (Soiuz frontovikov), which had more than one hundred local organizations throughout the Volga region. At this time the politics of the Unions were predominantly maximalist (Left SR or Bolshevik), although during the late spring and early summer of 1918 they tended towards the Anarchists and the Right SRs (see ch. 4, sect. 1). In the *volost'* township of Krasnyi Kut (Novouzensk *uezd*) the Union organized an armed guard to confiscate peasant produce on its way to the market. The Bolshevik-dominated VIK endowed the Union with land, livestock, tools and grain from the estates, and levied a tax on the peasants to pay for the upkeep of the Union's headquarters.[268] Outside the network of the Unions there was a wide variety of local organizations of ex-servicemen. In Chernovka *volost'* (Buzuluk *uezd*) there were two. The Soldiers' Organization served as a revolutionary fighting force for the soviets (later it became the *boevaia druzhina*). It confiscated the produce of peasants and traders on the routes to the private markets. It requisitioned the surplus grain of the richest peasant farmers for redistribution among the landless population. And it combated the illegal felling of timber by the peasantry.[269] The second soldiers' organization, the Union of Wounded Veterans (Soiuz uvechnykh voinov), had sixty-one members and a three-man (salaried) executive with two secretaries. This was a more traditional and mainly economic organization. It arranged welfare schemes for the widows of

266 Lutskii, 'Krest'ianskie nakazy', pp. 139–41.
267 See e.g. *Protokoly novouzenskogo soveta*, n.p., 27 Jan. 1918, pp. 7–10.
268 TsGAOR, f. 393, op. 3, d. 325, ll. 244, 251, 255.
269 GAKO, f. 3134, op. 2, d. 21, ll. 5, 15, 76, 91, 95.

soldiers. It organized collective teams to cultivate the plots of the families whose principal adult male worker had not yet returned from the army (see further ch. 6, sect. 4).[270] It petitioned the district soviet authorities for pensions. It elected a 'commissar for the families of veterans', who regularly attended the meetings of the VIK. The latter granted the Union the right to levy a tax on the sales of shopkeepers in order to pay for the establishment of a crafts workshop employing wounded veterans.[271] This caused one shopkeeper to complain to the VIK that the tax was unjust, since the government in Moscow had 'not passed any law against the shops of small peasant traders, but only against criminals, speculators, and capitalists'.[272] A second plaintiff, the former land captain, was more outspoken in his petition against the confiscation of his typewriter by the Union: 'They call themselves invalids, but . . . if they really were invalids they would not treat their peasant brothers with such disrespect; the people have no sympathy for these so-called "invalids".'[273]

There is evidence to suggest that in many villages the power of the ex-servicemen caused resentment among the traditional peasant leaders, especially the old men whose position was challenged by this young revolutionary élite. The actions of the peasant-soldiers sometimes tended to be rather more zealous and violent than the situation perhaps warranted. The ex-servicemen were too ready to resort to military force in upholding the power of the soviet, and in some cases indulged themselves in a senseless 'red terror' against Tsarist officials, former landowners, or 'kulaks'.[274] The Bolshevik government, which was aware of the political dangers of releasing large numbers of ex-soldiers into the villages, tried to slow down the pace of the demobilization and to confiscate the soldiers' weapons.[275] But this only had the effects of increasing the rate of desertion from the garrisons and of encouraging the soldiers' organizations to move towards the Anarchists and the Right SRs. Despite these tensions, the ex-servicemen were superbly equipped to lead the villages during the early soviet period (see further ch. 5), and it is reasonable to assume that the majority of the peasantry was content to subordinate itself to their authority. The increased influence of the peasant-soldiers even

[270] GAKO, f. 81, op. 1, d. 127, l. 22; d. 119a, l. 5; TsGAOR, f. 393, op. 3, d. 333, l. 316; d. 336, l. 264; *PSG*, pp. 36, 40; *Protokoly zasedaniia kamyshinskogo uezdnogo ispolkoma* (5 Apr., 23 Apr.).

[271] GAKO, f. 3134, op. 2, d. 21, ll. 23, 33, 35, 68–9, 80, 92.

[272] Ibid., l. 92.

[273] Ibid., ll. 36–7.

[274] TsGAOR, f. 393, op. 3, d. 325, ll. 268, 294, 306.

[275] *PSS*, vol. 32, pp. 154, 160; vol. 43, pp. 10, 16–17, 153; O. H. Radkey, *The Unknown Civil War in Soviet Russia*, Stanford, 1976, p. 157. See also GAKO, f. 81, op. 1, d. 127, ll. 14–15.

began to penetrate the large family household, the most conservative of peasant institutions: during the early 1920s it was noted that in many large households the younger brother became the household elder, especially 'if he had served in the Red Army, was literate and had a good understanding of the law and current affairs'.[276]

The clergy

The typical parish priest (*pop*) of pre-revolutionary Russia barely rose above the peasantry in his standard of living and social status. As I. S. Belliutsin wrote in his *Description of the Clergy*, 'the farmer-priest is just a peasant, distinguished only by his literacy; otherwise he has a cast of thought, desires, aspirations, and even a way of life that are strictly peasant'.[277] Much of the priest's energy was spent tilling the household garden and arable strips assigned by the commune to the church-house. He was accustomed to negotiating the prices of his Christian services—if that is what they may be called, for the blessing of the harvest and the elaborate rituals which the parish priest performed in the fields and the peasant huts had a distinctly pagan feel.[278]

The revolution accentuated the 'peasant' nature of the parish priest. The attacks on the church and the monasteries by the Bolsheviks and the Decree on the separation of church and state (23 January 1918), which officially ended the right of the church to demand payment for religious services, forced the parish priest to support himself through agricultural labour. Many priests fled the countryside to join the anti-Bolshevik movement, or to find an alternative means of livelihood to agriculture. But the majority probably remained in the village, either because they had nowhere to go, or because they felt committed to the local peasantry. Some parish priests even became revolutionary activists: the editor of the Balashov *Izvestiia* and a leading member of the Ardatov district soviet had both been parish priests before 1917.[279] The priests who stayed in the village were invariably given an allotment of communal land. Sometimes the allotment was of particularly good quality, since it served in part payment for the priest's religious services. It was not unusual for the commune to

[276] *RR*, p. 231.

[277] I. S. Belliutsin, *Description of the Clergy in Rural Russia*, trans. G. L. Freeze, Cornell, 1985, p. 126.

[278] On pagan rituals and Christian rites in the Russian village see M. Lewin, *The Making of the Soviet System*, New York, 1985, pp. 57–71.

[279] *Izvestiia* (Kamyshin), no. 85, 29 Sept. 1918, p. 2; TsGAOR, f. 393, op. 3, d. 359, l. 266. See similarly *Kommuna* (Samara), no. 112, 27 Apr. 1919, p. 3; no. 138, 29 May 1919, p. 3.

organize a collective labour team to work the priest's allotment, in the nineteenth-century tradition of *pomoch'*.[280]

The politics of the rural clergy and the religious attitudes of the peasantry were put to the test by the legislation of January 1918 separating church and state. The church schools were to be brought under state (i.e. soviet) control. The church's official right to register births, deaths, and marriages, which formed an integral part of the traditional village political culture, was curtailed.[281] The same principles were applied to mosques in Tatar and Bashkir regions. How did the peasantry react to these measures? It is probably fair to assume that the majority of the VIKs lacked the means to enforce the new law in the villages. The affairs of the church and its schools were firmly in the domain of the commune and the parish (*prikhod*). The number of VIKs with their own department for the registration of births, deaths and marriages was tiny. As for the village soviets, they rarely made any effort to prevent the parish priest from collecting his dues in the traditional manner. The Soviet press regularly devoted columns to the denunciation of village soviets which allowed the priests to charge what were considered to be extortionate prices. In the village of Kliuchi (Buguruslan *uezd*) the soviet was reported to have paid the priest a monthly salary of 300 rb. to perform his services in church; it also gave him an annual flour ration of 200 *pud*. In the nearby village of Novo-Spasskoe the local priest was said to be making up to 8,000 rb. per month from marriages, christenings and funerals. He charged between 150 and 200 rb. for each service, according to the wealth of the client.[282] Some village soviets, it is true, did take measures to keep the profits of the clergy to a minimum: the most common method was to make the payment of religious services voluntary, 'according to belief', while levying a tax on the population to pay for the upkeep of the church, its property, and its personnel.[283] But for every such soviet there was another which bitterly opposed the separation of church and state, especially in the Tatar and Bashkir regions.[284]

280 TsGANKh, f. 478, op. 3, d. 1157, l. 46; TsGAOR, f. 393, op. 3, d. 325, ll. 76–7; *Rezoliutsii i tezisy priniatye na 7-om samarskom gubernskom s''ezde sovetov*, Samara, 1921, pp. 30–1; Kabanov, 'Oktiabr'skaia revoliutsiia', p. 125; Gimpel'son, *Sovety v pervyi god proletarskoi diktatury*, pp. 266–7.

281 M. M. Persits, *Otdelenie tserkvi ot gosudarstva i shkoly ot tserkvi v SSSR*, Moscow, 1958, pp. 99–103.

282 *Luch kommuny* (Buguruslan), no. 354, 27 May 1920, p. 2; *Kommuna* (Samara), no. 244, 5 Oct. 1919, p. 2; *Nabat* (Kamyshin), no. 36, 30 Mar. 1919, p. 3. There is journalistic evidence to suggest that the urban church councils, deprived of financial support from the state, collected flour from the local rural clergy: see *Kommunist* (Pugachev), no. 177, 17 Oct. 1920, p. 1.

283 GAKO, f. 3134, op. 2, d. 21, ll. 15, 30, 45; TsGAOR, f. 393, op. 3, d. 329, l. 64; d. 325, ll. 236, 259, 266; d. 337, ll. 154–5; d. 333, l. 89.

284 See e.g. *VI s''ezd kuznetskogo soveta*, Kuznetsk, 1919 ('Doklad otdela po delam natsional'nostei').

Tensions between the soviet authorities and the church community frequently arose over the issue of housing. The houses of the parish clergy officially became soviet property after the separation. The soviet was legally empowered to evict the clergy in order to turn these buildings into a social institution, such as a library, a reading hut (*izba chitatel'naia*), or a 'people's house' (*narodnyi dom*), or, indeed, into part of the soviet office itself. In the village of Durnikino (Balashov *uezd*) a conflict took place between the Bolshevik-dominated soviet and the church council (*tserkovnyi sovet*) when the former attempted to turn the priest's house into a *narodnyi dom*. The village soviet leaders were harassed and heckled by the peasantry until they agreed to accommodate the two village priests in the *narodnyi dom* itself. In the nearby village of Svinukha a similar conflict occurred when the soviet set itself up in one of the church houses, and turned the other one into a post office. The peasants, led by the church council, forced the soviet leaders to flee to the neighbouring village. The peasants then called a village gathering, at which it was resolved that the 'priests are needed in the village more than a post office or a soviet'.[285]

It is difficult to gauge any change in the peasantry's religiosity during the early years of the revolution. During the 1920s the church undoubtedly weakened its psychological hold over the peasantry, especially over the young peasant men whom the events of 1914–21 had taken out of the confined world of the village. But during the disturbed period of 1917–21 it is unlikely that any real weakening could have taken place in the religious attitudes of the peasantry, since this depended, above all, on a real increase in the level of peasant literacy. Indeed, if there was a change of attitudes then it was likely to be one that strengthened the position of the church, since the latter stood for tradition and certainty in a period when ordinary people were unsure or afraid of what the new order might bring. A. Okninsky, who was not a biased observer, detected a resurgence in church attendance in his village in Tambov province during 1918–20. The atheism of the peasant-soldiers on their return from the army in 1917–18 was, according to Okninsky, soon forgotten.[286]

The peasants' attachment to the parish church was reflected in petitions to the higher Soviet authorities for the return of the local priests whom the Red Army or the Cheka had conscripted for military service or some other arduous duty in the 'labour army' (e.g. road-sweeping, snow-clearing). In December 1918 the village commune in Bekovo (Serdobsk *uezd*) petitioned the district soviet military committee (*voenkom*) for the release of its priest and its deacon from the rear

[285] *Izvestiia* (Balashov), no. 117, 1 June 1919, p. 4; no. 121, 6 June 1919, p. 4.

[286] *DGS*, p. 231. From the Soviet perspective see Ia. A. Iakovlev, *Nasha derevnia*, pp. 127–31.

units of the Red Army, where they were said to be performing 'religious services'. The petition spoke of the two men as 'good people, excellent clergymen who satisfied all our moral and spiritual demands'. The priest had taken a keen interest in the peasantry's education, helping them to establish in 1917 a higher primary school (*vysshee nachal'noe uchilishche*). The school was becoming run-down and the one remaining priest in the locality was 'unable to serve all the 4,795 inhabitants of Bekovo as well as 1,000 inhabitants of Rogachevka 12 *versty* away'.[287]

Similar sentiments of support for the clergy were expressed in the numerous peasant uprisings of this period which were at least partly caused by the Bolsheviks' attack on the church.[288] One example will have to suffice here. In April 1918 a crowd of more than 500 peasants, most of them women, gathered in the village of Liubimovka (Buzuluk *uezd*) to protest against the removal of icons from the church by the Bolshevik party cell. The crowd set upon the Bolshevik leaders and carried out a *samosud*. When a detachment of the Buzuluk mounted police arrived in the village, the protesters attempted to disarm them and put them on trial too. Scuffles broke out and the brigade was forced to flee from the village.[289]

Schoolteachers

The Decree on the separation of church and state was hardest to implement in the field of education. The majority of the village schools in Russia were owned and run by the church. During the economic crisis of 1917–21 it was practically impossible for the soviet authorities to build new schools and train new teachers. The average village would have done well just to keep the old schoolhouse open during these years.

Many teachers fled to the towns after 1917. Some of them wanted to join the anti-Bolshevik movement. Others felt a decline in their influence among the peasantry during 1917, compared with the much more active role they had played during the revolution of 1905. Every village schoolteacher during these years was forced to live in some degree of poverty and was heavily dependent upon the support of the

[287] TsGAOR, f. 393, op. 3, d. 340, l. 268. See also d. 337, l. 161; GAKO, f. 81, op. 1, d. 10, l. 109; *Nabat* (Kamyshin), no. 39, 6 Apr. 1919, p. 3.

[288] The over-zealous confiscation of church property by rural Bolshevik officials was said by the higher authorities to have seriously threatened peasant–state relations during 1918–20 (*Vlast' Sovetov*, no. 5, Apr. 1919, p. 14).

[289] *Kommuna* (Samara), no. 100, 12 Apr. 1918, p. 3. See also *Samarskie eparkhial'nye vedomosti*, nos. 7–8, 14–28 Apr. 1918, p. 285; *Revoliutsionnaia armiia* (Samara/4th Army), no. 14, 21 Jan. 1919, p. 4; *Nabat* (Kamyshin), no. 33, 23 Mar. 1919, p. 3; *Sbornik 'Ves' Kuznetsk'*, Kuznetsk, 1927, p. 49.

communes, not all of which were as generous in the revolutionary period as they had been in peacetime. Where the teachers had fled, the schoolhouses generally closed down, though in some localities the peasants managed to find replacement teachers. Nadezhda Krupskaia (Lenin's wife), on agitational work in the Volga region during the summer of 1919, noticed that many of the village schoolteachers were young peasant girls. They were generally paid for their work in the form of a garden allotment near the schoolhouse, which the pupils cultivated.[290]

Many teachers of the pre-revolutionary period chose to remain in the village. Since the Bolshevik government was not known to be sympathetic towards the professional classes, they considered it safer to remain in the villages where they could rely upon the peasants to protect them from the Cheka. The materials of the village and *volost'* soviets during this period underline the peasantry's high estimation of the value of education, which Ben Eklof has described in relation to the nineteenth century.[291] The soviets levied taxes to pay for the upkeep of the schools and the teachers. They organized labour teams to repair the schoolhouse, and to fell timber to keep the classes heated. Some of the villages without a schoolhouse arranged for the lessons to be held in the fields or in the manor house. During the revolutionary period the peasantry closely associated literacy with the concept of liberty. As one peasant from Tambov province put it at the beginning of the 1920s, 'everyone needs to learn, since before we were not free, but now there are assemblies'.[292] The white-bearded sceptics who believed their sons would 'go soft' and would not want to work in the fields once they had learned to read were fast dying out. The younger peasants saw literacy as a 'badge of equality with the non-peasants'[293]—a way of ending the 'two Russias' of which Herzen had spoken, and the 'idiocy of rural life' to which Marx had referred. In the words of the Chernovka village soviet (Buzuluk *uezd*), only education would lead the peasantry 'out of the darkness and ignorance in which it has lived for hundreds of years'.[294]

In its dealings with the non-farming groups of the village, the Russian

290 N. K. Krupskaia, 'Po gradam i vesiam sovetskoi respubliki', *Novyi mir*, 11 (1960), pp. 118, 120–1, 123–4, 128.

291 B. Eklof, *Russian Peasant Schools: Officialdom, Village Culture and Popular Pedagogy, 1861–1914*, Berkeley, Calif., 1986.

292 Iakovlev, *Nasha derevnia*, p. 114.

293 T. Shanin, *The Roots of Otherness: Russia's Turn of Century*, vol. 2, *Russia, 1905–07: Revolution as a Moment of Truth*, London, 1986, p. 135.

294 GAKO, f. 3134, op. 2, d. 21, l. 42.

peasantry during the revolution applied many different moral standards and conceptions of social justice. These standards were used by the peasantry in a number of different forms, according to the perceived social value of the group in question. One set of rules was applied to people whose qualities were thought to be useful or necessary to the village community, while another was applied to those whose presence was unwelcome. The peasantry in this way drew up a circle of 'insiders', and assigned each of these social groups a different set of rights and duties within the community. It attempted to neutralize the political threat of the gentry by giving the squires a high economic status (without political rights) in the village community. On the other hand, the *khutoriane* and the *otrubniki* were given no more rights (and sometimes fewer) than the rest of the peasant farmers. The land rights of the landless labourers of the pre-revolutionary period were recognized, but only as long as the latter managed to sustain an independent family farm. The communes were rarely prepared to intervene in the labour market on behalf of those who were forced back into subordinate economic relations with the biggest peasant farmers, since this would be detrimental to the level of agricultural production in the community. The in-migrant population was supported by the peasants only as long as there was a need for extra labour, or only as long as there was a surplus of foodstuffs. On the other hand, the in-migrants with a valued social skill, such as craftsmen or *intelligenty*, might find a permanent place in the village community. It was the valuable social skills of the peasant-soldiers, the clergy and the schoolteachers that assigned them a leading role and a privileged status in the peasant community.

The village social system of 1918 was neither a peasant dictatorship, nor a village democracy. The farming peasantry decided the terms on which the other democratic elements of the village were given their rights. But these terms were also determined by external conditions. The socio-economic and political dislocation of 1917–21 necessitated the democratization of the village assembly, whereby the peasantry included in the process of decision-making the non-farming groups who had something to contribute. The social autonomy of the countryside during this period can only be understood if we take into account this growing interdependence between the farming peasantry and the other rural groups, whose social worth had been proven in the context of the revolution. The political system which arose from this interdependence was more traditional than democratic: the peasant patriarchs continued to wield a powerful influence; the peasant women were still excluded from power; and the 'free riders' (e.g. vagabonds, 'idlers', in-migrants) were in effect disenfranchised. Nevertheless, the system was more democratic than the village assembly of the nineteenth century: the younger peasants, especially those who had fought in the war, played a dominant role; the peasants who had not held land before the revolution were given a part to play for the first time; and the non-farming inhabitants played a more central role.

Was this political system stable? Was it capable of solving the problems of peasant Russia which had caused the revolution? The answer to both these questions must, in the long run, be no. The resolution of the land question by the communes satisfied the immediate aspirations of the peasantry, yet it was not able to remedy the fundamental problems of small-scale peasant farming. The rationalization of the communal land system required the assistance of the state in the form of agronomists, credit, and material aid. The regulation of the market by the communes and the local soviets managed to ease the food crisis of 1917–18, but could not have solved the broader problems of urban-rural trade, especially under the conditions of the civil war. As in the rest of post-war Europe, the reintegration of the rural and the urban economies required national market controls. The communes and the soviets were, for the most part, organs of the middle peasantry, yet they were unable to deal with the broader social problems of Russia, which had forced millions of townsmen into the countryside. The conflict between these two interests stood at the heart of the breakdown of the revolution in the village and the consolidation of the Soviet regime.

4
Counter-Revolution

> We do not want to spill blood in a war against our own brothers. We will send delegates to Samara to ask both the armies to lay down their arms.
>
> Resolution of Elshanka village (Khvalynsk *uezd*), July 1918

AFTER October 1917 it was commonly assumed by the political parties in Russia that the peasantry would align itself with the anti-Bolshevik movement. The SRs, for one, had high hopes of the peasantry, based on the party's strong traditions in the countryside. Since the majority of the peasants had voted for the SRs in the elections to the Constituent Assembly, it was expected that they would join them in their struggle against the Bolshevik regime for the restoration of political and social democracy. The Right SRs emphasized the defence of the Constituent Assembly. The Left SRs, who joined the Bolsheviks in government between December 1917 and March 1918, preferred to stress the defence of the local soviets against the *kombedy*, whose war against the 'kulaks' was seen to be misdirected against the middle peasantry. In contrast to the SRs, the Mensheviks believed that Russia was not ready for a socialist revolution: her industrial proletariat was tiny, while the 'contradictions' of bourgeois social development had not yet created the necessary conditions for socialism among the peasantry (the 'petty bourgeoisie'), whose interests were ultimately opposed to the goals of the Bolshevik revolution. As Marxists, the Bolsheviks also recognized the difficulties of staging a socialist revolution in a country where the 'proletariat' was still vastly outnumbered by the 'petty bourgeoisie'. However, their understanding of the dialectic enabled them to see beyond such theoretical problems. They reasoned that the civil war itself would raise the 'proletarian' consciousness of the poorest peasantry in opposition to the 'kulaks', thereby undermining the social base of the counter-revolution in the countryside.

History proved all the political parties wrong. The peasants failed to emerge as the main social force of the anti-Bolshevik movement. Their own struggle against the Bolshevik regime after 1919 (see ch. 7) proved too weak to overturn the new state structure in the provinces, which had been greatly strengthened by the civil war (see ch. 5). Marxist fears of a 'kulak' or 'petty-bourgeois' counter-revolution proved illusory: the traditional social structure of the central Russian countryside had not been fundamentally transformed by the development of capitalism prior to 1917; its pre-modern character had even been accentuated during the revolution as a result of the processes of socio-economic levelling among the peasantry.[1] The political outlook of the middle peasantry, which had emerged from the revolution as the dominant social force, was limited to the local institutions of the smallholding community—the communes and the *volost'* soviets—which had been made virtually autonomous during 1917–18. The middle peasants were prepared to leave their villages for the defence of the revolution against the landowners. They were ready to defend the autonomy of the communes and the soviets against the *kombedy* (see ch. 5, sect. 1). But they were not willing to leave their farms for the cause of political democracy at the national level.

1. THE 'KULAK COUNTER-REVOLUTION'

According to Soviet historians, the establishment of the 'food dictatorship' and the *kombedy* during May–June 1918 resulted in a 'wave of kulak revolts' against the soviets.[2] Lenin himself argued that if these two measures marked the beginning of the socialist revolution in the countryside, then the 'kulak' revolts marked the beginning of the counter-revolution.[3] The Leninist theory of the two stages of the revolutionary struggle can only be 'proved' if there is evidence of 'widespread kulak rebellion against the proletarian dictatorship' during the summer of 1918.[4]

There is little evidence to support the Leninist view. Soviet historians have selected diverse—and sometimes unreliable—reports of 'kulak revolts' without telling us anything about the scale of the uprisings. This may be gauged by the following figures. During the spring and summer of 1918 'disturbances' were reported in 12 out of 450 rural settlements in Saratov *uezd*; in 10 out of 450 rural settlements in Atkarsk *uezd*; in 20 out of 170 rural settlements in Vol'sk *uezd*; in 5 out of 150 rural settlements in Khvalynsk *uezd*; in 3 out of 450 rural settlements in Serdobsk *uezd*.[5] Saratov province was

[1] The socio-economic levelling effects of the agrarian revolution among the peasantry are not discussed in detail here. Although one or two Western historians (e.g. G. Yaney, *The Urge to Mobilize: Agrarian Reform in Russia, 1861–1930*, Urbana, Ill., 1982, pp. 470–1) have questioned the evidence of this levelling in the 1917 and 1919 censuses, it is reasonable to assume that the land redivisions and the increased tempo of household partitioning during 1917–21 did result in a relatively sharp increase in the number of middle peasant households at the expense of the number of rich and poor peasant households. The peasant household farming an average holding of land with its own labour and one horse became the typical figure of the Russian countryside after 1917 (see T. Shanin, *The Awkward Class*, Oxford, 1972, pp. 147–60; *KK*, pp.208–9, 219–40).

[2] The phrase was first used by Lenin in *PSS*, vol. 37, p. 313.

[3] Ibid., pp. 39–40, 176–7, 352–3.

[4] Shanin, *The Awkward Class*, p. 147.

[5] *Godovshchina sotsial'noi revoliutsii v Saratove*, Saratov, 1918, p. 29. The number of villages from: *Trudy TsSU: Itogi vserossiiskoi sel'sko-khoziaistvennoi perepisi 1920 g.*, vol. 2, vyp. 2, Moscow, 1921.

well known to the Whites and the moderate socialist parties as a centre of rich-peasant opposition to the Soviet regime. Other provinces must have been even less disturbed. An enquiry of the Moscow regional executive during May 1918 showed that only 46 out of 862 VIKs in 13 Russian provinces had witnessed any counter-revolutionary activity; a further 26 VIKs reported that such activity was limited to 'individual people'. The Soviet historian who published these results concluded that 'large-scale counter-revolutionary activity was almost totally absent' in the rural areas during the first half of 1918.[6]

What can we say about the social nature of these so-called 'kulak revolts'? The reports of Soviet officials should not be accepted at face value, for reasons outlined above (see pp. 82–3). There was a wide variety of rural protest in the summer of 1918, but only a small fraction of it may be said, without question, to have originated exclusively in the richest peasant stratum. The land redivisions, as we have seen, were accompanied by little direct opposition from the wealthy farmers, partly because they themselves managed to retain a great deal of influence in the communes and the *volost'* soviets (see ch. 3, sects. 3 and 4). The village uprisings against the *kombedy* and the requisitioning brigades generally united the peasant farmers, regardless of their socio-economic status (see ch. 5 sect. 1). The mutinies in the rear-army garrisons (e.g. in Kuznetsk on 7 March, in Samara at the beginning of May, and in Saratov on 16–19 May) were caused by the poor supply of food and uniforms, by delays in demobilization, and by rumours that the Bolsheviks intended to integrate the garrisons into the Red Army. The mutinies were led by Anarchist or Left SR officers; but 80% of the soldiers who had been arrested by the Cheka after the suppression of the Saratov mutiny were immediately released on the grounds that they had been 'politically unconscious' (*nesoznatel'nye*)—an epithet which the higher Soviet officials of that time usually reserved for the poorest peasantry.[7]

There is evidence to suggest that some of the reported cases of 'kulak' opposition may have resulted from the private denunciations written to the Cheka by one group of peasants against another. It was common for indebted peasants to denounce their 'kulak' creditor to the police, or for village feuds and vendettas to be settled in this manner. The Balakovo district Cheka complained in the summer of 1918 that its investigatory commission 'was forced to start every

[6] S. L. Makarova, 'Oprosnye listy Narodnogo Komissariata Zemledeliia i moskovskogo oblastnogo ispolnitel'nogo komiteta kak istochnik po istorii agrarnoi revoliutsii (noiabr' 1917–iiun' 1918)', kand. diss., Moscow, 1970, pp. 176–8.

[7] I. Sorin, 'Saratovskoe vosstanie 1918 g. (po chernovym zametkam)', *Letopis' revoliutsii*, Khar'kov, 1923, no. 5, p. 224.

investigation with extreme care, since it immediately ran up against attempts by the local inhabitants to use it to report their own private disputes and rivalries, sometimes even between close relatives'.[8] Less scrupulous local Chekas soon filled the prisons with the victims of peasant denunciations. A report by the Buguruslan district Bolshevik party lamented in December 1918 that 'at the beginning [during the early summer of 1918] the Cheka would make an arrest on the basis of virtually any anonymous accusation without bringing formal charges or collecting documentary evidence; consequently, there were far too many arrests'.[9] A report by the Kurmysh district Bolshevik party (Simbirsk province) confirmed in April 1918 that 'the district prisons are filled with innocent people'.[10] Many of these people must have been members of the village or *volost'* soviets who had been arrested as 'kulaks' by the higher Soviet authorities on the basis of private denunciations. The Soviet press encouraged such denunciations by running regular stories about the 'kulak' activities of some local soviet leaders; the detailed evidence in support of the claim (e.g. 'speculation' or vodka-brewing) was usually of the sort that could only have been provided by a fellow villager.

The village and *volost'* soviets generally did what they could to prevent these denunciations. The propaganda against the 'kulaks' was alien to the peasantry's own perception of the counter-revolution, which was seen to be located among the gentry landowners. A good illustration of this difference of understanding is from Chernovka *volost'* (Buzuluk *uezd*). The VIK had been ordered to arrest thirty listed inhabitants of Chernovka and send them to the district Cheka, following the suppression of an abortive 'kulak' revolt on 11 May. The *volost'* soviet assembly resolved on 14 June to write to the Buzuluk Cheka suggesting it come to Chernovka itself:

> most of the people who have been summoned do not even have their own horse, so the charges against them [i.e. participation in the 'kulak' revolt] cannot be right. The counter-revolutionary kulaks have been dealt with in the village, but now the supporters of the social revolution are being ordered to travel 20 *verstg*, and this is out of the question.[11]

A second example is from Zolotoe *volost'* (Kamyshin *uezd*), where the VIK had been ordered by the district Cheka to arrest three members of the soviet for 'kulak counter-revolutionary activities'. At a general *volost'* assembly the peasants resolved to protest to the district soviet.

[8] TsGAOR, f. 393, op. 3, d. 323, l. 12.
[9] Ibid., l. 355.
[10] Ibid., d. 359, l. 331.
[11] GAKO, f. 3134, op. 2, d. 21, l. 148.

The resolution of the assembly defended I. I. Menskii, one of the accused, on account of his 'uninterrupted and irreproachable service for fifty-five years as the scribe of our *volost'*, and in recent times as the secretary of our soviet executive'. The assembly sent the following petition to Kamyshin in defence of P. V. Kubasov, the head of the education department of the Zolotoe VIK:

we hereby guarantee that citizen P. V. Kubasov has in his whole life never exploited hired labour; until 1905 he was a teacher in the Zolotoe *zemstvo*-communal high school and was popular and trusted by everyone in not only the village, but also the whole *volost'* of Zolotoe; as a man who was without doubt trying to improve the lives of the peasants and the workers, he was elected by the people to stand as a representative in the first State Duma, and he proved a very popular representative. He took part in the famous electoral campaigns, for which he was imprisoned. He was denied the right to stand in public office and was persecuted by the Tsarist government. Since his release from prison, he has lived in his own village and has worked his household garden and his bee-hives with his own labour; his products have been used entirely for his own needs.[12]

A final example is the resolution of the Natal'in *volost'* soviet assembly (Samara *uezd*) on 19 March. The investigatory commission of the Samara district Revolutionary Tribunal had ordered the VIK in Natal'in to send four arrested 'counter-revolutionaries' to Samara. By forty-three votes to one, the *volost'* assembly resolved:

since the soviet knew nothing of the alleged counter-revolutionary propaganda of these people and received neither a written nor an oral complaint from the Natal'in village soviet, and since the order of the investigatory commission and the Samara district soviet executive was based only on the oral testimony of Andrei Gorodnov, we resolved to instruct the *volost'* soviet executive not to carry out the order of the investigatory commission, which is based upon the private accusation of one man and is therefore unjust and undermines the authority of the *volost'* soviet which carries out the will of all the people. People who make private denunciations unbeknown to the local organs of Soviet power are no better than the police spies under the reign of Nicholas II.[13]

Soviet historians have associated the 'kulak' revolts with the SRs, the Mensheviks, and the Anarcho-Maximalists (the so-called 'petty-bourgeois' political parties). Naturally, the Bolshevik party tried to discredit its socialist rivals during the civil war by accusing them of 'counter-revolutionary' activities. But is there any objective historical evidence in support of the Bolshevik claim?

[12] TsGAOR, f. 393, op. 3, d. 323, ll. 322–3.
[13] GAKO, f. 81, op. 1, d. 119a, ll. 73–4.

Roy Medvedev and Vladimir Brovkin have recently argued that there was an increase in popular support for the Mensheviks and the SRs during the spring and early summer of 1918.[14] The closure of the Constituent Assembly, the approach of the civil war, the worsening of the food crisis, the growth of urban unemployment, the weakening of workers' control in the factories, the increasing brutality of the red guards, the clamp-down on collective commodity exchange, and the start of the food requisitionings all undoubtedly alienated the masses from the Bolsheviks. But was this social discontent reflected in an increase of political opposition, or was it reflected, as William Rosenberg has suggested,[15] in general disillusionment with revolutionary politics?

Table 12 gives a rough idea of the extent of popular opposition to the Soviet regime at the beginning of summer 1918. It is based upon the reports of local NKVD officials on the 'attitude of the population towards Soviet power'.[16] Although the archival document was not dated, there is circumstantial evidence to suggest that it was compiled at the end of May or the beginning of June 1918.[17]

There is no direct evidence to suggest that the hostility towards the Soviet regime in Samara, Simbirsk, and Saratov provinces was articulated in the form of opposition party politics. But it is reasonable to assume that the opposition parties would attempt to take whatever advantage they could of the discontent. The Right SRs moved into the Volga countryside, one of their traditional strongholds, after the closure of the Constituent Assembly. The large majority for the SR parties in the elections to the Constituent Assembly, the strength of the SR party networks, and the security of the Volga in the event of a German invasion contributed to their preference of the Volga over the Don, Arkhangel'sk, and Kiev.[18] At the time of the Eighth (Right SR)

[14] R. Medvedev, *The October Revolution*, trans. G. Saunders, London, 1979, pp. 145–52; V. Brovkin, 'The Mensheviks' Political Comeback: The Elections to the Provincial City Soviets in Spring 1918', *Russian Review*, vol. 42, 1983, esp. pp. 37–8.

[15] W. G. Rosenberg, 'Russian Labor and Bolshevik Power: Social Dimensions of Protest in Petrograd after October', in D. H. Kaiser (ed.), *The Workers' Revolution in Russia, 1917: The View from Below*, Cambridge, Mass., 1987, pp. 98–131.

[16] It is not clear what the local population understood by the term 'Soviet power' at this time: the power of the *volost' soviet*, or the Soviet (Bolshevik) government in Moscow? I have assumed (perhaps contentiously) that the NKVD officials were primarily interested in gauging the attitude of the population towards the government in Moscow, and have therefore substituted the term 'Soviet regime' for 'Soviet power' in order to clarify this issue.

[17] The document is contained in the same file as a report on the uprising in Samara during 15–17 May.

[18] V. M. Chernov, *Pered burei: Vospominaniia*, New York, 1953, pp. 368–70. See further O. H. Radkey, *The Sickle under the Hammer: The Russian Socialist Revolutionaries in the Early Months of Soviet Rule*, New York, 1973, pp. 436–40.

Table 12. *Political mood of the Volga population, May–June 1918*

	Attitude of population towards the Soviet regime		
District	Good	Indifferent/uncertain	Hostile
Samara	workers ⅓ peasants		intelligentsia printers ⅔ peasants
Balakovo			all
Pokrovsk			all
Balashov	some townsmen all peasants	some townsmen	
Vol'sk	rural poor		townsmen kulaks
Kuznetsk	some peasants		most peasants townsmen
Serdobsk		all	
Petrovsk	workers		peasants
Simbirsk	workers		peasants
Ardatov	all		
Alatyr'			all
Buinsk			all
Karsun		rural	
Sengilei		weak	
Penza	all		
Insaro			all
Krasnoslobodsk	all		
Mokshan			majority
Nizhnelomov	all		
Narovchat	rural		urban
Chembar		all	
Menzelinsk	half		half
Kazan'		varied	
Mamadysh	all		
Laishevo	all		
Sviiazhsk	all		
Tetiushi	rural		urban
Tsivil'sk			majority
Cheboksary		all	
Chistopol'	majority		
Iadrinsk	rural	urban	

Source: TsGAOR, f. 393, op. 4, d. 22, l. 33.

Party Congress in May, only eight central committee members were still in Moscow: four were in the Volga provincial centres and two in the Urals. The Volga SR leaders increased their agitation in the rear army garrisons and the *soiuzy frontovikov*. A group of SR officers linked the party in Samara and Saratov with Dutov's Cossack army and the 'Union for the Rebirth of Russia' (*Soiuz vozrozhdeniia Rossii*).[19] Such efforts gained the Right SRs a certain level of support in the garrisons of Samara, Kuznetsk and, especially, Saratov.[20] But it was not enough to stage an open revolt. As the SR leader in Samara, P. D. Klimushkin, recalled, no one in the garrisons 'believed it was possible to overthrow the Bolshevik authorities. Everyone was sure they would hold onto power for a long time. One General with whom I spoke about this said that the power of the Bolsheviks was solid and that any attempt to overthrow it would be pure adventurism'.[21]

In the towns the influence of the Right SRs was very weak. The loyalties of the factory workers in Samara and Saratov still lay with the Bolsheviks, if with any party at all. The 'labour aristocracy' and the railway workers were more closely connected with the Mensheviks than the SRs. And the unskilled workers inclined towards the Anarcho-Maximalists. The latter were at the centre of the dockers' uprising in Samara on 15 May against the 'commissar dictatorship'. A Red Army commissar who had requisitioned the dockers' carts for military purposes was murdered and the city militia was disarmed. Some of the soldiers from the Red Army garrison together with a group of Anarchist sailors joined the revolt. The prison was opened. The post office and the telegraph and telephone stations were taken over. On 17 May the insurgents tried to arrest the Bolshevik leaders of the provincial Soviet executive and elect in its place a 'Constituent Assembly' (a policy which suggests that the revolt was well connected with the Right SRs). On the following morning, however, the insurgents were rounded up by 5,000 Red Army troops from Moscow with reinforcements from Penza, Balashov, Ufa, and Bugul'ma.[22]

Conscious of their weakness in the towns, the Right SRs sent the majority of their agitators into the rural areas. The main problem here

[19] K. V. Gusev, *Partiia eserov: Ot melkoburzhuaznogo revoliutsionarizma k kontrrevoliutsii*, Moscow, 1975, p. 229; V. Vladimirova, 'Rabota eserov v 1918 g.', *Krasnyi Arkhiv*, 1927, no. 20, pp. 154–5.

[20] I. M. Maiskii, *Demokraticheskaia kontrrevoliutsiia*, Moscow, 1923, p. 45; G. Semenov (Vasil'ev), *Voennaia i boevaia rabota partii sotsialistov-revoliutsionerov za 1917–18 gg.*, Berlin, 1922, p. 34. An indication of the strength of the Right SRs in the garrisons is given by an enquiry at the SR-staged conference of military organizations in December 1917: of the 89 military units represented at the conference, only 29 had their own Right SR organizations (Gusev, p. 242).

[21] Cited in Maiskii, pp. 45–6.

[22] V. V. Garmiza, *Krushenie eserovskikh pravitel'stv*, Moscow, 1970, pp. 16–17; TsGAOR, f. 393, op. 4, d. 22, l. 126.

was that most of the SR activists in the rural localities stood on the left wing of the party. The Left SRs strengthened their influence in the villages during the spring of 1918, mainly on account of the return of the peasant-soldiers. A Soviet historian has calculated that the Left SRs increased their representation at 100 district soviet assemblies from 18.9% before April to 23.1% between April and August (the Bolshevik representation dropped from 66% to 44.8%; and the non-party representation increased from 9.3% to 27.1%).[23] In the Saratov district soviet assembly the Left SRs increased their share of the delegation from 20% to 28% between March and July. The Left SRs were better represented in the more rural districts: the Vol'sk district soviet assembly in May 1918 was attended by 61 Left SRs (and 63 Bolsheviks); the Atkarsk district soviet assembly in July was attended by 11 Left SRs (and 19 Bolsheviks).[24]

The politics of the Left SRs were perhaps the closest reflection of the mood of the Volga peasantry during the spring and early summer of 1918. This did not bode well for the Right SRs in Samara, whose struggle against the Bolsheviks during the summer was to depend upon the political and military mobilization of the peasantry under the banner of the Constituent Assembly. The peasantry had rejected the Constituent Assembly as an alternative to Soviet power during the winter of 1917–18. They were not likely to change their minds now. The Left SR resolution passed by the 700 delegates at the Kazan' provincial peasant assembly in March was probably typical of the position of the peasantry during 1918:

> in view of the fact that the phase of the revolution which Russia is now passing through represents a higher stage than the one in which the idea of an all-national, classless Constituent Assembly prevailed, new elections to the Constituent Assembly as well as the convocation of the old and now defunct Assembly are to be considered unnecessary and efforts to convoke such an assembly, from whatever quarter they may emanate, are to be considered a counter-revolutionary act.[25]

Here was a clear warning that the peasantry would resist any 'counter-revolutionary' attempt by the Right SRs to substitute the Constituent Assembly for local soviet power.

2. THE PEASANTRY AND THE SAMARA GOVERNMENT (KOMUCH)

The failure of the Right SRs to stir the peasantry, the town population, and the soldiers into an uprising against the Bolsheviks led Klimush-

[23] L. M. Spirin, *Klassy i partii v grazhdanskoi voine v Rossii*, Moscow, 1968, p. 174.

[24] Gusev, p. 244; G. A. Gerasimenko and F. A. Rashitov, *Sovety Nizhnego Povolzh'ia v Oktiabr'skoi revoliutsii*, Saratov, 1972, pp. 291–2, 322–23.

[25] Cited in Radkey, *The Sickle under the Hammer*, p. 449.

kin to the recognition in May 1918 that 'unless there is a spur from the outside in the near future, then we can give up all hopes of a *coup d'état*'.[26] By one of the curious accidents of history, that spur came at the end of the same month when a legion of Czech soldiers became embroiled in a conflict with the Soviet authorities in eastern Russia.

The Czech legion numbered about 35,000 nationalist officers, workers, and peasants, most of them with democratic-socialist political sympathies. As war prisoners and deserters from the Austro-Hungarian Army on Russian soil, they had joined a small unit of resident Czech nationalists in 1917 to fight against Austria-Hungary as an independent corps of the Russian Army. After the Brest-Litovsk Treaty the Czech legion was determined to join the Czech Army fighting the Central Powers in France. Because of the rundown state of the shipping system and the dangers of crossing enemy lines, the legion decided to return to Europe via Vladivostok and the USA. An agreement was made with the Soviet authorities, with whom at that time the legion was on good terms, whereby the Czechs were allowed to travel eastward on the trans-Siberian railway 'not as fighting units, but as groups of free citizens who carry with them a specified number of weapons for self-defence against counter-revolutionary attacks'. All other weapons were to be turned over to the Soviet authorities in Penza. Had this agreement been adhered to by both sides, the history of the civil war would have taken a very different course. However, the passage of the Czech forces was marked by increasing mistrust and tension; the provincial soviets accused the Czechs of trying to conceal extra weapons in their railway compartments, and attempted to confiscate them. Events came to a head on 14 May when the Cheliabinsk town soviet in the Urals arrested several Czech soldiers who had become involved in a brawl with some Hungarian prisoners of war. The remaining Czech troops occupied the town and disarmed the red guard. Subsequently, Czech units occupied other towns on the trans-Siberian railway, including Penza on 28 May.

The Czech revolt raised the hopes of the Right SRs. Although the Eighth (Right SR) Party Assembly in May had resolved that the Russian people should fight the Bolsheviks without foreign intervention, the party's leaders in Samara convinced themselves that it would be possible to engage the support of the Czech legion against Germany without involving it in the struggle against the Bolshevik regime (indeed, the Czechs had made their intentions clear not to get involved in Russian internal affairs). Throughout the history of the Komuch the position of the SR leaders was highly ambiguous: were they fighting the Bolshevik regime in order to continue the war against the Central

[26] Cited in Maiskii, p. 46.

powers, or was their opposition to the Brest-Litovsk Treaty merely a bait to win the support of the Czech legion against the Bolsheviks? The truth probably includes both propositions, although the precise role of the Czech legion was never made clear.[27] The SR leaders spoke about its use against the Bolsheviks as an interim measure until the establishment of the People's Army (Narodnaia Armiia), but in fact they remained dependent upon the Czechs until the end because of the weakness of the military forces of the Komuch.

One of the SR leaders in Samara, I. M. Brushvit, went to Penza in the hope of persuading the Czech leaders to help in the overthrow of the Soviet regime in Samara. To begin with, the Czechs were unwilling to join the SRs. But Brushvit won them over, mainly on the basis of exaggerated reports of the connections between the Right SRs and the French government. The Czechs, whose main objective was to keep moving eastward, agreed to install the Right SRs in government in Samara. But they made it clear that they were not prepared to remain in the provincial capital. On 29 May the Czechs' armoured train, with Brushvit inside it, entered Syzran'. The town soviet, facing internal opposition from the local factory and railway workers, surrendered to the Czechs and signed a treaty which greatly facilitated the progress of the legion towards Samara.[28] Having assembled their forces in Syzran', the Czechs marched on Samara, which was still in a state of strikes and partial anarchy after the uprising of 15–18 May. The provincial soviet was able to mobilize only 2,000 party activists—many of them Latvian factory workers evacuated to Samara since 1915—to defend the city. Without military training, they stood no chance against 8,000 professional soldiers. The Reds lost 150 and the Czechs no more than six men during the battle for Samara on 7–8 June. Several Red officers who were sympathetic to the Left SRs joined the Czechs; and hundreds of soldiers deserted, as the superior forces of the enemy approached.[29]

The ease with which the small but well-disciplined Czech force was able to occupy the Volga towns underlined the military and political weaknesses of the Soviet regime during this period, when, as Trotsky put it, 'there was no food, there was no army, the railways were completely disorganized and the machinery of the state was just

[27] *Grazhdanskaia voina na Volge v 1918 godu: Sbornik pervyi*, Prague, 1930, pp. 38–9, 72.

[28] Ibid., p. 78; F. G. Popov, *Chekho-slovatskii miatezh i samarskaia uchredilovka*, Samara, 1932, pp. 55–64, 72; TsGAOR, f. 393, op. 13, d. 429, l. 76.

[29] F. G. Popov, *Chekho-slovatskii miatezh*, p. 73; N. N. Leitenant, 'Zapiski belogvardeitsa', *Arkhiv russkoi revoliutsii*, vol. 10, 1923, p. 72; B. N. Alekseev, 'Bor'ba s chekho-slovatskim miatezhom v Povolzh'e', *Proletarskaia revoliutsiia*, vol. 4, no. 75, 1928, p. 61. On the chaos among the Red forces during the Czech attack see *Sbornik vospominanii neposredstvennykh uchastnikov grazhdanskoi voiny*, kn. 2, Moscow, 1922, pp. 39–40.

beginning to take shape'.[30] Because of the hand-to-mouth nature of their regime, the Bolsheviks overlooked the dangers of the Czech legion getting bogged down in eastern Russia. Most of the soldiers in the Volga garrisons had been sent to the Ural'sk front during the spring, leaving the towns and the trans-Siberian railway open to Czech attack. In the event, the towns were defended almost exclusively by Bolshevik party activists—a reflection of the haste with which the defence had to be organized and the unwillingness of the non-party population to fight a civil war. Very few non-party inhabitants of the provincial towns were prepared to risk their lives for the soviet, especially in the towns (like Syzran') where the soviet had been over-zealous in seizing property and arresting anti-government agitators. Some of the town soviets were dominated by the SRs, and were ready to compromise with the Czechs. As for the peasants, they were quick to organize the defence of their own villages, but were reluctant to defend the towns or to join the Red Army, which in many areas was still associated with the vandalism of the urban red guards.[31] The localism of the rural soviets greatly complicated the organization of the Red Army and the defence of the Soviet Republic during the summer of 1918 (see ch. 6, sect. 4).

Because of the weakness of the Soviet authorities, the Komuch was soon able to extend its territory into the provinces of Samara, Ufa, Simbirsk, Kazan', and Saratov (see Map 3). The Czech legion and the White regiments, which formed the nucleus of the People's Army, brought the towns of Buzuluk, Buguruslan, Abdulino, and Khvalynsk under the rule of the Komuch during June. On 6 July they occupied Ufa. The capture of Simbirsk (22 July) was facilitated by the mutiny led by M. A. Murav'ev, the Left SR Commander on the Eastern Front, on 10–11 July, which severely disrupted the work of the Red Army in the provincial capital.[32] To the north and the south of this territory the influence of the Komuch was weaker. Kazan' was the last major provincial centre in the Volga to fall to the Komuch (6 August) and the

[30] L. Trotsky, *My Life*, Gloucester, Mass., 1970, p. 395.

[31] See TsGAOR, f. 393, op. 3, d. 327, l. 278; d. 334, l. 105.

[32] On 10 July Murav'ev arrived from Kazan' with 1,000 troops and arrested a number of Soviet, party, and Red Army leaders (including M. N. Tukhachevskii). The mutiny, which ended on 11 July with Murav'ev's arrest and execution, was influenced by the Left-SR uprising in Moscow on 6–7 July; its principal aim was to join with the Czechs and force a passage through western Russia in order to continue the war with Germany. Evan Mawdsley (*The Russian Civil War*, London, 1987, p. 57) has well described the danger posed by Murav'ev: 'On the night of 10 July Communist rule on the Volga, and perhaps ultimately in all of Russia, hung by a thread. Had Murav'ev kept control he would have taken with him the largest military force that the Bolsheviks had been able to assemble. The vital grain region of the Volga would have been lost . . . The Germans might have been encouraged to attack on the Soviet western front.'

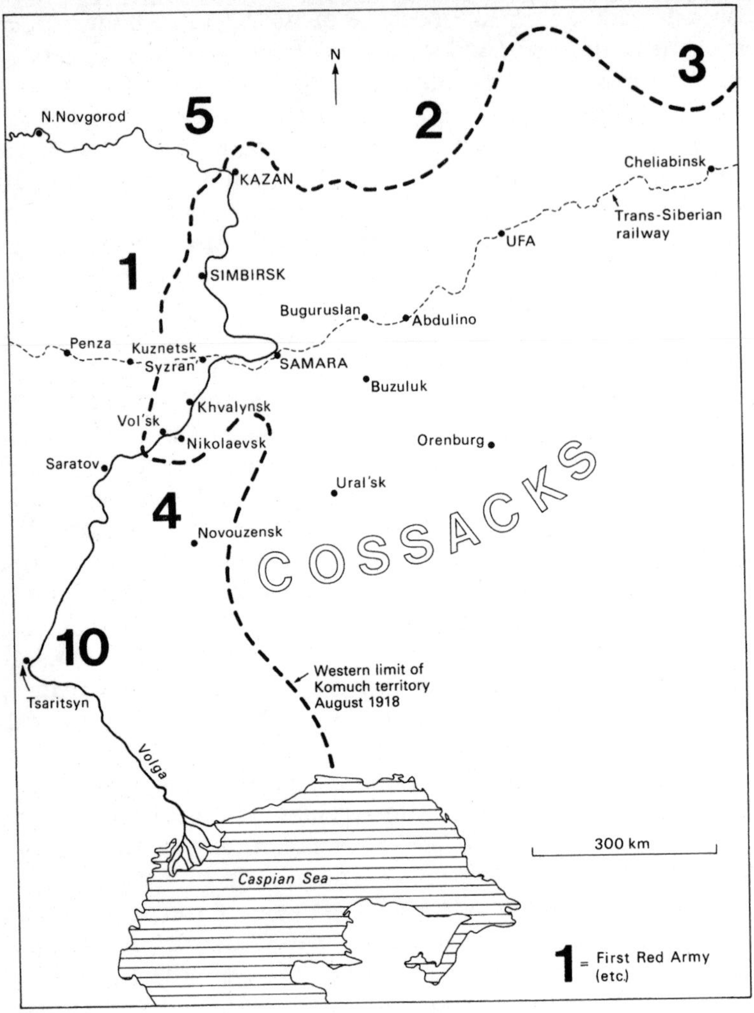

Map 3. *Territory of the Komuch*

first to be regained by the Red Army (10 September). Khvalynsk remained the southernmost point of Samara's influence, although there were major revolts in Balakovo and Vol'sk during June and July which were partly organized by Komuch agitators.[33] The Red Army retained the upper hand in the areas to the west and the south-east. The 1st Red Army, under the brilliant commander M. N. Tukhachevskii, controlled most of the right bank of the River Volga; smaller

[33] TsGAOR, f. 393, op. 3, d. 323, ll. 27–8; F. G. Popov, *1918 god v Samarskoi gubernii: Khronika sobytii*, Kuibyshev, 1972, pp. 151–2, 165, 171; *1917 god v Saratove*, p. 86.

partisan brigades, such as the one led by V. I. Chapaev, occupied the steppelands to the south of Nikolaevsk separating the forces of the Komuch from the Ural'sk Cossacks under Dutov.

After the capture of Samara on 8 June a new government was formed by the five resident members of the Constituent Assembly: Brushvit, Klimushkin, V. K. Vol'skii, I. P. Nesterov, and B. K. Fortunatov. In its early days, the government called itself the Samara Provincial Committee of Members of the Constituent Assembly, but the first two words were soon dropped as the territory of the new authority expanded. To the great irritation of its White allies in Siberia, the Committee thus presented itself as the legitimate heir of the all-Russian Constituent Assembly. The anti-Bolshevik members of the disbanded parliament were invited to join the Samara government: by the end of August forty-six members, including Viktor Chernov, had arrived from eighteen different provinces (seventeen members had been elected to the Assembly on the list of the Soviet of workers and peasant deputies; ten were SR representatives of the peasant soviets). By the end of September nearly 100 members of the Assembly had arrived in Samara.[34] The majority of the members were on the right wing of the SR party. The Kadets and the Mensheviks had few seats in the Constituent Assembly and were in any case hesitant to support the Komuch. The Kadets preferred their own alliance with the Whites in Siberia and south Russia. The Menshevik Central Committee in Moscow rejected the Samara government as 'just another SR adventure', although a conference of eleven provincial Menshevik organizations at the beginning of August supported a resolution in favour of the Komuch and appointed a regional committee to cover the area of its jurisdiction.[35]

The administrative structure of the Samara government was more solid in the towns than in the countryside. A significant portion of the lower-ranking bureaucracy of the town dumas and the district *zemstva* had remained in place during the Soviet period. The Samara provincial economic council (*sovnarkhoz*), which had been established under the Bolsheviks, was considered sufficiently reliable (or necessary) to remain in office under the Komuch. Elections to the town dumas were held in August and September. Between 30% and 40% of the electorate took part (mainly the propertied classes, the intelligentsia, and the skilled workers); the turn-out was roughly equal to that in the Soviet elections of 1919. The majority voted for the 'socialist bloc', although the liberal-conservative parties did well in Simbirsk and Ufa.[36] The

[34] *Vestnik Komiteta Uchreditel'nogo Sobraniia* (Samara), no. 41, 26 Aug. 1918, p. 2; Leitenant, p. 84.

[35] D. Footman, *Civil War in Russia*, London, 1961, pp. 102–3.

[36] Maiskii, p. 145; Garmiza, pp. 45–6.

influence of the conservatives, which was most noticeable in the army and the secondary institutions of the Samara government, contributed to the souring of relations between the Komuch and the workers and peasants. In the towns the new government encountered opposition from the factory workers; it was unable to maintain control without repressions and arrests; and it was forced to abuse the very political liberties which it had proclaimed on coming to power.[37] In the country areas the government was unable, from the outset, to extend its influence by democratic means. Because of the chronic shortage of reliable rural officials, the higher authorities were forced to depend upon provincial and district plenipotentiaries, who were given special powers under martial law to enforce all government orders, to remove officials from office, to break up public meetings, and to arrest suspected Bolsheviks. The government specified that the plenipotentiaries were to function in the manner of the provincial and district governors of the Provisional Government. Indeed, many of them had been governors or *zemstvo* chairmen during 1917.[38]

The weakness of the Samara government in the countryside was highlighted by its inability to re-establish the *volost'*-level *zemstva*, the official organs of rural administration under the Komuch. A Decree of 19 June ordered the re-election of the *volost'*-level *zemstva* on the lines set out by the Provisional Government. A meeting of at least one-quarter of the *zemstvo* electors was entitled to pass legally binding resolutions until the completion of the elections.[39] At the end of July the Komuch was forced to recognize in one of its own circulars that the *zemstva* 'have either lost all authority in the communes, or have lost touch with the needs of the moment'.[40] The representative responsible for the re-establishment of the *volost'*-level *zemstva* in Samara *uezd* complained in mid-August:

> in many *volosti* . . . the *zemstvo* administration is still not in fully working order and all the necessary work is being carried out by one man. As a result, many government orders on the establishment of the People's Army, on the maintenance of public order, on the regulation of the land, and on questions of food supply are either enforced very slowly or are not enforced at all.[41]

One of the main obstacles to the re-establishment of the *volost'*-level *zemstva* was the shortage of suitable officials. The village elders had, for the most part, been removed from office during 1917; no one

[37] G. Lelevich, *V dni samarskoi uchredilki*, Moscow, 1921.
[38] Maiskii, pp. 61–2; Garmiza, pp. 40–4.
[39] Garmiza, p. 44.
[40] *Vestnik Komiteta Uchreditel'nogo Sobraniia* (Samara), no. 24, 6 Aug. 1918, p. 1.
[41] Ibid., no. 34, 17 Aug. 1918, p. 4. See further *Chetyre mesiatsa uchredilovshchiny*, Samara, 1919, pp. 26–7.

wanted to take their place after the intervening period of Soviet rule. Some of the *volost' zemstvo* elections could not be completed because of communal boycotts. A large number of the communes refused to pay the *zemstvo* taxes, so that the *volost' zemstvo* floundered at an early stage because of financial difficulties: its schools and hospitals became run-down and its employees left their posts. In some places the VIK actually remained in power under the Komuch, but referred to itself in communiqués to the higher authorities as the '*zemstvo*'. Such deception was facilitated by the fact that during 1918 most of the VIKs still used the stationery of the former *zemstvo* administration. The Komuch was unable to stamp out this subterfuge, mainly on account of the shortages of rural instructors. The supervision of the *zemstva* had to be left to the Cossacks and the officers of the People's Army, whose tendency to use heavy-handed methods only worsened the government's relations with the peasantry. A good illustration of this is in the village of Pestravka (Nikolaevsk *uezd*), where the soviet had remained in power after the establishment of the Komuch. Two army officers who were sent in to condemn the soviet at a village gathering on 21 July were subjected by the peasants to a *samosud* and then brutally murdered. A complete brigade of the People's Army later arrived from Samara to substitute a *zemstvo* for the soviet. After the departure of the brigade, however, the peasants disbanded the *zemstvo* and elected a new soviet.[42]

Three main areas of policy determined the relationship between the Samara government and the peasantry: food procurement, land reform, and the organization of the People's Army. In each of these areas the government encountered an increasing level of opposition from the peasantry; it is misleading to suggest, as Stephen Berk has done, that the peasantry was 'the only group that did not pose a problem' for the Komuch.[43]

The Komuch repealed the Bolshevik state monopoly of food procurement, established in May 1918, in favour of a provisions policy similar to that of the Provisional Government. The government retained the right to fix the prices of grain but contracted rights of food procurement to private and co-operative organizations. The *zemstva*, which under the Provisional Government had been responsible for food distribution in the localities, played a similar role to that of the local soviets; they tended to retain as many foodstuffs as possible within their own areas and generally disrupted the operations of the centralized procurement agencies. The regional provisions assemblies

[42] F. G. Popov, *Chekho-slovatskii miatezh*, p. 157.

[43] S. Berk, 'The Democratic Counter-revolution: *Komuch* and the Civil War on the Volga', *Canadian-American Slavic Studies*, vol. 7, 1973, p. 450.

of the Samara government argued for greater centralization of the food procurement system, but it was recognized that the central food control agencies were paralysed by over-bureaucracy. The dominant procurement agency was the Grain Council (Khlebnyi sovet), which comprised three merchants, three representatives of the provincial Co-operative Union, one delegate from the state Grain Bank, and one from the provisions administration of the Samara government. The Grain Council organized food procurements through the co-operatives from the areas of Siberia under White control. It also subcontracted procurement rights in Siberia to small and medium-sized private traders with capital holdings up to the value of 50,000 rb. Since the traders were given a relatively high rate of commission by the Council, the period of the Komuch witnessed a rapid expansion of the private grain trade between Samara and Siberia. During the four months of Komuch rule the amount of grain imported privately from Siberia equalled the amount of grain procured directly by the government.[44]

The Komuch was blessed by the largest harvest in the Volga region since the pre-war period. People who arrived in Samara from Soviet Russia were invariably struck by the abundance and the cheap prices of peasant foodstuffs in the markets under the Komuch.[45] The liberal market policies of the Samara government undoubtedly helped to increase the movement of foodstuffs into the towns; the stable peasant farmers were eager to return to the free market system in view of the chronic shortages of manufactures, metals, kerosene, and other materials in the rural localities. But it would be wrong to jump from this to the conclusion that the provisions policies of the Komuch had tapped a deep source of political loyalty among the peasantry. The market controls of the first six months of Soviet power had been established by the local soviets themselves, in accordance with the consumption and production needs of the village communities; the oppressive effects of the Bolshevik grain monopoly, which were to cause widespread peasant resistance after 1918, had still not been registered in the majority of the rural localities by the time the Komuch came to power. The busy market in foodstuffs under the Komuch resulted not so much from the government's liberal policies as from the large size of the harvest surplus and the acute peasant demand for industrial consumer goods. The market in foodstuffs was just as busy during the autumn of 1918, under the Bolshevik grain

[44] *Vestnik Komiteta Uchreditel'nogo Sobraniia* (Samara), no. 26, 8 Aug. 1918, p. 4; *ISG*, no. 1, 1 Dec. 1918, p. 5; Maiskii, p. 87; Garmiza, pp. 151 ff.; K. M. Krasil'nikova, 'Bor'ba za khleb v Srednem Povolzh'e v period inostrannoi voennoi interventsii i grazhdanskoi voiny', kand. diss., Kuibyshev, 1968, pp. 108–9.

[45] See e.g. Maiskii, p. 32.

monopoly (see ch. 6, sect. 1). Indeed, it could even be argued that the fall of the Samara government and the establishment of a somewhat 'relaxed'[46] Bolshevik grain monopoly during the autumn of 1918 resulted in a more favourable market situation for the peasant farmers than the one immediately preceding it. The last days of the Samara government were marked by a growing food-supply crisis in the towns: the volume of free market imports declined sharply, on account of the shortages of industrial consumer goods. At the end of August bread had to be rationed in the provincial capital at ¼ *funt* per person per day. The provisions organs called for the compulsory procurement of grain and the requisitioning of livestock for the People's Army (12,000 horses were taken by the end of September).[47] The exigencies of the civil war had forced the Komuch to increase the level of state control of the peasant economy.

The Komuch supported the first ten points of the land reform passed at the first, and only, session of the Constituent Assembly on 5 January 1918. The determination of the Right SR leaders not to repeat their stand against the immediate redivision of the land, which had lost them so much peasant support during 1917, cost them the political alliance of the Kadet party in the Komuch.[48] The law of 5 January nationalized the land and prohibited all private land sales. The land was put under the control of the *zemstvo* land committees, which were officially re-established (though most of them were actually the former soviet land department). The peasantry gained nothing from this law which they had not already taken for themselves. On the other hand, a Decree passed by the Komuch on 22 July took away from the control of the communes all the winter arable fields which had been previously sown by the landowners (approximately one-third of the sown area in private ownership prior to the land redivisions). The landowners were entitled to reclaim this land from the communes; if the landowner was no longer present then the harvest was to belong to the provisions authorities of the government. A second directive on 25 July instructed the district plenipotentiaries to 'call for the help of the armed forces in the event of any trespass on the land'.[49] The purpose of the Samara government had been to find some 'temporary corrective'

[46] Lars T. Lih has noted a 'relaxation' of the Bolshevik grain monopoly during the autumn of 1918, compared with the previous summer ('Bolshevik Razverstka and War Communism', *Slavic Review*, vol. 54, 1986, pp. 673–88). The significance of this finding is discussed in ch. 6, sect. 1, below.

[47] *Vestnik Komiteta Uchreditel'nogo Sobraniia* (Samara), no. 38, 23 Aug. 1918, p. 2; *Grazhdanskaia voina na Volge*, p. 224.

[48] *Grazhdanskaia voina na Volge*, p. 61.

[49] F. G. Popov, *Za vlast' sovetov: Razgrom samarskoi uchredilovki*, Kuibyshev, 1959, pp. 131–2; Maisskii, pp. 81–3; Garmiza, pp. 179–80. A Decree of 1 Aug. 1918 extended

to the 'anarchic wave' of land redivisions following the October Decree on Land.[50] Instead, the impression had been given to the peasants, especially the poorest ones, among whom the largest portion of the winter-sown fields of the gentry had been divided, that the government intended to restore the property rights of the landowners in full. This impression was reinforced by the fact that in some localities the squires interpreted the Decree of 22 July as a license to take the law into their own hands: with the help of a Cossack brigade, or an *ad hoc* militia, they forcibly regained bits of their land and even some of their livestock. The effect of such actions on the mood of the peasantry was described by an eyewitness in Buzuluk district at the end of July:

> in the villages, especially near the large estates, the mood of the peasantry is depressed . . . The repressive measures against Bolshevik suspects and the return of the gentry squires has instilled an awkward sense of foreboding among the peasantry. This is clearly manifested in the return of the squires to their estates. The former landowners travel around the villages, interrogating the peasants; they establish guards on their land and threaten to send in the Cossacks to make the peasants knuckle down.[51]

In the village of Natal'in (Buguruslan *uezd*) a group of peasants who had refused to give back to the ex-landowner the grain which they had harvested from his winter fields were publicly flogged by a Cossack officer. In Miroliubovka *volost'* (Buzuluk *uezd*) the Black Hundreds threatened to shoot a group of peasant hostages if the commune did not return the winter fields to the former landowners. In Dubovo-Umet *volost'* (Samara *uezd*) the village communes of Kolyvan', Viazovka, and Kamenka were each fined 100,000 rb. for having harvested the winter fields of the landowner. When all the harvested grain had been confiscated from the communes, the peasants were given the chance to buy it back from the landowner.[52]

Of all the policies of the Samara government, the organization of the People's Army had the deepest effect on peasant–state relations. The survival of the Komuch depended upon the military mobilization of the Volga population. The Czech legion was unwilling to prop up the government indefinitely. From the end of August, its morale began to weaken as the prospects of a quick return to Europe grew more distant. The majority of the Czech soldiers became exhausted just at the moment when it first became clear that the period of easy victories

this right to the Orenburg Cossack region, outlawed the confiscation of livestock and tools (except harvesting implements), and restored private rental relations within the Cossack territory (Garmiza, p. 180).

50 *Grazhdanskaia voina na Volge*, p. 118.
51 Cited in F. G. Popov, *Za vlast' sovetov*, p. 132.
52 Ibid., p. 133; Garmiza, p. 181.

against disorganized Bolshevik partisans was coming to an end—the defeats at Kazan' (10 September) and Simbirsk (12 September) were a rude shock. The majority of the rank-and-file Czechs were alienated by the out-and-out monarchism of the military commanders in Samara and Ufa, which spread down into the officer corps of the People's Army.[53] Many began to doubt the support of the Entente powers for the Czech national cause; they questioned the whole purpose of their struggle against the Bolsheviks. The legion began to disintegrate. Some deserted to the Red Army. Others became more interested in selling the legion's vast quantities of military provisions to the surrounding population than in fighting the enemy.[54]

One of the first orders of the Samara government called upon volunteers for the People's Army. The length of the voluntary service was fixed at three months; there was a monthly salary of 15 rb. for a single man and a graded allowance starting at 100 rb. for men with families. The number of volunteers between June and September was estimated to have been no more than between 6,000 and 10,000 people, most of them townsmen. Officers and cadets of the Imperial Army, white-collar workers, students, isolated groups of workers, and Tatar or Bashkir nationalists (who were allowed to form their own army units) volunteered, for the most part, because they supported the anti-Bolshevik movement. But war-prisoners, refugees, and the unemployed more often joined because the material benefits of the army offered them the best possible means to support themselves and their families.[55]

In the country areas the number of volunteers was insignificant. Most of them must have come from the richest peasant stratum, especially in the south-eastern steppelands around Novouzensk, where some of the peasants had earlier supported the Ural'sk Cossacks.[56] This is reflected in the resolutions of the village and *volost'* soviets after the fall of the Samara government—especially in those concerning the confiscation of property from peasants who had volunteered for the People's Army. A resolution of the Androsovka

[53] See *Grazhdanskaia voina na Volge*, pp. 75–6; Maiskii, pp. 153–6.

[54] K. V. Sakharov, *Belaia Sibir': Vnutrennaia voina 1918–20 gg.*, Munich, 1923, pp. 216, 221–3; Leitenant, pp. 82–3; A. P. Stepanov, 'Simbirskaia operatsiia', *Beloe delo*, vol. 1, Berlin, 1926, pp. 85 ff.

[55] Maiskii, pp. 149–50, 158–9; N. N. Goleevskii, 'Leto na Volge: 1918 god', in *Russian Emigré Archives*, vol. 2, Fresno, Cal., 1973, p. 338; G. Stewart, *The White Armies of Russia*, New York, 1933, p. 145; Sakharov, p. 215; A. Zaitsev, *1918 god: Ocherki po istorii russkoi grazhdanskoi voiny*, n.p., 1934, pp. 169, 215, 200; *Krasnaia byl': Sbornik samarskogo gubernskogo biuro istparta*, no. 3, Oct. Samara, 1923, p. 99; *Grazhdanskaia voina na Volge*, pp. 79, 86; A. I. Denikin, *Ocherki russkoi smuty*, vol. 3, *Beloe dvizhenie i bor'ba dobrovol'cheskoi armii, mai–oktiabr' 1918 goda*, Berlin, 1924, pp. 96–7; *Vestnik Komiteta Uchreditel'nogo Sobraniia* (Samara), no. 35, 18 Aug. 1918, p. 4.

[56] See *Godovshchina sotsial'noi revoliutsii v Saratove*, pp. 52–3; I. Kutiakov, *S Chapaevym po ural'skim stepiam*, Moscow, 1928, pp. 27 ff.

volost' soviet (Nikolaevsk *uezd*) on 2 June 1920 gives a detailed account of the property confiscated from the Morev family during the autumn of 1918:

In Androsovka *volost'* the following property was confiscated from the kulaks who went off with the White Guards with counter-revolutionary intentions:

1. a semi-stone house with outbuildings situated in the village of Androsovka, valued at 30,000 rb. before the war, and belonging to the local kulak, a rich one, and his father-in-law, the big landowner, Mironov, who [the kulak] was also a petty wholesale trader and manufacturer—Nikolai Leont'ev Morev, whose son Vladimir volunteered for the White Guard and agitated during the period of the Czech rule in this *volost'*, and whose two daughters became nurses in the camp of the White Guard and then went off with the Whites.

2. a semi-stone house with outbuildings situated in the village of Androsovka, valued at 30,000 rb. before the war, and belonging to the brothers Andrei, Pavel, Mikhail, Gerasim, and Vasilii Leont'ev Morev, who all went off with the White Guards with the exception of Pavel. The Morev brothers are big farmers and exploiters of hired labour, who used to rent 1,000 *des.* of Crown land and who owned more than 500 *des.* of peasant land which they purchased in the Stolypinite manner, and who sowed every year up to 500 *des.* of grain with their own labour and tools and with the help of hired hands. The Morev brothers today have the use of a house and outbuildings in Studenets *volost'* on the Kamyshin *khutor*.

The house of Nikolai Morev is at the moment used by the Commandant of army Depot no. 291, and the house of the Morev brothers accommodates the *narodnyi dom*, the library, the party cell, the Komsomol, and the Land Department.[57]

Not all the volunteers from the rural areas came from the richest peasant stratum, of course. The middle peasants had good cause to join the People's Army in those villages where the Red Army had terrorized the population, or where the *kombed* had brutalized the peasant farmers during the collection of the food levy.[58] However, most villages in the Volga region had not yet experienced the full effects of the Red Terror, and were therefore unresponsive to the call to arms by the government in Samara. Other villages were frightened to align themselves with the People's Army because of the local influence of the Bolshevik partisans, or because it was rumoured that the Red Army would soon reach the village and there might be reprisals against the families of the peasants who had joined the anti-Bolshevik forces. The Red partisans were highly effective in spreading such rumours: the district plenipotentiaries in the outlying districts of the Komuch

[57] GAKO, f. 109, op. 4, d. 59, 11. 53–4.

[58] See e.g. Goleevskii, pp. 240–1; *Vestnik Komiteta Uchreditel'nogo Sobraniia* (Samara), no. 62, 21 Sept. 1918, p. 3.

territory were frequently calling upon the government to put down phantom Bolshevik uprisings.[59]

The primary concern of the vast majority of the peasantry was not to get itself involved in the civil war any more than it had to. The peasants were willing to fight against the landowners in their own localities: they formed their own peasant brigades; and they were, even ready to fight for the Red Army as long as it was seen to be defending the revolution in their own locality. But the peasants came to see the civil war increasingly as an alien political struggle between the socialist parties. Their attitude towards this struggle was one of indifference, as a recruiting officer of the People's Army in Simbirsk province pointed out:

> the mood of the peasants is indifferent, they just want to be left to themselves. The Bolsheviks were here—that's good, they say; the Bolsheviks went away—that's no shame, they say. As long as there is bread then let's pray to God, and who needs the Guards?—let them fight it out by themselves, we will stand aside. It is well known that playing it by ear is the best side to be on.[60]

At the Saratov provincial peasant soviet assembly on 30 May one of the delegates expressed a similar cynicism towards the struggles between the political parties:

> the cause of all this strife is our own stupidity, the fact that brothers are fighting each other. So many socialist parties were formed, nearly fifty different parties! You know their names . . . all of them are socialists! But just as the peasants were beginning to learn about all these parties, so they began to accuse one another of not representing the peasants' interests.[61]

The position of the delegates at the Samara peasant assembly, organized by the Komuch on 16 September, was similar to that of the Saratov peasant soviet delegates. One delegate underlined: 'the peasants say they will only fight enemies . . . they will not fight their own brothers'. A second delegate said: 'the peasants refuse to support a war between the political parties'. A third delegate proposed that the Komuch should 'try to come to an agreement with the Bolsheviks in order to bring this civil war to an end'. And a fourth delegate added: 'the continuation of the civil war ought to be decided by a referendum, and until we know the opinion of the whole population we do not have

[59] See Stepanov, p. 90; *Simbirskaia guberniia v gody grazhdanskoi voiny mai 1918–mart 1919 gg., Ul'ianovsk, 1958*, p. 100.

[60] Cited in Garmiza, p. 254.

[61] *PSG*, p. 67.

a moral right to vote on this resolution [put forward by Klimushkin to continue the war effort]'.[62]

The goals of the anti-Bolshevik movement, as presented by the Komuch, were incomprehensible to the majority of the peasantry. The nationalist call for the renewal of the war against Germany clashed with the peasantry's localist and pacifist attitudes. 'The war with Germany and all wars are bad,' resolved the Adelaidovka village assembly (Buguruslan *uezd*). 'If we do not fight, then the German soldiers will not take away our territory,' reasoned the peasants at the Bobrovka village assembly (Buzuluk *uezd*).[63] 'In our village nobody knows about [the Treaty],' a delegate from Buzuluk district informed the Samara peasant assembly on 16 September; 'We only know what we can see.'[64] Many peasant resolutions expressed confusion as to the reason why the Czechs and the foreign prisoners of war fought on the side of the 'patriots' in Samara.[65] A Komuch agitator in Simbirsk province claimed there was general confusion among the peasant-soldiers in the People's Army about the aims of the anti-Bolshevik movement: 'Many soldiers, especially the peasants, come on their own or in groups to see me at the provincial office and to complain that they do not understand what the new power is fighting for or who is leading it.'[66] The head of the Samara district police reached a similar conclusion:

> 'the population is poorly enlightened about the aims of the People's Army and misunderstands the course of events. The greater part of the toiling peasantry is completely indifferent to the present historic moment and is a long way from the correct viewpoint on the future political development of Russia. The idea has taken root among the population that the 'bourgeois' have again started a war and that the 'peace' signed by the Bolsheviks at Brest is unfavourable only to the 'bourgeois', while the peasantry, according to their expression, 'has suffered no harm and will not suffer any harm [from the peace], so let the bourgeois fight by themselves'.[67]

Such class hostilities must have been highlighted by the epaulettes and the ribbon of St George worn by the volunteer corps, which symbolized the disciplinarianism of the Imperial army, and the dominance within it of the landowners.

The poor response to the call for volunteers forced the Samara

[62] Garmiza, pp. 259–60; *Krasnaia byl'*, no. 3, pp. 59–60; F. G. Popov, *Chekho-slovatskii miatezh*, pp. 168–9, 171–2.
[63] Cited in *Krasnaia byl'*, no. 3, p. 53.
[64] Cited in F. G. Popov, *Chekho-slovatskii miatezh*, p. 169.
[65] See F. G. Popov, *Za vlast' sovetov*, pp. 135–6, Chernov, p. 383.
[66] Cited in Garmiza, p. 35.
[67] *Vestnik Komiteta Uchreditel'nogo Sobraniia* (Samara), no. 38, 23 Aug. 1918, p. 4.

government to introduce military conscription. On 30 June the Komuch authorities published the mobilization order for all able-bodied men born in 1897 and 1898 (aged between 20 and 21). The government mobilized these age groups, because it thought the older and more experienced soldiers were likely to be 'infected' by the radical socialism which had swept through the army in 1917; the army reserves, on the other hand, were not only politically unreliable, but also badly trained. The 20- and 21-year-olds were too young to have fought in the war: thus it was thought that, although they would require training, it would be easier to mobilize and discipline them.[68]

This turned out to be wishful thinking on the part of the military authorities. The proportion of the conscripted men who were actually recruited was small (although it is difficult to give precise figures). Ivan Maiskii, a Menshevik in the Komuch who later joined the Bolsheviks, estimated that no more than 15,000 out of the 50,000 conscripted men turned up at the recruiting stations.[69] Klimushkin, on the other hand, cited the testimony of his own military authorities in the Komuch that between 65% and 70% of the conscripts were recruited.[70] A third memoir account by an official of the Komuch estimated that only 21,000 of the 120,000 possible recruits were actually mobilized.[71] Whatever the figure, it was not enough. In the localities the rate of appearance was highly variable: in Samara district 7,894 out of 11,000 conscripts were recruited; whereas in Buzuluk district the figure was no more than 1,564 out of 14,441 conscripts. In Syzran' the appearance rate varied from 10% to almost 100%, according to the location of the village: the rates were much higher in the eastern *volosti*, closest to Samara, than in the western *volosti*, which bordered on the front.[72] Klimushkin believed that it was generally the case that the peasants could be mobilized in the centre of the Komuch territory, in the areas most fully integrated into the Samara administration, but not in the peripheral areas, where the Red Army was closest.[73] This is certainly confirmed by the available evidence: in Belebei district, in the far north-eastern corner of the Komuch territory, only nine conscripts were recruited during August; in the southern areas of Nikolaevsk district, where the Red partisans were active, the peasantry was said to

[68] P. P. Petrov, *Ot Volgi do Tikhogo Okeana v riadakh belykh (1918–22 gg.)*, Riga, 1930, pp. 25–6; Zaitsev, p. 172; *Grazhdanskaia voina na Volge*, p. 80. These principles were partly drawn from the experience of the Ural'sk Cossack army in the spring of 1918.

[69] Maiskii, p. 162.

[70] *Grazhdanskaia voina na Volge*, pp. 81–2.

[71] Ibid., pp. 198–9.

[72] Ibid., pp. 82–4.

[73] Ibid., p. 82.

be impossible to mobilize.[74] If it is generally applicable, then Klimushkin's theory may tell us a great deal about why the Bolsheviks won the civil war: the Red Army was generally able to mobilize the peasants in the villages immediately behind their front lines (on account of the peasantry's fear of the return of the landowners), but the People's Army was not (because of the influence of the Red partisans and the peasantry's fear of the Red Terror). This was a crippling disadvantage for the anti-Bolsheviks, given the tendency of the peasant recruits in both armies to desert as soon as the civil war began to take them a long way from their farms. It effectively meant that the People's Army, which was not able to put more than 10,000 capable soldiers in the field at any one time, had no chance to advance into Soviet territory.

The level of peasant desertion from the People's Army was at least as high as the level of desertion from the Red Army (see ch. 6, sect. 5). However, the disciplinary structure of the former was much inferior. The recruiting stations, according to Klimushkin, 'literally did not know what to do with the recruits', because they lacked the uniforms and guns to turn them into soldiers; many recruits had to remain at the station for several days before being assigned to units (some had to be sent home!). The soldiers received little military training before being put into battle, so that panic often broke out in the ranks at the first moment of danger.[75] Some of the recruits, especially the poorer ones, stayed only long enough to get their guns and uniforms before deserting (these items had a high market value in the countryside).[76] During the harvest period, when the Red Army began to advance eastwards, the peasant-soldiers deserted *en masse*: nearly 3,000 deserted from the Samara garrison during September; whole units were said to be deserting from the front lines, where the death penalty had to be introduced in a vain effort to stop the disintegration of the People's Army.[77]

The Komuch counteracted the peasant desertions with a series of repressive measures in the localities. The district plenipotentiaries and police departments were given sweeping legal powers against the deserters. Punitive (mainly Cossack) detachments were sent into the countryside, where they set up 'field courts' (reminiscent of the notorious field courts martial established during the suppression of the peasant uprisings in 1906) to enforce the mobilization order by any means, including the declaration of full-scale war on the deserters'

[74] *Grazhdanskaia viona na Volge*, p. 82; Garmiza, p. 36.
[75] Ibid., p. 87; Leitenant, p. 82.
[76] Denikin, p. 97.
[77] *Grazhdanskaia voina na Volge*, pp. 84–5, 88; Footman, p. 114.

villages. In some places the families and even the neighbours of the deserters were publicly flogged, beaten up or shot. In others the detachment threatened to mobilize random groups of peasants unless the deserters appeared; the village was surrounded by troops and then burned to the ground when the deserters failed to give themselves up. The punitive detachments sometimes organized *samosudy* for the Red partisans who had been caught; the villagers were often only too ready to see them punished for the troubles they 'had brought upon' the community. Hundreds of arbitrary arrests were made, especially after the government had banned any discussion of the mobilization order at the village assembly.[78] At the Samara peasant assembly in September a number of delegates complained that 'it has become impossible to speak freely in the village, there are spies and denunciations, and arrests are made on the basis of these denunciations'.[79]

Some of the punitive detachments were led by the former landowners, who knew the villages; it was hard to prevent them from using this opportunity to avenge the loss of their land to the peasants. In the village of Natal'in (Buguruslan *uezd*) a Cossack detachment flogged not only the relatives of the deserters, but also the leaders of the peasant commune who had organized the seizure of the gentry estate—a brutal act of repression deliberately designed to 'break the spirit' of the defiant peasants, and highly reminiscent of the gentry reaction of 1906–7. In the village of Dmitrievka (in the Orenburg region) another Cossack detachment flogged all the men of the village as a punishment for the division of the gentry land; over a period of three weeks 100 peasants were given a total of nearly 4,000 lashes. In the village of Prolei-Kasha (Tetiushi *uezd*) the former landowner S. I. Lapaev, as the leader of a punitive detachment, ordered the arrest of the deserters from the People's Army. The village assembly had recently passed a resolution not to send any conscripts to the recruiting station and had established a patrol to resist the punitive forces. Lapaev's detachment was repulsed from the village, but it returned later with fifty reinforcements and surrounded the village, whose patrol fled to the woods. The detachment entered the village and convoked a meeting of the old men, who finally betrayed the whereabouts of the patrol after Lapaev had threatened to burn the village; twenty-five members of the patrol were rounded up and shot.[80]

[78] Lelevich, pp. 19–20, 38–9; Garmiza, pp. 38–9, 56–8, 62, 264–6; *Krasnoe slovo* (Samara), no. 2, 9 Oct. 1918, p. 4; F. G. Popov, *Chekho-slovatskii miatezh*, pp. 160–7.

[79] Cited in Lelevich, p. 36.

[80] F. G. Popov, *Chekho-slovatskii miatezh*, pp. 117–19; *Za vlast' sovetov: Sbornik vospominanii uchastnikov revoliutsionnykh sobytii v Tatarii*, pt. 2, Kazan', 1960, pp. 113–15.

The punitive detachments encountered a wide variety of different forms of peasant resistance. The most common was for the village assemblies to pass a resolution refusing to carry out the mobilization order. These resolutions were sometimes firm enough to put off the punitive detachments: in Natal'in *volost'* (Samara *uezd*) the village communes all passed a resolution against the mobilization order, in spite of the fact that a punitive detachment had already arrested several village leaders; nevertheless, after a week of fruitless agitation the detachment decided to depart.[81] It was more common, however, for the punitive detachment to become engaged in an open struggle with the dissident villages. In some places the underground soviet provided the organization for the peasants. In the village of B. Kamenka (Nikolaevsk *uezd*) a brigade of Czech soldiers, led by the local police commander, arrested six members of the soviet for agitating against the mobilization order. A large peasant crowd assembled, disarmed the punitive brigade, and released the soviet members. The peasant conscripts then broke into the *volost' zemstvo* and destroyed the mobilization lists. The Czechs fled to the neighbouring village of Khoroshen'koe, where they arrested three other soviet activists; but here too the villagers managed to overcome the Czechs and killed the police commander. One week later a detachment of 100 Cossacks arrived in Khoroshen'koe and flogged the peasant leaders; in B. Kamenka they shot ten soviet activists. A similar White Terror was conducted in the neighbouring *volosti*.[82] Elsewhere, the village communes, rather than the underground soviets, organized the resistance. In Dubovo-Umet *volost'* (Samara *uezd*) an assembly of 900 peasants from the village communes of Kolyvan' and Viazovyi Gai agreed to combine their forces against the punitive detachments. The Kolyvan' village assembly confirmed the agreement on 25 August in the following resolution:

In view of the fact that the new government, having taken power in its own hands, is now trying to strengthen its power and is for this reason taking stringent measures against us, the peasants, and is demanding everything we have, that is our sons, our horses, and so on . . . ; in view of the fact that the present government is far from a kindred spirit to the peasantry, which we have already learned from experience; and in view of the fact that the peasantry can expect from it nothing but the destruction of all peasant rights—we decided to resolve the following: if anybody ventures to disrupt our peaceful existence then we, as one, will be obligated to defend our rights and interests; we will immediately form a peasant army which we should all join

[81] *Vestnik Komiteta Uchreditel'nogo Sobraniia* (Samara), no. 38, 23 Aug. 1918, p. 4; no. 39, 24 Aug. 1918, p. 4.
[82] *Krasnaia byl'*, no. 3, pp. 55–6.

> to repulse the enemy . . . In view of the fact that our village of Kolyvan' is threatened by the Czechs and other hired troops of the capitalists and the bourgeoisie, we must take measures to guard our village at night, and so all able-bodied men must take their turn as guards . . .
>
> Any person who tries to sow discord in our commune with the aim of returning to the old order, or claiming past rights, or even with the aim of spying on our commune—and any person who denounces us, will be declared an enemy of the toiling peasantry. Let every traitor remember that he will be strictly punished and will not be allowed to live in the territory of the Kolyvan' commune, but will be kicked out.[83]

A similar example of peasant organization was found in the villages around St Uzeli in Buguruslan *uezd*. At a communal assembly in the village of M. Balakino the peasants resolved to march on the neighbouring village of St Uzeli 'in order to save our peasant comrades from the thievery, the beatings, and the oppressions of the Czechs'. Messengers were sent to the surrounding villages, calling upon them to arm themselves and assemble at dawn at the Bezymianka ravine, near St Uzeli. The resolution of the M. Balakino commune threatened to deprive any peasant of his land allotment if he failed to take part in the 'uprising'; the rich peasants (*bogatye*) were to be fined an additional 100 rb. for every adult male member of their household who failed to participate. The peasant 'army' stormed the village of St Uzeli, taking the 250 Czechs by surprise. The latter fled to the neighbouring village of Korovino, but on the following day managed to regain the village of St Uzeli after a prolonged battle against the peasant partisans.[84]

It is not coincidental that the peasant resistance movement was strongest in the southern and eastern borderlands of the Komuch territory where the Red partisans were strongest. A number of the villages in these areas formed partisan brigades which were later to become regular units of the Red Army. The most famous was the Domashki village brigade, formed by the members of the local *soiuz frontovikov* and partisans of the soviets in the villages of Domashki and Utevskoe. The brigade defeated a Cossack detachment in the Domashki region at the beginning of October 1918 before joining the 1st Nikolaevsk Cavalry Regiment of the Red Army. This combined force continued to fight the Cossack units on the steppe long after the fall of Samara on 7 October. It was later reformed as the 219th Domashki Rifle Division—a regular detachment of the 4th Red Army.[85]

[83] Cited in F. G. Popov, *Za vlast' sovetov*, p. 149.

[84] B. Tal'nov, *Kratkie ocherki pervykh chetyrekh let proletarskoi revoliutsii v Buguruslanskom okruge (1917–1920 gg.)*, Buguruslan, 1929, pp. 19–20.

[85] F. G. Popov, *Za vlast' sovetov*, pp. 151–2.

The story of the Domashki brigade was a typical example of Red Army organization during the first few months of the civil war. Such brigades, whose military cohesion and enthusiasm were unmatched by any other peasant force in the Red or the White armies, played an important role in the military campaign against the Samara government during September and October.[86] It is important to emphasize, however, that they were initially established to defend their own villages and soviets, and not the Bolshevik government. D. A. Furmanov, the political commissar of Chapaev's 25th Division, underlined this point in *Chapaev*, his celebrated novel about this period of the civil war:

> In the steppe . . . every village is like a little republic: it feels independent, self-sufficient, and has a strong tendency towards separatism . . . These villages did not merely provide individual volunteers, they gave fully organized red regiments . . . For example, when the Cossacks captured the village of Kurilovo in 1918 and, with the help of the kulaks, began to arrest the workers in the soviet, the entire working population of the village rose up, armed itself with whatever came to hand, defeated the Cossacks, and decided to form its own special regiment: it was called the Kurilovo. Other local regiments were set up in similar circumstances: the Domashki, the Pugachev, the Sten'ka Razin, the Novouzensk, the Malouzensk, the Krasnokutsk, etc. They were established primarily to defend the villages, after which they had been named. The fighters and the commanders (at that time there were no commissars) came from the same village. The cohesion of these units was unparalleled: their members had known each other for dozens of years; many of them were old comrades or relatives. In the Kurilovo regiment, for example, there was a father with six sons.[87]

In military terms, the civil war was, to borrow the words of the Duke of Wellington, 'a damned close-run thing'. Had the leaders of the People's Army decided to concentrate their efforts in Saratov and Tsaritsyn, rather than Kazan', then perhaps the history of the civil war would have turned out very differently. The survival of the Samara government, and, arguably, the whole anti-Bolshevik movement, depended upon the union of the anti-Bolshevik forces on the Southern and Eastern Fronts. Denikin, Kolchak, and Dutov all recognized the military significance of this union, which they planned to take place in Saratov during 1918. Because of the strategic position and the economic importance of the Volga region within the Soviet Republic, the establishment of the Samara government offered the anti-Bolshevik forces one of the few opportunities they would get to

[86] See *Godovshchina pervoi revoliutsionnoi armii: Sbornik*, Moscow, 1920, pp. 56–76.

[87] D. Furmanov, *Chapaev*, Moscow, 1984, pp. 49–50.

consolidate a combined stronghold within striking distance of Moscow. Neither the Whites nor the military leaders in Samara fully appreciated the significance of this fact. The former mistrusted the socialist leaders in Samara and underestimated the strategic significance which the lower Volga, especially Tsaritsyn, would come to have in the civil war. The latter were diverted by the prospect of a union with the Entente powers in Arkhangel'sk, and by the chance of moving directly into the all-important heartland of central Russia, via Nizhegorod; they shied away from the 'separatist' south. In defiance of the SR leaders in Samara, who had ordered an attack towards Saratov with the aim of joining Denikin and Dutov, the leaders of the People's Army concentrated their forces in a campaign in Kazan' province that was almost doomed to failure, since the population of the latter was solidly behind the soviets (see Table 12).[88] This proved one of the most critical strategic errors of the anti-Bolshevik movement.

If the Samara government had managed to consolidate a military base, what would have been its chances of political survival? That question ultimately depended upon its relations with the Volga peasantry. The Right SR leaders in Samara were determined to disentangle themselves from the knot they had got themselves into on the land question during 1917. They were committed to supporting the land reforms, endorsed by the Constituent Assembly. Yet they were unable to convince the peasants that their own 'land and freedom' would be safer under the Komuch than under Soviet power. This was partly a problem of time, the inability of the Komuch to build up a relationship with the peasantry under peaceful conditions. It was also an outcome of the localization of the peasantry's attitudes which resulted from the revolution itself: the peasant communes already had the land, and as yet they had little reason to believe that the Bolsheviks would take it from them (as they were to during collectivization). But the failure of the Komuch to win over the peasantry was not merely a problem of communication; it was also a political problem. The unhappy alliance between the SR political leaders and the conservative commanders of the People's Army, whose social origins were manifestly in the old landowning class, ultimately ensured that the peasants would not support the Samara government.

[88] See Zaitsev, pp. 200–1; *Grazhdanskaia voina na Volge*, pp. 96–102, 150–1.

5

Rural Politics During the Civil War

> I will not join the *volispolkom*. I have said so many times. I will work for the *mir* here in the village: I will try to allocate the taxes in grain, poultry, carts, or in labour as fairly as possible. But I cannot do that in the *volost'* soviet. There they don't trouble themselves with any of that. There the secretary is the boss and everything is politics; I am not suited for that. And anyway there they could make me join the party, which I will not do—the Bolsheviks and I have parted company.
>
> Peasant of Moiseevo village (Tambov province), cited by A. Okninsky

AFTER the defeat of the Komuch the Bolsheviks were faced with the task of building their own apparatus of power in the Volga provinces. The forces of the Samara government had left the provincial towns in a state of utter chaos: banks, shops, military depots, and offices had been gutted by the departing troops, or pillaged by the residents during the brief interlude of anarchy preceding the arrival of the Reds. Most of the white-collar workers had fled with the anti-Bolsheviks; the Bolshevik partisans who had stayed behind in the underground *revkomy* were not nearly numerous enough to establish a new administration.[1] 'Apart from our own military forces', reported a Red Army official from Samara on 30 September, 'there are no local government workers at all; the entire city has been left without any political authority or organization.'[2]

The situation in the countryside was even worse. The departing forces had put out of action the key bridges, a large portion of the railways, and most of the system of communications. Many of the local SRs who had been active under the Komuch were now forced into hiding in the district towns and the villages, where they did their best to sabotage the work of the central authorities until the Bolsheviks tightened their grip on the district soviets (see Table 13). In the villages themselves there was no firm political base on which to

[1] After the capture of Samara the underground *revkom* (ten Bolsheviks under the leadership of V. V. Kuibyshev) took on the duties of 'accounting our forces, supplying the army, providing information, and controlling the local departments' until the establishment of the provincial department of administration (*otdel upravleniia*) and the Cheka. The *revkom* was not disbanded until February 1919: see N. F. Bugai, 'Revoliutsionnye komitety—chrezvychainye organy sovetskoi vlasti (1918–1921 gg.)', *Istoricheskie zapiski*, vol. 102, Moscow, 1978, pp. 21–2.

[2] TsGANKh, f. 1943, op. 3, d. 223, l. 81.

TABLE 13. *Bolshevik party representation in the district soviet assemblies of Samara, Saratov, and Simbirsk provinces, 1918–1919 (% of delegates)*

	Bolsheviks			
	Members	Sympathizers	Others	Non-party
July-December 1918	33.7	38.3	26.0	2.0
January-June 1919	47.0	33.7	4.6	14.7
July-December 1919	56.7	11.3	2.3	29.7

Source: M. Vladimirskii, *Sovety, ispolkomy i s"ezdy sovetov (materialy k izucheniiu stroeniia i deiatel'nosti organov mestnogo upravleniia)*, vyp. 2, *S"ezdy sovetov v 1917–1921 gg., ispolkomy v 1920–1921 gg., gorodskie sovety v 1920–1921 gg.*, Moscow, 1921, pp. 34–7.

construct a Bolshevik state apparatus. The soviets that had been established during the revolution were highly decentralized, non-party institutions, committed to the interests of the local communes. The number of Bolshevik party members in the rural localities was insignificant.[3] In his report on the food procurement campaign in Kazan' province during October and November 1918, the People's Commissar of Provisions, A. D. Tsiurupa, summarized the difficulties of establishing Bolshevik control in the countryside:

> there is complete economic dislocation in the localities. There is no political authority whatsoever; postal and telegraph communications have been disrupted; the technical infrastructure for the collection of grain has been destroyed; there is insufficient administrative personnel; the military authorities interfere in the procurement of grain; the peasants have been intimidated and say they are afraid to transport their grain.[4]

The civil war campaign brought into the countryside a large contingent of urban elements from central and northern Russia. The 'struggle for grain', which the Bolsheviks had launched during the summer as 'a ruthless and terrorist war' against the grain-hoarding peasantry,[5] was waged in the villages by an army of 'food brigades' (*prodotriady*) some 76,000 workers strong. Most of these workers (75%) came from the industrial centres of the north (Petrograd, Moscow, Ivanovo-Voznesensk); 10% of them were Bolshevik party members, and at least 20% were

[3] Figures may be found in *Saratovskaia oblastnaia organizatsiia KPSS v tsifrakh 1917–1975 gg.*, Saratov, 1977, p. 16; E. I. Medvedev, 'Partiinoe stroitel'stvo v Srednem Povol'zhe v period ustanovleniia i uprocheniia Sovetskoi vlasti', in *Problemy istorii Oktiabr'skoi revoliutsii i grazhdanskoi voiny v SSSR*, Tomsk, 1975, p. 278. See further sect. 3 below.

[4] TsGANKh, f. 1943, op. 1, d. 448, l. 68.

[5] Amendment by Lenin to Decree of 13 May 1918 on compulsory food procurements in *PSS*, vol. 36, p. 316.

Bolshevik 'sympathizers' (*sochuvstvuiushchie*).[6] Because of its importance as a grain-producing area, a large number of these brigades were sent into the Volga region: towards the end of 1918 there were an estimated 12,000 food-brigade workers in the four Volga provinces; more than 4,000 of them were in Simbirsk province.[7] The build-up of the Red Army in the western Volga districts during the summer of 1918 (in preparation for the campaign against the forces of the Komuch) brought in many more urban elements from the north, since the Red Army proved unable to mobilize enough troops from the local population of the Volga region (see ch. 6, sect.5). At the beginning of August, Lenin transferred more than 30,000 troops from the anti-German screens in the Don to the Volga Front on the assumption that the Germans would not attack: the Eastern Red Army Group grew from 53,000 on 21 June to 70,000 on 15 September, and to 103,000 on 7 October.[8]

The influx of these elements provided the Bolsheviks with a temporary solution to their political problems in the countryside. The urban food brigades were instructed to organize the *kombedy* and to help them in their work. The political departments of the Red Army also played a leading role in the establishment of the rural state apparatus,[9] although they were themselves sometimes inclined to act as autonomous military regimes in the localities (the Soviet authorities were constantly complaining about Red Army interference in their activities).[10] Some of these workers and soldiers were inevitably tempted to get themselves appointed to the *kombed* or the VIK in order to sit out the rest of the civil war in the countryside.[11] The whole

[6] V. M. Selunskaia, *Rabochii klass i Oktiabr' v derevne*, Moscow, 1968, pp. 171, 174–5.

[7] M. A. Molodtsygin, *Raboche-krest'ianskii soiuz 1918–20 gg.*, Moscow, 1987, p. 22; K. M. Krasil'nikova 'Bor'ba za khleb v Srednem Povolzh'e v period inostrannoi voennoi interventsii i grazhdanskoi voiny', kand. diss., Kuibyshev, 1968, p. 128.

[8] E. Mawdsley, *The Russian Civil War*, London, 1987, p. 66.

[9] See e.g. *Sovetskoe stroitel'stvo* (Samara) (henceforth referred to as *SS*), nos. 4–5, 6–7, 1919; *Revoliutsionnaia armiia* (Samara), no. 27 (1919); *Krasnoarmeets* (Saratov), nos. 8, 10 (1918); no. 2 (1919).

[10] See e.g. TsGANKh, f. 1943, op. 1, d. 448, l. 87; d. 223, ll. 113, 223, 224, 273, 351; d. 513, ll. 99, 242; op. 4, d. 116, l. 82; TsGAOR, f. 393, op. 3, d. 323, l. 355; GAKO, f. 193, op. 2, d. 159, l. 53; etc.

[11] On the presence of industrial workers and townsmen in the rural soviets see E. G. Gimpel'son, *Rabochii klass v upravlenii sovetskim gosudarstvom, noiabr' 1917–1920 gg.*, Moscow, 1982, pp. 190–6. During 1918–20 there were literally hundreds of reports of the VIKs and the *kombedy* hiding deserters from the Red and the White armies: see e.g. GAKO, f. 81, op. 1, d. 10, l. 74; TsGANKh, f. 1943, op. 1, d. 573, l. 155; *Doklad vol'skogo uezdnogo ispolkoma sovetov 15 oktiabria 1919 g.*, Vol'sk, 1919, pp. 29–30; *Stenograficheskii otchet 7-go syzranskogo uezdnogo soveta s 4-go po 5-e iiulia 1920 g.*, Syzran', 1920, pp. 26–7; *Serp i molot* (Kuznetsk), no. 226, 16 Oct. 1920, p. 2; *Kommuna* (Samara), no. 510, 31 Aug., 1920, p. 3; etc.

system of rural politics was thus put on a military footing. The urban and non-peasant rural elements in the *kombedy* and some of the VIKs were quick to resort to brutal repressions of the peasantry in the desperate struggle to procure foodstuffs and military supplies. The party bosses and police chiefs in the district centres and the *volost'* townships were sometimes known to set up their own *ad hoc* 'dictatorships', under which the local officials were permitted to operate networks of corruption and extortion from the peasantry. The local Chekas were left to run loose, rounding up suspected 'counter-revolutionaries' and imprisoning them without trial, until the party leadership began to curb their powers during the winter of 1918–19.[12] The exigencies of the civil war and the breakdown of political authority without doubt necessitated some of these terrorist methods, as William Chamberlin explained:

> No one, except under extreme compulsion, was willing to perform any state obligation. The old order had simply crumbled away; a new order, with new habits and standards of conduct, had not yet formed; very often the only way in which a governmental representative, whether he was a Bolshevik commissar or a White officer, could get his orders obeyed was by flourishing a revolver.[13]

It is equally clear that the hatred of the masses for the propertied classes, the plebeian desire for social revenge, only added fuel to the Terror, as Chamberlin again made clear: 'the course of the Revolution certainly indicated that the poorer classes derived a good deal of satisfaction from the mere process of destroying and despoiling the rich, quite irrespective of whether this brought about any improvement in their lot'.[14] Nevertheless, we need to be aware of the influence of the Red Terror on the general development of the Soviet regime. The civil war mentality of the Bolsheviks—the consciousness of fighting on an 'internal front' against large sections of the civilian population (e.g. the 'kulaks', the 'bourgeoisie'); the determination to bury all questions about representative government and the rule of law—established a powerful precedent for the use of political terror as a regular means of Soviet rule after 1921.[15]

[12] On the institutional struggle between the party and the Cheka see G. Leggett, *The Cheka: Lenin's Political Police*, Oxford, 1981, pp. 121–57.

[13] W. H. Chamberlin, *The Russian Revolution 1917–1921*, Princeton, 1987 (originally 1935), vol. 2, p. 81.

[14] Ibid., p. 460.

[15] On the relationship between Bolshevik methods of rule during the civil war and the evolution of the Soviet regime during the 1920s and 1930s see R. Pethybridge, *The Social Prelude to Stalinism*, London, 1974, pp. 73–131; S. Cohen, 'Bolshevism and Stalinism', in R. C. Tucker (ed.), *Stalinism: Essays in Historical Interpretation*, New York, 1977, pp. 15–21; M. Lewin, 'The Social Background to Stalinism', in Tucker, *Stalinism*, pp. 113–15; S. Fitzpatrick, 'The Civil War as a Formative Experience', in A. Gleason, P. Kenez, and R. Stites (eds.), *Bolshevik Culutre*, Bloomington, Ind., 1985.

The dangers of the Terror and the need to establish more broadly based organs of Soviet power in the rural localities were considered by the Bolshevik leadership during the winter of 1918–19, when it finally became clear that the activities of the *kombedy* and the Cheka were having a disastrous effect on the regime's relations with the middle peasantry. During the following two years, the Soviet government concentrated its efforts on the tasks of state-building in the countryside. The national soviet election campaign of 1919 witnessed a sharp increase in the number of Bolsheviks in the local soviets. This facilitated the bureaucratization and the gradual centralization of the VIKs during 1919–20. These developments undoubtedly strengthened the power of the Bolshevik state in the *volost'* townships. But they did very little to integrate the rest of the villages into the Soviet political order, and only exacerbated the old divide between the village communes and the *volost'* administration. This divide was to create serious problems for the Soviet regime in the countryside during the 1920s.

1. THE COMMITTEES OF THE RURAL POOR (*KOMBEDY*)

The soviets had completed the destruction of the old state apparatus in the rural localities during 1917–18. But they had not yet shown themselves to be a suitable base on which to construct a socialist state. They functioned in the interests of the local peasantry, but failed to carry out the orders of the higher authorities and proved unresponsive to the needs of the state during the grain crisis of spring and summer 1918. As the food supply in the cities deteriorated and the number of workers' protests increased, the Bolshevik leaders and the Soviet press began to call for a 'class war' against the 'kulak grain-hoarders' in the villages, who were said to be in control of the local soviets. The state grain monopoly and the fixed prices on cereals were to be tightened up by the declaration of a 'merciless struggle'[16] against the 'grain hoarders' and the private traders. Workers' brigades were to be sent into the rural areas to take from the peasantry—by ruthless force if necessary—any grain 'surpluses'. The rural poor were to be organized in Committees to wage this 'class war' against the 'kulaks' in the villages. Lenin heralded the institution of the *kombedy* on 11 June as the step by which 'the Russian proletariat passed the boundary separating the bourgeois-democratic revolution from the socialist revolution'.[17] The unification of the rural poor in hostile opposition to the 'kulaks' would align the class struggle in the villages with that in

[16] *SU*, 1918, no. 35, art. 468.
[17] *PSS*, vol. 37, pp. 314–15.

the towns, and provide the political base of a socialist state structure in the countryside.

Because of the occupation of the Volga region by the anti-Bolsheviks during the summer of 1918, the *kombedy* were not widely established in this region until the following autumn. In Saratov province, which was only partially affected by the civil war, no more than forty *kombedy* had been set up before the end of August; in Samara province, which was fully occupied by the anti-Bolsheviks, there were no *kombedy* at all before the beginning of October.[18] During the autumn the establishment of the *kombedy* in the Volga region progressed very slowly in comparison with the industrial and grain-consuming regions of central and northern Russia, which had not been affected by the civil war (see Table 14). This was partly due to the weakness of the state apparatus in the Volga immediately following the defeat of the anti-Bolsheviks; and to the influence of the Left SRs, who bitterly opposed the institution of the *kombedy*, at the district and *volost'* levels.[19] But it was mainly the result of the apathy of the Volga peasants themselves towards the new organs. The peasants were not enthusiastic about the idea of forming an extra layer of government in the villages—especially during the harvest season, which had already been delayed by the Volga military campaigns. A Bolshevik agitator reporting on the establishment of the *kombedy* in Samara district during November 1918 complained that 'in every village it was left entirely up to myself to organize the *kombed*': in some of the villages the male peasants were said to be constantly absent in the fields; in others the peasants seemed to be less interested in the *kombed* than in questioning the agitator about the shortages of industrial goods, or the meaning of 'all those decrees and commands from Lenin and Trotsky in the centre'. In nearly all of the villages the work of the soviet itself was found to have come to a standstill. The VIK in Bogdanovka claimed it had not received a copy of the instructions on the formation of the *kombed*; but the agitator later

18 P. F. Iakovlev, 'Komitety derevenskoi bednoty Saratovskoi gubernii', kand. diss., Saratov, 1952, p. 68; GAKO, f. 7, op. 1, d. 535, ll. 221–3. Silvana Malle (*The Economic Organization of War Communism, 1918–1921*, Cambridge, 1985, p. 367) is mistaken in stating that 'the mass of *kombedy*' in the Volga region 'were organized between June and September 1918'.

19 See e.g. TsGAOR, f. 393, op. 3, d. 330, l. 1; d. 331, ll. 2, 3, 19; d. 332, ll. 7, 16, 17; d. 334, l. 103; *Izvestiia* (Balashov), no. 166, 17 Sept., 1918, p. 2; no. 172, 24 Sept. 1918, p. 1; no. 173, 25 Sept. 1918, p. 4; no. 175, 27 Sept. 1918, p. 1. See further G. A. Gerasimenko and F. A. Rashitov, *Sovety Nizhnego Povolzh'ia v Oktiabr'skoi revoliutsii*, Saratov, 1972, pp. 266–70; E. I. Medvedev, *Oktiabr'skaia revoliutsiia v Srednem Povolzh'e*, Kuibyshev, 1964, pp. 181–5; P. F. Iakovlev, pp. 61, 70.

TABLE 14. Kombedy *in various provinces of Russia, December 1918*

Province	Number of *kombedy*	% villages with *kombed*	Rural population per *kombed*
Producing areas affected by civil war in summer 1918			
Simbirsk	507	38.6	2,750
Samara	1,105	35.4	2,243
Voronezh	1,428	53.7	2,121
Saratov	2,220	65.6	1,110
Kursk	2,766	84.3	1,017
Kazan'	2,274	64.7	989
Penza	2,227	95.0	726
Consuming areas not affected by civil war in summer 1918			
Tver'	8,612	64.4	442
Moscow	4,533	57.0	403
Petrograd	2,471	37.0	384
Tula	4,604	100.0	336
Vladimir	4,875	100.0	220
Vologda	5,000	55.1	187
Iaroslavl'	8,041	71.2	143
Viatka	15,988	86.0	128
Kostroma	6,711	93.0	111
Novgorod	5,000	75.9	78

Source: Calculated from V. V. Gerasimiuk 'Kombedy Rossiiskoi Federatsii v tsifrakh', *Istoriia SSSR*, vol. 4, 1960, p. 125. Also see his additions in 'Nekotorye novye statisticheskie dannye o kombedakh RSFSR', *Voprosy istorii*, vol. 6, 1963, p. 210.

found it in the office of the VIK on top of a pile of government decrees torn up for cigarette paper.[20]

A major obstacle to the formation of the *kombedy* in the agricultural regions was the tendency of the peasant fellow villagers to view themselves as members of one 'class', or 'family' (*krest'ianskaia sem'ia*). The notion of a separate organ for the poor peasants cut across the traditional political culture of the peasantry, embodied in the village commune, wherein the smallholding farmers were generally tied together by their common links to the land and the village community. Hence, in many villages all the peasants were allowed to join the *kombed* (which simply continued the work of the soviet). As a Bolshevik agitator in Nikolaevsk district explained, 'there are simply no lists of the poor peasants in the communes and so all the peasants at the assembly take part in the election of the *kombed*; the *kombedy* make no effort to develop a sense of party loyalty or class divisions

[20] GAKO, f. 7, op. 1, d. 535, l. 142–6.

among the peasantry'.[21] The following resolution (from an unnamed village in Serdobsk district) was typical: 'We the peasants of commune no. 4 welcome the committees of the rural poor, for in our commune no one speculates and no one is rich. We are all middle peasants and poor peasants and we will do all we can to help the poor peasants.'[22] Many village assemblies condemned the idea of a separate committee for the poor peasants as socially divisive. Thus the Kiselevo-Chemizovka *volost'* soviet assembly (Atkarsk *uezd*) resolved that the organization of the *kombed* was 'not seen by the local communes to be desirable, since the peasants are almost equal, and the poor peasants are already elected to the soviet ... so that the organization of separate committees for the poor peasants would only lead to unnecessary tensions between the citizens of the same commune'.[23] In some villages there were evidently informal social pressures inhibiting the poorest peasant stratum from forming their own committee. A *kombed* organizer reported from Obsharovka *volost'* (Samara uezd): 'the peasants categorically refused to organize a *kombed*; they claimed they were all rich peasants and that none of them were poor, so they should all join the *kombed*, though some later complained that the richer peasants had forbidden them [to form a committee] and had threatened them'.[24] In Novouzensk and Buzuluk districts it was widely reported that the poorer peasants, for fear of their richer neighbours, 'often refused to serve in the *kombed* on the most empty and flimsy excuses'.[25] In Samara district a *kombed* organizer noted a similar tendency:

> passing through the village of Smyshliaevka (Alekseev *volost'*), where there happened to be a general assembly in progress, I decided to attend the meeting, where it turned out they were electing a *kombed* . . . since I was not on official duty, I did not intervene, but simply watched this primitive and pitiful spectacle. On no less than three separate occasions, a number of candidates were put forward from the general gathering of the peasants to stand for election to the executive of the *kombed*; but on each occasion the peasants failed to complete the ballot, since none of the candidates was willing to join the *kombed* and each renounced his candidacy . . . I was shocked by this scene and could not explain it—whether the poor peasants were simply ignorant, or whether they had been terrified into submission by the local kulaks.[26]

It was common for the Soviet press to depict these all-peasant

[21] TsGAOR, f. 393, op. 3, d. 329, l. 36.
[22] Ibid., d. 340, l. 70. See also V. N. Aver'ev (ed.), *Komitety bednoty: Sbornik materialov*, Moscow/Leningrad, 1933, vol. 1, docs. 68, 87, 89, 121, 134, 135, 168, 169.
[23] Cited in Gerasimenko and Rashitov, p. 266.
[24] GAKO, f. 7, op. 1, d. 535, l. 164.
[25] TsGAOR, f. 393, op. 3, d. 325, l. 182; d. 323, l. 154.
[26] GAKO, f. 7, op. 1, d. 535, ll. 145–6.

kombedy as 'kulak' organs of power, especially if they had failed to bring about an improvement in the fulfilment of the grain levy.[27] Soviet historians have faithfully repeated these propaganda charges as historical fact.[28] But the failure of the *kombedy* to unite the poor peasantry can not be simply put down to the influence of the 'kulaks'. The 'proletarian class-consciousness' of the poorest peasantry failed to express itself in the *kombedy* not because it was repressed, but because it did not exist: the natural-patriarchal bonds of the peasant farmers in the village were still very much stronger than the socio-economic divisions between them. The majority of the richest peasant farmers were respected as well as feared by their poorest farming neighbours. They were looked up to as the best farmers in the village (whose agricultural knowledge was expected to serve the interests of the community), as the staunchest upholders of communal traditions, and as the most able mediators between the village and outside agents. Although the power of the rich was partly derived from their exploitation of the poor, it is important to note that the latter showed a marked preference for indebtedness to their well-to-do neighbours than to money-lenders in the neighbouring town, since the oral contract between the fellow-villagers could then at least be controlled by informal social pressures within the community (e.g. village opinion).

Because of the difficulties of establishing a *kombed* through the traditional institutions of the peasant community, it was common for the *kombed* organizers to establish the new institution through other channels, outside the commune or the village assembly. A survey by the NKVD in eight northern Russian provinces found that only 10.8% of the 3,900 registered *kombedy* had been elected at a general assembly of the village or the commune; the vast majority had been established at a factional meeting of the rural poor (the landless labourers and poorest peasants).[29] In some places these factional meetings were organized spontaneously, following the breakdown of a general gathering on the question of the *kombed*. In Chernovka village (Buzuluk *uezd*) a 'general meeting of the peasants and other citizens' was convened on 8 November and

> proceeded to the registration of members for the *kombed*; ninety-five householders were registered. Meanwhile, from the ranks of the rich

[27] See e.g. TsGANKh, f. 1943, op. 3, d. 223, l. 252; TsGAOR, f. 393, op. 3, d. 335, l. 68; d. 336, ll. 200, 202; *Krasnaia kommuna* (Atkarsk), no. 78, 27 Nov. 1918, p. 3; *Izvestiia* (Balashov), no. 195, 22 Oct. 1918, p. 3; *Izvestiia saratovskogo gubprodkoma* (Saratov), no. 13, 6 Apr. 1918, p. 15.

[28] See e.g. A. V. Shestakov (ed.), *Kombedy RSFSR*, Moscow, 1933, p. 201.

[29] V. V. Kabanov, 'Oktiabr'skaia revoliutsiia i krest'ianskaia obshchina', *Istoricheskie zapiski*, vol. 111, Moscow, 1984, p. 137.

peasants, who were all crowded together, the gibe was heard: 'Aha, so now these parasites want to live off the backs of the poor!' One by one, the peasants began to leave the meeting. At the end, only a very small number of the poorest peasants remained, and they quickly went on to elect an executive.[30]

Elsewhere such factional meetings tended to be organized by external agitators, sometimes after the latter had failed to unite the poor peasants at a general village meeting. A good illustration is in the village commune of Goliaev (Serdobsk *uezd*), where the chairman of the *volost' kombed* and a Bolshevik agitator from Serdobsk attempted to persuade the peasants to denounce their 'kulak' village soviet leaders and establish a *kombed*. The peasants shouted down the two agitators, who then put forward an alternative proposal to reduce the size of the village soviet from ten to four members. The peasants refused to cut the size of the soviet or alter its composition. This prompted the chairman of the *volost' kombed* to 'take full power into his own hands and close down the general meeting'. The two agitators then organized a separate meeting of the landless peasants to elect a *kombed*.[31]

It was a reflection of their methods of establishment that a large proportion of the *kombed* members were from social groups traditionally excluded from the smallholding peasant community (e.g. landless labourers, craftsmen, in-migrant townsmen). A study of more than 800 *kombedy* in Tambov province discovered that only 49.3% of the members of the *volost'*-level *kombedy* and 65.6% of the members of the village *kombedy* had been engaged in agriculture before 1914. The remaining members had been employed in urban industry (17.5% of the *volost'*-level members; 22.7% of the village members); white-collar professions (19.1% of the *volost'*-level members; 7.4% of the village members); and rural craft industries (10.5% of the *volost'*-level members; 4.3% of the village members). During the World War the majority of the *kombed* members who had previously been engaged in agriculture entered the army (a factor signifying their youth); this category included 30.2% of the *volost'*-level *kombed* members and 23.3% of the village *kombed* members. The non-agricultural social background of the *kombed* members was especially marked in the executives: 36.9% of the *volost'*-level *kombed* chairmen and 31.2% of the village *kombed* chairmen had been registered as urban or rural

[30] GAKO, f. 7, op. 1, d. 535, l. 141.

[31] TsGAOR, f. 393, op. 3, d. 340, l. 242. See similarly A. Ia. Pereverzev, 'Organizatorskaia pomoshch' promyshlennykh rabochikh derevne v 1918 g. (po materialam tsentral'no-chernozemnykh gubernii)'; *Trudy Voronezhskogo universiteta*, , vol. 87, Voronezh, 1969, p. 43.

industrialists before 1914; none of the bursars of the village *kombedy* had ever been a peasant (66.7% of them had been registered as urban factory workers before 1914). Finally, 33% of the *kombed* members (41.4% of the *kombed* chairmen) were registered as Bolshevik party members; a further 48% of the *kombed* members (and 41.4% of the *kombed* chairmen) were described as Bolshevik 'sympathizers'.[32]

The largely non-peasant social background of the *kombedy* is confirmed by looking more closely at fragmentary local materials. The *kombed* of Samoilovka *volost'* (Balashov *uezd*) comprised 120 members, described as cobblers, joiners, carpenters, blacksmiths, and 'only the very poorest peasants'. The *kombed* in the nearby *volost'* township of Mikhailovka comprised 70 members—all of them formerly domestic servants and agricultural labourers on the Sologubov estate.[33] In Zolotoe *volost'* there were 10 different village *kombedy*, whose executive staff of 30 (including 1 chairman, 1 assistant chairman, and 1 secretary in each *kombed*) comprised 17 poor peasants, 8 rural industrialists, and 5 soldiers. The bursars of the *kombedy* were all 'elected from the *intelligenty* in favour of Soviet power, and from the literate peasants'. All the *kombed* executive members were said to be members of the Bolshevik party, or Bolshevik 'sympathizers'.[34] The *kombed* in Aleksandrovka *volost'* (Samara *uezd*) was made up entirely of landless labourers, in-migrant townsmen and the 'poorest elements of the [German?] colonists'.[35] In the village of Aleksandrovka (Khilovka *volost'*, Samara *uezd*) the *kombed* comprised 25 landless labourers, 2 metal-workers, 2 carpenters, 1 blacksmith, 1 joiner, and 1 cobbler. Of the 32 *kombed* families (representing 145 family members), only 13 owned a horse, and only 4 owned a cow; 19 families did not have their own hut in the village—a certain indicator of their non-local origins.[36]

When the destructive effect of the *kombedy* on peasant–state relations finally became apparent, the Bolshevik leadership denounced them for having failed to win over the mass of the peasant smallholders. An article in *Pravda* on 5 December 1918 singled out the *kombedy* in Samara province for having 'forgotten completely about the middle peasantry, the smallholders, exploited by the kulak moneylenders'.[37] Lenin himself condemned the *kombedy* for not having 'tried hard enough to unite and satisfy the interests of the rural poor and the middle peasantry'.[38]

32 Aver'ev (ed.), *Komitety bednoty*, vol. 1, pp. 21–2, 34.
33 *Izvestiia* (Balashov), no. 170, 21 Sept. 1918, p. 4; no. 175, 27 Sept. 1918.
34 P. F. Iakovlev, p. 92.
35 GAKO, f. 7, op. 1, d. 535, l. 53b.
36 Ibid., l. 9.
37 Cited in E. I. Medvedev, *Oktiabr'skaia revoliutsiia*, p. 183.
38 *Leninskii sbornik*, 39 vols., Moscow, 1924–80, vol. 18, p. 184.

Disconnected from the peasant community, and lacking the know-how to account the agricultural surplus of the peasants (let alone to distinguish between the various socio-economic peasant subgroups), the *kombedy* proved unable to carry out their intended economic tasks—requisitioning food surpluses, expropriating the property of the 'kulaks', collecting government taxes, organizing peasant labour teams for government duties (*trudpovinnost'*), etc.—without resorting to the use of coercion and extortion. Some of the *kombedy*, especially those near the towns, the railways, and the civil war fronts, became associated with criminal or 'hooligan' elements from the urban working class and the Red Army.[39] These were destitute and brutalized people, whose livelihood had come to depend upon the use of the gun. The increasing presence of these elements in the countryside resulted in the militarization of a large number of the VIKs and the rural Bolshevik party cells, as well as the *kombedy* (see section 3 below). In many areas the *kombedy* set up road-blocks on the way to and from markets and forcibly requisitioned surpluses from the middle peasantry which were not in fact subject to the food tax at all (e.g. vegetables, dairy products). Elsewhere they made illegal arrests, confiscated the property of widows because they had employed hired labour, extorted home-brewed vodka from the peasants, and generally terrorized the villagers.[40] In Staro-Slavkino *volost'* (Petrovsk *uezd*) the *kombed* and the VIK were run as a 'mafia' by two brothers named Druzhaev, in alliance with the chief of the regional police. The Druzhaev gang ransacked barns, indiscriminately requisitioned property, and beat up men and women in the search for vodka and firearms (the Appendix presents a group of peasant petitions complaining about the activities of the gang).[41]

The corrupt and oppressive practices of these *kombedy* may be partly explained by their desperate financial position. Because of their weak connections with the peasant communes, the *kombedy* were unable to levy taxes from the local peasant farmers. Very few *kombedy* received any financial aid from the higher provisions authorities. The majority either financed themselves by taxes on local shops and craft enterprises, or had no formal source of revenue to speak of. Of the 65 *kombedy* in Atkarsk district at the end of September, only 8 received voluntary contributions from the village communes, and no more than

[39] See N. N. Leitenant, 'Zapiski belogvardeitsa', *Arkhiv russkoi revoliutsii*, vol. 10, 1923, pp. 63–4. On the debate about 'hooliganism' before 1914 (which partly influenced the writings of *intelligenty* about the *kombedy*) see N. Weissman, 'Rural Crime in Tsarist Russia: The Question of Hooliganism 1905–1914', *Slavic Review*, 37 (1978).

[40] TsGAOR, f. 393, op. 2, d. 59, l. 424; op. 3, d. 359, l. 176; TsGANKh, f. 478, op. 1, d. 330, ll. 51–2; GAKO, f. 7, op. 1, d. 535, l. 42; *SS*, nos. 6–7, 1919, pp. 54, 134; etc.

[41] See pp. 357–62.

12 levied taxes on the 'local rich' (*mestnye bogatye*); the remaining 45 *kombedy* had no source of financial support.[42] The declaration of the 10 milliard rouble Revolutionary Tax (Chreznalog) on the urban and rural bourgeoisie on 30 October 1918 offered the *kombedy*, as the organs officially in charge of the collection of the tax, a new opportunity to extort financial revenues from the farming peasantry.[43] The peasants complained that the level of the tax was too high. They pointed out that the richest peasant farmers had fled with the Whites.[44] In the majority of the villages the tax was left uncollected. In some villages the peasants collected a small fraction of the tax from the landless elements and the families of the soldiers in the Red Army, on whose behalf the Chreznalog had been imposed.[45] The village soviets and the VIKs did very little, on the whole, to enforce the collection of the tax. An investigation in Buzuluk district found that most of the VIKs had either ignored the Decree of 30 October, or had collected the tax exclusively for local soviet needs.[46] The *kombedy* were much more stringent. Many of them became involved in a bitter conflict with the communes and the soviets, as they proceeded to collect the Chreznalog without proper tax lists of the peasant households. Hundreds of peasant families had cause to complain to the soviet authorities about the repressive and unjust methods of the *kombed* during the collection of the tax: in many villages the *kombed* had collected the Chreznalog as a poll tax on all members of the village instead of on the bourgeoisie; some peasants had been forced to sell all their livestock in order to pay the tax; others had been beaten, whipped, or incarcerated in unheated quarters until they consented to pay.[47]

The coercive methods of the *kombedy* may also be explained by the fact that the higher Bolshevik authorities had granted them

42 *Izvestiia saratovskogo gubprodkoma* (Saratov), no. 13, 6 Apr. 1918, pp. 15–16. See also GAKO, f. 7, op. 1, d. 535, ll. 22, 34, 23, 57; TsGANKh, f. 1943, op. 3, d. 223, l. 307; *SEV*, vol. 1, p. 353; Aver'ev, vol. 2, pp. 250–69.

43 *DSV*, vol. 3, Moscow, 1964, p. 466; N. G. Sokolov, 'Nalogovaia politika v derevne v pervye gody sovetskoi vlasti (1917–1920 gg.)', *Istoricheskie zapiski*, vol. 113, Moscow, 1986, pp. 86 ff.

44 TsGAOR, f. 393, op. 3, d. 322, l. 31; d. 323, l. 96; *Zhurnal zasedaniia III-go samarskogo uezdnogo s''ezda sovetov krest'ianskikh i rabochikh deputatov*, Samara, 1918, p. 17; *Izvestiia* (Vol'sk), no. 21, 29 Jan. 1919, p. 3.

45 GAKO, f. 81, op. 1, d. 10, l. 73; *Krasnoarmeets* (Saratov), no. 8, 24 Nov. 1918, p. 16; no. 5, 23 Feb. 1919, p. 23; *Nabat* (Kamyshin), no. 35, 28 Mar. 1919, p. 4; *Izvestiia* (Balashov), no. 79, 11 Apr. 1919.

46 *SS*, nos. 6–7, 1919, pp. 127–8; TsGAOR, f. 393, op. 3, d. 323, ll. 136, 153–5, 166–8.

47 TsGAOR, f. 393, op. 13, d. 578, l. 250; op. 3, d. 323, l. 49; d. 337, l. 74; E. B. Skobelkina, 'Simbirskie bol'sheviki v bor'be s kulatskim miatezhom vesnoi 1919 g.', in *Uchenye zapiski ul'ianovskogo gosudarstvennogo pedagogicheskogo instituta*, vyp. 1, Ul'ianovsk, 1966, p. 206; *SEV*, vol. 2, p. 272; L. V. Maksakova, *Agitpoezd 'Oktiabr'skaia Revoliutsiia' (1919–1920)*, Moscow, 1956, p. 50; Aver'ev, vol. 2, pp. 43–51.

sweeping political powers in the belief that it was necessary to undermine the authority of the 'kulak-dominated' soviets. The *kombedy* were actively engaged in a wide variety of issues. Many of them tried to confiscate the property of the local churches, and to break down their hold over the village poor (e.g. by outlawing the charity schemes of the churches).[48] Some were known to combat vodka-brewing, gambling, prostitution, and musical parties at which anti-Bolshevik songs (*chastushki*) were sung.[49] A large number of the *kombedy* made it their business to hunt out and arrest on behalf of the Cheka local 'kulaks' or 'counter-revolutionaries'.[50] These arrests were bitterly resented by the peasants and the local soviets: they cut across the peasants' conception of social justice, and undermined the judicial institutions set up by the soviets during the revolution (see ch. 4, sect. 1).

Such institutional tensions lay at the heart of the bitter clashes between the *kombedy* and the peasant organs of power (the communes and most of the village and *volost'* soviets) during the autumn of 1918. One government official from Samara province claimed, with conscious irony, that the conflicts between the *kombedy* and the soviets represented the main form of 'class struggle' in the rural areas during this period.[51] Between July and November, the Cheka reported 108 large-scale peasant uprisings in European Russia; the local Cheka authorities reported innumerable peasant 'disturbances'.[52] Most of the uprisings (154 out of 200 armed village risings in Russia noted by one Soviet historian during July and August) were generally directed against the Bolshevik grain monopoly.[53] But the activities of the *kombedy* were undoubtedly one of the major catalysts. In Buguruslan district there were fifteen armed peasant uprisings against the

[48] GAKO, f. 7, op. 1, d. 535, ll. 111, 113, 123; TsGAOR, f. 393, op. 3, d. 359, ll. 325, 329; d. 337, ll. 128, 158, 160; d. 359, l. 221.

[49] TsGAOR, f. 393, op. 3, d. 359, l. 175; *Krasnaia kommuna*, no. 92, 13 Dec. 1918, p. 4; *Oktiabr'skaia revoliutsiia* (Khvalynsk), no. 612, 14 Jan. 1921, p. 4.

[50] See V. V. Romanenko, 'Sozdanie, razvitie i deiatel'nost' organov ChK i vnutrennikh voisk sovetskoi respubliki v Srednem Povolzh'e i Priural'e v 1918–22 gg.', kand. diss., Kuibyshev, 1977, p. 34.

[51] GAKO, f. 7, op. 1, d. 535, l. 2.

[52] For the Cheka figures see V. Vladimirova, *God sluzhby 'sotsialistov' kapitalistam: Ocherki po istorii kontrrevoliutsii v 1918 godu*, Moscow/Leningrad, 1927, p. 291. For other figures see *SS* nos. 6–7, 1919, pp. 134, 139; *Vlast' sovetov*, no. 10, Sept. 1919, p. 20; *Volia Rossii* (Prague), no. 8, 21 Sept. 1920; V. N. Aver'ev and S. Ronin, 'Kulatskie vosstaniia v epokhu kombedov', *Bor'ba klassov*, 3, 1935, pp. 86–100; Gerasimenko and Rashitov, pp. 239–40; Iu. K. Strizhkov, *Prodovol'stvennye otriady v gody grazhdanskoi voiny i inostrannoi interventsii 1917–1921 gg.*, Moscow, 1973, pp. 86 ff; E. G. Gimpel'son, *Sovety v pervyi god proletarskoi diktatury, oktiabr' 1917 g.–noiabr' 1918 g.*, Moscow, 1967, p. 390; etc.

[53] Strizhkov, p. 91.

kombedy during December 1918.[54] In Penza district there was a major peasant uprising beginning in June in the village of Kuchek. The peasants murdered eleven members of the *kombed* and a group of food brigade workers, and set up a military–political staff, including some local Left SR activists, who issued leaflets calling the neighbouring villages to arm against the 'alien food brigades, which have given power to hooligans calling themselves members of the "rural poor" '. The insurgents, who were joined by the villages of eight neighbouring *volosti*, organized a 'peasant army', which defeated several small brigades of Bolshevik volunteers from Penza before it was put down in August by red guard detachments from Petrograd and several other cities of central Russia.[55] During November there were peasant uprisings against the *kombedy* in seven out of the twelve districts of Tambov province. One of the most notable was in Ol'khin *volost'* (Morshansk *uezd*). At the beginning of the month the Morshansk soviet assembly had called for the abolition of the grain monopoly. After several weeks of further grain requisitionings by the *kombedy* and the food brigades, the Ol'khin peasants overthrew the *kombed*. The insurgents destroyed the railways and the lines of communication between Ol'khin and Morshansk; and distributed anti-Bolshevik propaganda among the neighbouring villages. The entire male population of Ol'khin *volost'* was mobilized in a peasant militia. Armed with pitch-forks, axes, and scythes, they stood little chance against the red guard detachments sent in from Tambov to suppress the revolt.[56]

These uprisings were neither 'kulak', nor counter-revolutionary in character. They commanded the support of the whole peasantry in those localities where, in the words of the Tambov provincial department of administration (*otdel upravleniia*), the *kombedy* had managed to 'terrorize not only the middle peasants, but also the poor peasants'.[57] Lenin himself saw the *kombedy*'s 'reckless destruction of the middle peasantry's interests' as the main cause of the peasant revolts in Penza province.[58] Iu. Steklov, the editor of *Izvestiia*, later concluded that 'the *kombedy* had mistakenly united a tiny minority of the countryside, but incited a series of "kulak risings" which were in fact the movement of the ordinary middle peasants'.[59]

The Sixth All-Russian Soviet Congress at the beginning of November 1918 called for the abolition of the *kombedy* and the re-election of

54 *SS*, nos. 6–7, 1919, p. 134.

55 *Leninskii sbornik*, vol. 18, pp. 201, 202, 206–7; *PSS*, vol. 35, p. 287; Strizhkov, pp. 89 ff.; E. I. Medvedev, *Oktiabr'skaia revoliutsiia*, pp. 192 ff.

56 Aver'ev and Ronin, pp. 87–90.

57 See *SEV*, vol. 1, p. 151; TsGAOR, f. 130, op. 2, d. 443, l. 33.

58 *Leninskii sbornik*, vol. 18, pp. 144, 206.

59 Cited in *Volia Rossii* (Prague), no. 207, 20 May 1921, p. 1.

the soviets on the franchise of the Soviet Constitution (see sect. 2 below). The Congress heralded a new party policy—officially endorsed at the Eighth Party Congress in March 1919—to improve relations with the middle peasantry. This was, to be sure, a 'timely retreat' from the 'untenable position' of the party during the autumn of 1918, when the mass opposition of the peasantry seriously endangered the Soviet government.[60] But was it not already too late to repair relations between the peasantry and the regime? Many peasants had become acquainted with the Bolshevik regime through the *kombedy*, whose reckless conduct could only have strengthened the peasantry's habitual mistrust of all government based in the towns. During the winter of 1918–19 the Bolsheviks must have feared that the failure of the *kombedy* would bring about a general rupture between the peasantry and the new regime.

2. THE VILLAGE AND *VOLOST'* SOVIET ELECTIONS OF 1919

On the eve of the first anniversary of the October revolution (6 November 1918) the Sixth All-Russian Soviet Congress assembled in Moscow. Of particular concern to the overwhelmingly Bolshevik delegation was the problem of government control in the countryside. The village and *volost'* soviets were still, for the most part, highly decentralized non-party organs of peasant self-rule, dominated by the village communes; but the attempt to supplant them with the *kombedy* had proved disastrous. The Congress was forced to abandon the *kombedy* and seek alternative methods to strengthen the power of the state in the rural localities. It was resolved to re-elect the village and *volost'* soviets on the 'proletarian franchise' of the Soviet Constitution of July 1918. The Congress ordered the provincial and district soviets to organize the elections without delay through the *kombedy*.[61] On 4 December detailed instructions by the VTsIK (All-Russian Central Executive Committee of the Soviets) were published in *Izvestiia*. At the end of the month the first national soviet election campaign commenced. By extending the influence of the Bolshevik party in the countryside at a crucial moment in the civil war, it was a campaign of historic importance.

The VTsIK instructions 'On procedures for the re-election of the *volost'* and village soviets'[62] stressed the need to broaden the popular

[60] E. H. Carr, *The Bolshevik Revolution 1917–1923*, vol. 2, Harmondsworth, 1966, p. 163.

[61] *Stenograficheskii otchet chrezvychainogo VI vserossiiskogo s''ezda sovetov*, Moscow, 1919, pp. 17–19.

[62] *SU*, no. 86, 1918, art. 901. The instructions were published in *Izvestiia*, no. 265, 4 Dec. 1918.

base of soviet representation (i.e. to turn the soviets into organs of 'proletarian' power in the countryside). All rural settlements with at least 100 adult inhabitants were to elect a soviet. The election was to take place on a non-working day. The entire population (including women) over 18 years of age was entitled to vote. Former landowners, Tsarist police officials, 'capitalists', 'kulaks', merchants, and others living on unearned income were to be disenfranchised. There was, however, some confusion over the electoral rights of the former village officials.[63] Each soviet member was to represent 100 franchised inhabitants, although no soviet was to comprise less than three members. One village soviet member in ten (and at least one member from every soviet) was to attend the *volost'* soviet assembly, where the VIK was to be elected. Within three days of the election of the VIK, the *kombedy*, which had helped to supervise the elections, were to be closed down; their official records were to be transferred to the soviets.

The instructions assigned a number of functions to the newly elected village soviets which the July Constitution had effectively left to the village communes: 'the account of the population and the land . . . seed, tools, cattle, and the harvest'; 'the correct management of agriculture . . . and cottage industry'; 'the resolution of all local matters'; and the raising of the general 'cultural and economic level' of the villages.[64] In addition, the soviets were to 'maintain revolutionary order in the village' and implement the instructions of the higher Soviet authorities, especially the food procurement organs. The elections, in short, were to move one step closer towards the realization of the ideal of the Soviet Constitution—a universal and uniform system of Soviet administration capable of superseding the autonomous village communes. 'Socialist construction', declared the Sixth Soviet Congress, 'will be completed only when Soviet organization is established everywhere in the countryside precisely according to the Soviet Constitution'.[65]

A centralized network of electoral commissions (*izbiratel'nye komissii*) was to supervise the elections. The village commissions

[63] Art. 65d of the Constitution did not specifically disenfranchise former village officials elected by the *skhod* (e.g. *starshiny, starosty, sotskie, desiatskie*), but M. Vladimirskii, a high-ranking official of the NKVD, warned electoral commissioners to make 'a thorough investigation' of their records. The Constitution did specify that pre-revolutionary *volost'* clerks were entitled to vote, but again Vladimirskii warned of their previous connections with the Tsarist secret police and suggested that 'according to the Constitution', such people 'should not be allowed to vote' (M. Vladimirskii, *Organizatsiia sovetskoi vlasti na mestakh*, Moscow, 1919, p. 11).

[64] On the Soviet Constitution and the land commune see D. Atkinson, *The End of the Russian Land Commune 1905–1930*, Stanford, 1983, pp. 197–8. On the new functions of the soviets see n. 62 above.

[65] *Stenograficheskii otchet chrezvychainogo VI s''ezda sovetov*, p. 18.

were either established by the village *kombed*, or nominated by the *volost'* electoral commission. The latter was established by the *volost'*-level *kombed*, or nominated by the district electoral commission. The village and *volost'* commissions were to provide ink and paper for the ballot, prepare the electoral lists, arrest anti-Soviet agitators, and conduct the election meeting. The chairman of the electoral commission opened the meeting by asking the peasants if anyone needed to be struck off, or added to, the electoral list; each proposal was debated in turn. The list of candidates—which was prepared by the peasants and, if it existed, the local party cell—was then read out, and any further nominations from the assembled peasants were discussed. A vote was then taken—usually by an open show of hands, or by standing in groups, or by the recording of 'voices' (i.e. by shouting), but in some places by a secret ballot—for each candidate in turn, or (especially where the Bolshevik cell had put forward its own nominations) for a slate of candidates. Complaints about the electoral procedures could then be voiced. Improperly elected candidates were sometimes replaced. If the whole election was deemed to have been unsatisfactorily conducted, then it was not uncommon for a new ballot to be ordered by the electoral commission.

The electoral commissions were to comprise three or four citizens who had 'clearly shown themselves, through their public activity, to be steadfast defenders of the interests of the working masses'.[66] Each commission was to include at least one member who had been nominated by the electoral commission at the higher level. Many commissions included higher Soviet officials, party 'instructors', and Red Army personnel. A commissioner could be removed from his post by a higher level soviet executive.[67] Such provisos did not, of course, guarantee that the electoral commissions would (or could) enforce the central directives in their organizational work. It was common for the village soviet, the VIK, or the *kombed* to act as the electoral commission—sometimes, no doubt, with the aim of ensuring that its own members were elected. It was also not unknown for a dozen or more peasants to sign the election document, in the manner of a communal resolution, as evidenced by the signatures of the Shamkinsk *volost'* electoral commission in Fig. 1.

[66] Vladimirskii, *Organizatsiia sovetskoi vlasti*, p. 11.

[67] It was not unknown for the higher authorities to clash with the peasants over the election of the commission. In Savruka village, Samara province, the district instructors attempted to nominate all the commissioners, but the peasants, supposedly swayed by 'kulak' agitation, refused to accept one of the Bolshevik candidates. The local party cell nominated nine candidates to the commission at an electoral meeting, while three were elected (*SEV*, vol. 2, p. 407).

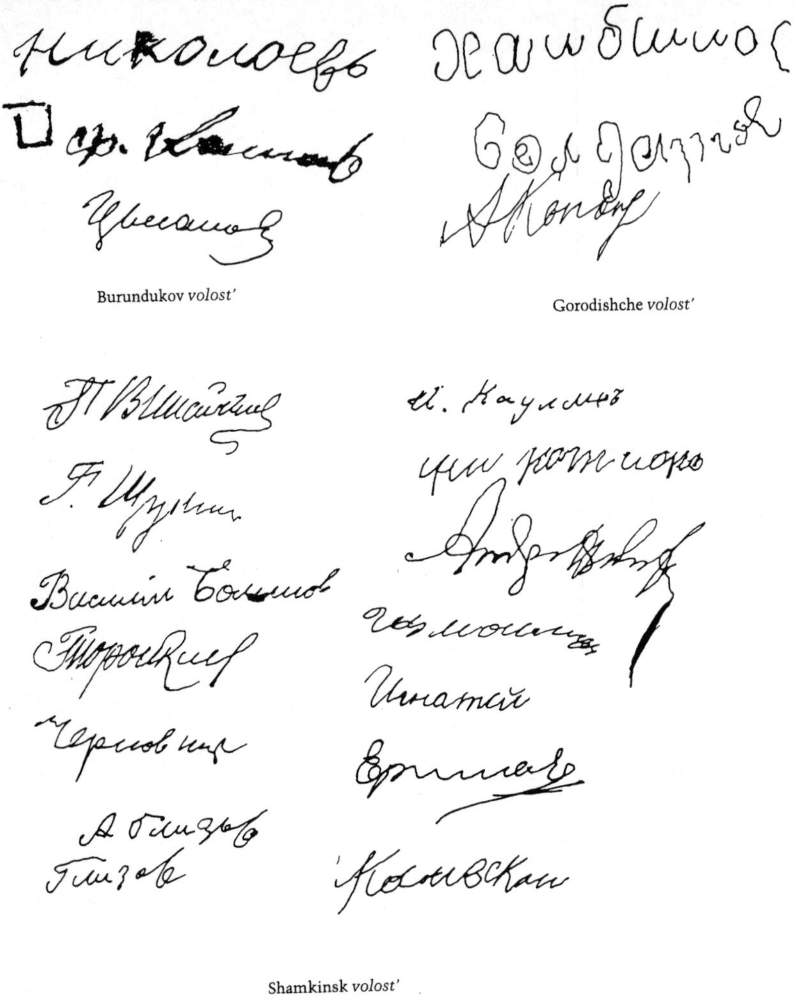

Fig. 1. *Signatures of* volost' *electoral commissioners, Buinsk* uezd

The low level of literacy displayed in the appearance of several hundred signatures and their proxies suggests that the electoral commissioners stood closer, in cultural terms, to the peasants at the head of the village communities than to the higher government authorities. Indeed, the VTsIK instructions were constantly infringed in the village elections by the traditional voting practices of the village assembly. The votes were not generally cast by secret ballot. The peasantwomen were rarely allowed to exercise their electoral rights granted by the Soviet Constitution. The villages continued to elect much larger soviets than permitted by the official regulations. During the election campaigns the NKVD frequently complained about the shortages—and the poor quality—of electoral commissioners: the latter were slow to deliver the election results to the higher authorities and frequently got themselves into hopeless disputes with the peasantry about the organization of the elections.[68]

The records of the 1919 election results, the *ankety o vyborakh v sovety*, are found in the Archives of the October Revolution (TsGAOR). They were completed by the soviet chairmen after the election, and were sent to the statistical department of NKVD. Information was requested on the date of the election; the population of the village or the *volost'*; the size of the electorate and its sexual, occupational, and party composition; and the breakdown of the elected soviet members by sex, occupation, education, age, and party membership. Although many of the *ankety* suffer from very low levels of literacy and numeracy, none of them manifests any signs of fraud.[69] They provide a genuinely valuable insight into the political culture of the village at a critical moment of its transformation during the civil war.

In view of their significance, it is perhaps surprising that only one Soviet historian, E. G. Gimpel'son, has ever studied the *ankety* in detail.[70] Gimpel'son counted the number of people taking part in the elections in each district, and gave a general breakdown (i.e. by district) of the sex, education, and party membership of the members of the village soviets and the VIKs. Such aggregates are of limited historical value, since they do not evaluate the influence of certain factors (e.g. the level of Bolshevik party organization) on others (e.g. the age structure of the soviet, or its educational background).

The following study of the soviet elections—mainly in Simbirsk province, but also in Tambov, Voronezh, Riazan', Saratov, and Severo-Dvinsk provinces—is the first to correlate such factors.[71] It analyses the *ankety* of 1,036 village soviet elections (representing at least 678,262 people) and 160 *volost'* soviet elections (representing at least 545,341 people). The province of Simbirsk comprised 1,357 villages and 179 *volost'* townships at the time of the 1920 census.[72] The *ankety* from

[68] See further R. Abrams, 'The Local Soviets of the RSFSR, 1918–1921', Ph.D. diss., Columbia University, 1966, pp. 166 ff.

[69] M. Frenkin (*Tragediia krest'ianskikh vosstanii v Rossii 1918–1921 gg.*, Jerusalem, 1987, pp. 54–5) writes without foundation that the elections were 'fictitious', since the successful candidates were pre-selected by the *kombedy*. This conflicts sharply with the evidence presented here.

[70] E. G. Gimpel'son, *Sovety v gody interventsii i grazhdanskoi voiny*, Moscow, 1968, pp. 48–69, 83–6, 97–8, 480–7.

[71] TsGAOR, f. 393, op. 13, d. 609 (Riazan', Saratov, Severo-Dvinsk, Tambov); f. 393, op. 13, d. 610, dd. 612–14 (Simbirsk); f. 393, op. 13, d. 618 (Tambov, Voronezh, Saratov); f. 393, op. 3, d. 334, ll. 377–85 (Saratov).

[72] *Trudy TsSU: Itogi vserossiiskoi sel'sko-khoziaistvennoi perepisi 1920 g. v granitsakh gubernii na 1 marta 1922 g.* Moscow, 1923, p. 70.

Simbirsk province analysed below relate to 842 different villages (62% of the total number in the province) and 91 different *volost'* centres (51%). The ethnic composition of the population of Simbirsk province in 1920 was relatively mixed: 64.8% Russian; 12.6% Chuvash; 11.7% Mordvinian; and 10.3% Tatar. The Tatar and Chuvash population was concentrated in Buinsk district[73]—a factor which greatly facilitates our analysis of the correlation between ethnic variations and other factors in the election results.

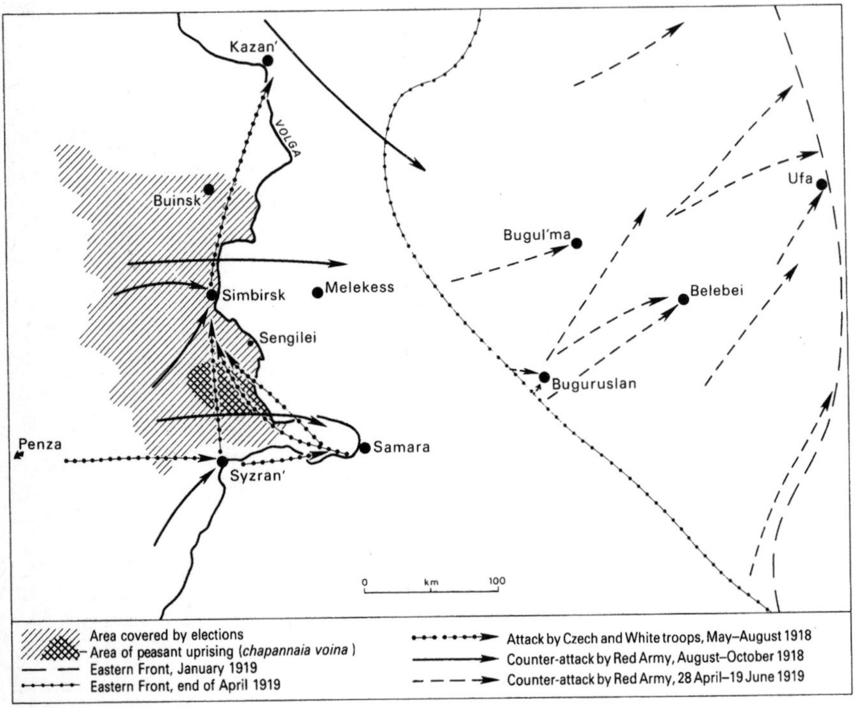

Map 4. *Area of Simbirsk elections and movement of civil war front, summer 1918 to summer 1919*

Map 4 illustrates the area covered by the election results in Simbirsk province and the movement of the civil war fronts. The towns which had been occupied by the Czech legion and the forces of the Komuch between May and August 1918 were recaptured by the Red Army between August and October. By the beginning of 1919, Kolchak's army had been pushed

[73] When the Tatar Republic and the Chuvash Autonomous Oblast were founded in May and June 1920, respectively, 239,000 people from Buinsk district (96 per cent of the population of the district) were transferred to the new administrative territories; this represents more than 80 per cent of the population from Simbirsk province transferred to the new administrative territories (*Vserossiiskaia perepis' naseleniia 1920 goda: Simbirskaia guberniia*, Simbirsk, 1923, pp. 106–9, 116–17).

back to Ufa and Orenburg, but during the following spring it counter-attacked towards the Volga. A major peasant uprising against the Bolsheviks (*chapannaia voina*) began behind the Red lines to the north of Syzran' at the beginning of March, and was suppressed later in the same month (see ch. 7, sect. 1). At the end of April the Red Army began to force Kolchak eastward again. By the time of the harvest of 1919, the Whites had retreated as far as the Urals.

The changing fortunes of the Reds, the Whites, and the 'Greens' (peasant armies fighting both the Whites and the Reds, so named because of their tendency to seek cover in woodland areas) had an enormous impact upon the voting patterns of the peasants, who were obviously concerned to curry favour with the winning side. For this reason, the records of the soviet elections will be divided into three seasons: 'spring' (January to April), when the Eastern Front was situated in the proximity of our area, and there was intense peasant discontent; 'summer' (May to August), when the Red Army pushed Kolchak towards the Urals, and the peasants were busy in the fields; and 'autumn' (August to December), when a large portion of the peasant-soldiers deserted the Red Army and returned to their villages (see ch. 6, sect. 5). The records relate to 448 village elections and 89 *volost'* elections during the 'spring'; 334 village elections and 43 *volost'* elections during the 'summer'; and 254 village elections and 28 *volost'* elections during the 'autumn'. To verify the seasonal variations we shall use the records of 70 village soviets and 16 *volost'* soviets elected in more than one of these seasons.

The Electorate

Participation in the peasant communal assembly was generally limited to the heads of the peasant households. The Statute of 1864 on the election of district *zemstvo* deputies from the villages, and the electoral law of 11 December 1905, which governed peasant curia elections to the Duma, reinforced this principle by making the *desiatidvorniki* (delegates representing ten households at the communal assembly) the smallest electoral units.[74]

During 1917–18 the communal assembly of peasant household heads began to be overshadowed by the general meetings of the village, where the younger men, especially those who had served in the war, tended to play a much greater part than they had done before 1914. This process of democratization did not fundamentally alter the patriarchal-traditional nature of village politics, however. Although

[74] K. E. McKenzie, 'Zemstvo Organization and Role within the Administrative Structure', in T. Emmons and W. S. Vucinich (eds.), *The Zemstvo in Russia: An Experiment in Local Self-Government*, Cambridge, 1982, p. 39; T. Emmons, *The Formation of Political Parties and the First National Elections in Russia*, Harvard, 1983, p. 241.

the elections to the *volost'*-level *zemstva* during the summer of 1917 and to the Constituent Assembly during the following winter were based on universal suffrage, the peasantwomen rarely exercised their electoral rights, while the influence of the household elders and the communal leaders remained dominant.[75]

The political influence of the commune on the development of the soviets was highlighted by the low turn-out in the elections of 1919. The vast majority of the village soviets were elected by a small male minority, often comprising no more than the peasant household elders.[76] In total, 26.1% of the *stated* adult population participated in the village soviet elections (26.4% in the Tatar and Chuvash villages of Buinsk). In 32.5% of the villages the soviet was elected by less than one-fifth of the stated adult population; in 55.5% of the villages it was elected by less than three-tenths; and in 75.7% of the villages the soviet was elected by less than half the stated adult population. It is unlikely that more than half the adult population actually took part in the remaining elections (24.3%), since the women were reported to have comprised only 9.5% of the voters in these elections. On the same principle, it should be underlined that the above figures may exaggerate the level of electoral participation, since the soviet chairmen sometimes counted only the men or only the household heads under the column for the 'adult population'.[77] In the 35 village elections where it was actually specified in the *anketa* that the adult

TABLE 15. *Size of village and electoral participation, Simbirsk and other provinces, 1919*

No. of adult inhabitants in village	% adults voting
100 or less	48.5
101–200	44.0
201–500	35.7
501–750	27.5
751 or more	22.6

[75] See W. G. Rosenberg, 'The Zemstvo in 1917 and its Fate under Bolshevik Rule', in Emmons and Vucinich (eds.), *The Zemstvo*, pp. 398–9; O. H. Radkey, *The Election to the Russian Constituent Assembly of 1917*, Harvard, 1950, pp. 63–9.

[76] It could be argued that the electorate was similar in size and composition to the one which had elected many of the *kombedy*. Although this was true in some of the larger *volost'* townships, it is very unlikely to have been the case in the majority of the villages, where the peasant commune dominated the election of the soviet. Nearly all the *ankety* specified that the soviet members were peasants by occupation.

[77] For this reason, the unqualified figure of 41 per cent given by Gimpel'son for the proportion of adults voting is misleading (Gimpel'son, *Sovety v gody interventsii*, p. 53).

population comprised both men and women no more than 8.7% of the franchised population turned out to vote.

The electoral turn-out declined slightly over the course of the year, from 27.8% in the 'spring', to 24.1% in the 'summer', and to 25% in the 'autumn'. The decline took place during the 'summer', when the peasants were busy in the fields.

The electoral turn-out also varied in accordance with the size of the village (see Table 15). It has been argued that the poor peasants were more likely to control the soviet in a large village.[78] If this is true, then the higher turn-out in the smaller villages may be partly explained by the supremacy and the greater organizational resources of the wealthy peasants. The main explanation, however, is probably related to the fact that the Soviet system tended to be more democratic in small units, where the people retained direct forms of control over their affairs, compared with the larger units, where more complex bureaucracies had to be organized and the people consequently tended to become indifferent about the soviet.[79]

Women took part in 31.5% of the village elections and, in total, comprised 10.1% of the electorate. There is evidence to suggest that in the villages where some women voted in the 'spring' or the 'summer', the number of women voting tended to increase in the subsequent election: this was the case in 5 out of 6 villages with elections in 'spring' and 'autumn'; and in 6 out of 7 villages with elections in 'summer' and 'autumn'. However, the aggregate female share of the vote dropped from 14.2% in the 'spring' to 6.1% in the 'autumn'. This is probably explained by the return of the peasant-soldiers from the Red Army during the latter half of 1919. The women who voted in the village elections tended to do so as a small minority (23.8% of the voters); they comprised less than 10% of the electorate in roughly half of the elections in which they took part. This suggests that the peasant-women voted only if their menfolk were away in the army, or if they headed a family household without adult male labour. One *anketa* from Malyi Chilim village (Buinsk *uezd*) stated that the soviet had been elected by '70 householders—69 men and one woman'. Another from Gorodetsk village (Sengilei *uezd*) stated that the soviet had been elected by 127 householders, two of them women.[80] In their own right,

[78] *RR*, p. 167.

[79] It has been noted (M. Dobb, *Russian Economic Development since the Revolution*, London, 1928, p. 359) that the young ex-servicemen tended to play a leading role in the establishment of hamlets (*vyselki, poselki*) after the revolution. They certainly played a prominent part in the establishment of collective farms in new settlements (see ch. 6, sect. 4). Their activism may explain the higher turn-out of the electorate in the smaller villages.

[80] TsGAOR, f. 393, op. 13, d. 612, l. 101; d. 613, l. 74.

female voters were not considered the equals of men. The *anketa* from Fedorovka village (Tambov *uezd*) recorded that the soviet had been elected by '69 people' and 'four women'. In Shirtany village (Buinsk *uezd*) it was reported that the soviet had been elected by '55 peasants' and 'eight women'.[81] Such comments echoed traditional peasant proverbs (e.g. 'A hen's no bird and a woman's no person!').

Women did not increase their role in village politics until the end of 1920, when a national campaign was launched to involve peasant-women in rural administration, especially in the field of social welfare (e.g. aid for the families of soldiers in the Red Army).[82] In our sample only 12 villages (out of a total of 1,036) contained a female Bolshevik party member. It is significant that the female share of the vote doubled (to 20.7%) in these 12 villages, although it did not increase at all in the villages with a Bolshevik party cell (between 3 and 15 members) consisting entirely of men. However, women did comprise 19.4% of the voters in the villages with resident 'workers',[83] which, on the whole, were closer to an urban centre.

In view of the unique political circumstances of the civil war, we need to be cautious in our interpretation of the data concerning peasant party allegiance (*partiinost'*). Four in five soviet chairmen declared the population in their village to be 'non-party' (*bespartiinyi*). This was no doubt a sensible thing to do during a civil war, but it does not tell us the whole truth about the political colours of the rural population. Many of the 'non-party' people must have been members of the opposition parties, hiding from persecution by the Cheka; although the Volga region was known as a stronghold of the moderate socialist parties before October 1917, none of them registered more than a handful of members in the soviet elections of 1919. Similarly, a large portion of the rural population was registered as 'sympathetic' to the Bolshevik party: many of these people may have been committed communists, and some may even have been awaiting registration as candidate party members; yet a large percentage must have been simply concerned to appear 'on the right side' before the higher Soviet authorities. This is highlighted by the fact that 55% (68 out of 124) of

81 Ts GAOR, f. 393, op. 13, d. 609, l. 191; d. 612, l. 206.

82 The majority of the reports from this campaign stressed the hostility of the peasant-men towards the politicized women. In Balashov district, Saratov province, for example, it was reported that bands of peasant fighters prevented women from being elected to the *volost'* soviets, where they were active in providing support schemes for the families of Red Army soldiers. The report added that the village soviets were unhappy about women being 'infiltrated' into the *VIKs*. Similar reports were made in Dergachi, Pokrovsk, and Novouzensk districts (Samara). See *Bor'ba* (Tsaritsyn), no. 36, 29 May 1921, p. 2.

83 Peasants sometimes referred to themselves as 'workers', in the sense that 'peasants work'. In such cases, they have been counted as peasants.

the village soviet chairmen registering 'sympathizers' claimed that the whole population of the village fell into this category. The proportion of the electorate registered as 'sympathizers' declined from 18.2% in the 'summer' (with 3 in 4 of the villages declaring all their inhabitants to be 'sympathizers') to a mere 4.1% in the 'autumn' (with over half of the villages registering no more than 5 individual 'sympathizers'). These changes may be explained by the subsidence of the civil war in the region, by mounting peasant discontent with war communism, and by the Bolshevik party registration of autumn 1919, which virtually eliminated the category of 'sympathizers'.[84]

The soviet chairmen who completed the *ankety* were not always clear about the status of the Bolshevik party members. It was not uncommon for a soviet chairman to register all his villagers as party members, or for the peasants who were counted as Bolshevik members at the *volost'* assembly to be registered only by name and patronymic in their own village soviet. More than a year after the Bolshevik party had changed its name to the Communist party (in March 1918), some village soviet chairmen continued to provide information on the membership of the two separate 'parties'.[85] Indeed, the slogan 'We are for the Bolsheviks, but against the Communists!' was widely noted in peasant uprisings during 1919–20 (the Bolsheviks were associated with the October Decree on Land, whereas the Communists were often confused with the *kommuny*—the collective farms).[86]

Bolshevik party members took part in 178 village elections (17.2% of the total number of elections) during 1919. In 33 of these elections only one Bolshevik member voted. In 41 of the elections 2 Bolsheviks voted. Small party cells (between 3 and 7 Bolsheviks) were registered in 72 village elections. Large party cells (between 8 and 15 Bolsheviks) were registered in 24 village elections. Eight soviet chairmen claimed, somewhat unconvincingly, that their village had more than 15 Bolshevik party members.[87] In total, Bolshevik party members comprised 0.6% of the voters in the village soviet elections during 1919.

The number of Bolshevik party members in the villages declined during the 'summer', largely on account of Red Army mobilizations, which, according to one survey, involved at least 30% of all party members in the Volga region at the end of 1918.[88] In the 'spring' 0.80%

[84] See Table 13.

[85] TsGAOR, f. 393, op. 13, d. 613, l. 179; d. 614, ll. 71–2; d. 612, l. 231, etc.

[86] *Izvestiia samarskogo gubernskogo soveta narodnogo khoziaistva*, no. 18, 22 Mar. 1919, p. 1.

[87] In this study rural inhabitants have been counted as party members only in villages claiming to have fewer than fifteen party members. Without access to party archives, this is unfortunately the best 'control' that can be imposed upon the data.

[88] Molodtsygin, p. 206. See further Iu. P. Petrov, *Partiinye mobilizatsii v krasnuiu armiiu 1918–20*, Moscow, 1956, pp. 64, 74, 76, 87–8.

of the electorate belonged to the Bolshevik party; and in the 'summer' only 0.27%; but by the end of the year, the Bolsheviks had increased their share of the village electorate to 0.69%, mainly as a result of the party recruitment campaigns (see sect. 3 below). E. G. Gimpel'son has noted a similar pattern nationwide, despite the constantly increasing levels of party recruitment. He concluded that 'the more Communists there were in a village, the more went off to the front'.[89] This is a useful thumb-rule, but it should be underlined that the number of villages with at least one party member remained buoyant in our sample at 15.4% in the 'spring' and 12.9% in the 'summer', thereafter rising steeply to 26.1% in the 'autumn'. This helps to explain why the rural party cells were able to gain control of the majority of the *volost'* soviets during 1919, in spite of the losses they incurred in the civil war (see Table 16).

TABLE 16. *Bolshevik party representation in rural soviets, Simbirsk and other provinces, 1919*

	Spring	Summer	Autumn	Overall
% registered as Bolsheviks				
Electorate	0.80	0.27	0.69	0.64
Village soviet members	3.13	1.99	2.90	2.75
Village soviet executive members	14.20	10.27	14.90	13.31
Volost' soviet assembly delegates	10.85	11.52	14.55	11.78
VIK members	52.94	21.48	66.66	49.43
% with registered Bolsheviks				
Village soviets	9.88	8.10	11.50	9.71
Village soviet executive committees	12.68	13.02	16.46	13.81
Volost' soviet assemblies	47.19	44.18	78.57	53.75
VIKs	38.20	25.58	71.43	38.75

Two final variations ought to be mentioned. First, there were fewer Bolsheviks in the Tatar and Chuvash villages (0.15% of the electorate), compared with the Russian ones, although the Bolsheviks did increase their share of the non-Russian vote from 0.08% in the 'spring' to 0.3% in the 'autumn'. Second, a higher proportion of the electorate was registered as Bolshevik (1.0%) in the 36 villages with resident 'workers'; 21 of these 36 villages (58.3%) had at least one resident Bolshevik party member. It is interesting to note that the 'workers', who represented only 15.4% of the adult population in these 21 villages, were found among the party members in 16 of the 21 villages.

[89] Gimpel'son, *Sovety v gody interventsii*, pp. 66–7.

Rural inhabitants engaged in non-agricultural occupations formed a major vanguard of the Bolshevik party.

The Village Soviets

In their social composition and character the village soviets closely resembled the rural electorate at large. Whereas the Bolshevik cadres were becoming increasingly influential in the *volost'* soviets during the civil war, most of the village soviets remained essentially 'peasant' organs of power.

The average village soviet comprised 10 members and represented 700 inhabitants. The Soviet Constitution stipulated that each soviet member was to represent 100 franchised inhabitants. But if we discount the villages with less than 300 inhabitants that were officially entitled to elect three soviet members, then it appears that each member of the average village soviet represented no more than 80 inhabitants (in the Chuvash and Tatar villages the average soviet member represented no more than 60 residents). The tendency of the villages to elect larger soviets than the size set out in the Constitution was, as we have already noted, rooted in traditional peasant customs (see ch. 3, sect. 1). Because the majority of the village soviet members were peasant farmers, they were not able to attend official meetings regularly during the summer months, so the peasants selected 'reserve' soviet members to share the burdens of public office. It was for this reason that the size of the village soviets tended to change between elections. Of the 57 villages with elections in more than one season, only 19 elected the same number of soviet members in consecutive elections; 28 villages elected a larger soviet the second time round, and 10 villages elected a smaller one.

The overwhelming majority of the village soviet members (97.7%) were peasantmen. Only 11 villages in our sample of 1,036 had a female member (none of the Chuvash or Tatar villages had a female member). Women comprised a mere 0.3% of the village soviet members. The peasantwomen in the electorate almost invariably voted for their men folk: women comprised only 1.2% of the members in the 325 village soviets, elected by men and women; and only 1.9% of the members in the soviets, containing a Bolshevik member and elected by men and women.

The remaining 2% of the village soviet members were registered as 'workers'. They were elected to the soviet in 20 of the 36 villages where 'workers' voted. They were members of the soviet in 9 villages where no 'workers' had voted in the elections (i.e. they were 'outsiders').

The vast majority of the village soviet members (86.3%) were registered as 'non-party', while 10.2% of the members declared themselves to be Bolshevik 'sympathizers'; in 8 out of 10 cases the latter may also be counted as 'non-party' (i.e. when all the village soviet members were registered as 'sympathizers').

Members of the opposition parties were registered in only 12 soviets. They were said to comprise, in total, only 0.72% of the village soviet members (2.0% in the Chuvash and Tatar villages). If we discount the improbable likelihood that a large number of the opposition party members were registered as members of the soviet, but not as franchised inhabitants of the village (the reverse was in fact more likely), then these figures may be said to constitute a very high rate of return. In the villages where an opposition party member had voted in the election, as many as 42.1% of the soviet members belonged to an opposition party. In the Chuvash and Tatar villages of Buinsk 85% of the opposition (mainly Muhammadan) party members who had voted in the elections were actually returned to their soviet. These figures suggest that there were some highly politicized centres of opposition to the Bolshevik government, particularly in the non-Russian areas. The NKVD report on the political mood of the rural population during the summer of 1918 (Table 12) characterized the whole population of Buinsk and the rural population of Simbirsk province, in general, as 'hostile' to the Soviet regime.

The Bolshevik party made slow but certain inroads into the village soviets. Its rural members represented 2.75% of the village soviet members during 1919 (0.6% in the Chuvash and Tatar villages). The number fell from 3.1% in the 'spring' to 2.0% in the 'summer', largely on account of the party mobilizations; but it recovered to 2.9% in the 'autumn'. Most of the soviets retained at least one Bolshevik party member during the 'summer': 9.9% of the soviets contained at least one party member during the 'spring'; 8.1% during the 'summer'; and 11.5% during the 'autumn'. A good indication of the growing influence of the Bolshevik party was the increasing likelihood of a party member getting elected to the soviet in his native village. In the 'spring' 17.1% of the Bolshevik residents in the villages were elected to their soviet; in the 'summer' the figure was 34.5%; and in the 'autumn' 23.8%. The decline during the 'autumn' may be largely explained by the absolute increase of Bolshevik party members in the villages as a result of the party recruitments. But peasant voting strategies against the party can not be discounted as a secondary factor: during this period there was an increasing level of conflict between the peasants and the party cells over the control of the soviet executives and the 'non-party' peasant assemblies (see sect. 4 below).

The role of the rural industrialists as a Bolshevik vanguard is confirmed by the data on soviet membership. Bolsheviks comprised 7.1% of the soviet members in the 36 villages where 'workers' had voted in the election (and only 2.6% in the villages where 'workers' had not participated). Whereas, in general, one in ten village soviets contained a Bolshevik, the figure in the villages with resident 'workers' was as high as one in three.

The educational background of the village soviet members was generally low, although the literacy rate of the members was probably higher than the rate among the rural male population as a whole (see Table 17). Only 1% of the members of the village soviets had attended

TABLE 17. *Education of rural soviet members and literacy of rural population, Simbirsk and other provinces, 1919* (%)

	Level of education			
	High	Mid	Low	None
Village soviet members	0.16	0.89	59.03	39.90
Village soviet executive members	0.31	1.28	75.09	23.32
Volost' soviet assembly delegates	0.22	0.69	72.95	26.14
VIK members	0.61	2.83	62.92	33.64
	Literate			Illiterate
Rural males aged 4 and over	40.89			59.11

Source: The rural male literacy rate in the last row is calculated from *Vserossiiskaia perepis' naseleniia 1920 goda: Simbirskaia guberniia*, Simbirsk, 1923.

a middle or a higher school. The majority of the soviet members (59%) had received some form of primary (including domestic) education—something which cannot be generally said for the rural population. The remaining 40% of the village soviet members had not received any education, and may be counted as illiterates. In 42% of the village soviets the majority of the members fell within this last category.

The educational background of the village soviet members varied according to ethnic and social factors. The majority of the soviet members in the Chuvash and Tatar villages (51.7%) had not received any education, although the proportion fell rapidly from 57% during the 'spring' to 44.4% during the 'autumn'. The soviets in the villages with resident 'workers', by contrast, registered only 23.9% of their members without education during the 'spring' and only 18.2% during the 'autumn'. Where women had voted in the village election there was a marked fall in the proportion of uneducated soviet members during the course of the year (from 38% to 30.3%). The soviets which included a female member contained significantly fewer members without education (22.5%).

The soviets which included at least one Bolshevik member were relatively (and increasingly) well educated. During the 'spring' 35.7% of the members of the village soviets which included a Bolshevik member were registered without education; by the end of the year the proportion had fallen to 24.1%. In the villages with a Bolshevik party cell the proportion of the soviet members without education fell from 29.5% during the 'spring' to 21% during the 'autumn'. Bolshevism, it appears, took root in the countryside among beardless peasant sons educated during the decade prior to 1914 and radicalized in the Imperial or the Red Army.

This is confirmed by the age structure of the village soviets. We have delineated the rural population aged between 18 and 35 years (born between 1884 and 1901) as a special cohort, broadly representing this generation of young men who benefited from the considerable advances in rural schooling prior to 1914, and who represented the majority of the conscripts in the Imperial and the Red armies. Table 18 shows that they played a vital role in the rural soviets and the Bolshevik party—a role out of all proportion to their demographic place within rural society at large. The 18- to 35-year-olds represented 31% of the adult rural population; 33.1% of the village soviet members; 37.9% of the soviet members in the villages where at least one Bolshevik party member had voted in the soviet election; 41.6% of the soviet members in the villages with a party cell; and 43.3% of the members of the soviets which included at least one Bolshevik party member.

The correlation between Bolshevism and youth was much stronger than that between any other social factor and the age structure of the village soviets. Where 'workers' had participated in the elections the village soviets were not markedly younger. In the Chuvash and Tatar villages, in which patriarchal attitudes were said to be stronger, the soviets were not noticeably older.

The Village Soviet Executive Committees

The Soviet Constitution of July 1918 stipulated that villages with over 1,000 inhabitants were to elect an executive committee (*ispolkom*) of up to five members. Lack of finance in fact prevented the majority of villages from electing more than three executive members. On the other hand, many villages with less than 1,000 inhabitants also elected an executive. In total, executives were elected by 58% of the village soviets in 1919. The proportion fell, due to Red Army mobilizations of

TABLE 18. *Age structure of adult rural population and soviet membership, Simbirsk and other provinces, 1919 (%)*

	18–20	20–5	25–30	30–5	35–40	40–5	45–50	50+	**18–35**
Rural population (18+)	6.07	11.09	9.18	20.34		20.29		33.00	**31.06**
Village soviets	0.62	3.68	10.04	18.76	23.06	22.04	14.57	7.14	**33.10**
with Bolshevik member	0.80	5.56	15.49	21.41	20.03	18.54	11.13	7.04	**43.26**
Village soviet executives	2.03	5.18	12.40	25.01	19.13	19.27	9.81	7.17	**44.62**
with Bolshevik member	2.17	3.62	17.39	31.88	21.01	13.76	5.79	4.38	**55.06**
Volost' soviet assemblies	1.28	7.36	15.53	24.30	23.92	12.13	8.76	6.72	**48.47**
with Bolshevik cell	1.41	10.61	21.10	26.17	22.78	8.64	5.11	4.23	**59.29**
VIKs	1.90	8.22	16.29	34.06	17.47	10.71	5.13	6.22	**60.47**
with Bolshevik member	2.81	10.42	19.71	30.14	17.18	12.11	4.50	3.13	**63.08**

Source: The age structure of the adult rural population in the first row is calculated from *Vserossiiskaia perepis' naseleniia 1920 goda: Simbirskaia guberniia*, Simbirsk, 1923.

leading soviet personnel, from 59.8% in the 'spring' to 51.6% in the 'summer'; but by the end of the year as many as 63.8% of the village soviets had their own separate executive committee.[90]

As expected, the larger villages were more likely to elect an executive. Only 28.9% of the villages with less than 100 adult inhabitants elected an executive, compared with: 43.4% of the villages with between 100 and 300 adult inhabitants; 63.1% of the villages with between 300 and 500 adult inhabitants; and 80.3% of the villages with more than 500 adult inhabitants. Village inhabitants engaged in non-agricultural occupations had a strong influence on the organization of an executive; 80.6% of the villages with resident 'workers' had a soviet executive. Bolshevik organization also strongly influenced the formation of the executives, which were elected in 75% of the villages with a Bolshevik party cell. If 80.3% of the villages with more than 500 adult residents elected an executive, then 93.6% of the villages of that size and with a Bolshevik party cell elected one. At the other end of the spectrum the influence of the Bolshevik party was even more marked: 37.4% of the villages with less than 300 adult residents elected an executive, whereas 63.6% of the villages of that size and with a Bolshevik party cell elected one.

There were three principal methods of electing a village soviet executive. Roughly one-fifth of the village soviet executives was elected at an open meeting of the village; three-fifths were elected at a meeting of the soviet; and one-fifth was elected at an enlarged meeting of either the village or (more commonly) the village soviet, attended by Red Army units, urban food brigades, Bolshevik party agents, or other agitators. The Bolshevik party was markedly better represented in the executives which had been established in the presence of these outsider agitators.

Bolshevik party members represented 13.3% of the village soviet executive members in 1919. Owing to party mobilizations, the proportion declined from 14.2% in the 'spring' to 10.3% in the 'summer'; but it rose to 14.9% by the end of the year. The Bolsheviks' growing influence in the executives is expressed most clearly in terms of the number of villages with Bolsheviks in the executive: the number of soviet executives with at least one Bolshevik member rose from 12.68% in the 'spring', to 13.02% in the 'summer', and to 16.46% in the 'autumn' (see Table 16). The increasing influence of the Bolshevik rural cadres is underlined by the finding that of the 21 village soviet

[90] Many of the soviet chairmen completed the sections on the executive committees by repeating the information they had already given on the soviet and the body of people electing the executive. Such information has not been included in the data on the executive committees.

executives elected in more than one season, 19 witnessed an increase in the number of Bolshevik executive members as a result of their second election. Moreover, the likelihood of a Bolshevik soviet member getting elected to his executive increased during the course of 1919: during the 'spring' 86.2% of the Bolsheviks in a village soviet were also in its executive; during the 'summer' the figure was 98.25%; and during the 'autumn' 94.74%.

In the Chuvash and Tatar villages the increase in the number of Bolshevik members of the soviet executives was particularly steep, largely because it rose from a low base. During the 'spring' only 2 of the 123 village soviet executives in these areas included a Bolshevik party member; by the 'summer' the number had increased to 7; and by the 'autumn' to 15. During the course of the year the Bolshevik rural cadres increased their share of the village soviet executive membership from 1.5% to 16.9%.

In the villages where the Red Army or Bolshevik party and other agitators had taken part in the establishment of the soviet executive, the latter contained a much higher proportion of Bolshevik party members. If, in general, 13.3% of the village soviet executive members were registered as Bolsheviks, then in the villages in which external agitators had taken part in the establishment of the executive as many as 32.6% of the soviet executive members belonged to the Bolshevik party (although these Bolsheviks accounted for only 3.6% of the soviet members in the corresponding villages). Evidently, a very large proportion of the Bolsheviks in these village soviets had been promoted to the executive. In fact, during the 'autumn' the number of Bolsheviks in these executives exceeded the number of Bolsheviks in the corresponding soviets by 14%—a figure that can only be explained if the Red Army and the Bolshevik party agitators appointed a number of Bolshevik outsiders to the village soviet executives.[91] This phenomenon, which was more commonly noted in the VIKs, was a key factor in the process whereby the Bolsheviks strengthened their grip on the soviets in the countryside during the civil war.

A good example of this 'placement' system was found in the area of the peasant uprising known as *chapannaia voina*. As a result of the soviet re-elections during the 'spring', shortly after the revolt had been put down, the Bolshevik party got its members elected to 36.4% of the places in the village soviet executives of this area. In the villages where

[91] It is unlikely that the Bolshevik party members were not registered as such by their soviet chairman in the columns for the soviet, but were counted as party members in the neighbouring columns relating to the village executives. The same point applies to the discrepancies between the number of Bolshevik party members registered at the *volost'* assemblies and in the VIKs.

Bolshevik party members had participated in the elections (24 out of 61 elections), they comprised 0.8% of the voters, but 78% of the village soviet executive members. The number of Bolsheviks in the village executives exceeded the number of Bolsheviks in the corresponding village soviets by 81.3%. In other words, the Bolshevik party appointed one outsider to the village soviet executives for nearly every local Bolshevik executive member elected by the soviet (or the village).

The village soviet executives were generally better educated and younger in composition than their soviets. This may have reflected the demand for energetic and literate administrators in the rural localities during the revolutionary period, when the villages were responsible more than ever before for the organization of their own affairs. Whereas 40% of the village soviet members were uneducated, only 23.3% of the village soviet executive members had not received any education (see Table 17). The proportion declined from 25.5% during the 'spring' to 17.3% during the 'autumn'. In the Tatar and Chuvash villages, where educational levels were generally lower, the contrast was less striking: 51.7% of the village soviet members and 42.7% of the soviet executive members were registered without education.

The educational level of the village executives was only marginally influenced by the presence of the Bolshevik party: 19.6% of the members of the village soviet executives with a Bolshevik member were uneducated; 20.6% of the members of the executives established in the presence of external agitators were uneducated. The influence of resident 'workers' had a much stronger impact on levels of education: only 7.3% of the members of the village executives elected by 'workers' had not received any education.

There was a very strong correlation between the age structure of the village soviet executives and the level of Bolshevik party organization (see Table 18). If 33.1% of the village soviet members were younger than 35, then 44.6% of the village soviet executive members came within this age group, as did 55.1% of the members of the village executives with a Bolshevik party member. Here, the crucial role was played by those aged between 25 and 35. This cohort comprised 28.8% of the village soviet members, 37.4% of the village executive members, and 49.3% of the members of the village executives with a Bolshevik party member. It was the peasants of this age group—those who had been taken outside the village by the World War—who took over the reins of Soviet power in the countryside after 1919.

The Volost' *Soviet Assembly*

The *volost'* soviet assembly was attended by delegates from the communes or the village soviets. It was, according to Article 57 of the

Soviet Constitution, the highest political authority within the *volost'*. During the civil war the VIKs and the Bolshevik party cells increasingly dominated the *volost'* assembly. Nevertheless, most of the directives of the VIKs and the higher Soviet authorities, especially those concerning the peasant economy, continued to prove impossible to implement without the approval of the *volost'* soviet assembly, or some other assembly of the peasants.

The *volost'* assemblies in our sample were attended, on average, by 35 peasants. Only 3 out of the 160 assemblies were attended by a female delegate. This says a great deal about the status of women in rural society.

The level of Bolshevik party representation at the *volost'* assemblies was slightly lower than in the village executives (see Table 16): only 11.8% of the assembly delegates were Bolshevik party members (2.3% in the Chuvash and Tatar areas). The proportion increased during the course of the year from 10.8% in the 'spring', to 11.5% in the 'summer', and to 14.5% in the 'autumn'. This may be explained by the party recruitment campaigns during the latter half of 1919 (see sect. 3 below), by the increasing domination of the village executives—particularly the Bolshevik-controlled ones—over their soviets in the selection of delegates, and, finally, by the growing indifference of the non-party peasants towards the *volost'* soviets in general (see sect. 4 below). It was the attendance of the delegates from the outlying villages which, for obvious reasons, tended to decline the most sharply, thereby increasing the influence of the delegates from the *volost'* township, who were generally more likely to be Bolshevik party members.

Although the Bolsheviks comprised a small minority at the *volost'* soviet assemblies, it should be borne in mind that it sometimes only required one or two committed Bolsheviks to sway the other delegates in favour of the resolutions supporting the Soviet government. Of the 160 *volost'* soviet assemblies in our sample, 86 (53.75%) were attended by at least one Bolshevik party member; the number increased sharply from 47.2% during the 'spring' to 78.6% during the 'autumn'. The Bolsheviks also benefited from the support of Bolshevik 'sympathizers' (registered at 19 assemblies during the 'spring' and the 'summer'). Finally, the absence of any opposition party members at all but five of the assemblies was to be of crucial importance to the consolidation of the Bolshevik regime in the *volost'* townships, since the VIKs tended to be elected on a party slate (see sect. 4 below).

On the whole, the village soviets sent their more literate and younger representatives to the *volost'* soviet assemblies, and this tendency increased during the course of 1919. Whereas 40% of the village soviet members were registered without education, only 26.1% of the delegates at the *volost'* soviet assemblies were registered in this category; the proportion declined from 30.1% during the 'spring' to 20.6% during the 'autumn' (see Table 17). As we have already noted in relation to the village executives, the educational level of the assembly delegates varied less in proportion to the influence of the Bolshevik party, than it did in proportion to the attendance of 'workers': where the latter attended the assembly only 14.9% of the delegates were registered without education.

There was a very strong correlation between the level of Bolshevik party organization and the age structure of the *volost'* soviet assemblies (see Table 18). The under-35-year-olds comprised 48.5% of the *volost'* soviet assembly delegates; 58% of the delegates at the assemblies with at least one Bolshevik delegate; 59.3% of the delegates at the assemblies with three or more Bolshevik delegates; 60% of the delegates at the assemblies attended by 'workers'; and 74.6% of the delegates at the assemblies attended by a female delegate. Whereas the village executives were dominated by those aged between 25 and 35, a much greater role was played at the *volost'* assemblies by those aged under 25 years, especially where the assembly was attended by a Bolshevik, a 'worker', or a female delegate. If only 7.2% of the village soviet executive members were aged younger than 25 years, then 12% of the delegates were in this age group at the assemblies attended by three or more Bolsheviks, as were 16.4% of the delegates at the assemblies attended by 'workers', and 26.9% of the delegates at the assemblies attended by a female delegate. This distinction may be explained by the idea that the younger brothers were considered the most mobile and went to the *volost'* assembly, whereas the elder brothers tended to form a stable administrative élite in the villages.

The Volost' *Soviet Executive Committees (VIKs)*

The transformation of the VIKs represented the central mechanism in the process of Bolshevik state-building in the rural areas during the civil war. The VIKs were the kernel of the soviet administrative structure in the countryside. During the early period of the revolution the majority of the VIKs comprised up to a dozen or more peasants, and perhaps one or two rural *intelligenty*, who met on an amateur and non-partisan basis to implement the resolutions of the *volost'* assembly (see ch. 3, sect. 1). By the end of 1920, most of the VIKs had become bureaucratized state organs, run by three to five executive members, most of them in the Bolshevik party, and a team of salaried officials (see sect. 4 below).

The representation of the Bolshevik party in the VIKs increased from

52.9% of the executive members during the 'spring' of 1919 to 66.7% during the 'autumn'. Considering the sharp decline in the number of Bolsheviks in the VIKs during the 'summer', as a result of the party mobilizations and the losses of the civil war, this may be said to represent a significant advance. The size of the advance is expressed most clearly in terms of the number of VIKs with Bolshevik representatives: during the 'spring' 38.2% of the VIKs contained at least one Bolshevik party member; during the 'summer' the proportion fell to 25.6%; but by the end of the year the Bolshevik party was represented in as many as 71.4% of the VIKs, almost twice as many as during the previous 'spring'.

Almost 1 in 3 of the VIKs (28 out of 90), compared with 1 in 5 of the village soviet executives, was established in the presence of the Red Army or Bolshevik party and other agitators. There is a strong correlation between the presence of the latter and the number of Bolshevik party members returned to the VIK. In the VIKs which had been established without the presence of outsider agitators, only 13.2% of the VIK members were registered as Bolshevik party members; but where such agitators had been present, as many as 89.2% of the VIK members were Bolsheviks.

Some of these party members were likely to have been appointed by the party cell, rather than elected by the *volost'* soviet assembly (see further sect. 4 below). Of the 28 VIKs which had been established with the help of outsider agitators, 23 contained at least one Bolshevik party member, although only 17 of the corresponding *volost'* assemblies included a Bolshevik delegate. In other words, 6 of the 23 Bolshevik executive cadres had either joined the party immediately upon entering the VIK (this did sometimes happen), or (more likely) had been appointed to the VIK as outsiders by the party cell or the agitators. Moreover, 16 of the 23 Bolshevik executives which had been established with the help of the outsider agitators included a larger number of Bolshevik party members than had been registered at the corresponding *volost'* assemblies: thus some of the Bolshevik executive members must have been appointed to the VIK by the agitators, provided they had not joined the party immediately upon their election to the VIK. The total number of Bolshevik party members returned to the VIKs in the presence of outsider agitators exceeded the number of Bolshevik delegates at the corresponding *volost'* assemblies by 83%.

Such discrepancies were not limited to the areas where the outsider agitators were active. The number of Bolshevik party members in the VIKs which had been elected without the help of these agitators exceeded the number of Bolshevik delegates at the corresponding assemblies by 6%. Bolshevik members of the VIKs who had not been registered at the corresponding *volost'* assembly (outsiders) were recorded in 32 of the 160 VIKs in our sample (20%). They were registered in 32 of the 62 VIKs (51.6%) which included more than one Bolshevik party member. This strengthens the argument that there were pressures on the newly elected members of the VIK to register as Bolshevik party members, especially in the VIKs where one member was already a party member. But it also lends weight to the hypothesis that it was becoming fairly common for the VIK to be elected from two separate lists of candidates—a list of assembly delegates, and a party slate (see sect. 4 below).

The educational background of the VIK members was very similar to that of the delegates at the *volost'* soviet assemblies: 33.6% of the executive members were registered without education (see Table 17). The level of education rose sharply, however, during the course of the year, as the percentage of VIK members without education fell from 36.9% during the 'spring' to 20.7% during the 'autumn'. It is interesting that whereas only 0.9% of the delegates at the *volost'* assemblies had been to middle or higher schools, as many as 3.4% of the VIK members had been to such schools—a small but certain sign of the new bureaucratic élite in the VIKs.

The average age of this élite was very young indeed (see Table 18). If 33.1% of the village soviet members and 48.5% of the *volost'* assembly delegates were younger than 35, then 60.5% of the VIK members—and 63.1% of the members of the VIKs which included a Bolshevik party member—fell in this age cohort. During the 'spring' 62.2% of the VIK members were in this cohort, with most of them (37.9%) aged between 30 and 35. During the 'summer' the size of the under–35 age group fell to 46.7%; but during the 'autumn' it recovered to 61.4%, as the peasant-soldiers returned from the front. The youngest age group (under 25) became increasingly influential in the VIKs during the course of the year: its representation in the VIKs increased from 6.5% during the 'spring' to 18.3% during the 'autumn'. Younger brothers evidently gained on their elders during the civil war.

The village and *volost'* soviet elections of 1919 represent an important turning-point in the social and political history of the Russian countryside during this formative period of the Soviet regime. The aim of the government had been to transform the 'kulak-dominated' soviets into organs of 'proletarian' (i.e. Bolshevik) power in the rural localities. By increasing the representation of the poor peasantry and the rural Bolshevik cadres in the local soviets and their executives, the Soviet government had hoped to tighten its political hold over the villages, partly in order to facilitate the mobilization of the peasantry's resources for the civil war campaign, and partly in order to begin the broader process of 'socialist transformation' in the rural areas. This, it was believed, could not be achieved until a network of 'proletarian' soviets had supplanted the autonomous village communes and integrated the rural areas into a national political system.

It cannot be said that the election campaign went entirely to plan. The electoral commissions and the Bolshevik propaganda campaigns[92] had only a marginal effect on the conduct of the elections, which tended to be organized according to the traditional voting practices of the village assembly. The peasantwomen generally did not take part in the elections, unless they headed a family household in the absence of their menfolk. The official regulations concerning the size of the local soviets were widely ignored because of practical considerations, such as the ability of the peasant members to attend the soviet meetings. The voting was carried out in the traditional open manner. Personal considerations must have had a much greater influence on the minds of the voters than Bolshevik ideology. It was not—as the Bolsheviks had intended—the socio-economic status of the candidates that determined the decision of the voters, so much as the influence of kinship ties and village factions. Many of the people whom the higher authorities would have labelled as 'kulaks' (e.g. entrepreneurial farmers, leaders of the 'localist' villages) were re-elected to the soviets by the peasantry; whereas most of those whom the peasants would have labelled as 'kulaks' (e.g. usurers, profiteers) had already left the village to join the counter-revolution. Apathy also played its part in determining the outcome of the elections. The villagers wanted 'one of their own people' to stand in the soviet; but none of them wanted to perform that role himself. There must have been many occasions when the village elected a Bolshevik to stand in the soviet for the sole reason that no one else was willing to take on the responsibilities of public office.

Nevertheless, there is no doubt that the election campaign achieved a major success in its principal objective—to increase the influence of the Bolshevik party in the rural soviets. The proportion of the VIKs in our sample with a Bolshevik party member almost doubled during the course of 1919 (from 38.2% in the 'spring' to 71.4% in the 'autumn'). By the end of the year, two-thirds of the VIK members had been

[92] On the Bolshevik propaganda campaigns at the time of the elections see P. Kenez, *The Birth of the Propaganda State*, Cambridge, 1985, pp. 50–69; R. Taylor, 'A Medium for the Masses: Agitation in the Soviet Civil War', *Soviet Studies*, vol. 22, no. 4, 1971, pp. 565–74; Ts. Gofman, 'K istorii pervogo agitparokhoda VTsIK "Krasnaia Zvezda" (iiul'–oktiabr' 1919 g.)', *Voprosy istorii*, 1948, no. 9, pp. 63–70; Maksakova, *Agitpoezd*; ead., 'Deiatel'nost' kollektiva agitpoezda "Oktiabr'skaia revoliutsiia" sredi krest'ianstva (1919–1920 gg.)', *Voprosy istorii*, 1956, no. 10, pp. 102–11.

registered as Bolshevik party members. This was a higher level of party representation than during the mid–1920s (see Table 19).

TABLE 19. *Officials of village soviets and VIKs, RSFSR, 1925–1926 (%)*

	Bolsheviks			
Posts	Total	Komsomol	Red Army ex-servicemen	Of peasant origin
Chairmen of VIKs	86.0	0.8	70.7	48.3
Members of VIKs	50.5	3.8	67.3	(70.0)
Chairmen of village soviets	18.0	3.7	53.1	95.3

Source: T. Shanin, *The Awkward class*, Oxford, 1972, p. 194.

Who were the new Bolshevik élites in the rural soviets? Were they simply the leaders of the former *kombedy*, which, as we have seen, had tended to be dominated by the non-peasant groups of rural society (e.g. landless labourers, rural craftsmen, in-migrant townsmen)? Gimpel'son has shown that 47.6% of the members of the village soviets in seven *volosti* of Viatka province during 1919 had previously belonged to their village *kombed*.[93] But this is a small empirical sample, and it does not necessarily tell us anything about the leaders of the village soviets, or the members of the VIKs. It is likely that the non-peasant types who had been dominant in the *kombedy* gained some influence in the VIKs of the larger *volost'* townships (see Table 19), some of which were industrial or market centres, rather than agricultural communities. The vast majority of the *volost'* townships in our sample, however, were predominantly agricultural. The dominant influence of the commune during the soviet elections must have made it very difficult for the non-peasant groups to dominate the soviets in the way they had previously dominated the *kombedy*. Indeed, a significant portion of the *kombed* members had left the rural localities to join the Red Army during the winter of 1918–19, following the abolition of the *kombedy* (see ch. 6, sect. 5). Finally, the level of party representation in the VIKs in our sample (53% to 67%) was significantly higher than the level of party representation in the *kombedy* of Tambov province (33% to 41%), which lends further weight to the argument that the Bolsheviks in the VIKs largely represented a new rural party cadre, recruited during 1919.

If the emergent Bolshevik élite of the rural soviets was not drawn from the groups which had dominated the *kombedy*, then from which rural groups was it drawn? Some of the Bolshevik members of the rural soviet executives had been appointed by outsider agitators; they

[93] Gimpel'son, *Sovety v gody interventsii*, p. 53.

probably originated from the local party cells, which we shall be looking at again in sections 3 and 4 below. However, it should be borne in mind that only one in five of the VIKs had been affected by this type of 'appointmentism', while the number of outsider (i.e. appointed) Bolshevik members in the VIKs represented no more than 28.3% of the insider (i.e. elected) Bolshevik members.

Most of the new rural soviet leaders—whether Bolsheviks or not—originated from the smallholding peasantry. The crucial point, however, is that they were not the sort of peasants who had previously dominated village politics. They tended to be younger and more literate than the traditional leaders of the commune and the village assembly. Many of them had served in the World War or the Red Army, a factor which, as we have already seen (see ch. 3, sect. 4), was likely to make the rest of the villagers hold them in high esteem, or at least leave in their hands the most difficult tasks of public office. It was the peasant ex-servicemen who formed the new élite in the rural soviets and the rank and file of the Bolshevik party in the countryside. After the civil war the Red Army ex-servicemen flooded into the rural soviets. By 1922 they represented 62.5% of the village soviet chairmen in Tsaritsyn province.[94] By 1925–6 they comprised 53% of the village soviet chairmen, 67% of the members of the VIKs, and 71% of the chairmen of the VIKs in the RSFSR (see Table 19). The psychological and material difficulties of readjustment to the dull and arduous routines of peasant toil following the wars of 1914–21 must have induced many ex-servicemen to seek a way out of the village through the ranks of the new state bureaucracy.[95] Working in the soviet and joining the Bolshevik party offered these men an escape from the narrow world of the peasants, an entry into the urban-orientated world of the rural bureaucratic élite. This first generation of Bolshevik officials in the countryside sought liberation from the customs of a peasant society which for generations had upheld the authority of white beards and callused hands.

3. THE BOLSHEVIK PARTY: A NOTE ON ITS MEMBERSHIP IN THE RURAL AREAS

The tasks of state-building in the rural localities of Soviet Russia were inextricably connected with the growth of the Bolshevik party. The

[94] M. G. Belogurov, 'Statisticheskie istochniki o sostave sel'skikh sovetov v pervye gody vosstanovitel'nogo perioda (1921–23 gg.)', in *Istochnikovedenie istorii sovetskogo obshchestva*, vyp. 3, Moscow, 1978, pp. 227–8.

[95] On the psychology of the ex-servicemen see Pethybridge, pp. 82–3, 109–10, 120–4; Shanin, *The Awkward Class*, pp. 190–2; S. S. Maslov, *Rossiia posle chetyrekh let revoliutsii*, Paris, 1922, pp. 111 ff.; 183 ff.

bureaucratization of the soviets, the subordination of the rural economy to the needs of the government, and the 'socialist transformation' of the countryside all to a large extent depended upon the spread of the Bolshevik party from its enclaves in the capital cities to the multitude of remote villages.

The Bolshevik party organization began to expand in the Volga region from the winter of 1918–19, simultaneously with the reconstruction of the Soviet regime after the defeat of the Komuch. At the end of 1918 there were approximately 670 party cells in the whole of the Volga region (one per thirty-six rural settlements), with 20,576 members (49.8% of them in rural party cells). For every hundred rural settlements in the region there were, on average, eighty-four party members.[96] In Samara province the number of party members was smaller in December 1918 (2,801) than it had been during the previous spring (approximately 3,500), mainly because of the losses resulting from the campaign against the Komuch. By the following March, however, the size of the provincial party had recovered to 7,628 members, largely owing to the party recruitment campaigns of early 1919. During the summer of 1919 more than 3,000 party members from Samara province were mobilized by the Red Army. But by the following November, on the eve of the first 'party week' (*partiinaia nedelia*), the Samara organization had recovered to the level of its membership during the previous March.[97] The effect of the 'party week' on the size of the Bolshevik party in Samara province is illustrated in Table 20. Bolshevik propaganda and the relaxation of the regulations governing the registration of party members resulted in a more than doubling of the party membership. The 'party weeks' of November–December 1919 had a similar effect in Saratov province.[98] In both provinces the size of the party was cut back during 1920–1 as a result of the mobilization of party members, party purges and re-registrations, peasant uprisings, and the famine crisis. The number of Bolshevik party members in Saratov province was halved between April 1920 (20,699) and September 1921 (10,383).[99] In Samara province the number fell from 17,177 at the end of 1919 to roughly 10,000 towards the end of 1920 (see Table 20).

A large proportion of those who joined the Bolshevik party during the civil war came from the countryside. The number of rural party cells in European Russia nearly doubled during 1919. The peasantry increased its representation in the Bolshevik party from 14.5% of the

96 Molodtsygin, p. 22
97 *Ocherki istorii kuibyshevskoi organizatsii KPSS*, Kuibyshev, 1960, pp. 264–5, 287.
98 *Biulleten' saratovskogo gubkoma RKP*, no. 15, 2 Apr. 1920, p. 3.
99 *Saratovskaia oblastnaia organizatsiia KPSS v tsifrakh 1917–1975 gg.*, p. 23.

TABLE 20. *Bolshevik party membership, Samara province, 1919–20*

	Urban	Rural	Total
Before 'party week' (November 1919)	—	—	7,709
After 'party week'	10,351	6,826	17,177
Left or purged between November 1919 and June 1920	—	—	3,299
Before party registration (July 1920)	—	—	13,878
November 1920	6,512	3,527	10,039

Source: *Izvestiia samarskogo gubkoma RKP* (Samara), no. 3 (15), 24 Feb. 1921, p. 3. See also L. M. Spirin, *Klassy i partii v grazhdanskoi voine v Rossii*, Moscow, 1968, pp. 404–5.

membership in 1918, to 21.8% in 1919, to 25.1% in 1920, and to a peak of 28.2% in 1921. During 1920 the party recruited even more peasants than workers—a fact that may be explained by the expansion of the Red Army into the predominantly agrarian zones of the south and the south-east.[100] The number of party cells in Saratov and Samara provinces grew to 541 and 632, respectively, by the end of 1920—that is, one for approximately every four rural settlements (compared with one per thirty-six rural settlements in the whole of the Volga region at the end of 1918). The number of rural party members per hundred rural settlements in the Volga region grew more slowly over the same period (from 84 to 121), which may be explained by the reduction in size of the average rural party cell (from 31 to 14 members). By 1921, the peasantry represented nearly one-third (32.8%) of the Bolshevik party membership in the Volga region.[101]

The rapid expansion of the party membership during 1919–20 gave rise to serious anxieties among the Bolshevik leaders about the quality of the new members, especially since so many of them had signed up during the 'party weeks', when little attention was paid to the 'socialist' credentials of the candidates. The Soviet press warned against 'careerist' elements, who, having sensed that the Bolsheviks would win the civil war, had only joined the party to take advantage of the power and prestige accruing to a member of the winning side.[102] The Saratov provincial party assembly complained in October 1919 that 'petty-bourgeois elements' had flooded into the local cells and

[100] *Vserossiiskaia perepis' chlenov RKP 1922 goda*, vyp. 4, Moscow, 1923, pp. 37–8; Iu. A. Poliakov, *Perekhod k NEPu i sovetskoe krest'ianstvo*, Moscow, 1967, p. 178.

[101] *Biulleten' saratovskogo gubkoma RKP*, no. 19, 17 Oct. 1920, p. 3; *Izvestiia samarskogo gubkoma RKP(b)*, no. 13 (25), 29 Oct. 1921, p. 22; Molodtsygin, pp. 162, 255.

[102] J. Arch Getty, *Origins of the Great Purges: The Soviet Communist Party Reconsidered, 1933–1938*, Cambridge, 1985, p. 40. See further T. H. Rigby, *Communist Party Membership in the USSR 1917–1967*, Princeton, 1968, pp. 70 ff.

lowered the standards of party discipline.[103] The leaders of the Simbirsk provincial party complained that the local rural party cells were 'ridiculously large'—up to eighty members—and included far too many 'kulaks and old men'; the rural party officials were socially and culturally 'indistinguishable from the mass of the non-party peasants'; and many of them had joined the party only to requisition foodstuffs from the peasants, or to petition the higher party authorities for material and financial support.[104]

It is difficult to gauge the social background and psychological motivations of those who joined the Bolshevik party at the village and *volost'* levels during the civil war, since there are no suitable records outside the archives of the Communist party. The evidence of the village and *volost'* soviet elections, which we examined in the last section, suggested that it was the younger and more literate peasant sons, especially those who had served in the Imperial or Red Army, who came to lead the rural soviet executives, and who would thus find it advantageous to join the Bolshevik party. Equally, there is evidence to suggest that the landless, marginal, and rootless elements who had dominated the *kombedy* (e.g. agricultural labourers, craftsmen, in-migrant workers) were also represented in the rural party cells. The Voronezh provincial party classified 87% of its rural members as poor or landless peasants (*bedniaki*), and only 13% as middle peasants (*seredniaki*).[105]

As far as the motivations of these Bolsheviks are concerned, we may conclude that ideological conviction, the desire for power, and economic gain must have all played their part to varying degrees.[106] The influence of ideology was probably greatest among the youngest, whose ways of thinking had been the most profoundly shaped by the war. The Bolshevik party gave them a simple theory to understand the injustices of the old world, and a disciplined organizational structure, reminiscent of the army itself, within which to change it. The desire for power was possibly strongest among the poorest elements, since they had most cause to seek revenge against those who had exploited and oppressed them. Where the latter had fled after the revolution, these new party officials were likely to vent their anger in acts of

103 *Saratovskaia partiinaia organizatsiia v gody grazhdanskoi voiny: Dokumenty i materialy 1918–1920 gg.*, Saratov, 1958, p. 182.

104 E. B. Skobelkina, 'Bor'ba partii bol'shevikov protiv melkoburzhuaznoi kontr-revoliutsii v 1918–19 gg. (po materialam Simbirskoi gubernii)', kand. diss., Voronezh, 1967, pp. 204–5.

105 Molodtsygin, p. 166. See further TsGANKh, f. 478, op. 3, d. 1157, ll. 44–50, 51–6; *Serp i molot* (Serdobsk), no. 204 (488), 23 Sept. 1920, p. 1; *Saratovskaia partiinaia organizatsiia v gody grazhdanskoi voiny*, p. 185.

106 For a discussion see Maslov, pp. 180 ff.

violence against the richer peasants. Finally, the motive of economic gain must have been most prevalent among the in-migrant elements (e.g. workers and military personnel), who depended upon the privileges afforded by their party position to support themselves. It was these types who were most commonly noted among those local party bosses whose acts of corruption and extortion from the peasants brought the new regime into increasing disrepute in the countryside.[107]

At the risk of a slight digression from our theme, it is worth stopping briefly to look at the background of the Bolsheviks in leading positions within the district and provincial soviets, since many of them were once members of a rural Bolshevik party cell. Their biographies tell us a great deal about the social and psychological 'make-up' of those who left the countryside to take up official positions in the new state apparatus during the civil war. According to the 1920 party census, 21.1% of the Bolshevik party members in the districts (i.e. excluding the provincial capital and its district) of Saratov, Simbirsk, and Penza provinces came from the peasantry, although only 17% of them worked in agriculture at the time of the party census. A large majority of the district party members in the three provinces were younger than 40 (77.5%), had received only primary or domestic education (82.5%), and had served in the army at some point (69.2%). Only 5% of these Bolsheviks had joined the party before the October Revolution, whereas 27.7% had joined between October 1917 and the end of 1918, 13.6% between January and August 1919, and as many as 53.7% after August 1919, when it was already becoming clear that the Bolsheviks would win the civil war.[108]

Reading through the autobiographies of leading Bolsheviks in the district and provincial soviets, written in the winter of 1918–19 and preserved in the NKVD archives of TsGAOR,[109] one cannot fail to notice how the majority—perhaps between 60% and 70%—shared a remarkably similar life experience, roughly characterized by the following.

The typical Bolshevik was born during the 1880s or early 1890s into a poor or landless peasant family, usually situated in the district or province where he was later to become a leading member of the soviet. He was unlikely to have received more than two years' education in

[107] See e.g. GAKO, f. 81, op. 1, d. 10, l. 94; D. A. Palagin, 'Rol' kommunisticheskikh fraktsii sovetov Srednego Povolzh'ia v ukreplenii diktatury proletariata v period inostrannoi interventsii i grazhdanskoi voiny (1918–20 gg.)', kand. diss., Moscow, 1972, pp. 33–4; *Kommuna* (Samara), no. 155, 20 June 1919, p. 4; *Saratovskaia partiinaia organizatsiia v gody grazhdanskoi voiny*, p. 123.

[108] *Lichnyi sostav RKP v 1920 g.*, Moscow, 1921, pp. 16–19.

[109] TsGAOR, f. 393, op. 11, dd. 183–210 (arranged alphabetically by surname).

the local village school, before being given away to a landowner as a shepherd or, more commonly, as an apprentice to a factory or workshop in the nearest town. The extreme poverty of his family or—curiously often—the death of his father were the most likely causes of this sacrifice. Thus, P. I. Lalov, a member of the Saratov city soviet executive, was born into a landless peasant-carpenter family in Saratov district and went to a church school for one year, until, at the age of 10, he was given away to a metal workshop as an apprentice.[110] S. S. Kosobokov, a Bolshevik member of the Kamyshin district soviet executive, was given away at the age of 2 to a rich peasant family on the death of his father, worked as a shepherd until the age of 11, and then went off to the town to find a job in a steam-mill; until the age of 24, he returned every summer to help his mother and six younger brothers and sisters by working on one of the estates.[111] R. I. Ziubalkin, secretary of the Chembar district party committee, was given away as a boy by his poor peasant parents to a childless couple in the same village, who employed him as a guard. After three years' village schooling and a period of work on his parents' farm, he ran away at the age of 16 to work as a kitchen-boy in the town of Penza, and later Moscow.[112]

The adolescence of the typical Bolshevik was spent moving from factory to factory, town to town, learning new trades, and occasionally returning to his native village during the harvest season. He was a peasant proletarian, moving between town and country, a marginal element to both. His ideal was to escape from the miserable life of his parents in the countryside and become a permanent worker or official in the town, a man with skills and education who could expect a reasonable wage. He was very likely to join a workers' self-education circle, or spend his evenings training to become an accountant or a clerk. 'From an early age', recalled one peasant-Bolshevik, 'education was my only opportunity to escape from . . . the impoverished and idiotic life of the village . . . and run away, anywhere, as far away from the village as possible.'[113]

Moving from factory to factory, the typical Bolshevik experienced the hardships and exploitation characteristic of Russian industry at the turn of the century. The socialist literature passed around workers' circles offered him simple, scientific answers to the problems he faced. For most of the generation of Bolsheviks born after 1880, it was the revolution of 1905 that first awakened their socialist consciousness. Joining the Social Democratic underground (very few Soviet leaders mentioned in their autobiography any Socialist Revolutionary

110 TsGAOR, f. 393, op. 11, d. 193, l. 9.
111 Ibid., d. 192, l. 105.
112 Ibid., d. 190, l. 26.
113 Ibid., d. 199, l. 60.

activities), our Bolshevik inevitably came under the surveillance of the secret police after the suppression of the workers' strikes in 1906–7, and probably spent the remaining years until 1914 in prison, exile, or movement from town to town, as one employer after the next dismissed him as a trouble-maker or political activist. Consequently, the mobility of many Bolsheviks during this period was extraordinary. I. A. Zemskov, a peasant son from Narovchat district and member of the district soviet executive, worked in Penza, Saratov, Samara, Petrograd, and Riga between 1906 and 1914.[114] V. V. Nikitin, a peasant son from Kamyshin district and member of the Saratov provincial soviet executive, spent his pre-war years in Saratov, Voronezh, Petrograd, Novgorod, and Peterhof.[115] N. N. Dreniakov, a peasant son from Penza province and military commissar of Narovchat district, worked as far afield as Tambov, Tiflis, and Novocherkassk before the First World War.[116]

The provincial Bolshevik leader of the civil war period learned his political manners in the Imperial army. For the typical Bolshevik, the army was a sort of political schooling, adding to the skills he had learned through the revolutionary underground a knowledge of new technologies and large-scale social organization. Having entered the ranks as an ordinary private, he was likely to gain promotion through the officers', engineers', or field-doctors' training course, perhaps being given a position of considerable responsibility. After February 1917, he was certain to be elected to the soldiers' committee of his regiment, and possibly to the committee of his battalion or division. He was also likely to be elected to the soldiers' soviet. If he had already joined the Bolshevik party, then he was bound to become much more active after February, competing against the SR activists for influence among the soldiers. Such activities might lead to his being delegated to soviet bodies in towns behind the front lines, where he was likely to play a leading part in the establishment of Soviet power.

However, during the winter of 1917–18, when the army was demobilized, nearly all the Bolsheviks returned to their native village or town, while the rest were sure to return to a place where they had spent at least some time before the war. The economic crisis and the redivision of the land were enough to attract even these hardened exiles back to the village from which they had fled in their youth. There they helped to organize the rural party cell or became leading members in the village soviet or the VIK, from which they were elected to the district or provincial soviet. The almost universal return of these Bolsheviks to their native village after 1917 supports the argument of

[114] Ibid., d. 190, l. 31.
[115] Ibid., d. 195, l. 22.
[116] Ibid., d. 187, l. 24.

the last section that it was the peasant sons and marginal elements from the army, rather than complete 'outsiders', who became the leading officials of the new regime in the countryside.

4. THE TRANSFORMATION OF THE SOVIETS

The problems of Bolshevik state-building in the countryside could not be simply resolved by expanding the rural party organizations and ensuring their numerical domination in the local soviets. The literacy and the discipline of the rural party cadres were of far too poor a standard for the Bolshevik authorities in Moscow to leave them a free hand in running the local state apparatus. The organization of the soviets and their relations with the party cadres had to be regulated within a bureaucratic structure that would ensure that the local organs of power continued to function in the interests of the Soviet regime.

The key component of the rural structure of power was the relationship between the party and the VIKs. The theoretical basis of this relationship was set out in the party programme at the Eighth Party Congress in March 1919: 'By practical daily dedication and work in the soviets, and by filling all the soviet positions with its best and most loyal members, the Russian Communist Party must win undivided political rule in the soviets and practical control over all their activities.'[117] The programme envisaged the party cadres 'leading' and 'controlling' the local soviets in every aspect of their work so that the latter would serve as efficient 'transmissions'—to use Lenin's term—of the 'proletarian dictatorship'. To what extent were the aims of the party programme fulfilled in the rural localities?

The influence of the rural party cadres in the VIKs was growing, as we have already seen (see sect. 2 above). The local party cells, the higher Soviet authorities, the Cheka, and the Red Army political departments were increasingly inclined to apply the right pressures to ensure that the rural Bolsheviks got 'elected' to the VIKs at the *volost'* soviet assemblies. This slide into 'appointmentism', which was widely noted in the urban representative bodies after 1919,[118] was facilitated by the common practice of voting by slate. The majority of the *volost'* soviet assemblies recognized the local party cell as a legitimate 'fraction'—with the right to nominate a slate of candidates for election to the VIK, alongside the list of non-party candidates nominated from the floor of the assembly. From this point, the election of the VIK became a process of negotiation between the rural party cell and the

117 *KPSS v rezoliutsiiakh i resheniiakh s''ezdov, konferentsii i plenumov TsK*, 9th edn., Moscow, 1983, vol. 1, p. 108.

118 See e.g. the account by E. Goldman of a factory election meeting in Moscow in 1920 in *My Disillusionment in Russia*, London, 1925, pp. 88–9.

delegates at the assembly over the size of the VIK and the ratio of party to non-party places within it. Thus, the VIK in Apraksino (Ardatov *uezd*) was elected on 18 December 1919 from a list of local Bolshevik candidates, nominated by the party cell, and a smaller list of non-party delegates.[119] In the nearby village of Kirzhemany (Ardatov *uezd*) the *volost'* soviet assembly on the same day resolved by a small majority 'to endorse without amendments the list [of candidates for election to the VIK] proposed by the Bolshevik party fraction'. The assembly was chaired by a member of the Ardatov district department of administration, and attended by the five members of the old VIK, and no more than sixteen peasant delegates.[120] Another example is from the Maresevo *volost'* soviet assembly (Ardatov *uezd*), where the VIK was elected from a list of four Bolshevik officials, nominated by the party cell, and nine peasant delegates at the assembly, nominated from the floor. After an open vote, two out of the four Bolshevik officials were elected to the VIK, along with five of the peasant delegates. The assembly was chaired by an official of the Ardatov district party committee, and attended by five representatives of the local party cell, and no more than ten peasant delegates.[121] A particularly detailed account is from the Tarkhanovo *volost'* soviet assembly (Ardatov *uezd*) on 14 December, where the Bolshevik party cell proposed a list of seven candidates for election to the VIK (three local party officials and four non-party delegates at the assembly). The acting chairman of the assembly, a member of the Ardatov district party committee, called for a fifteen-minute interval in the proceedings to enable the assembly delegates to discuss the list of candidates and make any alterations. After the break, the peasant delegates insisted on adding three more non-party names to the list of candidates. In the end it was decided to accept only four out of the seven party nominations (two of the local party officials and two of the non-party delegates) in order to accommodate the three additional candidates put forward by the assembly. Thus, the final composition of the VIK was: two Bolshevik officials; two party-nominated non-party delegates at the assembly; and three delegates nominated from the floor of the assembly.[122]

These negotiations between the party fractions and the peasant delegates sometimes ended in heated controversy. A good example is from the Komarov *volost'* soviet assembly (Ivanovo-Voznesensk province) on 2 February 1919. The acting chairman of the assembly, a member of the district electoral commission, urged the assembly delegates to divide themselves into two 'party' fractions (the Bolshevik

[119] TsGAOR, f. 393, op. 13, d. 429, l. 53.
[120] Ibid., l. 60.
[121] Ibid., l. 62.
[122] Ibid., l. 54.

party and the non-party delegates), so that each could formulate its own list of candidates for election to the VIK. The party fraction nominated fourteen candidates, and the non-party fraction nine candidates. But the former then claimed that all the members of the VIK should be party members, 'since the entire soviet structure and state apparatus was constructed by the forces of the Communist-Bolsheviks'. This claim infuriated some of the peasant delegates, who in turn demanded that they should retain a majority in the VIK. The party fraction was finally persuaded to accept a compromise list of three Bolsheviks and two non-party delegates for election to the VIK, which was reported to have been passed 'unanimously'.[123]

Similar conflicts took place at the district soviet assemblies. A good example is from the Kashir district soviet assembly (Tula province) on 17 August. A slate of three Bolshevik party officials, nominated by the forty-five-man Bolshevik fraction (including nine 'sympathizers'), and a competing slate of three non-party delegates, nominated by the sixty-eight-man non-party fraction, were put forward as candidates for election to the executive. The acting chairman of the district assembly, the chairman of the provincial soviet executive, spoke in favour of the three Bolshevik officials and reminded the assembly of the achievements of the Bolshevik party; he warned the delegates that 'weighty arguments' would have to be made to sustain any objections to the Bolshevik party candidates. The non-party vice-chairman of the district assembly intervened at this point to voice his objections: 'all of us are members of one single labouring family and we are all equally responsible for the achievements of the Revolution. We here [the non-party delegates] are as much responsible for the revolution as the representatives of the ruling party'. This rhetorical clash among the leaders of the assembly seems to have polarized the voting during the election of the executive: forty-three out of the forty-five pro-Bolshevik representatives voted in favour of the Bolshevik slate; forty-eight out of the sixty-eight non-party delegates voted in favour of the non-party slate. The Bolshevik fraction then objected to one of the non-party candidates on the grounds that he had once deserted his post in the VIK. A second roll-call vote had to be taken, which resulted in a majority in favour of the Bolshevik slate, since a large portion of the non-party delegates had abstained. The final composition of the executive was three Bolsheviks and two non-party members.[124]

A second example is from the Syzran' district soviet assembly on 5 July 1920. Before the assembly the Bolshevik fraction had nominated seventeen party candidates for election to the soviet executive, which

123 *SEV*, vol. 2, p. 410.
124 *SEV*, vol. 1, pp. 162–6.

was to comprise twenty members. The chairman of the assembly invited the non-party delegates to choose their own slate of candidates to occupy the three remaining places in the executive. One of the peasant delegates, Sedov, demanded an interval in the proceedings of the assembly 'so that the peasant group can confer'. But the Bolshevik leader, Stein, refused to allow this on the grounds that 'only a party fraction or an organized group' had the right to call an interval, whereas the peasants were neither a fraction nor a separate group, and did 'not bear the same responsibilities as the party'. This infuriated Sedov, the peasant delegate:

> Comrade Stein wants to make us out as being guilty of something, simply because the Communist party does not agree with it. He is trying to suggest that we want to incite a conflict, or that we want to do something bad! But the peasant group simply wants to confer, it wants to make sure that peasants are elected to the executive. If the peasants are to be given a place in the executive, then they must be given time to confer. But the comrade suspects us of plotting something illegal. Does comrade Stein not want to give the peasants any responsibilities? He is deliberately trying to frighten and intimidate the peasant delegates.

The chairman of the assembly intervened to defend the Bolshevik leader, and repeated that the Bolshevik slate had left open three places for the non-party workers and the peasants. He insisted that since these places were intended for any non-party group, it would be improper for a particular social group to confer about the election. He did concede, however, that the majority of the party candidates were urban workers, thus leaving the peasants under-represented. The Bolshevik fraction intervened at this moment to express its willingness to include Sedov and Kirushkin (who had also been actively voicing the peasants' demands) in the executive, provided they were nominated by the assembly floor. This failed to appease the peasants. They began to demand equality with the workers in the executive; and their increasingly noisy and disruptive behaviour forced the executive to concede an interval. During the break the peasant group compiled a slate of five candidates for election to the executive. But the chairman of the assembly rejected the two extra nominations on the grounds that the party slate, which had to be 'voted on in its entirety', left no more than three places for non-party nominations. Now the chairman made it clear where he stood:

> the Communist fraction, in compiling its slate, has in mind what each of its candidates is going to do in the executive; it has the advantage of party discipline to make sure that its members perform their duties. Besides, a Communist not only belongs to the party, he also belongs to the government,

and so he is obliged to carry out all their demands rigorously; that can not be said of the non-party delegates, who have no clear political outlook and no opinions.

The chairman concluded that Sedov, Kirushkin and a third peasant delegate might be considered suitable non-party candidates because they 'understand the policy of the Soviet government and know how to stand by the correct line'. At this point, the military commissar of the Simbirsk provincial soviet executive was brought on: he warned that ten of the district soviet executive members would be mobilized by the Red Army immediately following the election. This seems to have dampened the dissidence of the peasant delegates, who finally agreed to accept the slate of seventeen Bolshevik candidates along with the three non-party delegates proposed by the chairman. The party cell was also given the right to appoint six further Bolshevik officials to the executive, following the Red Army mobilization.[125]

Along with this trend of 'appointmentism' was the tendency of the VIKs to become increasingly bureaucratized. This was reflected most clearly in the declining size of the VIKs. The VIKs of 1917–18 tended to be larger than the size stipulated in the Soviet Constitution—a fact which, as we have already noted, reflected the peasant social background of the VIK members, (see ch. 3, sect. 1). By contrast, the VIKs of 1919–20 tended to be smaller than the size stipulated in the Constitution, largely on account of their financial weakness (their inability to pay the salaries of more than a small number of members). A survey by NKVD of 351 VIKs in European Russia during July 1919 found that only 33 (9.4%) of the executives included more than 5 members, whereas 314 (89.5%) contained between 3 and 5 members. The survey also showed that 67% of the VIK members had no other source of income but the salary which they received from the VIK (i.e. they were not engaged in any economic activity, such as peasant farming or craft production).[126] The centralization of the payment of the VIK members and the doubling of their wages (from 650 rb. to 1,300 rb. per month) after September 1919 increased the economic dependence of the VIK members on the state and enabled a broader range of declassed elements to enter the soviet administration in the rural localities. Indeed, this had been the intention of the NKVD, as set out by M. Vladimirskii, one of its highest ranking officials, in the summer of 1919:

the influx of the urban workers into the countryside, as a result of the closure of the factories, and the formation of these people into cadres of Soviet

125 *Stenograficheskii otchet 7-go syzranskogo uezdnogo soveta*, pp. 91–6.
126 Vladimirskii, *Organizatsiia sovetskoi vlasti*, pp. 25, 28.

> professionals, devoting all their energy and time to Soviet work in the villages, inevitably raises the question of the need to increase the salaries of these valuable specialists. Part of the solution must be the establishment of a set wage for officials in the VIKs.[127]

Another sign of the bureaucratization of the VIKs was their increasing professionalism. The VIKs of 1918 had been part-time, amateur organizations run by the peasant élites; those of 1920 were beginning to resemble complex structures of state administration run by a salaried and semi-permanent bureaucracy. The division of tasks between the VIK departments was becoming increasingly standardized. A Decree of July 1919 ordered the establishment by each VIK of: an administrative department (*otdel upravleniia*) with subdepartments for education and social welfare; a military department; and a land department. The departments were to share a general staff (*kantseliariia*) of one secretary, two clerks, one scribe, and a messenger. The staff was to be headed by the VIK secretary, who had sole control of the finances and, generally speaking, came to dominate the whole of the VIK. The secretary could be—and frequently was—appointed by the VIK executive from the rural party cadres; he did not necessarily have to come from within the *volost'* soviet administration (indeed, the stipulation of the higher Soviet authorities that a communal scribe of the pre-revolutionary period should not be allowed to be the VIK secretary discriminated against the latter being chosen from the local soviet administration).[128] These regulations were applied in general by the majority of the VIKs, although, as one might expect, there were still many local variations in the structural organization of the soviets.[129]

By the end of the civil war, the VIKs had superseded the village communes as the largest institutional employers in the countryside. The steady growth of the soviet administrative staff and the employees in the social institutions attached to the soviets (e.g. educational and political institutions, craft workshops, co-operatives, mills, postal services, etc.) assigned the VIKs an important socio-economic role, which in turn helped to transform the social and political structure of the countryside. The diverse—and, for the most part, declassed—social groups which came to depend upon the soviet for employment were by the end of the civil war beginning to resemble a sort of hybrid 'class' of bureaucrats, a 'rural salariat' (*sluzhashchie*), with its own

127 Ibid., pp. 12, 25, 27–8.
128 Ibid., p. 27; *SU*, 1919, no. 36, art. 356.
129 See e.g. *SEV*, vol. 1, pp. 192–6.

political and socio-economic interests separate from—and culturally in opposition to—the rural population at large.[130]

The transformation of the VIKs into a local governing cadre of the state bureaucracy was made possible by the decline of the *volost'* soviet assembly. The Seventh All-Russian Soviet Congress (December 1919) extended the minimum legal period between convocations of the *volost'* soviet assembly from one month (set by the Soviet Constitution) to three months; (the period was further extended to a year by the Ninth Soviet Congress in December 1921). Between convocations of the assembly the VIK was officially declared the highest organ of Soviet power within the *volost'*. The Seventh Congress set the period of office (*srok*) of the VIK members at three months; but this was extended to six months by a Decree of March 1920 on the grounds that it would improve the opportunity of the VIK officials to become experienced in administration.[131] These official developments were really only endorsing the existing practices of the party activists in the VIKs, who were becoming increasingly inclined to reappoint themselves every three months because of the problems of finding qualified and politically reliable peasants who were willing to act as officials.[132] The domination of the party activists in the VIKs, the bureaucratic and dictatorial nature of the latter (what the peasants termed *ispolkomshchina*—'rule by the executive'), the increasing preoccupation of the *volost'* soviets with the fulfilment of central government duties, and the deepening agricultural crisis of 1919–21 combined to dissuade the mass of the peasants from attending the *volost'* soviet assembly, let alone from becoming involved in the work of its executive. As the Bolshevik chairman of the VIK in Planskoe put it at the Kuznetsk district soviet assembly in January 1919, 'the peasant assemblies are very poorly attended, because the peasants presume that "they will only want to take some other tax from us" '.[133] The withdrawal of the peasantry from the *volost'* soviet assembly seriously weakened the authority of the government in the countryside. It reintroduced a fundamental duality in the power structure of the countryside—the

130 For a discussion see T. Shanin, *The Awkward Class*, Oxford, 1972, pp. 180 ff.

131 *SU*, 1919, no. 64, art. 578; 1920, no. 20, art. 108; Gimpel'son, *Sovety v gody interventsii*, pp. 179–80; Vladimirskii, *Organizatsiia sovetskoi vlasti*, p. 29. During 1920 the *srok* of village soviet executive members was also extended to six months (Belogurov, p. 210).

132 See e.g. GAKO, f. 185, op. 2, d. 89, ll. 56–7, 87, 100–1, 107; f. 3134, op. 2, d. 21, l. 289.

133 *VI s''ezd kuznetskogo soveta rabochikh i krest'ianskikh deputatov*, 2nd day, no page numbers, Kuznetsk, 1919. See also TsGAOR, f. 393, op. 3, d. 329, l. 36; *Sbornik materialov 12-mu vol'skomu uezdnomu s''ezdu sovetov 3 iiunia 1920 g.*, Vol'sk, 1920, p. 11; *SEV*, vol. 2, p. 97; *Izvestiia* (Kuznetsk), no. 157, 9 Oct. 1919, p. 2.

division between the village communes and the *volost'* administration—which would continue to haunt the Soviet regime throughout the 1920s.[134] The transformation of the VIKs during the civil war from, essentially, peasant organs into Bolshevik-dominated bodies, resembling a state administration, induced the peasantry to regroup politically within the village communes, which were still largely autonomous. The 'middle ground' between the VIKs and the village communes was vacated as peasant–state relations broke down: the *volost'* soviet assemblies, at which the VIKs were obliged to seek the agreement of the peasantry to fulfil the orders of the government, atrophied; the village soviets, whose allegiance was hopelessly divided between the VIK and the village commune, increasingly leaned towards the latter (from which they received nearly all of their finance), as the economy weakened and the level of state taxation became more burdensome. As a result of this institutional polarization, the Bolshevik-dominated VIKs found themselves increasingly isolated in the rural areas: they had no real authority outside the *volost'* township; and, as the social and economic power of the village communes strengthened in opposition to the Bolshevik regime, they began to find that they could get their way only by using force.

Because of the decline of the *volost'* soviet assembly and the growing institutional divide between the VIKs and the peasantry, the Soviet government began to encourage the organization of non-party peasant assemblies in the period following the Ninth Party Congress (March–April 1920). These assemblies were to become a permanent feature of rural politics during the 1920s. Lenin assigned great importance to them as a means of involving the peasants in government and overcoming soviet bureaucratization.[135] During the early period of their development, however, the conferences tended to suffer from the inclination of the local party activists to dominate all political matters. Some of the assemblies were closed down or infiltrated by the party, since it was feared that they were developing into peasant economic 'unions', or outright anti-Bolshevik organizations. Others became the scene of open clashes between the peasantry and the party over the composition of the assembly's executive and the formulation of its resolutions.[136]

[134] See D. J. Male, *Russian Peasant Organization before Collectivization*, Cambridge, 1971; Y. Taniuchi, *The Village Gathering in Russia in the Mid-1920s*, Birmingham, 1968; Atkinson, pp. 295–312; Shanin, *The Awkward Class*, pp. 162–9.

[135] *PSS*, vol. 39, p. 362; Gimpel'son, *Sovety v gody interventsii*, pp. 238–41; A. I. Lepeshkin, *Mestnye organy vlasti sovetskogo gosudarstva (1917–1920 gg.)*, Moscow, 1957, pp. 206–7; Molodtsygin, p. 171.

[136] Abrams, p. 176; Maslov, pp. 143 ff.

The Workers' and Peasants' Non-Party Conference in Alekseev

The minutes of the 'Workers' and Peasants' Non-Party Conference of the Alekseev Region' (Samara *uezd*) from 9 to 10 February 1920 highlight these tensions between the peasantry and the party.[137]

The Conference was attended by 162 delegates from Alekseev and Chernorech'e *volosti* as well as the local workers on the Samara–Zlatoust railway. It was convened during an especially oppressive period of the food procurement and labour duty (*trudpovinnost'*) campaigns. None of the village communes had delivered more than a tiny fraction of its grain quota to the collection point (*ssypnoi punkt*). The VIK in Alekseev had been inundated during the winter with petitions from the village soviets complaining that it would be 'absolutely impossible' and 'potentially catastrophic for the peasant economy' if the authorities attempted to squeeze any more food from the village communes.[138] The VIK did its best to dissuade the regional provisions committee (*raiprodkom*) from sending a food requisitioning brigade, pointing out that the recent arrival of more than 20,000 immigrant townsmen and refugees had put an unbearable burden on the food supply of Alekseev *volost'*; there were already several famine-stricken families in the village of Alekseev itself.[139] However, the VIK was becoming increasingly frustrated with the insubordination of the village soviets, which were doing nothing to mobilize the peasantry for the labour services (snow-clearing, timber-felling), or to punish those food-hoarding peasants whose illegal activities were being constantly brought to the attention of the VIK by one of the government's requisitioning brigades.[140] During the winter the VIK had begun to remove from office the non-party personnel of the key village soviets. The chairmen of the village soviets in Syreika, Chubovka, Smyshliaevka, and Alekseev were all purged on the grounds of 'inexperience' and replaced by VIK nominees. The Nikolaev village soviet was disbanded *in toto* and then 're-elected' under the supervision of the VIK. The newly appointed officials, however, proved just as incapable as their predecessors of forcing the peasantry to meet its tax obligations, and at the beginning of February the Cheka in Kinel'-Cherkasy was asked to arrest the chairmen of the village soviets in Chubovka, Alekseev, Smyshliaevka, and Syreika for 'inactivity' in the collection of the food levy and the organization of the labour duty.[141]

These arrests preoccupied the peasants during the opening of the

137 GAKO, f. 185, op. 3, d. 13, ll. 23–33.
138 Ibid., op. 2, d. 89, ll. 69–71, 78–98.
139 Ibid., l. 82.
140 Ibid., ll. 55, 65, 73, 76–80, etc.
141 Ibid., ll. 81, 104; op. 3, d. 13, ll. 9, 12.

Conference. The Bolshevik chairman of the VIK in Alekseev was attacked by the delegates on the grounds that the arrested village soviet chairmen 'had in fact taken stringent measures to fulfil the levies, but the peasants themselves are simply hostile to the demands that are made of them.[142] It was decided to petition the VIK for the release of the chairmen, and a committee was elected to draft the resolution. On the second day of the Conference the delegation from Syreika village interrupted the proceedings in order to read out a petition, signed by 250 peasants from the village, calling for the release of the chairman of their soviet on the grounds that his family had been struck down by typhus.[143]

Before the Conference was able to start on its main business there was a brief moment of high tension when it was declared that some Bolshevik party members had crept in at the back of the meeting. The peasant crowd began to shout and tried to eject the intruders. After a long period of disorder, the chairman of the meeting managed to restore some order, but the atmosphere remained very tense during the opening discussion on 'current affairs', when it appeared that the party cell had been granted rights to formulate and present resolutions to the assembly. Kadantsev, one of the peasant delegates, refused to give his opinion on the causes of the civil war and the role of the Bolshevik party until he had received an assurance that the 'members of the Conference will not be arrested for expressing their own views'.[144] This again incited a heated and disordered debate among the peasant delegates. When it died down, Kadantsev expressed his views directly to the Bolsheviks at the Conference: 'not everyone calling himself a Communist can be one, the Bolsheviks say; for example, a man with two horses cannot be a Communist. That sort of reasoning explains why the people cannot get on with the Bolsheviks.'[145]

Tensions between the peasant delegates and the Bolshevik members came to a head during the formulation of the resolution on 'current affairs'. The delegates on the floor complained that the Bolshevik resolution was 'incomprehensible' and did 'not agree with the opinions expressed at the Conference'. One of the delegates proposed that the Conference should elect a 'non-party' commission to frame its own resolutions, as an alternative to those of the Bolshevik group; the delegates would then be able to choose between the resolutions. This proposal was passed by a large majority, and a ten-man commission, consisting entirely of non-party peasants, was elected.[146]

[142] Ibid., op. 3, d. 13, l. 27.
[143] Ibid., l. 31.
[144] Ibid., l. 28.
[145] Ibid., l. 29.
[146] Ibid.

The contrast between the resolutions of the Bolshevik faction and those of the non-party commission—which, incidentally, were all passed by a large majority—is strikingly illustrative of the general political divide between the peasantry and the Bolsheviks during this period. The resolution of the non-party commission on 'current affairs' read as follows:

> Having heard the speech [of the leader of the Bolshevik faction] on the policy of the workers-peasants government in international affairs and particularly on the ending of the blockade of Soviet Russia, the Conference resolved that in future the government should try to bring about the quickest possible end to the war, since the country is living through terrible times, and, in this connection, since the lifting of the blockade can only be a result of the success of the Red Army, the Conference considered that this is a good time to start the negotiations for peace, especially since this can only have a good effect on the *tovaroobmen*, and so the workers and peasants should help the authorities to move in this direction, but only in so far as this is possible without harming the well-being of the peasants.
>
> The policies of the workers-peasants government inside Soviet Russia—that is, the improvement of the economic and legal position of the workers and peasants, and also the repeal of capital punishment—are correct in the view of the conference. As soon as the fronts are liquidated the Red Army should be dispersed and the soldiers allowed to go home, where they are needed on their farms.
>
> To carry out the measures of the workers-peasants government the Conference recognizes: (1) the need to involve all the toiling people in the administration of the country regardless of their political party; (2) the obligation of everyone to carry out the orders of the government, in so far as they meet the agreement of the ordinary people in the given locality; and (3) the need to organize as often as possible workers-peasants non-party conferences in order to discuss the general questions concerning internal and foreign policy.[147]

This highly conditional motion of support for the government stands in stark contrast to the bland and unconditional exclamations in favour of the Bolshevik government which one usually finds in the annals of the *volost'* soviets during this period. The majority of the delegates at the Conference were prepared to support the Bolshevik government only on the condition that it began negotiations with the Whites for the end of the civil war, that it demobilized the Red Army as quickly as possible, that it involved in the government all the democratic elements of the revolution—regardless of their political party—and, finally, that the local population agreed with the orders of the higher authorities.

[147] GAKO, f. 185, op. 3, d. 13, ll. 31–2.

The contrast between the resolution of the non-party commission and that of the Bolshevik faction on the question of social welfare, the subject of the second debate at the Conference, is equally interesting. The Bolshevik group argued that the families of the fallen soldiers who had volunteered for the anti-Bolshevik armies should not receive any social welfare benefits, while the families of those who had been conscripted by the anti-Bolshevik armies should only receive benefits after the families of the Red Army soldiers had been fully provided for (since the latter were everywhere said to be receiving only a small fraction of the benefits they were entitled to,[148] this would have effectively deprived the families of the soldiers conscripted by the anti-Bolshevik armies of any material benefits). The Conference voted for a series of amendments to the Bolshevik resolution. The most important concerned the families of the soldiers of the anti-Bolshevik armies, and read as follows: 'the Conference recognizes the obligation to provide for the families of those soldiers who were mobilized and taken away by the White Army'.[149] The Conference then moved a motion of support for the coming 'Week of the Front and Transport', when the peasants would be mobilized for labour service in aid of the Red Army and the families of its local soldiers.

On the land question, the third subject of debate at the Conference, there was, as one might expect, a much more direct confrontation between the Bolsheviks and the non-party delegates. Vasin, the leader of the Bolshevik group, spoke in favour of the collective farms (*arteli, kommuny*), 'because we cannot all work our own private farms'. The first delegate to oppose him was a peasant, named Kosnisarov, with a fine sense of irony:

> 'the last speaker talked about the establishment of the *kommuny* and so on. But the *kommuny* that have already been organized lay idle last summer, they didn't even harvest their own grain, potatoes, and other vegetables, and this is because these *kommuny* are full of Bolshevik activists who make a mess of things instead of setting a good example of farming, and also the last speaker said that the peasants should join the *kommuny*, but surely the peasants are only uneducated people not worthy to be in the *kommuny*![150]

Two other peasant delegates also spoke against the collectives, the first on the grounds that 'we cannot all live in the *kommuny*', and the second on the grounds that 'the peasantry can only work on separate family farms, not in the *kommuny*, because not everyone in the

[148] TsGAOR, f. 393, op. 3, d. 359, ll. 88–9, 232; op. 13, d. 429, l. 63; op. 13, d. 578, l. 290; TsGANKh, f. 478, op. 6, d. 2010, ll. 62–7; f. 1943, op. 6, d. 376, l. 9; *Kommuna* (Samara), no. 218, 4 Sept. 1919, p. 1; *Revoliutsionnaia armiia* (Samara/4th Army), no. 59, 16 Mar. 1919, p. 4; *Izvestiia* (Saratov), no. 230, 12 Oct. 1920, p. 3.

[149] GAKO, f. 185, op. 3, d. 13, l. 32.

[150] Ibid., l. 30.

peasantry is the same'.[151] The resolution of the non-party commission on the land question, which was passed in preference to the resolution of the Bolshevik group by a large majority, read as follows:

Having heard the speech of Vasin on the policy of the Soviet authorities on the question of land reorganization [*zemleustroistvo*], and having debated this question at length, the Conference came to the following conclusion: the best way to improve our agriculture is to eliminate strip-intermingling, but to carry on with private family household farming; at the same time the Conference is hostile towards the rise of the collective-communal farms on the basis of the Law on the Socialization of Land. The improvement of our agriculture requires agronomic assistance [to the peasant farmers] on a very broad scale.[152]

The final subject of debate at the Conference, the Bolshevik food procurement campaign, gave rise to a conflict between the Bolshevik and the non-party delegations on predictable lines. The former defended the forcible measures already taken by the VIKs to collect the grain levy, whereas the latter voiced its objections to these measures and insisted that it would be catastrophic for the local economy if the VIKs persisted with the food requisitionings. The resolution of the non-party commission, which was passed in preference to the resolution of the Bolshevik group by a large majority, read as follows:

Having heard the speech of Vasin on the provisions policy of the Soviet authorities, the Non-Party Conference decided that it [the policy] is correct, but it protests against the unfair repressions that have been carried out by the local organs of power against the peasantry. To improve the food situation, the Conference recognizes the need to combat speculation, but it requests a strict investigation of all those cases where the authorities have taken away the food which the peasants had saved for their own consumption, and [it requests that the authorities] should not carry out requisitionings from everyone indiscriminately, without proper grounds.

As regards the supply of livestock, the Conference believes that the peasants themselves should set a norm of livestock ownership to help support the farms, and should give up any surplus livestock to the provisions organs. In view of the acute needs of the population for essential goods, such as cotton, salt, matches, kerosene, soap, and sugar, the Conference agreed to draft a petition immediately to ask for the delivery of these goods, and also to increase the grain ration for the population to 2 *pud* per month and to 7½ *pud* per month for each working horse.[153]

Between 1917 and 1920 the system of peasant–state relations turned full circle. The war between the village communes and the state administration in the *volost'* townships, which had characterized rural

[151] GAKO, f. 185, op. 3, d. 13, l. 31.
[152] Ibid., l. 33.
[153] Ibid.

politics during the last period of the old regime, resulted in 1917–18 in the victory of the village communes: the old state organs in the *volost'* townships were destroyed; and the communes came to dominate the village and *volost'* soviets. The transformation of the VIKs into a part, albeit a weak one, of the Bolshevik-dominated state apparatus during 1918–20 reopened the old divisions between the village communes and the *volost'* administration. The communes adopted the same tactics of passive resistance and subterfuge against the Bolshevik state as they had previously used against the Tsarist regime. Yet, because of its disorganization on a national scale, the peasantry was incapable of generating an alternative to the Bolshevik state, and was indeed bound to become, sooner or later, one of its political victims. In the mean time, the new regime and the peasantry 'faced each other nationally in an uneasy truce'.[154]

The problem of governing the countryside after 1921 was in many ways more fundamental than it had been prior to 1917. The social autonomy and the economic power of the village communes had been greatly increased as a result of the revolution. The new state administrators in the VIKs and the village soviets were, unlike their predecessors under the Tsar, mainly drawn from the peasantry; they were, for the most part, barely literate, inexperienced in government, poorly disciplined, and strongly inclined towards localism. Even at the district and provincial levels the new regime continued to suffer from the power of local magnates during the 1920s and 1930s. The social background and the cultural outlook of the power-holders at the district and provincial levels were overwhelmingly urban-literate[155]—a factor which made it very difficult for the government to find realistic solutions to the problems of the rural sector. These structural weaknesses in the rural base of the new regime were to have a profound influence on the evolution of the Soviet system. As Teodor Shanin has concluded,

> With the political leadership committed to a misleading conception of rural society, with its local representatives out of touch with the peasantry in nearly all contexts other than coercive administrative force, with the power of the communes decisive in local affairs, yet unable to dictate national policy and bound to be defeated in a full-scale confrontation with a modern state, the stage was set already . . . for the drama of collectivization.[156]

[154] Shanin, *The Awkward Class*, p. 198.

[155] The (pre-1917) occupational background of the members of the district soviet executives in eighteen Russian provinces during 1920 was as follows: industrial workers 33.3 per cent; white-collar professionals 25.5 per cent; peasants 20.6 per cent; schoolteachers 8.4 per cent; other professionals 7.8 per cent; students 1.4 per cent; technicians with high-school education 1.3 per cent (Vladimirskii, *Sovety, ispolkomy i s''ezdy sovetov*, vyp. 2, p. 13).

[156] Shanin, *The Awkward Class*, p. 199.

6

The Rural Economy under War Communism

> More and more often one hears not only bourgeois and kulaks, but also members of the rural poor and workers comparing Soviet power unfavourably with the old regime . . . The enormous number of government orders, the proliferation of official institutions and commissions, the thousands of party bosses with lists of warrants and orders three yards long who travel around the country terrorizing the peasants—all this has placed a heavy burden on the population, and has caused the people to grumble and curse and become bitter. It has even driven some of the peasants to destroy their grain, meat, and other foodstuffs rather than give them to the Communists.
>
> Provisions Commissar of Kozlov *uezd* (Tambov Province), Summer 1919

THE victory of the Red Army in the civil war was ultimately dependent upon the ability of the Bolsheviks to mobilize the rural economy behind the state. Without the conscription of the rural population for military and labour services, the Red Army would have been unable to defeat the Whites and the Allied interventionary forces. Without a regular supply of foodstuffs in the towns and the garrisons, there was a serious danger that the workers and the servicemen would turn against the Bolsheviks, whom they had helped to bring to power.

The political economy of the Bolsheviks was bound to be complicated by the economic dislocation of the post-war period, which affected the whole of Europe. On the one hand, government borrowing and the collapse of manufacturing industry during the First World War had resulted in hyperinflation of industrial prices, a food supply crisis, and the rapid depopulation of the major industrial cities.[1] Emma Goldman described the former capital of Russia

> in ruins, as if a hurricane had swept over it. The houses looked like broken old

[1] On the depopulation of the cities during 1918–20 see D. Koenker, 'Urbanization and Deurbanization in the Russian Revolution and Civil War', *Journal of Modern History*, vol. 57, no. 3 (1985); E. G. Gimpel'son, *Sovetskii rabochii klass 1918–20 gg.*, Moscow, 1974, pp. 76 ff.; D. A. Baevskii, *Rabochii klass v pervye gody Sovetskoi vlasti (1917–1921 gg.)*, Moscow, 1974, pp. 248 ff.; V. Z. Drobizhev, A. K. Sokolov, and V. A. Ustinov, *Rabochii klass Sovetskoi Rossii v pervyi god proletarskoi diktatury (opyt strukturnogo analiza po materialam professional'noi perepisi 1918 g.)*, Moscow, 1975, pp. 109 ff.; W. J. Chase, *Workers, Society and the Soviet State: Labour and Life in Moscow, 1918–29*, Urbana, Ill., 1987, pp. 33–5. It is a good indication of the relative economic position of the countryside and the towns that the process of deurbanization was reversed after 1920.

tombs upon neglected and forgotten cemeteries. The streets were dirty and deserted; all life had gone from them. The population of Petrograd before the war was almost two million; in 1920 it had dwindled to five hundred thousand. The people walked about like living corpses; the shortage of food and fuel was slowly sapping the city . . .[2]

On the other hand, the inflation of industrial prices and the chronic shortages of consumer goods encouraged the peasants to withdraw from the market and retreat into autarky. The rural economy became geared towards the consumption needs of the peasants in opposition to the government's increasing market controls. The black market, closely related to systems of natural exchange and barter in foodstuffs and consumer goods, flourished. Even rural industry, contrary to the general opinion, began to play a more important role than before, as the rural population, now swelled by the urban in-migrants, attempted to manufacture on a local and domestic basis all those consumer goods which the towns and the government were no longer able to supply. The localism of the soviets and the village communes during the revolutionary period politically and culturally reinforced this 'primitive peasant capitalism'[3]—the 'capitalism' of smallholding family farms with 'egalitarian land allocation, connected and surrounded by a world of commodity exchange'.[4]

The increasing authoritarianism of the state in the rural economy under war communism (1918–21) needs to be viewed in the context of this growing divide between town and country, rather than in the context of Bolshevik ideology versus military exigency.[5] The extreme centralization of war communism—the increasing reliance of the government on the local economic councils (*sovnarkhozy*), the Commissariats, the military authorities, the requisitioning brigades, and the 'thousands of party bosses with lists of warrants and orders three yards long'[6]—was made necessary by the unreliability of the local soviets as organs of Communist power. These new government agents were quick to use coercive and arbitrary powers, because they were themselves without political roots in the localities, and because the militarized culture of the civil war had 'induced some people to confront economic problems as military goals'.[7]

[2] E. Goldman, *My Disillusionment in Russia*, London, 1925, p. 8.

[3] Lenin commonly used this phrase in his descriptions of the Russian countryside after the October Revolution. See e.g. *PSS*, vol. 29, p. 178.

[4] *RR*, pp. 32–3.

[5] For a survey of the long-standing debate on the origins of war communism (ideology or pragmatism?) see S. Malle, *The Economic Organization of War Communism 1918–1921*, Cambridge, 1985, pp. 1–28.

[6] TsGANKh, f. 1943, op. 1, d. 447, l. 96.

[7] Malle, p. 506.

The Bolshevik assault on the rural economy slowly developed into a full-scale war between the state and the peasantry, with the majority of the local soviets caught unhappily in between. The Bolsheviks saw themselves during the civil war as a socialist bastion surrounded by a hostile sea of ('capitalist') market relations in the countryside: a constant battle had to be fought against the market to save the regime from drowning. To begin with, the peasantry fought back with the weapons of economic subterfuge. They sabotaged the food monopoly by reducing their productivity to a minimun subsistence level, by concealing their grain from officials, by feeding it to their livestock, or by selling it privately. They delayed the fulfilment of the labour and military conscriptions by writing petitions to the higher authorities and simply by refusing to co-operate. But such tactics only worsened the conflict, thereby strengthening the—for the most part illusory—conviction of the higher authorities that the villages were filled with 'kulak' saboteurs. The food requisitionings and the punitive campaigns against Red Army deserters became increasingly violent as the economic crisis deepened and military discipline broke down. Once the requisitionings began to take away the food and seed supplies of the peasants, and the danger of famine approached, once the Whites had been defeated so that the requisitionings and punitive measures against deserters could no longer be easily justified, the peasantry put down its weapons of passive economic resistance and picked up those of armed struggle against the Bolshevik regime.

1. FOOD PROCUREMENT

The story of the Bolshevik food procurement campaigns is one of the most gruesome episodes in the history of the civil war. Like many notorious historical incidents, it has been subject to an uncommon degree of mystification and misunderstanding. Relatively little is known, for example, about the mechanics of the food procurement campaigns—how the levy was allocated and collected, and what the obstacles were to the fulfilment of the levies. Some historians in the West have been rather too quick to condemn the campaigns in general as an undisciplined and brutal assault on the peasantry, without discriminating between the various characteristics of the different procurement campaigns, or, indeed, without stopping to wonder whether 'rule by the gun' could have been effective enough on a national scale to explain the achievements of the campaigns. Soviet historians, on the other hand, have deliberately played down the adverse effects of the campaigns on the peasant economy and peasant–state relations. It is particularly unclear—and in any case very difficult to prove—whether the Bolsheviks knowingly or unknowingly requisitioned the basic food and seed of the peasants, as opposed to their surplus, and thereby helped to bring about the terrible famine of 1921–2, which was concentrated in the Volga region. This section aims to account for the changes in the organization of the procurement campaigns during 1918–21 and for the effects of the latter on the general position of the peasant economy.

The Grain Procurement Campaign of Autumn 1918

During the first procurement campaign (1918–19) under the grain monopoly (declared in May 1918) the Soviet regime was heavily dependent upon the Volga region. The other main grain-producing areas of the former Russian Empire—the northern Caucasus, the Kuban', the Don, the Ukraine, and western Siberia—were all in the hands of the Whites. Because of the political and infrastructural weaknesses of the Soviet regime outside the cities, the Bolsheviks decided to concentrate their forces for the procurement campaign. The decisive factor in determining where the grain was to be taken was not so much the location of the biggest surpluses (which the Bolsheviks did not know) as the location of the strongest political structures that were the least likely to be captured by the Whites. As Lenin put it in a letter to Tsiurupa, the Commissar for Provisions, in the early summer of 1918, 'In view of the critical food situation, we must not spread our forces too wide, but concentrate the mass of our forces on one centre where *it is possible* to take *a large amount* of grain' (emphasis in source).[8] Saratov, Samara, Penza, and Tambov provinces, which Lenin himself had suggested as a suitable location for this 'centre', were heavily overburdened in the subsequent allocation of the grain levy (*nariad, razverstka*), especially in comparison with Simbirsk and Kazan' provinces, where the Soviet state apparatus had still not been built up after the defeat of the Komuch. The four Volga provinces (Samara, Saratov, Penza, Simbirsk) in general were asked to pay a very large share (44.1%) of the total grain levy on the thirteen grain-producing provinces of the RSFSR (see Table 21).

The *razverstki* were calculated on the basis of estimates by the provincial provisions authorities of the harvest surplus (the gross harvest in all cereals minus a fixed consumption norm for food, feed, and seed). The inequalities of the *razverstki* were largely explained by the poor statistical 'methods' of the provisions authorities. The statistical departments of the provisions authorities were only able to make very rough estimates of the harvest in each *volost'*, since the

[8] *PSS*, vol. 50, p. 137.

TABLE 21. *Estimated cereal surplus and levy for 1918–1919, producing provinces of Soviet Russia ('000 pud)*

Province	Estimated cereal surplus of 1918 harvest	Cereal levy for 1918–19
Samara	50,000	60,000
Saratov	22,143	31,100
Simbirsk	50,011	12,000
Penza	2,467	11,600
Kazan'	46,020	13,500
Tambov	16,157	36,000
Voronezh	18,059	15,500
Tula	15,225	13,800
Viatka	33,040	30,500
Orel	13,524	14,100
Riazan'	3,304	5,000
Kursk	—	17,000
Total	[269,950]	260,100

Source: A. Mikhailovskii, 'Khlebnaia kampaniia 1918–1919 gg.', *Vestnik statistiki*, 1919, nos. 8–12, Moscow, 1920, p. 87; *Obzor deiatel' nosti khlebnogo otdela samarskogo gubernskogo prodovol'stvennogo komiteta s oktiabria 1918 g. po 1 marta 1919 g.*, Samara, 1919, p. 27; *Izvestiia saratovskogo gubprodkoma*, no. 12, 31 Mar. 1919, p. 17.

existing data on the sown area had been compiled before 1914 and there was no information on the current area occupied by the different crops. As the provisions commissar of Simbirsk province put it: 'We knew that there was grain, but how much and where it was found—that was unknown. The exact area of peasant land use, the area under different crops, the harvest yield, the amount of cattle—that is, everything we needed to know for our daily work—were completely unknown factors.'[9] The *kombedy* and the food brigades were unable to improve the accounting of the harvest, since they had little access to the records of the village communes and were themselves inclined to adopt 'mechanical' accounting methods (e.g. estimating the total harvest 'by eye', or inventing a harvest yield and multiplying it by the total land area, as opposed to the sown arable, to arrive at some fantastic 'surplus').[10] Narkomprod itself admitted in an undated report that 'the majority of the figures for the *razverstki* were fictional and unfulfillable'; they were said to have had 'a purely formal . . . and even

[9] Cited in L. N. Kritsman, *Probtarskaia revoliutsiia i derevnia*, Moscow/Leningrad, 1929, p. 100.

[10] TsGANKh, f. 1943, op. 1, d. 448, l. 131; op. 4, d. 339, l. 52; *Izvestiia saratovskogo gubprodkoma* (Saratov), no. 20, 1 Dec. 1918, p. 13; no. 12, 31 Mar. 1919, p. 8. See also TsGANKh, f. 3429, op. 1, d. 857, l. 94.

an abstract theoretical value'. The report concluded that 'there can hardly be a more important explanation of the chronic failure of the procurement campaigns than the poor accounting of the actual production and consumption of cereals'.[11] The Saratov provincial provisions committee estimated that '99% of the misunderstandings with the peasantry' during the procurement campaign of 1918–19 had arisen on the basis of the incorrect accounting of the peasantry's harvest by government officials.[12]

The calculations of the *razverstki* made no allowance for the long-term production needs of the peasant farms. The consumption norm left the peasant farms without any grain reserves for collateral, or insurance against harvest failure. Consequently, the peasants were very reluctant to part with their surplus before the corn-stalks of the next harvest had grown high. This partly explains the slow pace of the grain procurements during the autumn and winter of 1918–19, and the decision of the provisions authorities in January 1919 to put back the targeted date for the fulfilment of the levy from 1 March to 1 June.[13]

The conflict between the peasantry and the provisions authorities over the production needs of the family farm came to a head on the issue of the consumption norms. The official consumption norm set by Narkomprod for the 1918–19 agricultural year (12 *pud* of cereals per person; 15 to 18 *pud* of fodder and cereals per work-horse; 7 *pud* of fodder and cereals per cow) was considered unrealistically low by the mass of the peasantry (as well as a number of the Narkomprod officials themselves).[14] Thus on 2 October 1918 the Sinodka *volost'* soviet assembly (Vol'sk *uezd*) passed the following resolution on the official norm:

> The cereal norm in the articles of the Decree is not enough to meet the needs of the peasant household and cannot be implemented, since it would lead to the ruin of our farms . . . The peasant is constantly working hard, especially during the summer months, when he works night and day reaping and threshing, etc. His horse is also hard-working and needs more than 18 *pud* of grain, because . . . at the beginning of the sowing season the peasant must strengthen his horse . . . or the fields will not all get ploughed.

The assembly agreed to petition the Vol'sk provisions authority for an increase of the norm to 18 *pud* per person, 40 *pud* per work-horse, and

[11] TsGANKh, f. 1943, op. 1, d. 448, ll. 130–1.
[12] *Iubileinyi sbornik saratovskogo gubprodkomiteta 7 noiabria 1917 g.–7 noiabria 1919 g.*, Saratov, 1919, p. 41.
[13] *SS*, nos. 6–7, 1919, p. 152; *Samarskaia guberniia v gody grazhdanskoi voiny (1918–1920 gg.): Dokumenty i materialy*, Kuibyshev, 1958, pp. 450–2. See also *DSV*, vol. 4, Moscow, 1968, pp. 292–4.
[14] See Malle, p. 377.

12 *pud* per milk-cow.[15] Dozens of village and *volost'* soviets formulated similar resolutions and petitions during the autumn of 1918. The Iur'ev *volost'* soviet (Vol'sk *uezd*) petitioned the district provisions committee for an increase of the norm to 24 *pud* per person, and 60 *pud* per work-horse.[16] The Zhdamirovka *volost'* soviet (Simbirsk *uezd*) petitioned for an increase of the norm to 18 *pud* per person and 60 *pud* per work-horse.[17] The Neverkin *volost'* soviet (Kuznetsk *uezd*) petitioned for an increase of the norm to 27.5 *pud* per person, and 70 *pud* per work-horse.[18] The Samara district soviet assembly (November 1918) and the Saratov provincial assembly of land departments (January 1919) both endorsed the view that the consumption norms were dangerously low.[19]

Without firm control in the rural localities, the higher provisions authorities could do little to prevent the flagrant infringement of the official consumption norms by the peasantry. The Samara provincial provisions authorities carried out a budget study in 1918–19 which showed that the average peasant household used on the farm between 20% and 50% more than the amount of grain and fodder allowed by the Narkomprod norm. The average member of the peasant household ate (or used for the distillation of vodka) between 19 and 22 *pud* of cereals, and between 5 and 6 *pud* of potatoes. The average household used to feed and bed its horses: 7 *pud* of oats; 50 *pud* of chaff; 2.5 *pud* of flour; 3 *pud* of bran; 40 *pud* of hay; and 40 *pud* of straw. On its cows the average household used: 35 *pud* of chaff; 0.3 *pud* of flour; 5 *pud* of bran; 8 *pud* of hay; and 50 *pud* of straw. The study concluded with this prophetic warning:

> the peasantry is not used to self-deprivation and it is unrealistic to suppose that he will feed himself according to the Narkomprod norms . . . Naturally, by using coercive measures it would be possible to take the entire surplus of the peasantry, but that would be highly damaging for the whole of the economy in the region: a shortage of provisions would force the peasantry to eat part of its seed material and this would mean a smaller harvest next year. We must proceed with care. The estimate of the grain surplus in Samara province [50 million *pud*] should be reduced by 20 million *pud*.[20]

Table 22 shows the monthly results of the 1918–19 grain procure-

[15] TsGAOR, f. 393, op. 3, d. 332, l. 195.
[16] Ibid., ll. 4, 201, 253.
[17] Ibid., d. 359, l. 152.
[18] Ibid., d. 334, l. 161; d. 339, l. 39.
[19] *Zhurnal zasedaniia III-go samarskogo uezdnogo s''ezda sovetov krest'ianskikh i rabochikh deputatov*, Samara, 1918, pp. 14–15; TsGANKh, f. 478, op. 6, d. 1015, l. 96.
[20] *Obzor deiatel'nosti khlebnogo otdela samarskogo gubernskogo prodovol'stvennogo komiteta s oktiabria 1918 g. po 1 marta 1919 g.*, Samara, 1919, pp. 27–9; GAKO, f. 7, op. 1, d. 802, l. 3.

ment campaign (*zagotovka*) in Samara, Saratov, and Simbirsk provinces, and in sixteen grain producing provinces of the RSFSR. The volume of grain procured was quite heavy during the October-December period, but thereafter fell steadily. In view of the large size of the 1918 harvest, these were very disappointing results for the Soviet government.

TABLE 22. *State procurement of rye, wheat, groats, and fodder in Samara, Saratov, Simbirsk, and sixteen producing provinces of the RSFSR, 1918–1919*

	Samara		Saratov		Simbirsk		RSFSR	
	'000 *pud*	levy[a]	'000 *pud*	levy[a]	'000 *pud*	levy[a]	'000 *pud*	levy[a]
August 1918	1,040	1.7	45	0.1	—	—	1,584	0.6
September	1,040	3.4	1,911	6.2	—	—	7,647	3.5
October	1,383	5.7	4,505	20.7	936	7.8	15,835	9.6
November	4,977	14.0	1,330	25.0	459	11.6	14,727	15.3
December	4,803	22.0	982	28.2	775	18.0	14,735	20.9
January 1919	3,737	28.3	625	30.2	620	23.2	12,629	25.8
February	2,273	32.0	794	32.7	477	27.2	7,496	28.7
March	1,748	35.0	952	35.8	313	29.8	13,481	33.8
April	504	35.8	1,460	40.5	311	32.4	4,178	35.4
May	86	36.0	302	41.5	134	33.5	1,376	36.0
June	371	36.6	427	42.8	329	36.2	2,274	36.9
July	976	38.2	418	44.2	300	38.7	3,420	38.2
Total	22,938	38.2	13,751	44.2	4,654	38.7	99,382	38.2

[a] Cumulative percentage procured of total levy

Source: TsGANKh, f. 1943, op. 4, d. 339, ll. 169–77.

How are we to explain the failure of the procurement campaign? The Bolshevik leaders and the Soviet press placed the blame squarely on the shoulders of the 'kulak grain-hoarders' and 'speculators', who were said to have buried their surplus grain underground, sold it on the black market, or squandered it on their own farms. Modern Soviet historians have reproduced these arguments without an objective evaluation of the available evidence. In fact, evidence from the Narkomprod archives suggests that grain-hoarding and the black market did not become a major problem until the beginning of 1919, and that during the previous autumn the peasants, in general, were 'wildly enthusiastic to sell as much grain as possible' to the government.[21] The harvest of 1918 had been so large in the Volga region that until the end of the year the government price for rye (14 rb. 25 kop. per *pud*) remained higher than the black-market one (between

[21] TsGANKh, f. 1943, op. 3, d. 127, ll. 11, 108, 109; op. 1, d. 573, l. 11; op. 3, d. 223, ll. 51, 168, 304; op. 4, d. 116, l. 217; etc.

7 and 8 rb. per *pud*). In parts of Samara province it was reported that the private traders were even buying up grain which the peasants were unable or afraid to transport to the government collection points (*ssypnye punkty*), or which the infrastructure at the *ssypnye punkty* was too slow to collect, in order to resell it at government prices to the local units of the Red Army.[22] The prices of the private traders began to exceed those of the government only at the beginning of the following year, when—in the mistaken assumption that it would accelerate the peasants' grain deliveries—Narkomprod reduced its fixed prices by 25%.[23] It was only at this point, when the food stocks of the peasant farms began to run down, and it became apparent that the new government would be unable to pay for the grain procurements in industrial goods, that the peasants began to retain their grain on the farms, or sell it to the private traders in preference to the government.

What went wrong? Why did the government squander its best opportunity, during the autumn of 1918, to procure a larger share of the harvest? The answer lies in the breakdown of the state infrastructure at every stage of the procurement process.

First, a large portion of the 1918 harvest was left unreaped or unthreshed, on account of the delays in field work caused by the civil war, and the difficulties of transportation. The worst-affected areas were in the eastern steppe regions of Samara, where the Red Army was located until the end of the year; the distances between the villages and the fields, especially those of the former estates, were particularly large in this region. Much of the grain was ruined by the first snows before it could be harvested. A report of the military provisions bureau (*voenprodbiuro*) in Novouzensk district in the third week of November estimated that only one-quarter of the harvest in the area had been threshed: the rest of the crop was still in damp stacks in the fields. The harvests of the private estates had been abandoned, partly because of the physical separation of the estates from the villages and the difficulties of transport, and partly because the White Army had threatened to take reprisals against the peasants if they reaped the harvest.[24]

The *ssypnye punkty* were ill prepared to cope with the heavy volume of peasant grain coming in during the autumn. The mills were constantly being shut down for lack of fuel, or because the mill-

[22] Ibid., op. 3, d. 223, l. 304; op. 4, d. 116, l. 95; *Kommuna* (Petrovsk), no. 50, 17 Oct. 1918, p. 4. See also Malle, p. 394 n. 297. Free trade cereal prices were much lower in the Volga region than in other areas of Soviet Russia during 1918–19. See *KK*, p. 160.

[23] TsGANKh, f. 1943, op. 4, d. 116, ll. 210–18; op. 1, d. 448, l. 67; *Iubileinyi sbornik saratovskogo gubprodkomiteta*, pp. 69–70.

[24] TsGANKh, f. 1943, op. 3, d. 223, ll. 247–50; op. 4, d. 116, ll. 210–11. See also *Izvestiia saratovskogo gubprodkoma*, no. 16, 29 Oct. 1918, p. 6.

workers were found to be taking bribes. The Mills Department of the Saratov *sovnarkhoz* reported in January 1919 that no more than 97 of the 525 state-controlled mills in the province were still in working order; the turnover of the mills had been cut from 4.370 million *pud* per month during the pre-1914 period to 0.900 million *pud.*[25] Nearly all of the *ssypnye punkty* lacked sufficient barn-space to store the peasant grain. Most of them did not have enough experienced administrators to co-ordinate the payment of the peasants and the dispatch of the grain to the railway depots. Some even lacked the necessary weights and scales to weigh the peasants' grain. Long delays inevitably resulted in the processing of the grain; queues of up to 500 carts were not uncommon at the *ssypnye punkti.* The peasants had to wait several days to process their grain delivery. Since the *ssypnye punkty* serviced villages within a radius of up to 50 km., many peasants had to camp out by their carts. They wandered into the nearest settlement in search of a drink, some food, and a place to sleep.[26]

The transport system was chronically broken down in the Volga region immediately after the defeat of the Komuch. The shortages of horses and carts meant that a large portion of the grain at the *ssypnye punkty* never got to the railway depots. The shortages of fuel and rolling stock meant that much of the grain had to be left at the railway stations to freeze during the winter because it could not be transported. Chaos and corruption on the rivers and roads further slowed down the transport system.[27] The railway system presented the greatest problems. The two central rail links between the Volga and Moscow—the Riazan'-Ural'sk and the Moscow-Kazan' railways—had both been reserved for military transportation. The Samara-Buguruslan railway had been severely damaged by the retreating Whites; for much of the winter it had to be kept going by teams of peasants felling timber for fuel. The three railways, between them, required nearly 1 million cubic *sazhen'* of timber to replace the tracks and bridges destroyed during the Volga campaign.[28] All but one of the bridges across the Volga River, and most of those across its major tributaries, had been destroyed by the Whites. The loss of the Syzran' bridge forced the trains from the grain-rich areas of the south-east to make a long detour

[25] *Ekonomicheskaia zhizn'* (Saratov), nos. 1–2, 1920, p. 15.

[26] N. Orlov, *Deviat' mesiatsev prodovol'stvennoi raboty Sovetskoi vlasti,* Moscow, 1918, p. 299; TsGANKh, f. 1943, op. 1, d. 448, l. 132; d. 573, l. 12; op. 3, d. 223, l. 304; op. 4, d. 116, ll. 116, 165.

[27] TsGAOR, f. 130, op. 2, d. 443, l. 35; f. 5451, op. 4, d. 103, l. 25; TsGANKh, f. 1943, op. 1, d. 448, ll. 58–9; op. 3, d. 223, l. 306; op. 4, d. 116, l. 104; f. 3429, op. 1, d. 920, l. 69; *Izvestiia saratovskogo gubprodkoma,* no. 12, 31 Mar. 1919, p. 15.

[28] TsGANKh, f. 1943, op. 1, d. 447, l. 10; op. 4, d. 116, l. 204; *SS,* nos. 6–7, 1919, pp. 150–3.

north-eastwards to join up with the Simbirsk–Bugul'ma railway, the only major line not to have been seriously damaged during the civil war. The latter snowed up in November, however, and the requests of the local authorities for teams of snow-clearers were turned down by Narkomtrud.[29] On the smaller rivers the railway tracks could be laid directly onto the ice; this was a time-consuming exercise and had to be replaced by an even slower ferry system after the thaw.[30]

To add to its problems, the transport system was heavily over-burdened by the *polutorapudniki*, the 'one-and-a-half-pooders',[31] who were temporarily permitted to resume their journeys into the country-side following the harvest of 1918.[00] The Saratov provincial provisions commissar informed Narkomprod that the mass influx of these 'bag-men' (*meshochniki*) into the province had totally disrupted the transport system and the state procurement of grain; some of the peasants were said to be under the illusion that free trade had been restored.[33] The provisions authorities in Petrovsk district had to compete with more than 50,000 in-migrant workers buying up food from the peasants at free trade prices during February 1919.[34] The attempts of the government to bring these independent procurements to a halt after January 1919 by prohibiting passenger transport on the railways, and by setting up special brigades (*zagraditel'nye otriady*) to combat private food sales, proved unsuccessful. The country-bound trains from the major cities continued to be overcrowded by *polutora-pudniki* during 1919–20, especially in the harvest period. Countless reports were made to the effect that railway-workers were running an illicit private trade with the 'bag-men' in opposition to the special brigades.[35] The *zagraditel'nye otriady* in Simbirsk province en-countered daily up to five different teams of 'bag-men', most of them railwaymen, during August 1919.[86] Some of the 'bag-men' teams were

[29] TsGANKh, f. 1943, op. 4, d. 116, l. 204.

[30] Ibid., op. 3, d. 223, ll. 294, 304; op. 4, d. 116, ll. 104, 133–4, 204.

[31] City inhabitants authorized by their provisions authority to travel into the countryside and purchase, at free market prices, up to 1½ *pud* of food for their families; sometimes referred to as 'bag-men' (*meshochniki*).

[32] V. M. Andreev, 'Prodrazverstka i krest'ianstvo', *Istoricheskie zapiski*, vol. 97, Moscow, 1976, p. 9; L. T. Lih, 'Bolshevik Razverstka and War Communism', *Slavic Review*, vol. 54, 1986, p. 675. Sovnarkom ordered a new clamp-down on the *meshochniki* on 1 Oct. 1918 (TsGAOR, f. 130, op. 3, d. 93, l. 143).

[33] Andreev, 'Prodrazverstka i krest'ianstvo', pp. 9–10.

[34] *Izvestiia saratovskogo gubprodkoma*, no. 12, 31 Mar. 1919, p. 15.

[35] TsGAOR, f. 130, op. 2, d. 443, l. 35; f. 5451, op. 4, d. 103, l. 25; TsGANKh, f. 1884, op. 28, d. 1, l. 27; *Doklad ot narodnogo komissara putei; soobshchenii*, Moscow, 1919, pp. 8–9; etc.

[36] TsGANKh, f. 1943, op. 1, d. 573, l. 103. For a graphic description of the chaos on the railways see *DGS*, pp. 8–23, 80–6.

said to be highly organized, travelling in armed units with up to 100 men, and leaving the local authorities powerless to stop them.[37]

The administration of the grain procurement was notoriously unreliable. The *kombedy* proved even less effective as agencies of state grain procurement than as organs of 'proletarian power'. Tsiurupa, the head of *Narkomprod*, later complained:

> the *kombedy* worked at much too primitive a level for our purposes; almost everywhere they disrupted our work by pursuing their own local interests at the expense of the state. They often directly prevented the export of grain surpluses from their own *volost'*; they handed out food rations to the village poor far in excess of the Narkomprod norms; they set their own local prices for bread, which were generally far too low and forced the peasant farmers to bury their grain.[38]

The food brigades (*prodotriady*) came out no better in Tsiurupa's view:

> the food brigades carried out most of their work in a blind manner, without the slightest hint of a plan. They often used coercive measures; they seized not only foodstuffs but also private property for their own profit; and they indulged in other criminal activities. At times, they skilfully copied the methods of the Tsarist police in extracting arrears.[39]

A second source described the urban food brigades in the autumn of 1918 as a 'horde of kulak speculators on extended leave' from their factories.[40] The railway-workers, who were one of the few groups of the working class to grow in size during the civil war,[41] were well known for their black-market activities: wagon-loads of food left standing in the railway depots were gradually emptied and their produce sold off; trains which left the Volga region replete with food arrived empty in Moscow and Petrograd.[42] The provisions departments of the local soviets were constantly rebuked by the higher authorities for putting their own interests above those of the state. Some of them attempted to conceal the size of the grain surplus in their locality. Others petitioned the higher authorities for a lowering of the levy. Some physically prevented the export of surpluses by setting up

[37] TsGAOR, f. 130, op. 2, d. 443, l. 36.

[38] TsGANKh, f. 1943, op. 1, d. 448, l. 65. Similar statements may be found in ibid., op. 3, d. 223, l. 82; *Izvestiia saratovskogo gubprodkoma*, no. 17, 7 Nov. 1918, p. 23; no. 24, 31 Dec. 1918, p. 7; no. 6, 9 Feb. 1919, p. 16; no. 8, 23 Feb. 1919, p. 9; *Izvestiia* (Kuznetsk), no. 139, 27 Feb. 1919, p. 3; *Obzor deiatel'nosti khlebnogo otdela*, pp. 46–7; *Iubileinyi sbornik saratovskogo gubprodkomiteta*, p. 71.

[39] TsGANKh, f. 1943, op. 1, d. 448, l. 70.

[40] GAKO, f. 193, op. 2, d. 159, l. 7 (report by the Stavropol' Military Commissar, 15 July 1919).

[41] Gimpel'son, *Sovetskii rabochii klass*, p. 81.

[42] TsGANKh, f. 1943, op. 1, d. 448, ll. 19–20; *Izvestiia saratovskogo gubprodkoma*, no. 5, 11 Aug. 1918, pp. 11, 13.

road blocks. The higher authorities responded by purging the provisions administration (the entire staff of the Simbirsk provincial provisions committee was arrested for 'localism' in the summer of 1919).[43] But this does not appear to have solved the problem, which it probably worsened as the food crisis deepened.

The breakdown of the supply infrastructure prevented not only the export of foodstuffs, but also the import of industrial manufactures. The shortage of consumer goods in the countryside, the rapid inflation of industrial prices, and the failure of the state-organized commodity exchange between town and country (*tovaroobmen*) induced the peasantry to cut back its grain sales to the government, and either retain the grain surplus on the farm or sell it privately. This tendency became noticeably more marked during the early months of 1919, as the peasants began to think about their cereal requirements for the coming agricultural season, and the grain prices on the black market began to soar above the government ones in response to the growing food crisis in the cities. The failure of the *tovaroobmen* became apparent in the countryside at about the same time. During the previous autumn the peasants had been given government receipts for their grain, which they were told they would be able to exchange for consumer goods up to the fixed money value of 40% of their grain (the rest was to be paid in cash), once they had gone through a complex series of administrative procedures in the local soviets and the district co-operatives.[44] But the supply of consumer goods fell a long way short of the amount required to pay the peasants, partly because of the shortage of industrial manufactures in the urban centres, and partly because of the problems of transportation already outlined.[45] In Saratov province it was estimated in December 1918 that the peasants had received only 15% of the value of their state-levied grain in consumer goods. In Samara province barely one-quarter of the manufactures sent from Moscow during the spring of 1919 ever reached the peasants.[46] The remotest villages were the worst to suffer (and the quickest to retreat into autarky), since they had not only transported their grain the furthest to the *ssypnoi punkt*, but had also,

[43] TsGANKh, f. 1943, op. 1, d. 448, l. 69; op. 4, d. 339, ll. 182–3.

[44] See TsGANKh, f. 1943, op. 1, d. 446, l. 28; Orlov, p. 299; *Krasnaia letopis': Materialy k istorii sovetskogo stroitel'stva v Samarskoi gubernii (oktiabr' 1917 g.–aprel' 1921 g.)*, Samara, 1921, pt. 3, p. 245.

[45] Another problem was the interception of goods deliveries by Red Army units and Soviet personnel (*Izvestiia saratovskogo gubprodkoma*, no. 24, 31 Dec. 1918, p. 5; *Iubileinyi sbornik saratovskogo gubprodkomiteta*, p. 120).

[46] *Izvestiia saratovskogo gubprodkoma*, no. 24, 31 Dec. 1918, p. 5; K. M. Krasil'nikova, 'Bor'ba za khleb v Srednem Povolzh'e v period inostrannoi voennoi interventsii i grazhdanskoi voiny', kand. diss., Kuibyshev, 1968, p. 223.

TABLE 23. *Grain procurement and distribution of industrial goods, various regions of Samara province, 1918–1919*

Region	Distance from *uezd* centre (km).	Value of grain receipts (rb.)	Value of received goods (rb.)	% grain receipts paid in kind
Samara *uezd*				
Samara suburb	5	108,867	59,843	55.0
Koshki	64	36,980	23,822	64.4
Obsharovka	109	108,497	41,434	38.2
Krasnyi Iar	38	63,965	17,409	27.2
Dubovo-Umet	—	423,192	46,288	10.9
Stavropol' *uezd*				
Stavropol'	—	27,849	11,956	42.9
Belyi Iar	53	65,000	19,533	30.0
Buzuluk *uezd*				
Bogatovskoe	132	67,263	20,341	30.2
Alekseev	110	82,503	12,613	15.3
Nikolaevsk *uezd*				
B. Glushitska	139	62,912	9,369	14.9
Petrovskoe	56	42,354	7,658	18.1
Bezenchuk	—	7,954	2,047	25.7
Spasskoe	—	67,141	17,193	25.6

Source: Krasnaia letopis': Materialy k istorii sovetskogo stroitel'stva v Samarskoi gubernii (oktiabr' 1917 g. – aprel' 1921 g.) k VIII gubernskomu s"ezdu sovetov r.k. i kr. dep., 18 iiunia 1921 g., Samara, 1921, pt. 3, pp. 246–8. Distances from the village to the *uezd* centre are from *Spisok naselennykh punktov Samarskoi gubernii*, Samara, 1928.

on the whole, received the lowest proportion of their payment in kind (see Table 23). Inequalities such as this only heightened the scepticism of the peasantry towards the *tovaroobmen*. During the spring the peasants were reported in many areas to have discarded their receipts 'as useless (and taxable) bits of paper'.[47] In some villages the farmers complained because the landless elements had been given a share of the consumer goods, although they had not contributed to the payment of the grain levy. The allocation of the goods on a *volost'*-by-*volost'* basis inevitably gave rise to disputes between the villages which had fulfilled their share of the levy and those which had not, since unless the whole of the *volost'* had fulfilled its levy the higher authorities refused to allocate it any consumer goods.[00]

Unable to meet their basic household needs (e.g. kerosene, cloth,

[47] *Obzor deiatel'nosti khlebnogo otdela*, p. 46.

[48] *Protokol 5-go s''ezda upolnomochennykh potrebitel'nykh obshchestv Serdobskogo uezda*, n.p., 1919, pp. 24–8.

soap, tea) through the *tovaroobmen*, the peasant farmers sold their surplus food on the black market, where such goods were more readily available. The growth of the black market was a universal and spontaneous response by urban and rural consumers to the breakdown of the supply system in essential goods between town and country. Lenin estimated that half the food consumed in the towns during 1918–19 had been supplied through private means.[49] It is reasonable to assume that during this period a similar proportion of the household goods in the countryside had been supplied by private exchange. It is nonsensical for Soviet historians to present this trade as 'speculative', a symptom, like all market relations, of some 'kulak' or 'petty-bourgeois' capitalism.[50] The black market grew naturally out of the struggle of ordinary people to meet their essential needs. It operated largely without the use of cash, through natural exchange and barter, since all types of money had been devalued by inflation. There was little point in trying to speculate on the rise of prices. The black market represented the naturalization, rather than the capitalization, of the rural economy. The shortage of consumer goods forced the peasantry to orientate its farm production towards its own consumption requirements (e.g. rye, potatoes, millet). Rural industries sprang up to replace those household goods that could no longer be obtained from the cities. It short, the rural economy slowly became independent of the entire urban-state sector. Yet, this only aggravated the economic situation in the towns, and provoked the Bolsheviks to take even more draconian measures during the requisitioning of the peasantry's foodstuffs.

The Prodrazverstka *(Food Levy)*

The introduction of the *prodrazverstka* in January 1919 aimed to reinforce the state system of food procurement.[51] Whereas the food monopoly of 1918 had been limited to cereals and fodder crops, the *prodrazverstka*, as the name suggests, covered all the main foodstuffs, including vegetables and dairy products, which the 'bag-men' had previously been allowed to buy at free market prices. Moreover, whereas the grain levies had been set during the autumn campaign in relation to local estimates of the cereal harvest, those of the *prodrazverstka* were set 'from above', according to the food needs of the state, rather than the actual size and location of the food surpluses.

[49] *PSS*, vol. 39, p. 168.

[50] A notable exception is the work of V. V. Kabanov, *Oktiabr'skaia revoliutsiia i kooperatsiia*, Moscow, 1973, pp. 224–35. See also *KK*, pp. 149–51.

[51] *SU*, 1919, no. 1, art. 10; *DSV*, vol. 4, Moscow, 1968, pp. 292–4.

The provincial provisions committees were given obligatory quotas to fulfil, which were only very loosely related to the productive capacity of the local economy; these, in turn, distributed the levy among the district provisions committees, and so on down the line. Accurate accounting methods were thus no longer required, although the lower-ranking officials were instructed to make sure that the households without a food surplus, or those with less than 4 *des.* for a family of six, were exempted from the levy. However, it was underlined that if the levy was not fulfilled then such households would also be forced to pay a share of the tax, for the *prodrazverstka* legally postulated the collective duty of the commune to pay the state's taxes (*krugovaia poruka*) left over from the period of serfdom.[52]

The higher Soviet authorities and the party assumed greater control of the procurement campaign under the *prodrazverstka* than during the previous autumn. A massive propaganda effort was launched during the spring, and then again on the eve of the 1919 harvest, to mobilize the support of the peasantry for the food levy, and to educate the urban personnel of the food brigades in the 'devious methods' of the 'kulak grain-hoarders'. The provincial and district provisions authorities were put under close supervision by the party cells. A conference of 2,500 provisions officials in Saratov province resolved on 10 January that only Bolshevik party members could be trusted to 'hold any position of authority' in the provisions organs.[53] A similar reform was carried out in Samara province: the main posts in the provisions organs were assigned to party members; and the *ssypnye punkty* were placed under the control of workers' organizations from the industrial regions.[54] Regional provisions authorities (*raiprodkomy*) were set up to provide closer control of the VIKs. Provisions conferences (*prodsoveshchaniia*) were organized at the provincial and district levels to co-ordinate the various elements of the food procurement campaign. And the organization of the food brigades was centralized under the control of the provincial provisions authorities.[55]

The 'food armies' (*prodarmii*) of the autumn 1918 campaign were large-scale organizations, many of them numbering several hundred recruits, affiliated to a specific town or factory. They were generally beyond the control of either the provincial or the central political authorities. The introduction of the *prodrazverstka* witnessed the

[52] *SU*, 1919, no. 1, art. 11; *Istoriia sovetskogo krest'ianstva*, vol. 1, *Krest'ianstvo v pervoe desiatiletie Sovetskoi vlasti 1917–1927*, Moscow, 1986, p. 112.
[53] *Izvestiia saratovskogo gubprodkoma*, no. 4, 26 Jan. 1919, p. 26.
[54] *SS*, nos. 6–7, 1919, p. 155.
[55] *Iubileinyi sbornik saratovskogo gubprodkomiteta*, pp. 40–3; *Kratkii otchet i rezoliutsii IX-go s''ezda sovetov Saratovskoi gubernii*, Saratov, 1921, p. 14.

rapid expansion of the 'military food brigades' (*voenprodotriady*), which had been instituted in August 1918. They numbered twenty-five members, led by two card-carrying party 'commissars', and were subordinated to the provisions authorities of the provinces in which they operated, as well as to the trade unions and the Voenprodbiuro (Military Provisions Bureau) in Moscow.[56] Table 24 shows the

TABLE 24. *Military food brigades in Simbirsk province, 30 June 1919*

Place of origin	Factory and trade-union brigades	Soviet provisions brigades	Others (e.g. peasant brigades)
Moscow	18	1	3
Moscow prov.	15	3	—
Petrograd	13	2	2
Briansk	5	—	—
Kronshtadt	1	—	—
Petrograd prov.	3	18	1
Tver' prov.	9	9	2
Arkhangel'sk prov.	—	3	—
Vladimir prov.	5	5	2
Severo-Dvinsk prov.	—	6	—
Ivanovo-Voznesensk prov.	5	7	1
Nizhegorod prov.	5	—	3
Cherepovets prov.	5	3	—
Kostroma prov.	4	7	—
Olonets prov.	—	11	—
Novgorod prov.	5	3	—
Iaroslavl' prov.	6	—	—
Smolensk prov.	1	—	—
Various transport workers' organizations	33		

Source: TsGAOR, f. 5556, op. 1, d. 35, ll. 43–6.

different types and geographical origins of the 225 military food brigades in Simbirsk province on the eve of the 1919 harvest. The small size of the brigades enabled them to penetrate the villages. Most of them carried out propaganda and political work among the peasants.[57] Others helped to harvest the fields and account the grain. They were sometimes joined by *ad hoc* harvest brigades of bourgeois townsmen conscripted by their soviet, migrant workers rounded up at

[56] TsGAOR, f. 5556, op. 1, d. 35, l. 6.
[57] Iu. K. Strizhkov, *Prodovol'stvennye otriady v gody grazhdanskoi voiny i inostrannoi interventsii 1917–1921 gg.*, Moscow, 1973, pp. 196–7.

railway stations, or Red Army soldiers on leave.[58] The food brigades usually operated within close proximity to one another, so that they could easily link up to put down peasant uprisings.[59]

The food brigades have come to be remembered mainly for the violent methods which they frequently employed against the peasantry. Much of this violence was engendered by the military language used by the Bolsheviks to rally the brigades behind the 'battle for bread', language later compared by one provincial leader to that of an army in an enemy country.[60] The *prodrazvertska* also invited repressive measures, since without any accounts of the harvest in the localities it would be difficult to enforce the collection of the levies without the use of a gun. Some of the provincial authorities illegally imposed regressive levies—such as 10 *funt* per head (Riazan' province), 10 *pud* per *des.* (Saratov province), or even 20 *pud* per *des.* (Kazan' province)[61]—whose collection was even more likely to require the use of coercion, since the levies were bound to take away the food and seed supplies of the poorer villages (in Saratov province, for example, the average yield of rye in 1919 was only 22.5 *pud* per *des.*).[62] G. A. Trofimov, an instructor of the food brigades in Balashov district, described the consequences of the attempt to collect, 'by ultimatum', the 10 *pud* per *des.* tax in Pada *volost'* during October 1919:

> The VIK in Pada passed a resolution to take [10 *pud*] per *des.*, regardless of the actual amount of the grain surplus. It was said there was not enough time to find out from whom the grain should be taken, and from whom it should not; everything would be sorted out later. Given the small size of the harvest in the *volost'*, the levy turned out to be an impossible burden on the poorer peasants, who were forced to give up most of their harvest. If there had been more time, the levy could have been collected more fairly, but it was all done by threats in order to collect the required amount of grain in the set time; we punished the poorer peasants. Now the peasantry is hostile to the Soviet regime; the peasants mistrust us and in some cases even hate us; everywhere you hear them complain 'How am I to feed myself and my cattle when they have taken away all my grain?' . . . These actions have brought little real benefit; yet, in psychological terms, they are already killing at its roots the creative spirit of the Revolution.[63]

If we are to explain the coercive actions of the food brigades then we

58 TsGAOR, f. 130, op. 2, d. 106, ll. 141, 223; f. 393, op. 3, d. 323, ll. 98, 102; GAKO, f. 81, op. 1, d. 10, ll. 194, 198, 204, 205; f. 193, op. 2, d. 159, l. 102,

59 TsGANKh, f. 1943, op. 1, d. 447, ll. 93–4.

60 Ibid., f. 3429, op. 1, d. 857, l. 94 (A. Chubarov, Skopin; Mar. 1920).

61 Ibid., f. 1943, op. 1, d. 448, l. 130; *Iubileinyi sbornik saratovskogo gubprodkomiteta*, p. 43; *Istoriia sovetskogo krest'ianstva*, vol. 1, p. 118.

62 *Trudy TsSU: Statisticheskii ezhegodnik 1918–1920 gg.*, vol. 8, vyp. 1, Moscow, 1921, p. 247.

63 TsGANkh, f. 1943, op. 1, d. 446, l. 80.

must look more closely at the social characteristics of their recruits and the context in which they operated. The majority of the food brigades comprised unemployed workers, demobilized soldiers, and other marginal elements without any experience of agriculture or tax collection.[64] Many of them, having arrived in the Volga region after a long journey, had to sell the items which they had brought with them from the cities (e.g. second-hand clothes, matches, soap) in order to feed themselves. In Melekess district it was reported in November 1919 that the provisions authorities could not employ all the workers' brigades which had arrived from the north: 'the workers were forced to sell everything they had, even their clothes. Some became beggars. Many became ill or contracted diseases. The mood of the workers is very bad and the atmosphere is ready for counter-revolution'.[65] Elsewhere it was reported that the food brigades had gone long periods without clothing, weapons, or wages. [66] In this state, it is not surprising that the discipline of the food brigades began to break down. A Narkomprod official in the German Volga region reported in September 1920: 'the food brigade workers are raggedly dressed and without shoes or weapons; autumn is approaching and they are totally unfit for work. I consider it my duty to report that half of the brigade workers are selfish scoundrels . . . one brigade has even been helping to hide the speculators'.[67]

The worst offences of the food brigades were committed in the areas closest to the civil war front, where the context of political action had already been militarized. A good example of the sort of local tyrants commonly found at the head of the brigades in these regions comes from the southern areas of Balashov district, behind the front against Denikin during the summer and autumn of 1919. Cheremukhin's brigade operated in the fashion of a feudal army. It was a large mounted force with its own 'headquarters' in the village of Samoilovka, where it stored the foodstuffs and property of the peasants, which it had collected, for the most part, by the use of mass terror. Several rival brigades in the area were either defeated and disarmed by Cheremukhin's gang, or co-opted into it. The Saratov provincial authorities sent a detachment of party workers to arrest Cheremukhin, but this

64 Soviet historians have argued that the brigades comprised exclusively factory workers, but this is not borne out by the evidence. The trade unions opposed the use of factory workers for grain procurement, because of labour shortages in industry. The brigades were often forced to accept recruits without any pre-selection (*fil'trovka*), so that discipline quickly broke down. See TsGAOR, f. 130, op. 2, d. 443, ll. 6, 13–15, 20, 33, 52, 55, 82; f. 5451, op. 4, d. 123, ll. 14, 36, 200, 208.

65 TsGAOR, f. 5556, op. 1, d. 35, l. 67.

66 Ibid., f. 130, op. 2, d, 443, ll. 5, 17, 33, 35.

67 TsGANkh, f. 1943, op. 6, d. 376, l. 1.

was defeated, and its members made to stand undressed in temperatures of −15°C. On the slightest rumour of Cheremukhin's approach, the peasants would flee to their huts or into the woods. The leader of a rival food brigade, on passing through one of the villages within Cheremukhin's fiefdom, caught a vivid impression of the mood of the peasantry:

> the peasants mistook us for some of Cheremukhin's assistants, and they all fell down onto their knees and bowed before us. One could feel that the spirit of the Revolution among the people of this village had been entirely suppressed. The slavery of Tsarism was again clearly visible on their faces. The effect upon us was one of overwhelming demoralization.[68]

Peasant complaints against the injustices of the *prodrazverstka* were voiced at virtually every assembly at the district and provincial levels during 1919–20. Let us look at two representative examples. At an assembly of officials of the consumer societies in Serdobsk district from 25 to 27 May 1919 the main grievance of the local delegates concerned the unfair terms of trade between town and country under the *prodrazverstka*. One delegate complained that his family had sold 100 *pud* of grain to the state, and had received 1,200 *rb.*—enough to buy one pair of shoes.[69] Others complained that the government payments were worthless, since there were no consumer goods available in the co-operative stores.[70] A delegate reminded the congress:

> the central authorities issued an order to provide the farmers with the tools which they need before anything else. In passing this order, the central authorities obviously had in mind the fact that without these tools it is impossible to fulfil the plan to sow all the arable. But we have still not seen any of these tools. What is more, they won't even give us any of the manufactures which are made right here in the district, such as wheels, for example, which we need very badly . . . The position is now so bad, that the peasant has to go around the village, asking his neighbours to lend him a wheel or two, before he can leave for the fields.[71]

The assembly was unanimous that the peasants had given up all their surplus grain. It agreed to appoint a commission to check the grain stores of the villages. The peasants were 'not trying to deny [their] obligation to give all the surplus grain to the government',[72] but it was now up to the authorities to explain why they could not

[68] Ibid., op. 1, d. 446, l. 85; see also ll. 72, 77–9, 81–4, 95–6, 100; d. 447, l. 48; op. 4, d. 167, ll. 24, 31; GAKO, f. 81, op. 1, d. 10, ll. 115, 118; etc.
[69] *Protokol 5-go s''ezda upolnomochennykh*, p. 18.
[70] Ibid., pp. 24–7, 31.
[71] Ibid., p. 24.
[72] Ibid., p. 26.

distribute the manufactures which had been promised to the peasantry. As the delegate from Cherkass *volost'* concluded,

it is clear that the workers won't give us their manufactures, and the peasants won't give up any more grain—not for some caprice, but simply because there is no grain left, the peasants have given it all already; we can see that there are manufactures in the co-operative, but they won't give us them; all we hear is the demand to give up more grain.[73]

At the Syzran' district soviet assembly from 4 to 5 July the *volost'* delegates were more concerned with the abuses of the provisions organs and the food brigades than with the unequal terms of trade. One of the delegates complained that his village soviet had taken no account of the needs of the peasant families in allocating the tax burdens, so that many households had been forced to give up their last food stores to pay their share of the levy.[74] A second delegate complained:

They always blame everything on the peasant, even if he has just delivered his last sack of grain to the *ssypnoi punkt* . . . The peasants gave their best in both the imperial war and the civil one: they gave both their sons and their products. But who cares about the peasants? We asked for more seed—but they didn't give it to us on time, and when they did it was already too snowed up to get to the fields. This also is wrong! [Cries: 'That's right!'].[75]

A third delegate complained that

only the commissars are able to do any trading. They take away our meat, but then let it rot. The district provisions committee should check to see if these rumours are true. Also, it is said that the workers in the factories are given jam and sausage, while the peasants see none of these. The instructors in the localities know nothing about peasant life, and are always doing everything wrong.[76]

This was supported by a Red Army commander, who was the next to speak:

It is painful for me, a Red Army commander, to see how the peasants are ordered around in the localities. When I was training, Lenin told us not to order the peasants around. You have to explain and prove things to the peasants, not simply use rigorous and iron discipline against them, not beat them into submission; you have to have the patience to talk to the peasants. You have to send comrades into the villages who know peasant life well, who can get close

[73] *Protokol 5-go s''ezda upolnomochennykh*, p. 26.
[74] *Stenograficheskii otchet 7-go syzranskogo uezdnogo soveta s 4-go po 5-e iiulia 1920 g.*, Syzran', 1920, p. 44.
[75] Ibid.
[76] Ibid., pp. 44–5.

to the peasants. It's no good just terrorizing the peasants. Is that not right, comrades? [Cries: 'That's right!' Applause].[77]

Emboldened by this speech, a number of the peasant delegates stood up to denounce the food brigades. One delegate said:

The brigades act improperly. They don't even take into account the opinions of the VIKs and the village soviets, but simply carry on as they please. This is not acceptable, comrades; by acting in this way, the brigades undermine the authority of the local powers. They make big promises, but give us nothing.[78]

A second delegate found his criticisms of the brigades developing into a general attack on the soviets:

the authorities take nothing into account, neither the needs of the peasants, nor anything else . . . Nobody trusts the peasants—neither the workers nor the speculators; they are treated like the lowest of the low. But nobody thinks about searching the people in the towns [for food] . . . although everyone knows there are speculators there. They ought to make sure that the people in the towns don't have one or two pounds of flour in store. They say there are no workers in the countryside. But in the war 50% were in the army and they were all workers . . . And now we have workers all right—they come into the countryside and sit about in the soviets doing nothing all day long.[79]

During the reading of the resolution, the party fraction clashed with the peasant delegates, who wanted the resolution to include a petition for higher fixed prices and an end to the 'abuses in the localities by the food brigades and the instructors'. When the party fraction rejected these demands there were cries from the floor to 'vote again on all the resolutions', and to elect a commission of the peasant delegates. In the end, a compromise was struck: the existing fixed prices were not to be challenged, but a resolution was passed calling for the punishment of the 'uneducated elements who do not understand the tasks of Soviet power' who had 'infiltrated into the food brigades and harmed the interests of the toiling peasantry'.[80] At midnight the assembly drew to a close.

The Prodrazverstka *and the Famine Crisis of 1920–1922*

Most famine crises result in part from natural causes and in part from man-made ones. The great Volga famine of 1920–2 was no exception to this rule. The crop failure of 1920, followed by a year of frost and drought, transformed the Volga steppelands into an arid wasteland. Cholera and typhus weakened the population and destroyed the

[77] Ibid., p. 45.
[78] Ibid.
[79] Ibid.
[80] Ibid., pp. 46–50.

draught livestock, bringing farming to a halt.[81] As soon as the impending catastrophe became clear from the pitiful appearance of the new corn-stalks during the spring of 1921, the peasants began to slaughter their cattle and flee the cursed region with their meagre belongings. Thousands of people and horses simply collapsed and died on the roads during the following eighteen months. These cracks in nature's moulds would not have proved so disastrous, however, had the peasant economy not already been debilitated by seven years of war and revolution. The economic losses of these years took away the food stores of the farms which otherwise might have helped a large portion of the peasants to withstand the crop failure and the drought. It is surely not coincidental that the famine took its greatest toll of human life in the Volga region, where the Bolsheviks had concentrated their efforts during the food procurement campaigns.

To establish a causal link between the food procurements and the famine we need to examine carefully the data concerning grain surpluses and seed stocks. If it could be shown that the provisions authorities overestimated the size of the grain surplus, and actually took away the seed of the peasants, then it would appear that the seriousness of the famine crisis could be in part explained by the effects of the food procurements. The problem is outlined in Table 25.

TABLE 25. *Grain procurement in Samara and Saratov provinces, 1919–1921 ('000 pud)*

	Samara		Saratov	
	1919–20	1920–1	1919–20	1920–1
Estimated harvest surplus	20,133	18,031	26,931	27,861
Grain levy	28,000	—	38,200	13,500
Grain procured	14,503	14,787	15,473	10,075
Seed procured	408	—	2,000	2,300
% of estimated harvest surplus procured	74.1	82.0	64.9	44.4

Source: TsGANKh, f. 1943, op. 4, d. 339, l. 264; *Sbornik statisticheskikh svedenii po Soiuzu SSR*, Moscow, 1924, pp. 424–5, 430–1; *Tri goda bor'by s golodom*, Moscow, 1920, p. 31.

The table shows that the grain levy deliberately exceeded the estimated harvest surplus, on the assumption that the peasantry would conceal from the state up to 30% of its actual surplus product. It also

[81] S. G. Wheatcroft ('Famine and Epidemic Crises in Russia, 1918–1922: The Case of Saratov', *Annales de démographie historique 1983*, pp. 339–40) has argued that more deaths were caused by cholera and typhus than by starvation during the 1920–2 crisis.

shows that a very large proportion of the estimated harvest surplus was actually procured, leaving a very small margin of error between surplus and seed. The proportion of the 'surplus' taken during these two campaigns (generally between 60% and 80%) was considerably greater than it had been in the campaign of 1918–19 (46% to 62%).

The records of the Samara provisions authorities suggest that the 1919 harvest surplus in the province was overestimated, and that the procurement campaign took away part of the basic food and seed stores of the peasantry. The estimate of the harvest surplus (20.133 million *pud*) included 8.051 million *pud* said to have been left over from the 1918–19 agricultural year. The calculation of this last figure is highly questionable. Firstly, it did not make adequate allowance for extra peasant consumption: the peasants were known to have used on their farms between 20% and 50% more grain than the amount allowed for by the Narkomprod norms; yet the Samara provisions authorities, in calculating the figure of 8.051 million, allowed for an increase of only 12.7% in the Narkomprod norm. Secondly, the calculation failed to make adequate allowance for the private export of foodstuffs from the province during 1918–19: whereas the TsSU budget studies suggested that several million *puds* of grain may have been exported through the 'bag-trade', the Samara provisions authorities allowed for no more than 2.567 million *pud* of private exports, on the questionable assumption that 'our province suffered much less than others' in this respect.[82] Thirdly, it was admitted that a large (but unspecified) portion of the 8.051 million *pud* surplus was situated in the southern steppelands, where, as we have already seen, the infrastructure of the 1918 procurement campaign had been particularly weak. But this area was transferred by Narkomprod in August 1919 to the newly established Pokrovsk provisions authority, which was allocated a separate grain levy (20.450 million *pud*) on top of the levy already imposed on Samara province (28 million *pud*).[83] Table 26 shows that 13.064 million *pud* of grain was procured in the Pokrovsk region during 1919–20—equal to 74% of the estimated 'surplus' (i.e. not including the deductions which ought to be made, but which cannot be quantified, on account of the extra consumption and private export of grain). In the rest of Samara province 14.503 million *pud* was collected, although the estimated 'surplus' here was only 11.253 million *pud*. On this calculation, the average peasant household in Samara province lost at least 7.2 *pud* from its basic food and seed stores as a direct result of the food procurement campaign.

[82] GAKO, f. 7, op. 1, d. 802, l. 3.
[83] TsGAOR, f. 393, op. 13, d. 578, l. 285.

TABLE 26. *Grain harvest, estimated surplus, grain levy and procurements, Samara province and Pokrovsk region, 1919–1920 ('000 pud)*

District (1919–20 administrative divisions)	Gross harvest in 1919	Estimated surplus (+) or deficit (−) until 1920 harvest	Grain Levy	Grain procured
Samara province				
Samara	12,577	+3,279	4,000	—
Bugul'ma	11,382	+2,534	3,000	—
Buguruslan	12,458	−1,364	4,000	—
Buzuluk	20,314	+2,754	7,000	—
Nikolaevsk	6,270	+1,108	5,000	—
Stavropol'	10,549	+2,942	5,000	—
Total	73,550	+11,253	28,000	14,503
Pokrovsk				
Nikolaevsk	12,540	+2,217	—	—
Novouzensk	29,325	+15,421	—	—
Total	41,865	+17,638	20,450	13,064

Source: GAKO, f. 7, op. 1, d. 802, l. 4. The levies are from *Kommuna* (Samara), no. 223, 10 Sept. 1919, p. 2.

The records of the Balashov district provisions authorities support the contention that the peasants lost a part of their basic food and seed stores as a result of the 1919–20 procurement campaign. The intensity of the 1918–19 campaign[84] and the civil war against Denikin during the following summer resulted in a sharp reduction of the sown area in Balashov district during 1918–19. The harvest yields of 1919 were sharply down on the previous year: 15.8 *pud* per *des.* (as opposed to 62 *pud* per *des.*) in rye; and 17.6 *pud* per *des.* (as opposed to 62 *pud* per *des.*) in wheat. The gross grain harvest in 1919 was a mere 6.990 million *pud* (as opposed to 19.060 million *pud* in 1918)—that is, 3.299 million *pud* less than the amount needed to meet the Narkomprod consumption norms for the district. And yet, in spite of this deficit, the provisions authorities proceeded to collect the 7.8 million *pud* grain levy, confident that it would be possible to take at least 5 million *pud*.[85] Virtually all the local reports on the grain collection stressed that the brigades were forcibly taking away the peasants' basic food

[84] More grain and fodder (3.6 million *pud*) was procured from Balashov than from any other district in Saratov province during 1918–19 (*Iubileinyi sbornik saratovskogo gubprodkomiteta*, p. 72).

[85] TsGANKh, f. 1943, op. 1, d. 446, ll. 71–7.

and seed.[86] Indeed, during the autumn of 1920 it was admitted by the Balashov authorities that there was 'practically no seed' to complete the sowing campaign. The autumn sown area of that year was a bare 34% of the sown area in 1918.[87]

It was one of the tragic ironies of the procurement campaigns that the poorest peasants suffered the greatest losses as a result of them. Because the village commune organized the collection of the grain levy among the individual households in the manner of a traditional communal tax (i.e. per capita or per unit of land), the poorest peasant households inevitably ended up losing a larger proportion of their farm income than the rich households. The local provisions authorities were powerless to enforce the collection of the levy on 'class [i.e. progressive] principles'. According to one budget study, the peasant household with 1 to 2 *des.* of arable in the grain-producing region of Russia lost, on average, 34.8% of its net farm income in the *prodrazverska*, whereas the middle peasant household lost between 13.8% and 20.5% of its income, and the household with over 8 *des.* of arable lost 34.5% of its farm income.[88] A similar set of results was obtained from other budget studies in Cherkass and Ulybovka *volosti* (Vol'sk *uezd*) in 1919 (see Table 27).

TABLE 27. *Grain levied in relation to sown area of peasant household, Cherkass and Ulybovka* volosti *(Vol'sk* uezd*), 1919 (pudy)*

	Household sown area (*des.*)			
Grain levied	1–2	2–4	4–8	8+
Per household				
Cherkass	14.2	22.1	38.9	57.2
Ulybovka	—	38.2	65.5	126.0
Per *des.*				
Cherkass	10.5	7.8	7.4	6.5
Ulybovka	—	12.7	12.4	13.6
Per soul				
Cherkass	5.2	4.7	5.0	5.3
Ulybovka	—	11.1	12.2	13.6

Source: *Tri goda bor'by s golodom*, Moscow, 1920, pp. xii–xv.

Why was the food requisitioning allowed to continue during the autumn of 1920 and the spring of 1921, when the civil war had already

[86] Ibid., l. 77–8.
[87] *Otchet saratovskogo gubernskogo ispolnitel'nogo komiteta 9-go sozyva 10-mu gubernskomu s''ezdu sovetov za oktiabr' 1920 g.–iiun' 1921 g.*, Saratov, 1921, pp. 280–1.
[88] A. Vainshtein, *Oblozhenie i platezhi krest'ianstva*, Moscow, 1924, p. 71.

been won and the famine crisis was already widespread? How could the people in power have justified to themselves the requisitioning of the peasants' seed materials during such a crisis? Why was the call of the Soviet government for international aid delayed until July 1921,[89] when the warning signs of the famine were already clear in the localities during the previous autumn? The grain passing through the state system had been declining in quality (i.e. there was an increasing level of chaff and dust) since the beginning of 1920. Many animals brought into the state slaughterhouses since the harvest failure of 1920 had had to be turned away because they were smaller than the minimum official size.[90] The district and provincial assemblies had passed dozens of resolutions against the continuation of the requisitionings, while the local procurement officials, like this one from the German Volga region in September 1920, had, with increasing alarm, been warning the central authorities of the consequences if they continued to do so:

> It is already clear that any measures to collect the levy will be doomed to failure from the start and that the results, if there are any at all, will be extremely insignificant: there is simply no grain left to take. The comrades who read my report will no doubt suspect me of localism; but that is not the point—I have lived through more than one year of hunger in Moscow, and I am just as eager as they are to take as much surplus grain as possible for the starving proletariat in the north; but I repeat, whatever measures are taken, IT WILL BE IMPOSSIBLE to achieve any positive results! [Emphasis as in source].[91]

Yet, in spite of these clear signals of the impending disaster—and perhaps even because of them—the Bolshevik leadership persisted with the requisitionings. Some provincial authorities even doubled the central food levies in order to meet the growing consumption needs of their own population, in addition to the demands of the government in Moscow.[92] In the German Volga region 41.9% of the gross cereal harvest was requisitioned under the *prodrazverstka* of 1920–1. Villages were ransacked, children were held to ransom, and groups of peasants were tortured.[93] The city of Saratov, recalled Alexis Babine, a professor in the University,

[89] H. H. Fisher, *The Famine in Soviet Russia 1919–1923*, New York, 1927, p. 51.

[90] TsGANKh, f. 1943, op. 1, d. 448, l. 59; *Kommuna* (Samara), no. 271, 6 Nov. 1919, p. 1; *Izvestiia saratovskogo gubprodkoma*, no. 9, 2 Mar. 1919, p. 10.

[91] TsGANKh, f. 1943, op. 6, d. 376, l. 1.

[92] *Istoriia sovetskogo krest'ianstva*, vol. 1, p. 115.

[93] *KK*, p. 188; *Trudy TsSU: Statisticheskii ezhegodnik 1921 g.*, vol. 8, vyp. 4, p. 226; *Volia Rossii* (Prague), 7 Sept. 1921, p. 2; K. Esselborn, *Aus den Leidenstagen der deutschen Wolga-Kolonien*, Darmstadt, 1922, p. 5; O Fisher, 'Über die heutige wirtschaftsliche Lage in den Wolgakolonien', *Wolgadeutsche Monatshefte*, Dec. 1922, p. 22; G. Loebsack, *Einsam kämpft das Wolgaland*, Leipzig, 1936, p. 314; A. Babine, 'The Bolsheviks in Russia', Library of Congress Manuscripts Division, p. 26.

was filled with destitute Germans who had abandoned their homes, put their families and belongings on to wagons and fled . . . without any other plan than to get away from the scenes of blood, torture and ruin. They camped on the banks of the Volga, sold their animals (a good horse was sold in one case for five loaves of bread) and later on stretched out their hands for alms. This was a sight that had never been seen before in Russia.[94]

To answer these difficult questions, we need to bear in mind the unbridled power of the requisitioning brigades, which managed to terrorize not only the peasantry, but also the local soviets; also, the strength of the Bolshevik party and its tendency, as Chamberlin put it, 'to produce a type of rank-and-file Communist who did what he was told, without questioning, who was content to leave all critical thinking to the Central Committee'.[95] It seems that the majority of the VIKs were prepared to take any necessary measure within their power to enforce the collection of the food levies during 1920–1, in spite of the allegiance of their members to the local population and the evidence of human suffering before their very eyes.[96] Finally, we need to bear in mind the fierce, and sometimes fanatical, loyalty of the local power-holders to the Revolution. The ruling cadres in the district towns and the mobile organs of power (e.g. the requisitioning brigades, the Red Army) were ready to do almost anything in defence of the new regime. They pretended to believe in the phantom threat of the 'kulaks', if only to legitimize their own needless acts of violence against the peasantry. This way of thinking was starkly summed up by the chairman of the Saratov provincial executive, Martynov, at the provincial soviet assembly in June 1921:

We had no choice but to break the alliance between the workers and the peasants, made during the October days . . . in order to save the Socialist Revolution, and we had to do it at the expense of the peasantry. We had no choice but to make this sacrifice. We now know what the consequences were. We will not try to hide them. We know the consequences of the *prodrazverstka* . . . We know how we took the peasants' last seed materials but we had to do it . . . We had our shortcomings and we made our mistakes, as we still do today and as we will continue to do for the next few years until we get out of this terrible situation . . . Nobody doubts that all those outrages by the Soviet authorities, that all those mistakes in assessing how much grain to take engendered the hatred of the peasantry towards the Soviet regime, and their hatred was justified; the peasants were right to protest.[97]

[94] Babine, p. 26.
[95] W. H. Chamberlin, *The Russian Revolution 1917–1921*, Princeton, 1987 (originally New York, 1935), vol. 2, p. 375.
[96] GAKO, f. 185, op. 3, d. 13, ll. 31–127.
[97] *Doklady i rezoliutsii 10-go saratovskogo gubernskogo s''ezda sovetov (190–13 iiunia 1921 g.)*, Saratov, 1921, p. 14.

2. PEASANT AGRICULTURE

The policies of the Soviet regime in the agrarian sector during the decade prior to collectivization were profoundly influenced by the economic consequences of the revolution and the civil war. The technical improvement of peasant agriculture, the integration of the peasant farms into the national economy, and the socialization of the primary sector were inevitably complicated by the economic devastation caused by seven years of war and revolution. The revolution liberated and strengthened the middle peasantry, the millions of small-scale commodity producers upon whom the new regime was almost entirely dependent for its agricultural surplus. But the collapse of manufacturing industry and the squeeze on the peasant economy under war communism encouraged the consumption orientation of the peasant smallholding farms. By directing their production towards the basic domestic needs of the peasant family, and by circumventing the official ban on market sales through natural exchange and barter, the peasant farms were able to make themselves virtually independent of the new regime in the towns. By the end of the civil war, peasant–state relations had broken down altogether; the grain-producing regions were taken over by peasant uprisings; the regime in the cities was nearly starved out of existence. The economic reconstruction of the Soviet regime obviously called for the reintegration and the socialization of the peasant economy through the market itself. However, the legacies of the civil war—the discrimination of the Soviet government in favour of industry, and the inclination of the peasant farms towards autarky—cast a long shadow over these tasks.

Because of the difficulties of collating reliable data on the peasant economy during the revolutionary period, it is not possible to give an accurate estimate of the decline of agricultural production during 1917–21. The TsSU estimates of the sown area in 1918–19, which were based upon information provided by the peasants themselves, were said by V. G. Groman to have underestimated the actual sown area by between 10% and 20%. Those of 1920–1 were said by other statisticians to have underestimated the actual sown area by between 20% and 40%.[98] The main problem was the determination of the peasants to conceal the extent of their taxable wealth. According to a well-known saying of this period, the peasantry owned 'by decree', but

[98] V. G. Groman, 'Neurozhai 1920 i 1921 gg. i ikh vliianie na russkoe narodnoe khoziaistvo', *Ekonomicheskaia zhizn'* (Moscow), no. 75, 21 Apr. 1922; S. G. Strumilin, 'K reforme urozhainosti', *Ekonomicheskoe obozrenie*, 1924, nos. 9–10; L. N. Kritsman (ed.), *Materialy po istorii agrarnoi revoliutsii v Rossii*, Moscow, 1928, vol. 1, pp. 56–7.

lived 'on the sly' (*my imeem po dekretam, no zhivem po sekretam*).[99] The communes deployed an almost infinite variety of statistical devices to 'hide' bits of land, or to turn fertile arable into 'wasteland'. A change in the course of a river, the clearing of a wood, the temporary flooding of a water-meadow, or the redrawing of the communal boundaries could all serve as a pretext for the commune to augment its agricultural area without the land officials discovering.[100]

TABLE 28. *Sown area of various crops, Samara and Saratov provinces, 1913–1921* (% of 1913 area)

		Wheat	Oats	Rye	Millet	Potatoes	Sunflower	Hemp	Flax
1913	Samara	100	100	100	100	100	100	100	100
	Saratov	100	100	100	100	100	100	100	100
1917	Samara	91.8	87.0	107.7	82.3	93.5	122.3	93.6	47.6
	Saratov	59.6	69.0	98.6	62.1	84.9	68.8	71.5	28.3
1918	Samara	86.1	87.3	135.8	74.1	79.3	112.4	54.4	96.4
	Saratov	66.9	77.2	103.9	132.9	87.9	104.7	83.1	16.8
1919	Samara	72.3	58.9	120.2	109.7	125.9	196.8	118.8	249.4
	Saratov	60.8	69.2	88.4	121.6	93.9	69.7	103.6	12.4
1920	Samara	64.5	60.1	112.6	109.3	66.3	128.6	76.9	265.1
	Saratov	52.2	69.3	78.2	143.7	94.2	47.3	113.4	46.9
1921	Samara	24.1	24.6	87.4	177.3	50.2	388.4	46.0	621.8
	Saratov	17.9	46.6	85.1	97.2	54.4	50.6	56.3	139.0

Source: *Sbornik statisticheskikh svedenii po Samarskoi gubernii*, Samara, 1924, p. 136; *Statisticheskii sbornik po Saratovskoi gubernii*, Saratov, 1923, pp. 134–5.

Table 28 shows the TsSU estimates of the arable area under the major crops in Samara and Saratov provinces during 1913 and 1917–21. The area under wheat, the main cash crop, fell by 35.5% in Samara province between 1913 and 1920; in Saratov province it fell by 47.8% over the same period. The area under rye, the staple consumption crop, declined only very slightly in Saratov province, while in Samara province it increased significantly until the agricultural crisis of 1920–1. The overall sown area during 1917–20 decreased by 17.1% in Samara province and by 24.1% in Saratov province between 1917 and 1920.[101]

[99] N. M. Vishnevskii, *Statistika i sel'sko-khoziaistvennaia deistvitel'nost'*, Moscow, 1922, p. 34.
[100] Ibid., pp. 32–4.
[101] *Trudy TsSU: Pouezdnye itogi vserossiiskoi sel'sko-khoziaistvennoi i pozemel'noi perepisi 1917 g.*, vol. 5, vyp. 2, Moscow, 1923, pp. 104–5, 108–9; *Trudy TsSU: Itogi vserossiiskoi sel'sko-khoziaistvennoi perepisi 1920 goda*, vol. 2, vyp. 2, Moscow, 1921, pp. 62, 87, 95; *Sbornik statisticheskikh svedenii po Samarskoi gubernii*, Samara, 1924, pp. 136–42.

Some studies have associated the fall in agricultural output with the 'parcelization' of the land system during the revolution.[102] It is true that the peasantry was unable to farm all the land gained from the gentry. But it must be noted that the number of peasant households did not increase as rapidly as the amount of land in peasant use after 1917, so that 'compared with pre-revolutionary times, no real parcelization of the peasant household economy occurred'.[103] A study of the Ukrainian steppe and Tambov province showed that only the richest peasant households (with means of production valued over 800 rb.) had smaller plots of land in 1924 than before the revolution; the average peasant household (with means of production valued between 501 and 800 rb.) increased its landholding by between 12% and 30%, while the poorest peasantry made significant gains in land.[104]

Other studies have correctly stressed the connections between the decline of the sown area, the *prodrazverstka*, and the civil war.[105] The recorded sown area decreased most sharply in the grain-producing regions directly affected by the food procurements and the civil war (e.g. the Volga, the Urals, the eastern Ukraine). However, government reports and the minutes of local soviet meetings suggest that a wide variety of secondary factors also inhibited peasant agricultural production, along with the civil war and the *prodrazverstka*: the problems of communal land organization, which had often been exacerbated by the land reforms (e.g. an increase in the distance between the village and the plots, or an increase of strip-intermingling); delays in field-work caused by the civil war, by food procurements, or by the communal land repartitions; the fear of the peasants to sow the gentry's land in case the revolution should be defeated; the shortages of means of production caused by the economic dislocation between town and country, or the unwise partitioning of the family household; the shortages of adult male labour resulting from military and labour mobilizations; the inadequate supply of seed materials, because of the economic crisis or excessive requisitioning; unfavourable climatic conditions (e.g. early snow in the autumn, spring hail storms); etc.[106]

Apart from the quantitative decline in the level of agricultural

[102] See e.g. P. Popov, *Proizvodstvo khleba v RSFSR i federiruiushchikhsia s neiu respublikakh*, Moscow, 1921, p. 29; Ia. A. Iakovlev, *Sel'skoe khoziaistvo i industrializatsiia*, Moscow/Leningrad, 1927, pp. 25–9.

[103] *RR*, p. 215.

[104] *RR*, p. 216.

[105] The classic statement is A. I. Khriashcheva, 'Krest'ianstvo v voine i revoliutsii', *Vestnik statistiki*, 1920, nos. 9–12. For a discussion of the rest of the literature see Malle, pp. 425–37; Iu. A. Poliakov, *Perekhod k NEPu i sovetskoe krest'ianstvo*, Moscow, 1967, pp. 54–69.

[106] TsGANKh, f. 478, op. 6, d. 1015, ll. 86–90, 97–8, 201; GAKO, f. 81, op. 1, d. 10, l. 79; *Protokol 5-go s''ezda upolnomochennykh*, p. 22; *Sel'sko-khoziaistvennyi listok* (Balashov), 4 May 1918, p. 1; *Izvestiia* (Saratov), no. 250, 3 Nov. 1920, p. 4; etc.

production, there was also a decline in the standards of cereal cultivation. This may help to explain why a decrease in the harvest yields was observed in the years following 1917 even after allowances had been made for climatic conditions.[107] Firstly, there was a sharp decline in the application of manure fertilizer on the peasant fields. This may be partly explained by the unsettled nature of land relations during the revolutionary period: it was not worthwhile for the peasants to fertilize the soil on their strips, or to make any other improvements (e.g. irrigation), as long as it was uncertain whether the strips would remain in their tenure. The decline of manure fertilization was also explained, however, by the shortages of fodder that resulted from the Red Army requisitionings and the decrease in the peasants' livestock. Secondly, the proportion of the spring fields prepared the previous autumn (*ziab'*)[108] fell dramatically on account of the shortages of peasant labour: in Samara province the proportion declined from 45% of the spring sown area in 1916 to a mere 6% in 1920.[109] Thirdly, there was a sharp increase in the proportion of seed sown by hand on account of the shortages of seed drills[110] and other sowing machines: in 1913 19% of the *volost'* respondents in Samara province had reported that more than half of the households in their area used mechanical means to sow the arable, whereas in 1920 only 10% of the respondents could make the same report.[111]

Let us return to Table 28 and consider some of the secondary peasant crops. The reduction of the area under oats was closely connected with the decrease of the peasants' livestock during the revolution (see Table 29), since the main fodder crop was oats. For similar reasons, there was a decline in the production of hay and other fodder means (maize, barley, oilcake). The decrease in the peasants' livestock was due to a number of factors. The sharp fall in the ownership of sheep and pigs was explained by the frequency with which small animals tended to be requisitioned, although goats and poultry were not subject to the *prodrazverstka* until 1920. The latter came to play a major role in the peasant household under war communism, providing a source of food

107 P. Popov, p. 29; *KK*, pp. 119–22.

108 By ploughing the spring fields in the autumn and leaving them under the snow, wheaten harvest yields could be increased by up to 33 per cent compared with the yields on spring fields ploughed immediately before sowing.

109 G. I. Baskin, 'Veroiatnye razmery posevnoi ploshchadi i urozhaev khlebov', in *Sbornik izbrannykh trudov G. I. Baskina po Samarskoi gubernii: Iubileinoe izdanie*, vyp. 1, Samara, 1925, p. 41; *Sostoianie ozimykh posevov i kolichestvo skota v Samarskoi gubernii vesnoiu 1919 g.*, Samara, n.d., pp. 1–2.

110 The use of a seed-drill was found to increase the harvest yield by up to 19% in rye and by up to 26% in wheat, compared with the yields on hand-sown fields.

111 Baskin, 'Vliianie tekhnicheskikh priemov na urozhainost' khlebov', in *Sbornik izbrannykh trudov*, vyp. 2, Samara, 1925, pp. 42–3.

TABLE 29. *Farm animals per peasant household, Samara and Saratov provinces, 1916 and 1920*

	1916	1920
Horses (aged over 1 year)		
Samara	2.09	1.58
Saratov	1.29	1.11
Horses (aged under 1 year)		
Samara	0.24	0.15
Saratov	0.15	0.13
Oxen and bullocks		
Samara	0.07	0.04
Saratov	0.16	0.10
Cows		
Samara	1.21	1.16
Saratov	0.90	0.99
Calves (aged under 1 year)		
Samara	0.81	0.38
Saratov	0.66	0.35
Sheep		
Samara	6.31	2.73
Saratov	4.61	2.38
Pigs		
Samara	0.87	0.47
Saratov	0.50	0.29

Source: *Trudy TsSU: Statisticheskii sbornik za 1913–1917 gg.*, vol. 7, vyp. 1, Moscow, 1921, pp. 186–9; *Trudy TsSU: Itogi vserossiiskoi sel'skokhoziaistvennoi perepisi 1920 g.*, vol. 2, vyp. 2, Moscow, 1921, pp. 58–60, 90–2.

(milk, cheese, eggs, meat) as well as wool, down, and feathers. The fall in the number of horses and oxen was mainly explained by the requisitioning of livestock transport by the Red and White armies. In Samara province the number of peasant oxen declined by 52.7% during 1918–19. The number of heavy cart-horses declined by 63.3%, whereas the number of geldings and mares (which were less suitable for draught-power) actually increased by 2.8% and 3.6%, respectively. It is not coincidental that the greatest losses of peasant draught livestock were incurred in Novouzensk district, immediately behind the Eastern Front.[112] The overall peasant ownership of cows did not decline between 1916 and 1920, although a large number of peasant cows was

[112] *Sostoianie ozimykh posevov i kolichestvo skota*, pp. 5–9.

slaughtered during the intervening years. This may be explained by the livestock gains of the peasantry during the revolution, and by the tendency of the peasants to hold on to their cows for as long as possible on account of the high value placed on dairy products (until March 1920 milk could be sold on the free market). The milking cow provided an essential food source for the peasant family in these difficult years. With a cow and a few poultry animals, the weakest peasant family could be confident of meeting its minimum subsistence needs. Some of the cattle slaughtering was no doubt a reaction by the richest peasants to the threat of expropriation or requisitioning. But the slaughtering was mainly explained by the cattle plague, which broke out in the Stavropol' region during December 1918 and, thanks to the movements of the civil war armies, spread throughout the Volga region, as well as Voronezh, Kursk, and Orel provinces, during the following spring. In Simbirsk province more than 100 cattle were slaughtered per day in the months of April and May 1919. In Saratov province 54,000 cattle were slaughtered between June 1919 and October 1920.[113]

The peasant farm economy under war communism was characterized by its consumption orientation and comprehensiveness. These two tendencies were reflected in the relative stability of the staple consumption crops (rye, millet, potatoes) in the production plan of the farm, compared with cash or fodder crops (Table 28). They were also reflected in the low commoditization of the peasant economy (the small proportion of the farm product sold or exchanged on the market) under war communism, as manifested in the budget studies of Tables 30 and 31. Table 30 shows that even the wealthiest peasant farms (e.g. no. 11) marketed a very small portion of their product. In all the peasant households dairy production was geared towards on-farm family consumption, but a small number of households (nos. 4, 7, 10, 11, 16, 27) marketed a sizeable share of their potatoes, vegetables, and fruits. The six *volosti* analysed in the Voronezh budget studies were characterized as 'suburban' (i.e. they were situated within a radius of 20 miles from the town of Voronezh itself, while many of the villages specialized in market gardening or domestic crafts). The Kazan' budget studies (Table 31) were carried out in a predominantly grain-producing area, by contrast. They revealed an even greater consumption orientation among the peasant households. The largest portion (72.3%) of the cereal product (including the grain stores) was used on the farm; only 6.2% of the grain was sold on the market. Most of the other products

[113] TsGAOR, f. 393, op. 13, d. 429, ll. 18–20; TsGANKh, f. 478, op. 3, d. 1157, ll. 61, 84–5; op. 6, d. 1015, l. 193.

TABLE 30. *Budget study of twenty-nine peasant households, Voronezh* uezd, *1920–1921*

No.	Family members	Sown area (*des.*)	Horses[a]	Cows[a]	Commodity product (Gold Rb.)	% value from craft production	% product value sold/exchanged			
							Grain	Potatoes	Other vegetables	Dairy products
1	8	5.5	1	1	201	52.1	—	3.0	3.9	4.8
2	5	2.5	1	2	140	47.7	2.2	—	—	29.4
3	5	2.5	1	1	151	32.4	2.5	2.1	2.8	21.3
4	6	4.4	1	1	126	25.5	—	59.0	0.9	12.6
5	7	1.9	2	2	178	47.0	6.3	1.1	—	2.7
6	9	5.6	2	3	190	82.2	—	2.5	—	1.0
7	8	3.9	1	1	119	12.6	—	65.2	16.5	8.1
8	10	5.2	2	1	53	14.0	—	35.0	6.0	3.4
9	3	4.1	1	2	202	9.4	—	26.0	8.5	6.5
10	11	6.6	1	1	245	6.8	—	0.8	66.4	2.0
11	5	5.8	2	2	465	7.8	—	30.5	58.6	1.7
12	6	2.7	0	2	89	19.1	0.4	—	3.6	18.1
13	12	3.1	0	1	55	16.5	7.6	26.6	5.4	5.8
14	9	3.5	1	1	21	7.8	—	36.2	7.3	46.8
15	8	2.7	1	1	94	76.0	1.7	—	6.1	16.2
16	8	5.8	1	1	199	2.2	2.7	63.2	18.5	4.8
17	6	4.3	3	1	137	9.4	—	—	32.0	—
18	5	2.2	1	1	93	22.5	—	10.1	17.1	12.4
19	4	2.3	0	1	43	—	3.6	—	4.9	27.3
20	8	2.7	1	1	77	11.0	—	—	—	23.0
21	8	5.6	1	1	228	57.3	2.5	5.3	—	9.5
22	4	2.1	1	1	41	71.0	0.7	4.3	1.7	3.9
23	8	7.5	1	1	74	6.0	3.0	—	—	6.5
24	7	3.3	1	2	34	34.0	15.0	—	—	22.6
25	8	3.5	1	1	93	57.4	—	—	—	1.2
26	4	4.8	1	1	175	36.0	1.1	0.2	19.2	4.5
27	16	9.5	3	1	252	5.1	—	4.8	70.0	5.1

28	8	3.3	1	1	119	21.0	—	—	22.5	12.0
29	4	2.6	2	1	58	19.9	—	2.0	49.0	23.1

[a] Figures given are for the beginning of the year, and exclude animals less than a year old.

Source: B. Bruk, *Krest 'ianskoe khoziaistvo v period prodrazverstki*, Voronezh, 1923, pp. 34–41, 44–7.

TABLE 31. *Budget study of twenty-eight peasant households, Kazan' province, 1918–1919*

Product	Gross product per household[a]				Various expenditure (% total product)					
	Farm product	Stores	Purchases	Total product[b]	Consumed	Seed	Feed	Sales	State taxes	Total expenditure[b]
Grains	103.6	7.8	7.1	139.8	48.5	13.8	10.0	6.2	10.6	97.3
Groats	23.0	—	—	23.2	44.0	22.0	—	2.1	4.3	87.1
Oats	39.0	0.1	0.6	39.9	5.5	26.3	30.8	7.0	19.8	92.7
Flax	1.8	—	—	1.8	16.7	5.5	—	27.8	—	88.9
Oil	0.1	—	—	0.1	100.0	—	—	—	—	100.0
Oilcake	0.9	—	—	0.9	—	—	100.0	—	—	100.0
Straw	262.1	1.0	0.9	285.5	—	—	93.5	5.5	—	99.0
Hay	36.7	—	12.1	51.5	—	—	96.5	—	0.8	97.3
Potatoes	39.8	—	0.4	40.4	82.2	7.9	3.5	1.7	—	98.5
Vegetables	27.6	—	0.6	28.2	75.5	—	2.1	20.9	—	98.6
Fruits	0.3	—	—	0.3	100.0	—	—	—	—	100.0
Meat	5.3	—	0.3	5.6	100.0	—	—	—	—	100.0
Lard (*funty*)	2.5	—	—	2.5	100.0	—	—	—	—	100.0
Poultry products	4.6	—	—	4.6	100.0	—	—	—	—	100.0
Hides (no.)	3.2	0.5	—	3.7	91.9	—	—	2.7	2.7	97.3
Wool (*funty*)	16.7	1.9	0.1	18.7	92.0	—	—	—	—	92.0
Down and feathers (*funty*)	1.2	—	—	1.2	83.3	—	—	—	—	83.3
Eggs (no.)	526.5	13.3	—	539.8	90.3	—	—	8.1	1.6	100.0
Milk	27.5	—	—	27.5	98.9	—	—	1.1	—	100.0
Butter	0.3	0.1	—	0.4	100.0	—	—	—	—	100.0
Curds and sour cream	1.1	—	—	1.1	90.9	—	—	9.1	—	100.0

TABLE 31. *(cont)*:

	Born	Stores	Purchases	Total product[b]	Slaughtered	Died	Feed	Sales	State taxes	Total expenditure[b]
Horses	0.01	1.29	0.03	1.33	—	—	—	3.0	7.5	10.5
Cattle	0.14	1.27	—	1.42	7.7	3.5	—	7.4	2.1	23.2
Sheep	3.3	6.4	—	9.9	24.2	5.0	—	1.0	1.0	31.2
Pigs	1.1	1.5	0.1	2.8	35.7	3.6	—	17.8	—	60.7
Goats	0.1	0.2	—	0.3	33.3	—	—	33.3	—	66.6
Poultry	8.2	12.9	—	21.1	21.8	17.5	—	1.4	—	42.2

[a] Livestock and poultry are counted by head; other amounts are in *pudy* unless stated otherwise.
[b] Includes receipts from exchange and other means not shown in the table.

Note: Average land area in household use = 5.6 *des.*; average size of family = 5.9 people.

Source: *Trudy TsSU: Statisticheskii ezhegodnik 1918–20 gg.*, vol. 8., vyp. 1, Moscow, 1922, pp. 78–9.

(sunflower oil, fruit, meat, butter, lard, poultry, wool, down and feathers) were exclusively used by the peasant family on the farm, or were used for the farm animals (oilcake, straw, hay). Pigs, goats, sheep, and poultry were an occasional source of meat for the peasant family (especially, no doubt, in the days immediately preceding the collection of the food levy). Garden vegetables, flax fibre, and the odd goat or pig provided the peasant farm with a very small cash income.

The rapid development of horticulture reflected the consumption orientation and comprehensiveness of the peasant economy under war communism.[114] The exemption of vegetables and fruit from the *prodrazverstka* encouraged the peasants to increase their production of these at the expense of cereals and livestock. Budget studies in the grain-producing regions showed that the field economy accounted for only 39.3% of peasant commodity production in 1920–1, compared with 62.6% in 1913; meanwhile, the garden economy increased its share of peasant commodities from 3.3% in 1913 to 12.7% in 1920–1.[115] The increase in the number of small and poor peasant households after 1917 was closely connected with the expanding role of horticulture and rural industry (see sect. 3 below). Many of the poorest or the newly partitioned households lacked the necessary transport and means of production to cultivate their arable land, especially if it was located a long way from the village. Such households often preferred to cultivate a small garden plot in the village itself, and this was sometimes arranged by the commune during the land repartition (see ch. 3, sect. 3). The increasing importance of the garden economy during the civil war may also be explained by the difficulties of commodity exchange, which encouraged the peasants to grow their own vegetables, fruit, and tobacco, rather than rely upon local markets, as they might have done previously. The shortages of consumer goods equally encouraged the peasants to experiment with their own home-grown alternatives. Bee-keeping and sugar-beet cultivation, which were encouraged by the land departments and the co-operatives after 1918, helped to relieve the shortages of sugar. The increased cultivation of oil-yielding crops (sunflower, cotton, flax) helped to sustain the rural soap-boiling industry and provided an alternative domestic fuel to

114 One source spoke in 1918 of 'an enormous increase in the number of newly created gardens and orchards over the last seven years': see *Sel'sko-khoziaistvennyi listok* (Balashov), 7 July 1918, p. 2. Similar reports may be found in *Rabochii i kooperativnyi mir* (Balashov), nos. 5–6, Mar. 1918, pp. 81–2; *Kooperativnaia mysl'* (Saratov), no. 12 (43), 28 Mar. 1919, p. 6. The budget study published by B. Bruk noted (*Krest'ianskoe khoziaistvo v period prodrazverstki*, Voronezh, 1923, pp. 25–6) a flourishing garden economy; the garden areas had been extended to occupy even the former meadows and the spring fields.

115 *Sbornik statisticheskikh svedenii po Soiuzu SSR*, Moscow, 1924, p. 421.

kerosene. The peasant huts during this period were commonly lit by a simple wick-and-pot contraption, burning sunflower oil or animal fat. These primitive lamps, which left a pungent smell and covered the ceiling with a black oil-stain, proved a serious fire hazard.[116]

3. RURAL INDUSTRY

In the debates about war communism during 1918 it was commonly assumed by the major Bolshevik theorists that cottage industry (*kustarnaia promyshlennost'*) would have no future under Socialism. As a form of 'petty-capitalist' production, the *kustar'* industry would have to be placed under the control of the soviets and the democratized co-operatives. The *kustari* would have to be reorganized into larger production units, integrated into the state distribution system, and, eventually, nationalized.[117] There was considerable disagreement within the Bolshevik party over the speed with which this transition could or should be achieved. However, it is probably fair to say that all the Bolshevik leaders underestimated the difficulties of implementing these policies. As Lenin was later to admit, 'we made the mistake of trying to bring about an immediate transition to communist production and distribution'.[118]

The censuses of 1917, 1919, and 1920 suggested that the *kustari* had been devastated during the 1914–18 war.[119] In 1920 the well-known statistician A. I. Khriashcheva explained this by the shortages of raw materials and the military conscription of skilled industrial workers.[120] Soviet historians have tended to reproduce Khriashcheva's arguments and data (see Table 32) without subjecting them to detailed analysis.

There are, however, a number of problems with the census data. Firstly, they did not differentiate between the organized industrial enterprises of the *kustari*, and the more widespread rural trades (*promysly*) of the peasant households, which included the domestic fabrication of any farm product (e.g. vodka distillation), as well as a wide range of labour services (e.g. carting, timber-felling). A second and more serious problem was that the peasants everywhere tried to

[116] TsGANKh, f. 478, op. 1, d. 330, ll. 24, 121; *Svobodnyi zemledelets* (Saratov), no. 10, 1 Apr. 1918, p. 31; *Tri goda raboty otdelov buguruslanskogo uezdnogo ispolnitel'nogo komiteta sovetov (1917–20 gg.)*, Buguruslan, 1921, p. 32; *Kooperativnaia mysl'* (Saratov), no. 9 (40), 2 Mar. 1919, p. 10; *Sel'sko-khoziaistvennyi listok* (Balashov), 1 Mar. 1918, pp. 5–6; *SGB*, no. 6, 1 Aug. 1918, p. 10; *Iubileinyi sbornik saratovskogo gubprodkomiteta*, pp. 45–6.

[117] On the nationalization of the *kustari* during this period see Malle, pp. 77–88.

[118] *PSS*, vol. 44, p. 157.

[119] According to the census data, the number of peasant households engaged in rural industries in the RSFSR declined from 23.5 per cent in 1917, to 14.7 per cent in 1920, and to 11.9 per cent in 1922 (*Sbornik statisticheskikh svedenii po Soiuzu SSR*, pp. 107–13).

[120] Khriashcheva, pp. 29–30.

TABLE 32. *Rural inhabitants engaged in domestic industrial production, 1912–1919*

Province		% households with *promysly*	People in *promysly* in each household	% women in *promysly*
Tula	1912	75.4	1.69	14.1
	1917	32.8	1.45	26.1
	1919	13.8	1.30	14.6
Tver'[a]	1912	76.8	1.88	17.5
	1917	41.0	1.53	28.3
Penza	1912	46.6	1.21	[no data]
	1917	18.6	1.40	29.8

[a] Seven *uezdy*.

Source: A. I. Khriashcheva, 'Krest' ianstvo v voine i revoliutsii', *Vestnik statistiki*, 1920, nos. 9–12, pp. 29, 42.

conceal from the census officials their industrial enterprises, since they were likely to be taxed and possibly expropriated by the Soviet authorities. The concealment of *kustar'* production was facilitated by the growing role of women in the rural industrial sector after 1914 (see Table 32), since peasant elders did not consider it necessary to register the economic activities of their womenfolk. It was widely acknowledged that the statistics of this period 'considerably underestimated' the number of domestic industrial producers.[121] The 1917 census, for example, registered 62,585 *kustari* in Saratov province, whereas Narkomzem estimated that there were 'approximately 150,000' *kustari* in Saratov province in January 1919.[122]

For different reasons, the statistics of Sovnarkhoz[123] also underestimated the significance of the rural industries. The industrial goods which the *sovnarkhozy* purchased from the *kustari* (e.g. woven cloth or finished leather) were registered as manufactures in the state sector (e.g. clothing, footwear). Some Soviet industrial production of this period was thus the unattributed work of the private *kustari*. It is impossible to estimate how much production was redirected in this manner, but the portion was undoubtedly large. An inspector of the *kustar'* section of Tsentrosoiuz warned in November 1920 that the

121 E. I. Shlifshtein, *Melkaia promyshlennost' Saratovskoi gubernii: Statistichesko-ekonomicheskii ocherk*, Saratov, 1923, p. 2.

122 *Tablitsy statisticheskikh svedenii po Saratovskoi gubernii po dannym vserossiiskoi sel'sko-khoziaistvennoi i gorodskoi perepisei*, Saratov, 1919, pp. 144–5; TsGANKh, f. 478, op. 10, d. 106, l. 21.

123 Sovnarkhoz and Narkomzem were both responsible for the *kustar'* industry until February 1920, when Glavkustprom was established. The latter was to combine the two *kustar'* departments.

'buying-up of wares from private craftsmen' was the main activity of the socialist organs in the field of rural industry.[124] A second source from Kuznetsk district stated that if the products which Sovnarkhoz had purchased from private craftsmen were to be added to the production figures of the craft co-operatives 'then the recorded level of production would be increased by a colossal amount'.[125]

Given the unreliability of the statistical data, we need to pay closer attention to the statements of contemporary observers on the position of the rural industries. Such statements present a more complex situation than the census data. Some rural industries were said to have experienced a sharp decline, while others were said to have increased their output. Regional variations were also commonly noted. The following report by V. Morgenshtern on the rural industries of the Volga region during 1914–21 was representative:

> it is possible to point out a number of handicrafts which have suffered during this period, but it would be a great mistake to conclude that the productivity of cottage industry as a whole has declined . . . Being able to find the necessary raw materials in the localities, many handicrafts have suffered relatively little from the economic collapse; and if one or two of the highly technical industries have suffered, then others have grown significantly by being able to satisfy those needs in the countryside that have been created by the collapse of large-scale industry. This is especially apparent in the production of household domestic goods—in the carpentry, pottery, and textile trades and even in the metal-working industry, where scythes, sickles, and other necessary tools have been forged out of any old scrap-iron.[126]

Indeed, the figures for tool production during these years show that the levels of production of small agricultural implements was sustained, while the production of advanced agricultural machinery collapsed (see Table 33). A report by Narkomzem admitted that this was due to the efforts of village blacksmiths, rather than the nationalized industries (as Soviet historians have maintained).[127]

Morgenshtern alluded to several widely noted reasons for the expansion of the rural industries. First of all, they tended to suffer less acutely than large-scale urban industry from the shortages of raw materials. The Tsaritsyn district *sovnarkhoz* agreed with this conclusion in its annual report of 1922: '[the rural industries] came to life during the civil war, since they required only small deliveries of raw materials which could easily be made by private individuals'.[128] In the

124 TsGAOR, f. 532, op. 1, d. 65, l. 11.

125 *Sbornik 'Ves' Kuznetsk'*, Kuznetsk, 1927, p. 29.

126 *Vosstanovlenie khoziaistva i razvitie proizvoditel'nykh sil iugo-vostoka RSFSR, postradavshego ot neurozhaia 1921 g.*, Moscow, 1921, pp. 110–11.

127 TsGANKh, f. 478, op. 3, d. 117, l. 113.

128 P. A. Barashevskii (ed.), *Istoricheskii ocherk Tsaritsynskogo uezda*, Tsaritsyn, 1922, p. 15.

TABLE 33. *Production of agricultural tools in the RSFSR, 1917–1921* ('000)

	1917	1918	1919	1920	1921
Ploughs	49.9	12.8	23.0	89.3	100.5
Harrows	6.5	0.1	1.0	2.6	6.2
Harvesters and mowers	7.6	0.6	1.0	2.3	5.5
Threshing machines	15.2	0.1	0.1	1.2	1.7
Winnowing machines and separators	3.2	0.5	0.8	3.3	2.0

Source: *Itogi desiatiletiia Sovetskoi vlasti v tsifrakh, 1917–1927*, Moscow, 1927, pp. 244–5. Narkomprod issued much higher production figures for 1918: 32,000 ploughs; 10,000 harrows; 72,000 sickles; and 104,000 scythes (TsGANKh, f. 3429, op. 1, d. 305, l. 15).

industries based upon agricultural raw materials the advantages of the rural domestic producers were obvious: the agricultural products that had failed to reach the towns on account of the breakdown of the transport system and the peasantry's opposition to the 'food dictatorship' could be used by the rural industrialists. The surplus grain and potatoes of the peasants were in part channelled into the *samogon* trade, which experienced a boom under the prohibition.[129] The leather-working industry flourished after 1919, as the peasantry began to slaughter its cattle on a large scale.[130] The wood-based industries also benefited from the high rate of peasant wood-cutting during the revolutionary period, in spite of the interdictions of the local soviets. In the industries based upon industrial raw materials (e.g. metal- and brick-working) the advantages of the rural producers were less obvious. The crucial determinant appears to have been the rapid depopulation of the cities in the wake of the food crisis and the collapse of large-scale industry. Skilled workers flooded into the countryside, bringing with them stolen materials from the factories, or any other industrial items which they had managed to fabricate by their own initiatives (*zazhigalochnichestvo*), in order to trade with the peasantry, or set up their own craft workshops.[131] As the Buguruslan authorities put it in July 1920, 'over the last three years literally hundreds of thousands of workers have been leaving the factories and mines and coming into the countryside; here they take up cottage crafts . . . Hundreds of thousands of peasants, who once went away on migrant labour, now remain in the villages.'[132] There was a

[129] See e.g. TsGAOR, f. 393, op. 3, d. 339, l. 16; d. 391, l. 21; d. 331, l. 91; GAKO, f. 81, op. 1, d. 119, l. 56; *Krasnyi nabat* (Balakovo), no. 203, 17 Dec. 1920, p. 2; *Izvestiia saratovskogo gubprodkoma*, no. 11, 19 Mar. 1919, p. 6; *Izvestiia* (Balashov), no. 174, 26 Sept. 1918, p. 4; *Kommuna* (Saratov), no. 160, 26 June 1918, p. 4; etc.

[130] TsGANKh, f. 478, op. 6, d. 1015, l. 193.

[131] See TsGAOR, f. 5451, op. 4, d. 123, l. 68; d. 148, ll. 13–14; d. 289, ll. 28–31, 52, 61; TsGANKh, f. 1637, op. 1, d. 361, ll. 21, 27; etc.

[132] *Luch kommuny* (Buguruslan), no. 402, 23 July 1920, p. 1.

marked regional variation in the level of in-migration, with the central black-earth and industrial regions and the areas closest to the railways bearing most of the burden. Eastern and south-eastern Russia also benefited, however, from the new markets for industrial raw materials in Kazakhstan and Central Asia. 'The entire industrial life of the country', noted one government official in 1918, 'has shifted to the east. It is there that the new markets are situated.'[133]

Some domestic industries, as Morgenshtern pointed out, were in a good position to benefit from the increased rural demand for household goods, following the collapse of large-scale industry and the economic dislocation between town and country. S. P. Sereda, the People's Commissar of Agriculture, informed the VTsIK on 20 April 1918 that 'cottage industry is at present providing the broad mass of the population with all those products which heavy industry is no longer able to produce'.[134] N. P. Speranskii, the head of the Kazan' section of the Narodnyi Bank, agreed in July 1919 that 'in Kazan' province over the last few years there has been an extraordinarily rapid development of the old cottage industries . . . on account of the rising needs of the rural population for industrial goods'.[135] The Mogilev provincial commissariat of agriculture (in White Russia) reported in a similar vein in 1919:

> the shortage of cloth has encouraged domestic textile production (flax, hemp, wool), spinning, and lace-making; the shortage of chinaware and earthenware has encouraged domestic pottery; there have been similar developments in the leather industry, in coopering, wheel-making, tar-working, rope-making, bee-keeping, basket-making, and shoe-making. Because of the difficulties of trade and the high internal demand for manufactures, all these products are swallowed up by the local provincial markets.[136]

In January 1919 V. V. Sklabinskii of the Volga Co-operative Union described, with more than a hint of sarcasm, the return of Soviet Russia to the Middle Ages idealized by K. S. Aksakov (1817–60), the Slavophile historian:

> at some point not so long ago we returned to those nice old days of Aksakov, when Rus' had neither railways nor steamboats, nor steam-mills, nor factories, nor any other 'European invention', when handicraftsmen fed, clothed, and heated the whole of Russia and made all its footwear, when everything was done by them on a tiny scale and very coarsely—with a hand chisel instead of a lathe, with an axe instead of a saw.[137]

Some rural industries fared better than others, as Morgenshtern

[133] A. Biriukov, *Kreditnaia kooperatsiia i kustarnaia promyshlennost'*, Saratov, 1918, p. 9.
[134] TsGANKh, f. 478, op. 10, d. 164, l. 24.
[135] TsGAOR, f. 532, op. 1, d. 65, l. 160.
[136] TsGANKh, f. 478, op. 10, d. 164, l. 5.
[137] *Kooperativnaia mysl'* (Saratov), no. 4 (35), 19 Jan. 1919, p. 10.

pointed out. The economic dislocation between town and country benefited those industries producing goods with a high transportation cost (e.g. furniture, wheels, barrels). It undermined those which were dependent upon sophisticated technology, or which were geographically separated from their raw materials. In most rural areas the 'heavier' rural industries (e.g. tar-distillation, charcoal-burning, brick-manufacture, soap-boiling, fulling) suffered acutely, although in some of these industries the producers formed co-operatives and artels (*arteli*), which were able to procure some of the means of production through the provincial *sovnarkhozy*.[138] The textiles industry suffered in many areas on account of the shortages of cloth and dye, although here, too, the situation could be eased by the organization of a textile producers' co-operative, by the substitution of locally produced (and generally inferior) dyes for the standard dyes, or by the local cultivation of flax and cotton to replace the loss of imported cloth. Generally speaking, the textiles industry was most successful in small domestic units, which could be easily integrated into the private supply networks of raw materials. The Volga German *sarpinka* textiles industry, for example, witnessed the closure of its larger mills on account of the shortages of fuel, but production was able to continue 'by the old hand methods'.[139] In November 1918 there were said to be as many as 30,000 household looms in production in Kamyshin district. Since the local demand for cloth was so great, these producers were willing to pay the black-market prices for the dyes and the cloth. The twenty-three socialist artels in the district, on the other hand, were forced to a standstill because they depended upon the less efficient distribution networks of the *sovnarkhozy*. Some artels did buy their materials from the private suppliers, but they could not afford to pay the top prices and were thus at a disadvantage against the private manufacturers.[140]

The most successful rural industries were those producing basic household utensils from readily obtainable raw materials: carpenters, builders, wicker-workers, coopers and wheelrights in areas near timber supplies; leather-workers, wool-weavers, and sheepskin workers in areas of pastoralism; and blacksmiths in areas near the main lines of

[138] TsGAOR, f. 532, op. 1, d. 65, ll. 157–8; *Vestnik kustarnoi promyshlennosti* (Petrograd), no. 6, Sept. 1921, p. 9; *Otchet pugachevskogo uezdnogo ekonomicheskogo soveshchaniia*, pp. 24, 31; *Otchet serdobskogo uezdnogo ekonomicheskogo soveshchaniia*, Serdobsk, 1921, p. 33.

[139] *Biulleten' saratovskogo gubernskogo soveta narodnogo khoziaistva* (Saratov), nos. 2–3, July 1918, p. 10.

[140] TsGANKh, f. 478, op. 10, d. 42, ll. 1–2; d. 104, l. 4; d. 106, ll. 4–6, 16–18; N. Bogdanov, 'Materialy po obsledovaniiu sarpinochno-tkatskogo proizvodstva kooperativnykh tovarishchestv i trudovykh artelei Kamyshinskogo kraia', *Vestnik kustarnoi promyshlennosti* (Petrograd), no. 12 (63), 1918, pp. 16–21.

transportation, where the in-migrant townsmen, bearing scrap metal, were concentrated.[141] The provincial *sovnarkhoz* reports of 1921–2 suggested that a significant portion of the local demand for these products had been satisfied by the *kustari* during the civil war. The Samara provincial *sovnarkhoz* estimated that up to two-fifths of the local demand for household goods had been satisfied in this way.[142] The Balashov district *sovnarkhoz* claimed that most of the local demand for earthenware pottery, agricultural tools, harnesses, ropes, wheels, carts, and sleighs could be satisfied by the local rural industries.[143] Similar reports were made by other authorities.[144]

A special place in the history of rural industry during the civil war belongs to the makers of agricultural tools. As we have noted, they were responsible for maintaining the production of small hand-tools (e.g. ploughs, sickles) while factory tool-making came to a halt. The handicraftsmen produced simple copies of modern tools, and adapted them to local conditions. In the Perm' area, for example, blacksmiths were reported to have developed simple harvesters copied from factory models but modified on the advice of the local peasants. The resulting machines were said to be very similar to those in use in the region thirty-five years previously. As one commentator concluded: 'experts on agricultural tool-making have been saying for a long time that hand-made harvesting tools would be squeezed out by large-scale production, yet these locally made tools have completely blocked out imported ones and, indeed, have themselves won markets in the neighbouring provinces'.[145]

Because of its integration into the peasant economy, small-scale rural industry enjoyed important advantages over the urban industrial sector during the civil war. Whereas the *kustari* were able to replace deficit raw materials from the local agricultural sector, the urban factories had to rely upon the sporadic importation of these materials through the state system. The rural textiles industry was supported by an increase in the local production of cotton and sheep. Cobblers,

[141] TsGAOR, f. 532, op. 1, d. 65, ll. 13, 26–7; *Biulleten' saratovskogo gubernskogo soveta narodnogo khoziaistva* (Saratov), nos. 3–4 (14–15), 20 Mar. 1919, p. 6; *Otchet melekesskogo uekonsoveshchaniia*, Melekess, 1921, pp. 18–19, 68–70; *Otchet buguruslanskogo uezdnogo ekonomicheskogo soveshchaniia sovetu truda i oborony 3-go iiunia po 1-e noiabria 1921 g.*, Buguruslan, 1921, p. 14.

[142] *Otchet samarskogo gubernskogo ekonomicheskogo soveshchaniia*, vyp. 1, Samara, 1921, p. 53.

[143] *Otchet balashovskogo uezdnogo ekonomicheskogo soveshchaniia iiun–sentiabr' 1921 g.*, Balashov, 1921, pp. 4, 22.

[144] TsGAOR, f. 532, op. 1, d. 65, l. 13; *Otchet buzulukskogo uezdnogo ekonomicheskogo soveshchaniia s 1-go iiulia po 1-e oktiabria 1921 g.*, Buzuluk, 1921, p. 3; *Otchet pugachevskogo uezdnogo ekonomicheskogo soveshchaniia*, Pugachev, 1921, pp. 5–6; etc.

[145] TsGAOR, f. 130, op. 2, d. 441, l. 89.

unable to obtain leather, manufactured bast sandals and wooden clogs instead of leather boots and shoes. The rope-making trade was kept alive by an expansion in the sown area of hemp and flax, whose cultivation, incidentally, also helped to maintain essential fuel supplies. The shortages of kerosene in the country areas gave rise to the production of various fuel substitutes, including alcohol, animal fat, straw-cake, and peat.[146]

Running parallel to this process of adaptation was the formation of localized market networks cutting across the main lines of urban-rural trade. One locality might specialize in vodka-distillation, another in furniture and wheels, and a third in harrows and ploughs. The spontaneous commodity exchange between the villages, which had been allowed to prevail in the period up to May 1918, continued to operate during the civil war, despite the attempt of the Soviet regime under war communism to control the distribution and exchange of commodities.

This localized system of commodity exchange is well illustrated in the records of the Androsovka *volost'* soviet (Nikolaevsk *uezd*).[147] The VIK resolved in January 1919 to build a new school and a *narodnyi dom*. A contract was signed with the village of Semenovka (Nizhegorod province), whereby the latter agreed to provide the timber (20 household timber rations) in exchange for 500 *pud* of grain (levied by a tax of 2.5 *funt* on each of the 9,543 souls in Androsovka *volost'*). A similar contract was drawn up with the village of Pokrovka (Simbirsk province) for the delivery of cement and nails. Local barge-haulers on the Volga River were paid in grain to collect the wood from Nizhegorod, while a soviet delegation was sent to Pokrovka. The VIK sent a petition to the provincial provisions authorities in Samara asking for further supplies of timber, but six months later it had still not received a reply. Consequently, the VIK decided to bypass the higher authorities and to draw up a new contract with Semenovka: 2,000 trees were to be sent down-river in exchange for 2,000 *pud* of grain (a considerable swing in the terms of trade in favour of grain). The grain would be levied by a tax of 10 *funt* per head, taken from the provisions norm of 8,000 residents in Androsovka *volost'*. The Samara provisions authority, having been told of this project, sent a telegram to the VIK in Androsovka forbidding them to proceed. The latter, however, resolved, in defiance of Samara, to go ahead with the exchange, while petitioning the provincial authorities to change their

[146] Ibid., f. 532, op. 1, d. 65, l. 93; *SGB*, no. 6, 1 Aug. 1918, p. 10; *Iubileinyi sbornik saratovskogo gubprodkomiteta*, p. 45; *Kooperativnaia mysl'* (Saratov), no. 9 (40), 2 Mar. 1919, pp. 10, 12; *DGS*, p. 60; *KK*, p. 115.

[147] GAKO, f. 109, op. 3, d. 52, ll. 2, 3, 20, 22–3, 31, 36.

mind, 'since forbidding us to export this grain will only postpone the building of the school and the *narodnyi dom* for an indefinite period and will therefore threaten the education of the people, which can only benefit the forces of darkness—the enemies of Soviet power'.[148]

In spite of the Bolsheviks' dislike of the *kustari*, the local soviets, the co-operatives, and the *sovnarkhozy* took a number of measures to help them. The most ambitious—and least effective—project was the co-operativization of the *kustari* in the socialist artels. The opposition of the rural industrialists to the artels was similar to that of the peasant farmers to the agricultural collectives (see sect. 4 below). The private *kustari* were, for the most part, willing to join the consumer societies (*potrebitel'skie obshchestva*) and the credit associations (*kreditnye tovarishchestva*), wherein the market relations of the industrialists were socialized. But very few were willing to join the artels, wherein the means of production and the management of the enterprises were both alienated from the family unit.[149]

A much more constructive role was played by the local government organs and the co-operatives in the procurement of raw materials, in the regulation of production relations, and in the negotiation of distribution outlets. The Kamyshin land department, for example, procured supplies of iron and steel through the *sovnarkhozy* for the local blacksmiths, and contracted with them the manufacture and sale of agricultural tools at fixed prices.[150] The Stavropol' district *sovnarkhoz* came to a similar arrangement with the local brick-makers.[151] In the village of Cherdym (Saratov province) the households were grouped into a union for the manufacture of baskets and chests from willow brushwood; these were purchased by the district consumer society and sold at fixed prices in the nearby villages and towns.[152] In the village of Bol'shie Sestrenki (Balashov *uezd*) the consumer society arranged the transfer of 3 *des.* of state woodland to the union of wheelrights; expert labour was hired from Penza (which was noted for its wheelrights); the wheels were sold to the society at 65 rb. each and to non-residents at 75 rb. each.[153] Similar arrangements were made in the villages of Ivanovka and Alekseevka (Samara *uezd*).[154] Finally, the VIK in Chernovka (Buzuluk *uezd*) hired two wheelrights from the city

148 GAKO, f. 109, op. 3, d. 52, l. 36.
149 On the avilable evidence it is impossible to estimate the number of *kustari* in artels. Informal estimates of the number integrated into the *sovnarkhoz* or the co-operative distribution system vary between 25 per cent and 50 per cent. The number of *kustari* in the artels was probably not higher than 10 per cent.
150 TsGANKh, f. 478, op. 6, d. 1015, ll. 95, 99–100.
151 GAKO, f. 193, op. 2, d. 159, l. 78.
152 *Kooperativnaia mysl'* (Saratov), no. 9 (40), 2 Mar. 1919, p. 11.
153 *Rabochii i kooperativnyi mir* (Balashov), no. 3, 30 June 1918, p. 12.
154 *Kooperativnaia mysl'* (Saratov), no. 9 (40), 2 Mar. 1919, p. 10.

of Simbirsk, procured the supplies of wood, and set the prices of the wheels. The VIK also established two 'communal workshops' (a forge and a tool-repair shop), and contracted craftsmen from the district trade union to manage the shops with local wage-labourers in the busy summer months.[155]

Many soviets organized the procurement of craft products for the Red Army. By the middle of 1919 a large number of textile- and leather-workers, in particular, had been integrated into the national system of military supply. In the village of Bazarnyi Karbulak (Saratov *uezd*)—a major centre of the leather-working industry—there were over 1,000 families engaged in the manufacture of bast shoes (*lapti*) for the Red Army: during the second half of 1918 they were producing over 100,000 pairs of *lapti* per month.[156] The Saratov provincial *sovnarkhoz* procured for the Red Army nearly 105,000 pairs of galoshes and over 60,000 pairs of *lapti* from the local *kustari* during January and February 1919. Between November 1920 and February 1921 the same department procured nearly 200,000 pairs of *lapti*; it argued that it had failed to procure another 750,000 pairs of *lapti* from Khvalynsk *uezd* only because it had not been given enough cash by the higher authorities.[157] The Samara provincial *sovnarkhoz* confidently claimed in October 1920 that it would be able to procure for the Red Army 500,000 pairs of *lapti* made by local craftsmen, provided it was given enough money.[158] The Melekess district *sovnarkhoz* procured for the Red Army during the first four months of 1919 the following *kustar'* products: 27,000 sleighs, 30,000 hempen sacks, 500 sets of harnesses, 700 shirts and 600 pairs of leather boots.[159] We could supply countless further examples of such procurements. The material support of the Red Army by the *kustari* was without doubt one of the key factors in the Bolshevik victory during the Civil War.

The resourcefulness of the *kustari* encouraged the Bolshevik party to reconsider their role. In 1919 and 1920 the Soviet leaders began to put forward arguments in favour of encouraging the rural industries. This change of policy was first manifested at the district and provincial levels and was only later adopted by the central authorities. The

155 GAKO, f. 3134, op. 2, d. 21, ll. 47, 68, 74, 83.

156 TsGAOR, f. 393, op. 3, d. 337, ll. 105–6; *Biulleten' saratovskogo gubernskogo soveta narodnogo khoziaistva*, no. 11, 20 Dec. 1918, p. 9.

157 *Izvestiia saratovskogo gubprodkoma* (Saratov), no. 8, 23 Feb. 1919, p. 15; *Otchet saratovskogo gubernskogo ispolkoma 9-go sozyva 10-mu gubernskomu s''ezdu sovetov*, p. 182.

158 *Izvestiia samarskogo gubernskogo soiuza potrebitel'nykh obshchestv* (Samara), no. 7, 15 Nov. 1920, pp. 2–3.

159 *Izvestiia samarskogo gubernskogo soveta narodnogo khoziaistva*, no. 19, May 1919, pp. 41–3.

Samara provincial soviet assembly passed a resolution as early as December 1918 to encourage the domestic production of industrial goods.[160] In 1919 the Simbirsk provincial commissar for agriculture proposed at a soviet assembly: 'all our attention ought to be turned towards cottage industry and the labouring artels. We ought to do everything possible to support small-scale domestic production until we can again rely upon our larger factories'.[161] The Saratov provincial commissariat of agriculture passed several measures during the spring of 1919 to collect data on the rural industries, to provide technical aid, to organize exhibitions, to establish model workshops, to distribute raw materials and to supply the *kustar* with financial credit.[162] Such measures were not repeated at the national level until the spring of 1921, when the government shelved its plans for the nationalization of the *kustari'* industry and began instead to encourage the private development of the rural industries as a stimulus to economic recovery under the NEP.[163] The contradiction between communist theory and economic pragmatism was thus mirrored during 1919–21 in the conflict between central and local policies.

The reappraisal of the rural industries played a significant part in the development of Lenin's thinking during the transition to the NEP. In his important article 'On the Tax in Kind' (April 1921) Lenin focused on the positive role that small-scale rural industry could play in the restoration of the economy and commodity exchange between town and country. This was of course the key element of the alliance between the workers and the peasants (the *smychka*), upon which Lenin placed such great emphasis:

> we do not deny that freedom of trade entails to a certain degree the development of capitalism, but we say: this capitalism will be controlled and supervised by the state. As long as the workers' state retains in its own hands the factories and the railways, this capitalism need not be feared. It will improve the economic exchange of the peasant products and the neighbouring craft manufactures, which cannot completely satisfy the needs of the peasant in industrial goods, but which nevertheless do partly satisfy these needs; all the same, the peasant economy will get better, and we desperately need to improve it.[164]

Lenin's positive attitude towards the *kustari* during the transition to the NEP was possibly influenced by the changes which had taken place

160 *Postanovleniia 4-go samarskogo gubernskogo s''ezda sovetov*, Samara, 1918, p. 8.
161 *Protokoly i doklady VII-go simbirskogo gubernskogo s''ezda sovetov*, Simbirsk, 1919, p. 102.
162 TsGANKh, f. 478, op. 10, d. 168, l. 153.
163 *SU*, 1921, no. 47, arts. 230, 240.
164 *PSS*, vol. 43, p. 160.

since 1914 in the production relations of the rural industrial sector. During the war women and dependants (e.g. children and the elderly) had increased their activities in the rural industries, since, with the menfolk in the army, it was difficult for these people to sustain a peasant farm. The economic crisis of the revolutionary period forced many of the weaker households to rent out their land allotment and take up handicrafts. This was especially prevalent among the households which had received an allotment for the first time during the revolution, yet which did not have adequate means of production to cultivate the land.[165] The dominance of natural exchange and barter after 1917 further weakened the capitalist orientation of the *kustari*, who were now interested in the production of cheap household goods (e.g. linen), rather than high-profit ones (e.g. lace). In short, it was no longer possible to argue that the predominant social nature of the rural industries was 'petty-capitalist'. Indeed, during the early 1920s a number of Soviet scholars began to stress the significance of pre-capitalist relations of production in the rural industrial sector, echoing the emphasis in Lenin's last writings on the traditional social structures of the Russian countryside.[166] Further study of the 1920s is required in order to evaluate the 'primitive peasant capitalism' of the *kustari*, and to assess the potential contribution of the latter to the industrialization of Soviet Russia as an alternative to the Stalinist path of economic development.[167]

4. COLLECTIVE AND STATE FARMS

Despite the Decree on Land of October 1917, the Bolsheviks were, in the long term, opposed to the system of small-scale peasant family farming. The 'illusory egalitarianism' of the commune during the revolution had, they maintained, merely reinforced the petty-proprietary and conservative instincts of the peasantry. The modernization of the agricultural sector and its 'socialist transformation' could only be achieved through collectivism, whose benefits—the

[165] TsGANKh, f. 478, op. 10, d. 106, ll. 20–1, 134; *Izvestiia samarskogo gubernskogo soiuza potrebitel'nykh obshchestv* (Samara), no. 5, 1 Nov. 1920, p. 2; *Izvestiia* (Saratov), no. 251, 5 Nov. 1921, p. 2.

[166] Shlifshtein's *Melkaia promyshlennost'* is a good example. It argues that 91 per cent of the households engaged in rural industries in Saratov province during 1913 had as few as one or two workers. The percentage of hired workers varied from 7.2 per cent in flax-based industries to 22.9 per cent in leather-working. The overall percentage of hired workers was only 11.6 per cent. The majority of the labourers had been hired on account of family labour shortages in the more complex industries. This was reflected in the fact that the rates of pay for the hired workers tended to be higher than the cash value of the family's own labour (pp. 44–50).

[167] It would be useful to have available in English the work on this subject of H. Okuda, of the University of Tokyo.

economies of large-scale farming with modern technology and labour co-operation, and the integration of the agricultural collectives into the state distribution system—had been clearly set out in Marxist theory.

Lenin envisaged the process of collectivization as the adoption of practical co-operative methods by the peasants in their own local environment: 'the more the peasantry is persuaded by example and by its own experience of the collectives, the more successful will the movement become'.[168] This transition, Lenin argued, could only be achieved 'patiently, as a series of gradual steps, awakening the consciousness of the labouring sections of the peasantry and moving forward only as their consciousness is awakened'.[169] The Eighth Party Congress (March 1919) confirmed the voluntarist and gradualist principles of collectivization: 'the only valuable associations are those which are established by the peasants on their own initiative, and whose advantages are discovered by the peasants in practice'.[170] As Lenin put it at the Eighth Congress, 'there is nothing more stupid than the very thought of coercion in our economic relations with the middle peasantry. Our task is not to expropriate the middle peasant, but to take account of the special circumstances of peasant life, to learn from the peasants the means of the transition to a better order without resorting to force!'.[171]

To aid the development of the agricultural collectives, the Soviet government passed a series of laws which provided the basis for a radical transformation of the system of land relations embodied in the October Decree on Land. The Law on the Socialization of Land (February 1918) and the Statute of 14 February 1919 on Socialist Land Organization both encouraged the development of socialist forms in agriculture. The former stipulated that the agricultural collectives (*kolkhozy, sovkhozy*) were to be formed 'at the expense of individual enterprises, in the interests of the transition to the Socialist economy'.[172] The collectives were to be allocated a special share of the property taken from the private estates during the land reforms. Some soviets took measures to retrieve the livestock, seed, and tools which the

168 *PSS*, vol. 37, p. 180.

169 Ibid., p. 356.

170 *KPSS v rezoliutsiiakh i resheniiakh s''ezdov, konferentsii i plenumov TsK*, 9th edn., vol. 2, Moscow, 1970, p. 78.

171 *PSS*, vol. 38, p. 201. Lenin was criticizing the policies put forward at the First All-Russian Congress of Land Departments, *Kombedy* and *Kommuny* in December 1918, which supported forcing the tempo of collectivization by administrative means (see *Trudy 1-go vserossiiskogo s''ezda zemotdelov, komitetov bednoty i kommun*, Moscow, 1919).

172 *Agrarnaia politika Sovetskoi vlasti (1917–1918 gg.)*, Moscow, 1954, p. 136.

communes had confiscated from the estates during the revolution, although this caused a great deal of peasant discontent.[173] The Statute on Socialist Land Organization declared all forms of peasant family farming 'transitional and obsolescent'.[174] The land was to be put in a single state reserve under the control of the soviets (rather than the communes, as set out in the October Decree on Land). Strict priority in the allocation of the land was to be given to the state (soviet) farms, the *sovkhozy*—the largest of the new collectives, which V. P. Miliutin, the Bolshevik leader, envisaged as 'factories producing grain, meat, milk and fodder, which will free the socialist order from its economic dependence on the petty-proprietary farms.'[175]

The biggest *sovkhozy* in Russia were situated in the south-east, in Samara, Saratov and Voronezh provinces (see Table 34). Some of them

TABLE 34. Sovkhozy *in Russia, 1919–1920*

Province	1919		1920	
	No. of *sovkhozy*	Average area (*des.*)	No. of *sovkhozy*	Average area (*des.*)
Moscow	201	225	201	160
Petrograd	185	118	140	246
Novgorod	106	471	68	735
Gomel'	252	647	244	678
Kursk	118	593	106	520
Voronezh	65	1,790	66	1,060
Samara	100	1,944	72	1,667
Saratov	66	2,597	82	2,548

Source: TsGANKh, f. 478, op. 3, d. 1157, l. 58.

were in effect agro-industrial cartels, producing a wide range of foodstuffs and handicraft goods. Thus, the Novo-Repin *sovkhoz* (Novouzensk *uezd*) united all the population of Novo-Repin *volost'* under the management of the VIK. It had 8,474 salaried members, divided into 508 working artels and 2,600 family 'cells' (households). It covered an area of 50,000 *des.* and owned collectively 2,979 head of draught cattle, 741 ploughs, 464 mowers, and 9 threshing machines. It had 10 blacksmiths, 5 metal-workers, 10 carpenters, 15 tailors, 10 cobblers, 24 schoolteachers, and 1

[173] GAKO, f. 81, op. 1, d. 10, ll. 79–82; TsGAOR, f. 393, op. 3, d. 329, l. 187; TsGANKh, f. 478, op. 6, d. 1015, ll. 194–5; etc.

[174] B. N. Knipovich, 'Napravlenie i itogi agrarnoi politiki 1917–1920 gg.', in *O zemle*, p. 30. For the legislation see *Agrarnaia politika Sovetskoi vlasti*, pp. 417–31; and *KK*, pp. 93–5.

[175] V. P. Miliutin, *Sotsializm i sel'skoe khoziaistvo*, Moscow, 1919, p. 54.

agronomist. The Novo-Khoper *sovkhoz* (Novouzensk *uezd*) was equally complex. It had 8,524 members (mainly described as 'rural proletarians') and covered an area of 55,000 *des.*[176]

Whereas the *sovkhozy* were mainly established on the directives of the Soviet authorities, the collective farms (*kolkhozy*) developed, for the most part, on the spontaneous initiatives of various social groups. There were three main types of *kolkhoz* during this period, although in the early stages it was not always possible to distinguish between them. The earliest were the *kommuny*, which also tended to be the most socialistic and 'pioneering' in spirit. Most of them were established on the land of the ex-gentry estates[177] by groups of poor peasants, landless labourers, or in-migrant townsmen. A study of eight *kommuny* in Simbirsk province carried out in September 1920 discovered that the main social groups in the collectives were: 'the very poorest peasants'; 'peasants formerly engaged in migrant labour'; 'barge haulers on the Volga'; and 'in-migrant carpenters, blacksmiths, and factory workers'.[178] A national survey of 500 *kommuny* found that only half of the members had originally been peasant farmers; the majority of the remaining members had been either rural craftsmen or in-migrant workers.[179] Some *kommuny* were set up by demobilized soldiers whose own farms had been ruined by the war, or who were eager to break away from the households of their fathers.[180] Others were established by the richest peasant stratum, sometimes as a means of evading the requisitioning brigades, or the levelling policies of the soviets, and sometimes as a means of restoring the *khutora* and the *otruba* which had been broken up by the communes during the revolution.[181] In general, the membership of the *kommuny* was young, with a large proportion of dependants (mainly children). The Simbirsk study found that 50% of the members of the *kommuny* were of working age (over 12 years), whereas 65% of the rural population in Simbirsk province was in this age-group.[182] Women represented a large proportion of the workforce, since many of the men had been mobilized by the Red Army. A similar pattern was noted by a study of 35 *kommuny* in Samara province during June 1919 (see Table 35). A typical *kommuna* in this

176 TsGAOR, f. 130, op. 2, d. 441, l. 69; E. I. Medvedev, *Oktiabr'skaia revoliutsiia v Srednem Povolzh'e*, Kuibyshev, 1964, pp. 121, 197.

177 In Saratov province 86 per cent of the land in the *kommuny* was formerly estate land (*KK*, p. 85).

178 TsGANKh, f. 478, op. 3, d. 1157, l. 46.

179 V. V. Grishaev, *Sel'skokhoziaistvennye kommuny Sovetskoi Rossii 1917–1929 gg.*, Moscow, 1976, p. 20.

180 TsGAOR, f. 130, op. 2, d. 441, ll. 27–8, 60.

181 TsGANKh, f. 478, op. 6, d. 1015, ll. 115–16, 193; op. 3, d. 1157, l. 55.

182 Ibid., op. 3, d. 1157, l. 46; *Trudy TsSU: Statisticheskii ezhegodnik 1921 g.*, vol. 8, vyp. 3, Moscow, 1922, pp. 24–5.

TABLE 35. *Population of thirty-five* kommuny, *Samara province, June 1919*

	Men	Women	Boys	Girls	Total
Number	629	616	653	635	2,533
% of whole	24.8	24.3	25.8	25.0	100
Dependants as % of their sex group	—	—	50.9	50.7	50.8

Source: *Samarskaia guberniia v gody grazhdanskoi voiny (1918–1920 gg.): Dokumenty i materialy*, Kuibyshev, 1958, pp. 407–12.

sample—the Bratskaia ('Brotherly') in Titovka *volost'*, Samara *uezd*—comprised three families: the Mizovatkins (9 adults, 12 children); the Sumbaevs (2 adults); and the Chavkins (2 adults, 4 children). Of the 6 men, 3 were registered as 'unskilled workers'; 1 as a cobbler; 1 as a blacksmith; and 1 as a bee-keeper. The movable property of the *kommuna*, included: 5 horses, 5 cows, 1 calf, 11 sheep, 4 harrows; 3 carts; and 372 *pud* of grain.[183]

Of the eight *kommuny* in the Simbirsk study, seven had been organized by 'party workers and ex-members of the *kombed*, many of whom are now leading party activists and important officials in the soviet institutions'.[184] The exception was an all-women's *kommuna*, formed by twenty-four nuns of the Kievo-Nikolaev Convent in Alatyr' district. The others all had their own party cell—ranging in size from four to fifteen members—which provided the 'ideological leadership of the *kommuna*'. Some of the *kommuny* held regular political meetings and reading sessions. One even had its own school (the rest sent their children to neighbouring village schools). The influence of the Orthodox Church was said to be in decline among the members, although most of the latter had entered the *kommuna* as believers:

> in almost all the *kommuny* religion has become less important. People are permitted to go to church, but the performance of religious ceremonies is becoming less popular. Religious fasting is no longer practised . . . Some members of the Kazneevka *kommuna* do not even christen their children; nor do they perform religious burial services for their dead; they bury them on the hill or near the *kommuna* without a religious ceremony.[185]

The seven *kommuny* all had their own soviet and Red Army brigade: 12% of the *kommuna* members (39% of the able-bodied men) were reported absent in the Red Army. In some *kommuny* the women had

[183] GAKO, f. 236, op. 1, d. 141, l. 4.
[184] TsGANKh, f. 478, op. 3, d. 1157, l. 45.
[185] Ibid., l. 49.

had to defend themselves against the Whites and peasant bandits. Generally speaking, the women played a critical role in the *kommuny*, according to the Simbirsk study:

> If the *kommuny* have not yet fallen apart, then this is in large part due to the women. All the field work, including the ploughing, and all the pastoral duties, fall exclusively upon the women and the youths. The woman in the *kommuna* works even harder than she does in the village; she never has a rest-day; in the autumn she no longer has the time to spin or to weave, so that she and her children walk about in rags. The women curse Communism when they see that in all the huts in the village the peasants are scutching their tow and preparing their looms.[186]

In all the *kommuny* the women complained about the lack of a crèche, since they had to carry their infants around with them during field-work.

The typical *kommuna* functioned as a microcosm of the new communistic lifestyle. According to the first model charter of the *kommuny*, issued by Narkomzem on 21 July 1918, there was to be no private ownership of property (other than personal belongings) in the collectives.[187] The residential buildings were co-inhabited by several families, usually because of the shortages of accommodation. Meals were taken in a communal cafeteria, run by the older women. In one or two of the larger *kommuny* in the Simbirsk sample the members ate and worked on different shifts in teams, organized according to the age of the members. The male adolescents were the most influential group, and, in one *kommuna*, even had their own 'chairman', who distributed the tasks among the work-teams. Disputes about work and pay were commonplace in the *kommuny*. In some collectives the members continued to live in their own family huts, retaining in private ownership their domestic animals (poultry, rabbits, milking cows). This sometimes caused further dissension between the members. In one of the *kommuny* in the Simbirsk sample the chairman of the party cell had his own rabbit-breeding business; he had requisitioned the rabbits from the other members of the *kommuna* and the surrounding villages.[188]

Smaller and more traditional than the *kommuna* was the artel (*artel'*), the most common type of *kolkhoz* during the civil war (see Table 36). In contrast to the *kommuny*, which were largely drawn from the landless elements of rural society, the artels mainly comprised ex-smallholding peasants who, for one reason or another, were dissatisfied

[186] TsGANKh, f. 478. op. 3, d. 1157, l. 48.
[187] *Agrarnaia politika Sovetskoi vlasti*, pp. 400–3, 433–41.
[188] TsGANKh, f. 478, op. 3, d. 1157, l. 49.

TABLE 36. Kolkhozy, *Samara and Saratov provinces, August 1920*

	Number		% rural population	
	Kommuny	Artels	*Kommuny*	Artels
Samara	29	55	0.075	0.189
Saratov	63	154	0.123	0.371

Source: Trudy TsSU: Itogi vserossiiskoi sel'sko-khoziaistvennoi perepisi 1920 g., vol. 2, vyp. 2, Moscow, 1921, pp. 58, 90.

with the communal system. A survey of thirty-two artels in Simbirsk province carried out in October 1920 discovered that the majority of the members in the artels had previously been poor peasants, or the farmers of an *otrub* or *khutor*. Peasants formerly engaged in migrant labour, village craftsmen, and members of the rural intelligentsia were also represented, of course. One of the main incentives to join an artel was said to have been the opportunity it afforded the peasant household to stabilize the holding of its arable strips:

the peasant household farmers in many of the larger village communes are prepared to unite in small groups of five or six family households and set up a farming settlement on a piece of land separated from the commune; the annual and even seasonal repartitions of the land in the commune are a terrible burden on all the peasants, who are interested in the improvement of their household economy . . . The most adventurous and energetic peasants are now leaving to form artels . . . All the peasants display a strong desire to base their household economy on an improved and rational basis, but they are not yet confident in the collective forms of agriculture.[189]

The general economic status of the artel members was comparable to that of the lower-to-middle stratum of the communal peasantry. The average family size of the artel household in the Simbirsk sample was large (9 members); 60% of the artel members were of working age (over 12 years). The arable land area per member was 2 *des.* (compared with the local communal average of 1.5 *des.*), mainly situated on the territory of the former estates.[190] About one-third of the family units did not have their own horse. The majority of the artels possessed the basic tools (which were invariably in need of repair), but few had any advanced machinery. In several artels the main material shortage was housing, especially if the collective had been set up on vacated land too

[189] Ibid., l. 56.

[190] A study of the artels in Saratov province showed that only 50 per cent of the land previously belonged to the estates; 34 per cent was formerly peasant allotment land (*KK*, p. 85).

far from any of the villages to make the removal of the peasant huts a feasible undertaking. Some members had to live in their native village and commute to the artel.[191]

The lifestyle and the social customs of the artels were broadly similar to those of the surrounding village communes. The model charter of the artels, adopted by Narkomzem on 19 May 1919, set an entrance fee for the households (e.g. a horse or some tools), but the latter were allowed to retain the rest of their property in private ownership. About 90% of the cattle, 50% of the working horses, and 30% of the ploughland was held in private tenure within the artels of Simbirsk province, according to a survey of 1919.[192] When a family left the artel, it could regain some of the entrance fee at the discretion of the rest of the members. The labour obligations of the family households were defined by a general agreement; once the household had performed its obligations it was free to work on its own allotment. The artel was run by an assembly of the members, which in turn elected a soviet and an artel *starosta*, a title borrowed from the village commune.[193] Few artels in the Simbirsk sample were large enough to have their own school, but the children were usually able to attend one of the neighbouring village schools, provided the villagers were not hostile. Some artels were dominated by their Bolshevik activists, who were known on occasion to employ coercive managerial techniques in the collectives and the neighbouring villages. But the majority of the artels were not connected in any way with the Bolshevik party. The Simbirsk study found that 6.5% of the artel members were absent in the Red Army, compared with 12.2% in the *kommuny*.[194]

The most informal types of collective farming during this period may be seen as predecessors of the TOZ (*tovarishchestvo po obshchestvennoi otrabotke zemli*), an association for the collective cultivation of the land. The communal cultivation of the land (*supriaga, obshchestvennye zapashki*) had developed during the nineteenth century, partly to pay the communal taxes, and partly to meet the welfare needs of the villagers themselves.[195] During the revolutionary period this practice was adopted by a much wider range of villages, mainly as a means of farming the arable which had been left untilled by the peasant-soldiers. Thus, in Pereliubov *volost'* (Nikolaevsk *uezd*) the soviet organized a scheme for the collective cultivation of the

[191] TsGANKh, f. 478, op. 3, d. 1157, ll. 52–4.
[192] *KK*, p. 247.
[193] *Agrarnaia politika Sovetskoi vlasti*, p. 462–70.
[194] TsGANKh, f. 478, op. 3, d. 1157, l. 53.
[195] O. Figes, 'Collective Farming and the 19th-Century Russian Land Commune: A Research Note', *Soviet Studies*, vol. 38, no. 1, 1986, pp. 89–97.

communal land in order to provide a food ration of 7 *pud* per head for the family members of the 121 peasant-soldiers in the Red Army.[196] In Staro-Slavkino *volost'* (Petrovsk *uezd*) a special village committee was set up for the sowing campaign of spring 1919 to organize the collective cultivation of the vacant land in the communes. The tools were to be provided from the estates, but the peasants were ordered to supply their own horses.[197] Similar collective practices were found in the small, informal associations (e.g. *piatidvorki, sosedskie arteli*) commonly established by demobilized soldiers, in-migrant townsmen, and members of ethnic minorities and religious sects on the vacant steppeland of Nikolaevsk and Novouzensk districts. Two to five families would pool their resources, farm collectively, and share the harvest during one or more agricultural seasons.[198] According to a survey by the Moscow *oblast'* executive committee in spring of 1918, as many as 5% of the *volost'* soviets in the thirteen Russian provinces reported the cultivation of *obshchestvennye zapashki* in their localities; a further 19% stated that the communes were planning to institute collective cultivation during 1918.[199] It was from these simple forms of labour co-operation that the TOZy later developed.[200]

The smallholding peasantry was, for the most part, hostile to the new agricultural collectives, as we have already had cause to discover (see pp. 243–4). This should be seen in the general context of the peasantry's cultural and technological conservatism and its attachment to the concepts and the social institutions of family ownership, which were seen to be threatened by the new collectives. Such fears were reinforced by the peasantry's habitual mistrust of the state, under whose auspices the collectives had emerged. As a delegate at the Penza provincial assembly of land departments in September 1919 pointed out in relation to the state farms, 'we have to take into account the psychology of the peasant family farmer, who sees in the *sovkhozy* and their bureaucratic administration the restoration of the old gentry regime'.[201] The predominance of party officials and non-peasant groups in the larger collectives also played a part. 'In the *sovkhozy*', complained a peasant delegate at the Syzran' district soviet assembly in July 1920, 'there are people who know nothing about agriculture;

[196] *Kommunist* (Pugachev), no. 191, 26 Nov. 1920, p. 2.

[197] TsGAOR, f. 393, op. 3, d. 336, l. 264. See also TsGANKh, f. 478, op. 6, d. 1015, l. 128; d. 2010, l. 60; TsGAOR, f. 393, op. 3, d. 325, l. 153; d. 333, ll. 39, 316.

[198] *KK*, pp. 100–2, 145–6.

[199] S. L. Makarova, 'Oprosnye listy Narodnogo Komissariata Zemledeliia i moskovskogo oblastnogo ispolnitel'nogo komiteta kak istochnik po istorii agrarnoi revoliutsii (noiabr' 1917–iiun' 1918)', kand. diss., Moscow, 1970, p. 257.

[200] See further *KK*, pp. 100–2, 145–6; V. V. Kabanov, 'Oktiabr'skaia revoliutsiia i krest'ianskaia obshchina', *Istoricheskie zapiski*, vol. 111, Moscow, 1984, pp. 130 ff.

[201] TsGANKh, f. 478, op. 6, d. 1015, l. 193.

they cannot cope with it.'[202] V. A. Antonov-Ovseenko, the Bolshevik leader, came to a similar conclusion in his report on the causes of the peasant uprising in Tambov province during 1920–1:

Both the state farms and the collective farms have quite frequently had former landowners, estate managers, and household servants and such like people setting down in them. The collective farms no less than the state farms became places of refuge for disabled men and slackers; only very few of them are of any value in the running of the farms and can successfully stand up to the carping criticism of individual peasant farmers.[203]

Many of the *sovkhozy* and *kommuny* were so badly run that they relied upon the conscription of the surrounding peasantry under the labour duty (*trudpovinnost'*). This only strengthened the peasantry's association of the collectives with the former gentry regime, since it was obviously reminiscent of the *barshchina*. As a peasant delegate at the Syzran' assembly put it, 'the *sovkhozy* are always forcing the peasantry to work; they make the peasants weed their fields. And they don't even give us bread or water. What will come of all this? It is like *barshchina* all over again'.[204]

The inefficiency of the collectives would not have caused such offence had the Soviet regime not granted them so many privileges at the expense of the peasant farms. V. V. Kabanov has argued that the collective farms suffered from heavy requisitioning of foodstuffs and livestock, which partly explains their poor economic performance. But a secret directive of Sovnarkom on 21 August 1919 forbad the requisitioning of collective farm property in cases where this would have had a detrimental effect on the potential of the collectives. Strict limits were set on the amount of property that could be requisitioned from the collectives.[205] The peasantry also objected to the collective farms occupying the former estates, since this land was deemed to belong to the communes. Nearly all the sources noted a close correlation between the level of the peasantry's opposition to the collectives and the proximity of the latter to the village settlement. One land official in Serdobsk district noted:

In general, the population is indifferent towards the *sovkhozy*, but as soon as a *sovkhoz* is organized near a village so as to utilize its outlying buildings then the population begins to complain bitterly, arguing that the *sovkhoz* should be

202 *Stenograficheskii otchet 7-go syzranskogo uezdnogo soveta*, p. 71.
203 V. A. Antonov-Ovseenko, 'O banditskom dvizhenii v Tambovskoi gubernii', in J. M. Meijer (ed.), *The Trotsky Papers*, 2 vols., The Hague, 1971, vol. 2, p. 489.
204 *Stenograficheskii otchet 7-go syzranskogo uezdnogo soveta*, p. 71.
205 *KK*, p. 269; TsGAOR, f. 130, op. 3, d. 106, l. 256.

organized on vacant land, far away from the village, which in the present economic crisis is of course impossible.[206]

The artels suffered especially on this account, since much of their land was taken from peasant allotments. In some places the communes and the village soviets prohibited the separation of any allotment land from the commune for the establishment of an artel. A study in Simbirsk province found that only 38 out of 120 artels had been properly allocated land by 1920.[207] Thus, the artels were sometimes forced to seize land by force 'regardless of its suitability'. For this reason, a large portion of the land in the artels suffered from strip-intermingling, lack of water supplies, ill-defined boundaries, etc. In some of the smaller artels the members had to take their rifles with them into the fields, since they were likely to be attacked by the peasantry from the neighbouring villages.[208]

TABLE 37. *Means of production and economic performance of* sovkhozy, kolkhozy, *and peasant farms, Samara province, 1920*

	Sovkhozy	*Kolkhozy*	Peasant family farms
Means of production per 100 souls			
Sown area (*des.*)[a]	66.2	165.3	83.6
Working horses	18.5	27.1	20.4
Cows	13.6	29.9	16.8
Sheep	26.4	72.7	66.0
Ploughs	16.7	8.5	7.9
Iron harrows	11.9	4.1	0.9
Sowing machines	10.5	2.4	1.0
Harvest yields (pud *per* des.)			
Wheat	13.6	13.7	8.0
Rye	11.9	17.9	11.0
Oats	15.2	14.4	11.0
Millet	5.2	12.6	5.0
Barley	7.1	17.9	4.0
Potatoes	115.0	102.0	128.0

[a] The *sovkhozy* and *kolkhozy* were forced to leave a large share of their land fallow; this land is not recorded in the figures on sown area.

Source: *Otchet samarskogo gubernskogo ekonomicheskogo soveshchaniia*, Samara, 1921–2, vyp. 2, pp. 41–7, 50–1, 80–1.

[206] T. Galynskii, *Ocherki po istorii agrarnoi revoliutsii Serdobskogo uezda, Saratovskoi gubernii*, Serdobsk, 1924, p. 178. [207] *KK*, p. 87.

[208] GAKO, f. 236, op. 1, d. 3, l. 4; T. Shepelovaia, 'Sotsialisticheskie formy sel'skogo khoziaistva v 1918–1919 gg.', *Krasnyi Arkhiv*, no. 5 (96), 1939, p. 16.

The economic performance of the collective farms was, generally speaking, disappointing, considering the advantages they enjoyed over the peasant family farms in the supply of land, tools and livestock (see Table 37). V. V. Kabanov, the first Soviet historian to make a really objective study of the collectives during this period, was forced to admit that 'the economic successes of the earliest *kolkhozy* were modest'. Few collective farms made a profit, while there were many that ran at a loss to the state. Only 31.8% of the income of the collective farms in the RSFSR during 1919 was derived from productive activities, as opposed to membership dues and government loans (59.8%). In Saratov province only 17% of *kolkhoz* income was earned through productive activities, while 79.7% came from membership dues and state loans. In Simbirsk province the respective figures were 6.9% and 83.7%.[209] By the middle of 1920, it was widely acknowledged in official circles that the *sovkhozy* and the *kommuny* had failed to make any impact on the smallholding economy, while the artels—which had been formed mainly by peasants and were thus better equipped with means of production and agricultural expertise—had performed only slightly better. The harvest yields of the *kommuny* and *sovkhozy* were generally low. Their fallow area was large to the point of embarrassment (in the *kolkhozy* of Saratov province, for example, only 39.5% of the arable was sown during 1919–20).[210] And their working methods were, in Lenin's own words, 'an example of how not to farm: the neighbouring peasantry either poke fun at [the collectives] or pour scorn on them'.[211] In some *sovkhozy* the fallow area was reported to have increased between 1919 and 1920, because of the shortage of labour, horses, fodder, and seed, and the plain incompetence of the *sovkhoz* members.[212] The *sovkhozy*, the peasants complained, 'have got hold of the land, but do not know how to farm it'.[213] The chairman of the Penza provincial assembly of soviet land departments offered a similar explanation for the poor performance of the *kolkhozy*: 'only the urban proletariat joins the *kommuny* and artels, but they do not have tools, housing, or cash. They frequently demand footwear and clothes, etc. It is hardly surprising that of the twenty-four *kommuny* and artels established in Chembar *uezd*, only seven now remain'.[214]

A significant number of the collectives established during the civil war had to be liquidated within a short period, on account of their economic instability (see Table 38). The collectives began to fall apart

[209] *KK*, pp. 250, 267.
[210] Ibid., p. 268.
[211] *PSS*, vol. 43, p. 60.
[212] TsGANKh, f. 478, op. 3, d. 1175, l. 59.
[213] Cited in Antonov-Ovseenko, p. 521.
[214] TsGANKh, f. 478, op. 6, d. 1015, l. 198.

Table 38. *Organization and liquidation of* kolkhozy, *Saratov province, April – September 1919*

	Kommuny		Artels	
	Organized	Liquidated	Organized	Liquidated
April				
number	2	2	55	1
members	208	25	5,831	589
area (*des.*)	282	60	5,406	—
May				
number	3	2	24	2
members	165	105	978	91
area (*des.*)	87	105	1,191	96
June				
number	3	1	11	1
members	104	64	725	205
area (*des.*)	214	38	1,300	—
August				
number	20	—	26	14
members	1,573	—	3,036	1,206
area (*des.*)	2,343	—	5,376	1,506
September				
number	—	1	2	4
members	—	58	303	467
area (*des.*)	—	154	—	219

Source: TsGANKh, f. 478, op. 4, d. 132, ll. 1–5.

en masse during the autumn of 1920. In Samara province the number of *sovkhozy* declined from 71 in the summer of 1920 to a mere 19 at the end of 1921; in Saratov province the number declined over the same period from 150 to 45.[215] The drought and the famine crisis were mainly to blame, but the peasant uprisings of Antonov, Vakhulin, and Popov (see ch. 7, sect. 3) also took their toll. In Saratov province the peasant insurgents destroyed 15 *kommuny* and 34 *sovkhozy* during the first half of 1921, taking from them over 2,500 head of livestock and 50,000 *pud* of seed material. During the course of the year they annihilated 41 state farms (covering a total area of 434,000 *des.*) and took from them over 5 million roubles worth of property. The large *sovkhozy* on the open steppeland were the worst to suffer: those of Nikolaevsk district were said to have lost all their cattle by October

[215] *Trudy TsSU: Itogi vserossiiskoi sel'sko-khoziaistvennoi perepisi 1920 g. v granitsakh gubernii na. 1 marta 1922 g.*, vol. 2, vyp. 8, pp. 30, 34; *Trudy TsSU: Statisticheskii ezhegodnik 1921 g.*, vol. 8, vyp. 3–4, p. 298.

1921; those of the German Volga region were said to have been totally wiped out by the end of the following year.[216]

5. THE PEASANTRY AND THE RED ARMY

The organization of the Red Army as a regular mass army began in earnest on the Volga during the summer of 1918. The opening up of the Eastern Front underlined the weaknesses of the 'detachment system'—the loose network of volunteer brigades attached to an individual factory or village—which had formed the basis of the Red Army during the early days of the revolution. The brigades, which comprised anything between fifty and a thousand soldiers, usually under a 'commander' and two assistants elected from the ranks, functioned in a 'disorganized and egocentric' manner, according to M. N. Tukhachevskii, Commander of the First Army on the Eastern Front.[217] The elected officer corps was inexperienced and often dominated by careerist elements straight from the ranks of the Imperial Army. Without a command structure, military strategy was decided collectively, and chaos often ensued. Attacks were launched without adequate scouting of the enemy terrain, sometimes using no more than school geography maps. The brigades fought ineffectively and without discipline, shooting too early and breaking up on first sight of the well-disciplined Czech or Cossack troops.[218] The military defeats of May to June made it clear to a majority of the Bolshevik leadership that there was an urgent need to build up and reorganize the Red Army into proper regiments and divisions, instead of volunteer detachments, with a centralized chain of command—a general headquarters, a military staff, and iron discipline in the ranks, backed up by party controls.

The build-up of the Red Army after 1918 ran parallel with Bolshevik state construction in the political and economic fields. The integration of the partisan brigades into a centralized military structure was,

[216] *Otchet saratovskogo gubernskogo ispolnitel'nogo komiteta 9-go sozyva 10-mu gubernskomu s''ezdu sovetov za oktiabr' 1920 g–iiun' 1921 g.* Saratov, 1921, p. 153; *Otchet saratovskogo ekonomicheskogo soveshchaniia*, Saratov, 1922, pp. 17, 20; *Otchet pugachevskogo uezdnogo ekonomicheskogo soveshchaniia*, p. 19; *Nizhnee Povolzh'e* (Saratov), no. 10 (17), Oct. 1925, p. 18; *Izvestiia* (Saratov), no. 131, 15 June 1921, p. 1; *Otchet ekonomicheskogo soveshchaniia Oblasti Nemtsev Povolzh'ia na 1-oe aprelia 1922 g.*, p. 5.

[217] M. N. Tukhachevskii, 'Pervaia armiia v 1918 godu', in *Izbrannye proizvedeniia*, vol. 1, Moscow, 1964, p. 74.

[218] See *Izvestiia Narodnogo Komissariata po Voennym Delam*, no. 21, 2 Feb. 1919, p. 2; I. A. Onufriev, *Moi vospominaniia iz grazhdanskoi voiny na Urale*, Ekaterinburg, 1922, pp. 16–17; A. P. Nenarokov, 'Obrazovanie vostochnogo fronta i perekhod k massovoi reguliarnoi armii (mai–iiun' 1918 g.)', *Istoricheskie nauki*, no. 4, 1961; V. V. Kuibyshev, 'Pervaia revoliutsionnaia armiia', in *Simbirskaia guberniia v 1918–1920 gg. Sbornik vospominanii*, Ul'ianovsk, 1958, pp. 26–9.

indeed, itself an important aspect of the centralization and 'statization' of Soviet power. Established by the soviets as a local military guard, the brigades were slowly transformed into the regular units of a national army under the command of the Bolshevik party. As Trotsky later recalled:

> The Red Army was built from above, in accordance with the principles of the Dictatorship of the Proletariat. Commanders were selected and tested by the organs of Soviet power and the Communist party. Election of commanders by the units themselves—which were politically ill-educated, being composed of recently mobilized young peasants—would inevitably have been transformed into a game of chance ... The peasantry, taken by itself, is incapable of creating a centralized army. It cannot get beyond local guerrilla units, the primitive 'democracy' of which is often a screen for the personal dictatorship of their atamans ... In the first period guerrilla warfare was a necessary and adequate weapon ... But as the war grew in scope, it increasingly called for proper organization and discipline ... The year 1918 and a substantial part of 1919 were spent in constant ... struggle to create a *centralized, disciplined army* supplied and controlled from a single centre. In the military sphere this reflected, though in sharper forms, the process that was going forward in all spheres of the construction of the Soviet Republic. [Emphasis as in source][219]

Just as there are parallels between the growth of the Red Army and the Soviet state, so there are parallels in the response of the peasantry to these developments. During 1917 and the early months of 1918 the peasants had formed 'revolutionary' or 'soviet' brigades to defend the gains of the revolution against a Cossack or gentry reaction (see ch. 4, sect. 2). The first Red Army regiments, which were formed out of these brigades, retained a close relationship with the villages: the peasant-soldiers were fed and, to a large extent, clothed and armed by their own villages, to which they regularly returned between military campaigns. The reorganization of the Red Army on a national scale unavoidably threatened this reciprocal tie between the village and its regiment, since the peasant soldier was bound to be sent to fight on fronts too far away to return to his home. While the peasants were ready to defend the revolution in their own locality, they were slow to comprehend the need for a civil war—a 'war between brothers' (*bratoubiistvennaia voina*)—in distant parts of the country, not least because there were said to be revolutionaries and socialists fighting on the enemy's side. As the civil war spread and the Red Army grew in size, so the number of peasant volunteers declined, forcing the Bolsheviks to use coercive methods of military conscription.

According to a survey by the Supreme Military Inspectorate in the

[219] L. Trotsky, *How the Revolution Armed*, trans. B. Pearce, 3 vols., London, 1979, vol. 1, pp. 8–9.

autumn of 1918, 61.5% of the volunteers for the Red Army came from regions close to the civil war front. The proportion of adult men volunteering from these regions was nearly four times as high as in the regions further away from the fighting. A large number of the volunteers were urban or rural proletarians with weak ties to the land, since the peasant farmer was unwilling to leave the village during the land redivisions and the peak agricultural season. Trotsky recalled that the first Red Army volunteers tended to be 'vagabond, unstable elements', while others observed that the prospect of receiving food and clothing encouraged many volunteers 'who saw no alternative but starvation' (see ch. 3, sect. 4). These impressions were supported by the survey of the Supreme Military Inspectorate, which showed that even in the mainly agricultural districts of Voronezh and Kursk provinces peasants comprised only 49% of the Red Army volunteers, whereas industrial and unskilled workers comprised 43% (in the mainly industrial districts of Tver' and Moscow provinces the latter comprised 62% of the volunteers). Further, 68% of the volunteers joined the Red Army during the summer (May to September), when most of those with ties to the land would need to be on their farm. As many as 70% of the volunteers had previously taken part in the First World War; many of them had become accustomed to the army as a way of life. An almost identical proportion (68%) was aged between 18 and 31, while 63% of the volunteers were bachelors.[220]

In this context, the compulsory conscription of all peasants aged 21 to 25 (born between 1893 and 1897), declared in the Volga, Urals, and West Siberian Military Districts on 12 June 1918, stood little chance of success. Barely one-fifth of the enlisted peasant recruits were successfully mobilized during 1918.[221] The majority of the recruits, like the volunteers, comprised mobile elements from the margins of peasant society—the young ex-servicemen and rural proletarian elements with only weak ties to the land. According to a survey in January 1919, 68% of those enlisted from Vol'sk district had previously served in the Imperial Army.[222] The revolutionary enthusiasm of these young men, whose formative years had been spent in the army, made them

[220] *Izvestiia Narodnogo Komissariata po Voennym Delam*, no. 10, 16 Jan. 1919, p. 3. V. D. Polikarpov ('Dobrovol'tsy 1918 goda', *Voprosy istorii*, 1983, no. 2, p. 30) has argued that the large number of volunteers during the summer reflected a heightened sense of class struggle at that time, whereas I would stress the rootlessness of the summer recruits, and particularly their weak ties to the land. John Erickson ('The Origins of the Red Army', in R. Pipes (ed.), *Revolutionary Russia*, Harvard, 1968, p. 237) has pointed out that 20 per cent of the volunteers in Samara province were rejected on the first 'sifting' (*fil'tratsiia*), because of their poor health—a factor underlining the significance of the 'vagabond, unstable elements', highlighted by Trotsky.

[221] *DSV*, vol. 2, pp. 428–9; *Istoriia sovetskogo kres'tianstva*, vol. 1, p. 131.

[222] TsGAOR, f. 393, op. 3, d. 332, l. 14.

eminently recruitable. Knowing little of peacetime conditions, some of them must have welcomed the chance to re-enlist in the army rather than return to the dull routines of village life. Similar feelings were found among the landless rural types recruited by the *kombedy*. The *kombedy* in Samara province were ordered on 22 November to mobilize five members each for the Red Army.[223] By the following April, more than 40,000 former members of the *kombedy* had been mobilized in European Russia. The Red Army recruited a similar number of Bolshevik party members during the autumn of 1918.[224] The arrival on the Eastern Front of reinforcements from northern Russia and the anti-German screens during the autumn and winter of 1918 increased the dominance of proletarian elements in the Red Army within the Volga region.

The peasantry deployed a wide variety of tactics to sabotage the Red Army conscriptions. The communes, the village soviets, and the VIKs spent a great deal of energy petitioning the district authorities for an exemption of their members from military service, usually on the grounds of their 'indispensability' to the local community, but sometimes on the grounds of their religious beliefs (which were still a legitimate pretext not to serve in the Red Army).[225] For example, during 1919–20 the VIK in Androsovka (Nikolaevsk *uezd*) petitioned the military committee (*voenkom*) in the district town for an exemption on behalf of the following people, all of whom were said to be 'indispensable' (*ne zamenimy*) to the soviet: the assistant to the secretary of the VIK; a clerk in the provisions department of the VIK; a second clerk in the military department; a third clerk in the land department; a fourth clerk in the administrative department; the local station-master; three soviet postmen (and the brother of one of them, who was farming his allotment for him); two soviet firemen; five soviet millers; the stoker of a soviet steam-mill; two windmill operators; the head of the *volost'* co-operative shop; a shoe-maker; a leather-worker; four blacksmiths; two harness-makers; and fifty construction workers involved in the building of the school.[226] Most of these petitions had to be repeated every three months, since they only succeeded in getting the call-up delayed. Nevertheless, it was an effective counter-measure against the conscription, and certainly made a job in the soviet, or in one of the social institutions, an attractive proposition to the men in the village of recruitment age.

[223] *SS*, nos. 4–5, 1919, p. 13.
[224] *Istoriia sovetskogo krest'ianstva*, vol. 1, pp. 133–4.
[225] GAKO, f. 81, op. 1, d. 10, l. 244; *SS*, no. 10, 22 Oct. 1919, p. 6.
[226] GAKO, f. 109, op. 3, d. 52, ll. 4, 9–11, 26, 28–31, 36, 39, 42, 44, 47, 49, 62–3, 65–6, 70, 75; op. 4, d. 59, ll. 52, 55, 72, 79, 83.

A more general method of sabotage was for the VIK not to set up a *voenkom*, the organ locally reponsible for the registration and military training of the recruits. According to an NKVD survey in the RSFSR during 1919, only 27.9% of the VIKs had established a *voenkom*.[227] This was largely explained by the traditional domination of the *mir* in the field of military recruitment. Since they lacked detailed information on the rural population, the VIKs were forced to leave the military draft to the communes, which normally did whatever they could to limit the effects of the conscription.[228] Pacifist sentiments ran high among the peasantry after 1918 (see ch. 4, sect. 2). A general gathering of the peasants in Shirokopol' *volost'* (Petrovsk *uezd*) rejected the establishment of a *voenkom* on 30 June 1918 because 'to introduce military training in our *volost'* will threaten the peace in the whole of Europe, and we refuse to have anything more to do with war or human suffering, since this is against human rights and can only benefit the authorities [*vlasti*]'.[229] A general gathering in Dubovo-Umet *volost'* (Samara *uezd*) resolved in December 1918 not to fulfil the conscription order until the government had explained why 'it has not come to an agreement with the White-guard bands in order to bring the civil war to a peaceful conclusion. If the White guards refuse categorically to negotiate, then we will agree to conscript all the men in the *volost'* between the ages of 20 and 40.'[230]

The Soviet military authorities counteracted the passive resistance of the peasantry with a series of tighter controls of the recruitment process. A decree of 28 December 1918 stipulated that the chairman of the VIK was also to be the head of the *voenkom* in the *volost'*. During the call-up period the whole apparatus of the VIK was to be subordinated to the tasks of military recruitment.[231] This measure enabled the party organizations to establish closer supervision of the recruitment process. By 1919, it was estimated that half the personnel of the *volost' voenkomy* in twenty-one provinces of European Russia were members (24%) or sympathizers (26%) of the Bolshevik party, while as many as 22% were industrial workers. In the Volga region 22% were party members and 18% industrial workers, some of whom

227 A. I. Lepeshkin, *Mestnye organy vlasti sovetskogo gosudarstva (1917–1920 gg.)*, Moscow, 1957, p. 257.

228 See e.g. TsGAOR, f. 393, op. 3, d. 322, l. 4; d. 359, ll. 119, 214, 216, 218, 368, 369, 372; d. 332, ll. 73–5; op. 13, d. 578, ll. 96, 141, 160, 163.

229 Ibid., op. 3, d. 336, ll. 157, 158.

230 Ibid., d. 329, ll. 178–9.

231 E. G. Gimpel'son, *Sovety v gody interventsii i grazhdanskoi voiny*, Moscow, 1968, pp. 288–9; S. M. Kliatskin, *Na zashchite Oktiabria: Organizatsiia reguliarnoi armii i militsionnoe stroitel'stvo v Sovetskoi respublike, 1917–1920 gg.*, Moscow, 1965, pp. 333 ff.; TsGAOR, f. 393, op. 3, d. 359, l. 250.

had been sent by trade unions and urban party organizations to supervise the recruitment and agitate among the peasantry.[232] Where these outsiders dominated the recruitment process, coercive methods were frequently used. In some villages the recruiting brigade called a general meeting, where anyone refusing to obey the conscription order would be punished separately. Elsewhere, the brigade threatened to punish any member of the village soviet failing to enlist his quota of recruits during the specified period.[233]

The recruiting brigades were not infrequently met by open peasant resistance, as in the following incident, reported by a recruiting officer in Samara district during December 1918:

> in the village of Studenets a large crowd of 3,000 people had gathered; people from the crowd started to shout that they would not join the Red Army, and that they would arm their own brigade in the village instead. When we tried to arrest these trouble-makers the crowd surrounded us and tried to disarm us . . . Several of our men were beaten up . . . I realized that there was no choice but to run . . . The crowd moved off to the soviet building and tried to force the secretary of the VIK to give up the recruitment lists; next they went with torches around the huts and buildings in the villages [looking for the lists], but found nothing. Then someone suggested ringing the church bells and calling a village gathering . . .

The recruiting officer, having escaped to a neighbouring village, raised a small Red Army detachment, which returned to Studenets and put down the uprising.[234]

During 1919 the recruitment process was improved by shifting from the so-called '*volost'* mobilizations' (the mobilization of fifteen or twenty recruits from each *volost'*), which prevailed in the spring, to the universal mobilization of individual age cohorts, which became the norm from the autumn. The *volost'* mobilizations declared in May 1919 were supposed to enlist 30,100 recruits from five Volga provinces; yet only 4,203 (14%) turned up at the recruiting stations before the middle of June (the proportion for the whole of European Russia was 11.3%).[235] Part of the problem was that the *volost'* mobilizations naturally represented an unfairly heavy burden for the smaller *volosti*,

232 M. A. Molodtsygin, *Raboche-krest'ianskii soiuz 1918–20 gg.*, Moscow, 1987, pp. 64, 131.

233 *Vestnik Komiteta Uchreditel'nogo Sobraniia* (Samara), no. 34, 17 Aug. 1918, p. 4; E. B. Skobelkina, 'Bor'ba partii bol'shevikov protiv melkoburzhuaznoi kontrrevoliutsii v 1918–19 gg. (po materialam Simbirskoi gubernii)', kand. diss., Voronezh, 1967, pp. 180–1. See also N. N. Leitenant, 'Zapiski belogvardeitsa', *Arkhiv russkoi revoliutsii*, vol. 10, 1923, p. 63.

234 TsGAOR, f. 393, op. 3, d. 329, l. 178.

235 Molodtsygin, pp. 135, 254.

whose authorities thus felt justified in opposing the conscription orders.[236] The mobilization of all the male peasants born in one year was seen to be fairer, and was generally easier to administer (although conflicts frequently arose when a peasant had been unjustly conscripted because he could not produce his birth certificate).[237] The establishment of special departments at the district level during the autumn of 1919 to account more accurately the population eligible for recruitment, and the publicity presenting this measure as an alternative to the conscription of additional age groups, eased the mobilization of individual age groups.[238] A more serious problem of the *volost'* mobilizations was the tendency of the peasant communities to fulfil them in the manner of a traditional military draft, selecting recruits from the households with the largest number of eligible males. Since the largest households were usually the richest in terms of their sown area, this was said to have resulted in 'kulak' elements joining the Red Army. Some military authorities used this phenomenon to account for the poor discipline and high rate of desertion in the Red Army.[239]

The number of peasants conscripted by the Red Army increased during 1919–20, as the power of the VIKs and the party cells was strengthened, and Bolshevik propaganda—much of it associating the defeat of the counter-revolution with the defence of the Motherland—began to penetrate the countryside. The experience of the Volga peasantry under the Whites during 1918–19 undoubtedly influenced its support for the Red Army during 1919–20. More peasants were recruited from the Volga region during these years than from any other region of the Soviet Republic.[240] The youngest peasants proved the easiest to mobilize, and the government came increasingly to depend upon them. The mobilization of those aged between 29 and 30 (born in 1889 and 1890) on 22 April 1919 yielded only one-quarter of the eligible recruits in Samara province by the following July. By contrast, the call-up of 20-year-olds (born in 1899) on 1 March enlisted more than 280,000 recruits from the Volga and Urals regions by the beginning of June; and the call-up of 19-year-olds (born in 1900) on 20

[236] For this reason, the Penza authorities allowed some *volosti* to lower their recruitment quotas, provided the district quota was still fulfilled. This measure was subsequently adopted in several other provinces, and was approved in the general instructions on the *volost'* mobilizations published on 20 May 1919 (Molodtsygin, pp. 133–4).

[237] Gimpel'son, *Sovety v gody interventsii i grazhdanskoi voiny*, pp. 294–6; *DGS*, pp. 138–9.

[238] Molodtsygin, pp. 147–8.

[239] See e.g. I. Kutiakov, *S Chapaevym po ural'skim stepiam*, Moscow, 1928, p. 79; TsGAOR, f. 393, op. 3, d. 340, ll. 150, 268; *Izvestiia Narodnogo Komissariata po Voennym Delam*, no. 10, 16 Jan. 1919, p. 3; Molodtsygin, p. 155.

[240] N. Movchin, *Komplektovanie Krasnoi Armii*, Moscow, 1926, p. 110.

May yielded in total some 143,000 recruits by the end of July. Even more impressive was the mobilization of 18-year-olds (born in 1901) on 23 April 1919, which resulted in the appearance of 92.1% of the eligible recruits in the Volga region by the end of the year, of whom 68.2% (95,198) were actually enlisted and trained.[241] By the end of the civil war, when the Red Army had grown to a nominal size of 5 million men, the peasantry represented more than 75% of the recruits.[242]

Table 39 presents data from the 1920 census showing the participation of different age groups of the rural male population in the First

TABLE 39. *Age structure of rural male population participating in the wars of 1914–1918 and 1918–1920, Penza, Samara, and Saratov provinces and European Russia* (%)

Age	Penza		Samara		Saratov		European Russia	
	1914–17	1918–20	1914–17	1918–20	1914–17	1918–20	1914–17	1918–20
15–19	0.07	2.3	0.1	1.7	0.07	2.1	0.1	1.3
20–9	46.3	24.4	30.4	30.5	46.2	36.0	42.8	26.4
30–9	65.6	5.3	60.3	11.3	59.4	14.6	57.7	10.3
40–9	49.2	1.6	40.0	1.7	47.1	3.1	41.9	2.8
50–	1.6	0.05	1.6	0.1	1.5	0.1	1.3	0.1
Total	27.9	4.3	22.5	6.2	24.8	7.8	24.5	5.9

Source: *Itogi perepisi naseleniia 1920 g.*, Moscow, 1928, pp. 174–7.

World War and the civil war. The number of people involved in the civil war was small compared with the number taking part in the 1914-18 war. But since most of the participants in the civil war were aged in their twenties, a relatively large proportion of this age group was involved (up to 36%). Table 40 presents further evidence from the census in Samara province showing the distribution of the rural population registered as 'absent in the army' according to the size of the family household (the census did not give separate figures for the number of people in the White and Red armies). Whereas the average family household with four to six members lost 28.9% of its adult males to the army, the big family household with more than eleven members lost 41.5% of its adult males. This reflected the traditional criteria of the peasant communities in selecting recruits for the military draft. The biggest households were likely to be left by the

[241] GAKO, f. 81, op. 1, d. 10, l. 146; Molodtsygin, pp. 127, 146, 206.

[242] V. M. Andreev, *Pod znamenem proletariata*, Moscow, 1981, p. 179. According to the 1920 Red Army census, only 66 per cent of the Red Army and navy personnel had agricultural occupations (*Biulleten' Tsentral'nogo Statisticheskogo Upravleniia*, no. 66, 1922, p. 41).

TABLE 40. *Rural population registered in the army, Samara province, August 1920*

Family household members	Households	Total men in army	% adult men (18–60 years) in army
1	1,241	21	5.84
2–3	15,003	3,420	29.47
4–6	40,779	13,389	28.90
7–10	27,797	14,893	32.23
11 or more	5,165	5,893	41.49
Total	89,995	37,616	31.69

Source: *Sbornik statisticheskikh svedenii po Samarskoi gubernii*, Samara, 1924, table 20.

draft with a much less favourable ratio of consumers to workers than that of the smaller households, since they contained a large number of dependants.[243] Consequently, the military conscriptions were likely to contribute to the reduction of the sown area and to the high rate of household partitioning among the bigger family households—both factors helping socio-economic levelling among the peasantry.

Although the Red Army managed to enlist a large number of peasants, it suffered from astronomical rates of desertion, especially during the harvest period when the peasant-soldiers were naturally inclined to return to their farms. By the second half of 1919, there were estimated to be 1.5 million Red Army deserters in Russia. On some fronts up to 80% of the enlisted soldiers were registered as deserters during the harvest period.[244] Most of these were adolescents, who had simply failed to appear on time at the recruiting station.[245] They generally turned up at a later date (after the 1919 harvest 975,000 deserters gave themselves up to the recruiting authorities).[246] Others deserted from the ranks. They were known to form Green bands and

[243] Children under the age of 12 represented 38 per cent of the family members in households with more than 11 members, compared with 17 per cent in the households with only 2 to 3 members (*Sbornik statisticheskikh svedenii po Samarskoi gubernii*, Table 20).

[244] J. M. Meijer (ed.), *The Trotsky Papers*, The Hague, 1971, vol. 1, pp. 796–7, 799–800; TsGAOR, f. 393, op. 13, d. 578, l. 195; E. Wollenberg, *The Red Army*, trans. C. Sykes, London, 1978, p. 43.

[245] Many Soviet military authorities associated the high rate of desertion with the policies of extensive recruitment, i.e. mobilizing younger and younger age groups without regard for the quality of the recruits (see e.g. TsGAOR, f. 130, op. 3, d. 199, l. 12). On 8 Aug. 1919 the Revolutionary-Military Soviet of the Republic (Revvoensovet) resolved to delay the mobilization of the youngest age group (born in 1901), although this was reversed in Mar. 1920 (Molodtsygin, pp. 146–7).

[246] Molodtsygin, p. 145.

take to the woods, where they became engaged in a wide variety of activities, including brigandage and armed resistance to the requisitioning brigades and Red Army punitive detachments. The remote woodlands of the Volga region, situated behind the Southern and Eastern Fronts, attracted a large number of deserters, as shown by the data of Vol'sk *uezd* (Table 41). The number of deserters registered in

TABLE 41. *Number of registered deserters from the Red Army, Vol'sk* uezd, *1919–1921*

Period	Surrendered	Arrested	Total	Per day	As % of male population	
					Aged 18–60	In army
1/3/19–1/10/19	4,941	1,257	8,947[a]	41.6	20.03	70.71
23/11/19–26/6/20	3,140	1,632	8,648[a]	39.9	19.36	68.35
1/7/20–12/12/20	2,685	1,573	4,258	25.8	9.53	33.65
2/2/21–1/3/21	1,698	1,949	3,647	130.2	8.16	28.82
1/3/19–1/3/21	12,464	6,411	25,500	34.9	57.09	201.54

[a] Includes deserters from the Red Army garrisons, registered without specification of their method of capture.

Sources: *Doklad vol'skogo uezdnogo ispolkoma sovetov 15 oktiabria 1919 g.*, Vol'sk, 1919, pp. 29–30; *Sbornik materialov 12-mu vol'skomu uezdnomu s"ezdu sovetov 3 iiunia 1920 g.*, Vol'sk, 1920, p. 29; *Materialy k XIII-mu vol'skomu uezdnomu s"ezdu sovetov 12 dekabria 1920 g.*, Vol'sk, 1920, p. 165; *Materialy k XIV-mu vol'skomu uezdnomu s"ezdu sovetov 1 iiunia 1921 g.*, Vol'sk, 1921, p. 47.

Vol'sk during the two years following March 1919 was at least 25,500—a number equal to 57% of the adult rural male population of the district, and twice the number of people from the district registered in the army. The daily number of detected desertions peaked in February 1921, the climax of the Vakhulin–Popov anti-Bolshevik uprising, which was centred in the woodlands of Khvalynsk and Vol'sk after February (see ch. 7, sect. 3). Throughout the Volga region, in the woodland and non-woodland areas, there were very high rates of desertion during this period. The Samara authorities registered 28,808 Red Army deserters in the province during June and July 1920. The military authorities in the Tatar Republic registered 75,681 deserters during 1920, and as many as 99,339 in 1921.[247]

According to the data in Table 41, the number of deserters voluntarily giving themselves up was twice as high as the number arrested by Soviet authorities. The relatively small number of arrests

[247] *Kommunist* (Pugachev), no. 166, 22 Sept. 1920, p. 2; L. M. Iakubova, 'Likvidatsiia kontrrevoliutsionnykh sil v Srednem Povolzh'e 1918–1922 gg. (Na materialakh Kazanskoi, Samarskoi i Simbirskoi gubernii)', kand. diss., Kazan', 1981, p. 189.

reflects the difficulties of tracking down Red Army deserters under the lawless, near-anarchic conditions of the civil war. Hundreds of local soviets were accused—often with justification—of concealing deserters, or failing to take adequate measures against them.[248] On the other hand, the large number of deserters surrendering voluntarily highlights the economic, as opposed to the political, motivation of the majority of the peasant desertions—what the Soviet authorities termed desertions of a 'non-malicious' (*nezloe*) or 'politically unconscious' (*nesoznatel'noe*) kind. Whereas the deserters from the White Army rarely returned to it, or even joined the Reds, those from the Red Army could sometimes be persuaded to return to the front, as illustrated by the famous incident at Sviiazhsk in the autumn of 1918, when Trotsky persuaded a group of deserters to return to the ranks.[249] Also known to be effective in this respect were the 'amnesty weeks', declared during special propaganda campaigns in aid of the Red Army, when deserters were given the opportunity to return to the ranks without punishment.[250]

The mainly economic character of the peasant desertions was reflected in the causes of the latter. The primary motivation of the peasant deserters was to return to their farm for the harvest. According to one survey, the number of deserters in the Volga region at the peak of the 1919 harvest season (August) was five to seven times greater than during the previous April. The same survey found that 43.7% of the deserters from Tambov, Riazan', Tula, and Moscow provinces during January to May 1919 had run away because their unit was close to their home village, while a further 23.2% had deserted because their unit had been assigned to leave for the front.[251] A second common motivation was the deserters' concern for the well-being of their families, most of whom never received the welfare benefits (state pensions, food and clothing rations) promised by the government during the recruitment campaigns. A third major cause of desertion from the Red Army was the chronic supply of food, tobacco, soap,

[248] See e.g. GAKO, f. 81, op. 1, d. 10, l. 74; TsGANKh, f. 1943, op. 1, d. 573, l. 155; *Doklad vol'skogo uezdnogo ispolkoma sovetov 15 oktiabria 1919 g.*, Vol'sk, 1919, pp. 29–30; *Serp i molot* (Kuznetsk), no. 226, 16 Oct. 1920, p. 2; *Kommuna* (Samara), no. 510, 31 Aug. 1920, p. 3; *Stenograficheskii otchet 7-go syzranskogo uezdnogo soveta*, pp. 26–7.

[249] L. Trotksy, *My Life*, Gloucester, Mass., pp. 411–12.

[250] A telegram to Lenin from the Moscow region on 8 Aug. 1919 gave a more negative appraisal of the amnesties: 'the amnesty week went badly, and few appeared. The best agitators were sent . . . but the population did not respond to the call . . . In the countryside there are thousands of provocative rumours. The population is sceptical, and in places hostile, both to the Soviet regime and to communists' (TsGAOR, f. 130, op. 3, d. 199, l. 11).

[251] Molodtsygin, pp. 141, 145. See also Gimpel'son, *Sovety v gody interventsii i grazhdanskoi voiny*, pp. 297, 301; *Istoriia sovetskogo krest'ianstva*, vol. 1, p. 137.

uniforms, boots, guns, and medicine in the ranks and, especially, the rear garrisons. Such shortages sometimes resulted in military units refusing new recruits. The physical conditions of the garrisons were so bad (cholera, typhus, and venereal diseases were widespread) that it was not unknown for soldiers to desert to the front, where the rations were generally better and the chances of getting shot probably not much worse than those of becoming fatally ill in the garrison.[252]

It is probably fair to say that the causes of the peasant desertions became more 'political' in the course of 1920 (according to Table 41, the proportion of deserters voluntarily surrendering fell during 1920). This coincided with the beginning of several major peasant uprisings against the Bolshevik regime in Tambov province, the Volga region, western Siberia, and other areas. Once the Whites had been defeated in the summer and autumn of 1920, the peasantry saw little justification for the continuation of military conscription, food requisitioning, and the other coercive measures of war communism. A growing number of peasants deserted from the ranks and formed themselves into Green bands in order to fight the Red Army recruiting brigades, the food brigades, and the other detachments of Soviet power. Unable to stem the tide of desertion through the local soviets, whose authority in the countryside was rapidly declining, the Red Army dispatched punitive detachments into the strongholds of peasant desertion to carry out a brutal campaign of repression. The detachments occupied whole villages, threatening to confiscate the property of anyone concealing deserters, or taking as hostages the relatives of deserters. In a number of villages the leaders of the soviet were shot as an example to the rest of the peasants. Some villages suspected of harbouring a large number of deserters were surrounded by the Red troops and razed to the ground when the deserters failed to give themselves up.[253] Such measures inevitably strengthened the opposition of the deserters—and the whole of the rural population—to the Bolshevik regime. The small peasant armies turned their localities into 'no-go' areas, tearing up the

[252] TsGAOR, f. 130, op. 3, d. 105, ll. 207–8; f. 393, op. 3, d. 322, l. 534; d. 329, l. 20; d. 359, ll. 88–9; op. 13, d. 429, l. 63; d. 578, l. 290; TsGANKh, f. 3429, op. 1, d. 1586, l. 8; f. 1943, op. 6, d. 376, l. 9; f. 478, op. 6, d. 2010, ll. 62–3; *Izvestiia Narodnogo Komissariata po Voennym Delam*, no. 8, 14 Jan. 1919, p. 4; *Protokoly i doklady VII-go simbirskogo gubernskogo s''ezda sovetov*, Simbirsk, 1919, p. 74 and app. 2, pp. 18–25; *Voennaia mysl'*, no. 3, 30 Apr. 1919, pp. 40, 43; *Krasnoarmeets* (Saratov), no. 8, 24 Nov. 1918, p. 16; no. 10, 13 Dec. 1918, p. 14; no. 5, 23 Feb. 1919, p. 23; *Revoliutsionnaia armiia* (Samara), no. 59, 16 Mar. 1919, p. 4; *DGS*, pp.183–4; D. D. F. White, *The Growth of the Red Army*, Princeton, 1944, pp. 100–3, 114; Chamberlin, vol. 2, p. 30; Molodtsygin, p. 63.

[253] GAKO, f. 81, op. 1, d. 10, l. 109; *DGS*, pp. 114–47; Iakubova, pp. 137–9; *Izvestiia* (Atkarsk), no. 139, 8 Oct. 1920, p. 2; *Luch Kommuny* (Buguruslan), no. 473, 25 Nov. 1920, p. 1; *Kommuna* (Petrovsk), no. 101, 23 Dec. 1920, p. 2; *Kommuna* (Samara), no. 529, 22 Sept. 1920, p. 2.

railway lines, pulling down the telegraph poles, terrorizing local party and soviet officials, and setting ambushes for passing Red troops.[254] It was from these local wars that the mass peasant uprisings against the Bolshevik regime took shape after 1919. The latter will form the subject of the next chapter.

[254] See TsGAOR, f. 393, op. 13, d. 582, l. 26; d. 578, l. 278; *Izvestiia* (Balashov), no. 133, 22 June 1919, p. 2; *Stenograficheskii otchet 7-go syzranskogo uezdnogo soveta*, pp. 26–7; *Vestnik Komiteta Uchreditel'nogo Sobraniia*, no. 31, 14 Aug. 1918, p. 2.

7

Peasant Wars

Boga net, tsaria ne nado,
Komissarov razob'em,
Krasnuiu armiiu razgonim
Muku sami my voz'mem.

There is no God, we don't need a Tsar,
We're going to smash the Commissars,
We'll drive away the Red Army
And take the flour for us.

Peasant song (*chastushka*) at the time of the civil war.

A MAP of the Russian civil war in any standard history shows the main battle lines between the Reds and the Whites, with the most important offensives marked out in a series of arrows. The destiny of the thousands of unmarked villages appears to be tied to the fortunes of the dominant army in the given region, an army which the peasants were obliged to feed and equip with transport and soldiers. Yet, if we were to look in greater detail at any one area behind the main battle lines in the eastern Ukraine, in western Siberia, in the northern Caucasus, in parts of White Russia and Central Asia, in the Volga region and Tambov province, then we would find a series of smaller 'peasant wars' against the Reds and the Whites. These wars, which aimed to establish peasant rule in the localities against the authority of the central state, were in Lenin's estimation 'far more dangerous than all the Denikins, Yudeniches, and Kolchaks put together, since we are dealing with a country where the proletariat represents a minority'.[1] Together with the Kronshtadt mutiny and a series of workers' revolts, they forced the Bolshevik leadership in March 1921 to abandon the unpopular policies of war communism in favour of a free trade under the NEP. Having defeated the White Army, backed by eight Western powers, the Bolshevik government surrendered before its own peasantry.

It would be interesting to compare all the various peasant wars during this period. What did the uprisings in the Ukraine and Siberia, in White Russia and the Caucasus, have in common, in spite of the huge geographical distances between them? Soviet historians, unable to admit the existence of popular resistance to the Bolshevik regime, have dismissed these uprisings as 'kulak revolts', stage-managed by the

[1] *PSS*, vol. 43, p. 18.

opposition parties and their allies abroad.[2] The empirical poverty of this interpretation is such that it does not warrant a detailed critique. Suffice to say that the few Western studies so far completed of the Makhno uprising in the Ukraine and the Antonov uprising in Tambov province have established beyond doubt the mass appeal of these movements among the peasantry.[3]

The uprisings in the Volga region during 1919–21 (see Map 5) shared a number of common features with those in the Ukraine and Tambov province. They broke out in response to the social and political changes outlined in Chapters 5 and 6: an intolerable increase in the tax burden on the rural economy as a result of the civil war; a sharp swing in the urban-rural terms of trade against the peasantry; and a process of political centralization, which undermined the influence of the peasants in the local soviets, destroyed the power-base of the opposition parties, and gave rise to a dictatorship of the Bolshevik cadres in the *volost'* townships and the provincial towns, along with the Red Army, the requisitioning brigades, and the other mobile organs of the state. The peasant struggles became more violent only as the passive forms of economic resistance to the state failed to meet their objectives: the sabotage of the food requisitionings and the sporadic village riots of 1918–19 developed into the mass peasant wars of 1920–1 as the economic crisis deepened. The appearance of the 'peasant armies' in the field awaited the final defeat of the Whites: because they supported the October revolution, the peasants dared not endanger the Bolshevik government until the counter-revolution had been defeated; indeed, the peasants could only hope to defeat the Bolshevik regime after it had been exhausted by the civil war.

The Volga uprisings shared common features in their aims, objectives, and tactics. They sought, for the most part, to restore the localized village democracy of the revolution, which had been lost as a result of the civil war and the emergence of the Bolshevik state. They aimed not to march on Moscow so much as to cut themselves off from

[2] The classic Soviet account is I. Ia. Trifonov, *Klassy i klassovaia bor'ba v SSSR v nachale NEPa (1921–23 gg.)*, vol. 1, *Bor'ba s vooruzhennoi kulatskoi kontrrevoliutsiei*, Leningrad, 1964. In the 1920s some Soviet historians saw the uprisings as rural wars against the towns: see e.g. M. I. Kubanin, 'Anti-sovetskoe krest'ianskoe dvizhenie v gody grazhdanskoi voiny (voennogo kommunizma)', *Na agrarnom fronte*, 1926, no. 2; A. Kazakov, 'Obshchie prichiny vozniknoveniia banditizma i krest'ianskikh vosstanii', *Krasnaia armiia*, 1921, no. 9; N. Kakurin, 'Organizatsiia bor'by s banditizmom po opytu tambovskogo i vitebskogo komandovanii', *Voennaia nauka i revoliutsiia*, 1922, no. 1.

[3] See e.g. M. Malet, *Nestor Makhno in the Russian Civil War*, London, 1982; O. H. Radkey, *The Unknown Civil War in Soviet Russia*, Stanford, 1976. For a general survey of the peasant revolts see M. Frenkin, *Tragediia krest'ianskikh vosstanii v Rossii 1918–1921 gg.*, Jerusalem, 1987.

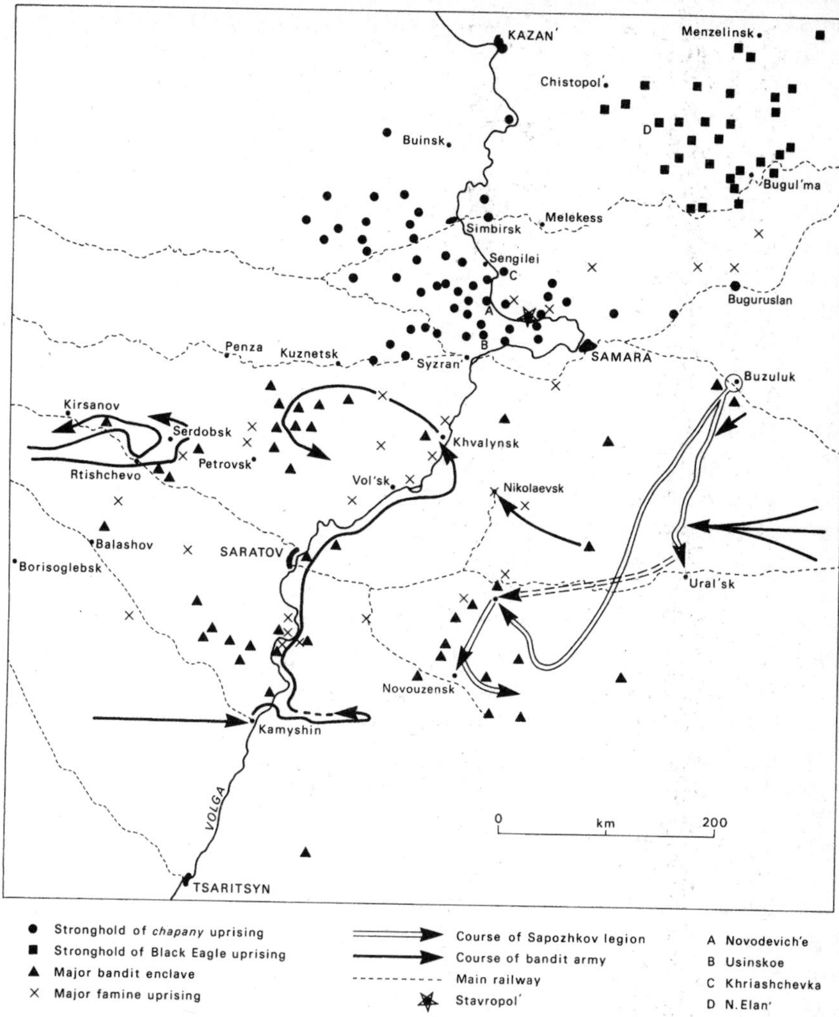

Map 5. *Peasant wars in the Volga region, 1919–22*

its influence by fighting a guerrilla and terrorist war against the Red Army and the state officials in the countryside.

Each uprising developed in its own form, according to the context in which it operated. Four main types of peasant armed resistance to the Bolshevik regime may be delineated in the Volga region during this period:

1. The spontaneous village uprising, or riot, against the local officials, often accompanied by lynch law (*samosud*), pillage, and violent acts of vengeance. Such uprisings were generally short-lived

and easily suppressed, although they recurred frequently and were, in Lenin's own words, 'a permanent feature of the general Russian picture' under war communism.[4]

2. The general peasant uprising, similar in form to the village riot, but on a broader scale and with better organization. Such uprisings (e.g. the wars of the *chapany* and the Black Eagle) began with the peasants in one of the villages ousting the local officials, electing their own soviet, forming a militia, and spreading the word of revolt to the neighbouring villages. As they expanded, these uprisings developed sophisticated forms of political and military organization, within which the local SRs and the odd White Army officer were able to play a subsiduary role. They were most commonly noted in areas where the mass of the peasantry had been heavily overburdened by taxes during the civil war.

3. The Red Army mutiny or *guerrilla* by Green bands of deserters. These usually took a specifically military form, although they often espoused an anti-Bolshevik ideology similar to that of the peasant uprisings, and developed close links with the rural population. The bands of deserters played a key role in the *chapany* uprising, for example, while A. P. Sapozhkov's mutinous Red Army division enjoyed a broad base of peasant support.

4. Banditry. Soviet historians have used the term 'political banditism' to describe virtually any form of peasant resistance to the Bolshevik regime after 1920. This is misleading, since banditry, in its 'social' and criminal forms,[5] played a number of different insurrectionary roles, especially during the famine crisis, and these merit special attention.

1. THE WARS OF THE *CHAPANY* AND THE BLACK EAGLE

The term for a tunic or caftan (*chapan*, pl. *chapany*) was used by the peasants of the Volga region to distinguish themselves from townsmen. The *chapan* was a familiar badge of the peasantry, instantly identifying its wearer as a humble farmer, and setting him apart from the *intelligenty* in suits, the workers in overalls, and the Bolsheviks in black leather jackets. The peasant called his neighbour a *chapan* when he wanted to poke fun at his 'rustic' simplicity. If a peasant had done something foolish, he might be called a *lapot'* (a bast-sandal) or a *chapan* by his peers. Thus, by christening their anti-Bolshevik uprising of March 1919 a 'war of the *chapany*' (*chapannaia voina*), the peasants

4 *PSS*, vol. 45, p. 285.

5 For a discussion of 'social banditry' see in particular E. J. Hobsbawm, *Primitive Rebels*, London, 1959; id., *Bandits*, London, 1969.

were underlining its distinctively rural character in opposition to the towns.

The war of the *chapany* took place in the deeply rural districts of Syzran', Sengilei, and Stavropol', immediately behind the Eastern Front (see Map 5). The Bolshevik party reports on the uprising compiled after its suppression in April 1919 were unanimous that it had been caused by the ruthless requisitioning of the peasantry's grain and property by the Bolshevik authorities during the autumn and winter of 1918–19.[6] Some peasant households had lost their last cow to the requisitioning brigades. Others had lost farmyard animals and domestic property, although the law prohibited such exactions. Entire villages had been left without food and seed stores, because the Red Army had indiscriminately seized farm produce from the villages before its departure in February 1919. The peasants had been commandeered to transport military personnel to and from the front, to fell timber in the surrounding forests, and to repair the Volga bridges destroyed by the Whites. They had lost an inordinate number of horses and carts to the army. And it was later discovered that the Syzran' garrison had mobilized a much larger number of peasant conscripts from these regions than was officially permitted. During the winter the *kombedy* and the party cells had carried out a violent campaign to exact the Chreznalog, which, it was admitted, had been set far in excess of the wealth of this 'overwhelmingly middle-peasant region'.[7] When the local soldiers in the Syzran' garrison read in their mail and heard it confirmed by anti-Bolshevik agitators that their own families had been forced illegally to pay the Chreznalog, they deserted in large numbers and returned to their villages to help in the organization of the uprising.

Apart from these economic factors, the uprising had been caused by a growing political conflict between the peasantry and the Bolsheviks. The Syzran' party was small, dominated by Latvians, and inclined towards dictatorial methods. The party coup of April 1918, which had temporarily overthrown Soviet power in the district,[8] had been followed by a series of party repressions during the autumn and winter of 1918–19. The district party instructors who had been sent into the villages to re-establish Soviet power after the defeat of the Komuch had removed icons from schools and social institutions, and had generally

[6] TsGAOR, f. 393, op. 13, d. 429, ll. 67–8, 76–81; op. 3, d. 339, l. 16; TsGANKh, f. 1943, op. 4, d. 116, ll. 168–9; op. 1, d. 448, ll. 134–5; N. V. Gur'ev, *Chapannaia voina*, Syzran', 1924, pp. 20–31.

[7] TsGAOR, f. 393, op. 3, d. 339, l. 16.

[8] Ibid., op. 13, d. 429, ll. 76–9.

abused their positions.[9] The Bolshevik-dominated VIKs had been accused of dictatorial methods (*ispolkomshchina*). 'In the localities', admitted R. E. Zirin, the chairman of the Syzran' district soviet, in his report on the uprising, 'the impression had been given that the Soviet regime knew only how to demand and command, but not how to give.'[10]

The political dimension was important during the events leading up to the outbreak of the uprising on 3 March in the big trading village of Novodevich'e (Sengilei *uezd*). For some time, the local party cell and the VIK had been engaged in a power struggle against the village soviets, the communes and the co-operative institutions, which had remained under the influence of the richest peasants and local traders. The January soviet elections had been accompanied by scuffles between the rival village groups, ending in the murder of the assistant to the chairman of the VIK and the arrest of four peasants by the district Cheka. This had been followed by a conflict between the peasants and a Red Army punitive detachment searching for deserters in the villages. On 6 March the peasantry finally rose up when a food brigade arrived and began, with the help of the VIK, to requisition livestock from the peasants.[11]

Soviet historians have depicted the *chapany* uprising as a 'counter-revolutionary kulak' revolt, carefully orchestrated by the SRs and Kolchak's spies.[12] Although these allegations are not supported by source citations, it is reasonable to assume that there may have been some SRs or White agents among the *chapany*. During the summer of 1918 the Novodevich'e region had been occupied by the Czech legion and the People's Army, which on their retreat were likely to have left behind agents for underground work.[13] None the less, this need not alter the fact that the uprising was a popular and spontaneous one. The SRs and the White agents in the crowd were far too few to affect the basic character of the peasant movement.

The mass, spontaneous nature of the uprising was reflected in the speed with which it spread. The rising in Novodevich'e—a wealthy

[9] E. B. Skobelkina, 'Simbirskie bol'sheviki v bor'be s kulatskim miatezhom vesnoi 1919 g.', in *Uchenye zapiski ul'ianovskogo gosudarstvennogo pedagogicheskogo instituta*, vyp. 1, Ul'ianovsk, 1966, p. 208.

[10] TsGAOR, f. 393, op. 13, d. 429, l. 78.

[11] Ibid., op. 3, d. 339, ll. 16–17; Gur'ev, pp. 5–6, 14–16, 21, 27; *Voennaia mysl'*, no. 3, 30 Apr. 1919, pp. 12–13; Skobelkina, 'Simbirskie bol'sheviki', pp. 221–5.

[12] See e.g. A. L. Litvin, *Krest'ianstvo Srednego Povolzh'ia v gody grazhdanskoi voiny*, Kazan', 1972, pp. 172 ff.; E. I. Medvedev, *Krest'ianstvo Srednego Povolzh'ia v gody grazhdanskoi voiny (1918–19 gg.)*, Saratov, 1974, p. 205; L. M. Spirin, 'Kommunisticheskaia partiia—organizator razgroma Kolchaka', *Voprosy istorii*, 1956, no.6, p. 101.

[13] A. Zaitsev, *1918 god: Ocherki po istorii russkoi grazhdanskoi voiny*, n.p., 1934, p. 169.

village with many peasant institutions—developed relatively slowly, in comparison with the subsequent village uprisings in Simbirsk and Samara provinces. The peasantry's clash with the food brigade had occurred on 3 March, when a general *skhod* was called to discuss further action. On 4–5 March the postal-telegraph office was captured and the *volost'* provisions commissar and local Cheka boss were murdered. On 6 March the chairman of the VIK was arrested by the peasant crowd, which then elected its own soviet and set up a military staff (*shtab*). The young men of the village were conscripted, and the blacksmiths mobilized to manufacture pikes. A proclamation was drawn up and sent around the neighbouring villages calling upon them to join the uprising. On 7 March the Novodevich'e peasant army—a force of several hundred men with more than a hundred supply carts—advanced 20 km. southwards to establish the military headquarters of the uprising at Usinskoe, a predominantly middle-peasant village, 25 km. north of Syzran'. Within twenty-four hours of this march, uprisings had broken out in the following *volosti*: Russkie Bektiashi, Gorodishche, Sobakino, Terengul', and Popovka (Sengilei *uezd*); Usol'e, Zhiguli, Pecherskoe, and Shigoni (Syzran' *uezd*); and Iagodnoe, St Binaradka, Eriklin, Cherdaklin, and Khriashchevka (Stavropol' *uezd*). At its zenith, during the second week of March, the uprising had spread to at least 24 of the 45 *volosti* in Syzran' district; to 5 of the 14 *volosti* in Sengilei district; to 10 of the 24 *volosti* in Karsun district; and to 7 of the 13 *volosti* in Stavropol' district. It was a major presence in the neighbouring districts of Ardatov, Alatyr', Buinsk, Simbirsk, Samara, Buzuluk, and Buguruslan. The only town to fall to the peasant insurgents was Stavropol' (7 March), an agricultural and small-craft town, which remained the political centre of the rising until its capture by the Red Army on 12 March. Syzran', like Karsun, never fell, despite several offensives. But the political situation in the town remained volatile: the garrison, which comprised local peasant soldiers, had to be disarmed; and hundreds of arrests were made in the town. The total number of participants in the uprisings was estimated to be approximately 150,000 people, a figure which puts beyond doubt the mass nature of this anti-Bolshevik war.[14]

The institutional and social forms of the uprising displayed a remarkable uniformity, stemming from the common traditions of

[14] TsGAOR, f. 393, op. 13, d. 429, ll. 67–8, 79; Gur'ev, pp. 5–8, 20–31; Skobelkina, 'Simbirskie bol'sheviki', pp. 228–9; *Simbirskaia guberniia v 1918–1920 gg.: Sbornik vospominanii*, Ul'ianovsk, 1958, p. 390; L. M. Iakubova, 'Likvidatsiia kontrrevoliutsionnykh sil v Srednem Povolzh'e 1918–1922 gg. (Na materialakh Kazanskoi, Samarskoi i Simbirskoi gubernii)', kand. diss., Kazan', 1981, pp. 88–96; V. V. Romanenko, 'Sozdanie, razvitie i deiatel'nost' organov ChK i vnutrennikh voisk sovetskoi respubliki v Srednem Povolzh'e i Priural'e v 1918–22 gg.', kand. diss., Kuibyshev, 1977, p. 129.

Russian peasant organization and the general context of rural unrest, rather than any preconceived plan of co-ordinated action. At every point of the uprising the crowd played a dominant role. On the arrival of the messengers from a neighbouring insurgent village, the peasants convened a general village *skhod* to decide whether to join the uprising. The voice of a local priest or a Left SR occasionally tipped the balance of opinion in favour of an uprising, but the messengers often found that they only had to communicate the news to get the peasants to rise up. This decision was expressed in a communal resolution. Tough social pressures were put on the waverers to get into line: men who refused to join the village militia were known to lose their land rights in the village; peasants who objected to the uprising were subjected to 'rough music' (*charivari*), or even a *samosud*. Similar methods were used against the victims of the uprising—party officials, members of the collective farms, the personnel of the requisitioning brigades, and local residents seen to be in alliance with the Bolsheviks (e.g. millers, co-operative workers, minor soviet officials). The anger of the crowd often spilled over into personal acts of vengeance and gory murders. In the village of Khriashchevka (Stavropol' *uezd*) nine members of a food-requisitioning brigade were drowned under the ice on the Volga River. In the village of Repinskoe (Karsun *uezd*) the chairman of the district party was beheaded agitating against the revolt; his body was thrown into the river and his head put on top of a stake.[15]

The military organization of the uprising was sophisticated. The headquarters at Usinskoe decided military strategy and distributed the few pieces of advanced weaponry in the hands of the rebels (e.g. cannon, machine-guns). It divided the forces on a territorial basis (one regiment per *volost'*) and issued detailed operational orders. At the height of the uprising the 'peasant army' numbered approximately 20,000 armed conscripts between the ages of 18 and 36 (in some places 18 and 50). The territorial basis of the army facilitated the procurement of military supplies, since each *volost'* was responsible for feeding and equipping its own regiment. This link between the regiments and the villages was essential for the guerrilla-type operations carried out by the peasant army ordinary peasants could serve as spies in the Red-controlled villages, while armed insurgents could be disguised as peasants before surprise attacks and ambushes. The first Red Army

[15] TsGAOR, f. 393, op. 13, d. 429, l. 79; Gur'ev, p. 7; N. F. Lysikhin, 'Razgrom kontrrevoliutsionnogo miatezha na srednem Volge v 1919 g.', in *Kraevedcheskie zapiski*, Kuibyshev, 1963, p. 120; Skobelkina, 'Simbirskie bol'sheviki', p. 230; Romanenko, p. 129.

units sent to suppress the uprising were utterly trounced by the peasant army for this reason.[16] At Usinskoe, where the Reds were surrounded by the guerrillas on 7 March, twenty Bolshevik officers were taken hostage (the rank and file were released). At Khriashchevka, on 11 March, 200 peasant rebels, fighting, in the words of one Red commander, 'with indescribable heroism', repulsed a force of 700 Red Army soldiers, having turned the centre of the village into a deadly ambush.[17] The effectiveness of such guerrilla tactics, which had not been previously encountered by the Soviet military, was in large part due to the influence of the peasant deserters from the civil war armies and the ex-servicemen of the First World War, who were prominent in the insurgent village bands. The vast majority of the rebel fighters, however, were ordinary peasants—a fact suggested by the primitive nature of their weaponry (pikes, axes, clubs, boat-hooks, pitchforks, and hoes).[18]

The insurgent bands shunned direct conflict with the Red Army and sought to cut off the strongholds of the uprising from the Bolshevik-controlled towns. Telegraph poles were cut down, railway tracks were pulled up, and roads were made impassable by ambushes. The offensives against Stavropol', Syzran', and Karsun aimed to paralyse the nearest urban centres of Bolshevik power and establish peasant control of the town infrastructure. In Stavropol', the only town to fall to the insurgents, a soviet was established on 9 March with peasant, trade-unionist, and urban representatives. The trade unions were organized into a 'soviet of unions' (*sovet soiuzov*), which conscripted its members for the insurgent army. The capture of the town was accompanied by the looting of shops and attacks on the bakeries and mills, since the insurgents were unable to resist this opportunity to avenge their losses during the requisitioning campaigns.[19]

The main political objective of the uprising was to re-establish the soviets without the party cadres. All the slogans of the movement revolved around this theme: 'Down with the domination of the Communists and Anarchists! Long live the power of the soviets on the platform of the October revolution!' (Usol'e *volost'*, Syzran' *uezd*);

[16] The Red Army experienced similar difficulties against the guerrillas in Tambov, whom Antonov-Ovseenko described as 'scarcely vulnerable, extraordinarily invisible, and, so to speak, ubiquitous', ('O banditskom dvizhenii v Tambovskoi gubernii', in J. M. Meijer (ed.), *The Trotsky Papers*, The Hague, 1971, vol. 2, p. 504).

[17] Kubanin, 'Anti-sovetskoe krest'ianskoe dvizhenie', p. 41; B. N. Chistov, 'Krakh chapannogo miatezha', *Volga*, vol. 4 (100), 1974, pp. 157 ff.; TsGAOR, f. 393, op. 13, d. 429, l. 79; *Voennaia mysl'*, no. 3, 30 Apr. 1919, p. 11; Lysikhin, pp. 119–20, 122.

[18] TsGAOR, f. 393, op. 13, d. 429, l. 67; Lysikhin, p. 120; Gur'ev, pp. 7, 11.

[19] Lysikhin, pp. 121–5.

'Down with the Communists! Long live the soviets!' (various districts).[20] The politics of the uprising were couched in terms of the restoration of the soviet democracy established during the October revolution. The transformation of the VIKs and the district soviets into state organs for the taxation of the peasantry was seen to contravene the principle of 'All power to the soviets', whereby the peasants would be left to control their own villages, their own system of land use, and their own market sales. The peasants did not need the Left SRs to tell them this; we may safely discount the claim of Soviet historians that the Left SRs formulated the slogans of the uprising in an effort to win the peasantry over to counter-revolution. It is difficult to imagine the Left SRs approving the slogan 'Down with the Communists! Long live the Bolsheviks!', under which many of the peasant insurgents, evidently confused by the renaming of the party, went into battle.[21] It is equally unlikely that the Left SRs would have formulated either of these slogans, widely noted among the *chapany*: 'Long live Lenin! Down with Trotsky!' (some villages had this slogan reversed);[22] 'Down with the power of the Communist party in the soviets! Long live the Russian Federative Republic headed by the Bolshevik party, which is the only true defender of our All-Russian revolution!'[23] The meaning of these slogans is not hard to disentangle: whereas the 'Bolsheviks' had carried out the October revolution and had issued the Decree on Land, the 'Communists' had sent the requisitioning brigades into the villages and had set up the *kommuny*. By appealing to an established structure of revolutionary power (the soviets), the peasant insurgents were seeking to legitimize and give a legal form to their own complaints against the Bolsheviks. The proclamations of the *chapany* often expressed outrage against the 'communist-violators and hooligans' (*kommunisty-nasil'niki i bezobrazniki*) in the district soviets and the VIKs. The insurgent villagers of Beketovka (Sengilei) resolved, for example:

> some individuals in power, having forgotten about the resolutions of the central authorities and having cast aside their own conscience, are carrying out an illegitimate government of their own, which undermines the whole authority of Soviet power. They make illegal threats like: 'we'll take the sheep's hides of the peasants', or 'we'll pour away the peasants' kerosene and burn it'. They ride around on the horses they have taken from the peasants. We, citizens, consider such actions to be not only offensive, but also unjust and

20 Gur'ev, p. 6; TsGAOR, f. 393, op. 13, d. 429, l. 68.
21 *Voennaia mysl'*, no. 3, 30 Apr. 1919, p. 13.
22 Ibid.
23 Skobelkina, 'Simbirskie bol'sheviki', p. 237.

illegal; these people have made all of us indignant, to which we sign below. . .[24]

A similar proclamation was issued by the political leadership of the Stavropol' town soviet in its newspaper, *Izvestiia*:

Comrades, peasants, and citizens of Soviet Russia! You are right to resist the domination of a few Communists since this political party of Bolsheviks and Communists contains many tramps and hooligans, in the spiritual and physical sense, who are not even able to look after themselves and their own comrades honourably. Peasants, now you are eager to fight and if necessary die in the struggle against these rascals, but remember that you still have the soviets. The soviets are your flesh and blood, they are the means by which you threw off the chains of servitude.

The former defenders of the Constituent Assembly also recognize that only the power of the soviets, of the poorest peasants and workers, will consolidate our achievements . . .

Citizens-intelligentsia! Help the peasants understand their movement; direct them towards the wisest path! Join the peasants and help them in their difficult task![25]

In so far as the Communists were seen to have betrayed the October revolution, the *chapany* believed their protest was just and legitimate. Wherever the Communists were ousted from power the soviets were re-elected on a democratic basis. In some villages, such as Usol'e and Berezovka (Syzran' *uezd*), the Communist chairman of the VIK was allowed to remain in office, provided he agreed to carry out the resolutions of the *volost'* soviet assembly. The *chapany* established local *sovnarkhozy*, elected *prodkomy*, and called their military departments *voenkomy*. As a Red Army commander put it, the *chapany* in every respect aimed to reconstruct their own local '*sovdepia*' (soviet apparatus).[26]

The military defeat of the *chapany* was to be expected, given their primitive weaponry, their poor organizational resources, and their weak links with the anti-Bolshevik forces in other regions. The *chapany* might have continued to fend off small Red Army cavalry units, but they were unable to resist the steady advance of a large modern army with cannon, machine-guns, and armoured vehicles. After the first round of humiliating defeats at the hands of the peasant rebels, the party authorities in Samara and Simbirsk carried out a general mobilization of party workers and students, and called for reinforcements from Moscow and the neighbouring provinces. The

24 *Voennaia mysl'*, no. 3, 30 Apr. 1919, p. 14.
25 Ibid.
26 Ibid. See also Gur'ev, pp. 7, 9.

Samara authorities raised 10,000 soldiers and the Simbirsk authorities 3,000. Frunze dispatched part of the 4th Army to Syzran'. Smaller district towns, such as Karsun, Alatyr', and Kuznetsk, raised armed units of between 100 and 300 men each. The Red offensive was launched simultaneously from the four closest district towns under Bolshevik control: Samara, Melekess, Syzran', and Sengilei. It was controlled by the *revkomy* and a special Revolutionary Field Headquarters in Samara, which operated under martial law. A combined Red Army force of cavalry and infantry with machine-guns took just over four days to complete a pincer movement from Samara to Stavropol', which fell on 13 March. The same day marked the third and last assault on Khriashchevka, the most resilient *chapany* stronghold. The village was attacked from the north and the south by a combined force of engineers and students from Melekess and Samara. After a five-hour battle in the market square, this 'fortress' of the peasant resistance was finally taken. The combined Red forces of Syzran', Samara, and Penza were less successful against the peasant rebels in Usinskoe, the military headquarters of the *chapany* uprising. A battle on 14 March ended in heavy losses for the Red Army and no prospect of victory. The village was surrounded and set on fire, its inhabitants gunned down as they fled for their lives. Novodevich'e, the last remaining stronghold of the uprising, was taken by a regiment of workers from Samara on 15 March. Minor operations had to be continued against the *chapany* in parts of Syzran', Karsun, Ardatov, and Alatyr' until the end of the month.[27]

The military suppression of the *chapany* was followed by a period of intense political work and agitation in the insurgent area. On Lenin's instructions, an enquiry was carried out into the soviet and party institutions of Simbirsk province.[28] Workers from the provincial and district levels were sent into the countryside to carry out propaganda work and reorganize the local soviets and party cells. The Bolshevik party recovered its influence in the VIKs during the soviet re-elections of April, largely on account of the low electoral turn-out and the heavy presence of the Red Army and party agitators: 77.3% of the VIK members after April belonged to the Bolshevik party in the eight

[27] TsGAOR, f. 393, op. 3, d. 359, l. 308; op. 13, d. 429, l. 67–8; GAKO, f. 81, op. 1, d. 10, l. 57; Romanenko, p. 130; *10 let Oktiabria v Alatyrskom uezde, Chuvashskoi respubliki: Sbornik statei*, Alatyr', 1927, pp. 22–3; *M. V. Frunze na frontakh grazhdanskoi voiny*, Moscow, 1941, p. 76; K. M. Krasil'nikova, 'Bor'ba za khleb v Srednem Povolzh'e v period inostrannoi voennoi interventsii i grazhdanskoi voiny', kand. diss., Kuibyshev, 1968, p. 203; *Samarskaia guberniia v gody grazhdanskoi voiny mai 1918–mart 1919 gg.*, pp. 252–4; Chistov, pp. 157–61; Lysikhin, pp. 127–8; *Simbirskaia guberniia v 1918–1920 gg.*, p. 391.

[28] *Leninskii sbornik*, vol. 24, p. 173.

volosti of the insurgent region whose electoral records have survived in the archives.[29] Trotsky visited the Syzran' area shortly after the elections in order to organize the political campaign for the Eastern Front and explain the conciliatory policies of the Eighth Party Congress towards the middle peasantry.[30] The middle peasants arrested during the suppression of the uprising were released shortly after, and a promise was made (but not kept) to replace the horses which the Red Army had requisitioned from the poor and middle peasants.[31]

Depite these efforts to patch up its relations with the peasantry, the Bolshevik regime in this region remained in a precarious position. The requisitionings of livestock and the campaign to retrieve the tools taken from the *kommuny* during the *chapany* uprising both had to be shelved during the summer of 1919 for fear of another 'counter-revolutionary uprising'.[32] The peasantry continued its passive economic resistance to the food procurements with renewed determination. And the local woodlands were filled with Green bands of deserters, the largest and best known being Nikita Ukhachev's, which retained a dominant influence over the peasantry in Syzran' and Sengilei districts during the two years following the suppression of the uprising.[33] Many of these bands contained *chapany*, who were determined to carry on their war against the Bolsheviks through isolated acts of banditry and terrorism.

The war of the Black Eagle and the Farmer (*voina chernogo orla i zemledel'tsa*) took place during February and March 1920 in Bugul'ma and Menzelinsk districts and the northern areas of Buguruslan district (see Map 5). The Union of the Black Eagle and the Farmer was an organization of Right SRs and ex-Kolchak officers committed to the restoration of the Constituent Assembly and a 'third all-nationality peasant revolution against the White reaction and Bolshevik commissarocracy'.[34] The peasant war in the Bugul'ma region which inherited the name of this organization certainly benefited from the political and military expertise of the Right SRs and former White officers, but it started as a spontaneous peasant uprising against the Bolshevik requisitionings and, like the *chapany* uprising, was directed in the villages by the peasants and deserters from the civil war armies.

29 See ch. 5, n. 71.
30 TsGAOR, f. 393, op. 13, d. 429, l. 80.
31 GAKO, f. 81, op. 1, d. 10, ll. 75, 134; f. 193, op. 2, d. 159, ll. 12, 46.
32 GAKO, f. 193, op. 2, d. 159, l. 6.
33 *Stenograficheskii otchet 7-go syzranskogo uezdnogo soveta s 4-go po 5-e iiulia 1920 g.*, Syzran', 1920, pp. 26–7; Romanenko, p. 159.
34 *Zashchishchaia revoliutsiiu*, Kazan', 1980, p. 162.

The uprising began in the village of Novyi Elan' (Troitskoe *volost'*, Menzelinsk *uezd*) on 7 February 1920. A requisitioning brigade of thirty-five workers from Menzelinsk had placed the village under its own martial law because of the refusal of the peasantry to fulfil the food levy (which, it was later admitted, had been set far too high). Twenty suspected 'kulaks', including two women, had been incarcerated in unheated quarters at −30°C. The villagers attacked the brigade with pitchforks, axes, and pikes, disarmed it, and chased it out of the village. Some of the nearby villages rose up in a similar fashion against other brigades. On 9 February a major uprising broke out in the small market town of Zainsk, where the main headquarters of the uprising were subsequently established. The chairman of the Menzelinsk Cheka, which had recently conducted a brutal campaign against the deserters in the woodland regions, was murdered, along with twenty-eight food-brigade workers from Petrograd. The police building was ransacked. On the steps of the town church a 'parliament' was established, headed by the bandit A. I. Borisov, several Right SRs, and deserters from Kolchak's army.[35]

From Zainsk, the uprising spread rapidly in three main directions: south-east towards Ufa, winning over a large proportion of the Bashkir population (pastoralists, poor peasants); south towards Bugul'ma and Buguruslan, taking in a broad cross-section of the Russian and Tatar peasants, especially in the areas near the Simbirsk–Ufa railway; and west towards Chistopol', where Mordvin, Chuvash, Tatar, and Russian peasants all joined the insurrection. Despite this ethnic diversity, nationalist opposition does not appear to have played a prominent role in the uprising, which was squarely based upon peasant opposition to the requisitionings. The slogans of the movement were preoccupied with political and economic issues similar to those of the *chapany* uprising: 'Down with the Communists!'; 'Down with the *prodrazverstka*!'; 'Long live Soviet power without the Communists!'; 'Long live the Bolsheviks and free trade!'; 'Down with the seizures of grain, smash the collection points!'; 'Long live peasant power!'; etc. It is true, however, that in some of the non-Russian areas, particularly among the Tatars, hatred of the requisitioning brigades had been stirred up by the inability of the latter to distinguish between the different socio-economic groups of the population—a failure no doubt explained by the fact that the brigades comprised mainly Russians.[36]

[35] *Zashchishchaia revoliutsiiu* p. 163; *Byli plamennykh let*, Kuibyshev, 1963, p. 221; Iakubova, p. 101; *Kommuna* (Samara), no. 526, 18 Sept. 1920, p. 1.

[36] Krasil'nikova, pp. 326–7; *Bol'sheviki Tatarii v gody inostrannoi voennoi interventsii i grazhdanskoi voiny: Sbornik dokumentov*, Kazan', 1961, p. 438; F. G. Popov, *1920 god v Samarskoi gubernii: Khronika sobytii*, Kuibyshev, 1977, p. 31; *Samarskaia guberniia v gody grazhdanskoi voiny*, pp. 385–6; *Zashchishchaia revoliutsiiu*, pp. 165–6.

The armed forces of the Black Eagle rising were, like the *chapany*, organized on a territorial basis. Each insurgent village established and maintained its own regiment. The entire male population between the ages of 18 and 45 was subject to conscription. The large number of deserters in the region endowed the rebel units with a natural officer class and a relatively advanced supply of weaponry, including rifles and machine-guns. At the height of its influence, on 12 March, this 'peasant army' numbered 26,000 armed men, organized on three main 'fronts'—Chistopol'–Kazan', Bugul'ma–Samara, and Menzelinsk. The army could count on the support of the peasantry in twenty-five *volosti* in Menzelinsk district, twenty-two *volosti* in Bugul'ma district, and twelve *volosti* in Chistopol' district.[37] Within these woodland regions, the rebel units were difficult to combat, since they had built up very close ties with the rural population. The main channels of Bolshevik influence within the insurgent region were all destroyed: the lines of communication were cut; the railways were torn up; the party cells, the police and the Cheka were terrorized. Over 600 party and soviet officials were murdered in Menzelinsk, Belebei, and Bugul'ma districts during the uprising.[38]

The remoteness of the insurgent areas, which had only been under Soviet power since the previous spring, weakened the early initiatives of the Bolshevik authorities and allowed the uprising to take root. The Red Army reserve forces in the region seriously underestimated the extent of the uprising and, with inadequate troops, made little headway against it until the middle of March.[39] The Reds would overcome a village stronghold and arrest the suspected ringleaders, only to find that the core of the rebel forces had dispersed and fled to the woods. Officially, the uprising was said to have been suppressed by the end of March, but until the end of the year small bandit groups surviving from the February uprising continued to harass the party authorities and disrupt the requisitioning campaigns. Participants of the Black Eagle uprising were noted in the armies of Sapozhkov, Antonov, and Popov during 1920–1.[40]

2. SAPOZHKOV

One of the many ironies of the history of the Russian civil war is that a large number of the peasant uprisings against the Bolshevik regime were led by former Soviet officials and heroes of the Red Army. A. S. Antonov had been chief of police in Kirsanov district during 1917–18

[37] *Menzelinskaia byl'*, Kazan', 1970, pp. 137–9; Litvin, p. 219; Iakubova, pp. 102 ff.; *Zashchishchaia revoliutsiiu*, pp. 166–7.

[38] *Zashchishchaia revoliutsiiu*, p. 169.

[39] Litvin, p. 215.

[40] *Zashchishchaia revoliutsiiu*, pp. 173–9; Iakubova, pp. 109, 162.

before turning the same area into a stronghold of his peasant uprising. Nestor Makhno had been the commander of a brigade, and then a full division, of the Red Army against the Whites in the Ukraine during the first half of 1919, before leading the peasant movement at Huliai Pole. The various peasant bands which roamed the Volga steppe and terrorized the Bolshevik food procurement organs counted a number of former Soviet officials among their leadership (see sect. 3 below). Yet, none of these small bandit atamans in the Volga region matched the distinguished revolutionary record of Sapozhkov and Serov, who together led an ill-fated Red Army mutiny in Samara province during the summer of 1920.

The son of a peasant farmer in Samara province, A. P. Sapozhkov served in the Imperial Army from 1914 to 1917, joining the SR party at the front. In 1917 he returned to Novouzensk where he organized the Left SRs. Sapozhkov played a leading role in the establishment of the Novouzensk town soviet, and became the first chairman of the district soviet executive. During the campaign against the Ural'sk Cossacks in April and May 1918, he was elected not only the military commissar of Novouzensk district, but also the chairman of the district *sovnarkom* presidium.[41] He organized the defence of Novouzensk against the Cossacks and, along with Chapaev, led the military campaign which eventually broke through from the Red bases at Ozinki and Altata towards Ural'sk itself. A Soviet account of the first Ural'sk campaign later admitted that Sapozhkov, who led the largest Red Army force (2,450 bayonets, 150 sabres, 92 machine-guns, 4 cannon, and 5 aeroplanes), did most of the fighting, although Chapaev, who commanded a force less than half the size of Sapozhkov's, made his name during this campaign. By suppressing the 'kulak' uprisings in the Orlov-Gai region, by diverting the Cossacks from Chapaev's offensive troops, and by covering the latter during his assaults on Shipovo and Ural'sk, Sapozhkov helped to ensure the success of the Red Army counter-offensive.[42]

During the campaign against the Komuch Sapozhkov served as a member of the Bolshevik *revkom* in Samara, which assumed full power in the provincial capital after its liberation in October 1918.[43] During the following autumn Sapozhkov put down a series of 'kulak

[41] TsGAOR, f. 393, op. 3, d. 325, ll. 86–7, 120; *Otchet novouzenskogo soveta soldatskikh, rabochikh i krest'ianskikh deputatov*, Novouzensk, 1918, pp. 1–2, 10–11, 16; R. A. Taubin, 'Razgrom kulatskogo miatezha Sapozhkova', *Bor'ba klassov*, no. 12, 1934, p. 56.

[42] I. Kutiakov, *S Chapaevym po ural'skim stepiam*, Moscow, 1928, pp. 27, 34, 38–9, 58, 60, 72, 79; *Godovshchina sotsial'noi revoliutsii v Saratove*, Saratov, 1918, pp. 51–3.

[43] *Vestnik informatsionno-instruktorskogo podotdela otdela upravleniia Samarskoi gubernii* (Samara), no. 1, 15 Nov. 1918, p. 2.

revolts' in Novouzensk district, and forestalled a revolt by a faction of the Bolshevik party in the district town. In February 1919 he was given the command of the 22nd (southern) Division of the 4th Army; its former commander, Dement'ev, had failed to suppress a mutiny in the Division. Sapozhkov continued in command of the 22nd Division during 1919, although his political convictions were slowly moving towards a rupture with the Bolshevik party. In the summer he resigned from the Novouzensk soviet, after losing a campaign to halt the food requisitionings. In February 1920 he was released from the 22nd Division 'on account of [his] unreliable policies and support for the peasantry's looting of the grain collection stations'.[44] Surprisingly, he was given the task of forming a new division—the 2nd Turkestan Cavalry Division—from deserters in Buzuluk district. This was the division, established in May 1920, which Sapozhkov led into mutiny.

Appointing his Left SR associates to its officer ranks, Sapozhkov turned the 2nd Turkestan Division into a powerful ally of the Buzuluk peasantry in its efforts to sabotage the food requisitionings. The Division diverted the food brigades, disrupted the export of grain, and refused to suppress peasant riots against the requisitionings. In June 1920 the Volga Military Command warned Sapozhkov against any further 'anti-Soviet' activities. At the beginning of July he was ordered to resign his command of the Turkestan Division in favour of a former Tsarist officer, N. Stasov. Sapozhkov refused to go. After a meeting of its officers in the town of Buzuluk on 13 July, the Turkestan Division declared itself in opposition to the Bolshevik government, mobilized the peasants from the surrounding villages, and, without loss of blood, captured the town of Buzuluk on the following night. All lines of communication were cut. The neighbouring stations on the Samara–Orenburg railway were put out of action. The party and soviet officials in the town who refused to join the uprising were arrested. The town co-operative was ransacked and 350 million roubles worth of goods, designated for the families of Red Army soldiers, was taken. The bread shops and grain stores were emptied and their contents distributed among the townsmen and peasants of the nearby villages.[45]

Having mobilized and equipped from the surrounding villages a force of 1,800 bayonets, 900 sabres, 10 machine-guns, 4 cannon, and 400 carts of supplies and ammunition, Sapozhkov's army moved south in two directions on 17 July (see Map 5). Serov, Sapozhkov's right-hand man, a former leading member of the Novouzensk soviet executive and commander of the 193rd Rifle Division of the Red Army during the

44 Taubin, 'Razgrom', pp. 56–7.
45 Ibid.; F. G. Popov, *1920 god*, pp. 98–100.

Ural'sk campaign of May 1919,[46] led a squadron of cavalry southwards towards Ural'sk. Sapozhkov led the main force south-westwards towards Novouzensk; he was joined *en route* by hundreds of deserters from the 4th Red Army. Counting on rumours of growing discontent among the town population of Novouzensk, Sapozhkov was evidently hoping to set up a stronghold in his old power-base.[47] It is also possible that he was intending to break through to the lower Volga and Ural'sk, as Lenin feared at the beginning of August.[48] However, Sapozhkov's plan was foiled. On 30 July he was forced off course by an infantry brigade of military students (*kursanty*), and retreated to the remote lake districts of Chizhinki. After a second defeat on 1 August in the region of Shil'naia Balka, Sapozhkov's army began to disperse. A company of perhaps 3,000 men followed Sapozhkov to Altata, where they were joined by Serov's legion, which had failed to capture Ural'sk. Together they assaulted the town of Novouzensk on 6 August; but the city, whose garrison had recently been reinforced by a large number of troops from central Russia, held firm. A second assault on 11 August was also repulsed. Sapozhkov, whose forces were rapidly dwindling, retreated to the remote steppelands of Lake Bak-Baul, where he fell in battle on 6 September after his small scouting party of 60 men had been routed by a battalion of the 4th Red Army.[49] The command of his remaining troops was taken over by Serov, whose remarkable history will be related in the next section.

Given the mobility of Sapozhkov's rebel army and the dearth of information about the peasantry in the remote eastern steppelands of Samara province, our comments on the social basis of this resistance movement ought to be treated with caution. We know that Sapozhkov's army grew considerably in size during its march from Buzuluk to Novouzensk. Many of the new recruits were deserters from the 4th Army and small bandit groups (e.g. the band of Kireev). But a contingent of the Ural'sk Cossacks, who were to become widely involved in banditry after 1921, also joined the rebel army.[50] The booty captured from Sapozhkov's forces by the Reds suggests that the former enjoyed considerable support among the local population. The rebels moved in a train of wagons with up to 2,000 head of cattle, taken

[46] TsGAOR, f. 393, op. 3, d. 325, l. 133; Kutiakov, pp. 27, 49.

[47] See Taubin, 'Razgrom', p. 60; id., 'Iz istorii bor'by s menshevistskoi i esero-kulatskoi kontrrevoliutsiei v period grazhdanskoi voiny v b. Saratovskoi gubernii', *Uchenye zapiski saratovskogo gos. universiteta im. N. G. Chernyshevskogo*, vol. 1 (14), vyp. 1, 1939, p. 22; *Saratovskaia partiinaia organizatsiia v gody grazhdanskoi voiny: Dokumenty i materialy 1918–1920 gg.*, Saratov, 1958, p. 316.

[48] *PSS*, vol. 51, p. 348.

[49] Taubin, 'Razgrom', pp. 61–2; *Boevye podvigi chastei krasnoi armii (1918–1922 gg.)*, Moscow, 1957, p. 86.

[50] Taubin, 'Razgrom', p. 59; *Kommuna* (Samara), no. 606, 21 Oct. 1920, p. 2.

largely from the collective farms, and an enormous array of supplies for distribution among the peasantry in those villages where Sapozhkov's forces intended to mobilize recruits and horses. This connection with the peasantry explains the capacity of Sapozhkov's army to recover very quickly after a seemingly hopeless defeat. It also explains the speed and versatility of Sapozhkov's cavalry, which, having abandoned its wagon train under attack, could outstrip the Red cavalry on fresh horses mobilized from the villages.

Although the basic character of Sapozhkov's movement was military, it had a strong ideological bias towards the peasant struggle against war communism. Sapozhkov's proclamations in Buzuluk on 13 July were directed against the food requisitionings, and the employment of bourgeois 'specialists' (*spetsy*) in the Soviet and military institutions (Sapozhkov himself had been ordered to surrender his post to a former Tsarist officer). The original declaration of the mutiny on 13 July read as follows:

> In view of the unjust policies of the Centre, which are clearly and deliberately beginning to resemble the ideas and methods of the White guards, we propose an immediate armed uprising to protest and demand a change of policy, which ought to be properly conducted in the interests of the poor population of the Republic. All specialist personnel must be removed immediately, as they are the enemies of the working people; all political prisoners must be released with the exception of the Whites. We demand a just and equitable distribution of essential provisions among the people.[51]

The *Declaration of the Rights of Man—Citizens of the RSFSR*, issued by Sapozhkov's officers in Buzuluk on 14 July as Order No. 1 of the rebel government, declared the Communist party unfit to govern and called for the re-election of the soviets, the abolition of the requisitioning brigades and the Cheka, and the declaration of free trade.[52] The slogans of Sapozhkov's movement combined the grievances of the lower officer class of the Red Army with those of the farming peasantry: 'Down with the commissars, the specialists, and the regional provisions committees! Long live free trade!'; 'Down with the Tsarist officers, who hold commanding positions in the Red Army! Down with the *prodotriady* and all specialists!'[53]

The military character of the Sapozhkov movement made it relatively easy to suppress, compared with the other resistance

51 Taubin, 'Razgrom', p. 58.
52 Ibid., p. 59; F. G. Popov, *1920 god*, p. 98.
53 Taubin, 'Razgrom', p. 58; B. Tal'nov, *Kratkie ocherki pervykh chetyrekh let proletarskoi revoliutsii v buguruslanskom okruge (1917–1920 gg.)*, Buguruslan, 1929, p. 28.

movements of this period, which, on the whole, had deeper connections with the rural population. If it took the Bolsheviks of Samara and Saratov provinces the best part of two months to put down the mutiny, then this was the result of their own bureaucratic incompetence, as S. S. Kamenev, the Main Commander-in-Chief, himself pointed out:

> the main reason for the early failures against Sapozhkov actually turned out to be the bureaucratism and the very poor discipline [of the Bolsheviks], which were revealed later. Sapozhkov was not uncatchable, but he was lively. His bands would be overtaken by our forces and defeated, only to come to life again very quickly. On closer examination, it turned out that they had been revived with the help of our own ammunition stores.[54]

Eventually, Sapozhkov's 'army', a force of perhaps 3,000 men, was bound to be cut down to the size of the small band which Serov inherited after Sapozhkov's death. The Bolsheviks in Samara, Saratov, Ural'sk, and Orenburg assembled an army of 7,166 bayonets, 974 sabres, 70 machine-guns, and 9 cannon, which sooner or later had to get the better of Sapozhkov's forces.[55] Nevertheless, without a radical change of policy and a series of measures to improve socio-economic conditions in the countryside, the Bolsheviks would not be able to continue indefinitely to eliminate resistance movements, such as Sapozhkov's, in the military field alone, since the latter represented a fundamental dissatisfaction among the peasantry with the Soviet regime. The defeat of Sapozhkov's legion was soon followed by the appearance of a multitude of small-scale bands, which roamed across the steppe during the winter of 1920–1 and merged with the peasantry in widespread famine uprisings.

3. BANDITRY

Banditry represents a more widespread and complex social phenomenon than the other forms of peasant struggle which we have so far considered in this chapter. The Soviet press reported the presence of 'bandits' in thousands of villages during the famine years of 1920–2. The Soviet and party authorities declared whole regions to be under the control of various 'bandit groups'. However, to build these fragments of information into a coherent historical picture is an almost impossible task, on account of the inconsistencies and ideological prejudices in the Soviet records.

To analyse the banditry we must first understand the people who wrote about it. The 'bandit' was defined by Soviet officials responsible for the maintenance of revolutionary law: policemen, army personnel,

[54] *Vospominaniia o V. I. Lenine*, vol. 2, Moscow, 1968, pp. 307–8.
[55] Romanenko, p. 227.

magistrates, soviet and party workers, etc. During the civil war, when special vigilance was required, such officials were inclined to interpret virtually any act of civil disobedience as a form of 'banditry', or 'counter-revolutionary sabotage' against the Soviet regime. Any law infringement, any case of drunken hooliganism, any assault on a state official, or any famine riot could have been seen as 'banditry' under these circumstances. This is not to deny that some 'banditry' was, in reality, directed towards the overthrow of the Bolshevik regime: the large bandit armies which swept through the Volga famine region during the spring of 1921 espoused political goals which could be described in these terms. Nor is it to argue that all 'banditry' should be seen as a form of social protest by the oppressed, as Hobsbawm is inclined to argue: some bandits were, by any criteria, criminals, and were never seen—or saw themselves—as avengers of the poor. However, it is to argue that people became 'bandits' for a wide variety of reasons, and that we therefore need to distinguish between several different 'banditries'. One 'bandit' group could have been formed by deserters from the Red Army, who resisted the punitive detachments and supported themselves through brigandage and attacks on state institutions (e.g. grain-elevators, distilleries, *sovkhozy*). A second 'bandit' group could have been formed by steppeland pastoralists, displaced by the civil war, who supported themselves by cattle-thefts from the settled farmers and *kolkhozy*. And a third 'bandit' group could have been formed by impoverished peasants, forced to support themselves through begging and brigandage.

Broadly speaking, four pure types of banditry may be delineated. The most common was simple brigandage by 'robber bands' (*razboinich'i shaiki*), numbering up to a dozen, predominantly young, men from the margins of peasant society (impoverished peasants and pastoralists, Red Army deserters, landless labourers, refugees, etc.). A permanent feature of the Russian countryside before the revolution, such brigandage flourished amidst the chaos of the civil war and the famine crisis.[56] Some of the brigands supported themselves by robbing the masses who fled the famine region during 1920–1. Others made a living by posing as police officials, and confiscating property from the peasantry.[57] These criminal bands were often held together only by the personal prestige of the brigand leader; if he was killed, the band was likely to disperse.

The second form of banditry was the 'raiding bands' (*naletnye bandy*) and bandit armies which besieged the eastern steppe regions of

[56] See *Kommunist* (Pugachev), no. 180, 24 Oct. 1920, p. 2; no. 182, 29 Oct. 1920, p. 2.
[57] *Krasnyi nabat* (Balakovo), no. 21, 25 Feb. 1921, p. 2.

Buzuluk, Nikolaevsk, and Novouzensk (see Map 5). These mounted brigades were associated with the in-migration of famine-stricken Cossacks and pastoralists from the Ural'sk steppelands and Central Asia. They had been a traditional breeding-ground for banditry since Razin and Pugachev. During 1920–1 thousands of pastoralists were ruined by the drought and forced to migrate westward in a desperate search for food. It was not long before they took to raiding the large, well-stocked *sovkhozy* on the steppelands of the Volga. The ChON (*chasti osobogo naznacheniia*, party military formations) in Samara province registered the arrival of twelve bands, comprising 1,304 bandits, from the Ural'sk and Orenburg steppe during September and October 1921; during April–June 1922 the arrival of thirteen bands, comprising 1,288 bandits, was registered.[58] The most notable bands were led by Aistov, Gorin, Katushkov, Dalmatov, Sarafanov, and Ivanov. They numbered between 200 and 500 cavalrymen each, were well organized, and, according to a report of the Buzuluk district party committee in April 1921, 'knew exactly where and when to strike'. They raided the *sovkhozy* and the *kommuny*. They burned bridges and tore up railway tracks. And they murdered Bolshevik officials. But, the Buzuluk party report underlined, 'the property of the peasant farmers was very rarely stolen'. This greatly complicated the suppression of the bands, since the 'poor and ignorant peasant youths' of the region were said to have been keen to join the bandits and develop their own forms of brigandage.[59]

A third pure type of banditry was conducted in settled enclaves mainly in the steppeland and forest regions, whose seclusion favoured brigandage (see Map 5). These bandit strongholds resembled those of the Tambov peasant uprising, or the *chapany*, in character. The bandits formed small armies; cut the lines of communication with the towns; held up the goods traffic on the roads; disrupted the requisitionings of peasant foodstuffs by the state; attacked the *sovkhozy* and the *kolkhozy*; terrorized party and soviet officials; and set up independent (mostly 'soviet') forms of peasant rule in the bandit strongholds. These bandit groups, led by Nosaev (Leninskii *uezd*, Tsaritsyn province), Sarafankin (Nikolaevsk *uezd*), Osiankin (Samara *uezd*), Shokhin (Serdobsk and Balashov *uezdy*), Borodaev (Kamyshin *uezd*), Safonov (Novouzensk *uezd*), Korshunov (Bugul'ma *uezd*), Kolob (Novouzensk *uezd*), and a multitude of lesser-known peasant atamans, varied in size

[58] Iakubova, pp. 185–6.

[59] *Izvestiia samarskogo gubkoma RKP(b)*, no. 13 (25), 29 Apr. 1921, pp. 18–19. See further *Krasnyi Ural* (Ural'sk), no. 87, 22 Apr. 1921, p. 1; no. 88, 23 Apr. 1921, p. 1; no. 92, 29 Apr. 1921, p. 2; no. 169, 9 Aug. 1921, p. 2; no. 176, 17 Aug. 1921, p. 2; no. 178, 19 Aug. 1921, p. 2; no. 179, 21 Aug. 1921, p. 3.

between 50 and 1,000 men. With the exception of Shokhin's (which joined Antonov's army on its raid into Saratov and Penza provinces) and Nosaev's (which joined the Novikov band), these bands rarely ventured out of their local strongholds, or showed the slightest desire to combine their forces with neighbouring bandit groups. Their outlook was introspective. Their military organization was unprepared to expand into Bolshevik territory. They were blind to any ideological influences beyond their own local horizons. And their policies, in so far as they had any, were evidently limited to the immediate tasks of keeping those inside the bandit movement alive, at whatever costs, during the famine crisis.[60]

The fourth pure type of banditry was the large 'bandit' army fighting a full-scale 'peasant war' against the Bolsheviks. The longest-surviving bandit army in the Volga region was Serov's, formed by the survivors of the Sapozhkov mutiny in the autumn of 1920 (see Map 5). Its size constantly fluctuated as battles were lost and won, but at the height of its influence, in January 1922, the army numbered over 3,000 sabres. This was after Serov's capture of Nikolaevsk in mid-November 1921—a short-lived success, but one which brought with it great fame and a large number of recruits and supplies. Combining his forces with the bands of Usov and Dalmatov, Serov went on to capture the market town of Uil' and threatened the city of Ural'sk during January and February 1922. After several defeats by the Red Army during the following June (which the Soviet press prematurely celebrated as Serov's end), the band dispersed. But it remained a subversive presence on the eastern steppelands until the middle of August 1922, when Serov negotiated his own surrender.[61]

The largest and most threatening bandit army was Vakhulin's. Like Sapozhkov, Vakhulin had a fine revolutionary past record when he led the Red Army mutiny which was to set in motion his bandit sortie into the Volga famine region during the winter of 1920–1. He had served in Makhno's brigade against the Whites in the Ukraine during 1919, and became the commander of a Red Army cavalry battalion at Mikhailovka in the far north-eastern corner of the Don Cossack territory.[62]

[60] See Iakubova, pp. 121, 163–4; *Stepnoi rabotnik* (Novouzensk), no. 15, 17 July 1921, p. 2; *Trudovaia pravda* (Pokrovsk), no. 91, 2 Aug. 1922, p. 2; no. 92, 4 Aug. 1922, p. 2; *Bor'ba* (Tsaritsyn), no. 257, 16 Nov. 1920, p. 2; *Kommunist* (Pugachev), no. 238, 21 Apr. 1921, p. 1; *Izvestiia* (Saratov), no. 143, 30 June 1921, p. 2; *Nabat* (Kamyshin), no. 436, 8 June 1921, p. 2; *Kommuna* (Samara), no. 784, 30 July 1921, p. 4; *Krasnyi Ural* (Ural'sk), no. 92, 29 Apr. 1921, p. 2; *Volia Rossii* (Prague), no. 264, 27 July 1921, p. 3.

[61] Taubin, 'Iz istorii bor'by', p. 28; Trifonov, pp. 260–2; Iakubova, pp. 165–7; *Izvestiia* (Saratov), no. 189, 19 Aug. 1922, p. 1; no. 191, 23 Aug. 1922, p. 2.

[62] Romanenko, p. 164; Iakubova, p. 158; *Kommunist* (Pugachev), no. 238, 21 Apr. 1921, p. 1.

After the garrison mutiny at Mikhailovka in December 1920, Vakhulin's battalion (500 sabres, 4 machine-guns) moved eastward towards the Volga, joined *en route* by over 1,000 (mainly Cossack) recruits. On 5 February Vakhulin's army captured Kamyshin after a battle on the streets of the town lasting several hours. Fresh supplies and a further 2,000 recruits, many of them political prisoners, were acquired from the town.[63] Chased by reinforcements of the Red Army, Vakhulin crossed the Volga a little up-river from Kamyshin near Razin's legendary burial-mound (*kurgan*) between Lapot and Danilovka. He then moved into the steppe, possibly intending to join forces with Serov in Novouzensk. On 12 February Vakhulin's army surrounded a Red Army force of more than 1,000 men, taking 800 prisoners.[64] On 17 February Vakhulin fell in battle against the Red Army.

The command of his remaining troops (6,000 cavalry bayonets and sabres) passed to F. Popov, a Don Cossack, who immediately ordered a retreat to the Volga. Pursued by the 26th and 58th Divisions of the Red Army, Popov's cavalry rode northwards through the famine-stricken villages on the left bank of the Volga River, from which it acquired hundreds of horses and recruits. The Bolsheviks, on the other hand, were delayed in the German areas by a series of famine uprisings and a number of small bandit legions closely resembling Popov's. One such band was led by Piatakov, the former provisions commissar of the Rovnoe district (midway between Saratov and Kamyshin). It ransacked the government grain stores; blocked the movement of government troops; murdered over 100 party officials; and turned the surrounding area into an 'occupied region'.[65] Meanwhile, Popov's army passed between Balakovo and Nikolaevsk, crossed back to the right bank of the Volga River, and occupied the town of Khvalynsk on 17 March. With fresh horses and weapons and several cartloads of *samogon*, Popov left Khvalynsk on 19 March and moved westward into the old bandit ravines and woods of Kuznetsk and Petrovsk districts.[66] It has been suggested that Popov was planning to link up with Antonov's army.[67] It is known that Antonov was forced out of his woodland

[63] Romanenko, p. 164; Iakubova, p. 158; *Kommunist* (Pugachev), no. 238, 21 Apr. 1921, p. 1., Trifonov, p. 260.

[64] Trifonov, pp. 260–2.

[65] E. Gross, *Avtonomnaia Sovetskaia Sotsialisticheskaia Respublika Nemtsev Povolzh'ia*, Pokrovsk, 1926, pp. 19–21; *Krest'ianskaia pravda* (Tsaritsyn), no. 27, 11 Sept. 1921, p. 4.

[66] This was traditional bandit country during the 19th cent. See the article on the 'woodland brotherhoods' of this region in *Russkie vedomosti*, 15 Oct. 1911, p. 5.

[67] Radkey (*The Unknown Civil War*, p. 398) has argued that if the two leaders had combined their forces, they 'could conceivably have shaken down the regime' in both Saratov and Tambov. This is doubtful. S. S. Kamenev was convinced that 'Popov obviously has no intention of joining up with Antonov' (J. M. Meijer (ed.), *The Trotsky Papers*, The Hague, 1971, vol. 2, p. 414).

strongholds in Kirsanov and Borisoglebsk districts by the threat of Red Army encirclement during February–March and May–June 1921; he moved eastward into the neighbouring districts of Balashov, Serdobsk, and Chembar to within 100 km. of Popov's westernmost strongholds in Petrovsk district (see Map 5). That Antonov stayed long enough during his second sortie into Serdobsk district to establish insurgent political structures in Karpovka, Kurakino, Elan', and several other *volosti* suggests that he may have been waiting for Popov's army to join him there and consolidate a combined territorial base for the peasant movement, which was close to defeat in Tambov province. Indeed, rumours were said to be circulating around the villages of Serdobsk during the spring that a bandit by the name of 'Hungry Vanya' was on his way from Petrovsk district, and this was likely to have been Popov.[68] Intended or not, the rendezvous between the two peasant leaders never took place. Antonov's forces suffered a series of heavy defeats in June at Elan' and Bakury, before dispersing into a dozen or more small bandit units spread across six different districts.[69] Popov's forces, meanwhile, suffered a heavy defeat by the Red Army at Bazarnyi Karbulak (Saratov *uezd*) and then dispersed in a similar fashion. Soviet sources suggest that Popov escaped to the Don with several hundred bandits, and was captured in a battle near Mikhailovka (the starting-point of the revolt), where he was shot on the orders of a Revolutionary Tribunal at the beginning of May 1921.[70] The story is difficult to credit, since in March and April the Soviet military authorities had been clueless about the whereabouts of Popov's army and had reported its presence in peasant uprisings throughout the Volga region. Why should we now believe that these same authorities had tracked down Popov? A more likely ending to the story is that Popov simply ceased to be a serious danger, yet remained locally active in the bandit enclaves of Petrovsk and Kuznetsk districts.

None of the four pure types of banditry existed by itself, of course. The brigands were frequently employed to protect the fringes of the settled bandit enclaves, or to provide spy networks for the bandit armies. The Cossack and pastoralist cavalrymen were known to work in conjunction with the larger forces of Serov, Usov, and Sarafankin. And the large bandit armies stuck closely to the settled enclaves of peasant insurrection (see Map 5). Indeed, their progress was commonly

68 *Serp i molot* (Serdobsk), no. 39 (562), 22 Apr. 1921, p. 2. See also no. 33 (556), 5 Apr. 1921, p. 1; no. 34 (557), 7 Apr. 1921, p. 2; no. 38 (561), 20 Apr. 1921, p. 4; no. 78, 23 June 1921, p. 1; *Izvestiia* (Saratov), no. 142, 29 June 1921, p. 2; *1917 god v Saratove*, Saratov, 1927, pp. 87–88; *Antonovshchina: Sbornik statei*, Tambov, 1923, p. 49.

69 Radkey, *The Unknown Civil War*, pp. 275 ff.

70 *Serp i molot* (Serdobsk), no. 109, 26 May 1921, p. 1; *1917 god v Saratove*, p. 95.

described as a 'blazing trail' of peasant uprisings. The bandit armies grew and shrank in size as recruits from the surrounding countryside joined and left it: some returned to their villages, perhaps to set up their own local bands, once the bandit army left the vicinity; others became full-time members of the bandit army and did not return. These connections with the rural population made the bandit armies swift, versatile, and pervasive.

As soon as it entered a village, the bandit army hunted out and eliminated the soviet and Bolshevik leaders. Popov's army dispatched spies, disguised as priests and beggars, into the villages it was about to occupy in order to recruit supporters and mark out with a chalk cross the huts of the party and soviet members.[71] Most of the local officials managed to flee before the arrival of the bandit army.[72] But some stayed in order to fight a brave, if hopeless, battle against the guerrillas before meeting their end. In Nikolaevsk district over 300 party members were killed by the bandits before October 1921. In the Pokrovsk region more than 100 were killed before April.[73] Some party members were put through a *samosud*, and subjected to gruesome tortures: eyes and tongues were cut out; bodies were dismembered; crosses were branded on foreheads and torsos; heads were cut off; men were burned alive or drowned in ice-packed rivers and ponds; etc.[74] Such excesses could not have taken place without the participation of the village population. The bandit armies, to be sure, murdered Bolsheviks, but these terrible mutilations could only have stemmed from the villagers' hatred and desires for vengeance, and must be seen in the context of the terrible conditions at the end of the civil war, when the famine crisis reduced some people to murderous cannibalism (see Plate 12). As Babine wrote in 1921, 'people have witnessed so much wanton destruction of human life in the past few years that they are no longer startled by the sight of a pool of blood . . . People have grown to be unresponsive and callous to the suffering of others . . . [and] seem to have acquired a taste for agonizing forms of death.'[75]

Having dealt with the local officials, the bandits proceeded to

[71] *V boiakh za diktaturu proletariata: Sbornik vospominanii*, Saratov, 1933, pp. 35–6; Trifonov, p. 80; Romanenko, p. 166.

[72] *Izvestiia melekesskogo uezdnogo komiteta RKP(b)*, no. 5, 27 Nov. 1921, pp. 6–7; *Vestnik saratovskogo gubkoma RKP* (Saratov), no. 11, 15 Oct. 1921, pp. 6, 9–11.

[73] *Izvestiia samarskogo gubkoma RKP(b)*, no. 13 (25), 29 Oct. 1921, p. 18; A. I. Strel'tsova, 'Partiinaia organizatsiia Saratovskoi gubernii v bor'be za provedenie politiki partii v derevne v vosstanovitel'nyi period (1921–25 gg.)', kand. diss., Moscow, 1953, p. 46.

[74] *Kommuna* (Petrovsk), no. 24, 29 Mar. 1921, p. 1; no. 25, 2 Apr. 1921, pp. 1–2; no. 26, 6 Apr. 1921, p. 1; no. 27, 9 Apr. 1921, p. 2; no. 28, 13 Apr. 1921, p. 2; *Otchet saratovskogo gubispolkoma 9-go sozyva 10-mu gubernskomu s''ezdu sovetov za oktiabr' 1920–iiun' 1921 gg.*, Saratov, 1921, pp. 276–7; *1917 god v Saratove*, pp. 89–94.

[75] A. Babine, 'Bolsheviks in Russia', p. 52.

destroy the remaining symbols of the state. The party and soviet offices were turned upside-down, the tax sheets burned, and the cash boxes emptied. The post office and the police headquarters were 'occupied', the typewriters and telephones used for the bandits' military purposes. The railways and the telegraph lines were destroyed. And the soviet schools and propaganda centres were assaulted.[76] The bandits, or the peasant crowd itself, were also known to attack *sovkhozy* and *kolkhozy*, soviet barns, *ssypnye punkty*, railway depots, mills, co-operative stores, craft workshops, wine distilleries, beer factories, bread shops, offices, and banks.[77] Antonov's band made off from Kniazeva *volost'* (Serdobsk *uezd*) with the contents of the costume and props department of the local theatre, including magic lanterns, dummies, and bustles.[78] The appearance of the bandit armies, with their vast herds of stolen livestock and their caravans of military hardware, furniture, liquor barrels, and bags of grain, must have been striking. One eyewitness described Popov's band in the town of Khvalynsk as a long train of machine-gun carriers drawn by six horses each:

> the carriers were covered with blood stains and the horses were decorated with brightly coloured ribbons and material. Ten of the carriers also bore gramophones, while others carried barrels of beer and vodka. All day long the bandits sang and danced to the music and the town was taken over by an unimaginable din.[79]

Incidentally, these bandit songs (*chastushki*), usually accompanied by an accordion, played an important role in the resistance movement. They united the bandits and the peasant population in a common underground culture, whose popular heroes were the *samogon* drinker and the deserter from the Red Army. The basic emotions of the anti-Bolshevik movement were voiced in these songs.[80]

Before leaving a village, the bandit armies usually set up their own form of political organization. Popov and Serov established five-man soviets (*sovety piati*) in the insurgent villages with a population of

[76] E. E. Gershtein, 'Bor'ba za osushchestvlenie leninskogo dekreta o likvidatsii negramotnosti v Saratovskoi gubernii (1920–21 gg.)', in *Iz istorii saratovskogo Povolzh'ia*, Saratov, 1968, pp. 68–9; *Kommunist* (Pugachev), no. 244, 11 May 1921, p. 2.

[77] *Kommunist* (Pugachev), no. 276, 14 Aug. 1921, p. 2; no. 280, 26 Aug. 1921, p. 2; *Izvestiia* (Saratov), no. 64, 24 Mar. 1921, p. 1; no. 74, 5 Apr. 1921, p. 2; no. 79, 12 Apr. 1921, p. 4; no. 82, 15 Apr. 1921, p. 3; no. 85, 19 Apr. 1921, pp. 5–6; no. 131, 15 June 1921, p. 2; no. 132, 16 June 1921, p. 1; *Serp i molot* (Serdobsk), no. 78, 23 June 1921, p. 2.

[78] *Kommuna* (Petrovsk), no. 48, 22 June 1921, p. 3.

[79] *1917 god v Saratove*, pp. 92–3.

[80] Some of these *chastushki* are transcribed in *Antonovshchina*, pp. 57–64; A. M. Bol'shakov, *Sovetskaia derevnia za 1917–24 gg.*, Leningrad, 1924, p. 131; M. Lidin (M. Fomichev), 'Antonovshchina: Iz vospominanii antonovtsa', MS, Bakhmatiev Archive, Columbia University (pp. 16, 24).

more than 2,000 people, and three-man soviets (*sovety trekh*) in villages with less than 2,000 inhabitants.[81] The armies of Maslakov, Savinkov, Volchanskii, and Chernov in the Tsaritsyn region established village 'Committees for the Liquidation of Communism'.[82] Antonov's army instituted Unions of the Toiling Peasantry (STK), as in Tambov province and western Siberia.

The influence of the SRs was only superficially reflected in the bandit movement. True, the basic form of the *sovety piati* and the STK had been approved by the Left SRs. The proclamations of the bandit armies espoused free trade, the Constituent Assembly, and the rights of the opposition socialist parties, which could be said to reflect the general political orientation of the Right SRs. The SR central committee had moved to Saratov in January 1921 and was propagandizing the idea of an 'anti-Bolshevik Saratov Republic',[83] as reported in the Paris *émigré* press. And there was some, albeit very questionable, Cheka evidence that the Right SRs had tried to link the factory strikes and the workers' uprisings, which brought the city of Saratov to a standstill in March 1921, with Popov's bandit army.[84] There were, indeed, rumours in Saratov at the end of March that Popov was about to attack the city.[85] It would be absurd, however, to argue, as Soviet historians have done, on the basis of this evidence that the bandit movement in the villages was no more than a means for the 'counter-revolutionary' ends of the SR party. The SR central committee openly disapproved of the peasant uprisings, because of their 'anarchic' tendencies and their avowed support of the soviets.[86] Although the Left SRs supported the peasant uprisings, they were able to shape neither their strategy, nor their political orientation. Whereas the Left SRs aimed to substitute an all-socialist alliance for the Bolshevik regime in Moscow, the peasant uprisings were localist in their aspirations, and hostile to any form of central government. Hence, while recognizing the rights of the political parties which had supported the February Revolution, Popov's 'manifesto' warned that 'their activities must be limited to the political-parliamentary sphere,

[81] *1917 god v Saratove*, p. 97; Trifonov, p. 98.

[82] *Kommunist* (Tsaritsyn), no. 11, Oct. 1921, p. 11.

[83] Iu. Steklov, *Partiia SR-ov*, Moscow, 1922, pp. 24–5; Trifonov, p. 57; *Izvestiia* (Saratov), no. 62, 22 Mar. 1921, p. 1; no. 66, 26 Mar. 1921, p. 1; etc.

[84] It was claimed that the evidence had been fabricated by the Cheka on the basis of a confession extracted from the chairman of the investigatory department of the Saratov *Komendant* (*Volia Rossii* (Prague), no. 299, 7 Sept. 1921, p. 2). On the workers' uprising in Saratov see ibid.; *Izvestiia* (Saratov), no. 68, 29 Mar. 1921, p. 1; no. 74, 5 Apr. 1921, p. 2.

[85] *1917 god v Saratove*, p. 93; A. Babine, 'Journal', 23 Mar. 1921.

[86] *Volia Rossii*, no. 218, 2 June 1921, p. 3. See also Radkey, *The Unknown Civil War*, pp. 111–27.

so that any encroachment by the parties into the sphere of government [soviet] power will be considered a most illegitimate usurpation'.[87] The power of the local soviets was thus placed above the authority of a national parliament (e.g. the Constituent Assembly); the soviets were to be free from the intervention of the state bureaucracy. As Popov's manifesto put it,

The bureaucratic-Communist apparatus of power, which has founded an army of new bureaucrat-commissars, and which can bring only harm, is henceforth abolished in favour of a simple system of soviets of five and soviets of three which are better suited to the ways of life of the Russian people, and which are elected at general gatherings; all power in the localities is transferred to these soviets, which are not to be subject to any limitations of their power.[88]

Who joined the bandit armies? Soviet historians have argued that the majority of the bandit fighters were 'kulaks' and rich peasants, but the available evidence suggests the contrary. A number of eyewitnesses noted the beggarly state of the bandits. Popov's men were said to be dressed 'in rags and felt boots soaked through with the rain'; in the town of Khvalynsk they were reported to have made it one of their priorities to rob the rich inhabitants of their clothes.[89] A report by the Buguruslan district party committee in April 1921 stated that it was 'characteristic' that the bands from the Orenburg steppe were

joined by people who have been completely displaced through poverty and hunger. The kulaks help the bandits materially, but themselves take up arms only very rarely indeed . . . The bands find it very easy to enlist supporters. The slogan 'Kill the Communists! Smash the *kommuny*!' is very popular among the ignorant and poor peasants, searching for any escape from their desperate situation. It must be frankly admitted that the most backward and downtrodden strata of the peasantry, which suffer the most acutely from the famine and other deprivations, blame their plight entirely on the Communists.[90]

A report by the Buzuluk district party in the same month described the local bandits as 'ignorant peasant youths, reduced to desperate actions by hunger; this was confirmed by our own questioning of the captured bandits'.[91] Examining the lists of arrested bandits published in the Soviet press, it is, indeed, impossible not to notice their very young age (mostly between 16 and 25).[92] A large portion of them must have been deserters from the Red or the White army, since the booty captured

[87] *1917 god v Saratove*, p. 97.
[88] Ibid.
[89] Ibid., p. 91; *Serp i molot* (Kuznetsk), no. 62, 23 Mar. 1921, p. 1.
[90] *Izvestiia samarskogo gubkoma RKP(b)*, no. 13 (25), 29 Apr. 1921, p. 18.
[91] Ibid., p. 19.
[92] *Krasnyi Ural* (Ural'sk), no. 158, 19 Sept. 1920, p. 2; *Izvestiia* (Saratov), no. 189, 19 Aug. 1922, p. 3; *Kommuna* (Samara), no. 565, 3 Nov. 1920, p. 2.

from the bandit forces invariably included a large quantity of rifles, revolvers, and machine-guns, while many bandits had their own military horses.[93] The bandit armies of Popov and Serov contained a large contingent of Cossacks, Tatars, and Kirghiz. Some of them were no doubt attracted by the 'Asiatic Soviet nationalism', propagandized by the two bandit leaders as part of their opposition to rule from Moscow.[94]

The attitude of the stable peasantry was ambivalent. The richest peasants and the *khutoriane*, contrary to the assumptions of Soviet historians, tended to be the most hostile to the bands, since the latter usually mobilized their horses from them. The middle peasants gave neither the bandits nor the Bolsheviks more than the minimum assistance. Their position was summed up by a report of the Buzuluk district party committee in April 1921:

> In the spring, when the bands pillaged the villages indiscriminately, the attitude [of the peasantry] towards them was negative; but as soon as the bands attacked the property of the state the attitude of the peasantry changed in their favour. There were occasions when our brigades, in pursuit of the bands, were mistaken for a bandit force; many people wanted to join. It is true that the population does not see a solution to its problems in banditry. They do not believe it is possible to overthrow the authorities, and they take into account the negative aspects of trying to do so. But it is characteristic that the struggle against the bandits has to be carried out by the Communist forces on their own. There is no real peasant support for this struggle. Even the non-party workers cannot be involved in the campaign.[95]

It was commonly noted that the villagers used the opportunity afforded by the breakdown of law and order following the bandit occupation to retrieve their property from the soviet barns, the *ssypnye punkty*, and other state institutions.[96] The Novouzensk district soviet reported in June 1921 that 'in some places the visit of the bandits was followed by a peasant uprising in which the entire adult male population was, albeit primitively, armed.'[97] The trail of Popov's army

[93] *Oktiabr'skaia revoliutsiia* (Khvalynsk), no. 663, 15 June 1921, p. 2; no. 714, 4 Sept. 1921, p. 4; *Krasnyi nabat* (Balakovo), no. 68, 8 June 1921, p. 2; *Krasnyi Ural* (Ural'sk), no. 73, 14 Apr. 1922, p. 1.

[94] *Krasnyi Ural* (Ural'sk), no. 88, 23 Apr. 1921; Taubin, 'Iz istorii bor'by', p. 12; *1917 god v Saratove*, p. 96.

[95] *Izvestiia samarskogo gubkoma RKP(b)*, no. 13 (25), 29 Apr. 1921, p. 19.

[96] See e.g. *Izvestiia* (Saratov), no. 73, 3 Apr. 1921, p. 1; *Izvestiia samarskogo gubernskogo soiuza potrebitel'nykh obshchestv* (Samara), nos. 8–9, 22 Nov.–1 Dec. 1920, p. 13; *Biulleten' simbirskogo gubernskogo otdela upravleniia* (Simbirsk), nos. 5–6, 2 Mar. 1922, p. 9; *Krest'ianin* (Menzelinsk), no. 35, 4 June 1921, p. 2; Iakubova, pp. 161–2.

[97] *Otchet saratovskogo gubernskogo ispolnitel'nogo komiteta 9-go sozyva 10-mu gubernsskomu s''ezdu sovetov za oktiabr' 1920–iiun' 1921 gg.*, Saratov, 1921, p. 290.

along the Volga River was marked by dozens of famine uprisings (see Map 5), in which the peasants ransacked government food stores. On 23 March 1921 the Saratov Cheka reported 'huge crowds of peasants on horseback and on foot ... removing piecemeal the grain from the granaries at the *ssypnye punkty*'. The Volga Military Command added that 'peasant famine uprisings have flared up throughout the middle and lower Volga regions, especially in those places where the largest quantities of grain were extracted ... hungry peasants collect in the volosts in crowds of several thousands and demand grain from the food supply organs'.[98] The report mentioned in particular the region around Krasnyi Kut, Rovnoe, and Zolotoe in the German Volga which Popov's army had traversed. A large peasant crowd ransacked the *ssypnoi punkt* at Krasnyi Kut at the end of February; they were fired upon by 300 Red Army cavalrymen with two machine-guns. It is not known how many died in the massacre, but an eyewitness estimated that 'the first 300 peasants the Red Army could find were shot without trial', and that 'after the military tribunal had cleared the executioners of any fault in this action, at least another 300 were shot'.[99] An even uglier massacre took place at Balzer (Goloi Karamysh), a small German market town 100 km. north of Kamyshin, on Sunday 15 March. A crowd of 6,000 hungry peasants from the surrounding villages marched on the town with clubs, pitchforks, hoes, and scythes in order to protest against the export of requisitioned foodstuffs. As the peasants approached, Red Army soldiers opened machine-gun fire upon them from the Balzer church tower. A troop of cavalry, followed by infantry with fixed bayonets, charged the crowd. Hundreds of peasants were cut down or shot. The people of Balzer were forbidden to help the wounded, who were later rounded up and executed. This incident, which is not recorded in the Soviet literature, was to become known in the annals of the Volga Germans as the 'war of the clubs' (*Knüppelkrieg*).[100]

During the spring of 1921 there was panic in Moscow and the Volga cities about the scale of the banditry, and a number of counter-measures were taken. The Saratov authorities warned Moscow on 19 March that the situation in the province was 'intolerable':

the whole work of the province is paralysed; in those places where the bandits

[98] Meijer (ed.), *The Trotsky Papers*, vol. 2, pp. 415, 417.
[99] *The Hardships of Our Co-Religionists in the German Volga Colonies*, Pokrovsk, 1921.
[100] G. Loebsack, *Einsam kämpft das Wolgaland*, Leipzig, 1936, pp. 320–1; F. C. Koch, *The Volga Germans in Russia and the Americas from 1763 to the Present*, Pennsylvania, 1977, p. 262.

have passed through the Soviet regime is not recognized; towns are completely sacked by the bandits; the levies of grain cannot be met; the towns of the province are threatened by hunger riots; the working masses are demoralized . . . and there are signs of ferment and strikes and a sharp decline in productivity . . . The position of the whole province is menacing. All possible steps must be taken immediately, otherwise the province will be a total loss to the Republic.[101]

A similar plea was relayed to Moscow on 25 March by the Saratov provisions authorities, which added the alarming report that Lunacharskii, the Commissar for Education, had almost been taken prisoner by Antonov at Rtishchevo.[102] Although Trotsky was unsympathetic to the Saratov authorities and wanted to leave them to cope with the situation, Lenin took a more serious view and replied to Trotsky: 'It is *essential* to support the local organizations. Moscow *must* send help to Saratov *ultra-urgently*. The Voenkom of the Republic must concentrate its energies on this, or else we are in trouble' (emphasis as in source).[103]

The military forces used to combat the bandit armies in the Volga region were considerable. Moscow assigned for this task the 48th, 26th, 58th, and 50th Divisions of the Red Army, together with the celebrated 81st Rifle Brigade of the 27th Omsk Division, which had played such a prominent role in the suppression of the Kronshtadt mutiny. Penza, Tver', Kursk, and Petrograd sent various brigades and regiments, while the Volga authorities carried out a full-scale mobilization of the party, the Cheka, and the Komsomol.[104] The military offensive made little headway during the spring. As the Saratov authorities were forced to admit during March, 'the struggle against the bandits . . . has not led to the desired results . . . The lack of cavalry and infantry in adequate numbers allows the bands to roam at will in any direction . . . Fighting the bandits with small detachments has simply enabled them to arm themselves.'[105] The absence of any major towns or railways in the steppeland regions complicated the equipping and transportation of troops. Further problems were caused by the huge losses in the membership of the VIKs and the Bolshevik party as a result of the famine crisis and the widespread fear of the bandits.[106] The situation began to improve only during the summer, when a

[101] Meijer (ed.), *The Trotsky Papers.*, vol. 2, p. 409.
[102] TsGANKh, f. 1943, op. 1, d. 1016, l. 1. I am indebted to Russell Gerard, who deciphered this coded telegram.
[103] Meijer (ed.), *The Trotsky Papers*, vol. 2, p. 409.
[104] Taubin, 'Iz istorii bor'by', pp. 40–1; Trifonov, pp. 260–1; TsGANKh, f. 1943, op. 1, d. 1016, l. 25.
[105] Meijer (ed.), *The Trotsky Papers*, vol. 2, p. 409.
[106] *Vestnik saratovskogo gubkoma RKP*, no. 11, 15 Oct. 1921, p. 4.

number of new military tactics were employed by the Reds: larger units were formed; aeroplanes were used to track the movement of the bandit armies; greater co-ordination was achieved between the units in the field; military commands were established within the regions of peasant unrest; and the bandit strongholds were occupied and subjected to cruel deprivations (e.g. confiscations of property, hostage-taking, deportations to concentration camps, torture of families, and the burning of whole villages) in the struggle to stamp out insurrection and lawlessness.[107]

These initiatives were accompanied by an extensive campaign to reconsolidate the position of the regime in the countryside in the wake of the peasant uprisings. *Revkomy* were established in the troubled regions, and given the task of combining the military campaign against the bandits with the political one for the support of the peasantry. Amnesties for the bandits were declared. The soviets were re-elected and replenished with new party cadres, fresh from the Red Army. Initiatives were taken to recruit the youths of the villages into the Komsomol. A propaganda campaign was launched to advertise the NEP and the party programme for economic recovery. And 'weeks for the peasantry' were organized, when the sowing committees (*posevkomy*) distributed seed in a last-ditch effort to avert the famine crisis, and townsmen were conscripted to help with famine relief for the skin-and-bone children.[108]

By the late summer of 1921, the main peasant rebellions in the Volga region, as in most of Soviet Russia, had been crushed. Although small-scale brigandage continued to trouble the Soviet authorities until the end of 1922, the bandit armies had been militarily defeated and socially undermined. The famine crisis had exhausted the peasantry's strength and will-power to resist the new regime.

[107] Romanenko, pp. 157, 174; Iakubova, pp. 145, 165, 187–8; *Volia Rossii* (Prague), no. 299, 7 July 1921, p. 2; *Otchet saratovskogo gubernskogo ispolnitel'nogo komiteta 9-go sozyva*, p. 44; *Kommuna* (Petrovsk), no. 37, 14 May 1921, pp. 2–3.

[108] *Otchet saratovskogo gubernskogo ispolnitel'nogo komiteta 9-go sozyva*, pp. 29, 32; Taubin, 'Iz istorii bor'by', pp. 34, 38–9; *Serp i molot* (Kuznetsk), no. 67, 29 Mar. 1921, p. 2; no. 94, 8 May 1921, p. 3; *Izvestiia* (Saratov), no. 274, 3 Dec. 1921, p. 1.

8
Conclusion

In the long run, the defeat of the peasant rebellions was unavoidable. Although the rebels had helped to force the government into retreat from war communism, they had little prospect of bringing about a fundamental change in the nature of Soviet power. Against the might of the Bolshevik regime the bandit armies could not hope to achieve more than fleeting military victories. The gap in the edifice of state power, which in 1917–18 had enabled the peasantry to become a national political force, had since been closed by the organization of the Red Army and the construction of a centralized party–state apparatus in the provinces. The political impotence of the peasantry, which had characterized and shaped the course of Russian history under the Tsars, became a basic precondition of the Soviet regime after 1921.

The consolidation of the Bolshevik dictatorship was inextricably connected with the social and political transformation of the countryside during 1917–21. The peasant revolution of 1917–18 destroyed the power of the old regime in the countryside and undermined the anti-Bolshevik movement based upon the restoration of the Constituent Assembly. But the peasantry was too weak by itself to defend its revolutionary gains against the gentry reaction. The civil war necessitated the establishment of a strong state apparatus in the provinces to organize the resources of the peasantry for the struggle against the counter-revolution. As long as the peasants feared the Whites, they would go along, feet dragging, with the demands of the Soviet regime. Centuries of illiteracy and Tsarist rule had not bred in the peasantry a high level of democratic expectation from its own national government. Provided the old ruling class was seen to be dispossessed and removed from power, the peasants would not ask too many questions about their new political masters. Thus the Bolshevik dictatorship climbed up on the back of the peasant revolution.

The rural official élite of the emergent party–state apparatus was formed as the village democracy of the peasant revolution disintegrated under the social pressures of the civil war. The communal system of egalitarian land use, which had been reinforced by the agrarian revolution, proved incapable of providing a material base for all the villagers during the socio-economic crisis of 1917–21. The breakdown of market relations between town and country, the mass influx of urban residents into the countryside, and the impoverishment of large sections of the rural population weakened the social cohesion of the village community and placed intolerable burdens on the democratic soviets. The stable peasant farmers, who dominated the communes, sought to isolate themselves from the outside world by turning their backs on the soviets, which were increasingly seen as organs of government taxation and Communist rule. On the other hand, many of the marginal and landless elements of rural society (ex-servicemen, general labourers, craftsmen, migrants, rural youth, and even women) sought to break away from the confined world of the peasantry—with its primitive daily routines, its patriarchal hierarchies and traditions—by joining the ranks of the rising state bureaucracy in the *volost'* townships. The Soviet regime was consolidated through the institutionalization of these social divisions—the divisions between the traditional world of the farming peasantry, embodied in the village commune, and the modern world, the world of school and industry, represented by the officialdom of the VIKs and the party cells. It was precisely these divisions that delimited the power of the new regime during the 1920s, and ensured that Communist control in the countryside would only be established once the communes had been destroyed and the peasant farms collectivized.

From the perspective of the peasantry, the events of 1917–21 were in many ways a revolution lost. The autonomy and democracy of the local soviets, consolidated in the peasant revolution of 1917–18, were both undermined by the erection of a centralized state apparatus with a massive standing army, and a greatly enlarged bureaucracy under Communist domination. The balance of power within the new regime was—even more than under the old one—heavily weighted against the peasantry. The Neo-Populists, who would undoubtedly have attracted considerable peasant support under a pluralist-socialist system were forced underground or into exile during the civil war. The Bolshevik dictatorship was centred in—and largely limited to—the urban centres of peasant Russia. The higher levels of the government and party bureaucracy were dominated by workers and intellectuals, whose political and cultural disposition towards the peasantry ranged from guarded toleration to open hostility and imperious contempt. The basic long-term goals of the regime—the collectivization of agriculture, socialist industrialization, and the universal establishment of Communist rule —were incompatible with the market orientation of the peasantry, its attachment to the customs and institutions of family ownership, and its quasi-anarchist traditions of social organization. The experience of the civil war merely reinforced Bolshevik prejudices about the peasantry, and established a precedent for the use of mass terror as a means of socialist transformation in the countryside.

But in 1921 the terrors of collectivization were still in the distant future. Once the famine crisis had been overcome and the economy restored to peaceful conditions, the Russian peasantry enjoyed a period of unparalleled freedom and well-being during the 1920s. Although it had amassed a formidable array of means of coercion during the civil war, the new regime was still in the early stages of state formation in the countryside. The village communes remained virtually autonomous in the supervision of land relations, the organization of the agricultural economy and the maintenance of peasant culture. The power of the landowners had been destroyed by the revolution, and the influence of capitalist elements substantially reduced. The extremes of rural poverty had been eliminated, and the social dominance of the middle peasantry greatly strengthened. Favourable market conditions and the improvement of agricultural technology helped to bring about an expansion of peasant commodity production. The level of literacy among the rural population, especially the women, rose rapidly. Hospitals, theatres, cinemas, libraries, and the other trappings of urban civilization at last began to appear in the countryside. For the mass of the peasantry, these were the precarious fruits of a revolution gained.

APPENDIX

Peasant Petitions from Staro-Slavkino Village, May 1919[1]

1. To the representative of NKVD

I have the honour to attest that last autumn the punitive detachment (*karatel'nyi otriad*) took from me my horse and harnesses, a cow, 20 *funt* of butter, 200 eggs, 8 *vershok* of wooden board. None of these articles was paid for and the horse is now with fellow villager I. A. Bubanov. I have been left with only one horse for a family of ten which I am not able to feed. My son is in the Red Army and my other son only recently came back from captivity in the war and I am 65 years old and so am practically unable to feed my family, since I have no hired labourers but work with my own callused hands (*mozol'nymi rukami*), and therefore I humbly ask you . . . to petition whomever necessary to make an order for the return of my horse.

Ivan Ivanovich Taganov (signed)

2. To the representative of NKVD

In August of last year 1918 I had my cow taken from me, which at the moment is with the citizen of this village Larion Nikolaevich Abmakin. Taking away my cow is undoubtedly not correct and is unjust because I have never exploited the labour of another man, but work day and night with my own hands and barely eat enough since my harvest was small . . .

Semen E. Doraev (illiterate, signed by scribe)

3. To the representative of NKVD

On 8 May last the chairman of the Staro-Slavkino VIK, Petr Druzhaev, together with a policeman (*militsioner*), took from me, Zubanov, 26 rb. 90 kop. in silver cash and 3 rb. 3 kop. in coppers, left to me by my mother on her death. This money was acquired by her honestly and I kept it openly because I do not exploit the labour of others, and with my father, a cobbler, have nothing but our own house and labour . . .

A. Zubanov (illiterate, signed by scribe)

4. To the instructor

The chairman of the Staro-Slavkino village soviet, comrade Bateikin, wrote to me, Lachev, ordering me to give 25 *pud* of rye to Anton Bateikin (the brother of the chairman) and threatening to punish me if I did not . . . I gave him the 25 *pud* but was never paid for it and therefore I humbly and obediently ask you, comrade instructor, to punish the chairman of the Staro-Slavkino village soviet, Bateikin, according to the law, or at least make him pay me for the 25 *pud* of rye which I gave to his brother . . .

Vasilii Nikitich Lachev (illiterate, signed by scribe)

[1] TsGAOR, f. 393, op. 3, d. 336, ll. 237–85.

5. To the representative of the central authorities

I write to draw your attention to the following: Petr Druzhaev together with some members of the village soviet requisitioned goods from my home and my small shop without paying me for them, without a receipt, and without witnesses. My shop itself was smashed to pieces by order of the *volost'* soviet and the iron and the boards from it were stolen. The goods from my shop were taken to the co-operative shop and the money received from their sale, 712 rb. 95 kop., was handed over to Petr Druzhaev.

Vasilii Nikolaevich Romanov (written and signed)

6. To the representative of NKVD

On 5 October of last year at 11 o'clock at night Petr Druzhaev, Ivan Nikushin, and Evsai Maiorov burst into my home with guns and side-arms and whips. They threatened me and took from me without witnesses the following items: about 1 *pud* 20 *funt* of pig fat, 30 eggs. For these items they did not give me a receipt and, of course, they shared them between themselves afterwards. Seven days later, on 12 October, the same comrades, together with comrade Fomin, returned at midnight and ordered me to give them a revolver which they claimed I had, but which I did not have. Putting a gun to my chest, they demanded vodka from me, but since I had none and refused to buy any for them, they beat me and then beat my wife. I asked them to allow my five-year-old son, who was shaking with fear, to go, but they refused, at which my wife became so petrified that she defecated there and then. As a result of this ordeal at the hands of these aliens (*inoplemenniki*), I was arrested, but was told that I would be released if I gave them half a bottle of vodka, but would be shot if I did not . . .

E. Doraev (illiterate, signed by scribe)

7. To the instructor

In November of last year 1918 at about 12 o'clock at night I was summoned by Petr Druzhaev, Fedor Vasin, and Vasilii Leksin to the house of Pavel Kudoshkin, where the above comrades ordered me to give them a bottle of vodka, and when they realized that I did not have any vodka they asked for money to buy some. I had no choice but to give them 80 rb., since they threatened to kill my wife and me if I refused. They also took my best horse, leaving me only one old horse. I am not a kulak and not even a middle peasant, but belong to the small peasantry . . .

A.S. Semenov (illiterate, signed by scribe)

8. To the instructor

In August of last year they took without just cause my horse and my harnesses, my cow, 1 *pud* of butter, 5 *vershok* of wooden boards . . . In January of this year the same people took 28 *arshin* of wool, which I consider to be unfair since I have always worked with my own callused hands and so I ask you as a representative of the government to return my horse and harnesses, which are in the yard of Dmitrii Listratov of this village, and also to punish the people who have done this.

Akima Akimovna Ruslikina (written and signed)

9. To our comrade delegate in the *volost'* soviet

A complaint: I have the honour to inform you, comrade delegate, of the following: the Staro-Slavkino village soviet took from me last year, 1918, without any payment or reason, 29 sheep and 39 *arshin* of wool. Since my feet are lame and I cannot see properly, I ask you to go to those on high and to do what lies in your power to do, since I am now in a very poor condition.

Fedor Lomovtsev (written and signed)

10. To the instructor

At various times they took from me 20 *pud* of rye, 10 *funt* of butter, 80 eggs, and 16 *arshin* of wool, all taken at night by comrade Pavel Druzhaev and other comrades who are unknown to me, but who had guns and who threatened to shoot me if I did not give them vodka; since I didn't have any they took my eggs instead and gave them to citizen Aleksandr Sumboev, who returned the dish from the eggs to me the other day.

I have never exploited the labour of others, and have never even hired one day-labourer; I have not lived in need only because I have not let one day go by without working; in my free time I work as a copper-smith and a log-cutter, which helps me to save money. I, a working peasant, am offended to have the products of my own labour, the products made by my own callused hands, taken away from me, and so I ask you to do what you can so that I may be paid for the goods taken from me.

(illiterate, written and signed by a neighbour)

11. To the representative of NKVD

On 2 June [1918] my sons Il'ia and Vasilii were mobilized into the ranks of the famous Red Army, one of them into the Serdobsk artillery regiment, the other into the Petrograd cavalry regiment, and they have been gone for almost a year now; but here the comrade chairman took from me without payment a horse, with all its harnesses, a cow, 12 *funt* of cow's butter, 24 *funt* of wool, 100 rb. in money. If I was some sort of exploiter of the labour of others, then in any case my sons would not have been called into the ranks of the Red Army and would not have defended the interests of the Socialist Republic; if only for that reason, I do not understand how it came to pass that the local comrades could allow evil abuse to mock the ideas proposed by comrade Lenin. I ask you, comrade representatives, to make an order for the return of my horse with its harnesses, which are now with citizen Vasilii Suslin, and for the payment of the remaining items, since this is a scandalous crime against me, a member of the middle peasantry, and therefore the guilty people should be called to account.

N. A. Ruslikin (signed by two neighbours)

12. To the comrade representative

Last year comrade Druzhaev and others took from us, the Spirins, one cow, all our household utensils, and other household and domestic property, and we were kicked out of our own home and had to move to our brother's in the town of Petrovsk and live there in his flat. Having farmed in Serdobinka village and then moving to Staro-Slavkino village, we made a living to begin with by producing leather sandals. Our family never belonged to the kulak class, since we always worked with our own callused hands and never exploited the labour of others, although if we did sometimes hire others, it was only because we were in desperate need of labour, as you will probably understand, comrade repesentative.

N. S. Spirina (signed)

13. To comrade Pal'kin

In August 1918 a punitive detachment from the town of Petrovsk came and took from me, Kudoshkin, 2,000 rb. in money, a cow, 20 *funt* of cow's butter.

Then on the authority of Druzhaev they took my horse and his harnesses without payment and 20 *pud* of rye, also without payment, and they took 23 *pud* of rye and 10 *pud* of hay and 5 *pud* of hemp oilcake, stored in the communal barn, and all this was taken for the soviet's horses without payment. I most humbly ask you, comrade Pal'kin, to look into this matter according to the law, and I would like to get something in payment for the 43 *pud* of rye and the other things, including also 17 *funt* of wool, which were all taken without payment.

Stepan Trofimovich Kudoshkin (signed)

14. To the instructor

I, Doraev, a working peasant, below the average means and with a family of seven people, had confiscated from me two horses . . . and they did not pay me a single kopeck. They also took 11 *funt* of wool and 20 *funt* of butter. They paid me nothing for these things. I, a working peasant who have never exploited the labour of others, do not understand why the higher authorities of the workers and peasants government say very clearly in their decrees that the middle working peasantry is not subject to any taxes, if our own local authorities make their own decrees and pay no attention to the orders of the higher authorities, so I call upon you, comrade representatives, as representatives of the higher authorities, to defend my rights, the rights of a working peasant, having worked with my own horse and callused hands, and I ask you, comrades, to make an order for the return of my horse, which is now in the yard of D. Piataev, citizen of this village, and to punish the guilty people.

Iakov Iakovlevich Doraev (illiterate, signed by scribe)

15. Petition

I, a working peasant, working only with my family and my own callused hands, had one of my two horses confiscated, leaving me only one horse, and they also took 16 *funt* of wool, all without payment.

I ask you, comrade representatives, to defend my rights as you should defend the interests of all working peasants, and I ask you to consider why the comrade leaders took my horse and wool, when I have only two horses, and whether I can really be a kulak with only two horses, and whether I can exploit the labour of others when I do not even have enough animals and tools for myself.

Surely my interests, the interests of a working peasant, will be defended by comrade Lenin, surely I will be defended by you, representatives of the higher authorities. I think the voice of the working peasant will be heard by you and that you will make an order for the return of my horse, which is now in the yard of Fedor Trifonov, and the wool must be paid for and the guilty people brought to justice.

Stepan Efimovich Iakitin (signed)

16. To the chairman of the people's commissariat, comrade Lenin!

I served as a member of the *kombed* in the autumn of last year 1918, in September. I left after one month because of the behaviour of Petr Akimovich Druzhaev and his brother Pavel Akimovich Druzhaev, who at that time served as chairman of the *volost'* soviet and Pavel as the chairman of the *kombed.* The two brothers worked in the same way: instead of bringing together the working people, they committed terrible crimes against them and created a state of panic. Their normal work consisted of drinking and robbing. The Druzhaev brothers usually carried out their robberies at night. If a man was not able to give them vodka, then they killed him and raped his wife. Because of such behaviour, the people loathe the Druzhaev brothers and instead of unity there is now dissension and, despite the fact that our village of 8,000 people and our *volost'* of 15,000 are the poorest in the whole of Saratov province, the people live in the shade of ignorance and the darkness of distrust. When the central authorities decided to call for the re-election of the soviets among the middle peasants, the people as one fulfilled the plans of the central authorities and elected my son, Grigorii Iakovlevich Kudoshkin, and gave him the task of informing the central authorities about the abuses of the Druzhaev brothers described in the people's petitions, although these petitions got no further and have been left on a shelf until now. The office of Grigorii Kudoshkin, which seemed to the people more like three days than three months, came to an end. On 29 March 1919, at the end of Kudoshkin's period, the soviet was re-elected under threat of force by the chief of the regional police, comrade Varlamov, who threatened to shoot people and so dispersed the people in panic, which enabled him to get re-elected those elements who have already terrorized the entire working people and who have by their actions alienated the whole population from the authorities and therefore, by such actions, have destroyed the authority of Soviet power among the middle peasants, since the army consists entirely of those masses whom they have desecrated. Encouraged by comrade Varlamov, these elements used force to get comrade Druzhaev elected to the soviet, which at present worships terror against the people instead of struggle against the exploiters. They spend most of their time drunk and one night . . . comrade Druzhaev, the present chairman of the *volost'* soviet, got so drunk that he smashed the windows of the soviet building. A protocol was passed against him by the chief of the police, Kachkurin, for disturbing the peace . . . But instead of punishing Druzhaev for his drunken behaviour, the chief of the regional police, comrade Varlamov, arrested Kachkurin himself. The people, seeing this, are beginning to say that life was better under the Tsar Nicholas than under the soviets, which by their actions have driven life itself into the grave. One week after his unjust re-election, that is on 5 April 1919, Druzhaev and his police comrades confiscated from my household 25 hides and 4 lambskins, 2 *pud* of butter, 1 *pud* of meat, and about 20 *funt* of mutton fat, leaving my family of ten to starve on bread and water . . . All the confiscated goods were, as before, sent to the chief of the regional police, Varlamov, who lives in the village of Serdoba, Petrovsk *uezd*, Saratov province. My son Grigorii and myself were imprisoned for three days and were subjected to various interrogations and torture. Druzhaev demanded 8,000 rb. from me under the Chreznalog. My entire property is 2 old horses, a two-year-old foal, 2 cows, 20 sheep, and buildings insured under the *zemstvo* for 590 rb. I have a family of ten and am 60 years old and have two working sons, one in the army and the other a wounded veteran. My wife works in the fields. I have never worked in trade, have never had any sort of factory or workshop, have never made profits at the expense of the working people, have never hired labourers. In addition, I consider it my duty to say that I took part in the revolutionary movement, distributed revolutionary leaflets among the people, for which I was arrested on several occasions during the well-known persecutions carried out in the province in 1905 and 1906 . . . Stolypin arrested my brother, Efim Kudoshkin, and me for spreading the ideas of the Petrovsk soviet. I was released on bail, but my brother was exiled and now lives in the town of Balakovo in Samara province. On the basis of the above, I humbly ask the chairman of the people's commissariat to make an order for the return of my property and for the lifting of the *kontributsiia* on me of 8,000 rb. since I am really a middle peasant, and was elected to the *kombed*, and my son, Grigorii, served in the soviet after the abolition of the *kombed*.

Iakov Gavriilovich Kudoshkin (written and signed)

BIBLIOGRAPHY

1. SOVIET ARCHIVAL SOURCES

(a) TsGAOR

(i) *fond* 130 (Sovnarkom)
opis' 2 (1918)
dela 441 (Narkomzem); 442–3 (procurement brigades)
opis' 3 (1919)
dela 93, 104–07a (resolutions); 199 (Red Army desertion, 1919)

(ii) *fond* 393 (Narodnyi Komissariat Vnutrennikh Del)
opis' 2 (Otdel mestnogo upravleniia)
dela 59 (Nizhegorod, 1918); 80 (Saratov, 1918)
opis' 3 (Otdel mestnogo upravleniia)
dela 322 (Samara, 1918); 323 (Buzuluk, 1918); 324 (Samara, 1918); 325 (Melekess, Novouzensk, Nikolaevsk, 1918); 326 (Syzran', 1918); 327 (Saratov, 1918); 328 (Atkarsk, 1918); 329 (Nikolaevsk, Samara, Stavropol', 1918–19); 330 (Atkarsk, 1918); 331 (Balashov, 1918); 332 (Novouzensk, Vol'sk, 1918–19); 333 (Kamyshin, 1918); 334 (Kuznetsk, 1918); 335–6 (Petrovsk, 1918); 337–9 (Saratov, 1918); 340 (Serdobsk, 1918); 359 (Ardatov, Alatyr', 1918–19)
opis' 4 (Biuro pechati)
dela 22 (various regions, 1918–19); 110 (various regions, 1918)
opis' 11 (Informatsionnyi)
dela 183–210 (autobiographies of provincial and district soviet leaders, 1918–19)
opis' 13 (Otdel upravleniia; Podotdel informatsionnyi)
delo 429 (Simbirsk, 1919)
opis' 13 (Biuro pechati)
dela 578 (various regions, 1919); 581 (various regions, 1919); 582 (various regions, 1919–20)
opis' 13 (Informatsionno-statisticheskii otdel)
dela 609 (Riazan', Saratov, Severo-Dvinsk, Tambov, 1919); 610 (Alatyr', Ardatov, 1919); 612 (Buinsk, 1919); 613 (Alatyr', Ardatov, 1919); 614 (Simbirsk, 1919); 618 (Tambov, Voronezh, Saratov, 1919)

(iii) *fond* 484 (Vserossiiskii Tsentral'nyi Soiuz Potrebitel'skikh Obshchestv)
opis' 9 (Lesopromyshlennyi otdel)
dela 94 (Saratov, 1918); 207 (Samara, 1920–1)

(iv) *fond* 531 (*Sel'skosektsiia, Tsentrosoiuz*)
opis' 1 (Organizatsionno-tekhnicheskaia chast')
delo 43 (various regions, 1920)

(v) *fond* 532 (*Kustarnaia sektsiia, Tsentrosoiuz*)

opis' 1 (Otdel organizatsionno-inspektorskii)
delo 65 (various regions, 1920)

(vi) *fond* 5451 (Vserossiiskii Tsentral'nyi Sovet Professional'nykh Soiuzov)
opis' 4
dela 103, 123, 148 (provincial trade union councils, 1920); 289 (labour discipline, 1920)

(vii) *fond* 5556 (Voenno-prodovol'stvennoe Biuro VTsSPS)
opis' 1 (*Organizatsionnoe upravlenie, Instruktorskii otdel*)
dela 35a (various regions, 1918–19); 50 (various regions, 1919–20)

(b) TsGANKh

(i) *fond* 478 (Narodnyi Komissariat Zemledeliia)
opis' 1 (Upravlenie zemleustroistva i melioratsii)
dela 149–50 (Penza, 1918); 154 (Saratov, 1918); 202 (Saratov, Tsaritsyn, 1918)
opis' 1 (Biuro pechati)
delo 330 (various regions, 1919)
opis' 3 (Administrativno-finansovoe upravlenie)
dela 116 (Samara, 1918); 117 (Saratov, 1918); 384–5 (various regions, 1919); 387 (various regions, 1919)
opis' 3 (Glavsel'khoz)
delo 1157 (various regions, 1921)
opis' 4
delo 132 (various regions, 1918–19)
opis' 6 (Upravlenie zemleustroistva i melioratsii, OZU)
dela 101 (various regions, 1918); 224 (various regions, 1919–20); 1015 (various regions, 1918–19); 1701 (various regions, 1918–20); 2010 (various regions, 1920)
opis' 10 (Otdel kustarnoi promyshlennosti)
dela 42 (various regions, 1918–21); 104 (no title-page); 106 (Saratov, 1918–19); 164 (various regions, 1919); 168 (various regions, 1919); 240 (Saratov, 1919–20)

(ii) *fond* 1637 (Gosudarstvennoe Ob"edinenie Mashinostroitel'nykh Zavodov, 'GOMZA')
opis' 1 (Administrativnyi)
dela 358–62 (labour conscription, 1920)

(iii) *fond* 1881 (Narodnyi Komissariat Putei Soobshcheniia)
opis' 28 (Kollegiia)
delo 1 (protocols, 1919–20)

(iv) *fond* 1943 (Narodnyi Komissariat Prodovol'stviia)
opis' 1 (Glavnyi sekretariat)
dela 446–8 (various regions, 1919); 513 (various regions, 1919); 573 (Simbirsk, 1919); 1016 (Saratov, 1921)
opis' 3 (Organizatsionnyi otdel)
dela 127 (various regions, 1918); 223 (Samara, 1918)
opis' 4 (Khlebofurazhnoe upravlenie)

dela 116 (Samara, 1918); 117 (Saratov, 1918–19); 167 (various regions, 1919); 339 (various regions, 1918–21)
opis' 5 (Upravlenie skoroportiashchikhsia produktov)
delo 339 (various regions, 1920–1)
opis' 6 (Upravlenie zagotovok)
dela 330 (various regions, 1918–20); 347 (various regions, 1918–20); 376 (German Volga, Tsaritsyn, Nikolaevsk, 1920–1); 468 (various regions, 1921); 1225 (Samara, Severo-Dvinsk, Smolensk, 1919–20); 1420 (various regions, 1920)

(v) *fond* 3429 (Vysshii Sovet Narodnogo Khoziaistva)
opis' 1 (presidium)
dela 305 (food distribution, 1918); 857–9 (military procurements, 1919–20); 920 (various military affairs, 1919); 1485 (military inspection and procurements, 1920); 1527 (labour conscription, 1919–20); 1586 (military procurements, 1920–1)

(c) GAKO

(i) *fond* 7 (Samara Provincial Provisions Committee (*gubprodkom*))
opis' 1
dela 535 (*kombedy*, 1918); 802 (grain campaign, 1919)

(ii) *fond* 81 (Samara Provincial Soviet Executive Committee (*gubispolkom*))
opis' 1
dela 1–2 (Samara Provincial Soviet Assembly, 1917); 10 (Samara Provincial Soviet Executive Committee, 1919); 119–119a (various *volost'* soviets, Samara *uezd*, 1918); 127 (Buguruslan *uezd* soviet, 1918)

(iii) *fond* 109 (Androsovka VIK, Nikolaevsk *uezd*)
opis' 3
delo 52 (1919)
opis' 4
delo 59 (1920)

(iv) *fond* 185 (Alekseev VIK, Samara uezd)
opis' 2
delo 89 (1919–20)
opis' 3
delo 13 (1919–20)

(v) *fond* 193 (Samara Provincial Department of Administration (*otdel upravleniia*))
opis' 2 (Samara Provincial Soviet Executive Committee)
delo 159 (Stavropol' *sovnarkhoz*, 1919)

(vi) *fond* 236 (Samara *uezd* Land Department (*zemel'noe upravlenie*))
opis' 1
dela 3 (collective farms, 1918–19); 141 (collective farms, 1918–19); 159–60 (collective farms, 1918–19); 230 (collective farms, 1918–19)

(vii) *fond* 1241 (Mokshchan' VIK, Nikolaevsk *uezd*)

opis' 2
delo 1 (1919–20)

(viii) *fond* 3134 (Chernovka VIK, Buzuluk *uezd*)
opis' 2
delo 21 (1918–19)

2. ARCHIVAL SOURCES IN THE USA

(A) COLUMBIA UNIVERSITY RUSSIAN ARCHIVE

American Relief Association (A. E. Blomquist)
T. K. Chugunov
S. L. Frank
M. Lidin (M. Fomichev), 'Antonovshchina: Iz vospominanii antonovtsa'
A. Wardell

(b) LIBRARY OF CONGRESS MANUSCRIPTS DIVISION

A. Babine, 'The Bolsheviks in Russia'; 'Journal'

3. NEWSPAPERS AND PERIODICALS

Biulleten' saratovskogo gubernskogo soveta narodnogo khoziaistva (Saratov), 1918–19.
Biulleten' saratovskogo gubkoma RKP (Saratov), 1920.
Biulleten' saratovskogo gubprodkoma (statisticheskii otdel) (Saratov), 1918 [*SGB*].
Biulleten' simbirskogo gubernskogo otdela upravleniia (Simbirsk), 1921–2.
Biulleten' Tsentral'nogo Statisticheskogo Upravleniia, 1922.
Bor'ba (Tsaritsyn), 1918–22.
Bugul'minskaia gazeta (Bugul'ma), 1918.
Ekonomicheskaia zhizn' (Moscow), 1921–2.
Ekonomicheskaia zhizn' (Saratov), 1920.
Iunyi kommunar (Serdobsk), 1920–1.
Izvestiia, 1918–21.
Izvestiia (Atkarsk), 1919–20.
Izvestiia (Balakovo), 1919.
Izvestiia (Balashov), 1918–19.
Izvestiia (Kamyshin), 1918.
Izvestiia (Kuznetsk), 1917–19.
Izvestiia (Samara), 1919.
Izvestiia (Saratov), 1917–21.
Izvestiia (Vol'sk), 1918–19.
Izvestiia gosudarstvennogo kontrolia (Moscow), 1919.
Izvestiia melekesskogo uezdnogo komiteta RKP(b) (Melekess), 1921.
Izvestiia samarskogo gubernskogo soveta narodnogo khoziaistva (Samara), 1918–19.
Izvestiia samarskogo gubkoma RKP (Samara), 1920–1.
Izvestiia samarskogo gubprodkoma (Samara), 1918–19 [*ISG*].

Izvestiia samarskogo gubernskogo soiuza potrebitel'nykh obshchestv (Samara), 1920–1.
Izvestiia saratovskogo gubprodkoma (Saratov), 1918–19.
Kommuna (Petrovsk), 1918–21.
Kommuna (Samara), 1918–22.
Kommunist (Pugachev), 1920–21.
Kommunist (Tsaritsyn), 1921.
Kommunisticheskii put' (Saratov), 1923–
Kooperativnaia mysl' (Saratov), 1919.
Krasnaia armiia (Samara), 1919.
Krasnaia kommuna (Atkarsk), 1918–19.
Krasnoarmeets (Saratov), 1918–19.
Krasnoarmeets (Tambov), 1921.
Krasnoe slovo (Samara), 1918.
Krasnoe znamia (Khvalynsk), 1920.
Krasnyi nabat (Balakovo), 1919–22.
Krasnyi pakhar' (Pugachev), 1921.
Krasnyi Ural (Ural'sk), 1920–2.
Krest'ianin (Menzelinsk), 1920–1.
Krest'ianskaia pravda (Tsaritsyn), 1921.
Luch kommuny (Buguruslan), 1919–22.
Nabat (Kamyshin), 1919–21.
Nabat (Pokrovsk), 1919.
Nizhnee Povolzh'e (Saratov), 1921– .
Oktiabr'skaia revoliutsiia (Khvalynsk), 1920–2.
Partiinyi sputnik (Tsaritsyn), 1922.
Plennyi i bezhenets (Saratov), 1918.
Pravda, 1918–21.
Privolzhskaia pravda (Samara), 1917–18.
Proletarskaia revoliutsiia (Istpart), 1921.
Rabochii i kooperativnyi mir (Balashov), 1918.
Revoliutsionnaia armiia (Samara/4th Army), 1919.
Samarskie eparkhial'nye vedomosti (Samara), 1918.
Samarskii zemledelets (Samara), 1918.
Saratovskii listok (Saratov), 1917.
Sel'sko-khoziaistvennyi listok (Balashov), 1918.
Serdobskaia zhizn' (Serdobsk), 1918.
Serp i molot (Kuznetsk), 1920–2.
Serp i molot (Samara), 1918.
Serp i molot (Serdobsk), 1920–2.
Sovetskaia derevnia (Saratov), 1920.
Sovetskoe stroitel'stvo (Samara), 1918–19[SS].
Stepnoi rabotnik (Novouzensk), 1921.
Svobodnyi zemledelets (Saratov), 1918.
Trudovaia pravda (Pokrovsk), 1921–2.
Vestnik informatsionno-instruktorskogo podotdela otdela upravleniia Samarskoi gubernii (Samara), 1918.

Vestnik Komissariata Vnutrennikh Del (*Vlast' sovetov* after November 1918), 1917–18.
Vestnik Komiteta Uchreditel'nogo Sobraniia (Samara), 1918.
Vestnik kustarnoi promyshlennosti (Petrograd), 1921–2.
Vestnik saratovskogo gubkoma RKP (Saratov), 1921.
Vlast' sovetov (*Vestnik Komissariata Vnutrennikh Del* before November 1918,) 1919.
Voennaia mysl' (Revvoensovet vostochnogo fronta), 1919.
Volia Rossii (Prague), 1920–1.

4. CONTEMPORARY GOVERNMENT AND PARTY PUBLICATIONS

Biulleten' gubotnaroba k gubernskomu s"ezdu po narodnomu obrazovaniiu, Saratov, 1921.
Chetvertyi vserossiiskii s"ezd sovetov. Stenograficheskii otchet, Moscow, 1919.
Chislennost' naseleniia Saratovskoi gubernii po dannym demografichesko-professional'noi perepisi 1920 g., Saratov (Saratovskoe gubernskoe statisticheskoe biuro), 1921.
Chislennost' sel'skogo naseleniia v Samarskoi gubernii, Samara, 1920.
Doklad samarskogo gubispolkoma 9-go sozyva o politicheskom i ekonomicheskom sostoianii i o prodelannoi rabote za god 10-mu gubernskomu s"ezdu sovetov za 1922 god, Samara, 1922.
Doklad vol'skogo uezdnogo ispolkoma sovetov 15 oktiabria 1919 g., Vol'sk, 1919.
Doklady i rezoliutsii 10-go saratovskogo gubernskogo s"ezda sovetov (10–13 iiunia 1921 g.), Saratov, 1921.
Godovshchina sotsial'noi revoliutsii v Saratove, Saratov, 1918.
Itogi desiatiletiia Sovetskoi vlasti v tsifrakh, 1917–1927, Moscow, 1927.
Itogi perepisi naseleniia 1920 goda, Moscow, 1928.
Iubileinyi sbornik saratovskogo gubprodkomiteta 7 noiabria 1917 g.–17 noiabria 1919 g., Saratov, 1919.
Krasnaia byl': Sbornik samarskogo gubernskogo biuro istparta, Samara, 1923.
Krasnaia letopis': Materialy k istorii sovetskogo stroitel'stva v Samarskoi gubernii (oktiabr' 1917 g.–aprel' 1921 g.) k VIII gubernskomu s"ezdu sovetov r.k. i kr. dep., 18 iiunia 1921 g., Samara, 1921.
Kratkii otchet i rezoliutsii IX-ogo s"ezda sovetov Saratovskoi gubernii, Saratov, 1921.
Krest'ianstvo i trudovaia povinnost', n.p., 1920.
Kriticheskaia otsenka materialov vserossiiskoi perepisi i sistema ee razrabotki, Samara (Samarskoe gubernskoe zemstvo), 1916.
Lichnyi sostav RKP v 1920 g., Moscow, 1921.
Materialy dlia otsenki zemel' Saratovskoi gubernii, vyp. 6, *Osnovaniia otsenki i normy dokhodnosti zemel'nykh ugodii*, Saratov (Saratovskoe gubernskoe zemstvo), 1908.
Materialy k XIII-mu vol'skomu uezdnomu s"ezdu sovetov 12 dekabria 1920 g., Vol'sk, 1920.

Materialy k XIV-mu vol'skomu uezdnomu s"ezdu sovetov 1 iiunia 1921 g., Vol'sk, 1921.

Materialy po zemel'noi reforme 1918 goda, vyp. 1, *Raspredelenie zemli v 1918 godu*, Moscow, 1919 [*MZR 1*].

Materialy po zemel'noi reforme 1918 goda, vyp. 6, *Otchuzhdenie i ispol'zovanie sel'sko-khoziaistvennogo inventaria*, Moscow, 1918 [*MZR 6*].

O zemle: Sbornik statei o proshlom i budushchem zemel'no-khoziaistvennogo stroitel'stva, Moscow, 1921.

Obvinitel'noe zakliuchenie po delu Tsentral'nogo Komiteta i otdel'nykh chlenov inykh organizatsii partii s.-r. po obvineniiu ikh v vooruzhennykh ogrableniiakh i izmennicheskikh snosheniiakh s inostrannymi gosudarstvami, Moscow, 1922.

Obzor deiatel'nosti khlebnogo otdela samarskogo gubernskogo prodovol'stvennogo komiteta s oktiabria 1918 g. po 1 marta 1919 g., Samara, 1919.

Otchet balakovskogo uezdnogo ekonomicheskogo soveshchaniia, Balakovo, 1921.

Otchet balashovskogo uezdnogo ekonomicheskogo soveshchaniia iiun'–sentiabr' 1921 g., Balashov, 1921.

Otchet buguruslanskogo uezdnogo ekonomicheskogo soveshchaniia sovetu truda i oborony 3-go iiunia po 1-e noiabria 1921 g., 2 vols., Buguruslan, 1921.

Otchet buzulukskogo uezdnogo ekonomicheskogo soveshchaniia s 1-go iiulia po 1-e oktiabria 1921 g., Buzuluk, 1921.

Otchet ekonomicheskogo soveshchaniia Oblasti Nemtsev Povolzh'ia na 1-oe aprelia 1922 g., Pokrovsk, 1922.

Otchet khvalynskogo uezdnogo ekonomicheskogo soveshchaniia (za 1921–1923 gg.), 3 vols., Khvalynsk, 1923.

Otchet melekesskogo uekonsoveshchaniia, Melekess, 1921.

Otchet novouzenskogo soveta soldatskikh, rabochikh i krest'ianskikh deputatov, Novouzensk, 1918.

Otchet petrovskogo uezdnogo ekonomicheskogo soveshchaniia (iiul'-sentiabr' 1921 g.), Petrovsk, 1921.

Otchet pugachevskogo uezdnogo ekonomicheskogo soveshchaniia, Pugachev, 1921.

Otchet samarskogo gubernskogo ekonomicheskogo soveshchaniia, vyp. 1–3, Samara, 1921–2.

Otchet saratovskogo ekonomicheskogo soveshchaniia, Saratov, 1922.

Otchet saratovskogo gubernskogo ispolnitel'nogo komiteta 9-go sozyva 10-mu gubernskomu s"ezdu sovetov za oktiabr' 1920 g.-iiun' 1921 g., Saratov, 1921.

Otchet saratovskogo uezdnogo ispolnitel'nogo komiteta 10-go sozyva 11-mu uezdnomu s"ezdu sovetov za dekabr' 1921 g.-dekabr' 1922 g., Saratov, 1922.

Otchet serdobskogo uezdnogo ekonomicheskogo soveshchaniia, Serdobsk, 1921.

Otchet vol'skogo uezdnogo ekonomicheskogo soveshchaniia, 2 vols., Vol'sk, 1922.

Otchet vol'skogo uezdnogo ispolkoma sovetov, 2 vols., Vol'sk, 1919–24.

Pervaia vseobshchaia perepis' naseleniia Rossiiskoi Imperii 1897 g., St Petersburg, 1903–4.
Ploshchadi sadov, ogorodov i bakhchei v sel'skikh khoziaistvakh Samarskoi gubernii v 1919 godu, Samara, 1920.
Posevnye ploshchadi, kolichestvo senokosov raznykh vidov i chislennost' mertvogo inventaria, Samara, 1919.
Postanovleniia 4-go samarskogo gubernskogo s"ezda sovetov, Samara, 1918.
Prodovol'stvennaia statistika: Samarskaia guberniia 1917 goda, Samara, 1918.
Protokol kamyshinskogo uezdnogo s"ezda krest'ianskikh deputatov i predstavitelei razlichnykh politicheskikh grupp, uchrezhdenii i organizatsii, 10-go marta 1918 g., Kamyshin, 1918.
Protokol 5-go s"ezda upolnomochennykh potrebitel'nykh obshchestv Serdobskogo uezda, n.p., 1919.
Protokol zasedaniia 11-go pugachevskogo uezdnogo s"ezda sovetov 6 dekabria 1921 g., Pugachev, n.d.
Protokoly i doklady VII-go simbirskogo gubernskogo s"ezda sovetov, Simbirsk, 1919.
Protokoly i doklady VI-go atkarskogo uezdnogo s"ezda sovetov 15–19 oktiabria 1918 g., Atkarsk, 1918.
Protokoly novouzenskogo soveta, n.p., 1918.
Protokoly saratovskogo gubernskogo s"ezda sovetov krest'ianskikh deputatov, proiskhodivshego v g. Saratove s 25-go maia po 2 iiunia 1918 g., Saratov, 1918 [*PSG*].
Protokoly saratovskogo s"ezda sovetov, Saratov, 1918.
Protokoly 2-go samarskogo gubernskogo krest'ianskogo s"ezda s 20 maia po 6 iiunia 1917 g. i protokoly obshchegubernskogo vsesoslovnogo s"ezda s 28 maia po 6 iiunia 1917 g., Samara, 1917 [*PVS*].
Protokoly zasedaniia kamyshinskogo uezdnogo ispolkoma soveta s 22 marta po 1 iiunia 1918 g., Kamyshin, 1918.
Protokoly zasedanii saratovskogo voennogo komiteta: Protokoly zasedanii prezidiuma saratovskogo voennogo komiteta, Saratov, 1921.
Rezoliutsii i postanovleniia 7-go buzulukskogo uezdnogo s"ezda sovetov 20–24 oktiabria 1919 g., Buzuluk, 1919.
Rezoliutsii i tezisy priniatye na 7-om samarskom gubernskom s"ezde sovetov,, Samara 1921.
Rezoliutsii priniatye pervym gubernskim krest'ianskim s"ezdom posevkomov Samarskoi gubernii proiskhodivshim v g. Samare 10–14 marta 1921 g., Samara, 1921.
Rezul'taty obsledovaniia pitaniia gorodskogo naseleniia Samarskoi gubernii, Samara, 1919.
Sbornik materialov 12-mu vol'skomu uezdnomu s"ezdu sovetov 3 iiunia 1920 g., Vol'sk, 1920.
Sbornik statisticheskikh svedenii po Samarskoi gubernii, Samara, 1924.
Sbornik statisticheskikh svedenii po Soiuzu SSR, Moscow, 1924.
Sbornik 'Ves' Kuznetsk', Kuznetsk, 1927.
Sed'moi Vserossiiskii s"ezd Sovetov: Stenograficheskii otchet, Moscow, 1920.

VI s"ezd kuznetskogo soveta rabochikh i krest'ianskikh deputatov, Kuznetsk, 1919.
Sobranie uzakonenii i rasporiazhenii raboche-krest'ianskogo pravitel'stva, Moscow, 1917–24 [*SU*].
Sostoianie ozimykh posevov i kolichestvo skota v Samarskoi gubernii vesnoiu 1919 g., Samara (Samarskoe gubernskoe statisticheskoe otdelenie), n.d.
Spiski naselennykh mest Saratovskoi gubernii: Saratovskii uezd Saratov, 1912.
Spisok naselennykh punktov Samarskoi gubernii, Samara, 1928.
Statisticheskii sbornik po Saratovskoi gubernii, Saratov, 1923.
Statistika zemlevladeniia 1905 g., 50 vols., St Petersburg, 1906.
Stenograficheskii otchet chrezvychainogo VI vserossiiskogo s"ezda sovetov, Moscow, 1919.
Stenograficheskii otchet 11-go saratovskogo gubernskogo s"ezda sovetov 16–17 dekabria 1921 g., Saratov, 1921.
Stenograficheskii otchet 7-go syzranskogo uezdnogo soveta s 4-go po 5-e iiulia 1920 g., Syzran', 1920.
Tablitsy statisticheskikh svedenii po Saratovskoi gubernii po dannym vserossiiskoi sel'sko-khoziaistvennoi i gorodskoi perepisei, Saratov, 1919.
Tretii otchet vol'skogo uezdekonomsoveshchaniia za vremia aprel'–oktiabr' 1922 goda, n.p., n.d. (typed MS).
Tri goda bor'by s golodom, Moscow, 1920.
Tri goda raboty otdelov buguruslanskogo uezdnogo ispolnitel'nogo komiteta sovetov (1917–20 gg.), Buguruslan, 1921.
Trudy 9-go buguruslanskogo s"ezda sovetov 1-go dekabria 1921 g.: Sekretarskaia zapis', Buguruslan, 1922.
Trudy 1-go vserossiiskogo s"ezda zemotdelov, komitetov bednoty i kommun, Moscow, 1919.
Trudy TsSU: Itogi vserossiiskoi sel'sko-khoziaistvennoi perepisi 1920 g., vol. 2, vyp. 2, Moscow, 1921.
Trudy TsSU: Itogi vserossiiskoi sel'sko-khoziaistvennoi perepisi 1920 g. v granitsakh gubernii na 1 marta 1922 g., vol. 2, vyp. 8, Moscow, 1923.
Trudy TsSU: Pogubernskie itogi vserossiiskoi sel'sko-khoziaistvennoi i pozemel'noi perepisi 1917 g., vol. 5, vyp. 1, Moscow, 1921.
Trudy TsSU: Pouezdnye itogi vserossiiskoi sel'sko-khoziaistvennoi i pozemel' noi perepisi 1917 g., vol. 5, vyp. 2, Moscow, 1923.
Trudy TsSU: Ekonomicheskoe rassloenie krest'ianstva v 1917 i 1919 g., vol. 6, vyp. 3, Moscow, 1922.
Trudy TsSU: Statisticheskii sbornik za 1913–1917 gg., vol. 7, vyp. 1, Moscow, 1921.
Trudy TsSU: Statisticheskii ezhegodnik 1918–1920 gg., vol. 8, vyp. 1–2, Moscow, 1922.
Trudy TsSU: Statisticheskii ezhegodnik 1921 g., vol. 8, vyp. 3–4, Moscow, 1922.
Trudy TsSU: Gruppovye itogi sel'sko-khoziaistvennoi perepisi 1920 goda, vol. 9, vyp. 1a, Moscow, 1926.

Urozhai khlebov v 1918 godu, Samara (Samarskoe gubernskoe statisticheskoe biuro), 1918.

Vos'moi vserossiiskii s"ezd sovetov 21–29 dekabria 1920 g.: Stenograficheskii otchet, Moscow, 1921.

Vosstanovlenie khoziaistva i razvitie proizvoditel'nykh sil iugo-vostoka RSFSR, postradavshego ot neurozhaia 1921 g., Moscow, 1921.

Vserossiiskaia perepis' chlenov RKP 1922 goda, vyp. 1–5, Moscow, 1922–4,

Vserossiiskaia perepis' naseleniia 1920 goda: Simbirskaia guberniia, Simbirsk (Simbirskoe gubernskoe statisticheskoe biuro), 1923.

Vtoroi otchet vol'skogo uezdekonomsoveshchaniia za vremia oktiabr' 1921 g.–mart 1922 g., n.p., n.d. (typed MS).

Vtoroi plenum saratovskogo gubkoma RKP, 5–7 oktiabria 1921 g. (Doklady i rezoliutsii), Saratov, 1921.

Zasedanie saratovskogo soveta s uchastiem predsedatelia VTsIK, tov. Kalinina: Stenograficheskii otchet, Saratov, 1921.

Zemel'nyi fond Samarskoi gubernii, Samara, 1918: vyp. 1, *Zemel'nye obrochnye stat'i kazni*; vyp. 2, *Zemli samarskogo otdeleniia byvshego krest'ianskogo pozemel'nogo banka*; vyp. 3, *Zemli byvshego udel'nogo vedomstva*; vyp. 4, *Svod dannykh o vydelennykh nadel'nykh zemliakh*; vyp. 5, *Zemli tserkovnye i monastyrskie*; vyp. 8, *Kachestvennyi sostav zemel'nogo fonda po materialam mestnykh otsenochno-statisticheskikh obsledovanii*; vyp. 9, *Kazennye lesnye dachi*; vyp. 10 (appendix), *Raspredelenie zemel' po ugod'iam* (1919).

Zhurnal zasedaniia III-go samarskogo uezdnogo s"ezda sovetov krest'ianskikh i rabochikh deputatov, Samara, 1918.

5. SECONDARY SOURCES

Abramov, P. N., 'K voprosu o vremeni sozdanii pervykh volostnykh sovetov', *Istoriia SSSR*, 1960, no. 5.

—— 'Oprosnyi list volostnogo soveta (1918 g.)'. *Istoricheskii Arkhiv*, 1960, no. 3.

—— 'Sovetskoe stroitel'stvo na sele v dokombedskii period', *Voprosy Istorii KPSS*, 1960, no. 6.

Abrams, R., 'The Local Soviets of the RSFSR, 1918–1921', Ph.D. diss., Columbia University, 1966.

'Agitpoezdki M. I. Kalinina v gody grazhdanskoi voiny', *Krasnyi Arkhiv*, vol. 1 (86), 1938.

Agrarnaia politika Sovetskoi vlasti (1917–1918 gg.), Moscow, 1954.

Agrarnoe dvizhenie v Rossii v 1905–1906 gg., St Petersburg, 1908.

Alaverdova, A, 'Ocherk agrarnoi politiki vremennogo pravitel'stva (fevral'-oktiabr' 1917 g.)', *Sotsialisticheskoe khoziaistvo*, vol. 2, 1925.

Aleksandrov, V. A., *Sel'skaia obshchina v Rossii (XVII v.–nachalo XIX v.)*, Moscow, 1976.

Alekseev, B. N., 'Bor'ba s chekho-slovatskim miatezhom v Povolzh'e', *Proletarskaia revoliutsiia*, vol. 4, no. 75, 1928.

Altrichter, H., *Die Bauern von Tver: Vom Leben auf dem russischen Dorfe zwischen Revolution und Kollektivierung*, Munich, 1984.

ANDREEV, V. M., 'Prodrazverstka i krest'ianstvo', *Istoricheskie zapiski*, vol. 97, Moscow, 1976.
—— *Pod znamenem proletariata*, Moscow, 1981.
ANDREIUK, I. M., 'Bor'ba krest'ian za zemliu v Penzenskoi gubernii v 1917 godu', in *Uchenye zapiski penzenskogo pedag. instituta. Seriia istoricheskaia*, Saratov/Penza, 1966, no. 16.
ANFIMOV, A. M., 'K voprosu o kharaktere agrarnogo stroia Evropeiskoi Rossii XX v.', *Istoricheskie zapiski*, vol. 65, Moscow, 1959.
—— *Zemel'naia arenda v Rossii v nachale XX veka*, Moscow, 1961.
—— *Rossiiskaia derevnia v gody pervoi mirovoi voiny*, Moscow, 1962.
—— *Krupnoe pomeshchich'e khoziaistvo Evropeiskoi Rossii*, Moscow, 1969.
—— *Krest'ianskoe khoziaistvo Evropeiskoi Rossii 1881–1904*, Moscow, 1980.
—— *Ekonomicheskoe polozhenie i klassovaia bor'ba krest'ian Evropeiskoi Rossii 1881–1904*, Moscow, 1984.
—— and MAKAROV, I. F., 'Novye dannye o zemlevladenii Evropeiskoi Rossii', Istoriia SSSR, 1974, no. 1.
ANIKEEV, V. V., 'Svedeniia o bol'shevistskikh organizatsiiakh s marta po dekabr' 1917 goda', *Voprosy istorii KPSS*, 1958, nos. 2–3.
ANISTRATENKO, V. P., 'Kommunisty Urala vo glave bor'by trudovogo krest' ianstva protiv kulachestva v 1921–23 godakh', kand. diss., Sverdlovsk, 1971.
ANTONOV-OVSEENKO, V. P., 'O banditskom dvizhenii v Tambovskoi gubernii', in Meijer (ed.), *The Trotsky Papers*, vol. 2.
ANTONOV-SARATOVSKII, V. P., *Pod stiagom proletarskoi bor'by: Otryvki iz vospominanii o rabote v Saratove za vremia s 1915 g. do 1918 g.*, Moscow/Leningrad, 1925.
—— (ed.), *Sovety v epokhu voennogo kommunizma (1918–1921): Sbornik dokumentov*, 2 vols., Moscow (Communist Academy), 1928–9 [*SEV*].
Antonovshchina: Sbornik statei, Tambov, 1923.
ANWEILER, O., *The Soviets: The Russian Workers, Peasants and Soldiers Councils, 1905–1921*, trans. R. Hein, New York, 1974.
ATKINSON, D., *The End of the Russian Land Commune 1905–1930*, Stanford, 1983.
AVER'EV, V. N. (ed.), *Komitety bednoty: Sbornik materialov*, 2 vols., Moscow/Leningrad, 1933.
—— 'Likvidatsiia burzhuaznykh organov mestnogo samoupravleniia', *Sovetskoe gosudarstvo*, 1936, no. 4.
—— and RONIN, S., 'Kulatskie vosstaniia v epokhu kombedov', *Bor'ba klassov*, 1935, no. 3.
AVRICH, P., *The Russian Anarchists*, Princeton, 1967.
BAEVSKII, D. A., *Rabochii klass v pervye gody Sovetskoi vlasti (1917–1921 gg.)*, Moscow, 1974.
BARASHEVSKII, P. A. (ed.), *Istoricheskii ocherk Tsaritsynskogo uezda*, Tsaritsyn, 1922.
BASKIN, G. I., *Printsipy zemel'nogo naseleniia v sviazi s otnosheniem naseleniia k raznym formam zemlevladeniia i zemlepol'zovaniia*, Samara, 1917.

Baskin, G. I., *Sbornik izbrannykh trudov G. I. Baskina po Samarskoi gubernii: Iubileinoe izdanie*, vyp. 1–6, Samara, 1925.

Bazarov, V. K., 'K voprosu o razvitii batrachestva v poslerevoliutsionnye gody', in *Sel'skoe khoziaistvo na putiakh vosstanovleniia*, Moscow, 1925.

Belliutsin, I. S., *Description of the Clergy in Rural Russia*, trans. G. L. Freeze, Cornell, 1985.

Belogurov, M. G., 'Statisticheskie istochniki o sostave sel'skikh sovetov v pervye gody vosstanovitel'nogo perioda (1921–23 gg.)', in *Istochnikovedenie istorii sovetskogo obshchestva*, vyp. 3, Moscow, 1978.

Berk, S., 'The Democratic Counter-Revolution: *Komuch* and the Civil War on the Volga', *Canadian-American Slavic Studies*, vol. 7, 1973.

Berkevich, A., *Petrogradskie rabochie v bor'be za khleb 1918–20 gg.*, Leningrad, 1941.

Berzin, A., 'Itogi i blizhaishie perspektivy zemleustroistva', in *O zemle.*

Biriukov, A., *Kreditnaia kooperatsiia i kustarnaia promyshlennost'*, Saratov, 1918.

Bliakher, Ia., 'Sovremennoe zemlepol'zovanie po dannym spetsial'noi ankety TsSU 1922 g.', *Vestnik statistiki*, vol. 13, 1923, nos, 1–3.

Bliumental', I. I., *Revoliutsiia 1917–1918 gg. v Samarskoi gubernii (Khronika sobytii)*, Samara, 1927.

Boevye podvigi chastei krasnoi armii (1918–1922 gg.), Moscow, 1957.

Bogdanov, N., 'Materialy po obsledovaniiu sarpinochno-tkatskogo proizvodstva kooperativnykh tovarishchestv i trudovykh artelei Kamyshinskogo kraia', *Vestnik kustarnoi promyshlennosti* (Petrograd), no. 12 (63), 1918.

Bol'shakov, A. M., *Sovetskaia derevnia za 1917–24 gg.*, Leningrad, 1924.

—— 'The Soviet Countryside 1917–24', in R. E. F. Smith (ed.), *The Russian Peasant*, London, 1977.

Bol'sheviki Tatarii v gody inostrannoi voennoi interventsii i grazhdanskoi voiny: Sbornik dokumentov, Kazan', 1961.

Bor'ba za ustanovlenie i uprochenie sovetskoi vlasti v Simbirskoi gubernii: Sbornik dokumentov, Ul'ianovsk, 1958.

Brovkin, V., 'The Mensheviks' Political Comeback: The Elections to the Provincial City Soviets in Spring 1918', *Russian Review*, vol. 42, 1983.

Bruk, B., *Krest'ianskoe khoziaistvo v period prodrazverstki*, Voronezh, 1923.

Bugai, N. F., 'Revoliutsionnye komitety—chrezvychainye organy sovetskoi vlasti (1918–1921 gg.)', *Istoricheskie zapiski*, vol. 102, Moscow, 1978.

Bushnell, J., *Mutiny and Repression: Russian Soldiers in the Revolution of 1905–1906*, Indiana, 1985.

Butyl'kin, P. A., and Gerasimenko, P. A., 'Osushchestvlenie agrarnykh preobrazovanii v Nizhnem Povolzh'e', in *Leninskii Dekret o zemle v deistvii.*

Byli plamennykh let, Kuibyshev, 1963.

Bystrova, A. S., *Komitety bednoty v Viatskoi gubernii*, Kirov, 1956.

Carr, E. H., *The Bolshevik Revolution 1917–1923*, 3 vols., Harmondsworth, 1966.

Chamberlin, W. H., *The Russian Revolution 1917–1921*, 2 vols., Princeton, 1987 (originally New York 1935).

CHANNON, J., 'Tsarist Landowners after the Revolution: Former Pomeshchiki in Rural Russia during NEP', *Soviet Studies*, vol. 39, no. 4, 1987.

CHASE, W. J., *Workers, Society and the Soviet State: Labour and Life in Moscow, 1918–1929*, Urbana, Ill., 1987.

CHAYANOV, A. V., *The Theory of Peasant Economy*, ed. D. Thorner, B. Kerblay, and R. E. F. Smith, Manchester, 1986.

CHEBAEVSKII, F. V., 'Stroitel'stvo mestnykh sovetov v kontse 1917 i pervoi polovine 1918 gg.', *Istoricheskie zapiski*, vol. 61, Moscow, 1957.

CHELINTSEV, A. N., *Teoreticheskie osnovaniia organizatsii krest'ianskogo khoziaistva*, Khar'kov, 1919.

CHERNOV, V. M., *Pered burei: Vospominaniia*, New York, 1953.

Chetyre goda prodovol'stvennoi raboty, Moscow, 1922.

Chetyre mesiatsa uchredilovshchiny, Samara, 1919.

CHISTOV, B. N., 'Krakh chapannogo miatezha', *Volga*, no. 4 (100), 1974.

CHUGAEV, D. A., and VASIUKOV, V. S. (eds.), *Ustanovlenie Sovetskoi vlasti na mestakh v 1917–1918 gg.*, Moscow, 1959.

COHEN, S., 'Bolshevism and Stalinism', in R. C. Tucker (ed.), *Stalinism: Essays in Historical Interpretation*, New York, 1977.

—— *Bukharin and the Bolshevik Revolution*, Oxford, 1980.

COLLINS, E. J. T., 'Labour Supply and Demand in European Agriculture 1800–1880', in E. L. Jones and S. J. Woolf (eds.), *Agrarian Change and Economic Development*, London, 1969.

COX, T., *Peasants, Class and Capitalism*, Oxford, 1986.

CZAP P., 'Peasant-Class Courts and Peasant Customary Justice in Russia, 1861–1912', *Journal of Social History*, vol. 1, 1967.

DANILOV, V. P., 'Zemel'nye otnosheniia v sovetskoi dokolkhoznoi derevne', *Istoriia SSSR*, 1958, no. 3.

—— 'O kharaktere sotsial'no-ekonomicheskikh otnoshenii sovetskogo krest'ianstva do kollektivizatsii sel'skogo khoziaistva', in *Istoriia sovetskogo krest'ianstva i kolkhoznogo stroitel'stva v SSSR*, Moscow, 1963.

—— 'K kharakteristike obshchestvenno-politicheskoi obstanovki v sovetskoi derevne nakanune kollektivizatsii', *Istoricheskie zapiski*, vol. 79, Moscow, 1966.

—— 'K voprosu o kharaktere i znachenii krest'ianskoi pozemel'noi obshchiny v Rossii', in *Problemy sotsial'no-ekonomicheskoi istorii Rossii*, Moscow, 1971.

—— 'Obshchina u narodov SSSR v posleoktiabr'skii period: K voprosu o tipologii obshchiny na territorii sovetskikh respublik', *Narody Azii i Afriki*, 1973, no. 3.

—— 'Ob istoricheskikh sud'bakh krest'ianskoi obshchiny v Rossii', *Ezhegodnik po agrarnoi istorii*, vyp.6, *Problemy istorii russkoi obshchiny*, Vologda, 1976.

—— 'Istochnikovedcheskie i arkheograficheskie problemy istorii russkoi obshchiny posle Oktiabr'skoi revoliutsii', in *Severnyi arkheograficheskii sbornik*, Syktyvkar, 1977.

—— *Rural Russia under the New Regime*, trans. with an introd. by O. Figes, London, 1988 (originally *Sovetskaia dokolkhoznaia derevnia: naselenie, zemlepol'zovanie, khoziaistvo*, Moscow, 1977) [*RR*].

DANILOV, V. P., 'Pereraspredelenie zemel'nogo fonda Rossii v rezul'tate Velikoi Oktiabr'skoi revoliutsii', in *Leninskii Dekret o zemle v deistvii.*

—— *Sovetskaia dokolkhoznaia derevnia: sotsial'naia struktura, sotsial'nye otnosheniia*, Moscow, 1979.

DEDOV, A. M., *Komitety derevenskoi bednoty i ikh rol' v ukreplenii sovetskoi vlasti*, Moscow, 1958.

Dekrety Sovetskoi vlasti, 10 vols., Moscow, 1957–9 [*DSV*].

DENIKIN, A. I., *Ocherki russkoi smuty*, vol. 3, *Beloe dvizhenie i bor'ba dobrovol'cheskoi armii mai–oktiabr' 1918 goda*, Berlin, 1924.

10 let Oktiabria v Alatyrskom uezde, Chuvashskoi respubliki: Sbornik statei, Alatyr', 1927.

DOBB, M., *Russian Economic Development since the Revolution*, London, 1928.

DROBIZHEV, V. Z., SOKOLOV, A. K., and USTINOV, V. A., *Rabochii klass Sovetskoi Rossii v pervyi god proletarskoi diktatury (opyt strukturnogo analiza po materialam professional'noi perepisi 1918 g.)*, Moscow, 1975.

DUBROVSKII, S. M., *Krest'ianstvo v 1917 g.*, Moscow/Leningrad, 1927.

—— *Die Bauernbewegung in der russischen Revolution 1917*, Berlin, 1929.

EISFELD, A., *Deutsche Kolonien an der Wolga 1917–1919 und das deutsche Reich*, Munich, 1985.

EKLOF, B., *Russian Peasant Schools: Officialdom, Village Culture and Popular Pedagogy 1861–1914*, Berkeley, Calif., 1986.

Ekonomicheskoe polozhenie Rossii nakanune Velikoi Oktiabr'skoi sotsialisticheskoi revoliutsii, Leningrad, 1967.

EMMONS, T., *The Formation of Political Parties and the First National Elections in Russia*, Harvard, 1983.

ERICKSON, J., 'The Origins of the Red Army', in Pipes (ed.), *Revolutionary Russia.*

ESSELBORN, K., *Aus den Leidenstagen der deutschen Wolga-Kolonien*, Darmstadt, 1922.

FALLOWS, T. S., 'Forging the Zemstvo Movement: Liberalism and Radicalism on the Volga, 1890–1905', Ph.D. diss., Harvard University, 1981.

FERRO, M., *October 1917: A Social History of the Russian Revolution*, trans. N. Stone, London, 1980.

FIGES, O., 'Collective Farming and the 19th-Century Russian Land Commune: A Research Note', *Soviet Studies*, vol. 38, no. 1, 1986.

—— 'V. P. Danilov on the Analytical Distinction Between Peasants and Farmers', in Shanin (ed.), *Peasants and Peasant Societies.*

—— 'The Village and *Volost* Soviet Elections of 1919', *Soviet Studies*, vol. 40, no. 1, 1988.

FISHER, H. H., *The Famine in Soviet Russia 1919–1923*, New York, 1927.

FISHER, O., 'Über die heutige wirtschaftsliche Lage in den Wolgakolonien', *Wolgadeutsche Monatshefte*, Dec. 1922.

FITZPATRICK, S., *The Russian Revolution 1917–1932*, Oxford, 1982.

—— 'The Civil War as a Formative Experience', in A. Gleason, P. Kenez, and R. Stites (eds.), *Bolshevik Culture*, Bloomington, Ind., 1985.

FOOTMAN, D., *Civil War in Russia*, London, 1961.

Frenkin, M., *Russkaia armiia i revoliutsiia 1917–1918, Munich, 1978.*
—— *Tragediia krest'ianskikh vosstanii v Rossii 1918–1921 gg.*, Jerusalem, 1987.
Frierson, C., 'Crime and Punishment in the Russian Village: Rural Concepts of Criminality at the End of the Nineteenth Century', *Slavic Review*, vol. 45, 1986.
M. V. Frunze na frontakh grazhdanskoi voiny, Moscow, 1941.
Fulin, Iu. V., 'Osushchestvlenie Dekreta o zemle v tsentral'no-zemledel' cheskom raione', in *Leninskii Dekret o zemle v deistvii.*
Furmanov, D., *Chapaev*, Moscow, 1984.
Gaisinskii, M., *Bor'ba bol'shevikov za krest'ianstvo v 1917 g.: Vserossiiskie s"ezdy Sovetov krest'ianskikh deputatov*, Moscow, 1933.
Galynskii, T., *Ocherki po istorii agrarnoi revoliutsii Serdobskogo uezda, Saratovskoi gubernii*, Serdobsk, 1924.
Gaponenko, L. S., (ed.), *Revoliutsionnoe dvizhenie v Rossii posle sverzheniia samoderzhaviia: Dokumenty i materialy*, Moscow, 1957.
Garmiza, V. V., *Krushenie eserovskikh pravitel'stv*, Moscow, 1970.
Gerasimenko, G. A., 'Klassovaia bor'ba v derevne i nizovye krest'ianskie organizatsii v 1917–pervoi polovine 1918 goda (Na materialakh Nizhnego Povolzh'ia)', kand. diss., Saratov, 1973.
—— *Nizovye krest'ianskie organizatsii v 1917–pervoi polovine 1918 gg. (Na materialakh Nizhnego Povolzh'ia)*, Saratov, 1974.
—— 'Vliianie posledstvii stolypinskoi agrarnoi reformy na krest'ianskie organizatsii 1917 goda (po materialam Saratovskoi gub.)', *Istoriia SSSR*, 1981, no. 1.
—— and Rashitov, F. A., *Sovety Nizhnego Povolzh'ia v Oktiabr'skoi revoliutsii*, Saratov, 1972.
—— and Sem'ianinov, V. P., *Sovetskaia vlast' v derevne na pervom etape Oktiabria (Na materialakh Povolzh'ia)*, Saratov, 1980.
Gerasimiuk, V. V., *Nachalo sotsialisticheskoi revoliutsii v derevne 1917–1918 gg.*, Moscow, 1958.
—— 'Kombedy Rossiiskoi Federatsii v tsifrakh', *Istoriia SSSR*, 1960, no. 6.
—— 'Nekotorye novye statisticheskie dannye o kombedakh RSFSR', *Voprosy istorii*, 1963, no. 6
Gerschenkron, A., 'Agrarian Policies and Industrialization in Russia, 1861–1917', in *Cambridge Economic History of Europe*, vol. 6, part 2, Cambridge, 1965.
Gershtein, E. E., 'Bor'ba za osushchestvlenie leninskogo dekreta o likvidatsii negramotnosti v Saratovskoi gubernii (1920–21 gg.)', in *Iz istorii saratovskogo Povolzh'ia*, Saratov, 1968.
Getty, J. A., *Origins of the Great Purges: The Soviet Communist Party Reconsidered, 1933–1938*, Cambridge, 1985.
Gill, G. J., *Peasants and Government in the Russian Revolution*, London, 1979.
Gimpel'son, E. G., *Sovety v pervyi god proletarskoi diktatury, oktiabr' 1917 g.–noiabr' 1918 g.*, Moscow, 1967.
—— *Sovety v gody interventsii i grazhdanskoi voiny*, Moscow, 1968.

GIMPEL'SON, E. G., *Sovetskii rabochii klass 1918–1920 gg.*,Moscow, 1974.
—— *Rabochi klass v upravlenii sovetskim gosudarstvom, noiabr' 1917–1920 gg.*, Moscow, 1982.
Godovshchina pervoi revoliutsionni armii: Sbornik, Moscow, 1920.
GOFMAN, TS., 'K istorii pervogo agitparokhoda VTsIK 'Krasnaia Zvezda' (iiul'–oktiabr' 1919 g.), *Voprosy istorii*, 1948, no. 9.
GOLDMAN, E., *My Disillusionment in Russia*, London, 1925.
GOLEEVSKII, N. N., 'Leto na Volge: 1918 god', in *Russian Emigré Archives*, vol. 2, Fresno, Calif., 1973.
GORODETSKII, E. N., *Rozhdenie sovetskogo gosudarstva 1917–1918 gg.*, Moscow, 1965.
GOROKHOV, V., 'Organizatsiia territorii sel'skikh sovetov', *Sovetskoe stroitel' stvo*, 1929, no. 2.
Grazhdanskaia voina i voennaia interventsiia v SSSR. Entsiklopediia, Moscow, 1983.
Grazhdanskaia voina na Volge v 1918 godu. Sbornik pervyi, Prague, 1930.
GREGORY, P., 'Grain Marketings and Peasant Consumption in Russia, 1885–1913', *Explorations in Economic History*, vol. 17, 1980.
—— 'Russian Living Standards during the Industrialization Era, 1885–1913', *Review of Income and Wealth*, vol. 26, 1980.
GRISHAEV, V. V., *Stroitel'stvo sovetov v derevne v pervyi god sotsialísticheskoi revoliutsii*, Moscow, 1967.
—— *Sel'ksokhoziaistvennye kommuny Sovetskoi Rossii 1917–1929 gg.*, Moscow, 1976.
GROMYKO, M. M., 'Territorial'naia krest'ianskaia obshchina Sibiri (30-e gg. XVIII v.–60-e gg. XIX v.)', in *Krest'ianskaia obshchina v Sibiri XVII v.—nachala XX v.*, Novosibirsk, 1977.
—— 'Obychai pomochei u russkikh krest'ian v XIX v. (K probleme kompleksnogo issledovaniia trudovykh traditsii)', *Sovetskaia etnografiia*, 1981, nos. 4–5.
GROSS, E., *Avtonomnaia Sovetskaia Sotsialisticheskaia Respublika Nemtsev Povolzh'ia*, Pokrovsk, 1926.
GUR'EV, N. V., *Chapannaia voina*, Syzran', 1924.
GUSEV, K. V., *Partiia eserov: Ot melkoburzhuaznogo revoliutsionarizma k kontrrevoliutsii*, Moscow, 1975.
HAMBURG, G. M., 'The Crisis in Russian Agriculture: A Comment', *Slavic Review*, vol. 37, 1978.
The Hardships of our Co-Religionists in the German Volga Colonies, Pokrovsk, 1921.
HAXTHAUSEN, A. F., *Studien über die innern Zustände, das Volksleben und insbesondere die ländlichen Einrichtungen Russlands*, vol. 2, Hannover, 1847.
HOBSBAWM, E. J., *Primitive Rebels*, London, 1959.
—— *Bandits*, London, 1969.
HOCH, S., *Serfdom and Social Control in Russia*, Chicago, 1986.
IAKOVLEV, IA. A., *Nasha derevnia: Novoe v starom i staroe v novom*, Moscow, 1924.
—— *Sel'skoe khoziaistvo i industrializatsiia*, Moscow/Leningrad, 1927.

IAKOVLEV, P. F., 'Komitety derevenskoi bednoty Saratovskoi gubernii', kand. diss., Saratov, 1952.

IAKUBOVA, L. M., 'Likvidatsiia kontrrevoliutsionnykh sil v Srednem Povolzh'e 1918–1922 gg. (Na materialakh Kazanskoi, Samarskoi i Simbirskoi gubernii)', kand. diss., Kazan', 1981.

IGRITSKII, I. V., *1917 god v derevne*, Moscow, 1967.

IONENKO, I. M., *Krest'ianstvo Srednego Povolzh'ia nakanune Velikogo Oktiabria*, Kazan', 1957.

Istoriia grazhdanskoi voiny v SSSR, 5 vols., Moscow, 1937–60.

Istoriia sovetskogo krest'ianstva, vol. 1, *Krest'ianstvo v pervoe desiatiletie Sovetskoi vlasti 1917–1927*, Moscow, 1986.

Itogi oktiabria 1917–1922, Buzuluk, 1922.

IUROVSKII, L. N., *Saratovskie votchiny*, Saratov, 1923.

Iz revoliutsionnogo proshlogo Kamyshina (1905–1920 gg.), Kamyshin, 1964.

KABANOV, V. V., *Oktiabr'skaia revoliutsiia i kooperatsiia (1917–mart 1919 g.)*, Moscow, 1973.

—— 'Oktiabr'skaia revoliutsiia i krest'ianskaia obshchina', *Istoricheskie zapiski*, vol. 111, Moscow, 1984.

—— *Krest'ianskoe khoziaistvo v usloviiakh 'voennogo kommunizma'*, Moscow, 1988 [*KK*].

KAKURIN, N., 'Organizatsiia bor'by s banditizmom po opytu tambovskogo i vitebskogo komandovanii', *Voennaia nauka i revoliutsiia*, 1922, no. 1.

KAUTSKY, K., *Die Agrarfrage*, Stuttgart, 1889.

KAZAKOV, A., 'Obshchie prichiny vozniknoveniia banditizma i krest'ianskikh vosstanii', *Krasnaia armiia*, 1921, no. 9.

KEEP, J. L. H., *The Russian Revolution: A Study in Mass Mobilization*, London, 1976.

KELLER, V., and ROMANENKO, I., *Pervye itogi agrarnoi reformy. Opyt issledovaniia rezul'tatov sovremennogo zemleustroistva na primere Zadonskogo uezda Voronezhskoi gubernii*, Voronezh, 1922.

KENEZ, P., *Civil War in South Russia, 1919–1920: The Defeat of the Whites*, Berkeley, Calif., 1977.

—— *The Birth of the Propaganda State*, Cambridge, 1985.

KHRIASHCHEVA, A. I., 'Krest'ianstvo v voine i revoliutsii', *Vestnik statistiki*, 1920, nos. 9–12.

KLIATSKIN, S. M., *Na zashchite Oktiabria: Organizatsiia reguliarnoi armii i militsionnoe stroitel'stvo v Sovetskoi respublike, 1917–1920 gg.*, Moscow, 1965.

KNIPOVICH, B. N., 'Napravlenie i itogi agrarnoi politiki 1917–1920 gg.', in *O zemle*.

KOCH, F. C., *The Volga Germans in Russia and the Americas from 1763 to the Present*, Pennsylvania, 1977.

KOENKER, D., 'Urbanization and Deurbanization in the Russian Revolution and Civil War', *Journal of Modern History*, vol. 57, no. 3, 1985.

KOLESNIKOV, V. I., *Voennye deistviia na territorii Samarskoi gubernii v 1918–1921 gg.*, Samara, 1927.

KONKOVA, A. S., 'Bor'ba partii bol'shevikov za trudiashcheesia krest'ianstvo

Samarskoi gubernii v period podgotovki Oktiabr'skoi revoliutsii', *Trudy moskovskogo istoriko-arkhivnogo instituta*, vol. 13, Moscow, 1959.

KOSENKO, M. IA., 'Agrarnaia reforma Stolypina v Saratovskoi gubernii', kand. diss., Saratov, 1950.

KOSTRIKIN, V. I., 'Iz istorii zemel'nykh komitetov Riazanskoi gubernii (mart–oktiabr' 1917g.)', *Trudy moskovskogo istoriko-arkhivnogo instituta*, vol. 9, 1957.

—— *Zemel'nye komitety v 1917 g.*, Moscow, 1975.

—— 'Krest'ianskoe dvizhenie nakanune Oktiabria', in *Oktiabr' i sovetskoe krest'ianstvo*, Moscow, 1977.

KOTEL'NIKOV, K. G., and MELLER V. L. (eds.), *Krest'ianskoe dvizhenie v 1917 g.*, Moscow/Leningrad, 1927.

KPSS v rezoliutsiiakh i resheniiakh s"ezdov, konferentsii i plenumov TsK, 9th edn., vol. 2, Moscow, 1983.

Kraevedcheskie zapiski, Kuibyshev, 1963.

KRASIL'NIKOVA, K. M., 'Bor'ba za khleb v Srednem Povolzh'e v period inostrannoi voennoi interventsii i grazhdanskoi voiny', kand. diss., Kuibyshev, 1968.

KRASNOV, V., 'Iz vospominanii o 1917–1920 gg.', *Arkhiv russkoi revoliutsii*, vol. 7, Berlin, 1923.

KRAVCHUK, N. A., *Massovoe krest'ianskoe dvizhenie v Rossii nakanune Oktiabria*, Moscow, 1971.

KRITSMAN, L. N., *Proletarskaia revoliutsiia i derevnia*, Moscow/Leningrad, 1929.

—— (ed.), *Materialy po istorii agrarnoi revoliutsii v Rossii*, vol. 1, Moscow, 1928.

KRUPSKAIA, N. K., 'Po gradam i vesiam sovetskoi respubliki', *Novyi mir*, vol. 11, 1960.

KUBANIN, M. I., 'Anti-sovetskoe krest'ianskoe dvizhenie v gody grazhdanskoi voiny (voennogo kommunizma)', *Na agrarnom fronte*, 1926, no. 2.

—— 'Predposylki kombedov', *Na agrarnom fronte*, 1934, no. 11.

KUCHUMOVA, L. I., 'Sel'skaia pozemel'naia obshchina Evropeiskoi Rossii v 60-e–70-e gody XIX v.', *Istoricheskie zapiski*, vol. 106, Moscow 1981.

KUIBYSHEV, V. V., 'Pervaia revoliutsionnaia armiia', in *Simbirskaia guberniia v 1918–1920 gg: Sbornik vospominanii*, Ul'ianovsk, 1958.

KUTIAKOV, I., *S Chapaevym po ural'skim stepiam*, Moscow, 1928.

LEBEDEFF, V. I., *The Russian Democracy and its Struggle against the Bolshevist Tyranny*, New York, 1919.

LEGGETT, G., *The Cheka: Lenin's Political Police*, Oxford, 1981.

LEITENANT, N. N., 'Zapiski belogvardeitsa', *Arkhiv russkoi revoliutsii*, vol. 10, 1923.

LELEVICH, G., *V dni samarskoi uchredilki*, Moscow, 1921.

LENIN, V. I., *Polnoe sobranie sochinenii*, 5th edn., 55 vols., Moscow, 1958–65 [*PSS*].

Leninskii Dekret o zemle v deistvii: Sbornik statei, Moscow, 1979.

Leninskii sbornik, 39 vols., Moscow, 1924–80.

LEPESHKIN, A. I., *Mestnye organy vlasti sovetskogo gosudarstva (1917–1920 gg.)*, Moscow, 1957.

LEWIN, M., *Russian Peasants and Soviet Power: A Study of Collectivization*, London, 1968.
—— 'The Social Background to Stalinism', in R. C. Tucker (ed.), *Stalinism: Essays in Historical Interpretation*, New York, 1977.
—— *The Making of the Soviet System*, New York, 1985.
LIH, L. T., 'Bolshevik Razverstka and War Communism', *Slavic Review*, vol. 54, 1986.
LITVIN, A. L., *Krest'ianstvo Srednego Povolzh'ia v gody grazhdanskoi voiny*, Kazan', 1972.
—— 'Itogi i zadachi izucheniia grazhdanskoi voiny v Povolzh'e', *Voprosy istorii*, 1988, no. 7.
LOEBSACK, G., *Einsam kämpft das Wolgaland*, Leipzig, 1936.
LONG, J., 'Agricultural Conditions in the German Colonies of Novouzensk District, Samara, 1864–1914', *Slavonic and East European Review*, vol. 57, no. 4, 1979.
LONGWORTH, P., 'The Subversive Legend of Stenka Razin', in V. Strada (ed.), *Russia*, vol. 2, Turin, 1975.
LOSITSKII, A. E., 'Publikatsii TsSu o zemlevladenii i ugod'iakh', *Sel'skoe i lesnoe khoziaistvo*, 1923, no. 7.
LUTSKII, E. A., 'Peredel zemli vesnoi 1918 goda', *Izvestiia AN SSSR: Seria istorii i filosofii*, vol. 6 (1949), no. 3.
—— 'Politika sovetskoi vlasti po otnosheniiu k zemel'nym komitetam', *Trudy moskovskogo istoriko-arkhivnogo instituta*, vol. 13, 1959.
—— 'Krest'ianskie nakazy 1917 g. o zemle', in *Istochnikovedenie istorii sovetskogo obshchestva*, Moscow, 1968.
—— 'Leninskii Dekret o zemle', in *Leninskii Dekret o zemle v deistvii*.
LYSIKHIN, N. F., 'Razgrom kontrrevoliutsionnogo miatezha na srednem Volge v 1919 g.', in *Kraevedcheskie zapiski*.
MACEY, D. A. J., *Government and Peasant in Russia 1861–1906*, De Kalb, Ill., 1987.
MCKENZIE, K. E., 'Zemstvo Organization and Role within the Administrative Structure', in T. Emmons and W. S. Vucinich (eds.), *The Zemstvo in Russia: An Experiment in Local Self-Government*, Cambridge, 1982.
MAISKII, I. M., *Demokraticheskaia kontrrevoliutsiia*, Moscow, 1923.
MAKAROV, N. P., *Krest'ianskoe khoziaistvo i ego evoliutsiia*, vol. 1, Moscow, 1920.
MAKAROVA, S. L., 'Oprosnye listy Narodnogo Komissariata Zemledeliia i moskovskogo oblastnogo ispolnitel'nogo komiteta kak istochnik po istorii agrarnoi revoliutsii (noiabr' 1917—iiun' 1918)', kand. diss., Moscow, 1970.
MAKSAKOVA, L. V., *Agitpoezd "Oktiabr'skaia Revoliutsiia" (1919–1920)*, Moscow, 1956.
—— 'Deiatel'nost' kollektiva agitpoezda 'Oktiabr'skaia revoliutsiia' sredi krest'ianstva (1919–1920 gg.)', *Voprosy istorii*, 1956, no. 10.
MALE, D. J., *Russian Peasant Organization before Collectivization*, Cambridge, 1971.
MALET, M., *Nestor Makhno in the Russian Civil War*, London, 1982.
MALIAVSKII, A. D., *Krest'ianskoe dvizhenie v Rossii v 1917 g. mart–oktiabr'*, Moscow, 1981.

MALLE, S., *The Economic Organization of War Communism 1918–1921*, Cambridge, 1985.
MANNING, R. T., *The Crisis of the Old Order in Russia: Gentry and Government*, Princeton, 1982.
MANUILOV, A., 'Melkaia arenda zemli', in *O zemle*.
MASLOV, S. S., *Rossiia posle chetyrekh let revoliutsii*, Paris, 1922.
MAWDSLEY, E., *The Russian Civil War*, London, 1987.
MEDVEDEV, E. I., 'Zavoevanie i uprochenie vlasti rabochikh i krest'ian v Samarskoi gubernii', in Chugaev and Vasiukov (eds.), *Ustanovlenie sovetskoi vlasti na mestakh*.
—— *Oktiabr'skaia revoliutsiia v Srednem Povolzh'e*, Kuibyshev, 1964.
—— *Krest'ianstvo Srednego Povolzh'ia v gody grazhdanskoi voiny (1918–19 gg.)*. Saratov, 1974.
—— 'Partiinoe stroitel'stvo v Srednem Povolzh'e v period ustanovleniia i uprocheniia Sovetskoi vlasti', in *Problemy istorii Oktiabr'skoi revoliutsii i grazhdanskoi voiny v SSSR*, Tomsk, 1975.
—— 'Agrarnye preobrazovaniia Oktiabr'skoi revoliutsii v Srednem Povolzh'e', in *Leninskii Dekret o zemle v deistvii*.
—— *Krest'ianstvo Srednego Povolzh'ia v bor'be za zemliu v mirnyi period revoliutsii 1917 goda*, Kuibyshev, 1981.
MEDVEDEV, R., *The October Revolution*, trans. G. Saunders, London, 1979.
MEIJER, J. M., (ed.), *The Trotsky Papers*, 2 vols., The Hague, 1971.
MELANCHON, M., 'Athens or Babylon: The Birth and Development of the Socialist-Revolutionary and Social-Democratic Parties in Saratov, 1890–1905', paper presented to Conference on the History of Saratov Province, University of Illinois, 1985.
MELGUNOV, S. P., *The Bolshevik Seizure of Power*, Oxford, 1972.
Menzelinskaia byl', Kazan', 1970.
MIKHAILOVSKII, A., 'Khlebnaia kampaniia 1918–1919 gg.', *Vestnik statistiki*, 1919, nos. 8–12, Moscow, 1920.
MILIUKOV, P., *Rossiia na perelome*, vol. 1, Paris, 1927.
MILIUTIN, V. P., *Sotsializm i sel'skoe khoziaistvo*, Moscow, 1919.
MINKH, A. N., *Istoriko-geograficheskii slovar' Saratovskoi gubernii*, vol. 1, Saratov, 1900.
MINTS, I. I., *Istoriia Velikogo Oktiabria*, 3 vols., Moscow, 1967–73.
MIRONOV, B., 'The Russian Peasant Commune after the Reforms of the 1860s', *Slavic Review*, vol. 44, 1985.
MITCHELL, B. R., *European Historical Statistics 1750–1970*, Columbia, 1978.
MIXTER, T., 'The Polarization of the Saratov Countryside: Peasants in the Revolution of 1905–1907', paper presented to Conference on the History of Saratov Province, University of Illinois, 1985.
MOISEEVA, O. N., *Sovety krest'ianskikh deputatov v 1917 g.*, Moscow, 1967.
MOLODTSYGIN, M. A., *Raboche-krest'ianskii soiuz 1918–20 gg.*, Moscow, 1987.
MOORE, B. JR., *Social Origins of Dictatorship and Democracy*, Harmondsworth, 1967.
MOROZOV, B. M., *Sozdanie i ukreplenie sovetskogo gosudarstvennogo apparata (noiabr' 1917 g.–mart 1919 g.)*, Moscow, 1957.

Movchin, N., *Komplektovanie Krasnoi Armii*, Moscow, 1926.
Müller, E., 'Der Beitrag der Bauern zur Industrialisierung Russlands, 1885–1930', *Jahrbücher für Geschichte Osteuropas*, no. 27, 1979.
Nemakov, N. I., 'K voprosu o zemlepol'zovanii byvshikh pomeshchikov v pervom desiatiletii sovetskoi vlasti', *Vestnik moskovskogo gosudarstvennogo universiteta*, 1961, no. 2.
Nenarokov, A. P., 'Obrazovanie vostochnogo fronta i perekhod k massovoi reguliarnoi armii (mai–iiun' 1918 g.)', *Istoricheskie nauki*, no. 4, 1961.
Ocherki istorii kuibyshevskoi organizatsii KPSS, Kuibyshev, 1960.
Okninsky, A., *Dva goda sredi krest'ian: Videnoe, slyshannoe, perezhitoe v Tambovskoi gubernii s noiabria 1918 goda do noiabria 1920 goda*, Newtonville, Mass., 1986 (originally Riga, 1936) [*DGS*].
Onufriev, I. A., *Moi vospominaniia iz grazhdanskoi voiny na Urale*, Ekaterinburg, 1922.
Orlov, N., *Deviat' mesiatsev prodovol'stvennoi raboty Sovetskoi vlasti*, Moscow, 1918.
Osipova, T. V., *Klassovaia bor'ba v derevne v period podgotovki i provedeniia Oktiabr'skoi revoliutsii*, Moscow, 1974.
Palagin, D. A., 'Rol' kommunisticheskikh fraktsii sovetov Srednego Povolzh'ia v ukreplenii diktatury proletariata v period inostrannoi voennoi interventsii i grazhdanskoi voiny (1918–20 gg.)', kand. diss., Moscow, 1972.
Perepiska sekretariata TsK RSDRP(b) s mestnymi partiinymi organizatsiiami: Sbornik dokumentov, 3 vols., Moscow, 1957.
Pereverzev, A. Ia., 'Organizatorskaia pomoshch' promyshlennykh rabochikh derevne v 1918 godu (po materialam tsentral'no-chernozemnykh gubernii)', *Trudy voronezhskogo universiteta*, vol. 87, Voronezh, 1969.
Perrie, M., 'The Russian Peasant Movement of 1905–07: Its Social Composition and Revolutionary Significance', *Past and Present*, vol. 57, 1972.
Pershin, P. N., *Uchastkovoe zemlepol'zovanie v Rossii*, Moscow, 1922.
—— 'Krest'ianskie zemel'nye komitety v period podgotovki Velikoi Oktiabr' skoi Sotsialisticheskoi Revoliutsii', *Voprosy istorii*, 1948, no. 7.
—— *Agrarnaia revoliutsiia v Rossii*, 2 vols., Moscow, 1966.
Persits, M. N., *Otdelenie tserkvi ot gosudarstva i shkoly ot tserkvi v SSSR*, Moscow, 1958.
Pethybridge, R., *The Social Prelude to Stalinism*, London, 1974.
Petrov, Iu. P., *Partiinye mobilizatsii v krasnuiu armiiu 1918–20*, Moscow, 1956.
Petrov, P. P., *Ot Volgi do Tikhogo Okeana v riadakh belykh (1918–22 gg.)*, Riga, 1930.
Pipes, R. (ed.), *Revolutionary Russia*, Harvard, 1968.
Pobeda Velikoi Oktiabr'skoi sotsialisticheskoi revoliutsii v Samarskoi gubernii: Sbornik dokumentov, Kuibyshev, 1957.
Podgotovka i pobeda Velikoi Oktiabr'skoi sotsialisticheskoi revoliutsii v Penzenskoi gubernii: Sbornik dokumentov, Penza, 1957.
Pokrovksii, M. N., *Kontrrevoliutsiia za 4 goda*, Moscow, 1922.
Poliakov, Iu. A., *Perekhod k NEPu i sovetskoe krest'ianstvo*, Moscow, 1967.
Polikarpov, V. D., 'Dobrovol'tsy 1918 goda', *Voprosy istorii*, 1983, no. 2.

PONTEN, J., *Der Sprung ins Abenteuer*, Stuttgart, 1932.

POPOV, F. G., *Chekho-slovatskii miatezh i samarskaia uchredilovka*, Samara, 1932.

—— *Za vlast' sovetov: Razgrom samarskoi uchredilovki*, Kuibyshev, 1959.

—— *1918 god v Samarskoi gubernii: Khronika sobytii*, Kuibyshev, 1972.

—— *1920 god v Samarskoi gubernii: Khronika sobytii*, Kuibyshev, 1977.

POPOV, P., *Proizvodstvo khleba v RSFSR i federiruiushchikhsia s neiu respublikakh*, Moscow, 1921.

PROKOF'EVA, L. S., *Krest'ianskaia obshchina v Rossii vo vtoroi polovine XVIII v.–pervoi polovine XIX v.*, Leningrad, 1981.

RADKEY, O. H., *The Election to the Russian Constituent Assembly of 1917*, Harvard, 1950.

—— *The Sickle under the Hammer: The Russian Socialist Revolutionaries in the Early Months of Soviet Rule*, New York, 1973.

—— *The Unknown Civil War in Soviet Russia*, Stanford, 1976.

RALEIGH, D., *Revolution on the Volga: 1917 in Saratov*, Cornell, 1986.

Revoliutsionnaia bor'ba krest'ian Kazanskoi gubernii nakanune Oktiabria: Sbornik dokumentov, Kazan', 1958.

RICKMAN, J., *An Eye Witness from Russia*, London, 1919.

RIGBY, T. H., *Communist Party Membership in the USSR 1917–1967*, Princeton, 1968.

ROBINSON, G. T., *Rural Russia under the Old Regime*, London, 1932.

ROMANENKO, V. V., 'Sozdanie, razvitie i deiatel'nost' organov ChK i vnutrennikh voisk sovetskoi respubliki v Srednem Povolzh'e i Priural'e v 1918–22 gg.', kand. diss., Kuibyshev, 1977.

ROSENBERG, W. G., 'The Zemstvo in 1917 and its Fate under Bolshevik Rule', in T. Emmons and W. S. Vucinich (eds.), *The Zemstvo in Russia: An Experiment in Local Self-Government*, Cambridge, Mass., 1982.

—— 'Russian Labor and Bolshevik Power: Social Dimensions of Protest in Petrograd after October', in D. H. Kaiser (ed.), *The Workers' Revolution in Russia, 1917: The View from Below*, Cambridge, Mass., 1987.

RUDNEV, S. P., *Pri vechernikh ogniakh: Vospominaniia*, Newtonville, Mass., 1978 (originally Kharbin, 1928) [*PVO*].

SAGRAD'IAN, M. O., *Osushchestvlenie leninskogo dekreta o zemle v Saratovskoi gubernii*, Saratov, 1966.

SAKHAROV, K. V., *Belaia Sibir': Vnutrennaia voina 1918–20 gg.*, Munich, 1923.

Samarskaia guberniia v gody grazhdanskoi voiny: (1918–1920 gg.): Dokumenty i materialy, Kuibyshev, 1958.

SANDERS, J. T., ' "Once More into the Breach, Dear Friends": A Closer Look at Indirect Tax Receipts and the Condition of the Russian Peasantry, 1881–1899', *Slavic Review*, vol. 43, 1984.

Saratovskaia oblastnaia organizatsiia KPSS v tsifrakh 1917–1975 gg., Saratov, 1977.

Saratovskaia partiinaia organizatsiia v gody grazhdanskoi voiny. Dokumenty i materialy 1918–1920 gg., Saratov, 1958.

Sbornik dokumentov po zemel'nomu zakonodatel'stvu SSSR i RSFSR, 1917–1954 gg., Moscow, 1954.

Sbornik vospominanii neposredstvennykh uchastnikov grazhdanskoi voiny, kn. 2, Moscow, 1922.

SCOTT, J. C., *The Moral Economy of the Peasant*, New Haven, 1976.

SELUNSKAIA, V. M., *Rabochii klass i Oktiabr' v derevne*, Moscow, 1968.

—— *Izmeneniia sotsial'noi struktury sovetskogo obshchestva, oktiabr' 1917–1920 gg.*, Moscow, 1976.

SEMENOV (Vasil'ev), G., *Voennaia i boevaia rabota partii sotsialistov-revoliutsionerov za 1917–18 gg.*, Berlin, 1922.

SEM'IANINOV, V. P., 'Volostnye sovety Srednego Povolzh'ia v dokombedskii period, noiabr' 1917–iiun' 1918 gg.', kand. diss., Saratov, 1977.

SERVICE, R., *The Bolshevik Party in Revolution: A Study in Organizational Change, 1917–1923*, London, 1979.

SHANIN, T., 'The Peasantry as a Political Factor', *The Sociological Review*, vol. 14, no. 1, 1966.

—— *The Awkward Class*, Oxford, 1972.

—— *The Roots of Otherness: Russia's Turn of Century*, vol. 1, *Russia as a 'Developing Society'*, London, 1985.

—— *The Roots of Otherness: Russia's Turn of Century*, vol. 2, *Russia, 1905–07: Revolution as a Moment of Truth*, London, 1986.

—— (ed.), *Peasants and Peasant Societies*, 2nd edn., Oxford, 1987.

SHARAPOV, G., *Razreshenie agrarnogo voprosa v Rossii posle pobedy Oktiabr'skoi revoliutsii*, Moscow, 1961.

SHEPELOVAIA, T., 'Sotsialisticheskie formy sel'skogo khoziaistva v 1918–1919 gg.', *Krasnyi Arkhiv*, vol. 5, 96, 1939.

SHESTAKOV, A. V. (ed.), *Sovety krest'ianskikh deputatov i drugie krest'ianskie organizatsii*, 2 vols., Moscow, 1929.

—— (ed.), *Kombedy RSFSR*, Moscow, 1933.

SHLIFSHTEIN, E. I., *Melkaia promyshlennost' Saratovskoi gubernii: Statistichesko-ekonomicheskii ocherk*, Saratov, 1923.

Simbirskaia guberniia v gody grazhdanskoi voiny mai 1918–mart 1919 gg., Ul'ianovsk, 1958.

Simbirskaia guberniia v 1918–1920 gg: Sbornik vospominanii, Ul'ianovsk, 1958.

SIMMS, J. Y., 'The Crisis in Russian Agriculture at the End of the Nineteenth Century: A Different View', *Slavic Review*, vol. 36, 1977.

SKOBELKINA, E. B., 'Simbirskie bol'sheviki v bor'be s kulatskim miatezhom vesnoi 1919 g.', in *Uchenye zapiski ul'ianovskogo gosudarstvennogo pedagogicheskogo instituta*, vyp. 1, Ul'ianovsk, 1966.

—— 'Bor'ba partii bol'shevikov protiv melkoburzhuaznoi kontrrevoliutsii v 1918–19 gg. (po materialam Simbirskoi gubernii)', kand. diss., Voronezh, 1967.

SKOCPOL, T., *States and Social Revolutions*, Cambridge, 1979.

SMIRNOV, A. S., 'Krest'ianskie s"ezdy Penzenskoi gubernii v 1917 g.', *Istoriia SSSR*, 1967, no. 3.

SMITH, R. E. F., *Peasant Farming in Muscovy*, Cambridge, 1977.
SMYKOV, IU. I., *Krest'iane Srednego Povolzh'ia v period kapitalizma*, Moscow, 1984.
SNOW, R. E., *The Bolsheviks in Siberia, 1917–1918*, Rutherford, 1977.
SOFINOV, P. G., *Ocherki istorii VChK (1917–1922 gg.)*, Moscow, 1960.
Soiuz rabochikh i krest'ian v pervye gody sovetskoi vlasti (1917–1922 gg.), Yaroslavl', 1958.
SOKOLOV, N. G., 'Nalogovaia politika v derevne v pervye gody sovetskoi vlasti (1917–1920 gg.)', *Istoricheskie zapiski*, vol. 113, Moscow, 1986.
Some Notes on Social Conditions in Soviet Russia, London (The Friends' Council), 1925.
SORIN, I., 'Saratovskoe vosstanie 1918 g. (po chernovym zametkam)', *Letopis' revoliutsii*, Khar'kov, 1923, no. 5.
Sovety v oktiabre: Sbornik dokumentov, Moscow, 1928.
SPIRIN, L. M., 'Kommunisticheskaia partiia—organizator razgroma Kolchaka', *Voprosy istorii*, 1956, no. 6.
—— *Klassy i partii v grazhdanskoi voine v Rossii*, Moscow, 1968.
STEKLOV, Iu., *Partiia SR-ov*, Moscow, 1922.
STEPANOV, A. P., 'Simbirskaia operatsiia', *Beloe delo*, vol. 1, Berlin, 1926.
STEWART, G., *The White Armies of Russia*, New York, 1933.
STONE, N., *The Eastern Front 1914–1917*, London, 1975.
Stranitsy zhizni: Iz istorii serdobskoi organizatsii KPSS, Penza, 1961.
STREL'TSOVA, A. I., 'Partiinaia organizatsiia Saratovskoi gubernii v bor'be za provedenie politiki partii v derevne v vosstanovitel'nyi period (1921–25 gg.)', kand. diss., Moscow, 1953.
STRIZHKOV, Iu. K., *Prodovol'stvennye otriady v gody grazhdanskoi voiny i inostrannoi interventsii 1917–1921 gg.*, Moscow, 1973.
STRUMILIN, S. G., 'K reforme urozhainosti', *Ekonomischeskoe obozrenie*, 1924, nos. 9–10.
—— 'Dinamika batratskoi armii v SSSR', in *Naemnyi trud v sel'skom khoziaistve: Statistiko-ekonomicheskii sbornik*, Moscow, 1926.
STUDENTSOV, A., *Saratovskoe krest'ianskoe vosstanie 1905 goda*, Penza, 1926.
SUSLOV, Iu. P., *Leninskaia agrarnaia programma i bor'ba bol'shevikov za ee osushchestvlenie, mart 1917 g.–mart 1918 g.*, Saratov, 1972.
TAL'NOV, B., *Kratkie ocherki pervykh chetyrekh let proletarskoi revoliutsii v buguruslanskom okruge (1917–1920 gg.)*, Buguruslan, 1929.
TANIUCHI, Y., *The Village Gathering in Russia in the mid–1920s*, Birmingham, 1968.
TAUBIN, R. A., 'Razgrom kulatskogo miatezha Sapozhkova', *Bor'ba klassov*, no. 12, 1934.
—— 'Iz istorii bor'by s menshevistskoi i esero-kulatskoi kontrrevoliutsiei v period grazhdanskoi voiny v b. Saratovskoi gubernii', *Uchenye zapiski saratovskogo gos. universiteta im. N. G. Chernyshevskogo*, vol. 1 (14), vyp. 1, 1939.
TAYLOR, R., 'A Medium for the Masses: Agitation in the Soviet Civil War', *Soviet Studies*, vol. 22, no. 4, 1971.
TEREKHIN, S. V., 'Prodovol'stvennye zagotovki v rabote saratovskoi kommun-

isticheskoi organizatsii v 1918–1920 gg.', in *Trudy saratovskogo ekonomicheskogo instituta*, vol. 4, Saratov, 1954.

—— *Gody ognevye: Saratovskaia organizatsiia bol'shevikov v period Oktiabr'skoi revoliutsii i grazhdanskoi voiny (1917–1920 gg.)*, Saratov, 1967.

Tri goda bor'by i stroitel'stva 1917–1920 gg., Samara, 1921.

TRIFONOV, I. Ia., *Klassy i klassovaia bor'ba v SSSR v nachale NEPa (1921–23 gg.)*, vol. 1, *Bor'ba s vooruzhennoi kulatskoi kontrrevoliutsiei*, Leningrad, 1964.

TROTSKII, V. V., and DEMIDOV, A. D., *1920 god v srednevolzhskom krae*, Samara, 1934.

TROTSKY, L., *1905*, 4th edn., Moscow, 1925.

—— *The History of the Russian Revolution*, trans. M. Eastman, London, 1965.

—— *My Life*, Gloucester, Mass., 1970.

—— *How the Revolution Armed*, trans. B. Pearce, 3 vols., London, 1979.

TUKHACHEVSKII, M. N., 'Pervaia armiia v 1918 godu', in *Izbrannye proizvedeniia*, vol. 1, Moscow, 1964.

1917 god v Saratove, Saratov, 1927.

UMNOV, A. S., *Grazhdanskaia voina i srednee krest'ianstvo (1917–1920 gg.)*, Moscow, 1959.

V boiakh za diktaturu proletariata: Sbornik vospominanii, Saratov, 1933.

VAINSHTEIN, A., *Oblozhenie i platezhi krest'ianstva*, Moscow, 1924.

VAS'KIN, V. V., and GERASIMENKO, G. A., *Fevral'skaia revoliutsiia v Nizhnem Povolzh'e*, Saratov, 1976.

VISHNEVSKII, N. M., *Statistika i sel'sko-khoziaistvennaia deistvitel'nost'*, Moscow, 1922.

VLADIMIROV, M., *Meshechnichestvo i ego sotsial'no-politicheskie otrazheniia*, Khar'kov, 1920.

VLADIMIROVA, V., *God sluzhby 'sotsialistov' kapitalistam: Ocherki po istorii kontrrevoliutsii v 1918 godu*, Moscow/Leningrad, 1927.

—— 'Rabota eserov v 1918 g.', *Krasnyi Arkhiv*, 1927, no. 20.

VLADIMIRSKII, M., *Organizatsiia sovetskoi vlasti na mestakh*, Moscow, 1919.

—— *Sovety, ispolkomy i s"ezdy sovetov (materialy k izucheniiu stroeniia i deiatel'nosti organov mestnogo upravleniia)*, vyp. 2, *S"ezdy sovetov v 1917–1921 gg., ispolkomy v 1920–1921 gg., gorodskie sovety v 1920–1921 gg.*, Moscow, 1921.

Vospominaniia o V. I. Lenine, vol. 2, Moscow, 1968.

WADA, H., 'The Inner World of Russian Peasants', *Annals of the Institution of Social Science*, vol. 20, Tokyo, 1979.

WADE, R. A., *Red Guards and Workers' Militias in the Russian Revolution*, Stanford, 1984.

WEISSMAN, N., 'Rural Crime in Tsarist Russia: The Question of Hooliganism 1905–1914', *Slavic Review*, vol. 37, 1978.

—— 'Prohibition and Alcohol Control in the USSR: The 1920s Campaign against Illegal Spirits', *Soviet Studies*, vol. 38, no. 3, 1986.

WHEATCROFT, S. G., 'Famine and Epidemic Crises in Russia, 1918–1922: The Case of Saratov', *Annales de démographie historique 1983*.

—— 'The Agrarian Crisis and Peasant Living Standards in Late Imperial

Russia: A Reconsideration of Trends and Regional Differentiation', paper presented to Conference on the Peasantry of European Russia, 1800–1917, University of Massachusetts at Boston, 1986.

WHITE, D. D. F., *The Growth of the Red Army*, Princeton, 1944.

WHITE, J. D., 'The Sormovo-Nikolaev zemlyachestvo in the February Revolution', *Soviet Studies*, vol. 31, no. 4, 1979.

WILBUR, E. M. W., 'Was Russian Peasant Agriculture Really That Impoverished?', *Journal of Economic History*, vol. 43, no. 1, 1983.

WILLIAMS, H. P., *The Czar's Germans*, Denver, 1975.

WOLLENBERG, E., *The Red Army*, trans. C. Sykes, London, 1978.

YANEY, G., *The Urge to Mobilize: Agrarian Reform in Russia, 1861–1930*, Urbana, Ill. 1982.

Za vlast' sovetov: Sbornik vospominanii uchastnikov revoliutsionnykh sobytii v Tatarii, pt. 2, Kazan', 1960.

ZAIONCHKOVSKY, P. A., *The Abolition of Serfdom*, Gulf Breeze, Fla., 1977.

ZAITSEV, A., *1918 god: Ocherki po istorii russkoi grazhdanskoi voiny*, n.p., 1934.

ZAKHAROV, N. S., *Oktiabr'skaia revoliutsiia i sovetskoe stroitel'stvo v Srednem Povolzh'e*, Kazan', 1970.

Zashchishchaia revoliutsiiu, Kazan', 1980.

ZASOV, A. F., *Bol'sheviki Povolzh'ia v bor'be s melkoburzhuaznymi partiiami v period uprocheniia sovetskoi vlasti*, Kuibyshev, 1967.

INDEX OF PLACE-NAMES

GENERAL INDEX